Rick

SCANDINAVIA

CONTENTS

To Östersund
To Boden &
Narvik
To Oulu
To Jyväskylä
Tampere
Pori
To St. Petersburg,
Russia
Rauma
Lahti
Porvoo
FINLAND
Mora
Rättvik
Gävle
Naantali
Turku
Salo
Helsinki
DALARNA
Falun
Åland
(Finland)
Borlänge
Mariehamn
Tallinn
Uppsala
ESTONIA
Sigtuna
Arlanda
Filipstad
E18
ARCHIPELAGO
Gulf of Finland
Västerås
Kärdla
Haapsalu
Örebro
DROTTNINGHOLM
Stockholm
Hiiumaa
Nynäshamn
Saaremaa
Göta Canal
Göta
Canal
Norrköping
E4
Nyköping
Lake
Vättern
Söderköping
Gotska
Sandön
Skovde
Linköping
To Riga, Latvia
Vimmerby
Västervik
Visby
Gotland
Jönköping
Ljugarn
SWEDEN
Byxelkrok
LATVIA
Oskarshamn
Burgsvik
KOSTA BODA
GLASS
Borgholm
Alvesta
GLASS
Öland
Växjö
Baltic
COUNTRY
Kalmar
Emmaboda
Sea
EKETORP
LITHUANIA
Karlskrona
Hässleholm
Kristianstad
Helsingborg
und
Malmö
Ystad
Trelleborg
To Gdynia,
Poland
Rønne
Bornholm
(Denmark)
Sassnitz
Rügen
Kołobrzeg
Koszalin
Stralsund
To
Berlin
Świnoujście
POLAND

Gulf
of
Bothnia

LEGEND

A-24	Freeway
	Major Rail Line
✈	Airport
■	Ruin, Museum, Other Point of Interest
⌘	Castle/Monument/Palace

0 km   50   100 km
0 mi   50   100 mi

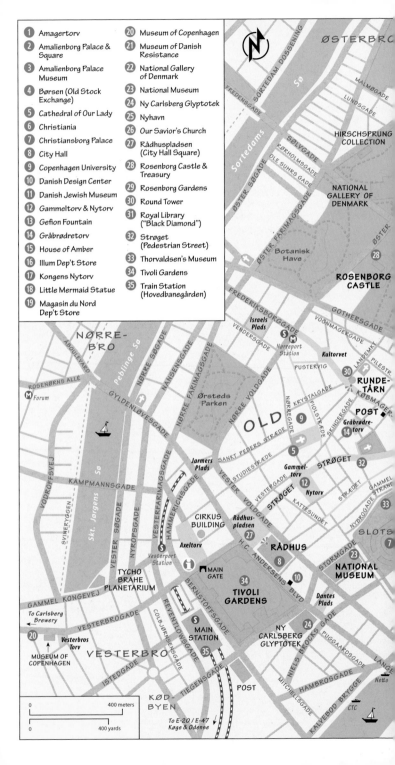

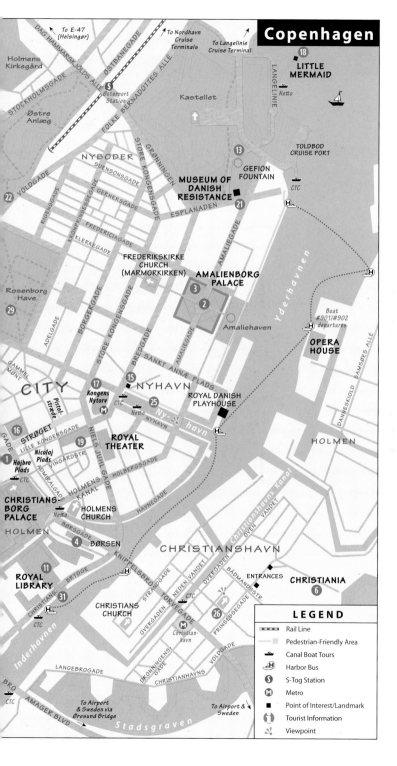

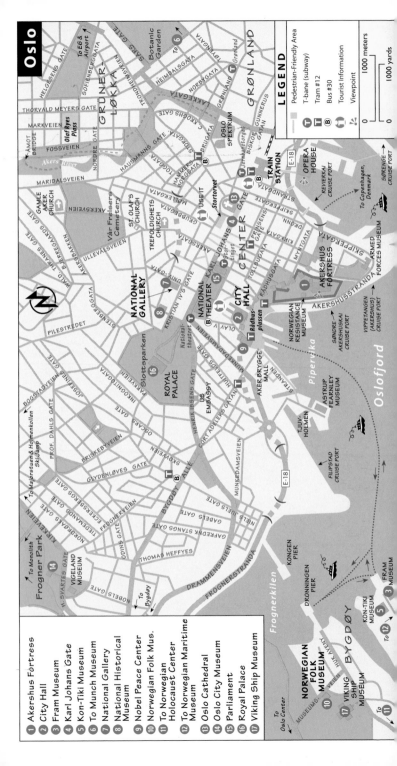

Oslo

1. Akershus Fortress
2. City Hall
3. Fram Museum
4. Karl Johans Gate
5. Kon-Tiki Museum
6. To Munch Museum
7. National Gallery
8. National Historical Museum
9. Nobel Peace Center
10. Norwegian Folk Mus.
11. To Norwegian Holocaust Center
12. To Norwegian Maritime Museum
13. Oslo Cathedral
14. Oslo City Museum
15. Parliament
16. Royal Palace
17. Viking Ship Museum

LEGEND

- Pedestrian-Friendly Area
- **T** T-bane (subway)
- **T** Tram #12
- **B** Bus #30
- ⓘ Tourist Information
- ⚲ Viewpoint

0 — 1000 meters
0 — 1000 yards

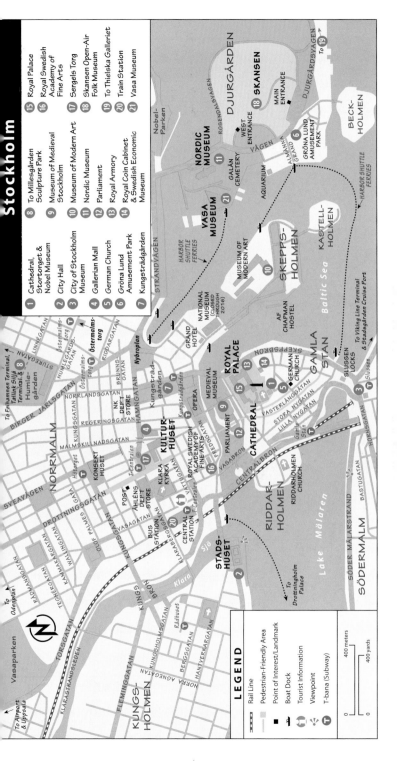

Stockholm

1. Cathedral, Stortorget & Nobel Museum
2. City Hall
3. City of Stockholm Museum
4. Gallerian Mall
5. German Church
6. Gröna Lund Amusement Park
7. Kungsträdgården
8. To Millesgården Sculpture Park
9. Museum of Medieval Stockholm
10. Museum of Modern Art
11. Nordic Museum
12. Parliament
13. Royal Armory
14. Royal Coin Cabinet & Swedish Economic Museum
15. Royal Palace
16. Royal Swedish Academy of Fine Arts
17. Sergels Torg
18. Skansen Open-Air Folk Museum
19. To Thielska Galleriet
20. Train Station
21. Vasa Museum

LEGEND

- Rail Line
- Pedestrian-Friendly Area
- ■ Point of Interest/Landmark
- Boat Dock
- Tourist Information
- Viewpoint
- T T-bana (Subway)

0   400 meters
0   400 yards

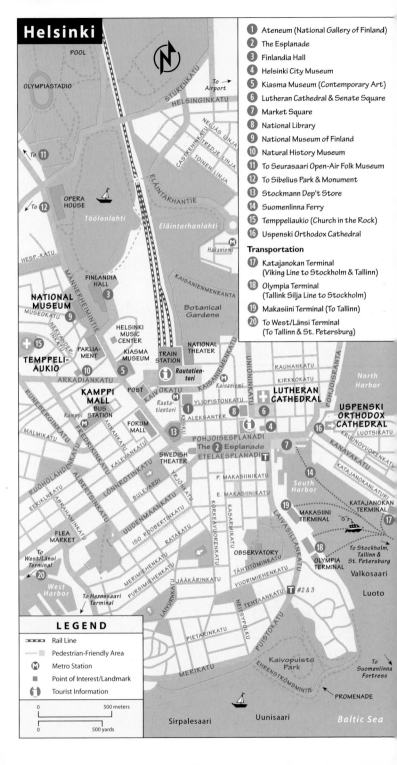

Helsinki

1 Ateneum (National Gallery of Finland)
2 The Esplanade
3 Finlandia Hall
4 Helsinki City Museum
5 Kiasma Museum (Contemporary Art)
6 Lutheran Cathedral & Senate Square
7 Market Square
8 National Library
9 National Museum of Finland
10 Natural History Museum
11 To Seurasaari Open-Air Folk Museum
12 To Sibelius Park & Monument
13 Stockmann Dep't Store
14 Suomenlinna Ferry
15 Temppeliaukio (Church in the Rock)
16 Uspenski Orthodox Cathedral

Transportation

17 Katajanokan Terminal
(Viking Line to Stockholm & Tallinn)
18 Olympia Terminal
(Tallink Silja Line to Stockholm)
19 Makasiini Terminal (To Tallinn)
20 To West/Länsi Terminal
(To Tallinn & St. Petersburg)

LEGEND

- Rail Line
- Pedestrian-Friendly Area
- M Metro Station
- Point of Interest/Landmark
- Tourist Information

0   500 meters

0   500 yards

Skansen Folk Museum, Stockholm

Copenhagen's Rosenborg Castle

Nyhavn, Copenhagen, Denmark

Join in the Viking fun

Roskilde Museum, Denmark

Gamla Stan, Stockholm, Sweden

Rick Steves'

SCANDINAVIA

AVALON
TRAVEL

Top Destinations in Scandinavia

MORE ON THE SOGNEFJORD

GUDBRANDSDAL & JOTUNHEIMEN

NORWAY IN A NUTSHELL

BERGEN

OSLO

HELSINKI

STOCKHOLM

TALLINN

SOUTH NORWAY

STOCKHOLM'S ARCHIPELAGO

SOUTHEAST SWEDEN

JUTLAND

COPENHAGEN

CENTRAL DENMARK

200 Kilometers

200 Miles

INTRODUCTION

Scandinavia—known for its stunning natural beauty, fun-loving cities, trend-setting design, progressive politics, high latitudes, and even higher taxes—is one of Europe's most enjoyable and most interesting corners. A visit here connects you with immigrant roots, modern European values, and the great outdoors like nowhere else. You'll gasp at breathtaking fjords, glide on a cruise ship among picturesque islands, and marvel at the efficiency and livability of its big cities. Yes, Scandinavia is expensive. But, delightfully, the best time to visit—summer—is also the best time to get great deals on the fancier hotels.

This book breaks Scandinavia into its top big-city, small-town, and rural attractions. It gives you all the information and opinions necessary to wring the maximum value out of your limited time and money. If you plan a month or less in Scandinavia, this book has all the information you'll need.

Experiencing the culture, people, and natural wonders of Scandinavia economically and hassle-free has been my goal throughout three decades of traveling, guiding tours, and travel writing. With this book, I pass on to you the lessons I've learned.

This book is balanced to include a comfortable mix of exciting capital cities and cozy small towns. It covers the predictable biggies and mixes in a healthy dose of Back Door intimacy. Along with seeing Tivoli Gardens, Hans Christian Andersen's house, and *The Little Mermaid,* you'll take a bike tour of a sleepy, remote Danish isle, dock at a time-passed fjord village, and wander among eerie, prehistoric monoliths in Sweden. And for an exciting Baltic side trip, I've added my vote for the most interesting city in that corner of Europe—Tallinn, Estonia.

INTRODUCTION

Map Legend

↳	Viewpoint	✈	Airport	)▭(	Tunnel
↟	Entrance	Ⓣ	T-Bana Stop		Pedestrian Zone
🛈	Tourist Info	🚋	Tram Stop		Railway
WC	Restroom	Ⓜ	Metro Stop	⋯⋯⋯	Ferry/Boat Route
🏰	Castle	Ⓑ	Bus Stop	⊢─┼─┤	Tram
⛪	Church	Ⓢ	S-Tog Station		Stairs
▪	Statue/Point of Interest	🚢	Harbor Bus	⋯⋯⋯	Walk/Tour Route
	Park	🅿	Parking	------	Trail
		)(	Mtn. Pass		

Use this legend to help you navigate the maps in this book.

The best is, of course, only my opinion. But after spending a third of my adult life exploring and researching Europe, I've developed a sixth sense for what travelers enjoy. Just thinking about the places featured in this book makes me want to belly up to a *smörgåsbord*.

About This Book

Rick Steves' Scandinavia is your smiling Swede, your Nordic navigator, and a personal tour guide in your pocket. This book is organized by destinations. Each destination is a mini-vacation on its own, filled with exciting sights, strollable neighborhoods, affordable places to stay, and memorable places to eat.

In the following chapters, you'll find these sections:

Planning Your Time suggests a schedule for how to best use your limited time.

Orientation includes specifics on public transportation, helpful hints, local tour options, easy-to-read maps, and tourist information.

Sights describes the top attractions and includes their cost and hours.

Self-Guided Walks take you through interesting neighborhoods, with a personal tour guide in hand.

Sleeping describes my favorite hotels, from good-value deals to cushy splurges.

Eating serves up a range of options, from inexpensive eateries to fancy restaurants.

Connections outlines your options for traveling to destinations by bus, train, plane, and boat. In car-friendly regions, I've also included route tips for drivers.

Country introductions give you an overview of each coun-

Key to This Book

Updates

This book is updated regularly. For the latest, visit www.rick steves.com/update. For a valuable list of reports and experiences—good and bad—from fellow travelers, check www .ricksteves.com/feedback.

Abbreviations and Times

I use the following symbols and abbreviations in this book:

Sights are rated:

▲▲▲	**Don't miss**
▲▲	**Try hard to see**
▲	**Worthwhile if you can make it**
No rating	**Worth knowing about**

Tourist information offices are abbreviated as **TI**, and bathrooms are **WCs.** To categorize accommodations, I use a **Sleep Code** (described on page 22).

Like Europe, this book uses the **24-hour clock**. It's the same through 12:00 noon, then keep going: 13:00, 14:00, and so on. For anything over 12, subtract 12 and add p.m. (14:00 is 2:00 p.m.).

When giving **opening times**, I include both peak season and off-season hours if they differ. So, if a museum is listed as "May-Oct daily 9:00-16:00," it should be open from 9 a.m. until 4 p.m. from the first day of May until the last day of October (but expect exceptions).

For **transit** or **tour departures**, I first list the frequency, then the duration. So, a train connection listed as "2/hour, 1.5 hours" departs twice each hour and the journey lasts an hour and a half.

try's culture, customs, money, history, current events, cuisine, language, and other useful practicalities.

The **Scandinavian History** chapter introduces you to some key people and events in these nations' complicated pasts, making your sightseeing that much more meaningful.

The **appendix** is a traveler's tool kit, with telephone tips, useful phone numbers, transportation basics (on trains, buses, boats, car rentals, driving, and flights), recommended books and films, a festival list, a climate chart, a handy packing checklist, a hotel reservation form, and survival phrases.

Browse through this book, choose your favorite destinations, and link them up. Then have a great trip! Traveling like a temporary local, you'll get the absolute most out of every mile, minute, and dollar. As you visit places I know and love, I'm happy that you'll be meeting some of my favorite Scandinavian people.

Planning

This section will help you get started on planning your trip—with advice on trip costs, when to go, and what you should know before you take off.

Travel Smart

Your trip to Scandinavia is like a complex play—easier to follow and really appreciate on a second viewing. While no one does the same trip twice to gain that advantage, reading this book in its entirety before your trip accomplishes much the same thing.

Design an itinerary that enables you to visit sights at the best possible times. Note holidays, festivals, specifics on sights, and days when sights are closed or most crowded (all covered in this book). To get between destinations smoothly, read the tips in this book's appendix on taking trains, buses, and boats, or renting a car and driving. A smart trip is a puzzle—a fun, doable, and worthwhile challenge.

Be sure to mix intense and relaxed periods in your itinerary. To maximize rootedness, minimize one-night stands. It's worth taking a long drive after dinner (or a train ride with a dinner picnic) to get settled in a town for two nights. Hotels are more likely to give a good price to someone staying more than one night. Every trip—and every traveler—needs slack time (laundry, picnics, people-watching, and so on). Pace yourself. Assume you will return.

Reread this book as you travel, and visit local tourist information offices (abbreviated as TI in this book). Upon arrival in a new town, lay the groundwork for a smooth departure; get the schedule for the train, bus, or boat that you'll take when you depart. Drivers can study the best route to their next destination.

Get online at Internet cafés or your hotel, and carry a mobile phone (or use a phone card) to make travel plans: You can find tourist information, learn the latest on sights (special events, tour schedule, etc.), book tickets and tours, make reservations, reconfirm hotels, research transportation connections, and keep in touch with your loved ones.

Enjoy the friendliness of the Scandinavian people. Connect with the culture. Set up your own quest for the best *kringle*, stave church, or *smörgåsbord*. Slow down and be open to unexpected experiences. Ask questions—most locals are eager to point you in their idea of the right direction. Keep a notepad in your pocket for noting directions, organizing your thoughts, and confirming prices. Wear your money belt, learn the currency, and figure out how to estimate prices in dollars. Those who expect to travel smart, do.

Budget Tips

While Scandinavia is expensive, transportation passes, groceries, alternative accommodations, and admissions are affordable (about what you'd pay in England or Italy). Being aware of your budget options will save you money.

It's fun to take advantage of midsummer hotel discounts, but keep in mind that these discounts are generally offered only by the more expensive hotels. You'll save much more by staying in hostels like the Scandinavians do (many hostels have double rooms and great breakfasts).

The breakfasts offered at your lodgings are all-you-can-eat, and so hearty that you'll need only a sandwich for lunch. If you'd prefer more of a meal, the good news is that many restaurants offer lunch specials under $20. At most restaurants, tap water is served free (except in Denmark), as are seconds on potatoes (so even if a restaurant's entrées cost $25, one entrée can easily make a complete dinner). Beer is very expensive, and wine is even more so (quench your thirst in Denmark, where alcohol isn't quite as pricey as it is farther north). Convenience and grocery stores offer a broad array of affordable to-go dishes, rescuing those shell-shocked by restaurant prices. You're never too far from a picnic-friendly park.

A Scandinavia railpass can make train travel one of your smaller expenses; bus travel is even cheaper—and sometimes faster. At sights, ask about discounted admission costs, as many aren't posted.

The great scenery is free. When things are pricey, remind yourself you're not getting less for your travel dollar. Up here there simply aren't any lousy or cheap alternatives to classy, cozy, sleek Scandinavia. Even youth-hostel toilets are flushed by electronic sensors.

This book will help you save a shipload of money and days of headaches. Read it carefully. Many of the skills and tricks that are effective in Copenhagen work in Oslo and Stockholm as well.

Trip Costs

Five components make up your trip costs: airfare, surface transportation, room and board, sightseeing and entertainment, and shopping and miscellany.

Airfare: A basic round-trip flight from the US to Copenhagen can cost $850-1,300, depending on where you fly from and when (cheaper in winter). Consider saving time and money in Scandinavia by flying into one city and out of another—for instance, into Copenhagen and out of Bergen.

Surface Transportation: For a three-week whirlwind trip of my recommended destinations, allow $650 per person for public

Scandinavia's Best
Three-Week Trip by Car

Day	Plan	Sleep in
1	Arrive in Copenhagen	Copenhagen
2	Copenhagen	Copenhagen
3	Copenhagen	Copenhagen
4	Sights near Copenhagen, into Sweden	Växjö
5	Växjö, Glass Country, Kalmar	Kalmar
6	Kalmar to Stockholm	Stockholm
7	Stockholm	Stockholm
8	Stockholm	Boat to Helsinki
9	Helsinki	Boat to Stockholm
10	Uppsala to Oslo	Oslo
11	Oslo	Oslo
12	Oslo	Oslo
13	Lillehammer, Gudbrandsdal Valley	Jotunheimen area
14	Jotunheimen Country	Lustrafjord area or Aurland
15	Sognefjord, Norway in a Nutshell	Bergen
16	Bergen	Bergen
17	Long drive south, Setesdal Valley	Kristiansand
18	Jutland, Aarhus, maybe Legoland	Aarhus (maybe Billund)
19	Jutland to Odense en route to Ærø	Ærøskøbing
20	Ærø	Ærøskøbing
21	Roskilde on the way into Copenhagen	Copenhagen

Flying into Copenhagen and out of Bergen (with a likely transfer in Copenhagen) can be wonderfully efficient; if you opt for this, you can see Jutland and Ærø sights near Copenhagen at the beginning of your trip.

transportation. This pays for a second-class Scandinavia Eurail pass (4-country, 10 days in 2 months; offers a 20-40 percent discount on Stockholm-Helsinki or Helsinki-Tallinn boat fares), and the extra boat rides that aren't discounted by the pass (such as Tallinn-Stockholm). Train passes normally must be purchased outside Europe, but aren't necessarily your best option—you may save money by simply buying tickets as you go. For more on public transportation and car rental, see "Transportation" in the appendix.

By car, figure $900 per person (based on two people sharing a car and related expenses) for a three-week car rental, tolls, fuel, and insurance; add about $180 per person for the round-trip boat fare between Stockholm and Helsinki. Ferrying to and from

Scandinavia's Best Three-Week Trip by Car

Jotunheimen

Sognefjord

Lillehammer

Aurland

SWEDEN

Åland Islands

FIN.

Bergen

NORWAY

To Helsinki & Tallinn

Oslo

LAKE COUNTRY

Uppsala

Setesdal Valley

Göta Canal

Stockholm

Söder-köping

Kristiansand

GLASS COUNTRY

Gotland

DENMARK

Växjö

Öland

North Sea

Aarhus

Kalmar

Copenhagen

Odense

Roskilde

Baltic Sea

R.U.S.

Ærø

● = Overnights
• = Other Stops

200 Kilometers

100 Miles

GERMANY

POLAND

Tallinn adds another $130. Leasing is worth considering for trips of three weeks or more. Car rentals and leases are cheapest if arranged from the US.

Consider flying. Hopping on a plane to zip from Tallinn (Estonia) to Copenhagen (Denmark) in an hour can be an excellent time-saver.

Room and Board: You can manage comfortably in Scandinavia on an average of $140 a day per person for room and board. A $140-a-day budget allows an average of $20 for lunch, $30 for dinner, and $90 for lodging (based on two people splitting the cost of a $180 double room that includes breakfast). Students and tightwads eat and sleep for $65 ($35 per hostel bed, $30 for

INTRODUCTION

groceries and snacks).

Sightseeing and Entertainment: In big cities, figure $10-20 per major sight (Oslo's Kon-Tiki Museum-$12, Copenhagen's Tivoli Gardens-$16), $5 for minor ones (climbing towers), and $25-30 for splurge experiences (such as folk concerts, bus tours, and fjord cruises). The major cities have cards giving you a 24-hour free run of the public transit system and entrance to many sights for about $50-60/day.

An overall average of $35 per day works for most people. Don't skimp here. After all, this category is the driving force behind your trip—you came to sightsee, enjoy, and experience Scandinavia.

Shopping and Miscellany: Shopping can vary in cost from nearly nothing to a small fortune. Good budget travelers find that this category has little to do with assembling a trip full of lifelong and wonderful memories.

Sightseeing Priorities

Depending on the length of your trip, and taking geographical proximity into account, here are my recommended priorities:

4 days:	Copenhagen, Stockholm (connected by a 5.5-hour express train)
6 days, add:	Oslo
8 days, add:	Norway in a Nutshell fjord trip, Bergen
10 days, add:	Overnight cruise from Stockholm to Helsinki
14 days, add:	Ærø, Odense, Roskilde, Frederiksborg (all in Denmark)
17 days, add:	Aarhus (Denmark), Kalmar (Sweden)
21 days, add:	Tallinn (Estonia) and more time in capitals
24 days, add:	More Norwegian countryside or Stockholm's archipelago

The map on page 7 and the three-week itinerary on page 6 include most of the stops in the first 21 days.

When to Go

Summer is a great time to go. Scandinavia bustles and glistens under the July and August sun; it's the height of the tourist season, when all the sightseeing attractions are open and in full swing. In many cases, things don't kick into gear until midsummer—about June 20—when Scandinavian schools let out. Most local industries take July off, and the British and southern Europeans tend to visit Scandinavia in August. You'll notice crowds during these times, but up here "crowds" mean fun and action rather than congestion. At these northern latitudes, the days are long—on June 21 the sun comes up around 4:00 in Oslo and sets around 23:00. Things really quiet down when the local kids go back to school, around August 20.

INTRODUCTION

Scandinavia's Best Three-Week Trip by Train and Boat

Day	Plan	Sleep in
1	Arrive in Copenhagen	Copenhagen
2	Copenhagen	Copenhagen
3	Copenhagen	Copenhagen
4	Roskilde, Odense, Ærø	Ærøskøbing
5	Ærø	Ærøskøbing
6	Ærø to Kalmar	Kalmar
7	Kalmar	Kalmar
8	Kalmar, early train to Stockholm	Stockholm
9	Stockholm	Stockholm
10	Stockholm, night boat to Helsinki	Boat
11	Helsinki	Helsinki
12	Helsinki, afternoon boat to Tallinn	Tallinn
13	Tallinn, night boat to Stockholm	Boat
14	Stockholm, afternoon train to Oslo	Oslo
15	Oslo	Oslo
16	Oslo	Oslo
17	Train and boat to Aurland	Aurland
18	Aurland to Bergen via fjord cruise	Bergen
19	Bergen	Bergen
20	Free day: more fjords, resting, or whatever	
21	Trip over	

If you want to see Legoland (near Billund) and the "bog man" (in Aarhus), visit these from Odense (closer) or Copenhagen. You could save lots of time by flying from Tallinn to Oslo.

"Shoulder-season" travel—in late May, early June, and September—lacks the vitality of summer but offers occasional good weather and minimal crowds. Norway in particular can be good from late May to mid-June, when the days are long but the tourist lines are short.

Winter is a bad time to explore Scandinavia unless winter sports are high on your agenda. Like a bear, Scandinavia's metabolism slows down, and many sights and accommodations are closed or open on a limited schedule (especially in remote fjord towns). Business travelers drive hotel prices way up. Winter weather can be cold and dreary. Days are short, and nighttime will draw the shades on your sightseeing well before dinner. Christmastime activities (such as colorful markets and Copenhagen's festively decorated Tivoli Gardens) offer a brief interlude of warmth at this chilly time of year.

Scandinavia at a Glance

Denmark

▲▲▲Copenhagen Vibrant Danish capital city, with *The Little Mermaid*, old-time Tivoli Gardens amusement park, excellent National Museum, Renaissance King Christian IV's Rosenborg Castle, delightful pedestrian Strøget, and eye-opening hippie enclave at Christiania.

▲Near Copenhagen Great day-trip options: West to the Viking Ship Museum and Royal Cathedral at Roskilde, and north to Frederiksborg Castle—the "Danish Versailles"—in Hillerød, the Louisiana modern-art museum in Humlebæk, the Karen Blixen Museum in Rungsted, and Kronborg Castle in Helsingør.

▲▲Central Denmark Peaceful isle of Ærø—perfect for a loop tour by bike or car—and home to Denmark's best-preserved 18th-century village—Ærøskøbing; and the busy town of Odense, with the Hans Christian Andersen Hus and the nearby Funen Village open-air folk museum.

▲Jutland Family-friendly region with Legoland kids' adventure park, and Denmark's second-largest city, Aarhus, with its stroll-able pedestrian center, ARoS art museum, and Den Gamle By open-air folk museum.

Norway

▲▲▲Oslo Norway's sharp capital city, with its historic and walk-able core, mural-lined City Hall, Vigeland sculptures at Frogner Park, and inspiring Nobel Peace Center, while the nearby Bygdøy district hosts museums dedicated to ships (Viking, *Fram*, and *Kon-Tiki*), the Holocaust, and traditional folk life.

▲▲Norway in a Nutshell A combination train, bus, and ferry trip to and through Norway's most spectacularly beautiful fjord, the Sognefjord, passing pristine waterfalls, verdant forests, and take-your-breath-away scenery.

▲More on the Sognefjord Fjordside hamlet of Balestrand, a cozy home base for exploring nearby sights (including a medieval stave church), plus the serene Lustrafjord, with more stave churches and a glacier you can walk on.

▲**Gudbrandsdal Valley and Jotunheimen Mountains** Lush green valley connecting northern and southern Norway, with touristy Lillehammer, the excellent Maihaugen Open-Air Folk Museum, and a rugged mountain range with some of this country's finest hikes and drives.

▲▲**Bergen** Salty port town and medieval capital of Norway, with lively fish market, colorful Hanseatic quarter (Bryggen), and a funicular to the top of Mount Fløyen with great views.

▲**South Norway** Harborside Stavanger—with its Norwegian Emigration Center, Petroleum Museum, and Pulpit Rock, time-passed and remote Setesdal Valley, and the resort town of Kristiansand with ferry connections to Denmark.

Sweden
▲▲▲**Stockholm** Bustling capital of Sweden, with its charming island core of Gamla Stan, Europe's original—and unsurpassed—Skansen open-air folk museum, the *Vasa* museum (17th-century warship), and the Nordic Museum's look at five centuries of Swedish lifestyles.

▲**Stockholm's Archipelago** Sweden's rocky garden of more than 30,000 islands, best seen on a boat trip from Stockholm.

▲**Southeast Sweden** Växjö, with a first-rate emigration museum and the Smålands Museum of glass-making; Kalmar, with its massive 12th-century Kalmar Castle and nearby holiday island of Öland; and the touristy "Kingdom of Crystal" Glass Country.

Finland
▲▲**Helsinki** Finland's capital city—an architectural delight for its Neoclassical and Art Nouveau buildings and churches—with the stirring "Chapel in the Rock," fine National Museum of Finland, and island fortress and open-air folk museum.

Estonia
▲▲**Tallinn** Russian-influenced, full-of-life capital of Estonia, with quaint Old Town center, remarkably intact medieval walls, and stirringly patriotic sights (Estonian art museum and the historic Song Festival Grounds).

INTRODUCTION

Know Before You Go

Your trip is more likely to go smoothly if you plan ahead. Check this list of things to arrange while you're still at home.

You need a **passport**—but no visa or shots—to travel in Scandinavia. You may be denied entry into certain European countries if your passport is due to expire within three to six months of your ticketed date of return. Get it renewed if you'll be cutting it close. It can take up to six weeks to get or renew a passport (for more on passports, see www.travel.state.gov). Pack a photocopy of your passport in your luggage in case the original is lost or stolen.

Book rooms well in advance if you'll be traveling during peak season (July and August) or any major holidays (see page 681). Try to schedule visits to the capitals outside of convention season, when hotels can be hard to find.

Call your **debit- and credit-card companies** to let them know the countries you'll be visiting, to ask about fees, request your PIN code (it will be mailed to you), and more. See page 16 for details.

Do your homework if you want to buy **travel insurance.** Compare the cost of the insurance to the likelihood of your using it and your potential loss if something goes wrong. Also, check whether your existing insurance (health, homeowners, or renters) covers you and your possessions overseas. For more tips, see www .ricksteves.com/insurance.

Consider buying a **railpass** after researching your options (see page 669 and www.ricksteves.com/rail for specifics).

If you plan to take an **overnight boat** between major Scandinavian cities in summer or on weekends, book it in advance (Copenhagen to Oslo, page 133; Stockholm to Helsinki, page 552; Stockholm to Tallinn, page 602). If you're doing the Norway in a Nutshell in July or August, make reservations for the Oslo-Bergen train (see page 296).

If you're planning on **renting a car** in Scandinavia, bring your US driver's license. An International Driving Permit is recommended, though not required (see page 671).

Border crossings between Norway, Sweden, Denmark, Finland, and Estonia are a wave-through (there are typically no border formalities at all). When you change countries, you change money (except between Finland and Estonia, which both use the euro), phone cards, and postage stamps.

If you plan to hire a **local guide,** reserve ahead by email. Popular guides can get booked up.

If you're bringing a **mobile device,** download any apps you might want to use on the road, such as translators, maps, and transit schedules. Check out **Rick Steves Audio Europe,** featuring hours of travel interviews and other audio content about Scandinavia (via www.ricksteves.com/audioeurope, iTunes, Google Play, or the

Rick Steves Audio Europe free smartphone app; for details, see page 678).

Check the **Rick Steves guidebook updates** page for any recent changes to this book (www.ricksteves.com/update).

Because **airline carry-on restrictions** are always changing, visit the Transportation Security Administration's website (www .tsa.gov) for an up-to-date list of what you can bring on the plane with you...and what you must check.

Practicalities

Emergency Telephone Numbers: In all the countries in this book, dial 112 for medical or other emergencies. If you get sick, go to a pharmacist for advice. Or ask at your hotel for help; they know of the nearest medical and emergency services.

For police, dial 112 in Denmark, Norway, Finland, and Sweden—but in Estonia, dial 110.

Theft or Loss: To replace a passport, you'll need to go in person to an embassy (see page 664). If your credit and debit cards disappear, cancel and replace them (see "Damage Control for Lost Cards" on page 17). File a police report, either on the spot or within a day or two; you'll need it to submit an insurance claim for lost or stolen railpasses or travel gear, and it can help with replacing your passport or credit and debit cards. For more information, see www.ricksteves.com/help. Precautionary measures can minimize the effects of loss—back up photos and other files frequently.

Time Zones: Norway, Sweden, and Denmark, which share the same time zone as continental Europe, are generally six/nine hours ahead of the East/West Coasts of the US. Finland and Estonia are one hour ahead of Norway, Sweden, and Denmark. The exceptions are the beginning and end of Daylight Saving Time: Europe "springs forward" the last Sunday in March (two weeks after most of North America) and "falls back" the last Sunday in October (one week before North America). For a handy online time converter, try www.timeanddate.com/worldclock.

Business Hours: Banks are generally open weekdays from 9:00 to 15:00 or 16:00, with retail shops open an hour or two later. Saturdays are virtually weekdays, with earlier closing hours and no rush hour. Sundays have the same pros and cons as they do for travelers in the US: Sightseeing attractions are generally open, while shops and banks are closed, public transportation options are fewer (for example, no bus service to or from the smaller towns), and there's no rush hour. Rowdy evenings are rare on Sundays. Many museums in Scandinavia are closed on Mondays.

Watt's Up? Europe's electrical system is 220 volts, instead of North America's 110 volts. Most newer electronics (such as laptops, battery chargers, and hair dryers) convert automatically, so you won't need a converter plug, but you will need an adapter plug with two round prongs, sold inexpensively at travel stores in the US. Avoid bringing older appliances that don't automatically convert voltage; instead, buy a cheap replacement in Europe.

Discounts: While discounts are generally not listed in this book, note that liberal Scandinavia is Europe's most generous corner when it comes to youths (under 18), students (with International Student Identity Cards, www.isic.org), seniors, and families. Children usually sleep and sightsee for half-price or free.

Money

This section offers advice on how to pay for purchases on your trip (including getting cash from ATMs and paying with plastic), dealing with lost or stolen cards, VAT (sales tax) refunds, and tipping.

What to Bring

Bring both a credit card and a debit card. You'll use the debit card at cash machines (ATMs) to withdraw local cash for most purchases, and the credit card to pay for larger items. Some travelers carry a third card, in case one gets demagnetized or eaten by a temperamental machine.

For an emergency stash, bring several hundred dollars in hard cash in easy-to-exchange $20 bills.

Because Scandinavian countries have different currencies, you'll likely wind up with leftover cash when you're leaving a country. Coins can't be exchanged once you leave the country, so try to spend them before you cross the border. But bills are easy to convert to the "new" country's currency. When changing cash, use exchange bureaus rather than banks. The Forex desks (easy to find at major train stations and airports) are considered reliable and fair.

Cash

Cash is just as desirable in Europe as it is at home. Small businesses (hotels, restaurants, shops, etc.) prefer that you pay your bills with cash. Some vendors will charge you extra for using a credit card, and some won't take credit cards at all. Cash is the best—and sometimes only—way to pay for bus fare, taxis, and local guides.

Throughout Europe, ATMs are the standard way for travelers to get cash. To withdraw money from an ATM, you'll need a debit card (ideally with a Visa or MasterCard logo for maximum usabil-

Exchange Rates

I've priced things in local currencies throughout the book. Here are the rough exchange rates for each country. (Check www.oanda.com for the latest rates.)

$1 equals about...
6 Danish kroner (1 krone equals about $0.17)
6 Norwegian kroner (1 krone equals about $0.17)
7 Swedish kronor (1 krona equals about $0.15)
0.77 euro in Finland and Estonia (€1 equals about $1.30)

Kroner are decimalized: 100 øre = 1 krone. Kroner from one Scandinavian country are not accepted in the next (except at foreign-exchange bureaus and banks, and then only bills). Standard abbreviations are Danish krone, DKK; Swedish krona, SEK; and Norwegian kroner, NOK. I'll keep it simple. For all three countries, I'll use the krone abbreviation "kr." Finland and Estonia's currency is the euro (€).

To roughly convert Danish and Norwegian prices into US dollars, multiply by two, then drop a zero (e.g., 15 kr = about $3, 100 kr = about $20). In Sweden, divide prices by 6 (100 kr = about $16). So, that 250-kr Norwegian sweater is about $50, and your 360-kr dinner in Stockholm is about $60. To roughly convert prices in euros to dollars, add 30 percent (€20 = about $26).

ity), plus a PIN code. Know your PIN code in numbers; there are only numbers—no letters—on European keypads. For security, it's best to shield the keypad when entering your PIN at an ATM. Although you can use a credit card for ATM transactions, it's generally more expensive (and only makes sense in an emergency) because it's considered a cash advance rather than a withdrawal. Try to withdraw large sums of money to reduce the number of per-transaction bank fees you'll pay.

Pickpockets target tourists. To safeguard your cash, use a money belt—a pouch with a strap that you buckle around your waist like a belt and tuck under your clothes. Keep your cash, credit cards, and passport secure in your money belt, and carry only a day's spending money in your front pocket.

Credit and Debit Cards

For purchases, Visa and MasterCard are more commonly accepted than American Express. Just like at home, credit or debit cards work easily at larger hotels, restaurants, and shops. I typically use my debit card to withdraw cash to pay for most purchases. I use my credit card only in a few specific situations: to book hotel reservations by phone, to cover major expenses (such as car rentals, plane tickets, and long hotel stays), and to pay for things near the end of my trip (to avoid another visit to the ATM). While you could use a debit card to make most large purchases, using a credit card offers a greater degree of fraud protection (because debit cards draw funds directly from your account).

Ask Your Credit- or Debit-Card Company: Before your trip, contact the company that issued your debit or credit cards.

• Confirm that your card will work overseas, and alert them that you'll be using it in Europe; otherwise, they may deny transactions if they perceive unusual spending patterns.

• Ask for the specifics on transaction **fees.** When you use your credit or debit card—either for purchases or ATM withdrawals—you'll often be charged additional "international transaction" fees of up to 3 percent (1 percent is normal) plus $5 per transaction. If your card's fees seem too high, consider getting a different card just for your trip: Capital One (www.capitalone.com) and most credit unions have low-to-no international fees.

• If you plan to withdraw cash from ATMs, confirm your daily **withdrawal limit,** and if necessary, ask your bank to adjust it. Some travelers prefer a high limit that allows them to take out more cash at each ATM stop (saving on bank fees), while others prefer to set a lower limit in case their card is stolen. Note that foreign banks also set maximum withdrawal amounts for their ATMs.

• Get your bank's emergency **phone number** in the US (but not its 800 number, which isn't accessible from overseas) to call collect if you have a problem.

• Ask for your credit card's **PIN** in case you need to make an emergency cash withdrawal or encounter Europe's "chip-and-PIN" system; the bank won't tell you your PIN over the phone, so allow time for it to be mailed to you.

Chip and PIN: If your card is declined for a purchase in Europe, it may be because Europeans are increasingly using chip-and-PIN cards, which are embedded with an electronic chip (rather than the magnetic stripe used on our American-style cards). Much of Europe, including Scandinavia, is adopting this system, and some merchants rely on it exclusively. You're most likely to encounter chip-and-PIN problems at automated payment machines, such as those at train and subway stations, toll roads, parking garages, luggage lockers, and self-serve gas pumps. If a machine won't take your card, find a cashier who can make your card work (they can print a receipt for you to sign), or find a machine that takes cash.

But don't panic. Most travelers who are carrying only magnetic-stripe cards never encounter any problems. Still, it pays to carry plenty of cash (you can always use an ATM with your magnetic-stripe debit card). Memorizing the PIN lets you use it at some chip-and-PIN machines—just enter your PIN when prompted.

If you're still concerned, you can apply for a chip card in the US (though I think it's overkill). While big US banks offer these cards with high annual fees, a better option is the no-annual-fee GlobeTrek Visa, offered by Andrews Federal Credit Union in Maryland (open to all US residents; see www.andrewsfcu.org).

Dynamic Currency Conversion: If merchants offer to convert your purchase price into dollars (called dynamic currency conversion, or DCC), refuse this "service." You'll pay even more in fees for the expensive convenience of seeing your charge in dollars.

Damage Control for Lost Cards

If you lose your credit, debit, or ATM card, you can stop people from using it by reporting the loss immediately to the respective global customer-assistance centers. Call these 24-hour US numbers collect: Visa (tel. 303/967-1096), MasterCard (tel. 636/722-7111), and American Express (tel. 336/393-1111). European toll-free numbers (listed by country) can be found at the websites for Visa and Mastercard.

At a minimum, you'll need to know the name of the financial institution that issued you the card, along with the type of card (classic, platinum, or whatever). Providing the following information will allow for a quicker cancellation of your missing card: full card number, whether you are the primary or secondary cardholder, the cardholder's name exactly as printed on the card, billing address, home phone number, circumstances of the loss or theft, and identification verification (your birth date, your mother's maiden name, or your Social Security number—memorize this, don't carry a copy). If you are the secondary cardholder, you'll also need to provide the primary cardholder's identification-verification details. You can generally receive a temporary card within two or three business days in Europe (see www.ricksteves.com/help for more).

If you report your loss within two days, you typically won't be responsible for any unauthorized transactions on your account, although many banks charge a liability fee of $50.

Tipping

Tipping in Europe isn't as automatic and generous as it is in the US—and Scandinavia is one part of Europe where tips are less common. But for special service, tips are appreciated, if not expected. As in the US, the proper amount depends on your resources, tipping philosophy, and the circumstances, but some general guidelines apply.

Restaurants: Tipping is an issue only at restaurants that have table service. If you order your food at a counter, don't tip.

Throughout Scandinavia, a service charge is typically included in your bill, and you aren't required to leave an additional tip. But don't assume that the service charge goes to your server— often it goes right to the restaurant owner. In fancier restaurants or whenever you enjoy great service, round up the bill (about 5-10 percent of the total check). Rounding up for good service is especially common in Estonia (though never more than 10 percent).

Taxis: To tip the cabbie, round up. For a typical ride, round up your fare a bit (for instance, if the fare is 85 kr, pay 90 kr). If the cabbie hauls your bags and zips you to the airport to help you catch your flight, you might want to toss in a little more. But if you feel like you're being driven in circles or otherwise ripped off, skip the tip.

Special Services: In general, if someone in the service industry does a super job for you, a small tip (the equivalent of a euro or two) is appropriate...but not required. If you're not sure whether (or how much) to tip for a service, ask your hotelier or the TI.

Getting a VAT Refund

Wrapped into the purchase price of your Scandinavian souvenirs is a Value-Added Tax (VAT) of 20-25 percent (among the highest rates in Europe). You're entitled to get most of that tax back if you make a purchase of a certain amount (300 kr in Denmark, 315 kr in Norway, 200 kr in Sweden, €40 in Finland, and €38 in Estonia) at a store that participates in the VAT refund scheme (look for signs in store windows—VAT is called MVA in Norway and MOMS in Denmark, Finland, and Sweden). Typically, you must ring up the minimum at a single retailer—you can't add up your purchases from various shops to reach the required amount.

Getting your refund is usually straightforward and, if you buy a substantial amount of souvenirs, well worth the hassle. If you're lucky, the merchant will subtract the tax when you make your purchase. (This is more likely to occur if the store ships the goods to your home.) Otherwise, you'll need to:

Get the paperwork. Have the merchant completely fill out the necessary refund document. You'll have to present your passport. Get the paperwork done before you leave the store to ensure you'll have everything you need (including your original sales receipt).

Get your stamp at the border or airport. If you've made purchases in Denmark, Sweden, Finland, and/or Estonia, process your VAT document at your last stop in the European Union by the customs agent who deals with VAT refunds. If you've shopped hard in Norway (a non-EU country), get your document(s) stamped at the border or at your point of departure from Norway.

Before checking in for your flight, find the local customs office, and be prepared to stand in line. Keep your purchases readily available for viewing by the customs agent (ideally in your carry-on bag—don't make the mistake of checking the bag with your purchases before you've seen the agent). You're not supposed to use your purchased goods before you leave. If you show up at customs wearing your new Norwegian sweater, officials might look the other way—or deny you a refund.

Collect your refund. You'll need to return your stamped document to the retailer or its representative. Many merchants work with a service, such as Global Blue or Premier Tax Free, that has offices at major airports, ports, or border crossings (either before or after security, probably strategically located near a duty-free shop). These services, which extract a 4 percent fee, can usually refund your money immediately in cash, or credit your card (within two billing cycles). If the retailer handles VAT refunds directly, it's up to you to contact the merchant for your refund. You can mail the documents from home, or more quickly, from your point of departure (using an envelope you've prepared in advance or one that's been provided by the merchant). You'll then have to wait—it could take months.

Customs for American Shoppers

You are allowed to take home $800 worth of items per person duty-free, once every 30 days. You can also bring in duty-free a liter of alcohol. As for food, you can take home many processed and packaged foods: vacuum-packed cheeses, dried herbs, jams, baked goods, candy, chocolate, oil, vinegar, mustard, and honey. Fresh fruits and vegetables and most meats are not allowed. Any liquid-containing foods must be packed in checked luggage, a potential recipe for disaster. To check customs rules and duty rates, visit www.cbp.gov.

Sightseeing

Sightseeing can be hard work. Use these tips to make your visits to Scandinavia's finest sights meaningful, fun, efficient, and painless.

Plan Ahead

Set up an itinerary that allows you to fit in all your must-see sights. For a one-stop look at opening hours in the bigger cities, see this book's "At a Glance" sidebars for Copenhagen, Oslo, Stockholm, Helsinki, and Tallinn. Most sights keep stable hours, but you can easily confirm the latest by checking with the TI or visiting museum websites.

Don't put off visiting a must-see sight—you never know when a place will close unexpectedly for a holiday, strike, or restoration. On holidays (see list on page 681), expect reduced hours or closures. In summer, some sights may stay open late. Off-season, many museums have shorter hours.

Going at the right time helps avoid crowds. This book offers tips on the best times to see specific sights. Try visiting popular sights very early or very late. Evening visits are usually peaceful, with fewer crowds. When possible, visit the major sights in the morning (when your energy is best), and save other activities for the afternoon. At sights, hit the highlights first, then go back to other things if you have the time and stamina.

Study up. To get the most out of the sight descriptions in this book, read them before your visit.

At Sights

Here's what you can typically expect:

Some important sights require you to check daypacks and coats. To avoid checking a small backpack, carry it under your arm like a purse as you enter. From a guard's point of view, a backpack is generally a problem, while a purse is not.

Flash photography is often banned, but taking photos without a flash is usually allowed. Flashes damage oil paintings and distract others in the room. Even without a flash, a handheld camera will take a decent picture (or buy postcards or posters at the museum bookstore).

Museums may have special exhibits in addition to their permanent collection. Some exhibits are included in the entry price, while others come at an extra cost (which you may have to pay even if you don't want to see the exhibit).

Expect changes—artwork can be on tour, on loan, out sick, or shifted at the whim of the curator. To adapt, pick up any available free floor plans as you enter, and ask museum staff if you can't find a particular item.

Many sights rent audioguides, which generally offer excellent recorded descriptions in English (about $8). If you bring your own earbuds, you can enjoy better sound and avoid holding the device to your ear. To save money, bring a Y-jack and share one audioguide with your travel partner.

Important sights may have an on-site café or cafeteria (usually a handy place to rejuvenate during a long visit). The WCs at sights are free and nearly always clean.

Many places sell postcards that highlight their attractions. Before you leave a sight, scan the postcards and thumb through the biggest guidebook (or skim its index) to be sure you haven't overlooked something that you'd like to see.

Most sights stop admitting people 30 to 60 minutes before closing time, and some rooms may close early (often about 45 minutes before the actual closing time). Guards usher people out, so don't save the best for last.

Every sight or museum offers more than what is covered in this book. Use the information in this book as an introduction—not the final word.

Sleeping

Accommodations in Scandinavia are fairly expensive, but normally very comfortable and come with breakfast. When budgeting, plan on spending about $180 per hotel double in big cities, and $100 in towns and in private homes.

I favor accommodations and restaurants that are handy to your sightseeing activities. Rather than list hotels scattered throughout a city, I choose two or three favorite neighborhoods and recommend the best accommodation values in each, from dorm beds to fancy doubles with all the comforts.

A major feature of this book is its extensive listing of good-value rooms. I like places that are clean, central, relatively quiet at night, reasonably priced, friendly, small enough to have a hands-on owner and stable staff, run with a respect for Scandinavian traditions, and not listed in other guidebooks. (In Scandinavia, for me, six out of these eight criteria means it's a keeper.) I'm more impressed by a convenient location and a fun-loving philosophy than flat-screen TVs and shoeshine machines. I've also thrown in a few hostels, private rooms, and other cheap options for budget travelers.

Book your accommodations well in advance if you'll be traveling during busy times. See page 681 for a list of major holidays and festivals in Scandinavia; for tips on making reservations, see page 24.

To get the most sleep for your dollar at these northern latitudes, pull the dark shades (and even consider bringing your own night shades) to keep out the early-morning sun.

Rates and Deals

I've described my recommended accommodations using a Sleep Code (see the sidebar). Prices listed are for one-night stays in peak

Sleep Code

Price Rankings

To help you easily sort through my hotel listings, I've divided the accommodations into three categories based on the price for a standard double room with bath during high season:

$$$ **Higher Priced**
$$ **Moderately Priced**
$ **Lower Priced**

Prices can change without notice; verify the hotel's current rates online or by email.

Abbreviations

To pack maximum information into minimum space, I use the following code to describe accommodations in this book. Prices listed are per room, not per person. When a price range is given for a type of room (such as double rooms listed for 1,050-1,250 kr), it means the price fluctuates with the season, size of room, or length of stay; expect to pay the upper end for peak-season stays.

- **S** = Single room (or price for one person in a double).
- **D** = Double or twin room. Double beds (which can be two twins sheeted together) are usually big enough for nonromantic couples.
- **T** = Triple (generally a double bed with a single bed moved in).
- **Q** = Quad (usually two double beds; adding an extra child's bed to a T is usually cheaper).
- **b** = Private bathroom with toilet and shower or tub.
- **s** = Private shower or tub only (the toilet is down the hall).

According to this code, a couple staying at a "Db-1,050 kr" hotel in Sweden would pay a total of 1,050 kr (about $175) for a double room with a private bathroom. Unless otherwise noted, breakfast is included, hotel staff speak English, and credit cards are accepted.

There's almost always Wi-Fi and/or Internet access available, either free or for a fee. "Wi-Fi only" means there's no public computer available.

season, include breakfast, and assume you're booking directly (not through a TI or online hotel-booking engine). Using an online booking service costs the hotel about 20 percent and logically closes the door on special deals. Book direct.

Most Scandinavian business hotels use "dynamic pricing," which means they change the room rate depending on demand—just like airlines change their fares. This makes it extremely difficult to predict what you will pay. For many hotels, I list a range of prices. If the rate you're offered is at or near the bottom of my printed range, it's likely a good deal. Check several hotel websites to see what they're offering, or email establishments that don't have an online reservation system and ask for their best prices. Comparison-shop and make your choice.

As you look over the listings, you'll notice that some accommodations promise special prices to my readers who book directly with the hotel or proprietor. To get these rates, you must mention this book when you reserve, and then show the book upon arrival. Rick Steves discounts apply to readers with ebooks as well as printed books. Discounts may not apply to promotional rates.

In general, prices can soften if you do any of the following: offer to pay cash, stay at least three nights, or mention this book. You can also try asking for a cheaper room or a discount, or offer to skip breakfast.

Many places keep an odd misfit room (100 kr cheaper than the others) lashed to a bedpost in the attic, but will only tell you if you ask. Backpacker places have a range of rooms, blurring the distinction between "hotel" and "hostel." Money-conscious travelers should consider doubles in hostels and rooms in simple hotels with shared baths—a respectable option in clean and wholesome Scandinavia.

A triple is much cheaper than a double and a single. While hotel singles are most expensive, private accommodations have a flat per-person rate. Hostels and dorms always charge per person. Families can get a price break; normally a child can sleep free or for very little in the parents' room.

Types of Accommodations
Hotels
Hotels are expensive ($150-250 doubles), with some exceptions. Business-class hotels often drop prices to attract tourists with sum-

mer rates (late June-early Aug) and weekend rates (Fri, Sat, and sometimes Sun). You need to ask about these—receptionists don't volunteer the information. When a classy, modern $200 place has a $150 summer special that includes two $10 buffet breakfasts, the dumpy $100 hotel room without breakfast becomes less exciting.

Many modern hotels have "combi" rooms (singles with a sofa that turns the room into a perfectly good double), which are cheaper than a full double. And if a hotel is not full, any day can

Making Hotel Reservations

Given the good value of the accommodations I've found for this book, I'd recommend that you reserve your rooms several weeks in advance—or as soon as you've pinned down your travel dates—particularly if you'll be traveling during peak times (especially in the capitals during conventions). Note that some national holidays jam things up and merit your making reservations far in advance (see the "Holidays and Festivals" on page 681).

Requesting a Reservation: It's usually easiest to book your room through the hotel's website; many have a reservation-request form built right in. (For the best rates, be sure to use the hotel's official site and not a booking agency's site.) Just type in your preferred dates and the website will automatically display a list of available rooms and prices. Simpler websites will generate an email to the hotelier with your request. If there's no reservation form, or for complicated requests, send an email. Other options include calling (see "Phoning" next page, and be mindful of time zones) or faxing.

The hotelier wants to know these key pieces of information (also included in the sample request form in the appendix):

- number and type of rooms
- number of nights
- date of arrival
- date of departure
- any special needs (such as bathroom in the room or down the hall, twin beds vs. double bed, air-conditioning, quiet, view, ground floor, etc.)

When you request a room, use the European style for writing dates: day/month/year. For example, for a two-night stay in July of 2014, I would request: "1 double room for 2 nights, arrive 16/07/2014, depart 18/07/2014." Consider in advance how long you'll stay; don't just assume you can tack on extra days once you arrive. Make sure you mention any discounts—for Rick Steves readers or otherwise—when you make the reservation.

If you don't get a response to your email, it usually means the hotel is already fully booked—but try sending the message again or call to follow up.

Confirming a Reservation: Most places will request your credit-card number to hold the room. To confirm a room using a hotel's secure online reservation form, enter your contact information and credit-card number; the hotel will email a confirmation.

If you sent an email to request a reservation, the hotel will reply with its room availability and rates. This is not a confirmation. You must email back to say that you want the room at the given rate. While you can email your credit-card information (I do), it's safer to share that confidential info via phone call, two emails (splitting your number between them), or the hotel's secure online reservation form.

Canceling a Reservation: If you must cancel your reservation, it's courteous to do so with as much advance notice as possible. Simply make a quick phone call or send an email. Family-run places lose money if they turn away customers while holding a room for someone who doesn't show up. Understandably, many hoteliers bill no-shows for one night.

Cancellation policies can be strict: For example, you might lose a deposit if you cancel within two weeks of your reserved stay, or you might be billed for the entire visit if you leave early. Internet deals may require prepayment, with no refunds for cancellations. Ask about cancellation policies before you book.

If canceling via email, request confirmation that your cancellation was received to avoid being accidentally billed.

Reconfirming a Reservation: Always call to reconfirm your room reservation a few days in advance. Smaller hotels and B&Bs appreciate knowing your estimated time of arrival. If you'll be arriving late (after 17:00), let them know. On the small chance that a hotel loses track of your reservation, bring along a hard copy of their confirmation.

Reserving Rooms as You Travel: You can make reservations as you travel, calling hotels a few days to a week before your arrival. If everything's full, don't despair. Call a day or two in advance and fill in a cancellation. If you prefer the flexibility of traveling without any reservations at all, you'll have greater success snaring rooms if you arrive at your destination early in the day. When you anticipate crowds (weekends are worst), call hotels at about 9:00 or 10:00 on the day you plan to arrive, when the receptionist knows who'll be checking out and just which rooms will be available.

Phoning: To make international calls to Scandinavia to line up hotel reservations, you'll need to know the country codes. For detailed instructions on telephoning, see page 657.

bring out summer discounts.

If you're arriving early in the morning, your room probably won't be ready. You can safely drop your bag at the hotel and dive right into sightseeing.

Hoteliers can be a great help and source of advice. Most know their city well, and can assist you with everything from public transit and airport connections to finding a good restaurant, the nearest launderette, or an Internet café.

Even at the best places, mechanical breakdowns occur: Air-conditioning malfunctions, sinks leak, hot water turns cold, and toilets gurgle and smell. Report your concerns clearly and calmly at the front desk. For more complicated problems, don't expect instant results.

If you suspect night noise will be a problem (if, for instance, your room is over a nightclub), ask for a quieter room in the back or on an upper floor. To guard against theft in your room, keep valuables out of sight. Some rooms come with a safe, and other hotels have safes at the front desk. I've never bothered using one.

Checkout can pose problems if surprise charges pop up on your bill. If you settle up your bill the afternoon before you leave, you'll have time to discuss and address any points of contention (before 19:00, when the night shift usually arrives).

Above all, don't expect things to be the same as back home. Keep a positive attitude. Remember, you're on vacation. If your hotel is a disappointment, spend more time out enjoying the city you came to see.

Private Rooms
Throughout Scandinavia, people rent rooms in their homes to travelers for about $85 per double (or about $95 for a double with private bath). While some put out a *Værelse, Rom, Rum,* or *Hus Rum* sign, many operate solely through the local TI (which occasionally keeps these B&Bs a secret until all hotel rooms are taken). You'll get your own key to a clean, comfortable, but usually simple private room (sometimes without a sink), with access to the family shower and WC if the room doesn't have its own bath. When possible, I've listed direct contact information for B&Bs—booking direct saves both you and your host the cut the TI takes. The TIs are very protective of their lists. If you enjoy a big-city private home that would like to be listed in this book, I'd love to hear from you.

Hostels
Scandinavian hostels, Europe's finest, are open to travelers of all ages. They offer classy facilities, members' kitchens (making your own meals is a great way to save money), cheap hot meals

(often breakfast buffets), plenty of doubles (for a few extra kroner), Internet access, Wi-Fi, self-service laundries, and great people experiences. Nowadays, concerned about bedbugs, hostels are likely to provide all bedding, including sheets. Family and private rooms may be available on request. Hostels are also a tremendous source of local and budget travel information. Note that many hostels close in the off-season.

You'll find lots of Volvos in hostel parking lots, as Scandinavians know that hostels provide the best (and usually only) $35 beds in town. Hosteling is ideal for families who fit into two sets of bunk beds (4-bed rooms, kitchens, washing machines, discount family memberships). Pick up each country's free hostel directory at any hostel or TI.

Independent hostels tend to be easygoing, colorful, and informal (no membership required); see www.hostelz.com, www.hosteleurope.com, www.hostels.com, and www.hostelbookers.com. **Official hostels** are part of Hostelling International (HI) and share an online booking site (www.hihostels.com). HI hostels typically require that you either have a membership card or pay extra per night. Many hostels in Norway regularly promote nonmember prices—if you have a membership card, be sure to ask about a discount.

Camping

Scandinavian campgrounds are practical, comfortable, and cheap (about $10/person with $20 camping card, available on the spot). This is the middle-class Scandinavian family way to travel: safe, great social fun, and no reservation problems. Campgrounds are friendly, safe, more central and convenient than rustic, and rarely full.

The national tourist office websites have campground listings, but for more comprehensive guides, visit these websites: www.camping.se (Sweden), www.camping.dk (Denmark), and www.camping.no (Norway). Your hometown travel bookstore should also have guidebooks on camping in Europe. You'll find campgrounds just about everywhere you need them.

Most campgrounds provide **huts** *(hytter)* for wannabe camp-

ers with no gear. Huts normally sleep four to six in bunk beds, come with blankets and a kitchenette, and charge one fee (about 500 kr, plus extra if you need sheets). The toilet and shower may be in a nearby shared washhouse. Because locals typically move in for a week or two, many campground huts are booked for summer long in advance. You can book these ahead as well, or try your chances on the road.

Eating

When restaurant-hunting, choose a spot filled with locals, not tourists. Venturing even a block or two off the main drag leads to higher-quality food for less than half the price of the tourist-oriented places. Locals eat better at lower-rent locales.

Most Scandinavian nations have one inedible dish that is cherished with a perverse but patriotic sentimentality. These dishes, which often originated during a famine, now remind the young of their ancestors' suffering. Norway's penitential food, lutefisk (dried cod marinated for days in lye and water), is used for Christmas and for jokes.

Breakfast

Hotel breakfasts are a huge and filling buffet, generally included but occasionally a $12-or-so option. They feature fruit, cereal, and various milks (look for words like *skummet* for skim, *lett* for low-fat, *sød* or *hel* for whole, *filmjölk* for buttermilk). Grab a drinkable yogurt and go local by pouring it in the bowl and sprinkling your

cereal over it. The great selection of breads and crackers comes with jam, butter *(smør)*, margarine (same word), and cheese *(ost)*. And you'll get cold cuts, pickled herring, caviar paste (in a squeeze tube), and boiled eggs *(æg—bløt* is soft-boiled, *kokt* is hard-boiled); use the plastic egg cups and small spoons provided to eat your soft-boiled egg Scandinavian-style.

The brown cheese with the texture of earwax and a slightly sweet taste is called *geitost* ("goat cheese") or *brunost* ("brown cheese"). Popular in Norway, it's not really a cheese—it's made from boiled-down, slightly sweetened whey—and it's more often made from cow's milk. Try to develop a taste for this odd but enjoyable dairy product. Swedes prefer a spreadable variety called *messmör*.

For beverages, it's orange juice (the word for orange is *appelsin*, so OJ is AJ) and coffee or tea. Coffee addicts can buy a thermos and get it filled in most hotels and hostels for around $5. While it's bad form to take freebies from the breakfast buffet to eat later, many hotels will provide you with wax paper and a plastic bag to pack yourself a lunch, legitimately, for $7-8. Ask for a *matpakke* (packed lunch).

If you skip your hotel's breakfast, you can visit a bakery to get a sandwich and cup of coffee. Bakeries have wonderful inexpensive pastries. The only cheap breakfast is the one you make yourself. Many simple accommodations provide kitchenettes or at least coffeepots.

Lunch

Many restaurants offer cheap daily lunch specials *(dagens rett)* and buffets for office workers. Scandinavians, not big on lunch, often

just grab a sandwich *(smørrebrød)* and a cup of coffee at their work desk.

Especially in Denmark, you'll find *smørrebrød* shops turning sandwiches into an art form. These open-face delights taste as good as they look. My favorite is the one piled high with *rejer*

(shrimp). The roast beef is good, too. Shops will wrap sandwiches up for a perfect picnic in a nearby park.

If you want to enjoy a combination of picnics and restaurant meals on your trip, you'll save money by eating in restaurants at lunch (when there's usually a special and food is generally cheaper) and picnicking for dinner.

Picnics

Scandinavia has colorful markets and economical supermarkets. Picnic-friendly mini-markets at gas and train stations are open late. Samples of picnic treats: *Wasa* cracker bread (Sport is my

INTRODUCTION

favorite; Ideal *flatbrød* is ideal for munchies), packaged meat and cheese, brown "goat cheese" *(geitost),* drinkable yogurt, freshly cooked or smoked fish from markets, fresh fruit and vegetables, lingonberries, squeeze tubes of mustard and sandwich spreads (shrimp, caviar), rye bread, and boxes of juice and milk. Grocery stores sell a cheap, light breakfast: a handy yogurt with cereal and a spoon. Most places offer cheap ready-made sandwiches. If you're bored with sandwiches, some groceries and most delis have hot chicken, salads by the portion, and picnic portables.

Dinner

The large meal of the Nordic day is an early dinner. Most Scandinavians eat dinner at home, and restaurant dinners are expensive

treats. Alternate between picnic dinners (outside or in your hotel or hostel); cheap, forgettable, but filling cafeteria or fast-food dinners ($20); and atmospheric, carefully chosen restaurants popular with locals ($40 and up). One main course and two salads or soups fill up two travelers without emptying their pocket-

books. If potatoes came with your main dish, most servers are happy to give you a second helping. Booze is pricey: A beer costs about $10 in Oslo. Water is served free with an understanding smile at most restaurants (though in Denmark, there is a charge for water if you don't order another beverage).

In Scandinavia, a $40 meal in a restaurant is not that much more than a $30 American meal, since tax and tip are included in the menu price.

Smörgåsbord

The *smörgåsbord* (known in Denmark and Norway as the *store koldt bord*) is a Scandinavian culinary tradition. Though locals reserve the *smörgåsbord* for festive times such as the Christmas season, anyone can dig into this all-you-can-eat buffet any time of year at certain hotels and on overnight ferries. While the word originally referred to a spread of cold cuts, the *smörgåsbords* you'll find usually include hot dishes, too.

Seek out a *smörgåsbord* at

least once during your trip, just for the high of seeing so much wholesome Nordic food spread out in front of you. Good *smörgås-bord* opportunities covered in this book are at the Grand Hotel in Stockholm; on the overnight boats between Stockholm and Helsinki or Copenhagen and Oslo; and at Kviknes Hotel in the Norwegian fjordside town of Balestrand.

Follow these simple steps to enjoy a *smaklig* (tasty) *smörgåsbord:*

1. Browse the buffet before you begin, so you can budget your stomach space. Think of the *smörgåsbord* as a five- or six-course meal.

2. Don't overload your plate. Instead, make several trips, taking a fresh plate and cutlery each time. To signal the waiter that you're finished with each round, lay your fork and knife side-by-side on the plate. If you're getting up but are not finished with your plate, place your fork and knife in the shape of an *X* on the plate.

3. Begin with the herring dishes, along with boiled potatoes and *knäckebröd* (Swedish crisp bread).

4. Next, sample the other fish dishes (warm and cold) and more potatoes. *Gravlax* is salt-cured salmon flavored with dill, served along with a sweet mustard sauce *(gravlax senap)*.

5. Move on to salads, egg dishes, and various cold cuts.

6. Now for the meat dishes—it's meatball time! Pour on some gravy as well as a spoonful of lingonberry sauce, and have more potatoes. Reindeer and other roast meats and poultry may also tempt you.

7. Still hungry? Make a point to sample the Nordic cheeses—try creamy Havarti, mild Castello (a soft blue cheese), and in Norwegian buffets, goat cheese. Sample the delicious seasonal fruits and *franskbrød* white bread. And there are racks of traditional desserts, cakes, and custards (see "Dessert," later). Cap the meal with coffee.

Smaklig måltid! Enjoy your meal!

Drinking

Purchasing heavily taxed wine, beer, and spirits in Scandinavia can put a dent in your vacation budget. In Sweden and Norway, spirits, wine, and strong beer (more than 3.5 percent alcohol) are sold in state-run liquor stores: Systembolaget in Sweden, and Vinmonopolet in Norway. Buying a beer or glass of wine in a bar or restaurant in Sweden or Norway is particularly expensive. Therefore, many Scandinavians will have a drink or a glass of wine at home (or in their hotel room) before going out, then limit themselves to one or two glasses at the restaurant. If taking an overnight cruise during your trip, you can get a good deal on a bottle of wine or spirits in the onboard duty-free shop. Liquor laws are much more relaxed in Denmark, where you can buy wine, beer, and spirits at any supermarket or corner store. Prices are a bit lower as well. Public drinking is acceptable in Denmark, while it is illegal (although often done) in Norway and Sweden. Throughout Scandinavia, drinking and driving is not tolerated.

Some local specialties are *akvavit,* a strong, vodka-like spirit distilled from potatoes and flavored with anise, caraway, or other herbs and spices—then drunk ice-cold (common in Norway, Sweden, and Denmark). *Lakka* is a syrupy-sweet liqueur made from cloudberries, the small orange berries grown in the Arctic (popular in Norway, Sweden, and Finland). *Salmiakka* is a nearly black licorice-flavored liqueur (Finland, Norway, and Denmark). *Gammel Dansk* can be described as Danish bitters for the adventurous (Denmark only).

Dessert

Scandinavians love sweets. A meal is not complete without a little treat and a cup of coffee at the end. Bakeries *(konditori)* fill their

window cases with all varieties of cakes, tarts, cookies, and pastries. The most popular ingredients are marzipan, almonds, hazelnuts, chocolate, and fresh berries. Many cakes are covered with entire sheets of solid marzipan. To find the neighborhood bakery, just look for a golden pretzel hanging above the door or windows.

Scandinavian chocolate is some of the best in Europe. In Denmark, seek out Anthon Berg's dark chocolate and marzipan treats, as well as Toms' chocolate-covered caramels (Toms Guld are the best). Sweden's biggest chocolate producer, Maribou, makes huge bars of solid milk chocolate, as well as some with dried fruits or nuts. *Daim* are milk chocolate-covered hard toffees, sold in a variety of sizes, from large bars to bite-size pieces, all in bright-red wrappers. The Freia company, Norway's chocolate goddess (named for the Norse goddess Freya), makes a wonderful assortment of delights, from *Et lite stykke Norge* ("A little piece of Norway"—bars of creamy milk chocolate wrapped in pale-yellow paper) and *Smil* (chocolate-covered soft caramels sold in rolls) to *Firkløver* (bars of

How Was Your Trip?

Were your travels fun, smooth, and meaningful? If you'd like to share your tips, concerns, and discoveries, please fill out the survey at www.ricksteves.com/feedback. I value your feedback. Thanks in advance—it helps a lot.

milk chocolate with hazelnuts). For those who can't decide on one type, the company sells bags of assorted chocolates called *Twist* and red gift boxes of chocolates called *Kong Haakon,* named after Norway's first king.

While chocolate rules, licorice and gummy candies are also popular. Black licorice *(lakrits)* is at its best here, except for *salt lakrits* (salty licorice), which is not for the timid. Black licorice flavors everything from ice cream to chewing gum to liqueur (see "Drinking," earlier). Throughout Scandinavia, you'll find stores selling all varieties of candy in bulk. Fill your bag with a variety of candies and pay by the gram. Look around at the customers in these stores...they aren't all children.

Traveling as a Temporary Local

We travel all the way to Scandinavia to enjoy differences—to become temporary locals. You'll experience frustrations. Certain truths that we find "God-given" or "self-evident," such as cold beer, ice in drinks, bottomless cups of coffee, hot showers, and bigger being better, are suddenly not so true. One of the benefits of travel is the eye-opening realization that there are logical, civil, and even better alternatives.

While the materialistic culture of the US is sneaking into these countries, simplicity has yet to become subversive. Scandinavians are into "sustainable affluence." They have experimented aggressively in the area of social welfare—with mixed results. Travel in high-tax/high-government-service Scandinavia can rattle capitalist Americans. The people seem so happy and the society seems so genteel. Fit in, don't look for things American on the other side of the Atlantic, and you're sure to enjoy some thought-provoking stimulation and a full dose of Scandinavian hospitality.

Europeans generally like Americans. But if there is a negative aspect to their image of Americans, it is that we are loud, wasteful, ethnocentric, too informal (which can seem disrespectful), and a bit naive. While Europeans look bemusedly at some of our Yankee excesses—and worriedly at others—they nearly always afford us individual travelers all the warmth we deserve.

Judging from all the happy feedback I receive from travelers who have used this book, it's safe to assume you'll enjoy a great, affordable vacation—with the finesse of an independent, experienced traveler.

Thanks, and happy travels!

Back Door Travel Philosophy
From *Rick Steves' Europe Through the Back Door*

Travel is intensified living—maximum thrills per minute and one of the last great sources of legal adventure. Travel is freedom. It's recess, and we need it.

Experiencing the real Europe requires catching it by surprise, going casual..."through the Back Door."

Affording travel is a matter of priorities. (Make do with the old car.) You can eat and sleep—simply, safely, and enjoyably—anywhere in Europe for $120 a day plus transportation costs. In many ways, spending more money only builds a thicker wall between you and what you traveled so far to see. Europe is a cultural carnival, and time after time, you'll find that its best acts are free and the best seats are the cheap ones.

A tight budget forces you to travel close to the ground, meeting and communicating with the people. Never sacrifice sleep, nutrition, safety, or cleanliness to save money. Simply enjoy the local-style alternatives to expensive hotels and restaurants.

Connecting with people carbonates your experience. Extroverts have more fun. If your trip is low on magic moments, kick yourself and make things happen. If you don't enjoy a place, maybe you don't know enough about it. Seek the truth. Recognize tourist traps. Give a culture the benefit of your open mind. See things as different, but not better or worse. Any culture has plenty to share.

Of course, travel, like the world, is a series of hills and valleys. Be fanatically positive and militantly optimistic. If something's not to your liking, change your liking.

Travel can make you a happier American, as well as a citizen of the world. Our Earth is home to seven billion equally precious people. It's humbling to travel and find that other people don't have the "American Dream"—they have their own dreams. Europeans like us, but with all due respect, they wouldn't trade passports.

Thoughtful travel engages us with the world. In tough economic times, it reminds us what is truly important. By broadening perspectives, travel teaches new ways to measure quality of life.

Globetrotting destroys ethnocentricity, helping us understand and appreciate other cultures. Rather than fear the diversity on this planet, celebrate it. Among your most prized souvenirs will be the strands of different cultures you choose to knit into your own character. The world is a cultural yarn shop, and Back Door travelers are weaving the ultimate tapestry. Join in!

SCANDINAVIA

SCANDINAVIA

Scandinavia is Western Europe's least populated, most literate, most prosperous, most demographically homogeneous, most highly taxed, most socialistic, and least church-going corner. For the visitor, it's a land of Viking ships, brooding castles, salty harbors, deep green fjords, stave churches, and farmhouses—juxtaposed with the sleek modernism of its people-friendly cities.

Denmark, Norway, and Sweden are Scandinavia's core. They share a common linguistic heritage with Iceland, and a common history, religion, and culture with Finland and the Baltic nation of Estonia (both former Swedish colonies).

Emerging only slowly from under the glacial ice sheets, Scandinavia was the last part of Europe to be settled (its land mass is still rising from the ocean, rebounding from the press of the glaciers). Later, it was almost the last part of Europe to accept Christianity, and it's never quite forgotten its pagan roots, which live on in literature, place names, and the ancient runic alphabet. (For more background, see the Scandinavian History chapter.)

Scandinavia is blessed with natural beauty. The cavernous fjords of Norway's west coast are famous. Much of the region has mountains, lakes, green forests, and waterfalls. By contrast, low-lying Denmark has its rugged islands, salty harbors, and wind-swept, sandy coasts.

Climate-wise, Scandinavia has four distinct seasons. With Alaska-like latitudes, it's the "land of the midnight sun" in summer (18 hours of daylight) and of mid-afternoon darkness in winter (when there are just six hours between sunrise and sunset).

Most of Scandinavia is sparsely populated and very big. Sweden is the size of California, but has only a quarter the people (9.5 million). Nearly 5 million Norwegians stretch out in Norway, where Oslo is as far from the northern tip of Norway as it is from Rome. The exception is Denmark, which packs 5.5 million fun-loving Danes into a flat land the size of Switzerland.

Though each of the Scandinavian countries has its own language, there are some common threads. Danes and Norwegians can read each other's newspapers and can converse somewhat (but with difficulty because of thick accents). Swedes (whose written language is different) have a hard time with printed Danish and Norwegian, but can carry on simple conversations in those languages. Finns (whose language is not related at all) learn Swedish in school, thanks to Sweden's long historical presence in Finland. Estonian is similar to Finnish. Despite these common denominators, communication can be difficult due to one more factor—national pride. A Dane may simply pretend not to understand a Swede's request, and vice versa. If there's ever a language barrier, though, most Scandinavians can easily revert to their common second language—English.

It's not easy (and probably unwise) to make sweeping generalizations about a region's people, but here goes: In general,

Scandinavians are confident, happy, healthy, and tall. They speak their minds frankly, even about taboo subjects like sex. They're strong individualists who cut others slack for their own eccentricities. They don't fawn on the rich and famous or look down on the down and out. At work, they're efficient and conscientious. They don't take cuts in line. They're well-educated, well-traveled, and worldly. Though reserved and super-polite at first, they have a good sense of humor and don't take life or themselves too seriously.

Scandinavians work hard, but they guard their leisure time fiercely. They like the out-of-doors, perhaps in keeping with the still-rural landscape they live in. For many, a weekend with the family at a (well-furnished) country cottage is all they need. Cycling, boating, and fishing are popular. Internationally, they're known for skiing, speed skating, hockey, and other winter sports. And, as with the rest of Europe, they're wild about football (soccer).

The region is a leader in progressive lifestyles, including recognizing same-sex partnerships. More than half the heterosexual couples in Denmark are "married" only because they've lived together for so long and have children. Wives and mothers generally have a job outside the home. While the state religion is Lutheran, only a small percentage of Scandinavians actually attend church other than at Easter or Christmas. Most are either indifferent or assertively secular.

Scandinavia is rich, with a very high standard of living (as American tourists learn the hard way). Norway has been blessed with offshore oil, Denmark with farmland, and Sweden and

SCANDINAVIA

Scandi-hoovians You Might Know

Famous Danes
Hans Christian Andersen, writer of *The Ugly Duckling*, *The Little Mermaid*, etc.
Søren Kierkegaard, proto-existentialist philosopher
Bertel Thorvaldsen, sculptor
Karen Blixen, who wrote *Out of Africa* under pen name Isak Dinesen
Niels Bohr, physicist who described the atom as a tiny planetary system
Victor Borge, classical-music comedian
Arne Jacobsen, architect
Lars Ulrich, drummer for rock band Metallica
Brigitte Nielsen and Viggo Mortensen (half Danish), movie actors
Carl Nielsen, composer
Lars von Trier, movie director
Morten Andersen, NFL placekicker and all-time leading scorer

Famous Norwegians
Eric the Red, first European settler in Greenland and father of Icelander Leif Eriksson, the Viking who discovered America
Edvard Grieg, Romantic composer
Edvard Munch, *The Scream* painter
Henrik Ibsen, playwright
Roald Amundsen, Antarctic explorer
Gustav Vigeland, sculptor
Sonja Henie, figure skater and movie actress
Thor Heyerdahl, explorer of *Kon-Tiki* fame
Jan Stenerud, NFL placekicker
Liv Ullmann, movie actress and director
Rick Steves, travel writer

Finland with lush forests. They are all rich in fish. Alternative energy sources are important, especially hydroelectric and wind power. Given such pristine natural surroundings, the Scandinavians are environmentalists, committed to preserving their resources for future generations (except for the Norwegians' stubborn appetite for whaling).

Scandinavian society, carefully organized to maximize prosperity and happiness for everyone, is the home of cradle-to-grave security. Residents pay hefty taxes but get a hefty return. Chil-

SCANDINAVIA

Famous Swedes
Anders Celsius, inventor of the temperature scale
Carolus Linnaeus, botanist who developed taxonomic naming
    system
August Strindberg, playwright
Alfred Nobel, inventor of dynamite and the Nobel Peace Prize
Carl Milles, sculptor
Astrid Lindgren, children's author who created *Pippi
    Longstocking*
Ingmar Bergman, movie director
Greta Garbo and Noomi Rapace, actresses
Max von Sydow and Stellan Skarsgård, actors
Dag Hammarskjöld, UN Secretary General
Björn Borg and Stefan Edberg, tennis players
Hans Blix, UN weapons inspector
Annika Sörenstam and Jesper Parnevik, golfers
ABBA, pop-rock supergroup
Stieg Larsson, author of the *Millennium* trilogy

Famous Finns
Jean Sibelius, Romantic composer
Alvar Aalto, Modernist architect
Eliel Saarinen and son Eero, Modernist architects (the father
    known for his work in Finland, the son for his work in the
    US)
Esa-Pekka Salonen, classical conductor
Tove Jansson, author of the *Moomin* books
Linus Torvalds, creator of the Linux operating system

dren are educated. The old and sick are cared for. Cities are carefully planned to be clean, green, crime-free, and built on a human scale—with parks, fountains, public art, and pedestrian zones.

Generally speaking, citizens willingly share the burden for the common good. High taxes mean there's less of a gap between the very rich and the very poor, resulting in a less class-oriented society. Scandinavians are proud of this. If they seem a bit smug, you can't fault them, because statistics verify that they live longer, healthier, happier lives.

Scandinavia is also on the high-tech edge of the global economy. They practice a mix of free-market capitalism and enlightened socialism. In international business, they make their mark with telecommunications (Nokia from Finland, Ericsson from Sweden), Ikea furniture (originally from Sweden), Electrolux appliances (Sweden), and Lego toys (Denmark).

Politically, Denmark, Norway, and Sweden are constitutional monarchies with a figurehead monarch who cuts ribbons, works with parliament and a prime minister, and tries to stay out of the tabloids. Finland and Estonia have democratically elected presidents. The Scandinavian nations maintain close ties with each other. To some degree or other, they all participate in the European Union (though Norway is not a member, and only Finland uses the euro). Every election brings another debate about how closely they want to tie themselves to the rest of Europe. The Scandinavian nations have a reputation for international cooperation, exemplified by their leading role in the United Nations, and Sweden and Norway's Nobel Peace Prize.

All of Scandinavia's monarchs are descended from Oscar I, King of Sweden and Norway (and son of King Karl Johan XIV), through the House of Bernadotte: Denmark's Queen Margrethe II and Crown Prince Frederik (b. 1968), Sweden's King Carl XVI Gustaf and Crown Princess Victoria (b. 1977), and Norway's King Harald V and Crown Prince Håkon (b. 1973).

Artistically, Scandinavia is known for its serious playwrights (Henrik Ibsen and August Strindberg), brooding filmmakers (Ingmar Bergman), and gloomy painters (Edvard Munch), and most recently for its crime-thriller author, Stieg Larsson. Nordic mythology is familiar to the English-speaking world for its *Lord of the Rings*-style roots. Hans Christian Andersen and Astrid Lindgren (creator of *Pippi Longstocking*) brought us children's tales. Less familiar are Scandinavia's people-friendly sculptors— Bertel Thorvaldsen, Gustav Vigeland, and Carl Milles—whose noble, realistic statues evoke the human spirit. Architecturally, Scandinavia continues to lead the way, with sleek modern buildings that fit in with the natural landscape. Late-20th-century Modernism (or Functionalism) had several Scandinavian champions, including Eero Saarinen and Alvar Aalto (Finland) and Arne Jacobsen (Denmark). Musically, Scandinavia is known for classical composers like Grieg (Norway) and Sibelius (Finland) who celebrate the region's nature and folk tunes. Scandinavia's cities have thriving jazz scenes that rival America's. Oh yes, and then there's Scandinavia's biggest musical export—the '70s pop band from Sweden named ABBA.

The Scandinavian flair for art shines best in the design of everyday objects. They fashion chairs, lamps, and coffeemakers to be both functional and beautiful: sleek, with no frills, where the "beauty" comes from how well it works. In their homes, Scandinavians strive for a coziness that mixes modern practicality with traditional designs—carved wood and old flower-and-vine patterns.

Despite its ultra-modern, progressive outlook, Scandinavia still honors its traditions. Parents tell kids the old folk tales about grumpy, clever trolls, and gardeners dot their yards with friendly garden gnomes. At midsummer, you'll see locals in traditional clothes dancing around a maypole to the tunes of a folk band. At winter solstice and Christmas, they enjoy Yule cakes and winter beer. Scandinavia is sailing into the high-tech future on the hardy ship of its Viking past.

DENMARK

DENMARK

Danmark

Denmark is by far the smallest of the Scandinavian countries, but in the 16th century, it was the largest—at one time, Denmark ruled all of Norway and the three southern provinces of Sweden. Danes are proud of their mighty history and are the first to remind you that they were a lot bigger and a lot stronger in the good old days. And yet, they're a remarkably mellow, well-adjusted lot—organized without being uptight, and easygoing with a delightfully wry sense of humor.

In the 10th century, before its heyday as a Scan-superpower, Denmark was, like Norway and Sweden, home to the Vikings. More than anything else, these fierce warriors were known for their great shipbuilding, which enabled them to travel far. Denmark's Vikings journeyed west to Great Britain and Ireland (where they founded Dublin) and brought back various influences, including Christianity.

Denmark is composed of many islands, a peninsula (Jutland) that juts up from northern Germany, Greenland, and the Faroe Islands. The two main islands are Zealand (Sjælland in Danish), where Copenhagen is located, and Funen (Fyn in Danish), where Hans Christian Andersen (or, as Danes call him, simply "H. C.") was born. Out of the hundreds of smaller islands, ship-in-bottle-cute Ærø is my

favorite. The Danish landscape is gentle compared to the dramatic fjords, mountains, and vast lakes of other Scandinavian nations. Danes (not to mention Swedes and Norwegians) like to joke about the flat Danish landscape, saying that you can stand on a case of beer and see from one end of the country to the other. Denmark's highest point in Jutland is only 560 feet above sea level, and no part of the country is more than 30 miles from the ocean.

In contrast to the rest of Scandinavia, much of Denmark is arable. The landscape consists of rolling hills, small thatched-roof

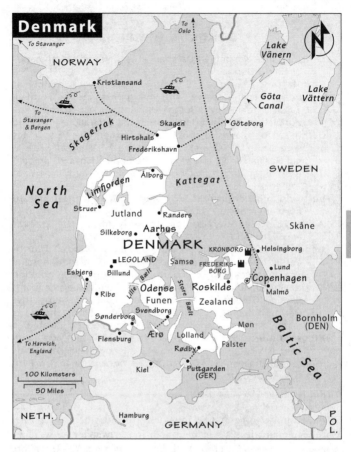

farmhouses, beech forests, and whitewashed churches with characteristic stairstep gables. Red brick, which was a favorite material of the nation-building King Christian IV, is everywhere—especially in major civic buildings such as city halls and train stations.

Like the other Scandinavian countries, Denmark is predominantly Lutheran, but only a small minority attend church regularly. The majority are ethnic Danes, and many (but certainly not all) of them have the stereotypical blond hair and blue eyes. Two out of three Danes have last names ending in "-sen." The assimilation of ethnic groups into this homogeneous society, which began in earnest in the 1980s, is a source of some controversy. But in general, most Danes have a live-and-let-live attitude and enjoy one of the highest standards of living in the world. Taxes are high in this welfare state, but education is free and medical care highly subsidized. Generous paternity leave extends to both men and women.

DENMARK

Denmark Almanac

Official Name: Kongeriget Danmark—the Kingdom of Denmark—or simply Denmark.

Population: Denmark's 5.5 million people are mainly of Scandinavian descent, with immigrants—mostly German, Turkish, Iranian, and Somali—making up 10 percent of the population. Greenland is home to the indigenous Inuit, and the Faroe Islands to people of Nordic heritage. Most Danes speak both Danish and English, with a small minority speaking German, Inuit, or Faroese. The population is 90 percent Protestant—mostly Evangelical Lutheran—and 10 percent "other."

Latitude and Longitude: 56°N and 10°E, similar latitude to northern Alberta, Canada.

Area: 16,600 square miles, roughly twice the size of Massachusetts.

Geography: Denmark includes the Jutland peninsula in northern Europe. Situated between the North Sea and the Baltic Sea, it shares a 42-mile border with Germany. In addition to Greenland and the Faroe Islands, Denmark also encompasses 400 islands (78 of which are inhabited). Altogether Denmark has 4,544 miles of coastline. The mainland is mostly flat, and nearly two-thirds of the land is cultivated.

Biggest Cities: Denmark's capital city, Copenhagen (pop. 1 million), is located on the island of Zealand (Sjælland). Aarhus (on the mainland) has 243,000 and Odense (on Funen/Fyn) has 168,000.

Denmark, one of the most environmentally conscious European countries, is a front-runner in renewable energy, recy-

cling, and organic farming. You'll see lots of modern windmills dotting the countryside. Since the country lacks other sources of power, wind power accounts for 20 percent of Denmark's energy today, with a goal of 50 percent by 2030. Half of all waste is recycled. In grocery stores, organic products are shelved right alongside non-organic ones—for the same price.

Denmark's Queen Margrethe II is a very popular and talented woman who, along with her royal duties, has designed coins, stamps, and book illustrations. Danes gather around the TV on New Year's Eve to hear her annual speech to the nation and flock to the Royal Palace in Copenhagen on April 16 to sing her "Happy Birthday." Her son, Crown Prince Frederik, married Australian Mary Donaldson in 2004. Their

Economy: Denmark's modern economy is holding its own, with a Gross Domestic Product of just under $210 billion. Denmark's top exports include pharmaceuticals, oil, machinery, and food products. It is also one of the world's leaders in exports of wind turbine technology. The GDP per capita is about $37,600.

Currency: 6 Danish kroner (kr, officially DKK) = about $1.

Government: Denmark is a constitutional monarchy. Queen Margrethe II is the head of state, but the head of government is the prime minister, a post held since October 2011 by Helle Thorning-Schmidt. The 179-member parliament (Folketinget) is elected every four years.

Flag: The Danish flag is red with a white cross.

The Average Dane: He or she is 41 years old, has 1.74 children, and will live to be 78. About 74 percent of Danish women are employed outside the home. About 53 percent of Danes own a home or apartment, 83 percent own a mobile phone, and 90 percent have Internet access.

DENMARK

son Christian's birth in 2005 was cause for a national celebration.

The Danes are proud of their royal family and of the flag, a white cross on a red background. Legend says it fell from the sky during a 13th-century battle in Estonia, making it Europe's oldest continuously used flag. You'll see it everywhere—decorating cakes, on clothing, or fluttering in the breeze atop government buildings. It's as much a decorative symbol as a patriotic one.

You'll also notice that the Danes have an odd fixation on two animals: elephants and polar bears, both of which are symbols of national (especially royal) pride. The Order of the Elephant is the highest honor that the Danish monarch can bestow on someone; if you see an emblematic elephant, you know somebody very important is involved. And the polar bear represents the Danish protectorate of Greenland—a welcome reminder to Danes that their nation is more than just

Jutland and a bunch of flat little islands.

From an early age, Danes develop a passion for soccer. You may see red-and-white-clad fans singing on their way to a match. Despite the country's small size, the Danish national team does well in international competition. Other popular sports include sailing, cycling, badminton, and team handball.

The Danish language, with its three extra vowels (Æ, Ø, and Å), is notoriously difficult for foreigners to pronounce. Even seemingly predictable consonants can be tricky. For example, the letter "d" is often dropped, so the word *gade* (street)—which you'll see, hear, and say constantly—is pronounced "gah-eh." Luckily for us, almost everyone also speaks English and is heroically patient with thick-tongued foreigners. Danes have playful fun teasing tourists who make the brave attempt to say Danish words. The hardest phrase, *rød grød med fløde* (a delightful red fruit porridge topped with cream), is nearly impossible for a non-Dane to pronounce. Ask a local to help you.

Sample Denmark's sweet treats at one of the many bakeries you'll see. The pastries that we call "Danish" in the US are called *wienerbrød* in Denmark. Bakeries line their display cases with several varieties of *wienerbrød* and other delectable sweets. Try *kringle, snegle,* or *Napoleonshatte,* or find your own favorite. (Chances are it will be easier to enjoy than to pronounce.)

For a selection of useful Danish survival phrases, see page 689. Two important words to know are *skål* ("cheers," a ritual always done with serious eye contact) and *hyggelig* (pronounced HEW-glee), meaning warm and cozy. Danes treat their home like a sanctuary and spend a great deal of time improving their gardens and houses—inside and out. Cozying up one's personal space (a national obsession) is something the Danes do best. If you have the opportunity, have some Danes adopt you while you are in Denmark so you can enjoy their warm hospitality.

Heaven to a Dane is returning home after a walk in a beloved beech forest to enjoy open-faced sandwiches washed down with beer among good friends. Around the *hyggelig* candlelit table, there will be a spirited discussion of the issues of the day, plenty of laughter, and probably a few good-natured jokes about the Swedes or Norwegians. *Skål!*

COPENHAGEN

København

Copenhagen, Denmark's capital, is the gateway to Scandinavia. It's an improbable combination of corny Danish clichés, well-dressed executives having a business lunch amid cutting-edge contemporary architecture, and some of the funkiest counterculture in Europe. And yet, it all just works so tidily together. With the Øresund Bridge connecting Sweden and Denmark (creating the region's largest metropolitan area), Copenhagen is energized and ready to dethrone Stockholm as Scandinavia's powerhouse city.

A busy day cruising the canals, wandering through the palace, and taking an old-town walk will give you your historical bearings. Then, after another day strolling the Strøget (STROY-et, Europe's first and greatest pedestrian shopping mall), biking the canals, and sampling the Danish good life (including sampling a gooey Danish), you'll feel

right at home. Live it up in Scandinavia's cheapest and most fun-loving capital.

Planning Your Time

A first visit deserves a minimum of two days. Note that many sights are closed on Monday year-round or in the off-season.

Day 1: Catch a 10:30 city walking tour with Richard Karpen (Mon-Sat mid-May–mid-Sept; described later under "Tours in

The Story of Copenhagen

If you study your map carefully, you can read the history of Copenhagen in today's street plan. København (literally, "Merchants' Harbor") was born on the little island of Slotsholmen—today home of Christiansborg Palace—in 1167. What was Copenhagen's medieval moat is now a string of pleasant lakes and parks, including Tivoli Gardens. You can still make out some of the zigzag pattern of the moats and ramparts in the city's greenbelt.

Many of these fortifications—and several other land-marks—were built by Denmark's most memorable king. You need to remember only one character in Copenhagen's history: Christian IV. Ruling from 1588 to 1648, he was Denmark's Renaissance king and a royal party animal (see the "King Christian IV" sidebar, later). The personal energy of this "Builder King" sparked a Golden Age when Copenhagen prospered and many of the city's grandest buildings were erected. In the 17th century, Christian IV extended the city fortifications to the north, doubling the size of the city, while adding a grid plan of streets and his Rosenborg Castle. This old "new town" has the Amalienborg Palace and *The Little Mermaid* site.

In 1850, Copenhagen's 140,000 residents all lived within this defensive system. Building in the no-man's-land outside the walls was only allowed with the understanding that in the event of an attack, you'd burn your dwellings to clear the way for a good defense.

Most of the city's historic buildings still in existence were built within the medieval walls, but conditions became too crowded, and outbreaks of disease forced Copenhagen to spread outside the walls. Ultimately those walls were torn down and replaced with "rampart streets" that define today's city center: Vestervoldgade (literally, "West Rampart Street"), Nørrevoldgade ("North"), and Østervoldgade ("East"). The fourth side is the harbor and the island of Slotsholmen, where København was born.

Copenhagen"). After lunch at Riz-Raz, catch the relaxing canal-boat tour out to *The Little Mermaid* site and back. Enjoy the rest of the afternoon tracing Denmark's cultural roots in the National Museum and visiting the Ny Carlsberg Glyptotek art gallery (Impressionists and Danish artists). Spend the evening strolling the Strøget (follow my self-guided walk).

Day 2: At 10:00, go Neoclassical at Thorvaldsen's Museum (closed Mon), and tour the royal reception rooms at the adjacent Christiansborg Palace. After a *smørrebrød* lunch, spend the afternoon seeing the Rosenborg Castle/crown jewels and the Museum of Danish Resistance. Spend the evening at Tivoli Gardens.

Christiania—the hippie squatters' community—is not for everyone. But it's worth considering if you're intrigued by alternative lifestyles, or simply want a break from the museums. During a busy trip, Christiania fits best in the evening.

Budget Itinerary Tip: Remember the efficiency and cost-effectiveness of sleeping while traveling in and out of town (saving time and hotel costs). Consider taking an overnight train to Stockholm or Oslo, or cruise up to Oslo on a night boat. Kamikaze sightseers on tight budgets see Copenhagen as a useful Scandinavian bottleneck. They sleep heading into town on a train, tour the city during the day, and sleep heading north into Scandinavia on a boat or train to their next destination. At the end of their Scandinavian travels, they do the same thing in reverse. The result is two days and no nights in Copenhagen (you can check your bag and take a shower at the train station). Considering the joy of Oslo and Stockholm, this isn't all that crazy if you have limited time and can sleep on a moving train or boat.

Orientation to Copenhagen

Copenhagen is huge (with a million people), but for most visitors, the walkable core is the diagonal axis formed by the train station, Tivoli Gardens, Rådhuspladsen (City Hall Square), and the Strøget pedestrian street, ending at the colorful old Nyhavn sailors' harbor. Bubbling with street life, colorful pedestrian zones, and most of the city's sightseeing, the Strøget is fun (and most of it is covered by my self-guided walk in this chapter). But also be sure to get off the main drag and explore. By doing things by bike or on foot, you'll stumble onto some charming bits of Copenhagen that many travelers miss.

Outside of the old city center are three areas of interest to tourists:

1. To the north are Rosenborg Castle and *The Little Mermaid* area (Amalienborg Palace and Museum of Danish Resistance).

COPENHAGEN

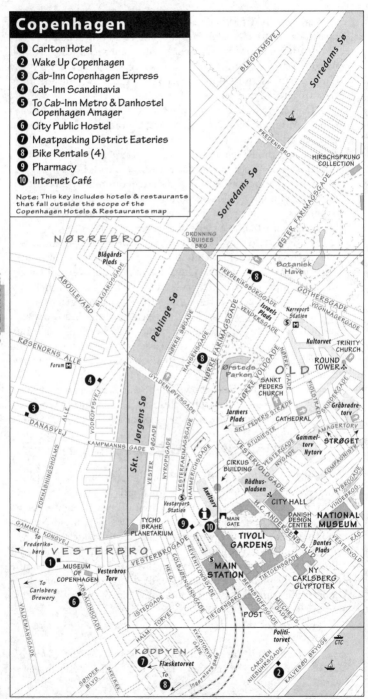

Copenhagen

1. Carlton Hotel
2. Wake Up Copenhagen
3. Cab-Inn Copenhagen Express
4. Cab-Inn Scandinavia
5. To Cab-Inn Metro & Danhostel Copenhagen Amager
6. City Public Hostel
7. Meatpacking District Eateries
8. Bike Rentals (4)
9. Pharmacy
10. Internet Café

Note: This key includes hotels & restaurants that fall outside the scope of the Copenhagen Hotels & Restaurants map

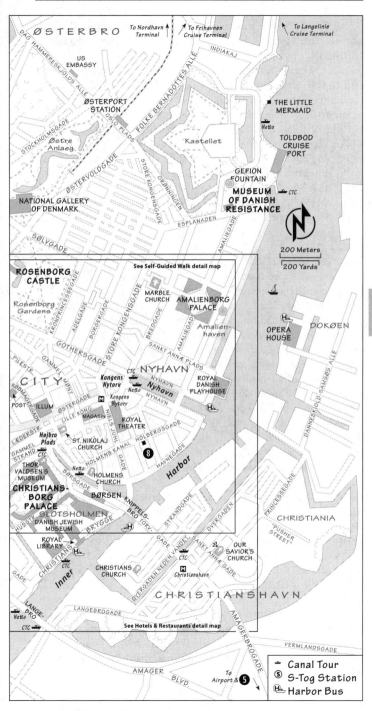

ØSTERBRO

To Nordhavn Terminal

To Frihavnen Cruise Terminal

To Langelinie Cruise Terminal

DAG HAMMERSKJOLDS ALLE

US EMBASSY

INDIAKAJ

THE LITTLE MERMAID

ØSTERPORT STATION

Netto

Østre Anlæg

STOCKHOLMSGADE

FOLKE BERNADOTTES ALLE

Kastellet

TOLDBOD CRUISE PORT

GEFION FOUNTAIN

ØSTERVOLDGADE

STORE KONGENSGADE

GRØNNINGEN

MUSEUM OF DANISH RESISTANCE

CTC

NATIONAL GALLERY OF DENMARK

ESPLANADEN

AMALIEGADE

N

SØLVGADE

200 Meters
200 Yards

COPENHAGEN

See Self-Guided Walk detail map

ROSENBORG CASTLE

Rosenborg Gardens

KRONPRINSESSEGADE

ADELGADE

BORGERGADE

MARBLE CHURCH

BREDGADE

AMALIENBORG PALACE

Amalien-haven

OPERA HOUSE

DOKØEN

GOTHERSGADE

STORE KONGENSGADE

SANKT ANNÆ PLADS

GAMMEL MONT

CITY

PILESTR.

Kongens Nytorv

Netto

CTC

NYHAVN

Kongens Nytorv

NYHAVN

Nyhavn

NYHAVN

ROYAL DANISH PLAYHOUSE

DANNESKIOLD-SAMSØS ALLE

KØBMAGERGADE

POST

ILLUM

ØSTERGADE

LILLE KONG

M

ROYAL THEATER

NIELS JUEL GADE

H

LÆDERSTR.

MAGASIN

Hejbro Plads

ST. NIKOLAJ CHURCH

HOLMENS KANAL

HOLBERGSGADE

HAVNEGADE

Harbor

GAMMEL STRAND

CTC

8

THOR VALDSEN'S MUSEUM

Netto

BØRSGADE

HOLMENS CHURCH

CHRISTIANS-BORG PALACE

SLOTSHOLMEN

BØRSEN

KNIPPELS-BRO TORV

STRANDGADE

PRINCESSEGADE

CHRISTIANIA

HUSSTR.

CHRISTIANS BRYGGE

DANISH JEWISH MUSEUM

H

OVERGADEN

"PUSHER STREET"

ROYAL LIBRARY

H

CHRISTIANS CHURCH

OVERGADEN NEDEN VANDET

SANKT ANNÆ GADE

CTC

OUR SAVIOR'S CHURCH

Inner

CTC

Christianshavn

CHRISTIANSHAVN

GADE

LANGE-BRO

Netto

CTC

LANGEBROGADE

AMAGERBROGADE

See Hotels & Restaurants detail map

VERMLANDSGADE

AMAGER BLVD.

To Airport & 5

Canal Tour

Ⓢ S-Tog Station

Harbor Bus

2. To the east, across the harbor, are Christianshavn (Copenhagen's "Little Amsterdam" district) and the alternative enclave of Christiania.

3. To the west (behind the train station) is Vesterbro, a young and trendy part of town with lots of cafés, bars, and boutiques (including the hip Meatpacking District, called Kødbyen); the picnic-friendly Frederiksberg park; and the Carlsberg Brewery.

All of these sights are walkable from the Strøget, but taking a bike, bus, or taxi is more efficient. I rent a bike for my entire visit (for about the cost of a single cab ride per day) and park it safely in my hotel courtyard. I get anywhere in the town center literally faster than by taxi (nearly anything is within a 10-minute pedal). In good weather, the city is an absolute delight by bike (for more on biking in Copenhagen, see "Getting Around Copenhagen: By Bike," later).

Tourist Information

Copenhagen's questionable excuse for a TI, which bills itself as "Wonderful Copenhagen," is actually a blatantly for-profit company. As in a (sadly) increasing number of big European cities, it provides information only about businesses that pay a hefty display fee of thousands of dollars each year. This colors the advice and information the office provides. While they can answer basic questions and have a room-booking service (for a 100-kr fee), the office is worthwhile mostly as a big rack of advertising brochures—you can pick up the free map at many hotels and other places in town (May-June Mon-Sat 9:00-18:00, closed Sun; July-Aug Mon-Sat 9:00-20:00, Sun 10:00-18:00; Sept-April Mon-Fri 9:00-16:00, Sat 9:00-14:00, closed Sun; just up the street from train station—to the left as you exit the station—at Vesterbrogade 4A, good Lagkagehuset bakery in building, tel. 70 22 24 42, www.visit copenhagen.com).

The **Copenhagen Card,** which includes free entry to many of the city's sights (including expensive ones, like Tivoli and Rosenborg Castle) and all local transportation throughout the greater Copenhagen area, can save busy sightseers some money; if you're planning on visiting a lot of attractions with steep entry prices, do the arithmetic to see if buying this pass adds up (249 kr/24 hours, 479 kr/72 hours, 699 kr/120 hours—sold at the TI and some hotels).

Alternative Sources of Tourist Information: As the TI's bottom line competes with its mission to help tourists, you may want to seek out other ways to inform yourself. The local English-language newspaper, *The Copenhagen Post,* has good articles about what's going on in town (comes out each Thursday, often available free at TI or some hotels, or buy it at a newsstand, www.cph

post.dk). The witty alternative website, **www.aok.dk,** has several articles in English (and many more in Danish—readable and very insightful if you translate them in Google Translate).

Arrival in Copenhagen
By Train
The main train station is called Hovedbanegården (HOETH-bahn-gorn; look for *København H* on signs and schedules). It's

a temple of travel and a hive of travel-related activity (and 24-hour thievery). Kiosks and fast-food eateries cluster in the middle of the main arrivals hall. The **ticket office** is on the left (as you face the front of the hall), and a **train information** kiosk is right in the middle of the hall.

Within the station, you'll find **baggage storage** (go down stairs at back of station marked *Bagagebokse;* lockers cost 40-50 kr/day, and the checkroom/*garderobe* costs 45-55 kr/day per bag; both open Mon-Sat 5:30-1:00 in the morning, Sun 6:00-1:00 in the morning); pay **WCs** (right side of station, near ticket offices); a **post office** (back of station, Mon-Fri 8:00-21:00, Sat-Sun 10:00-16:00); a branch of the recommended **Lagkagehuset** bakery; and lots more. At both the front and the back of the station, you'll find **ATMs** and **Forex** exchange desks (the least expensive place in town to change money, daily 8:00-21:00).

The tracks at the back of the station (tracks 9-10 and 11-12) are for the suburban train (S-tog).

Tickets: While you're in the station, you can plan for your departure by reserving your overnight train seat or *couchette* at the *Billetsalg* office (daily 9:30-18:00). Some international rides and high-speed InterCity trains require reservations (usually 25-55 kr), but railpass-holders can ride any Danish train without a reservation. The *Kviksalg* office, with longer hours, sells tickets within Denmark (plus the regional train to Malmö, Sweden). This "quick sale" office will also help you with reservations for international trips if the *Billetsalg* office is closed, or if you're departing by train within one hour or early the next day. If you're heading into Sweden, you can also buy tickets at the *SJ Rejsebutik* (Swedish Railways) office, near the back of the station.

Getting into Town: If you want to get right to sightseeing, you're within easy walking distance of downtown. Just walk out the front door and you'll run into one of the entrances for Tivoli amusement park; if you go around its left side and up a couple of blocks, you'll be at Rådhuspladsen, where my self-guided walk begins.

Hotels are scattered far and wide around town. It's best to get arrival instructions from your hotelier, but if you're on your own, here are some tips:

To reach hotels **behind the station,** slip out the back door—just go down the stairs at the back of the station marked *Reventlowsgade.*

For hotels **near Nørreport** (Ibsens and Jørgensen), ride the S-tog from the station two stops to Nørreport, within about a 10-minute walk of the hotels.

For hotels **near Nyhavn** (71 Nyhavn and Bethel Sømand-shjem), you can take the S-tog to Nørreport, then transfer to the Metro one stop to Kongens Nytorv, within a 10-minute walk of Nyhavn. Or you can take bus #11A or #15 (or #26 from around the corner) to Kongens Nytorv, next to Nyhavn.

Note: If you're staying near Nørreport (or near Nyhavn, an easy Metro connection from Nørreport), check your train schedule carefully; many local trains (such as some from Roskilde) continue through the main train station to the Nørreport station, saving you an extra step.

By Plane

Kastrup, Copenhagen's international airport, is a traveler's dream, with a TI, baggage check, bank, ATMs, post office, shopping mall, grocery store, bakery, and more. There are three check-in terminals, within walking distance of each other (departures screens tell you which terminal to go to). But on arrival, all flights feed into one big arrivals lobby in Terminal 3. When you pop out here, there's a TI kiosk on your left, taxis out the door on your right, trains straight ahead, and shops and eateries filling the atrium above you. You can use dollars or euros at the airport, but you'll get change back in kroner (airport code: CPH, airport info tel. 32 31 32 31, www.cph.dk).

To get from the airport to downtown, your options include the Metro, trains, and taxis. There are also buses into town, but the train/Metro is generally better.

The **Metro** runs directly from the airport to Christianshavn, Kongens Nytorv (near Nyhavn), and Nørreport, making it the best choice for getting into town if you're staying in any of these areas (36-kr three-zone ticket, yellow M2 line, direction: Vanløse, 4-10/hour, 11 minutes to Christianshavn). The Metro station is located at the end of Terminal 3 and is covered by the roof of the terminal.

Convenient **trains** also connect the airport with downtown (36-kr three-zone ticket, covered by railpass, 4/hour, 12 minutes). Buy your ticket from the ground-level ticket booth (look for *DSB:*

Tickets for Train, Metro & Bus signs) before riding the escalator down to the tracks. Track 2 has trains going into the city (track 1 is for trains going east, to Sweden). Trains into town stop at the main train station (signed *København H;* handy if you're sleeping at my recommended hotels behind the train station), as well as the Nørreport and Østerport stations. At Nørreport, you can connect to the Metro for Kongens Nytorv (near Nyhavn) and Christianshavn.

With the train/Metro trip being so quick, frequent, and cheap, I see no reason to take a taxi here. But if you do, **taxis** are fast, civil, accept credit cards, and charge about 250 kr for a ride to the town center.

By Boat
For information on Copenhagen's cruise terminals, see the end of this chapter.

Helpful Hints
Emergencies: Dial 112 and specify fire, police, or ambulance. Emergency calls from public phones are free.

Pharmacy: Steno Apotek is across from the train station (open 24 hours, Vesterbrogade 6C, tel. 33 14 82 66).

Blue Monday: As you plan, remember that most sights close on Monday, but these attractions remain open: Amalienborg Palace Museum (closed Mon Nov-April), Christiansborg Palace (closed Mon Oct-April), City Hall, Danish Design Center, Museum of Copenhagen, Rosenborg Castle (closed Mon Nov-April), Round Tower, Royal Library, Our Savior's Church, Tivoli Gardens (generally closed late Sept-mid-April), canal tours, and walking or bike tours. You can explore Christiania, but Monday is its rest day ("resting" from what, I'm not sure), so it's unusually quiet and some restaurants are closed.

Telephones: Use the telephone liberally—everyone speaks English. Calls anywhere in Denmark are cheap; calls to Norway and Sweden cost 6 kr per minute from a booth (half that from a private home). Get a phone card (sold at newsstands, starting at 30 kr). To make inexpensive international calls, buy an international phone card. There are a variety to choose from, varying in price. (7-Eleven stores give you a voucher that acts as the calling card, with instructions and your PIN code.)

Internet Access: Wi-Fi is easy to find in Copenhagen (available free at virtually all hotels and many cafés). **Telestation,** tucked behind the train station kitty-corner from the TI, is a call shop with several Internet terminals (10 kr/15 minutes,

15 kr/30 minutes, 25 kr/1 hour; Mon-Sat 10:00-21:00—until 19:00 in winter, Sun 11:00-20:00—until 18:00 in winter, Banegårdspladsen 1, tel. 33 93 00 02). Additionally, several places offer free Internet access (designed for quick info and email checks): **Copenhagen Central Library** (most terminals, least wait, midway between Nørreport and the Strøget at Krystalgade 15, Mon-Fri 10:00-19:00, Sat 10:00-14:00, closed Sun); **"Black Diamond" library** (2 stand-up terminals on the skyway over the street nearest the harbor, see page 93); and the main **university building** (corner of Nørregade and Sankt Peders Stræde, 2 terminals just inside the door).

Laundry: **Pams Møntvask** is a good coin-op laundry near Nørreport (31 kr/load wash, 6 kr for soap, 2 kr/minute to dry, daily 6:00-21:00, 50 yards from Ibsens Hotel at 86 Nansensgade). **Tre Stjernet Møntvask** ("Three Star Laundry") is a few blocks behind the train station at Istedgade 45, near the Meatpacking District (wash-27 kr/load, soap-5 kr, dry-1 kr/1.5 minutes, daily 6:00-21:00). *Vaskel* is wash, *torring* is dry, and *sæbe* is soap.

Ferries: Book any ferries now that you plan to take later in Scandinavia. Visit a travel agent or call direct. For the Copenhagen-Oslo overnight ferry described on page 133, call **DFDS** (Mon-Fri 9:30-17:00, tel. 33 42 30 00, www.dfdsseaways.com) or visit the **DSB Resjebureau** at the main train station. For the boat from Stockholm to Helsinki described on page 552, contact **Viking Line** (08/452-4000, www.vikingline.fi) or **Tallink Silja** (tel. 08 22 21 40, www.tallinksilja.com). For the boat to St. Petersburg described on page 595, contact **St. Peter Line** (www.stpeterline.com).

Jazz Festival: The Copenhagen Jazz Festival—10 days in early July—puts the town in a rollicking slide-trombone mood. The Danes are Europe's jazz enthusiasts, and this music festival fills the town with happiness. The TI prints up an extensive listing of each year's festival events, or get the latest at www.jazz.dk. There's also a winter jazz festival in February.

Updates to This Book: For news about changes to this book's coverage since it was published, see www.ricksteves.com/update.

Getting Around Copenhagen

By Public Transit: It's easy to navigate Copenhagen, with its fine buses, Metro, and S-tog (a suburban train system with stops in the city; Eurail valid on S-tog). For a helpful website that covers public-transport options (nationwide) in English, consult www.rejseplanen.dk.

The same **tickets** are used throughout the system. A 24-kr, two-zone ticket gets you an hour's travel within the center—pay as you board buses, or buy from station ticket offices or vending machines for the Metro. (Automated ticket machines may not accept American credit cards, but I was able to use an American debit card with a PIN, and most machines also take Danish cash; if you want to use your credit card and the machine won't take it, find a cashier.) Assume you'll be within the middle two zones unless traveling to or from the airport, which requires a three-zone ticket (36 kr).

One handy option is the blue, two-zone *klippekort*, which can be shared—for example, two people can take five rides each (145 kr for 10 rides, insert it in the validation box each time you board a train and it'll snip off one of your rides).

If you're traveling exclusively in central Copenhagen, the **City Pass** is a good value (75 kr/24 hours, 190 kr/72 hours, covers travel within zones 1-4, including the airport). To travel throughout the greater Copenhagen region—including side-trips such as Roskilde, Frederiksborg Castle, Louisiana, and Kronborg Castle—you'll need to pay more for a **"24-hour ticket"** (130 kr) or a **"7-day flexicard"** (225 kr—can be a good value even for less than a week). All passes are sold at stations, the TI, 7-Elevens, and other kiosks. Validate any all-day or multi-day ticket by stamping it in the yellow machine on the bus or at the station.

While the train system is slick (Metro and S-tog, described later), its usefulness is limited for the typical tourist—but **buses**

serve all of the major sights in town every five to eight minutes during daytime hours. If you're not riding a bike everywhere, get comfortable with the buses. Bus drivers are patient, have change, and speak English. City maps list bus routes. Locals are usually friendly and helpful. There's also a floating "Harbor Bus" (described on page 62).

Bus lines that end with "A" (such as #1A) use quiet, eco-friendly, electric buses that are smaller than normal buses, allowing access into the narrower streets of the old town. Designed for tourists, these provide an easy overview to the city center. Among these, the following are particularly useful:

Bus **#1A** loops from the train station up to Kongens Nytorv (near Nyhavn) and then farther north, to Østerport.

Bus **#2A** goes from Christianshavn to the city center, then onward to points west.

Bus **#5A** connects the station more or less directly to Nørreport.

Bus **#6A** also connects the station to Nørreport, but on a much more roundabout route that twists through the central core (with several sightseeing-handy stops).

Bus **#11A** does a big loop from the train station through the core of town up to Nørreport, then down to Nyhavn before retracing its steps back via Nørreport to the train station.

Other, non-"A" buses, which are bigger and tend to be more direct, can be faster for some trips:

Bus **#14** runs from Nørreport (and near my recommended hotels) down to the city center, stopping near the Strøget and Slotsholmen Island, and eventually going near the main train station.

Buses **#15** and **#26** run a handy route right through the main tourist zone: train station/Tivoli to Slotsholmen Island to Kongens Nytorv (near Nyhavn) to the Amalienborg Palace/*Little Mermaid* area. Bus #26 continues even farther northward to the city's cruise ports, but the line splits, so pay attention to which bus you're on: Those marked *Langelinie* go to the Langelinie Pier, while *Færgehavn Nord* heads for Frihavnen. Note that bus #26 does not run on weekends.

Bus **#29** goes from Nyhavn to Slotsholmen Island to Tivoli.

Copenhagen's **Metro** line, while simple, is super-futuristic and growing. For most tourists' purposes, only the airport and three consecutive stops within the city matter: Nørreport (connected every few minutes by the S-tog to the main train station), Kongens Nytorv (near Nyhavn and the Strøget's north end), and Christianshavn. Nearly all recommended hotels are within walking distance of the main train station or these three stops.

The city is busy at work on the new Cityringen (City Circle) Metro line. When it opens in 2018, the Metro will instantly become far handier for tourists—linking the train station, Rådhuspladsen, Gammel Strand (near Slotsholmen Island), and Kongens Nytorv (near Nyhavn). In the meantime, you can expect to see massive construction zones at each of those locations. Eventually the Metro will also extend to Ørestad, the industrial and business center created after the Øresund Bridge was built between Denmark and Sweden (for the latest on the Metro, see www.m.dk).

The **S-tog** is basically a commuter line that links stations on the main train line through Copenhagen; for those visiting the city, the most important stops are the main train station and Nørreport (where it ties into the Metro system). However, the S-tog is very handy for reaching many of the outlying sights described in the Near Copenhagen chapter.

By Boat: The hop-on, hop-off "Harbor Bus" (Havnebus) boat stops at the "Black Diamond" library, Christianshavn (near Knippels Bridge), Nyhavn, the Opera House, and Nordre Tolbod, which is a short walk from *The Little Mermaid* site. The boat is actually part of the city bus system (lines #901 and #902) and covered by the tickets described earlier. Taking a long ride on this boat—from the library to the end of the line—is the "poor man's cruise," without commentary, of course (runs 6:00-19:00). Or, for a true sightseeing trip, consider a guided harbor cruise (described later under "Tours in Copenhagen").

By Taxi: Taxis are plentiful, easy to call or flag down, and pricey (26-kr pickup charge and then 13 kr/kilometer). For a short ride, four people spend about the same by taxi as by bus. Calling 35 35 35 35 will get you a taxi within minutes...with the meter already well on its way.

By Bike: Cyclists see more, save time and money, and really feel like locals. With a bike, you have Copenhagen at your command. I'd rather have a bike than a car and driver at my disposal. Virtually every street has a dedicated bike lane (complete with bike signal lights). Police issue 500-kr tickets to anyone riding on sidewalks or through pedestrian zones. Note also that bikes can't be parked just anywhere. Observe others and park your bike among other bikes. The simple built-in lock that binds the back tire is adequate.

Your best bet for renting a bike is to ask your hotelier first. Many rent decent bikes at reasonable rates to their guests, saving you a trip to a bike-rental outlet and letting you hit the road the moment you arrive.

For an (often) better-quality bike and advice from someone with more cycle expertise, consider one of these rental outfits in or near the city center:

• **Baisikeli Bike Rental,** behind Ørsteds Park just south of Nørreport (budget bike: 50 kr/6 hours, 80 kr/24 hours, 35 kr/extra day; better "standard" bike: 80 kr/6 hours, 110 kr/24 hours, 50 kr/extra day; daily 10:00-18:00; Turesensgade 10—see map on page 54, tel. 53 71 02 29, this location closed in winter; second location tucked behind the Kødbyen district and train station at Ingerslevsgade 80; www.cph-bike-rental.dk). *Baisikeli* means "bike" in Swahili, and this company donates their refurbished used bikes to Africa.

• **Københavens Cyklebørs,** also near Nørreport (75 kr/1 day, 140 kr/2 days, 200 kr/3 days, 350 kr/week, Mon-Fri 9:00-17:30, Sat 10:00-13:30-but you can return bike until 21:00, closed Sun, Gothersgade 157—see map on page 116, tel. 33 14 07 17, www.cykelborsen.dk).

• **Gammel Holm Cykler,** near Nyhavn (Holbergsgade 12—see map on page 116, tel. 33 33 83 84).

From May through November, 2,400 clunky but practical little **free bikes** are scattered around the old town center (basically

the terrain covered in the Copenhagen map in this chapter). Simply locate one of the hundred-some racks, unlock a bike by popping a 20-kr coin into the handlebar, and pedal away. When you're done, plug your bike back into any other rack, and your deposit coin will pop back out; if you can't find a rack, just abandon your bike and someone will take it back and pocket your coin. These simple bikes come with theft-proof parts (unusable on regular bikes) and—they claim—embedded computer chips so that bike patrols can trace and retrieve strays. The bikes are funded by advertisements painted on the wheels and by a progressive electorate. Copenhagen's radical city-bike program is a clever idea, but in practice, it doesn't work great for sightseers. It's hard to find bikes in working order, and when you get to the sight and park your bike, it'll be gone by the time you're ready to pedal on. (The 20-kr deposit coin acts as an incentive for any kid or homeless person to pick up city bikes not plugged back into their special racks.) Use the free bikes for a one-way pedal here and there. For efficiency, pay to rent one.

Tours in Copenhagen

On Foot

Copenhagen is an ideal city to get to know by foot. You have two good options:

▲▲**Hans Christian Andersen Tours by Richard Karpen**— Once upon a time, American Richard Karpen visited Copenhagen and fell in love with the city. Now, dressed as Hans Christian Andersen in a 19th-century top hat and long coat, he leads one-hour tours that wander in and out of buildings, courtyards, back streets, and unusual parts of the old town. Along the way, he gives insightful and humorous background on the history, culture, and contemporary life of Denmark, Copenhagen, and the Danes.

Richard offers three entertaining and informative walks: "Castles and Kings," "Royal Copenhagen," and "Romantic Copenhagen." Each walk includes a stroll of a little more than a mile (with breaks) and covers different parts of the historic center (100 kr apiece, kids under 12 free; departs from the TI, up the street from the main train station at Vesterbrogade 4A—at the corner with Bernstorffsgade and directly across from Hard Rock Café; mid-May–mid-Sept Mon-Sat at 10:30, none on Sun; departs promptly—if you miss him try to catch up with the tour at the next stop on Rådhuspladsen). Richard's tours, while all different, complement each other and are of equal introductory value. Go whichever day is convenient for you. The earlier you take this tour, the earlier you'll have a good historical orientation.

Richard also does excellent tours of Rosenborg Castle (80 kr, doesn't include castle entry, mid-May–mid-Sept Mon and Thu at 13:30, one hour, led by dapper Renaissance "Sir Richard," meet outside castle ticket office). You can also hire him for a private tour of the city or of Rosenborg Castle (1,000 kr, or save a bit by paying $165 in US dollars, May-Sept, advance notice required, mobile 60 43 48 26, copenhagenwalks@yahoo.com).

For details, see www.copenhagenwalks.com. No reservations are needed for Richard's scheduled tours—just show up.

▲▲**Copenhagen History Tours**—Christian Donatzky, a charming young Dane with a master's degree in history, runs a walking tour on Saturday mornings. Themes vary by month: In April and May, Christian offers "Reformed Copenhagen" (covering the period from 1400-1600); in June and July, he runs the "King's Copenhagen" (1600-1800); and in August and September, he leads special themed tours—in 2013, he will focus on Danish philosopher Søren Kierkegaard (in honor of the thinker's 200th birthday), while in 2014 and beyond, the tour will feature "Hans Christian Andersen's Copenhagen" (1800-present). The tours are thoughtfully designed, and those with a serious interest in Danish history find them time well spent. Strolling with Christian is like walking with your own private Danish encyclopedia (80 kr, Sat at 10:00, approximately 1.5 hours, small groups of 5-15 people, tours depart from statue of Bishop Absalon on Højbro Plads between the Strøget and Christiansborg Palace, English only, no reservations necessary—just show up, tel. 28 49 44 35, www.history tours.dk, info@historytours.dk).

By Boat

For many, the best way to experience the city's canals and harbor is by canal boat. Two companies offer essentially the same live, three-language, one-hour cruises. Both

COPENHAGEN

Hans Christian Andersen
(1805-1875)

The author of such classic fairy tales as *The Ugly Duckling* was an ugly duckling himself—a misfit who blossomed. Hans Christian

Andersen (called H. C., pronounced "hoe see" by the Danes) was born to a poor shoemaker in Odense. As a child he was gangly, high-strung, and effeminate. He avoided school because the kids laughed at him, so he spent his time in a fantasy world of books and plays. When his father died, the 11-year-old was on his own, forced into manual labor. He loved playing with a marionette theater that his father had made for him, sparking a lifelong love affair with the theater. In 1819, at the age of 14, he moved to Copenhagen to pursue an acting career and worked as a boy soprano for the Royal Theater. When his voice changed, the director encouraged him to return to school. He dutifully attended—a teenager among boys—and eventually went on to the university. As rejections piled up for his acting aspirations, Andersen began to shift his theatrical ambitions to playwriting.

After graduation, Andersen won a two-year scholarship to travel around Europe, the first of many trips he'd make and write about. His experiences abroad were highly formative, providing inspiration for many of his tales. Still in his 20s, he published an (obviously autobiographical) novel, *The Improvisatore*, about a poor young man who comes into his own while traveling in Italy. The novel launched his writing career, and soon he was hobnobbing with the international crowd—Charles Dickens, Victor Hugo, Franz Liszt, Richard Wagner, Henrik Ibsen, and Edvard Grieg.

Despite his many famous friends, Andersen remained a

boats leave at least twice an hour from Nyhavn and Christiansborg Palace, cruise around the palace and Christianshavn area, and then proceed into the wide-open harbor. Best on a sunny day, it's a relaxing way to see *The Little Mermaid* and munch on a lazy picnic during the slow-moving narration.

▲**Netto-Bådene**—These inexpensive cruises cost about half the price of their rival, Canal Tours Copenhagen. Go with Netto; there's no reason to pay double (45 kr, mid-March–mid-Oct daily 10:00-17:00, runs later in summer, sign at dock shows next departure, generally every 20 minutes, dress warmly—boats lonely soul who never married. Of uncertain sexuality, he had very close male friendships and journaled about unrequited love affairs with several women, including the famous opera star of the day, Jenny Lind, the "Swedish Nightingale." (For more on this aspect of his life, see the sidebar on page 81.) Without a family of his own, he became very close with the children of his friends—and, through his fairy tales, with a vast extended family of kids around the world.

Though he wrote novels, plays, and travel literature, it was his fairy tales, including *The Ugly Duckling*, *The Emperor's New Clothes*, *The Princess and the Pea*, *The Little Mermaid*, and *The Red Shoes*, that made him famous in Denmark and abroad. They made him Denmark's best-known author, the "Danish Charles Dickens." Some stories are based on earlier folk tales, and others came straight from his inventive mind, all written in an informal, conversational style that was considered unusual and even surprising at the time.

Andersen's compelling tales appeal to children and adults alike. They're full of magic and touch on strong, universal emotions—the pain of being different, the joy of self-discovery, and the struggle to fit in. The ugly duckling, for example, is teased by his fellow ducks before he finally discovers his true identity as a beautiful swan. In *The Emperor's New Clothes*, a boy is derided by everyone for speaking the simple, self-evident truth that the emperor is fooling himself. Harry Potter author J. K. Rowling recently said, "The indelible characters he created are so deeply implanted in our subconscious that we sometimes forget that we were not born with the stories." (For more on Andersen's famous story *The Little Mermaid*—and what it might tell us about his life—see page 81.)

By the time of his death, the poor shoemaker's son was wealthy, cultured, and had been knighted. His rise through traditional class barriers mirrors the social progress of the 19th century.

are open-top until Sept, tel. 32 54 41 02, www.havnerundfart .dk). Netto boats often make two stops where passengers can get off, then hop back on a later boat—at the bridge near *The Little Mermaid*, and at the Langebro bridge near Danhostel. Not every boat makes these stops; check the clock on the bridges for the next departure time.

Don't confuse the cheaper Netto and pricier Canal Tours Copenhagen boats: At Nyhavn, the Netto dock is midway down the canal (on the city side), while the Canal Tours Copenhagen dock is at the head of the canal. Near Christiansborg Palace, the

Netto boats leave from Holmen's Bridge in front of the palace, while Canal Tours Copenhagen boats depart from Gammel Strand, 200 yards away. Boats leaving from Christiansborg are generally less crowded than those leaving from Nyhavn.

Canal Tours Copenhagen—This more expensive option does the same cruise as Netto for 70 kr (daily March-late Oct 9:30-17:00, until 20:00 late June-late Aug; late-Oct-Dec 10:00-15:00, no tours Jan-Feb, boats are sometimes covered if it's raining, tel. 32 96 30 00, www.stromma.dk).

In summer, Canal Tours Copenhagen also runs unguided hop-on, hop-off **"water bus"** tours (40 kr/single trip, 70 kr/24 hours, daily late May-early Sept 10:15-18:45) and 1.5-hour evening **jazz cruises** (see "Nightlife in Copenhagen," page 113).

By Bus

Hop-on, Hop-off Bus Tours—These offer a basic 1.25- to 1.5-hour circle of the city sights, allowing you to get on and off as you like: Tivoli Gardens, Gammel Strand near Christiansborg Palace, *The Little Mermaid* site, Rosenborg Castle, Nyhavn sailors' quarter, and more, with recorded narration. The options include **City Sightseeing** (red buses, 155 kr, 185 kr includes Carlsberg and Christiania routes, ticket good for 24 hours, 2/hour, May-Aug daily 10:00-16:30, shorter hours off-season, bus departs City Hall below the *Lur Blowers* statue—to the left of City Hall—or at many other stops throughout city, pay driver, tel. 25 55 66 88, www.city-sightseeing.dk) and **Open Top Tours** (green buses, 175 kr, 35 kr more to add cruise on Canal Tours Copenhagen, ticket good for 24 hours, 2/hour, departures 10:00-16:00, www.stromma .dk/en/opentoptours). Another operation—called **Step On Step Off**—does a similar route with slightly lower frequency (every 45 minutes in summer, hourly in winter; 170 kr/1 day, 200 kr/2 days, www.steponstepoff.dk).

City Sightseeing also runs jaunts into the countryside, with themes such as Vikings, castles, and Hamlet. There are other companies as well; a variety of guided bus tours depart from Rådhuspladsen in front of the Palace Hotel.

By Bike

▲**Bike Copenhagen with Mike**—Mike Sommerville offers a good three-hour, guided tour of the city daily at 10:30 (with a second departure at 14:30 Tue-Wed, Fri, and Sat in June-Aug, and on Sat in Sept; 290 kr including bike rental, cash only). A Copenhagen native, Mike enjoys showing off his city to visitors by biking at a leisurely pace, "along the high roads, low roads, in-roads, and off-roads of Copenhagen." All tours are in English, and depart from the Bike Copenhagen with Mike tour base at Sankt Peders Straede 47, in the Latin Quarter (see the map on page 116). Mike also offers a night tour, a countryside tour, and private tours; see the details at www.bikecopenhagenwithmike.dk.

Self-Guided Walk

The Strøget and Copenhagen's Heart and Soul

Start from Rådhuspladsen (City Hall Square), the bustling heart of Copenhagen, dominated by the tower of the City Hall. Today this square always seems to be hosting some lively community event, but it was once Copenhagen's fortified west end. For 700 years, Copenhagen was contained within its city walls. By the mid-1800s, 140,000 people were packed inside. The overcrowding led to hygiene problems. (A cholera outbreak killed 5,000.) It was clear: The walls needed to come down...and they did. Those formidable town walls survive today only in echoes—a circular series of roads and the remnants of moats, now people-friendly city lakes (see "The Story of Copenhagen" sidebar, earlier).

• *Stand 50 yards in front of City Hall and turn clockwise for a...*

Rådhuspladsen Spin-Tour

The **City Hall,** or Rådhus, is worth a visit (described on page 84). Old **Hans Christian Andersen** sits to the right of City Hall, almost begging to be in another photo (as he used to in real life). Climb onto his well-worn knee. (While up there, you might take off your shirt for a racy photo, as many Danes enjoy doing.)

The wooded area behind Andersen is **Tivoli Gardens.** In 1843, magazine publisher Georg Carstensen convinced the king to let him build a pleasure garden outside the walls of crowded Copenhagen. The king quickly agreed, knowing that happy people care less about fighting for democracy. Tivoli became Europe's first great public amusement park. When the train lines came, the station was placed just beyond Tivoli.

The big, broad boulevard is **Vesterbrogade** ("Western Way"), which led to the western gate of the medieval city (behind you, where the pedestrian boulevard begins). Here, in the traffic hub of this huge city, you'll notice...not many cars. Denmark's 180 percent tax on car purchases makes the bus, Metro, or bike a sweeter option.

Down Vesterbrogade towers the **SAS building,** Copenhagen's only skyscraper. Locals say it seems so tall because the clouds hang so low. When it was built in 1960, Copenhageners took one look and decided—that's enough of a skyline.

COPENHAGEN

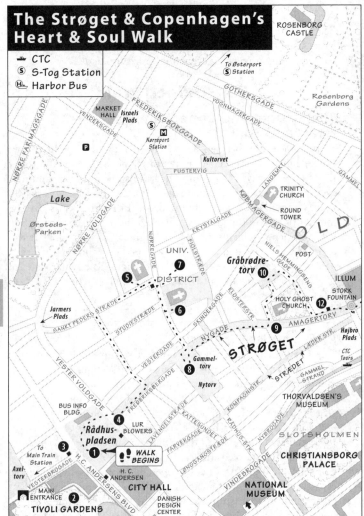

The Strøget & Copenhagen's Heart & Soul Walk

- CTC
- Ⓢ S-Tog Station
- Ⓗ Harbor Bus

ROSENBORG CASTLE

To Østerport Ⓢ Station

GOTHERSGADE

Rosenborg Gardens

NØRRE FARIMAGSGADE

VENDERSGADE

MARKET HALL

Israels Plads

FREDERIKSBORGGADE

VOGNMAGERGADE

Ⓟ

Ⓢ Ⓜ Nørreport Station

Kultorvet

PUSTERVIG

LANDEMÆRKET

GAMMEL

Lake

Ørsteds-Parken

NØRRE VOLDGADE

KRYSTALGADE

KØBMAGERGADE

TRINITY CHURCH

ROUND TOWER

O L D

NØRREGADE

FIOLSTRÆDE

UNIV. ⑦ DISTRICT

⑤

⑥

NIELS HEMMINGSENS GADE

POST

Gråbrødre-torv ⑩

ILLUM

HOLY GHOST CHURCH

STORK FOUNTAIN

⑫

Jarmers Plads

SANKT PEDERS STRÆDE

STUDIESTRÆDE

SKINDERGADE

KLOSTERSTR.

AMAGERTORV

NYGADE ⑨

Højbro Plads

STRØGET

LÆDER STR.

CTC Tours Ⓗ

VESTERGADE

Gammel-torv ⑧

STRÆDET

GAMMEL STRAND

VESTER VOLDGADE

FREDERIKSBERGGADE

Nytorv

KOMPAGNISTR.

THORVALDSEN'S MUSEUM

BUS INFO BLDG.

④ LUR BLOWERS

LAVENDELSTRÆDE

KATTESUNDET

RÅDHUS-STR.

NYBROGADE

SLOTSHOLMEN

③ Rådhus-pladsen ①

WALK BEGINS

CHRISTIANSBORG PALACE

To Main Train Station

FARVERGADE

LØNGANGSTRÆDE

VINDEBROGADE

Axeltorv

VESTERBROGADE

H.C. ANDERSENS BLVD

H.C. Andersen

CITY HALL

NATIONAL MUSEUM

MAIN ENTRANCE ②

TIVOLI GARDENS

DANISH DESIGN CENTER

The golden **weather girls** (on the corner, high above Vesterbrogade) indicate the weather: on a bike (fair weather) or with an umbrella. These two have been called the only women in Copenhagen you can trust, but for years they've been stuck in almost-sunny mode...with the bike just peeking out. Notice that the red temperature dots max out at 28° Celsius (that's 82° Fahrenheit).

To the right, just down the street, is the Tiger Store (a popular local dime store...everything is priced at 10 or 20 kr). The next street (once the local Fleet Street, with the big newspapers) still

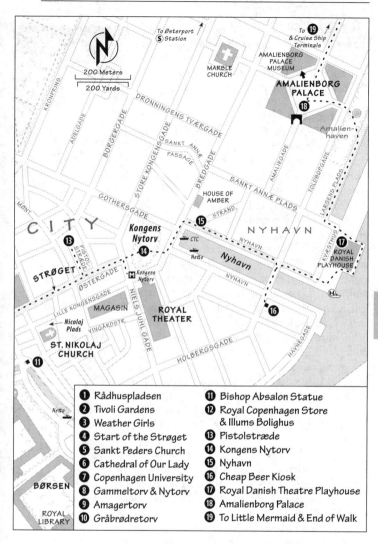

1 Rådhuspladsen
2 Tivoli Gardens
3 Weather Girls
4 Start of the Strøget
5 Sankt Peders Church
6 Cathedral of Our Lady
7 Copenhagen University
8 Gammeltorv & Nytorv
9 Amagertorv
10 Gråbrødretorv
11 Bishop Absalon Statue
12 Royal Copenhagen Store & Illums Bolighus
13 Pistolstræde
14 Kongens Nytorv
15 Nyhavn
16 Cheap Beer Kiosk
17 Royal Danish Theatre Playhouse
18 Amalienborg Palace
19 To Little Mermaid & End of Walk

COPENHAGEN

has the offices for *Politiken* (the leading Danish newspaper) and the best bookstore in town, Boghallen.

As you spin farther right, three fast-food joints stand at the entry to the Strøget (STROY-et), Copenhagen's grand pedestrian boulevard—where we're heading next. Just beyond that and the Art Deco-style Palace Hotel (with a tower to serve as a sister to the City Hall) is the *Lur Blowers* **sculpture,** which honors the earliest warrior Danes. The *lur* is a curvy, trombone-sounding horn that was used to call soldiers to battle or to accompany pagan religious processions. The earliest bronze *lurs* date as far back as 3,500 years

ago. Later, the Vikings used a wood version of
the *lur.* The ancient originals, which still play,
are displayed in the National Museum. (City
tour buses leave from below these Vikings.)

• *Now head down the pedestrian boulevard.*

The Strøget
The American trio of Burger King, 7-Eleven,
and KFC marks the start of this otherwise
charming pedestrian street. Finished in 1962,
Copenhagen's experimental, tremendously
successful, and much-copied pedestrian shop-
ping mall is a string of lively (and individually named) streets and
lovely squares that bunny-hop through the old town from City
Hall to the Nyhavn quarter, a 20-minute stroll away.

As you wander down this street, remember that the commercial focus of a historic street like the Strøget drives up the land
value, which generally trashes the charm and tears down the old
buildings. Look above the modern window displays and street-
level advertising to discover bits of 19th-century character that still
survive. Though the Strøget has become hamburgerized, historic
bits and attractive pieces of old Copenhagen are just off this commercial cancan.

After one block (at Kattesundet), make a side-trip three blocks
left into Copenhagen's colorful **university district.** Formerly the
old brothel neighborhood, later the heart of Copenhagen's hippie
community in the 1960s, today this "Latin Quarter" is Soho chic.
At Sankt Peders Stræde, turn right and walk to the end of the
street.

Along the way, look for large mansions that once circled
expansive **courtyards.** As the population grew, the city walls con-
stricted Copenhagen's physical size. The courtyards were gradually
filled with higgledy-piggledy secondary buildings. Today throughout the old center, you can step off a busy pedestrian mall and
back in time into these characteristic half-timbered time warps.
Replace the parked car with a tired horse and the bikes with a line
of outhouses, and you're in 19th-century Copenhagen. If you see
an open courtyard door, you're welcome to discreetly wander in
and look around.

You'll also pass funky shops, and the big brick **Sankt Peders
Church**—the old German merchant community's church, which
still holds services in German. Its crypt (filling a ground-floor
building out back due to the boggy nature of the soil) is filled with
fancy German tombs (fee to enter).

• *When Sankt Peders Stræde intersects with Nørregade, look right to
find the big, Neoclassical...*

Cathedral of Our Lady (Vor Frue Kirche)

The obelisk-like **Reformation Memorial** across the street from the cathedral celebrates Denmark's break from the Roman Catholic Church to become Lutheran in 1536.

Walk around and study the reliefs of great Danish reformers protesting from their pulpits. The relief facing the church shows King Christian III presiding over the pivotal town council meeting when they decided to break away from Rome. As a young man, Prince Christian had traveled to Germany, where he was influenced by Martin Luther. He returned to take the Danish throne by force, despite Catholic opposition. Realizing the advantages of being the head of his own state church, Christian confiscated church property and established the state Lutheran Church. King Christian was crowned inside this cathedral. Because of the reforms of 1536, there's no Mary in the Cathedral of Our Lady.

The cathedral's **facade** looks like a Greek temple. (Two blocks to the right, in the distance, notice more Neoclassicism—the law courts.) You can see why Golden Age Copenhagen (early 1800s) fancied itself a Nordic Athens. Old Testament figures (King David and Moses) flank the cathedral's entryway. Above, John the Baptist stands where you'd expect to see Greek gods. He invites you in...to the New Testament.

The **interior** is a world of Neoclassical serenity. Go inside (free, open daily 8:00-17:00). This pagan temple now houses Chris-

tianity. The nave is lined by the 12 apostles, clad in classical robes—masterpieces by the great Danish sculptor Bertel Thorvaldsen (see sidebar, page 92). Each strikes a meditative pose, carrying his identifying symbol: Peter with keys, Andrew with the X-shaped cross of his execu-

tion, Matthew and John writing their books, and so on. They lead to a statue of the *Risen Christ* (see photo next page), standing where the statue of Zeus would have been: inside a temple-like niche, flanked by columns, and topped with a pediment. Rather than wearing a royal robe, Jesus wears his burial shroud, opens his arms wide, and says, "Come to me." (Mormons will recognize this statue—a replica stands in the visitors center at Salt Lake City's

Temple Square and is often reproduced in church publications.) The
marvelous acoustics are demonstrated
in free organ concerts Saturdays in
July and August at noon. Notice
how, in good Protestant style, only
the front half of the pews are "revers-
ible," allowing the congregation to
flip around and face the pulpit (in the
middle of the church) to better hear
the sermon.

• *Head back outside. If you face the
facade and look to the left (across the
square called Frue Plads), you'll see...*

Copenhagen University

Now home to 30,000 students, this university was founded by the
king in the 15th century to stop the Danish brain drain to Paris.

Today tuition is free (but room,
board, and beer are not). Locals
say it's easy to get in, but, given
the wonderful lifestyle, very hard
to get out.

Step up the middle steps of
the university's big building and
enter a colorful lobby, starring
Athena and Apollo. The frescoes
celebrate high thinking, with themes such as the triumph of wisdom over barbarism. Notice how harmoniously the architecture,
sculpture, and painting work together. (Just inside the door are
two stand-up terminals offering free Internet access.)

Outside, busts honor great minds from the faculty, including
(at the end) Niels Bohr, a professor who won the 1922 Nobel Prize
for theoretical physics. He evaded the clutches of the Nazi science
labs by fleeing to America in 1943, where he helped develop the
atomic bomb.

• *Rejoin the Strøget (down where you saw the law courts) at the twin
squares called...*

Gammeltorv and Nytorv

This was the old town center. In Gammeltorv ("Old Square"), the
Fountain of Charity (Caritas) is named for the figure of Charity on
top. It has provided drinking water to locals since the early 1600s.
Featuring a pregnant woman squirting water from her breasts
next to a boy urinating, this was just too much for people of the
Victorian Age. They corked both figures and raised the statue to

what they hoped would be out of view. The Asian-looking kiosk was one of the city's first community telephone centers from the days before phones were privately owned. Look at the reliefs ringing its top: an airplane with bird wings (c. 1900) and two women talking on the newfangled phone. (It was thought business would popularize the telephone, but actually it was women.)

While Gammeltorv was a place of happiness and merriment, Nytorv ("New Square") was a place of severity and judg-

ment. Walk to the small raised area in front of the old ancient-Greek-style former City Hall. Do a 360. The square is Neoclassical (built mostly around 1800). Read the old Danish on the City Hall facade: "With Law Shall Man Build the Land." Look down at the pavement and read the plaque: "Here stood the town's *Kag* (whipping post) until 1780."

• *Now walk down the next stretch of the Strøget to reach...*

Amagertorv

This is prime real estate for talented street entertainers and pickpockets. Walk to the stately brick Holy Ghost church (Helligåndskirken). The fine spire is typical of old Danish churches. Under the stepped gable was a medieval hospital run by monks (one of the oldest buildings in town, dating from the 12th century).

A block behind the church (walk down Valkendorfsgade—the street just before the church—and through a passage under the rust-colored building at #32) is the leafy and caffeine-stained **Gråbrødretorv.** This "Grey Friars' Square," surrounded by fine

old buildings, is a popular place for an outdoor meal or drink in the summer. At the end of the square, the street Niels Hemmingsens Gade returns (past the recommended Copenhagen Jazz House, a good place for live music nightly) to the Strøget.

Once at the Strøget, turn left and continue down Amagertorv, with its fine inlaid Italian granite stonework, to the next square with the "stork" fountain (actually three herons). From the fountain, you can see the imposing Parliament building, Christiansborg Palace (with its "three crowns" spire) and an equestrian statue of Bishop Absalon, the city's founder (canal boat tours depart

Copenhagen at a Glance

▲▲▲**Tivoli Gardens** Copenhagen's classic amusement park, with rides, music, food, and other fun. **Hours:** Mid-April-late Sept daily 11:00-22:00, later Fri-Sat and mid-June-late Aug, also open daily 11:00-22:00 for a week in mid-Oct and mid-Nov-late Dec. See page 82.

▲▲▲**National Museum** History of Danish civilization with tourable 19th-century Victorian Apartment. **Hours:** Museum—Tue-Sun 10:00-17:00, closed Mon; Victorian Apartment—tours June-Sept Sat at 14:00. See page 86.

▲▲▲**Rosenborg Castle and Treasury** Renaissance castle of larger-than-life "warrior king" Christian IV. **Hours:** June-Aug daily 10:00-17:00; May and Sept-Oct daily 10:00-16:00; Nov-Dec Tue-Sun 11:00-14:00 (treasury until 16:00), closed Mon; Jan-April Tue-Sun 11:00-16:00, closed Mon. See page 97.

▲▲▲**Christiania** Colorful counterculture squatters' colony. **Hours:** Always open. See page 106.

▲▲**Christiansborg Palace** Royal reception rooms with dazzling tapestries. **Hours:** Palace—daily 10:00-17:00 except closed Mon Oct-April; stables—daily 13:30-16:00 except closed Mon Oct-April. See page 89.

▲▲**Museum of Danish Resistance** Chronicle of Denmark's struggle against the Nazis. **Hours:** May-Sept Tue-Sun 10:00-16:00, Oct-April Tue-Sun 10:00-15:00, closed Mon year-round. See page 95.

▲▲**Thorvaldsen's Museum** Works of the Danish Neoclassical sculptor. **Hours:** Tue-Sun 10:00-17:00, closed Mon. See page 91.

▲**City Hall** Copenhagen's landmark, packed with Danish history and symbolism and topped with a tower. **Hours:** Mon-Fri 8:30-

nearby). The Victorian WCs here (steps down from fountain, 2 kr, free urinals) are a delight.

Amagertorv is a highlight for shoppers, with the Royal Copenhagen store—stacked with three floors of porcelain—and Illums Bolighus' three floors of modern Danish design (see "Shopping in Copenhagen," later). A block toward the canal—running parallel to the Strøget—starts Strædet, which is a "second Strøget" featuring cafés, antique shops, and no fast food.

North of Amagertorv, a broad pedestrian mall called **Købmagergade** leads past a fine modern bakery (Illum Bager,

16:30, some Sat 10:00-13:00, closed Sun. See page 84.

▲**Ny Carlsberg Glyptotek** Scandinavia's top art gallery, featuring Egyptians, Greeks, Etruscans, French, and Danes. **Hours:** Tue-Sun 11:00-17:00, closed Mon. See page 85.

▲**Museum of Copenhagen** The story of Copenhagen, displayed in an old house. **Hours:** Daily 10:00-17:00. See page 89.

▲**Danish Jewish Museum** Exhibit tracing the 400-year history of Danish Jews, in a unique building by American architect Daniel Libeskind. **Hours:** June-Aug Tue-Sun 10:00-17:00; Sept-May Tue-Fri 13:00-16:00, Sat-Sun 12:00-17:00; closed Mon year-round. See page 94.

▲**Amalienborg Palace Museum** Quick and intimate look at Denmark's royal family. **Hours:** May-Oct daily 10:00-16:00; Nov-April Tue-Sun 11:00-16:00, closed Mon. See page 95.

▲**Rosenborg Gardens** Park surrounding Rosenborg Castle, filled with statues and statuesque Danes. **Hours:** Always open. See page 103.

▲**National Gallery of Denmark** Good Danish and Modernist collections. **Hours:** Tue-Sun 10:00-17:00, Wed until 20:00, closed Mon. See page 104.

▲**Our Savior's Church** Spiral-spired church with bright Baroque interior. **Hours:** Church—daily 11:00-15:30 but may close for special services; tower—July-mid-Sept Mon-Sat 10:00-19:00, Sun 10:30-19:00; April-June and mid-Sept-Nov daily until 16:00, closed Dec-March and in bad weather. See page 105.

COPENHAGEN

next to McDonald's; salads, sandwiches, and traditional pastries) to Christian IV's Round Tower and the Latin Quarter (university district). The recommended Café Norden overlooks the fountain—a good place for a meal or coffee with a view. The second floor offers the best vantage point.

The final stretch of the Strøget leads to **Pistolstræde** (leading off the Strøget to the left from Østergade at #24, just after crossing the busy street), a cute lane of shops in restored 18th-century buildings. Wander back into the half-timbered section.

• *Continuing along the Strøget, passing major department stores (see "Shopping in Copenhagen," later), you'll come to the biggest square in town...*

Kongens Nytorv

The "King's New Square" is home to the National Theater, French embassy, and venerable Hotel d'Angleterre. In the mid-1600s the city expanded, pushing its wall farther east. The equestrian statue in the middle of the square celebrates Christian V, who made this square the city's geographical and cultural center. In 1676, King Christian rode off to reconquer the southern tip of Sweden and reclaim Denmark's dominance.

He returned empty-handed and broke. Denmark became a second-rate power, but Copenhagen prospered. In the winter this square becomes a popular ice-skating rink.

Before entering the square, walk to the right, toward the small glass pyramids (marking the Metro). Wander into **Hviids Vinstue,** the town's oldest wine cellar (from 1723, before the Metro station, at #19, under the Bali Restaurant) to check out its characteristic interior and fascinating old Copenhagen photos. It's a colorful spot for an open-face sandwich and a beer (three sandwiches and a beer for 65 kr at lunchtime). Their wintertime *gløgg* (hot spiced wine) is legendary. Across the street, towering above the Metro station, is Magasin du Nord, the grandest old department store in town.

The **Metro** that runs underground here features state-of-the-art technology (automated cars, no driver...sit in front to watch the tracks coming at you). As the cars come and go without drivers, compare this system to the public transit in your town.

• *Back up at ground level, walk across the square to the trendy harbor of...*

Nyhavn

Established in the 1670s along with Kongens Nytorv, Nyhavn ("New Harbor") is a recently gentrified sailors' quarter. (Hong Kong is the last of the nasty bars from the rough old days.) With its trendy cafés, jazz clubs, and tattoo shops (pop into Tattoo Ole at #17—fun photos, very traditional), Nyhavn is a wonderful place to hang out. The canal is filled with glamorous old sailboats of all sizes. Historic sloops are welcome to moor here in Copenhagen's ever-changing boat museum. Hans Christian Andersen lived and wrote his first stories here (in the red double-gabled building on the right at #20). A miniscule amber museum is above the House of Amber at the head of the canal (see "Shopping in Copenhagen," page 112).

Wander the quay, enjoying the frat-party parade of tattoos (hotter weather reveals more tattoos). Celtic and Nordic mythological designs are in (as is bodybuilding, by the looks of things). The place thrives—with the cheap-beer drinkers dockside and the richer and older ones looking on from comfier cafés.

A note about all this public beer-drinking: There's no more beer consumption here than in the US; it's just out in public. Many

young Danes can't afford to drink in a bar, so they "picnic drink" their beers in squares and along canals, spending a quarter of the bar price for a bottle from a nearby kiosk. Consider grabbing a cold 10-kr beer yourself and joining the scene (the kiosk is on Holbergsgade, just over the bridge and on the left, open daily until 24:00).

From the end of Nyhavn canal, turn left around the **Royal Danish Theatre's Playhouse.** Continuing north along the har-

bor, you'll stroll a delightful waterfront promenade to the modern fountain of Amaliehaven Park, immediately across the harbor from Copenhagen's slick Opera House. The Opera House is bigger than it looks because much of it is underground. Its striking design is controversial. Completed in 2005 by Henning Larsen, it was a $400 million gift to the nation from an oil-shipping magnate.

• *A block inland (behind the fountain) is the orderly...*

Amalienborg Palace and Square

Queen Margrethe II and her husband live in the mansion to your immediate left as you enter the square from the harborside. (If the flag's flying, she's home.) Her son and heir to the throne, Crown Prince Frederik, recently moved into the mansion across the

COPENHAGEN

street with his wife, Australian businesswoman Mary Donaldson, and their four children.

Though the guards change with royal fanfare at noon only when the queen is in residence, they shower every morning. The royal guard often has a police escort when it marches through town on special occasions—leading locals to joke that theirs is "the only army in the world that needs police protection."

The small **Amalienborg Palace Museum** offers an intimate look at royal living (far side of square, described on page 95).

The equestrian statue of Frederick V is a reminder that this square was the centerpiece of a planned town he envisioned in 1750. It was named for him—Frederikstaden. During the 18th century, Denmark's population grew and the country thrived (as trade flourished and its neutrality kept it out of the costly wars impoverishing much of Europe). Frederikstaden, with its strong Neoclassical harmony, was designed as a luxury neighborhood for the city's business elite. Nobility and other big shots moved in, but the king came here only after his other palace burned down in a 1794 fire.

Just inland, the striking Frederikskirke—better known as the **Marble Church**—was designed to fit this ritzy new quarter. If it's open, step inside to bask in its vast, serene, Pantheon-esque atmosphere (free, Mon-Thu 10:00-17:00, Fri-Sun 12:00-17:00).

• *From the square, Amaliegade leads two blocks north to...*

Kastellet Park

In this park, you'll find some worthwhile sightseeing. Just before the park's entrance, look for Denmark's fascinating (and free) WWII-era **Museum of Danish Resistance** (see page 95). Beyond that is the 1908 **Gefion Foun-tain,** which illustrates the myth of the goddess who was given one night to carve a hunk out of Sweden to make into Denmark's main island, Sjælland (or "Zealand" in English), which you're on. Gefion transformed her four sons into oxen to do the job, and the chunk she removed from Sweden is supposedly Vänern, Sweden's largest lake. If you look at a map showing Sweden and Denmark, the island and the lake are, in fact, roughly the same shape.

Next to the fountain is an Anglican church built of flint. Climb up the stairs by the fountain and continue along the top of the rampart about five minutes to reach the harborfront site

The Little Mermaid and Hans Christian Andersen

"Far out in the ocean, where the water is as blue as a corn-flower, as clear as crystal, and very, very deep..." there lived a young mermaid. So begins one of Hans Christian Andersen's (1805-1875) best-known stories. The plot line starts much like the Disney children's movie, but it's spiced with poetic description and philosophical dialogue about the immortal soul.

The mermaid's story goes like this: One day, a young mermaid spies a passing ship and falls in love with a handsome human prince. The ship is wrecked in a storm, and she saves the prince's life. To be with the prince, the mermaid asks a sea witch to give her human legs. In exchange, she agrees to give up her voice and the chance of ever returning to the sea. And, the witch tells her, if the prince doesn't marry her, she will immediately die heartbroken and without an immortal soul. The mermaid agrees, and her fish tail becomes a pair of beautiful but painful legs. She woos the prince—who loves her in return—but he eventually marries another. Heartbroken, the mermaid prepares to die. She's given one last chance to save herself: She must kill the prince on his wedding night. She sneaks into the bedchamber with a knife...but can't bear to kill the man she loves. The mermaid throws herself into the sea to die. Suddenly, she's miraculously carried up by the mermaids of the air, who give her an immortal soul as a reward for her long-suffering love.

The tale of unrequited love mirrors Andersen's own sad love life. He had two major crushes—one of them for the famous opera singer, Jenny Lind—but he was turned down both times, and he never married. Scholars with access to Andersen's diary believe he was bisexual and died a virgin. The great author is said to have feared he'd lose his artistic drive if he ever actually made love to another person. His dearest male friend, Edvard Collin, inherited Andersen's entire estate (which was not unusual in the Romantic 19th century, when men tended to have more emotional and intimate friendships than today).

of the overrated, overfondled, and overphotographed symbol of Copenhagen, **Den Lille Havfrue—The Little Mermaid.** *The Little Mermaid* statue was a gift to the city of Copenhagen in 1909 from brewing magnate Carl Jacobsen (whose art collection forms the basis of the Ny Carlsberg Glyptotek). Inspired by a ballet performance of Andersen's story, Jacobsen hired the young sculptor Edvard Eriksen to immortalize the mermaid as a statue. Eriksen used his wife Eline as the model.

For the non-Disneyfied *Little Mermaid* story—and insights into Hans Christian Andersen—see the sidebar.

• *Our walking tour is finished. You can get back downtown on foot, by taxi, or on bus #1A or #15 from Store Kongensgade on the other side of Kastellet Park, or bus #26 from farther north, along Folke Bernadottes Allé.*

Sights in Copenhagen

Near the Train Station

Copenhagen's great train station, the Hovedbanegården, is a fascinating mesh of Scandinavian culture and transportation efficiency. From the station, delightful sights fan out into the old city. The following attractions are listed roughly in order from the train station to Slotsholmen Island.

▲▲▲**Tivoli Gardens**—The world's grand old amusement park—since 1843—is 20 acres, 110,000 lanterns, and countless ice cream

cones of fun. You pay one admission price and find yourself lost in a Hans Christian Andersen wonderland of rides, restaurants, games, marching bands, roulette wheels, and funny mirrors. A roller coaster screams through the middle of a tranquil Asian food court, the Small-World-inspired Den Flyvende Kuffert ride floats through Hans Christian Andersen fairy tales, and a fancy pavilion hides one of the most respected restaurants in Copenhagen. It's a children's fantasyland midday, but it becomes more adult-oriented later on. With or without kids, this place is a true magic kingdom. Tivoli doesn't try to be Disney. It's wonderfully and happily Danish. I find it worth the admission just to see Danes—young and old—at play.

Cost: 95 kr, free for kids under 8. To go on rides, you'll buy ride tickets from the automated machines (25 kr, color-coded rides cost 1, 2, or 3 tickets apiece); or you can buy an all-day ride pass for 199 kr. If you'll be using at least eight tickets, buy the ride pass

instead. To leave and come back later, you'll have to buy a 15-kr re-entry ticket before you exit. Tel. 33 15 10 01, www.tivoli.dk.

Hours: Mid-April-late Sept daily 11:00-22:00, later Fri-Sat and mid-June-late Aug. In winter, Tivoli opens daily 11:00-22:00 for a week in mid-October for Halloween, then again from mid-November to New Year's Day for a Christmas market with *gløgg* (hot spiced wine) and ice-skating on Tivoli Lake. Dress warm for chilly evenings any time of year. There are lockers by each entrance.

Getting There: Tivoli is across Bernstoffsgade from the train station. If you're catching an overnight train, this is *the* place to spend your last Copenhagen hours.

Entertainment at Tivoli: Upon arrival (through main entrance, on left in the service center), pick up a map and look for the events schedule. Take a moment to sit down and plan your entertainment for the evening. Events are spread between 15:00 and 23:00; the 19:30 concert in the concert hall can be as little as 50 kr or as much as 1,200 kr, depending on the performer (box office tel. 33 15 10 12). If the Tivoli Symphony is playing, it's worth paying for. The ticket box office is outside, just to the left of the main entrance (daily 10:00-20:00; if you buy a concert ticket you get into Tivoli for free).

Free concerts, pantomime theater, ballet, acrobats, puppets, and other shows pop up all over the park, and a well-organized visitor can enjoy an exciting evening of entertainment without spending a single krone beyond the entry fee. Friday evenings feature a (usually free) rock or pop show at 22:00. People gather around the lake 45 minutes before closing time for the "Tivoli Illuminations" (except on Fri, when there's no show). Fireworks blast a few nights each summer. The park is particularly romantic at dusk, when the lights go on.

Eating at Tivoli: Inside the park, expect to pay amusement-park prices for amusement-park-quality food. Still, a meal here is part of the fun. **Søcafeen** serves only traditional open-face sandwiches in a fun beer garden with lakeside ambience. They allow picnics if you buy a drink (and will rent you plates and silverware for 10 kr per person). The *pølse* (sausage) stands are cheap, and there's a bagel sandwich place in the amusements corner. **Færgekroen** offers a quiet, classy lakeside escape from the amusement-park intensity, with traditional dishes washed down by its own microbrew (190-265-kr hearty pub grub). They host live piano on Thursday, Friday, and Saturday evenings from 20:00, often

COPENHAGEN

resulting in an impromptu sing-along with a bunch of very happy Danes. **Wagamama,** a modern pan-Asian slurpathon from the UK, serves healthy noodle dishes (at the far back side of the park, also possible to enter from outside, 100-130-kr meals). **Nimb's Terrasse** has dignified French food in a garden setting (175-225-kr dishes). **Café Georg,** to the left of the concert hall, has tasty 75-kr sandwiches and a lake view (also 100-kr salads and omelets). The kid-pleasing **Piratiriet** lets you dine on a pirate ship (140-170-kr main dishes).

For something more upscale, consider the complex of Nimb restaurants, in the big Taj Mahal-like pavilion near the entrance facing the train station. **Nimb's Louise** is Tivoli's big splurge, with seasonal menus that are well-regarded even by non-parkgoers (lunch: three courses-495 kr; dinner: four courses-750 kr, eight courses-1125 kr). **Nimb's Brasserie,** sharing the same lobby, has more affordable prices (175-235-kr main dishes).

If it's chilly, you'll find plenty of **Mamma Mokka** coffee take-away stands. If you get a drink "to go," you'll pay an extra 5-kr deposit for the cup, which you can recoup by inserting the empty cup into an automated machine (marked on maps).

▲**City Hall (Rådhus)**—This city landmark, between the train station/Tivoli and the Strøget, is free and open to the public; you can wander throughout the building and into the peaceful garden out back. It also offers private tours and trips up its 345-foot-tall tower.

Cost and Hours: Free, Mon-Fri 8:30-16:30; you can usually slip in Sat 10:00-13:00 when weddings are going on, or join the Sat tour; closed Sun. Guided English-language tours-30 kr, 45 minutes, gets you into more private, official rooms; Mon-Fri at 15:00, Sat at 10:00. Tower-20 kr, 300 steps for the best aerial view of Copenhagen, June-Sept Mon-Fri at 11:00 and 14:00, Sat at 12:00, closed Sun and Oct-May. Tel. 33 66 33 66.

Visiting City Hall: It's draped, inside and out, in Danish symbolism. The city's founder, Bishop Absalon, stands over the door. Absalon (c. 1128-1201)—bishop, soldier, and foreign-policy wonk—was King Valdemar I's right-hand man. In Copenhagen, he drove out pirates and built a fort to guard the harbor, turning a miserable fishing village into a humming Baltic seaport. The polar bears climbing on the rooftop symbolize the giant Danish protectorate of Greenland. Six night watchmen flank the city's gold-and-green seal under the Danish flag.

Step inside. The info desk

(on the left as you enter) has racks of tourist information (city maps and other brochures). The building and its huge tower were inspired by the city hall in Siena, Italy (with the necessary bad-weather addition of a glass roof). Enormous functions fill this grand hall (the iron grate in the center of the floor is an elevator for bringing up 1,200 chairs), while the busts of four illustrious local boys—fairy-tale writer Hans Christian Andersen, sculptor Bertel Thorvaldsen, physicist Niels Bohr, and the building's architect, Martin Nyrop—look on. Underneath the floor are national archives dating back to 1275, popular with Danes researching their family roots.

Danish Design Center—This center shows off the best in Danish design as well as top examples from around the world, including architecture, fashion, and graphic arts. A visit to this low-key display for sleek Scandinavian objects offers an interesting glimpse into a culture that takes pride in functionalism and minimalism. The ground and upper floors are filled with changing exhibits; the basement houses the "semipermanent" Denmark by Design exhibit (likely through sometime in 2013), with samples of Danish design from 1950 to 2000. The boutique next to the ticket counter features three themes: travel light (chic travel accessories and gadgets), modern Danish classics, and books and posters. Sometimes it feels a bit like an Ikea showroom—suggesting the prevalence of Scandinavian design in our everyday lives. But perusing the exhibits here, you'll come to see design not just as something pleasing to the eye, but as an invaluable tool that can improve lives and solve problems.

Cost and Hours: 55 kr, Mon-Fri 10:00-17:00, Wed until 21:00, Sat-Sun 11:00-16:00—July-Aug until 17:00, across from Tivoli Gardens and down the street from City Hall at H. C. Andersen Boulevard 27, tel. 33 69 33 69, www.ddc.dk.

Eating: The café on the main level, under the atrium, serves light lunches (55-65-kr sandwiches and salads, three *smørrebrød* for 125 kr).

▲**Ny Carlsberg Glyptotek**—Scandinavia's top art gallery is an impressive example of what beer money can do. Brewer Carl Jacobsen (son of J. C. Jacobsen, who funded the Museum of

National History at Frederiksborg Castle) was an avid collector and patron of the arts. (Carl also donated *The Little Mermaid* statue to the city.) His namesake museum has intoxicating artifacts from the ancient world, along with some fine art from our own times. The next time you sip a

Carlsberg beer, drink a toast to Carl Jacobsen and his marvelous collection. *Skål!*

Cost and Hours: 75 kr, free Sun; open Tue-Sun 11:00-17:00, closed Mon, classy cafeteria under palms, behind Tivoli at Dantes Plads 7, tel. 33 41 81 41, www.glyptoteket.com.

Visiting the Museum: Pick up a floor plan as you enter to help navigate the confusing layout. For a chronological swing, start with Egypt (mummy coffins and sarcophagi, a 5,000-year-old hippo statue), Greece (red-and-black painted vases, statues), the Etruscan world (Greek-looking vases), and Rome (grittily realistic statues and portrait busts). The sober realism of 19th-century Danish Golden Age painting reflects the introspection of a once-powerful nation reduced to second-class status—and ultimately embracing what made them unique. The "French Wing" (just inside the front door) has Rodin statues. A heady, if small, exhibit of 19th-century French paintings (in a modern building within the back  courtyard) shows how Realism morphed into Impressionism and Post-Impressionism, and includes a couple of canvases apiece by Géricault, Delacroix, Monet, Manet, Millet, Courbet, Degas, Pissarro, Cézanne, Van Gogh, Picasso, Renoir, and Toulouse-Lautrec. Look for art by Gauguin—from before Tahiti (when he lived in Copenhagen with his Danish wife and their five children) and after Tahiti. There's also a fine collection of modern (post-Thorvaldsen) Danish sculpture.

Linger with marble gods under the palm leaves and glass dome of the very soothing winter garden. Designers, figuring Danes would be more interested in a lush garden than in classical art, used this wonderful space as leafy bait to cleverly introduce locals to a few Greek and Roman statues. (It works for tourists, too.) One of the original *Thinker* sculptures by Rodin (wondering how to scale the Tivoli fence?) is in the museum's backyard.

▲▲▲**National Museum**—Focus on this museum's excellent and curiously enjoyable Danish collection, which traces this civilization from its ancient beginnings. Its prehistoric collection is the best of its kind in Scandinavia. Exhibits are laid out chronologically and are eloquently described in English.

Cost and Hours: Free, Tue-Sun 10:00-17:00, closed Mon, mandatory lockers take a 10-kr coin that will be returned, enter at Ny Vestergade 10, tel. 33 13 44 11, www.natmus.dk. The café overlooking the entry hall serves coffee, pastries, and lunch (90-145 kr).

❍ **Self-Guided Tour:** Pick up the museum map as you enter, and head for the Danish history exhibit. It fills three floors, from the bottom up: prehistory, the Middle Ages and Renaissance, and modern times (1660-2000).

Start before history did, in the **Danish Prehistory** exhibit (on the right side of the main entrance hall). Recently updated, this collection is slick and extremely well-presented.

In the Stone Age section, you'll see primitive tools and still-clothed skeletons of Scandinavia's reindeer-hunters. The oak coffins were originally covered by burial mounds (called "barrows"). People put valuable items into the coffins with the dead, such as a folding chair (which, back then, was a real status symbol). In the farming section, ogle the ceremonial axes and amber necklaces.

The Bronze Age brought the sword (several are on display).

The "Chariot of the Sun"—a small statue of a horse pulling the sun across the sky—likely had religious significance for early Scandinavians (whose descendants continue to celebrate the solstice with fervor). In the same room are those iconic horned helmets. Contrary to popular belief (and countless tourist shops), these helmets were not worn by the Vikings, but by their predecessors—for ceremonial purposes, centuries earlier. In the next room are huge cases filled with still-playable *lur* horns (see page 71). Another room shows off a bitchin' collection of well-translated rune stones proclaiming heroic deeds.

This leads to the Iron Age and an object that's neither Iron nor Danish: the 2,000-year-old Gundestrup Cauldron of art-textbook fame. This 20-pound, soup-kitchen-size bowl made of silver

was found in a Danish bog, but its symbolism suggests it was originally from Thrace (in northeast Greece) or Celtic Ireland. On the sides, hunters slay bulls, and gods cavort with stags, horses, dogs, and dragons. It's both mysterious and fascinating.

Prehistoric Danes were fascinated by bogs. To make iron, you need ore—and Denmark's many bogs provided that critical material in abundance, leading people to believe that the gods dwelled there. These Danes appeased the gods by sacrificing valuable items (and even people) into bogs. Fortunately for modern archaeologists, bogs happen to be an ideal environment for preserving fragile objects. One bog alone—the Nydam bog—has yielded thousands of items, including three whole ships.

No longer bogged down in prehistory, the people of Scandinavia came into contact with Roman civilization. At about this time, the Viking culture rose; you'll see the remains of an old warship. The Vikings, so feared in most of Europe, are still thought of fondly here in their homeland. You'll notice the descriptions straining to defend them: Sure, they'd pillage, rape, and plunder. But they also founded thriving, wealthy, and cultured trade towns. Love the Vikings or hate them, it's impossible to deny their massive reach—Norse Vikings even carved runes into the walls of the Hagia Sophia church (in today's Istanbul).

Next, go upstairs. You'll enter (awkwardly) right between the **Middle Ages and Renaissance** sections; to go in chronologi-

cal order, go left, cover your eyes, and walk through the exhibits to the start of the Middle Ages and the coming of Christianity. Then retrace your steps through the Middle Ages (eyes open this time). Here you'll find lots of bits and pieces of old churches, such as golden altars and *aquamaniles*, pitchers used for ritual hand-washing. The Dagmar Cross is the prototype for a popular form of crucifix worn by many Danes (Room 102, small glass display case, smallest of the three crosses in this case—with colorful enamel paintings). Another cross in this case (the Roskilde Cross, studded with gemstones) was found inside the wooden head of Christ displayed high on the opposite wall. There are also exhibits on tools and trade, weapons, drinking horns, and fine, wood-carved winged altarpieces. Carry on to find fascinating material on the Reformation, an exhibit on everyday town life in the 16th and 17th centuries, and, in Room 126, a unique "cylinder perspective" of the noble family (from 1656) and two peep shows. (Don't get too excited—they're just church interiors.)

The next floor takes you into **modern times,** with historic toys and a slice-of-Danish-life (1600-2000) gallery where you'll see everything from rifles and old bras to early jukeboxes. You'll learn that the Danish Golden Age (which dominates most art museums in Denmark) captured the everyday pastoral beauty of the countryside, celebrated Denmark's smallness and peace-loving

nature, and mixed in some Nordic mythology. With industrialization came the labor movement and trade unions. After delving into the World Wars, Baby Boomers, creation of the postwar welfare state, and the "Depressed Decade" of the 1980s (when Denmark suffered high unemployment), the collection is capped off by a stall that, until recently, was used for selling marijuana in the squatters' community of Christiania.

The Rest of the Museum: If you're eager for more, there's plenty left to see. The National Museum also has exhibits on the history of this building (the Prince's Palace), a large ethnology collection, antiquities, coins and medallions, temporary exhibits, and a good children's museum. The floor plan will lead you to what you want to see.

▲**National Museum's Victorian Apartment**—The National Museum (listed above) inherited an incredible Victorian apartment just around the corner. The wealthy Christensen family managed to keep its plush living quarters a 19th-century time capsule until the granddaughters passed away in 1963. Since then, it's been part of the National Museum, with all but two of its rooms looking just as they did around 1890.

Cost and Hours: 50 kr, required one-hour tours in English leave from museum reception desk, June-Sept Sat only at 14:00.

▲**Museum of Copenhagen (Københavns Museum)**—This fine old house is filled with an entertaining and creative exhibit telling the story of Copenhagen. The ground floor covers the city's origins, the upper floor is dedicated to the 19th century, and the top floor includes a fun year-by-year walk through Copenhagen's 20th century, with lots of fun insights into contemporary culture.

Cost and Hours: 20 kr, daily 10:00-17:00, behind the train station at Vesterbrogade 59, tel. 33 21 07 72, www.copenhagen.dk.

On Slotsholmen Island

This island, where Copenhagen began in the 12th century, is a short walk from the train station and Tivoli, just across the bridge from the National Museum. It's dominated by Christiansborg Palace and several other royal and governmental buildings.

▲▲**Christiansborg Palace**—A complex of government buildings stands on the ruins of Copenhagen's original 12th-century fortress: the Parliament, Supreme Court, prime minister's office, royal reception rooms, royal library, several museums, and royal stables. Although the current palace dates only from 1928 and the

COPENHAGEN

royal family moved out 200 years ago, this building—the sixth to stand here in 800 years—is rich with tradition.

Three palace sights (the reception rooms, old castle ruins, and stables) are open to the public, giving us commoners a glimpse of the royal life.

Cost and Hours: Reception rooms-80 kr, ruins-40 kr, stables-40 kr, combo-ticket for all three-110 kr; reception rooms and ruins open daily 10:00-17:00 except closed Mon Oct-April, reception rooms may close at any time for royal events; stables and carriage museum daily 13:30-16:00 except closed Mon Oct-April; tel. 33 92 64 92, www.christiansborgslot.dk.

Visiting the Palace: From the equestrian statue in front, go through the wooden door; the entrance to the ruins is in the corridor on the right, and the door to the reception rooms is out in the next courtyard, also on the right.

Royal Reception Rooms: While these don't quite rank among Europe's best palace rooms, they're worth a look. This is still the place where Queen Margrethe II impresses visiting dignitaries. The information-packed 50-minute English tours of the rooms are excellent (included in ticket, daily at 15:00). At other times, you'll wander the rooms on your own, reading the sparse English descriptions. As you slip-slide on protect-the-floor slippers through 22 rooms, you'll gain a good feel for Danish history, royalty, and politics. For instance, the family portrait of King Christian IX illustrates why he's called the "father-in-law of Europe"—his children eventually became or married royalty in Denmark, Russia, Greece, Britain, France, Germany, and Norway. You'll see the Throne Room; the balcony where new monarchs are proclaimed (most recently in 1972); the Velvet Room, where royals privately greet VIP guests before big functions; and the grand Main Hall lined with boldly colorful (almost gaudy) tapestries. The palace highlight is this dazzling set of modern tapestries—Danish-designed but Gobelin-made in Paris. This gift, given to the queen on her 60th birthday in 2000, celebrates 1,000 years of Danish history, from the Viking age to our chaotic times...and into the future. Borrow the laminated descriptions for blow-by-blow explanations of the whole epic saga.

Castle Ruins: An exhibit in the scant remains of the first fortress built by Bishop Absalon, the 12th-century founder of Copenhagen, lies under the palace. A long passage connects to another set of ruins, from the 14th-century Copenhagen Castle. There's precious little to see, but it is, um, old and well-described.

A video covers more recent palace history.

Royal Stables and Carriages Museum: This facility is still home to the horses that pull the Queen's carriage on festive days, as well as a collection of historic carriages.

Old Stock Exchange (Børsen)—The eye-catching red-brick stock exchange was inspired by the Dutch Renaissance, like much of 17th-century Copenhagen. Built

to promote the mercantile ambitions of Denmark in the 1600s, it was the "World Trade Center" of Scandinavia. The facade reads, "For the profitable use of buyer and seller." The dragon-tail spire with three crowns represents the Danish aspiration to rule a united Scandinavia—or at least be its commercial capital. The Børsen (which is not open to tourists) symbolically connected Christianshavn (the harbor, also inspired by the Dutch) with the rest of the city, in an age when trade was a very big deal.

▲▲Thorvaldsen's Museum—This museum, which has some of the best swoon-worthy art you'll see anywhere, tells the story

and shows the monumental work of the great Danish Neoclassical sculptor Bertel Thorvaldsen (see sidebar). Considered Canova's equal among Neoclassical sculptors, Thorvaldsen spent 40 years in Rome. He was lured home to Copenhagen with the promise to showcase his work in a fine museum, which opened in the revolutionary year of 1848 as Denmark's first public art gallery. Of the 500 or so sculptures Thorvaldsen completed in his life—including 90 major statues—this museum has most of them, in one form or another (the plaster model used to make the original, the original marble, or a copy done in marble or bronze).

Cost and Hours: 40 kr, free Wed, includes excellent audio-guide on request, Tue-Sun 10:00-17:00, closed Mon, located in Neoclassical building with colorful walls next to Christiansborg Palace, tel. 33 32 15 32, www.thorvaldsensmuseum.dk.

Visiting the Museum: The ground floor showcases his statues. After buying your ticket, go straight in and ask to borrow a free iPod audioguide at the desk. This provides a wonderful statue-by-statue narration of the museum's key works.

Just past the audioguide desk, turn left into the Great Hall,

Bertel Thorvaldsen
(1770-1844)

Bertel Thorvaldsen was born, raised, educated, and buried in Copenhagen, but his most productive years were spent in Rome. There he soaked up the prevailing style of the time: Neoclassical. He studied ancient Greek and Roman statues, copying their balance, grace, and impassive beauty. The simple-but-noble style suited the patriotism of the era, and Thorvaldsen got rich off it. Public squares throughout Europe are dotted with his works, celebrating local rulers, patriots, and historical figures looking like Greek heroes or Roman conquerors.

In 1819, at the height of his fame and power, Thorvaldsen returned to Copenhagen. He was asked to decorate the most important parts of the recently bombed, newly rebuilt Cathedral of Our Lady: the main altar and nave. His *Risen Christ* on the altar (along with the 12 apostles lining the nave) became his most famous and reproduced work—without even realizing it, most people imagine the caring features of Thorvaldsen's Christ when picturing what Jesus looked like.

The prolific Thorvaldsen depicted a range of subjects. His grand statues of historical figures (Copernicus in Warsaw, Maximilian I in Munich) were intended for public squares. Portrait busts of his contemporaries were usually done in the style of Roman emperors. Thorvaldsen carved the *Lion Monument*, depicting a weeping lion, into a cliff in Luzern, Switzerland. He did religious statues, like the *Risen Christ*. Thorvaldsen's most accessible works are from Greek mythology—*The Three Graces*, naked *Jason with the Golden Fleece*, or Ganymede crouching down to feed the eagle Jupiter.

Though many of his statues are of gleaming white marble, Thorvaldsen was not a chiseler of stone. Like Rodin and Canova, Thorvaldsen left the grunt work to others. He fashioned a life-sized model in plaster, which could then be reproduced in marble or bronze by his assistants. Multiple copies were often made, even in his lifetime.

Thorvaldsen epitomized the Neoclassical style. His statues assume perfectly balanced poses—maybe even a bit stiff, say critics. They don't flail their arms dramatically or emote passionately. As you look into their faces, they seem lost in thought, as though contemplating deep spiritual truths.

In Copenhagen, catch Thorvaldsen's *Risen Christ* at the Cathedral of Our Lady, his portrait bust at City Hall, and the full range of his long career at the Thorvaldsen's Museum.

which was the original entryway of the museum. It's filled with replicas of some of Thorvaldsen's biggest and grandest statues—national heroes who still stand in the prominent squares of their major cities (Munich, Warsaw, the Vatican, and others). Two great equestrian statues stare each other down from across the hall; while they both take the classic, self-assured pose of looking one way while pointing another (think Babe Ruth calling his home run), one of them

(Jozef Poniatowski) is modeled after the ancient Roman general Marcus Aurelius, while the other (Bavaria's Maximilian I) wears modern garb.

Then take a spin through the smaller rooms that ring the central courtyard. Each of these is dominated by one big work—

mostly classical subjects drawn from mythology. At the far end of the building stand the plaster models for the iconic *Risen Christ* and the 12 Apostles (the final marble versions stand in the Cathedral of Our Lady—see page 73). Peek into the central courtyard to see the tomb of Thorvaldsen himself. Speaking of which, continuing into the next row of rooms, look for Thorvaldsen's (very flattering) self-portrait, leaning buffly against a partially finished sculpture.

Upstairs, get into the mind of the artist by perusing his personal possessions and the private collection of paintings from which he drew inspiration.

Royal Library—Copenhagen's "Black Diamond" (Den Sorte Diamant) library is a striking, supermodern building made of shiny black granite, leaning over the harbor at the edge of the palace complex. From the inviting lounge chairs, you can ponder this stretch of harborfront, which serves as a showcase for architects. Inside, wander through the old and new sections, catch the fine view from the "G" level, read a magazine, surf the Internet (free terminals in the skyway lobby over the street nearest the harbor), and enjoy a classy—and pricey—lunch.

Cost and Hours: Free, special exhibitions generally 30 kr; reading room open generally Mon-Fri 9:00-21:00, Sat 10:00-17:00, closed Sun; different parts of the library have varying hours, tel. 33 47 47 47, www.kb.dk.

▲**Danish Jewish Museum (Dansk Jødisk Museum)**—This museum, which opened in 2004 in a striking building by American architect Daniel Libeskind, offers a very small but well-exhibited display of 400 years of the life and impact of Jews in Denmark.

Cost and Hours: 50 kr; June-Aug Tue-Sun 10:00-17:00; Sept-May Tue-Fri 13:00-16:00, Sat-Sun 12:00-17:00; closed Mon year-round; behind the Royal Library's "Black Diamond" branch at Proviantpassagen 6—enter from the courtyard behind the red-brick, ivy-covered building; tel. 33 11 22 18, www.jewmus.dk.

Visiting the Museum: Frankly, the architecture overshadows the humble exhibits. Libeskind—who created the equally conceptual Jewish Museum in Berlin, and whose design is the basis for redeveloping the World Trade Center site in New York City—has literally written Jewish culture into this building. The floor plan, a seemingly random squiggle, is actually in the shape of the Hebrew characters for *Mitzvah*, which loosely translated means "act of kindness."

Be sure to watch the two introductory films about the Jews' migration to Denmark, and about the architect Libeskind (12-minute loop total, English subtitles, plays continuously). As you tour the collection, the uneven floors and asymmetrical walls give you the feeling that what lies around the corner is completely unknown...much like the life and history of Danish Jews. Another interpretation might be that the uneven floors give you the sense of motion, like waves on the sea—a reminder that despite Nazi occupation in 1943, nearly 7,000 Danish Jews were ferried across the waves by fishermen to safety in neutral Sweden.

Near the Strøget

Round Tower—Built in 1642 by Christian IV, the tower con-

nects a church, library, and observatory (the oldest functioning observatory in Europe) with a ramp that spirals up to a fine view of Copenhagen (though the view from atop Our Savior's Church is far better—see page 106).

Cost and Hours: 25 kr, nothing to see inside but the ramp and the view; tower—daily June-Sept 10:00-20:00, Oct-May 10:00-17:00; observatory—summer Sun 13:00-16:00 and mid-Oct-mid-March Tue-Wed 19:00-22:00; just off the Strøget on Købmagergade.

Amalienborg Palace and Nearby

For more information on this palace and nearby attractions, including the famous *Little Mermaid* statue, see the end of my self-guided walk (page 82).

▲**Amalienborg Palace Museum (Amalienborgmuseet)**— While Queen Margrethe II and her husband live quite privately in one of the four mansions that make up the palace complex, another mansion has been open to the public since 1994. It displays the private studies of four kings of the House of Glucksborg, who ruled from 1863-1972 (the immediate predecessors of today's Queen). Your visit is short—six or eight rooms on one floor—but it affords an intimate and unique peek into Denmark's royal family. You'll see the private study of each of the last four kings of Denmark. They feel particularly lived-in—with cluttered pipe collections and bookcases jammed with family pictures—because they were. It's easy to imagine these blue-blooded folks just hanging out here, even today. The earliest study, Frederik VIII's (c. 1869), feels much older and more "royal"—with Renaissance gilded walls, heavy drapes, and a polar bear rug. Temporary exhibits fill the larger halls.

Cost and Hours: 80 kr, or 110-kr combo-ticket with Rosenborg Palace; May-Oct daily 10:00-16:00; Nov-April Tue-Sun 11:00-16:00, closed Mon; with your back to the harbor, the entrance is at the far end of the square on the right; tel. 33 15 32 86, www.dkks.dk.

Amalienborg Palace Changing of the Guard—This noontime event is boring in the summer, when the queen is not in residence—

the guards just change places. (This goes on for quite a long time—no need to rush here at the stroke of noon, or to crowd in during the first few minutes; you'll have plenty of good photo ops.) If the queen's at home (indicated by a flag flying above her home), the changing of the guard is accompanied by a military band.

▲▲**Museum of Danish Resistance (Frihedsmuseet)**—On April 9, 1940, Hitler's Nazis violated a peace treaty and invaded Denmark, overrunning the tiny nation in mere hours. This museum tells what happened next—the compelling story of Denmark's heroic Nazi-resistance struggle (1940-1945). While relatively small, the museum rewards those who take the time to read the English explanations and understand the fascinating artifacts. Video touchscreens let you hear interviews with the participants of history (dubbed into English).

Cost and Hours: Free; May-Sept Tue-Sun 10:00-16:00, Oct-April Tue-Sun 10:00-15:00, closed Mon year-round; hours likely to be reduced—call or check website to confirm; guided tours June-Aug Tue, Thu, and Sun at 14:00; on Churchillparken between Amalienborg Palace and *The Little Mermaid* site; bus #1A or #15 from downtown/Tivoli/train station stops right in front, a 10-minute walk from Østerport S-tog station, or bus #26 from Langelinie cruise port or downtown; tel. 41 20 62 91, www.friheds museet.dk.

◊ Self-Guided Tour: From the main hall, you'll take a counterclockwise spin through the collection. The first sec-

tion, **Adaptation to Avoid Nazification,** examines the unenviable situation in which the Danes found themselves in in 1940: Cooperate with the Nazis (at least symbolically) to preserve some measure of self-determination, or stand up to them and surely be crushed by their military might. Denmark opted for the first option, but kept a fierce resistance always at a rolling boil. Be sure to carefully examine the odd, sometimes macabre items from this period: A delicate, miniature rose made of chewed bread, given as a gift to an inmate at Ravensbrück Concentration Camp; Himmler's eye patch, worn as a disguise; actual human skin tattooed with the SS symbol, removed from a reformed Nazi after the war (at his own request); the pistol of the Danish Nazi leader, Fritz Clausen; RAF (British Royal Air Force) caps and stars-and-stripes bowties, worn as a symbol of resistance and rebellion by young people in the early days of Nazi occupation; cheaply made aluminum Nazi coins, crudely imprinted with messages of Danish resistance; and an old printing press used to produce anti-Nazi leaflets.

Moving down the hallway, you pass into the next section, **Resistance and Sabotage.** You'll learn how the Danish resistance, supported by the SOE (Special Operations Executive, a British governmental agency tasked with subverting Nazi control), bravely stood up to the Nazis, with occasional supplies airlifted in by the Allies. On display are many items used during the resistance, including slugs and bullet casings from a shootout between the resistance and Nazi-friendly forces, and a clandestine radio and telegraph. You'll also learn about everyday life (shortages and rationings for the Nazi war effort), and see a Nazi plate and cutlery emblazoned with a swastika.

The next section, **German Terror,** explains the Nazis' campaign of extermination against Jewish people, and details the valiant Danish effort to rescue some 7,000 Jews by ferrying them across the sea to neutral Sweden; only 481 were murdered by the Nazis (a tiny fraction of the toll in most countries). You'll see articles of the Jewish faith left behind by a refugee (who didn't want to be discovered with them, putting himself at greater risk), and some identification armbands from a concentration camp. You'll also see exhibits on industrial sabotage, and the growth of the underground army in the waning days of the war.

Finally we end at **The Liberation** (May 5, 1945). A giant stained-glass window in the lobby honors the victims of the Nazis. The moving, handwritten letters in the display cases in front (translated into English) are the final messages of Danes who had been sentenced to death by the Nazis.

Rosenborg Castle and Nearby

▲▲▲**Rosenborg Castle (Rosenborg Slot) and Treasury**—
This finely furnished Dutch Renaissance-style castle was built by King Christian IV in the early 1600s as a summer residence. Rosenborg was his favorite residence and where he chose to die. Open to the public since 1838, it houses the Danish crown jewels and 500 years of royal knickknacks. While the old palace interior is a bit dark and not as immediately impressive as many of Europe's later Baroque masterpieces, it has a certain lived-in charm. It oozes the personality of the fascinating Christian IV and has one of the

finest treasury collections in Europe. Notice that this is one of the only major sights in town open on Mondays (in summer only). For more on Christian, read the sidebar on page 98.

Cost and Hours: 80 kr, 110-kr ticket also includes Amalienborg Palace Museum, 20 kr for permission to take photos; June-Aug daily 10:00-17:00; May and Sept-Oct daily 10:00-16:00; Nov-Dec Tue-Sun 11:00-14:00 (treasury until 16:00), closed Mon; Jan-April Tue-Sun 11:00-16:00, closed Mon; mandatory lockers take 20-kr coin, which will be returned; Metro or S-tog: Nørreport, then 5-minute walk on Østervoldgade and through park; tel. 33 15 32 86, www.dkks.dk.

Tours: Richard Karpen leads fascinating one-hour tours in princely garb (mid-May-mid-Sept Mon and Thu at 13:30, 80 kr plus entry fee, see "Tours in Copenhagen," earlier). Or take the following self-guided tour that I've woven together from the

King Christian IV:
A Lover and a Fighter

King Christian IV (1577-1648) inherited Denmark at the peak of its power, lived his life with the exuberance of the age, and went to his grave with the country in decline. His legacy is obvious to every tourist—Rosenborg Castle, Frederiksborg Palace, the Round Tower, Christianshavn, and on and on. Look for his logo adorning many buildings: the letter "C" with a "4" inside it and a crown on top. Thanks to both his place in history and his passionate personality, Danes today regard Christian IV as one of their greatest monarchs.

During his 60-year reign, Christian IV reformed the government, rebuilt the army, established a trading post in India, and tried to expand Denmark's territory. He took Kalmar from Sweden and captured strategic points in northern Germany. The king was a large man who also lived large. A skilled horseman and avid hunter, he could drink his companions under the table. He spoke several languages and gained a reputation as outgoing and humorous. His lavish banquets were legendary, and his romantic affairs were numerous.

But Christian's appetite for war proved destructive. In 1626, Denmark again attacked northern Germany, but was beaten back. In 1643, Sweden launched a sneak attack, and despite Christian's personal bravery (he lost an eye), the war went badly. By the end of his life, Christian was tired and bitter, and Denmark was drained.

The heroics of Christian and his sailors live on in the Danish national anthem, "King Christian Stood by the Lofty Mast."

highlights of Richard's walk. If you have a mobile device, you can take advantage of the palace's free Wi-Fi signal, which is intended to let you follow the "Konge Connect" step-by-step tour through the palace highlights (with text explanations on your phone; for instructions, pick up the brochure at the ticket desk).

➔ **Self-Guided Tour:** Buy your ticket, then head back out and look for the *castle* sign. You'll tour the ground floor room by room, then climb to the third floor for the big throne room. After a quick sweep of the middle floor, finish in the basement (enter from outside) for the jewels. Begin the tour on the palace's ground floor (turn right as you enter), in the Winter Room.

Ground Floor: Here in the wood-paneled **Winter Room,**

all eyes were on King Christian IV. Today, your eyes should be on him, too. Take a close look at his bust by the fireplace (if it's not here, look for it out in the corridor by the ticket-taker). Check this guy out—earring and fashionable braid, hard drinker, hard lover, energetic statesman, and warrior king. Christian IV was dynamism in the flesh, wearing a toga: a true Renaissance guy. During his reign, Copenhagen doubled in size. You're surrounded by Dutch paintings (the Dutch had a huge influence on 17th-century Denmark). Note the smaller statue of the 19-year-old king, showing him jousting jauntily on his coronation day. In another case, the golden astronomical clock—with musical works and moving figures—did everything you can imagine. Flanking the fireplace (opposite where you entered), beneath the windows, look for the panels in the tile floor that could be removed to let the music performed by the band in the basement waft in. (Who wants the actual musicians in the dining room?) The audio holes were also used to call servants.

The **study** (or "writing closet," nearest where you entered) was small (and easy to heat). Kings did a lot of correspond-

ing. We know a lot about Christian because 3,000 of his handwritten letters survive. The painting on the right wall shows Christian at age eight. Three years later, his father died, and little Christian techni-cally ascended the throne, though Denmark was actually ruled by a regency until Christian was 19. A portrait of his mother hangs above the boy, and opposite is a portrait of Christian in his prime—having just conquered Sweden—standing alongside the incredible coronation crown you'll see later.

Going back through the Winter Room, head for the door to Christian's **bedroom.** Before entering, notice the little peephole in the door (used by the king to spy on those in this room—well-

camouflaged by the painting, and more easily seen from the other side), and the big cabinet doors for Christian's clothes and accessories, flanking the bedroom door (notice the hinges and keyholes). Heading into the bedroom, you'll see paintings showing the king as an old man...and as a dead man. (Christian died in this room.) In the case are the clothes he wore at his finest hour. During a naval battle against Sweden (1644), Christian stood directing the action when an explosion ripped across the deck, sending him sprawling and riddling him with shrapnel. Unfazed, the 67-year-old monarch bounced right back up and kept going, inspiring his men to carry on the fight. Christian's stubborn determination during this battle is commemorated in Denmark's national anthem. Shrapnel put out Christian's eye. No problem: The warrior king with a knack for heroic publicity stunts had the shrapnel bits removed from his eye and forehead and made into earrings as a gift for his mistress. The earrings hang in the case with his blood-stained clothes (easy to miss, right side). Christian lived to be 70 and fathered 25 children (with two wives and three mistresses). Before moving on, you can peek into Christian's private bathroom—elegantly tiled with Delft porcelain.

Proceed into the **Dark Room.** Here you'll see wax casts of royal figures. This was the way famous and important people were portrayed back then. (If the wax casts aren't here, they're likely out in the corridor.) The chair (possibly gone for restoration) is a forerunner of the whoopee cushion. When you sat on it, metal cuffs pinned your arms down, allowing the prankster to pour water down the back of the chair (see hole)—making you "wet your pants." When you stood up, the chair made embarrassing tooting sounds.

The **Marble Room** (which may be closed for restoration) has a particularly impressive inlaid marble floor. Imagine the king meeting emissaries here in the center, with the emblems of Norway (right), Denmark (center), and Sweden (left) behind him.

The end room, called the **King's Chamber,** was used by Christian's first mistress. You might want to shield children from the sexually explicit art in the case next to the door you just passed. Notice the tamer ceiling painting, with an orchestra looking down on you as they play.

The long **stone passage** leading to the staircase exhibits an intriguing painting (by the door to the King's Chamber) showing the crowds at the coronation of Christian's son, Frederick III. After Christian's death, a weakened Denmark was invaded, occupied, and humiliated by Sweden (Treaty of Roskilde, 1658). Copenhagen alone held out through the long winter of 1658-1659 (the Siege of Copenhagen), and Sweden eventually had to withdraw from the country. During

the siege, Frederick III distinguished himself with his bravery. He seized upon the resulting surge of popularity as his chance to be anointed an absolute, divinely ordained monarch (1660). This painting marks that event—study it closely for slice-of-life details. Next, near the ticket-taker, a sprawling family tree makes it perfectly clear that Christian IV comes from good stock. Notice the tree is labeled in German—the second language of the realm.

The queen had a hand-pulled elevator, but you'll need to hike up two flights of stairs to the throne room.

Throne Room (Third Floor): The **Long Hall**—considered one of the best-preserved Baroque rooms in Europe—was great

for banquets. The decor trumpets the accomplishments of Denmark's great kings. The four corners of the ceiling feature the four continents known at the time. (America—at the far-right end of the hall as you enter—was still considered pretty untamed; notice the decapitated head with the arrow sticking out of it.) In the center, of course, is the proud seal of the Danish Royal Family. The tapestries, designed for this room, are from the late 1600s. Effective propaganda, they show the Danes defeating their Swedish rivals on land and at sea. The king's throne—still more propaganda for two centuries of "absolute" monarchs—was made of "unicorn horn" (actually narwhal tusk from Greenland). Believed to bring protection from evil and poison, the horn was the most precious material in its day. The queen's throne is of hammered silver. The 150-pound lions are 300 years old.

The small room to the left holds a delightful **royal porcelain** display with Chinese, French, German, and Danish examples of the "white gold." For five centuries, Europeans couldn't figure out how the Chinese made this stuff. The difficulty in just getting it back to Europe in one piece made it precious. The Danish pieces, called "Flora Danica" (on the left as you enter), are from a huge royal set showing off the herbs and vegetables of the realm.

On your way back down, the middle floor is worth a look.

Middle Floor: Circling counterclockwise, you'll see more fine clocks, fancy furniture, and royal portraits. The queen enjoyed her royal lathe (with candleholders for lighting and pedals to spin it hidden away below; in the Christian IV Room). The small mirror room (up the stairs from the main hall) was where the king played Hugh Hefner—using mirrors on the floor to see what was under those hoop skirts. In hidden cupboards, he had a fold-out bed and a handy escape staircase.

Back outside, turn right and find the stairs leading down to the...

Royal Danish Treasury (Castle Basement): The palace was a royal residence for a century and has been the royal vault right up until today. As you enter, first head to the right, into the **wine cellar,** with thousand-liter barrels and some fine treasury items. The first room has a vast army of tiny golden soldiers, and a wall lined with fancy rifles. Heading into the next room, you'll see fine items of amber (petrified tree resin, 30-50 million years old) and ivory. Study the large box made of amber (in a freestanding case, just to the right as you enter)—the tiny figures show a healthy interest in sex.

Now head back past the ticket-taker and into the main part of the treasury, where you can browse through exquisite royal knickknacks.

The diamond- and pearl-studded **saddles** were Christian IV's—the first for his coronation, the second for his son's wedding. When his kingdom was nearly bankrupt, Christian had these constructed lavishly—complete with solid-gold spurs—to impress visiting dignitaries and bolster Denmark's credit rating.

The next case displays **tankards.** Danes were always big drinkers, and to drink in the top style, a king had narwhal steins (#4030). Note the fancy Greenland Inuit (Eskimo) on the lid (#4023). The case is filled with exquisitely carved ivory. On the other side of that case, what's with the mooning snuffbox (#4063)? Also, check out the amorous whistle (#4064).

Drop by the case on the wall in the back-left of the room: The 17th century was the age of **brooches.** Many of these are made of freshwater pearls. Find the fancy combination toothpick and ear spoon (#4140). Look for #4146: A queen was caught having an affair after 22 years of royal marriage. Her king gave her a special present: a golden ring—showing the hand of his promiscuous queen shaking hands with a penis.

Step downstairs, away from all this silliness. Passing through the serious vault door, you come face-to-face with a big, jeweled **sword.** The tall, two-handed, 16th-century coronation sword was drawn by the new king, who cut crosses in the air in four directions, symbolically promising to defend the realm from all attacks. The cases surrounding the sword contain everyday items used by the king (all solid gold, of course). What looks like a trophy case of gold records is actually a collection of dinner plates with amber centers (#5032).

Go down the steps. In the center case is Christian IV's **coronation crown** (from 1596, seven pounds of gold and precious stones, #5124), which some consider to be the finest Renaissance crown in Europe. Its six tallest gables radiate symbolism. Find

the symbols of justice (sword and scales), fortitude (a woman on a lion with a sword), and charity (a nursing woman—meaning the king will love God and his people as a mother loves her child). The pelican, which according to medieval legend pecks its own flesh to feed its young, symbolizes God sacrificing his son, just as the king would make great sacrifices for his people. Climb the footstool to look inside—it's as exquisite as the outside. The shields of various Danish provinces remind the king that he's surrounded by his realms.

Circling the cases along the wall (right to left), notice the fine enameled lady's goblet with traits of a good woman spelled out in Latin (#5128) and above that, an exquisite prayer book (with handwritten favorite prayers, #5134). In the fifth window, the big solid-gold baptismal basin (#5262) hangs above tiny oval silver boxes that contained the royal children's umbilical cords (handy for protection later in life, #5272); two cases over are royal writing sets with wax, seals, pens, and ink (#5320).

Go down a few more steps into the lowest level of the treasury and last room. The two **crowns** in the center cases are more modern (from 1670), lighter, and more practical—just gold and diamonds without all the symbolism. The king's crown is only four pounds, the queen's a mere two.

The cases along the walls show off the **crown jewels.** These were made in 1840 of diamonds, emeralds, rubies, and pearls from earlier royal jewelry. The saber (#5540) shows emblems of the realm's 19 provinces. The sumptuous pendant features a 19-carat diamond cut (like its neighbors) in the 58-facet "brilliant" style for maximum reflection (far-left case, #5560). Imagine these on the dance floor. The painting shows the coronation of Christian VIII at Frederiksborg Chapel in 1840. The crown jewels are still worn by the queen on special occasions several times a year.

▲**Rosenborg Gardens**—Rosenborg Castle is surrounded by the royal pleasure gardens and, on sunny days, a minefield of sunbathing Danish beauties and picnickers. While "ethnic Danes" grab the shade, the rest of the Danes worship the sun. When the royal family is in residence, there's a daily changing-of-the-guard mini-parade from the Royal Guard's barracks adjoining Rosenborg Castle (at 11:30) to Amalienborg Castle (at 12:00). The Queen's Rose Garden (across the moat from the palace) is a royal place for a picnic. The fine statue of Hans Christian Andersen in the park—erected while he was still alive (and approved by him)—is meant to symbolize how his stories had a message even for adults.

COPENHAGEN

▲National Gallery of Denmark (Statens Museum for Kunst)—The museum fills a stately building with Danish and European paintings from the 14th century through today. This is particularly worthwhile for the chance to be immersed in great art by the Danes, and to see its good collection of French Modernists.

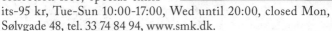

Cost and Hours: Permanent collection-free, special exhibits-95 kr, Tue-Sun 10:00-17:00, Wed until 20:00, closed Mon, Sølvgade 48, tel. 33 74 84 94, www.smk.dk.

Visiting the Museum: The ground floor holds special exhibits; the second floor has collections of Danish and Nordic artists from 1750 to 1900, and European art from 1300 to 1800; and the Danish and International Art after 1900 is spread between the second and third floors.

Head first to the Danish and Nordic artists section, and pick up the excellent floor plan that suggests a twisting route through

the collection. Take the time to read the descriptions in each room, which put the paintings into historical context. In addition to Romantic works by well-known, non-Danish artists (such as the Norwegian J. C. Dahl and the German Caspar David Friedrich), this is a chance to learn about some very talented Danish painters not well known outside their native land. Make a point to meet the "Skagen Painters," including Anna Ancher, Michael Ancher, Peder Severin Krøyer, and others (find them in the section called "The Modern Breakthrough I-II"). This group, with echoes of the French Impressionists, gathered in the fishing village of Skagen on the northern tip of Denmark, surrounded by the sea and strong light, and painted heroic folk-fishermen themes in the late 1800s. Also worth seeking out are the canvases of Laurits Andersen Ring, who portrayed traditional peasant scenes with modern style; and Jens Ferdinand Willumsen, who pioneered "Vitalism" (celebrating man in nature). Other exhibits are cleverly organized by theme, such as gender or the body.

In the 20th-century section, the collection of early French Modernism is particularly impressive (with works by Matisse, Picasso, Braque, and more). This is complemented with works by

COPENHAGEN

Danish artists, who, inspired by the French avant-garde, introduced new, radical forms and colors to Scandinavian art.

Christianshavn

Across the harbor from the old town, Christianshavn is one of the most delightful districts in town to explore. A little background helps explain what you'll see.

Copenhagen's planned port, Christianshavn, was vital to Danish power in the 17th and 18th centuries. Denmark had always been second to Sweden when it came to possession of natural resources, so the Danes tried to make up for it by acquiring resource-rich overseas colonies. They built Christianshavn (with Amsterdam's engineering help) to run the resulting trade business—giving this neighborhood a "little Amsterdam" vibe today.

Since Denmark's economy was so dependent on trade, the port town was the natural target of enemies. When the Danes didn't support Britain against Napoleon in 1807, the Brits bombarded Christianshavn. In this "blackest year in Danish history," Christianshavn burned down. That's why today there's hardly a building here that dates from before 1807.

Christianshavn remained Copenhagen's commercial center until the 1920s, when a modern harbor was built. Suddenly, Christianshavn's economy collapsed and it became a slum. Cheap prices attracted artsy types, giving it a bohemian flavor.

In 1971, several hundred squatters took over an unused military camp and created the Christiania commune (described later). City officials looked the other way because back then, no one cared about the land. But by the 1980s, the neighborhood had become gentrified, and today it's some of priciest real estate in town. (A small apartment costs around $300,000.) Suddenly developers are pushing to take back the land from squatters, and the very existence of Christiania is threatened.

Christianshavn prices are driven up by wealthy locals (who pay about 60 percent of their income in taxes) paying too much for apartments, renting them cheaply to their kids, and writing off the loss. Demand for property is huge. Prices have skyrocketed. Today the neighborhood is inhabited mostly by rich students and young professionals. Apart from pleasant canalside walks and trendy restaurants to enjoy, there are two things to see in Christianshavn: Our Savior's Church (with its fanciful tower) and Christiania (before it's gone).

▲Our Savior's Church (Vor Frelsers Kirke)

The church recently reopened after a restoration, which has left it gleaming inside and out. Its bright Baroque interior (1696) is shaped like a giant cube. The magnificent pipe organ is supported by elephants (a royal symbol of the prestigious Order of the Elephant). Looking up to the ceiling, notice elephants also sculpted into the stucco of the dome, and a little one hanging from the main chandelier. Best of all, you can climb the unique spiral spire (with an outdoor staircase winding up to its top—398 stairs in all) for great views of the city and of the Christiania commune below.

Cost and Hours: Church interior-free, open daily 11:00-15:30 but may close for special services; church tower-35 kr; July-mid-Sept Mon-Sat 10:00-19:00, Sun 10:30-19:00; April-June and mid-Sept-Nov daily until 16:00; closed Dec-March and in bad weather; bus #2A, #19, or Metro: Christianshavn, Sankt Annægade 29, tel. 41 66 63 57, www.vorfrelserskirke.dk.

Ⓞ Spin-Tour from the Top of Our Savior's Church: Climb up until you run out of stairs. As you wind back down, look for these landmarks:

The modern windmills are a reminder that Denmark generates 20 percent of its power from wind. Below the windmills is a great aerial view of the Christiania commune. Beyond the windmills, across Øresund (the strait that separates Denmark and Sweden), stands a shuttered Swedish nuclear power plant. The lone skyscraper in the distance—the first and tallest skyscraper in Scandinavia—is in Malmö, Sweden. The Øresund Bridge made Malmö an easy 35-minute bus or train ride from Copenhagen (it's become a bedroom community, with much cheaper apartments making the commute worthwhile).

Farther to the right, the big red-roof zone is Amager Island. Five hundred years as the city's dumping grounds earned Amager the nickname "Crap Island." Circling on, you come to the towering Radisson Blu hotel. The area beyond it is slated to become a forest of skyscrapers—the center of Europe's biomedical industry.

Downtown Copenhagen is decorated with several striking towers and spires. The tower capped by the golden ball is a ride in Tivoli Gardens. Next is City Hall's pointy brick tower. The biggest building, with the three-crown tower, is Christiansborg Palace. The Børsen (old stock exchange) is just beyond, with its unique dragon-tail tower. Behind that is Nyhavn. Just across from that and the new Playhouse is the dramatic new Opera House (with the flat roof and big, grassy front yard).

Christiania

If you're interested in visiting a freewheeling community of alternative living, Christiania is a ▲▲▲ sight.

In 1971, the original 700 Christianians established squatters' rights in an abandoned military barracks just a 10-minute walk from the Danish parliament building. A generation later, this "free city" still stands—an ultra-human mishmash of idealists, hippies, potheads, non-materialists, and happy children (600 adults, 200 kids, 200 cats, 200 dogs, 2 parrots, and 17 horses). There are even a handful of Willie Nelson-type seniors among the 180 remaining here from the original takeover. And an amazing thing has happened: The place has become the third-most-visited sight among tourists in Copenhagen. Move over, *Little Mermaid*.

"Pusher Street" (named for the sale of soft drugs here) is Christiania's main drag. Get beyond this touristy side of Christiania, and you'll find a fascinating, ramshackle world of moats and earthen ramparts, alternative housing, cozy tea houses, carpenter shops, hippie villas, children's playgrounds, peaceful lanes, and people who believe that "to be normal is to be in a straitjacket." (A local slogan claims, *"Kun døde fisk flyder med strømmen"*—"Only dead fish swim with the current.") Be careful to distinguish between real Christianians and Christiania's motley guests—drunks (mostly from other countries) who hang out here in the summer for the freedom. Part of the original charter guaranteed that the community would stay open to the public.

Hours and Tours: Christiania is open all the time (main entrance is down Prinsessegade behind the Our Savior's Church spiral tower in Christianshavn). You're welcome to snap photos, but ask residents before you photograph them. Guided tours leave from the front entrance of Christiania at 15:00 (just show up, 30 kr, 1.5 hours, daily late June-Aug, only Sat-Sun rest of year, in English and Danish, tel. 32 57 96 70).

The Community: Christiania is broken into 14 administrative neighborhoods on a former military base. The land is still owned by Denmark's Ministry of Defense. Locals build their homes but don't own the land; there's no buying or selling of property. When someone moves out, the community decides who will be invited in to replace that person. A third of the adult population works on the outside, a third works on the inside, and a third doesn't work much at all.

There are nine rules: no cars, no hard drugs, no guns, no

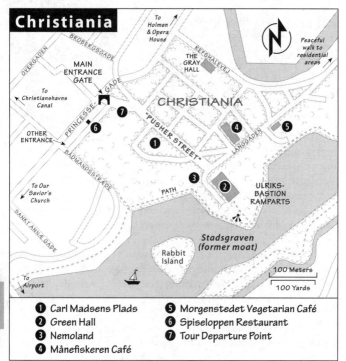

Christiania

To Holmen & Opera House

Peaceful walk to residential areas

BROBERGSGADE

OTERGADEN

MAIN ENTRANCE GATE

THE GRAY HALL

REFSHALEVEJ

To Christianshavns Canal

CHRISTIANIA

PRINCESSE GADE

"PUSHER STREET"

LANGGADEN

OTHER ENTRANCE

BADMANDSSTRADE

PATH

ULRIKS-BASTION RAMPARTS

To Our Savior's Church

SANKT ANN Æ GADE

Stadsgraven (former moat)

Rabbit Island

To Airport

100 Meters

100 Yards

❶ Carl Madsens Plads
❷ Green Hall
❸ Nemoland
❹ Månefiskeren Café
❺ Morgenstedet Vegetarian Café
❻ Spiseloppen Restaurant
❼ Tour Departure Point

COPENHAGEN

explosives, and so on. The Christiania flag is red and yellow because when the original hippies took over, they found a lot of red and yellow paint onsite. The three yellow dots in the flag are from the three "i"s in Christiania (or, some claim, the "o"s in "Love, Love, Love").

The community pays the city about $1 million a year for utilities and has about $1 million a year more to run its local affairs. A few "luxury hippies" have oil heat, but most use wood or gas. The ground here was poisoned by its days as a military base, so nothing is grown in Christiania. There's little industry within the commune (Christiania Cykler, which builds fine bikes, is an exception—www.pedersen-bike.dk). The community has one mailing address (for 25 kr/month, you can receive mail here). A phone chain provides a system of communal security (they have had bad experiences calling the police). Each September 26, the day those first squatters took over the barracks in 1971, Christiania has a big birthday bash.

Tourists are entirely welcome here, because they've become a major part of the economy. Visitors react in very different ways to the place. Some see dogs, dirt, and dazed people. Others see a haven of peace, freedom, and no taboos. Locals will remind judgmental Americans (whose country incarcerates more than a quarter of the world's prison inmates) that a society must make the choice: Allow for alternative lifestyles...or build more prisons.

Even since its inception, Christiania has been a political hot potato. No one in the Danish establishment wanted it. And no  one had the nerve to mash it. In the last decade, Christiania has connected better with the rest of society—such as paying for its utilities and taxes. But when Denmark's conservative government took over in 2001, they vowed to "normalize" Christiania (with pressure from the US), and in recent years police have regularly conducted raids on pot sellers. There's talk about opening the commune to market forces and developing posh apartments to replace existing residences, according to one government plan. But Christiania has a legal team, and litigation will likely drag on for many years.

Many predict that Christiania will withstand the government's challenge, as it has in years past. The community, which also calls itself Freetown, fended  off a similar attempt in 1976 with the help of fervent supporters from around Europe. *Bevar Christiania*—"Save Christiania"— banners fly everywhere, and locals are confident that their free way of life will survive. As history has shown, the challenge may just make this hippie haven a bit stronger.

Orientation Tour: Passing under the gate, take Pusher Street directly into the community. The first square—a kind of market square (souvenirs and marijuana-related stuff)—is named Carl Madsens Plads, honoring the lawyer who took the squatters' case to the Danish supreme court in 1976 and won. Beyond that is Nemoland (a food circus, on the right). A huge warehouse called the Green Hall (Den Gronne Hal) is a recycling center and hardware store (where people get most of their building materials) that does double duty at night as a concert hall and as a place where children work on crafts. If you go up the stairs between Nemoland and the Green Hall, you'll climb up to the ramparts that overlook the canal.

On the left beyond the Green Hall, a lane leads to the Måne-fiskeren café, and beyond that, to the Morgenstedet vegetarian restaurant. Beyond these recommended restaurants, you'll find yourself lost in the totally untouristy, truly local residential parts of Christiania, where kids play in the street and the old folks sit out on the front stoop—just like any other neighborhood. Just as St. Mark's Square isn't the "real Venice," the hippie-druggie scene on Pusher Street isn't the "real Christiania"—you can't say you've experienced Christiania until you've strolled these back streets.

A walk or bike ride through Christiania is a great way to see how this community lives. When you leave, look up—the sign above the gate says, "You are entering the EU."

Smoking Marijuana: Pusher Street was once lined with stalls selling marijuana, joints, and hash. Residents intentionally destroyed the stalls in 2004 to reduce the risk of Christiania being disbanded by the government. (One stall was spared and is on display at the National Museum.) Walking along Pusher Street today, you may witness policemen or deals being made—but never at the same time. You may also notice wafts of marijuana smoke and whispered offers of "hash" during your visit. And, in fact, on my last visit there was a small stretch of Pusher Street dubbed the "Green Light District" where pot was being openly sold (signs acknowledged that this activity was still illegal, and announced three rules here: 1. Have fun; 2. No photos; and 3. No running—"because it makes people nervous"). However, purchasing and smoking may buy you more time in Denmark than you'd planned—possession of marijuana is illegal. With the recent police crackdown on marijuana sales, the street price has skyrocketed, crime has crept into the scene, and someone was actually murdered in a drug scuffle near Christiania—problems unthinkable in mellower times.

About hard drugs: For the first few years, junkies were toler-

ated. But that led to violence and polluted the mellow ambience residents envisioned. In 1979, the junkies were expelled—an epic confrontation in the community's folk history now—and since then the symbol of a fist breaking a syringe is as prevalent as the leafy marijuana icon. Hard drugs are emphatically forbidden in Christiania.

Eating in Christiania: The people of Christiania appreciate good food and count on tourism as a big part of their economy. Consequently, there are plenty of decent eateries. Most of the restaurants are closed on Monday (the community's weekly holiday). **Pusher Street** has a few grungy but tasty falafel stands, as well as a popular burger bar. **Nemoland** is the hangout zone—a fun collection of stands peddling Thai food, burgers, *shawarma*, and other fast hippie food with great, tented outdoor seating (30-110-kr meals). Its stay-a-while atmosphere comes with backgammon, foosball, bakery goods, and fine views from the ramparts. **Månefiskeren** ("Moonfisher Bar") looks like a modern-day Brueghel painting, with billiards, chess, snacks, and drinks (Tue-Sun 10:00-23:00, closed Mon). **Morgenstedet** ("Morning Place") is a good, cheap vegetarian café with a mellow, woody interior and a rustic patio outside (75-100-kr meals, Tue-Sun 12:00-21:00, closed Mon, left after Pusher Street). **Spiseloppen** is *the* classy, good-enough-for-Republicans restaurant in the community (closed Mon, described on page 128).

Greater Copenhagen

Carlsberg Brewery—Denmark's beloved source of legal intoxicants, Carlsberg welcomes you to its visitors center for a self-guided tour and a half-liter of beer.

Cost and Hours: 65 kr, Tue-Sun 10:00-17:00, closed Mon, last entry one hour before closing; catch the local train to Enghave, or bus #18, #26, or #6A; enter at Gamle Carlsbergvej 11 around corner from brewery entrance, tel. 33 27 13 14, www.visit carlsberg.dk.

Open-Air Folk Museum (Frilandsmuseet)—This park, part of the National Museum, is filled with traditional Danish architecture and folk culture.

Cost and Hours: Free, late April-late Oct Tue-Sun 10:00-17:00, closed Mon and off-season, outside of town in the suburb of Lyngby, S-tog: Sorgenfri and 10-minute walk to Kongevejen 100, tel. 33 13 44 11.

Bakken—Danes gather at Copenhagen's *other* great amusement park, Bakken.

Cost and Hours: Free; late June-mid-Aug daily 12:00-24:00, shorter hours April-late June and mid-Aug-mid-Sept; closed mid-Sept-March; S-tog: Klampenborg, then walk 10 minutes through the woods; tel. 39 63 73 00, www.bakken.dk.

Dragør—If you don't have time to get to the idyllic island of Ærø (see the Central Denmark chapter), consider a trip a few minutes out of Copenhagen to the fishing village of Dragør (bus #350S from Nørreport). For information, see www.dragoer.dk.

Shopping in Copenhagen

Shops are generally open Monday through Friday from 10:00 to 19:00 and Saturday from 9:00 to 16:00 (closed Sun). While big department stores dominate the scene, many locals favor the characteristic, small artisan shops and boutiques.

Uniquely Danish souvenirs to look for include intricate paper cuttings with idyllic motifs of swans, flowers, or Christmas themes; mobiles with everything from bicycles to Viking ships (look for the quality Flensted brand); and the colorful artwork (posters, postcards, T-shirts, and more) by Danish artist Bo Bendixen.

For a street's worth of shops selling **"Scantiques,"** wander down Ravnsborggade from Nørrebrogade.

Copenhagen's colorful **flea markets** are small but feisty and surprisingly cheap (May-Nov Sat 8:00-14:00 at Israels Plads; May-Sept Fri and Sat 8:00-17:00 along Gammel Strand and on Kongens Nytorv). For other street markets, ask at the TI.

The city's top **department stores** (Illum at Østergade 52, and Magasin du Nord at Kongens Nytorv 13) offer a good, if expensive, look at today's Denmark. Both are on the Strøget and have fine cafeterias on their top floors. The department stores and the Politiken Bookstore on Rådhuspladsen have a good selection of maps and English travel guides.

The section of the Strøget called **Amagertorv** is a highlight for shoppers. The Royal Copenhagen store here sells porcelain on three floors (Mon-Fri 10:00-19:00, Sat 10:00-17:00, Sun 12:00-17:00). The first floor up features figurines and collectibles. The second floor has a free museum with demonstrations and a great video (10 minutes, plays continuously, English only). In the basement, proving that "even the best painter can miss a stroke," you'll find the discounted seconds. Next door, Illums Bolighus shows off three floors of modern Danish design (Mon-Fri 10:00-19:00, Sat 9:00-17:00, Sun 10:00-17:00, shorter hours off-season).

Shoppers who like jewelry look for amber, known as "gold of the North." Globs of this petrified sap wash up on the shores of all the Baltic countries. **House of Amber** has a shop and a tiny two-room museum with about 50 examples of prehistoric insects trapped in the amber (remember *Jurassic Park?*) under magnifying glasses. You'll also see remarkable items made of amber, from necklaces and chests to Viking ships and chess sets (25 kr, daily May-Aug 10:00-19:00, Sept-April 10:00-18:00, museum closes 30 minutes earlier, at the top of Nyhavn at Kongens Nytorv 2; 4 other locations sell amber, but only the Nyhavn location houses a museum as well). If you're visiting Rosenborg Castle, you'll see even better examples of amber craftsmanship in its treasury.

For stylish and practical items of Danish design, check out

the boutique in the **Danish Design Center** (see page 85).

If you buy anything substantial (300 kr, about $60) from a shop displaying the **Danish Tax-Free Shopping** emblem, you can get a refund of the Value-Added Tax, roughly 20 to 25 percent of the purchase price (VAT is "MOMS" in Danish). If you have your purchase mailed, the tax can be deducted from your bill. For details, call 32 52 55 66, and see "Getting a VAT Refund" in the Introduction.

Nightlife in Copenhagen

Neighborhoods: The **Meatpacking District,** which I've listed for its restaurants (see page 128), is also one of the city's most up-and-coming destinations for bars and nightlife. On warm evenings, **Nyhavn** canal becomes a virtual nightclub, with packs of young people hanging out along the water, sipping beers. **Christiania** always seems to have something musical going on after dark. **Tivoli** has evening entertainment daily from mid-April through late September (see page 83).

Venues: Copenhagen Jazz House is a good bet for live jazz (closed Mon, Niels Hemmingsensgade 10, tel. 33 15 26 00, check website for schedule, www.jazzhouse.dk). For blues, try the **Mojo Blues Bar** (70 kr Fri-Sat, otherwise no cover, nightly 20:00-5:00, music starts at 21:30, Løngangsstræde 21c, tel. 33 11 64 53, schedule in Danish on website, www.mojo.dk). For locations, see the map on page 116.

Jazz Cruises: Canal Tours Copenhagen offers 1.5-hour jazz cruises along the canals of Copenhagen. You can bring a picnic dinner and drinks on board and enjoy a lively night on the water surrounded by Danes (140 kr, June-Aug Thu and Sun at 19:00, Sept-Dec and April-May only Sun at 15:00, no tours Jan-March, departs from Canal Tours Copenhagen dock at Nyhavn, tel. 32 96 30 00). Call to reserve on July and August evenings; otherwise try arriving 20 to 30 minutes in advance.

Event and Live Music Listings: For the latest, check at the TI and pick up *The Copenhagen Post* (comes out on Thu, free at TI and some hotels, also sold at newsstands, www.cphpost.dk).

Sleeping in Copenhagen

I've listed a few big business-class hotels, the best budget hotels in the center, cheap rooms in private homes in great neighborhoods an easy bus ride from the station, and a few backpacker dorm options.

Big Copenhagen hotels have an exasperating pricing policy. Their high rack rates are actually charged only about 20 or 30 days a year (unless you book in advance and don't know better). As

COPENHAGEN

Sleep Code

(6 kr = about $1, country code: 45)
S = Single, **D** = Double/Twin, **T** = Triple, **Q** = Quad, **b** = bathroom, **s** = shower. Breakfast is generally included at hotels (unless you get a deeply discounted room rate), but not at private rooms or hostels. You can assume that staff speak English and credit cards are accepted unless otherwise noted.

To help you sort easily through these listings, I've divided the accommodations into three categories, based on the highest rack-rate price for a standard double room with bath during high season:

  $$$ Higher Priced—Most rooms 1,000 kr or more.
   $$ Moderately Priced—Most rooms between 600-1,000 kr.
    $ Lower Priced—Most rooms 600 kr or less.

Prices can change without notice; verify the hotel's current rates online or by email.

hotels are swamped at certain times, they like to keep their gouging options open. Therefore, you'll need to check their website for deals or be bold enough to simply show up and use the TI's booking service to find yourself a room on their push list (ask at their desk, 100-kr fee). The TI swears that, except for maybe 10 days a year, you can land yourself a deeply discounted room in a three- or four-star business-class hotel in the center. That means a 1,400-kr double with American-style comfort for about 900 kr, including a big buffet breakfast.

Note that at the big hotels, some rates include breakfast, while the cheapest rates may not (you'll pay extra if you want breakfast).

Hotels in Central Copenhagen
Prices include breakfast unless noted otherwise. All of these hotels are big and modern, with elevators and non-smoking rooms upon request, and all accept credit cards. Beware: Many hotels have rip-off phone rates even for local calls.

Near Nørreport
$$$ Ibsens Hotel is a stylish 118-room hotel in a charming neighborhood away from the main train station commotion and a short walk from the old center (on average Sb-1,000-1,200 kr, Db-1,100-1,400 kr, very slushy rates flex with demand—ask about discounts when booking or check website; higher prices are for larger rooms, third bed-300 kr, great bikes-150 kr/24 hours, entirely non-smoking, free Internet access and Wi-Fi, parking-185 kr/day,

Vendersgade 23, S-tog: Nørreport, tel. 33 13 19 13, fax 33 13 19 16, www.ibsenshotel.dk, hotel@ibsenshotel.dk).

$$ Hotel Jørgensen is a friendly little 30-room hotel in a great location just off Nørreport with some cheap, grungy rooms and some good-value, nicer rooms. A good budget option, it's a bit worn around the edges. While the lounge is welcoming, the halls are a narrow, tangled maze (basic S-575 kr, Sb-675 kr, very basic D-675 kr, nicer Db-850 kr, cheaper off-season, extra bed-200 kr, free Wi-Fi, Rømersgade 11, tel. 33 13 81 86, fax 33 15 51 05, www .hoteljoergensen.dk, hoteljoergensen@mail.dk). They also rent 175-kr dorm beds to those under 35 (4-12 beds per room, sheets-30 kr).

Near Nyhavn

$$$ 71 Nyhavn has 150 smallish, rustic, but very classy rooms in a pair of beautifully restored, early-19th-century brick warehouses located at the far end of the colorful Nyhavn canal. With a professional, polite staff, lots of old brick and heavy timbers, and plenty of style, it's a worthwhile splurge (Sb-1,000-1,500 kr, Db-1,500-2,000 kr, 200 kr more for canal-view "superior" rooms, 400 kr more for larger "executive" rooms, rates vary depending on demand, some rates include breakfast—otherwise 170 kr, air-con in one of the buildings, free Internet access and Wi-Fi, next to the new Playhouse at Nyhavn 71, tel. 33 43 62 00, fax 33 43 62 01, www.71nyhavnhotel.dk, 71nyhavnhotel@arp-hansen.dk).

$$ Hotel Bethel Sømandshjem ("Seamen's Home"), run by a Lutheran association, is a calm and stately former seamen's hotel facing the boisterous Nyhavn canal and offering 29 tired but cozy rooms at the most reasonable rack rates in town. While the decor is college-dorm-inspired, the hotel boasts a kind, welcoming staff and feels surprisingly comfortable once you settle in. Plus, the colorful Nyhavn neighborhood is a great place to "come home" to after a busy day of sightseeing. Book long in advance (Sb-645 kr, large Sb-845 kr, Db-845 kr, larger "good" Db-945 kr, biggest corner Db-1,045 kr, extra bed-200 kr, free Internet access and Wi-Fi, Metro to Kongens Nytorv, facing bridge over the canal at Nyhavn 22, tel. 33 13 03 70, fax 33 15 85 70, www.hotel-bethel.dk, info @hotel-bethel.dk).

Behind the Train Station

The area behind the train station mingles elegant old buildings, trendy nightspots, and a hint of modern sleaze. The main drag running away from the station, Iseldgade, has long been Copenhagen's red-light district; but increasingly, this area is gentrified and feels safe (in spite of the few remaining, harmless sex shops). These hotels are also extremely handy to the up-and-coming Meatpacking District restaurant zone.

COPENHAGEN

Copenhagen Hotels & Restaurants

- ⛵ Canal Tour
- Ⓢ S-Tog Station
- Ⓗ Harbor Bus

❶ Ibsens Hotel	⓫ Restaurant Schønnemann
❷ Hotel Jørgensen	⓬ Café Halvvejen
❸ 71 Nyhavn Hotel	⓭ Slagteren ved Kultorvet
❹ Hotel Bethel Sømandshjem	⓮ Rest. & Café Nytorv
❺ Axel Hotel	⓯ Sorgenfri
❻ Star Hotel	⓰ Domhusets Smørrebrød
❼ Hotel Nebo	⓱ Andersen Bakery
❽ Cab-Inn City	⓲ Lagkagehuset Bakeries (4)
❾ Danhostel Copenhagen City	⓳ Nansens Bakery
❿ Danhostel Copenhagen Downtown	⓴ Konditori La Glace

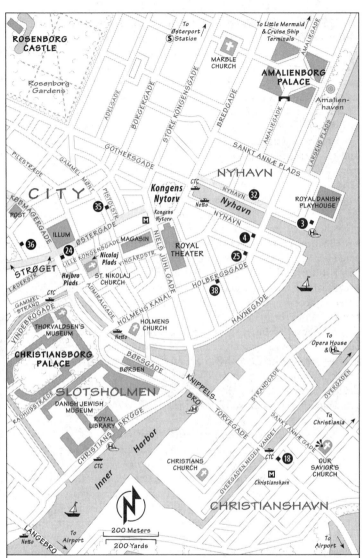

COPENHAGEN

21 Det Lille Apotek
22 Riz-Raz Veg. Buffet (2)
23 Tight Restaurant
24 Café Norden
25 Holberg No. 19
26 Københavner Caféen
27 The Ricemarket
28 Torvehallerne KBH
29 Café Klimt
30 Halifax Burgers (2)

31 To Meatpacking District Eateries
32 Nyhavn Eateries
33 Kompagnistræde Eateries
34 Gråbrødretorv Eateries
35 Netto Supermarket
36 Copenhagen Jazz House
37 Mojo Blues Bar
38 Bike Rentals (2)
39 Bike Copenhagen with Mike

$$$ Axel Hotel and **$$$ Carlton Hotel,** operated by the Guldsmeden ("Dragonfly") company, have more character than most—a restful spa-like ambience decorated with imported Balinese furniture, and an emphasis on sustainability and organic materials. I've listed average prices, but rates can change dramatically, depending on when you book—check their website for the best deals (Axel: Sb-845-975 kr, Db-985-1,145 kr, breakfast-165 kr, 129 rooms, request a quieter back room overlooking the pleasant garden, free Internet access and Wi-Fi, restful spa area with sauna and Jacuzzi-295 kr/person per stay, a block behind the train station at Helgolandsgade 7, tel. 33 31 32 66, fax 33 31 69 70, booking @hotelguldsmeden.com; Carlton: a bit cheaper than Axel, 64 rooms, Vesterbrogade 66, see map on page 54, tel. 33 22 15 00, fax 33 22 15 55, carlton@hotelguldsmeden.com). They share a website: www.hotelguldsmeden.com.

$$ Star Hotel has 134 charmless, cookie-cutter rooms at reasonable prices. Rates vary with the season and online specials (Sb-555-1,100 kr, Db-800-1,555 kr but usually around 950-1,000 kr, breakfast included in some rates—otherwise 65 kr, elevator, free Internet access and Wi-Fi, Colbjørnsensgade 13, tel. 33 22 11 00, star@copenhagenstar.dk).

$$ Hotel Nebo, a secure-feeling refuge with a friendly welcome and 84 comfy rooms, is a half-block from the station (S-420 kr, Sb-650-700 kr, D-650-845 kr, Db-950 kr, most rates include breakfast—otherwise 60 kr, cheaper Oct-April, periodic online deals, extra bed-150 kr, elevator, free Internet access, pay Wi-Fi, Istedgade 6, tel. 33 21 12 17, fax 33 23 47 74, www.nebo.dk, nebo @nebo.dk).

$$ Wake Up Copenhagen offers new, compact, slick, and stylish rooms (similar to but a notch more upscale-feeling than Cab-Inn, described next). The rates can range wildly (Db-600-2,400 kr), and their pricing structure is like the airlines' in that the further ahead and less flexibly you book, the less you pay (average rates are about Sb-500 kr, Db-800 kr). Rooms that are higher up—with better views and quieter—are also more expensive, and you can pay 200 kr extra for a larger room. It's in a desolate no-man's-land behind the station, between the train tracks and the harbor—about a 15-minute walk from the station or Tivoli, but ideal for biking (breakfast-60 kr, elevator, free Wi-Fi, bike rental, Carsten Niebuhrs Gade 11, see map on page 54, tel. 44 80 00 00, fax 44 80 00 01, www.wakeupcopenhagen.com—book on this site for best rates, wakeupcopenhagen@arp-hansen.dk).

A Danish Motel 6

$$ Cab-Inn is a radical innovation and a great value, with several locations in Copenhagen (as well as Odense, Aarhus, and

elsewhere): identical, mostly collapsible, tiny but comfy, cruise-ship-type staterooms, all bright, molded, and shiny, with TV, coffee-pot, shower, and toilet. Each room has a single bed that expands into a twin-bedded room with one or two fold-down bunks on the walls. It's tough to argue with this kind of efficiency (general rates: teensy "economy" Sb-485 kr, Db-615 kr; still small "standard" Sb-545 kr, Db-675 kr, flip-down bunk Tb-805 kr; larger "commodore" Sb-645 kr, Db-775 kr; relatively gigantic "captain's" Sb-745 kr, Db-875; larger family rooms also available, breakfast-60 kr, easy parking-60 kr, free Internet access and Wi-Fi, www.cabinn.com). The best of the bunch is **Cab-Inn City,** with 350 rooms and a great central location (no economy rooms here; a short walk south of the main train station and Tivoli at Mitchellsgade 14, tel. 33 46 16 16, fax 33 46 17 17, city@cab inn.com). Two more, nearly identical Cab-Inns are a 15-minute walk northwest of the station (for locations, see map on page 54): **Cab-Inn Copenhagen Express** (86 rooms, Danasvej 32-34, tel. 33 21 04 00, fax 33 21 74 09, express@cabinn.com) and **Cab-Inn Scandinavia** (201 rooms, some quads, Vodroffsvej 55, tel. 35 36 11 11, fax 35 36 11 14, scandinavia@cabinn.com). The newest and largest is **Cab-Inn Metro,** near the Ørestad Metro station (710 rooms, some quads, on the airport side of town at Arne Jakobsens Allé 2, tel. 32 46 57 00, fax 32 46 57 01, metro@cabinn.com).

Rooms in Private Homes

At about 600 kr or so per double, staying in a private home can be a great value. While these accommodations offer a fine peek into Danish domestic life, the experience can be as private or as social as you want it to be. Hosts generally speak English, and you'll get a key and can come and go as you like. Rooms generally have no sink, and the bathroom's down the hall. They usually don't include breakfast, but you'll have access to the kitchen. I've listed an agency with a website that represents scores of fine places and—if you'd rather book direct—a good B&B in Christianshavn.

$ Bed & Breakfast Denmark has served as a clearinghouse for local B&Bs since 1992. Peter Eberth and his staff take a 20-30 percent cut (the "deposit" you pay) but monitor quality. Given the high cost of hostels and hotels and the way local B&B hosts come and go, this is a fine and worthwhile service. Peter's website lets you choose the type and location of place best for you and gives you the necessary details when you pay. He has piles of good local

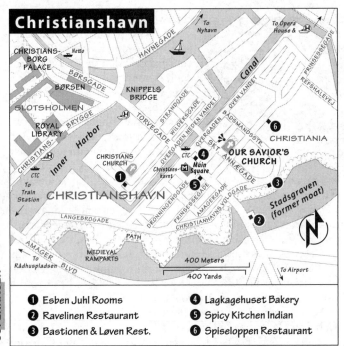

Christianshavn

① Esben Juhl Rooms
② Ravelinen Restaurant
③ Bastionen & Løven Rest.
④ Lagkagehuset Bakery
⑤ Spicy Kitchen Indian
⑥ Spiseloppen Restaurant

rooms in central apartments (D-400 kr, Db-500-600 kr). He's located near the station at Sankt Peders Stræde 41, but there's no reason to visit his office (tel. 39 61 04 05, www.bbdk.dk).

$ Esben Juhl rents two spic-and-span, bright rooms in his beautiful Christianshavn apartment, close to the harbor and canal. You'll be sharing Esben's bathroom, and if he books both rooms, he'll actually be sleeping out in the living room; if these sound like too-close quarters, look elsewhere. But Esben is soft-spoken and kind, and enjoys treating his guests like houseguests, making this a good opportunity to connect with a local (S-400 kr, D-500 kr, extra bed-150 kr, includes light breakfast, cash only, free Wi-Fi, David Balfours Gade 5, Metro: Christianshavn, tel. 32 57 39 08, mobile 27 40 12 15, mail@esju.dk).

Hostels

Copenhagen energetically accommodates the young vagabond on a shoestring. Hostels are the best value for those who travel alone, bring their own sheets, and make their own breakfast. Otherwise they can cost 250 kr per night per person.

$ Danhostel Copenhagen City, an official HI hostel, is the hostel of the future. This huge harborside skyscraper (1,004 beds on 16 stories) is clean, modern, non-smoking, and a 10-minute

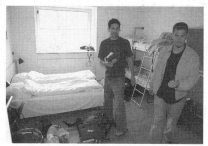

walk from the train station and Tivoli. Some rooms on higher floors have panoramic views over the city (available on a first-come, first-served basis). This is your best bet for a clean, basic, and inexpensive room in the city center (dorm beds in 6-bed rooms with bathrooms-135-195 kr—some co-ed, some separate; Sb/Db/Qb-495-720 kr, price depends on demand, sheets and towel-60 kr, breakfast-74 kr, nonmembers pay 35 kr/night extra, elevator, lockers, kitchen, self-service laundry, pay Internet access, free Wi-Fi, rental bikes, H. C. Andersen Boulevard 50, tel. 33 11 85 85, www.danhostelcopenhagencity .dk,copenhagencity@danhostel.dk).

$ Danhostel Copenhagen Downtown is beautifully located on a pleasant street right in the city center, a few steps from Slotsholmen Island and two blocks from the Strøget. Its 300 beds are a bit institutional, but it comes with a guest kitchen and a colorful, fun hangout bar, which doubles as the reception (rates vary with demand, bunk in 4- to 10-bed dorm-100-215 kr, D-250-450 kr, 100 kr more for a private bathroom, nonmembers pay 35 kr extra, sheets-30 kr, breakfast-65 kr, free Wi-Fi, Vandkunsten 5, tel. 70 23 21 10, www.copenhagendowntown.com, info@copen hagendowntown.com).

$ City Public Hostel houses travelers late May through August; the rest of the year, it's a latchkey program for local kids. It's well-run, welcomes people of all ages, and has a great location behind the Copenhagen City Museum on Vesterbrogade. With its sprawling grassy front yard, you can even forget you're in the middle of a big city (130 kr/bed in massive 66-bed room, 140 kr/ bed in 32- or 22-bed dorm, 160 kr/bed in 12-bed dorm, 170 kr/bed in 10- or 6-bed dorm, sheets-40 kr, no breakfast, relaxing lounge, 10-minute walk behind main train station at Absalonsgade 8, see map on page 54, tel. 33 31 20 70, www.citypublichostel.dk, info @citypublichostel.dk).

$ Danhostel Copenhagen Amager, an official HI hostel, is on the edge of town (dorm bed-145 kr, S-360 kr, Sb-460 kr, D-390 kr, Db-490 kr, T-520 kr, Tb-580 kr, Q-630 kr, Qb-680 kr, nonmembers pay 35 kr extra, sheets-45 kr, breakfast-55 kr, family rooms, no curfew, excellent facilities, Internet access, self-serve laundry, Vejlands Allé 200, tel. 32 52 29 08, fax 32 52 27 08, www.danhostelcopenhagen.dk, copenhagen@danhostel.dk). To get from downtown to the hostel, take the Metro (Metro: Bella Center, then 10-minute walk).

COPENHAGEN

Eating in Copenhagen

Cheap Meals

For a quick lunch, try a *smørrebrød*, a *pølse*, or a picnic. Finish it off with a pastry.

Smørrebrød

Denmark's 300-year-old tradition of open-face sandwiches survives. Find a *smørrebrød* take-out shop and choose two or three that look good (about 20 kr each). You'll get them wrapped and ready for a park bench. Add a cold drink, and you have a fine, quick, and very Danish lunch. Tradition calls for three sandwich courses: herring first, then meat, and then cheese. Downtown, you'll find these handy local alternatives to Yankee fast-food chains. They range from splurges to quick stop-offs.

Between Copenhagen University and Rosenborg Castle

My three favorite *smørrebrød* places are particularly handy when connecting your sightseeing between the downtown Strøget core and Rosenborg Castle.

Restaurant Schønnemann is the foodies' choice—it has been written up in international magazines and frequently wins awards for "Best Lunch in Copenhagen." It's a cozy cellar restaurant crammed with small tables—according to the history on the menu, people "gather here in intense togetherness." The sand on the floor evokes a bygone era when passing traders would leave their horses out on the square while they lunched here. You'll need to reserve to get a table, and you'll pay a premium for their *smørrebrød* (50-130 kr). At these prices, the sandwiches had better be a cut above...fortunately, they deliver (two lunch seatings Mon-Sat: 11:30-14:00 and 14:14-17:00, closed Sun, no dinner, Hauser Plads 16, tel. 33 12 07 85).

Café Halvvejen is a small mom-and-pop place serving traditional lunches and open-face sandwiches in a woody and smoke-stained café, lined with portraits of Danish royalty. You can eat inside or at an outside table in good weather (50-70 kr *smørrebrød*, 80-100-kr main dishes, food served Mon-Sat 12:00-15:00, closed Sun, next to public library at Krystalgade 11, tel. 33 11 91 12). In the evening, it becomes a hip and smoky student hangout, though no food is served.

Slagteren ved Kultorvet, a few blocks northwest of the university, is a small butcher shop with bowler-hatted clerks selling good, inexpensive sandwiches to go for about 35 kr. Choose from ham, beef, or pork (sorry—no vegetarian options, Mon-Thu 8:00-17:30, Fri 8:00-19:00, Sat 8:00-14:00, closed Sun, just off Kultorvet square at #4 Frederiksborggade, look for gold bull's head hanging outside).

Near Gammeltorv/Nytorv

Restaurant and Café Nytorv has pleasant outdoor seating on Nytorv (with cozy indoor tables available nearby) and a great deal on a *smørrebrød* sampler for about 179 kr—perfect for two people to share. This "Copenhagen City Plate" gives you a selection of the traditional sandwiches and extra bread on request (daily 9:00-22:00, Nytorv 15, tel. 33 11 77 06). **Sorgenfri** offers a local experience in a dark, woody spot just off the Strøget (80-100 kr, Mon-Sat 11:00-20:45, Sun 12:00-18:00, Brolæggerstræde 8, tel. 33 11 58 80). Or consider **Domhusets Smørrebrød** (Mon-Fri 8:00-15:00, closed Sat-Sun, off the City Hall end of the Strøget at Kattesundet 18, tel. 33 15 98 98).

The *Pølse*

The famous Danish hot dog, sold in *pølsevogne* (sausage wagons) throughout the country, is another typically Danish institution

that has resisted the onslaught of our global, prepackaged, fast-food culture. Study the photo menu for variations. These are fast, cheap, tasty, and, like their American cousins, almost worthless nutritionally. Even so, what the locals call the "dead man's finger" is the dog Danish kids love to bite.

There's more to getting a *pølse* than simply ordering a "hot dog" (which in Copenhagen simply means a sausage with a bun on the side, generally the worst bread possible). The best is a *ristet* (or grilled) hot dog *med det hele* (with the works). Employ these other handy phrases: *rød* (red, the basic boiled weenie), *medister* (spicy, better quality), *knæk* (short, stubby, tastier than *rød*), *brød* (a bun, usually smaller than the sausage), *svøb* ("swaddled" in bacon), *Fransk* (French style, buried in a long skinny hole in the bun with sauce). *Sennep* is mustard and *ristet løg* are crispy, fried onions. Wash everything down with a *sodavand* (soda pop).

By hanging around a *pølsevogn*, you can study this institution. Denmark's "cold feet cafés" are a form of social care: People who have difficulty finding jobs are licensed to run these wiener-mobiles. As they gain seniority, they are promoted to work at more central locations. Danes like to gather here for munchies and *pølsesnak*—the local slang for empty chatter (literally, "sausage

COPENHAGEN

talk"). And traditionally, after getting drunk, guys stop here for a hot dog and chocolate milk on the way home—that's why the stands stay open until the wee hours.

For sausages a cut above (and from a storefront—not a cart), stop by the little grill restaurant **Andersen Bakery,** directly across the street from the train station (next to the Tivoli entrance). The menu is limited—either pork or veal/beef—but the ingredients are high-quality and the weenies are tasty (50-kr gourmet dogs, daily 7:00-19:00, Bernstorffsgade 5, tel. 33 75 07 35).

Picnics

Throughout Copenhagen, small delis *(viktualiehandler)* sell fresh bread, tasty pastries, juice, milk, cheese, and yogurt (drinkable, in tall liter boxes). Two of the largest supermarket chains are **Irma** (in arcade on Vesterbrogade next to Tivoli) and **Super Brugsen. Netto** is a cut-rate outfit with the cheapest prices. And, of course, there's the ever-present **7-Eleven** chain, with branches seemingly on every corner; while you'll pay a bit more here, there's a reason they're called "convenience" stores—and they also serve pastries and hot dogs.

Pastry

The golden pretzel sign hanging over the door or windows is the Danes' age-old symbol for a bakery. Danish pastries, called *wienerbrød* ("Vienna bread") in Denmark, are named for the Viennese bakers who brought the art of pastry-making to Denmark, where the Danes say they perfected it. Try these bakeries: **Lagkagehuset** (multiple locations around town; the handiest options include one right in the train station, another nearby inside the TI, one along the Strøget at Frederiksborggade 21, and another on Torvegade just across from the Metro station in Christianshavn) and **Nansens** (on corner of Nansensgade and Ahlefeldtsgade, near Ibsens Hotel). For a genteel bit of high-class 1870s Copenhagen, pay a lot for a coffee and a fresh Danish at **Konditori La Glace,** just off the Strøget at Skoubogade 3.

Dine with the Danes

For a unique experience and a great opportunity to meet locals in their homes, consider having this organization arrange a dinner for you with a Danish family. You get a homey two-course meal with lots of conversation. Some effort is made to match your age and interests, but not occupations. Book online at least a week in advance (400 kr per person, www.dinewiththedanes.dk, tel. 26 85 39 61). Fill out an online questionnaire, and you'll be contacted by email a day or two later.

Restaurants

I've listed restaurants in three areas: the downtown core, the funky Christianshavn neighborhood across the harbor, and the trendy "Meatpacking District" behind the train station. Most of my suggestions in the high-rent downtown are tired but reliable Danish classics. For a broader range of Copenhagen's culinary scene of today, it's worth the short walk to the Meatpacking District.

Due to the high cost of water in Denmark, it's common to be charged for tap water with your meal if you do not order any other beverage. You'll often save money by paying with cash; many Danish restaurants charge a fee for credit-card transactions (about 2-5 percent).

In the Downtown Core

Det Lille Apotek ("The Little Pharmacy") is a reasonable, candlelit place. It's been popular with locals for 200 years, and now it's also quite touristy. Their specialty is "Stone Beef," a big slab of tender, raw steak plopped down and cooked in front of you on a scalding-hot soapstone. Cut it into smaller pieces and it's cooked within minutes (sandwich lunches, traditional dinners for 125-190 kr, nightly from 17:30, just off the Strøget, between Frue Church and Round Tower at Store Kannikestræde 15, tel. 33 12 56 06).

Riz-Raz Vegetarian Buffet has two locations in Copenhagen: around the corner from the canal boat rides at Kompagnistræde 20 (tel. 33 15 05 75) and across from Det Lille Apotek at Store Kannikestræde 19 (tel. 33 32 33 45). At both places, you'll find a healthy all-you-can-eat Middle Eastern/Mediterranean/vegetarian buffet lunch for 79 kr (cheese but no meat, great falafel, daily 11:30-16:00) and an even bigger dinner buffet for 99 kr (16:00-24:00). The wonderfully varied and very filling dinner buffet has to be the best deal in town. Use lots of plates and return to the buffet as many times as you like. They also offer à la carte and meat options for 65-95 kr. Tap water is 8 kr per jug.

Tight resembles a trendy gastropub, serving an eclectic international array of cuisine in a split-level maze of hip rooms that mix old timbers and brick with bright colors. You can only order a fixed-price meal here, unless you want their prizewinning burger (two courses-225 kr, three courses-275 kr, burger-140 kr; Mon-Thu 17:00-22:00, Fri 17:00-23:00, Sat 12:00-23:00, Sun 12:00-22:00, just off the Strøget at Hyskenstræde 10, tel. 33 11 09 00).

Café Norden, very Danish with modern "world cuisine" and fine pastries, is a big, venerable institution overlooking Amagertorv by the heron fountain. They have good light meals and salads, and great people-watching from window seats on the second floor (120-160-kr sandwiches and salads, 150-160-kr main dishes, huge splittable portions, daily 9:00-24:00, order at bar, Østergade 61, tel. 33 11 77 91).

Holberg No. 19, a cozy American-run café with classic ambience, sits just a block off the tourist crush of the Nyhavn canal. With a loose, friendly, low-key vibe, it offers more personality and lower prices than the tourist traps along Nyhavn (60-95-kr salads and sandwiches, order at the bar, Mon-Fri 10:00-22:00, Sat 10:00-20:00, Sun 10:00-18:00, sometimes opens at 8:00, Holberg 19, tel. 33 14 01 90).

Københavner Caféen, cozy and a bit tired, feels like a ship captain's dining room. The staff is enthusiastically traditional, serving local dishes and elegant open-face sandwiches for a good value. Lunch specials (80-100 kr) are served until 17:00, when the more expensive dinner menu kicks in (plates for 120-200 kr, daily, kitchen closes at 22:00, at Badstuestræde 10, tel. 33 32 80 81).

The Ricemarket, an unpretentious Asian fusion bistro, is buried in a modern cellar between the Strøget and Rosenborg Castle. It's the more affordable (and more casual) side-eatery of a popular local restaurant, and offers a break from Danish food (65-95-kr small dishes, 115-185-kr big dishes, 95-kr lunch special includes drink, Mon-Sat 11:00-22:00, Sun 11:00-21:00, Hausergade 38 near Kultorvet, tel. 35 35 75 30).

Illum and **Magasin du Nord** department stores serve cheery, reasonable meals in their cafeterias. At Illum, eat outside at tables along the Strøget, or head to the elegant glass-domed top floor (Østergade 52). Magasin du Nord (Kongens Nytorv 13) also has a great grocery and deli in the basement.

Also try **Restaurant and Café Nytorv** at Nytorv 15 or **Sorgenfri** at Brolæggerstræde 8 (both are described under *"Smørrebrød,"* earlier).

In Christianshavn

This neighborhood is so cool, it's worth combining an evening wander with dinner, even if you're not staying here. It's a 10-minute walk across the bridge from the old center, or a 3-minute ride on the Metro. Choose one of my listings (for locations, see map on page 120), or simply wander the blocks between Christianshavntorv, the main square, and the Christianshavn Canal—you'll find a number of lively neighborhood pubs and cafés.

Ravelinen Restaurant, on a tiny island on the big road 100 yards south of Christianshavn, serves traditional Danish food at reasonable prices to happy local crowds. Dine indoors or on the lovely lakeside terrace (which is tented and heated, so it's comfortable even on blustery evenings). This is like Tivoli without the kitsch and tourists (70-130-kr lunch dishes, 180-280-kr dinners, mid-April-late Dec daily 11:30-21:00, closed off-season, Torvegade 79, tel. 32 96 20 45).

The Latest Culinary Phe-noma-non

Foodies visiting Denmark probably already know that Copenhagen is home to the planet's top-rated restaurant. In 2010 and 2011, San Pellegrino and *Restaurant* magazine named noma the "Best Restaurant in the World." With the closure of El Bulli near Barcelona in 2011, noma has emerged as *the* reservation to get in the foodie universe. Chef René Redzepi is a pioneer in the burgeoning "New Nordic" school of cooking, which combines modern nouvelle cuisine and molecular gastronomy techniques with locally sourced (and, in some cases, foraged) ingredients from Denmark and other Nordic lands. So, while they use sophisticated cooking methods, they replace the predictable French and Mediterranean ingredients with Nordic ones. The restaurant's name comes from the phrase *nordisk mad* (Nordic food).

But noma, which is located at the northern edge of the trendy Christianshavn district (Strandgade 93, tel. 32 96 32 97), is not cheap. The seven-course *menu* runs 1,500 kr; accompanying wines add 950 kr to the bill. A couple going for the whole shebang is looking at spending close to $800. And even if you're willing to take the plunge, you have to plan ahead—noma is booked up around three months ahead. Check their website (www.noma.dk) for the latest procedure; you'll likely need to call on a specific date, at 10:00 in the morning Copenhagen time, about three months before your desired reservation...and hope you get through. You can also put your name on their waiting list, using their online form.

If you can't commit that far out (or don't want to spend that much), many of the top restaurants in Copenhagen (including Kødbyens Fisekebar, listed on page 129) are run by former chefs from noma—giving you at least a taste of culinary greatness.

COPENHAGEN

Bastionen & Løven, at the little windmill (Lille Mølle), serves gourmet Danish nouveau cuisine with a French inspiration from a small but fresh menu, on a Renoir terrace or in its Rembrandt interior. The classiest, dressiest, and most gourmet of all my listings, this restaurant fills a classic old mansion. Reservations for indoor dining are required; they don't take reservations for outdoor seating, as weather is unpredictable (65-165-kr lunches, 170-185-kr dinners, 325-kr three-course meal, daily 11:30-24:00, walk to end of Torvegade and follow ramparts up to restaurant, at south end of Christianshavn, Christianshavn Voldgade 50, tel. 32 95 09 40).

Lagkagehuset is everybody's favorite bakery in Christianshavn. With a big selection of pastries, sandwiches, excellent fresh-baked bread, and award-winning strawberry tarts, it's a great place for breakfast or picnic fixings (pastries for less than 20 kr, take-out coffee for 30 kr, daily 6:00-19:00, Torvegade 45). For other locations closer to the town center, see page 124 under "Pastry."

Ethnic Strip on Christianshavn's Main Drag: Torvegade, which is within a few minutes' walk of the Christianshavn Metro station, is lined with appealing and inexpensive ethnic eateries, including Italian, cheap kebabs, Mexican (thriving with a nightly 109-kr buffet), Chinese, and more. **Spicy Kitchen** serves cheap and good Indian food—tight and cozy, it's a hit with locals (55-70-kr plates, Mon-Sat 17:00-23:00, Sun 14:00-23:00, Torvegade 56).

In Christiania: Spiseloppen ("The Flea Eats") is a wonderfully classy place in Christiania. It serves great 135-165-kr vegetarian meals and 175-260-kr meaty ones by candlelight. It's gourmet anarchy—a good fit for Christiania, the free city/squatter town (Tue-Sun 17:00-22:00, closed Mon, occasional live music on weekends, reservations often necessary Fri-Sat; 3 blocks behind spiral spire of Our Savior's Church, on top floor of old brick warehouse, turn right just inside Christiania's main gate, enter the wildly empty warehouse, and climb the graffiti-riddled stairs; tel. 32 57 95 58). Other, less-expensive Christiania eateries are listed on page 111.

Near Nørreport

The following eateries are near the recommended Ibsens and Jørgensens hotels.

Torvehallerne KBH is in a pair of new, modern, glassy market halls right on Israel Plads. In addition to produce, fish, and meat stalls, it has several inviting food counters where you can sit to eat a meal, or grab something to go. I can't think of a more enjoyable place in Copenhagen to browse for a meal than this upscale food court (prices vary per place, Tue-Thu 10:00-19:00, Fri 10:00-20:00, Sat 9:00-17:00, Sun 10:00-15:00, most places closed Mon, Frederiksborggade 21).

Café Klimt is a tight and thriving place, noisy and lit with candles. A young, hip crowd gathers here under the funky palm tree for modern world cuisine—salads, big pastas, burgers, omelets, and brunch until 16:00 (80-150 kr, daily 9:30-24:00, later Fri-Sat, Frederiksborggade 29, tel. 33 11 76 70).

Halifax, part of a small local chain, serves up "build-your-own" burgers, where you select a patty, a side dish, and a dipping sauce for your fries (100-125 kr, daily 12:00-22:00, Sun until 21:00, Frederiksborggade 35, tel. 33 32 77 11). They have another location just off the Strøget (at Larsbjørnsstræde 9).

In the Meatpacking District (Kødbyen)

Literally "Meat Town," Kødbyen is an old warehouse zone huddled up against the train tracks behind the main station. There are three color-coded sectors—brown, gray, and white—each one a cluster of old industrial buildings. The brown zone, closest to the station, is a row of former slaughterhouses that has been converted into gallery space. At the far end is the white zone (Den Hvide Kødby), which has been overtaken by some of the city's most trendy and enjoyable eateries, mingling with surviving offices and warehouses for the local meatpacking industry. All of the places I list here are within a few steps of each other (except for the Mother pizzeria, a block away).

The curb appeal of this area is zilch (it looks like, well, a meatpacking district), but inside, these restaurants are bursting with life and flavor. While youthful and trendy, this scene is also very accessible—as much yuppie as it is avant-garde. Most of these eateries are in buildings with old white tile; this, combined with the considerable popularity of this area, can make the dining rooms quite loud. These places can fill up, especially on weekends (when it's virtually impossible to get a table if you just show up)—be sure to reserve ahead.

It's a very close stroll from the station: If you go south on the bridge called Tietgens Bro, which crosses the tracks just south of the station, and carry on for about 10 minutes, you'll run right into the area. Those sleeping in the hotels behind the station just stroll five minutes south. Or you can ride the S-tog to the Dybbølsbro stop, which is also just on the edge of this area.

Kødbyens Fisekebar ("Fish Bar"), one of the first and still the most acclaimed restaurant in the Meatpacking District, is run by a former chef from the famous noma restaurant (see sidebar). Focusing on small, thoughtfully composed plates of modern Nordic seafood, the Fiskebar has a stripped-down white interior with a big fish tank and a long cocktail bar surrounded by smaller tables. It's extremely popular (reservations are essential), and feels a bit too trendy for its own good. While the prices are high, so is the quality; diners are paying for a taste of the "New Nordic" style of cooking that's so in vogue here (100-145-kr small plates, 200-245-kr main dishes; Tue-Thu 17:30-24:00, Fri 15:30-24:00, Sat 12:00-2:00 in the morning, Sun 12:00-15:30, closed Mon; Flæsketorvet 100, tel. 32 15 56 56).

BioMio, in the old Bosch building, is a fresh take on an old cafeteria: First, claim a table (don't be afraid to share—Danes don't bite—and make a note of your table number). Then pick up a plastic card from the front desk to keep track of your purchases.

Select your meal from the 100 percent organic, eclectic menu (with "world fusion" food—curries, wok dishes, Moroccan meatballs, and so on). Survey the line of chefs working in the open kitchen, choose which one you want to cook your meal, and place your order directly with him or her. Buy your drinks at the bar, and return to your seat to wait for your food to be delivered. When you're finished, just bring your card to the cashier to settle up. While prices are high for a self-service model, it's a unique experience, with fun ambience and good, healthy food (55-kr small plates, 105-185-kr dinners with big portions, 100-kr two-course lunch available Mon-Fri, open daily 12:00-23:00, Halmtorvet 19, tel. 33 31 20 00).

Paté Paté, next door to BioMio, is a tight, rollicking bistro in a former pâté factory. While a wine bar at heart, it also has a full menu of pricey, carefully prepared modern cuisine and a cozy atmosphere rare in the Meatpacking District (85-115-kr starters, 165-195-kr main dishes, Mon-Sat 9:00-24:00, closed Sun, Slagterboderne 1, tel. 39 69 55 57).

Mother is a pizzeria named for the way the sourdough for their crust must be "fed" and cared for to flourish. You can taste that care in the pizza, which has a delicious tangy crust. Out front are comfortable picnic benches, while the interior curls around the busy pizza oven and chefs pulling globs of dough that will become the basis for your pizza (30-kr bruschetta, 75-140-kr pizzas, a block beyond the other restaurants listed here at Høkerboderne 9, tel. 22 27 58 98).

Nose2Tail Madbodega (*mad* means "food") prides itself on locally sourced, sustainable cooking, using the entire animal for your meal (hence the name). You'll climb down some stairs into an unpretentious white-tiled cellar (50-kr small plates, 70-180-kr large plates, Mon-Sat 18:00-24:00, closed Sun, Flæsketorvet 13A, tel. 33 93 50 45).

Other Central Neighborhoods to Explore

To find a good restaurant, try simply window-shopping in one of these inviting districts.

Nyhavn's harbor canal is lined with a touristy strip of restaurants set alongside its classic sailboats. Here thriving crowds are served mediocre, overpriced food in a great setting. On any sunny day, if you want steak and fries (120 kr) and a 50-kr beer, this can be fun. On Friday and Saturday, the strip becomes the longest bar in the world.

Kompagnistræde is home to a changing cast of great little eateries. Running parallel to the Strøget, this street has fewer tourists and lower rent, and encourages places to compete creatively for the patronage of local diners.

Gråbrødretorv ("Grey Friars' Square") is perhaps the most popular square in the old center for a meal. It's like a food court, especially in good weather. Choose from Italian, French, or Danish. Two respected steakhouses are **Jensen's Bøfhus** (100-kr burgers, 120-220-kr main dishes) and the pricier **Bøf & Ost** (170-250-kr main dishes). **Skildpadden** ("The Turtle") is a student hit, with make-it-yourself sandwiches (69 kr, choose the type of bread, salami, and cheese you want) and a 49-kr salad bar, plus draft beer (30 kr, or 22 kr after 16:00—sort of a reverse happy hour). It's in a cozy cellar with three little tables on the lively square (Mon-Fri 11:30-22:30, Sat-Sun 11:30-20:30, Gråbrødretorv 9, tel. 33 13 05 06).

Istedgade and the surrounding streets behind the train station (just above the Meatpacking District) are home to an assortment of inexpensive ethnic restaurants. You will find numerous kebab, Chinese, Thai, and pizza places. The area can be a bit seedy, especially right behind the station, but walk a few blocks away to take your pick of inexpensive, ethnic eateries frequented by locals.

Copenhagen Connections

By Train or Bus

From Copenhagen by Train to: Hillerød/Frederiksborg (6/hour, 40 minutes on S-tog), **Roskilde** (1-3/hour, 30 minutes), **Humlebæk** (Louisiana modern-art museum; 4/hour, 36 minutes), **Helsingør** (3/hour, 50 minutes), **Odense** (3/hour, 1.75 hours), **Ærøskøbing** (5/day, 2.75 hours to Svendborg with a transfer in Odense, then 1.25-hour ferry crossing to Ærøskøbing—see page 178 for info on ferry), **Billund/Legoland** (hourly, 2.25 hours to Vejle, then take buses #43, #143, #166, or #179 to Billund, allow 3.5 hours total), **Aarhus** (1-2/hour, 3 hours), **Malmö** (3/hour, 35 minutes), **Stockholm** (almost hourly, 5-6 hours on high-speed train, some with a transfer at Malmö or Lund, reservation required; overnight service available but requires a change in Lund), **Växjö** (8/day, 2.5-3 hours), **Kalmar** (12/day, 3.5-4 hours, transfer in Alvesta), **Oslo** (2/day, 8 hours, transfer at Göteborg; for night train—which runs in summer only—take 35-minute train to Malmö, Sweden, www.sj.se, then easy transfer to direct night train; see page 133 for overnight boat option), **Berlin** (5/day, 7 hours, reservation required, one direct, others change in Hamburg), **Amsterdam** (9/day, 11-18 hours, most require multiple changes, 1 direct night train), and **Frankfurt/Rhine** (4/day, 9-11 hours, most change in Hamburg). Train info tel. 70 13 14 15 (for English, press 1 for general information and tickets, and 2 for international trains). DSB (or Danske Statsbaner), Denmark's national railway, www.rejseplanen.dk.

By Bus: Taking the bus to **Stockholm** is cheaper but more time-consuming than taking the train (2/day, 9 hours, www.swe bus.se).

By Cruise Ship

More than half a million people visit Copenhagen via cruise ship each year. For a wealth of online information for cruise-ship passengers, see www.cruisecopenhagen.com. For more in-depth cruising information, pick up my *Rick Steves' Northern European Cruise Ports* guidebook.

Cruise Ports

Most cruise ships use one of two main terminals, both north of downtown—**Frihavnen** ("Freeport"), about three miles from the city center, and **Langelinie Pier,** about a mile closer to downtown (but a pleasant 10-minute walk north of *The Little Mermaid* site). A few cruises put in at **Toldbod,** even closer to town (just in front of Amalienborg Palace). The **Copenhagen Ferry Terminal,** located between the Frihavnen and Langelinie piers, serves DFDS ferries to and from Oslo (see "By Overnight Boat to Oslo," later).

Getting Downtown: Handy public **bus #26** connects both Langelinie and Frihavnen to downtown every 20 minutes (24 kr, buy ticket on board, possible to pay in euros or US dollars on this bus line only). Bus #26 does not run on weekends, when you'll have to consider one of the other options described next.

Langelinie and Frihavnen are both within about a 15-minute walk of a **train** station on Copenhagen's S-tog suburban rail line (Frihavnen is near the Nordhavn station, while Langelinie is near Østerport station). From either station, you can hop on a train headed downtown (buy a 24-kr ticket at machine on platform, then take any train headed in direction: Køge, Frederikssund, Ballerup, or Høje Taastrup; ride to the "København H" stop for the main train station).

From either terminal, you can also take a **taxi** (figure around 160 kr into downtown from Langelinie, or 200 kr from Frihavnen), or take a **hop-on, hop-off bus tour** (see page 68). From Frihavnen, most cruise lines offer a **shuttle bus** straight to Kongens Nytorv and/or Rådhuspladsen (City Hall Square), generally for a fee. From Langelinie, you can **walk** into town (explained later).

Port Details: Neither port area has much in the way of services (such as ATMs); make your way downtown, then find what you need there.

Langelinie Pier, closer to the city, is intuitive and user-friendly: a long, skinny pier with one road and a row of ships. Bus #26 (on weekdays) stops at three points along the road. Otherwise, you can walk: Head to the base of the pier, cross to the mainland, then either bear left to find *The Little Mermaid,* or right to circle around Kastellet Fortress and find Østerport train station for a speedy train downtown. From *The Little Mermaid,* you can walk in about 15 minutes to Amalienborg Palace, then 10 more minutes to the colorful Nyhavn canal.

Frihavnen, a bit farther out, is a sprawling industrial zone with several cruise piers (called Sundkaj, Orientkaj, Fortkaj, and—farther to the north—Levantkaj and a brand-new cruise terminal in the works). The first three piers are all within an easy 5- to 10-minute walk of the port gate (just follow the thick blue line painted on the sidewalk); from the more distant Levantkaj, the cruise line offers a free shuttle bus to the gate. Exiting the port gate, you can bear right to find the stop for bus #26; or bear left out to the main road, then turn left, walk a long block, cross the street, duck under the underpass, and turn left along a residential street to find the Nordhavn train station (for the speedy train downtown).

By Overnight Boat to Oslo

Luxurious DFDS Seaways cruise ships leave nightly from Copenhagen for Oslo, and from Oslo for Copenhagen. The 16-hour sailings leave at 17:00 and arrive at 9:30 the next day. So you can spend seven hours in Norway's capital and then return to Copenhagen, or take this cruise from Oslo and do Copenhagen as a day trip...or just go one-way in either direction (see page 289 for info on departing from Oslo).

Cruise Costs: Cabins vary dramatically in price depending on the day and season (most expensive on weekends and late June–mid-Aug; cheapest on weekdays and Oct-April). For example, a bed in a four-berth "Seaways" shoehorn economy cabin starts at 410 kr per person one-way for four people traveling together (500 kr with a window); a luxurious double "Commodore class" cabin higher on the ship starts at 950 kr per person one-way (and includes a TV, minibar, and free breakfast buffet). A "mini-cruise" round-trip with a day in Oslo and no meals starts at 598 kr per person in an economy double cabin. All cabins have private bathrooms inside.

Onboard Services: DFDS Seaways operates two ships on this route—the MS *Pearl of Scandinavia* and the MS *Crown of Scandinavia.* Both offer all the cruise-ship luxuries: big buffets for breakfast (129 kr) and dinner (239 kr), gourmet restaurants (359-kr three-course meals), a kids' playroom, pool (indoor on the *Crown,* indoor and outdoor on the *Pearl*), sauna, nightclubs, pay Wi-Fi, satellite phone, and tax-free shopping. There are no ATMs on board. Cash advances are available at the shipboard exchange desk. All shops and restaurants accept credit cards as well as euros, dollars, and Danish, Swedish, and Norwegian currency.

Reservations: Reservations are smart in summer and on weekends. Advance bookings get the best prices. Book online or call DFDS Seaway's Danish office at 33 42 30 10 (Mon-Fri 8:30-17:00, www.dfdsseaways.us), or, in the US, call 800-533-3755 (www.dfdsseawaysusa.com).

Port Details: The **Copenhagen Ferry Terminal** (a.k.a. DFDS Terminalen) is a short walk north of *The Little Mermaid* site. The terminal is open daily 9:00-17:00 (luggage lockers available).

Getting Downtown: Shuttle bus #20E meets arriving ships from Oslo (daily 9:30-10:15). It goes first to Østerport station (far from downtown but on the S-tog line—easy connection to the main train station, with some recommended hotels and the start of my self-guided walk), then to Kongens Nytorv (on the Metro line and near Nyhavn and other recommended hotels); from either stop, you can connect to Nørreport station (with additional recommended hotels).

To reach the ferry terminal *from* the city center, catch bus #20E at Kongens Nytorv (free for cruise passengers, coordinated with sailing schedule; daily 14:00-16:00, departs every 10-30 minutes, arrives at the terminal 11 minutes later). Or take the S-tog from downtown in the direction of Hellerup or Hillerød to the Nordhavn station. Exit the station, cross under the tracks, and hike toward the water; you'll see the ship on your right.

NEAR COPENHAGEN

Roskilde • Frederiksborg Castle • Louisiana •
Karen Blixen Museum • Kronborg Castle

Copenhagen's the star, but there are several worthwhile sights nearby, and the public transportation system makes side-tripping a joy. Visit Roskilde's great Viking ships and royal cathedral. Tour Frederiksborg, Denmark's most spectacular castle, and slide along the cutting edge at Louisiana—a superb art museum with a coastal setting as striking as its art. Blixen fans can get *Out of Africa* at the author's home. At Helsingør, do the dungeons of Kronborg Castle before heading on to Sweden.

Planning Your Time

Roskilde's Viking ships and Frederiksborg Castle are the area's essential sights. Each one takes a half-day, and each one is an easy commute from Copenhagen in different directions (30-40-minute train ride, then a 20-minute walk or short bus ride). You'll find fewer tour-bus crowds in the afternoon. While you're in Roskilde, you can also pay your respects to the tombs of the Danish royalty.

If you're choosing between castles, Frederiksborg is the beautiful showpiece with the opulent interior, and Kronborg—darker and danker—is more typical of the way most castles really were. Both are dramatic from the outside, but Kronborg—overlooking the raging sea channel to Sweden—has a more scenic setting. Castle collectors can hit both in a day (see the two-castle day plan, later).

Louisiana is the obvious choice for art-lovers; the Karen Blixen Museum is for her admirers.

Drivers can visit these sights on the way into or out of Copenhagen. By train, do day trips from Copenhagen, then sleep while

traveling to and from Copenhagen to Oslo (by boat, or by train via Malmö, Sweden) or Stockholm (by train via Malmö). Consider getting a Copenhagen Card (see page 56), which covers your transportation to all of the destinations in this chapter, as well as admission to Roskilde Cathedral, Frederiksborg Castle, and the Karen Blixen Museum (but not the Roskilde Viking Museum, Kronborg Castle, or Louisiana).

A Two-Castle Day (plus Louisiana) by Public Transportation: You can see both Frederiksborg and Kronborg castles, plus Louisiana Art Museum, in one busy day. (This works best on Tue-Fri, when Louisiana is open until 22:00.) Ride the 9:05 train from Copenhagen to Hillerød, then hop on the awaiting bus to Frederiksborg Castle; you'll hear the 10:00 bells and be the first tourist inside. Linger in the sumptuous interior for a couple of hours, but get back to the station in time for the 12:30 (weekdays only) or 13:00 (any day) train to Helsingør, a 15-minute walk from Kronborg Castle. Either munch your picnic lunch on the train, or—if it's a nice day—save it for the ramparts of Kronborg Castle. If you're castled out, skip the interior (saving the ticket price, and more time for Louisiana) and simply enjoy the Kronborg grounds and Øresund views before catching a train south toward Copenhagen. Hop off at Humlebæk for Louisiana.

Getting Around

All of these sights except Roskilde are served by Copenhagen's excellent commuter-train (S-tog) system (covered by the Copenhagen Card and by the "24-hour ticket" and "7-day flexi-card" that cover greater Copenhagen; not covered by the City Pass, which includes only zones 1-4—see page 61). All of the train connections (including the line to Roskilde) depart from the main train station; but be aware that most lines also stop at other Copenhagen stations, which may be closer to your hotel (for example, the Nørreport station near Ibsens and Jørgensen hotels). Check the schedules carefully to avoid needlessly going to the main train station.

At the main train station, the S-tog lines do not appear on the overhead schedule screens (which are for longer-distance destinations); simply report to tracks 9-10 to wait for your train (there's a schedule at the head of those tracks).

Roskilde

Denmark's roots, both Viking and royal, are on display in Roskilde (ROSS-killa), a pleasant town 18 miles west of Copenhagen. Eight hundred years ago, Roskilde was the seat of Denmark's royalty— its center of power. Today the town that introduced Christianity to Denmark in A.D. 980 is most famous for hosting northern Europe's biggest annual rock/jazz/folk festival (early July, www.roskilde-festival .dk). Wednesday and Saturday are flower/flea/produce market days (8:00-14:00).

Getting There: Roskilde is an easy side-trip from Copenhagen by train (1-3/hour, 30 minutes). Trains headed to Ringsted, Nykøbing, or Lindholm all stop in Roskilde (which is an intermediate stop you won't see listed on departure boards).

Orientation to Roskilde

Tourist Information

Roskilde's helpful TI is on the main square, not far from the cathedral (Mon-Fri 10:00-17:00—closes Fri at 16:00 in off-season, Sat 10:00-13:00, closed Sun; Stændertorvet 1, tel. 46 31 65 65, www .visitroskilde.com).

Arrival in Roskilde

There are no lockers at the train station (or nearby), but the TI—about a 5-minute walk away—will take your bags for a few hours if you ask nicely (they'll likely charge 25 kr).

From the train station, consider this circular route: First you'll head to the TI, then the nearby cathedral, and finally down to the harborfront museum. Exit straight out from the station, and walk down to the bottom of the square. Turn left (at the Kvickly supermarket) on the pedestrianized shopping street, Algade. After about four blocks, you emerge into the main square, Stændertorvet. The TI is straight ahead, and the cathedral is to your right. After visiting the cathedral, you'll head about 10 minutes downhill (through a pleasant park) to the Viking Museum: Facing the cathedral facade, turn left and head down the path through the park. When you emerge at the roundabout, continue straight through it to reach the museum.

If you want to go directly from the station to the Viking Museum, you can ride a bus; see page 142.

Sights in Roskilde

▲▲Roskilde Cathedral

Roskilde's imposing 12th-century, twin-spired cathedral houses the tombs of all of the Danish kings and most of the queens (38 royals in all; pick up the essential map as you enter). If you're a fan of Danish royalty or of evolving architectural styles, it's thrilling; even if you're neither, Denmark's "Westminster Abbey" is still interesting. It's a stately, modern-looking old church with great marblework, paintings, wood carvings, and an engaged congregation that makes the place feel very alive (particularly here in largely unchurched Scandinavia).

Cost and Hours: 60 kr; April-Sept Mon-Sat 9:00-17:00, Sun 12:30-17:00; Oct-March Tue-Sat 10:00-16:00, Sun 12:30-16:00, closed Mon; often closed Sat and

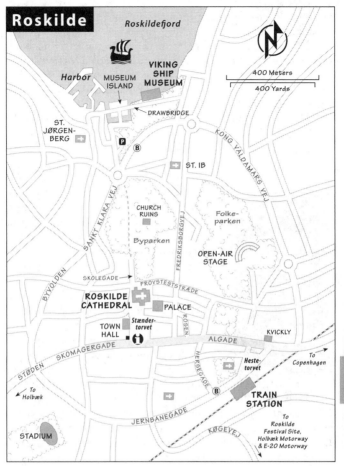

Roskilde
Roskildefjord
Harbor
VIKING SHIP MUSEUM
MUSEUM ISLAND
DRAWBRIDGE
ST. JØRGEN-BERG
P
B
KONG VALDAMARS VEJ
ST. IB
SANKT KLARA VEJ
CHURCH RUINS
Folke-parken
Byparken
FREDRIKSBORGVEJ
OPEN-AIR STAGE
BYVOLDEN
SKOLEGADE
PRØVSTESTSTRÆDE
ROSKILDE CATHEDRAL
PALACE
Stænder-torvet
TOWN HALL
RØSEN
ALGADE
KVICKLY
SKOMAGERGADE
HERSEGADE
To Copenhagen
STØDEN
To Holbæk
Heste-torvet
B
JERNBANEGADE
TRAIN STATION
KØGEVEJ
To Roskilde Festival Site, Holbæk Motorway & E-20 Motorway
STADIUM
400 Meters
400 Yards

NEAR COPENHAGEN

Sun afternoons for baptisms and weddings; free organ concerts offered July-Aug Thu at 20:00; tel. 46 35 16 24, www.roskildedom kirke.dk.

⊘ Self-Guided Tour: Begun in the 1170s by Bishop Absalom (and completed in 1280), Roskilde Cathedral was cleared of its side chapels and altars by the Reformation iconoclasts—leaving a blank slate for Danish royals to fill with their tombs. The highlight here is slowly strolling through a half-millennium's worth of royal chapels, representing a veritable textbook's worth of architectural styles.

Before entering, face the towering facade. The main door—called the **King's Door**—was installed only in 2010, and depicts the 12 apostles (each with a symbol that hints at his identity). This door is used by the congregation only to leave special services; the only people who may enter through this door are members of the royal family.

Notice the freestanding brick chapel to the left. This holds the remains of Denmark's last king, **Frederik IX** (1899-1972), and his wife Ingrid. While all of the other monarchs are inside, Frederik—who was an avid sailor in his youth—requested to be buried here, with a view of the harbor.

Now go around the right side, buy a ticket, and go inside. We'll take a clockwise spin through the interior to see the significant royal burial chapels. While this tour is not chronological, neither are the tombs.

First head to the middle of the nave and look at the **inside of the King's Door**—a glittering-gold, highly stylized relief showing the scene after the Resurrection when Jesus breaks bread in the company of some apostles—who until this point, had not recognized him (their mouths hang agape at their realization).

Walking a few steps to the right, then looking high above, you can see the silly little **glockenspiel** that makes a racket at the top of every hour.

Continue through the left aisle and into the big chapel housing some of the cathedral's most recent additions (from the late 19th through early 20th centuries). The next chapel toward the front will eventually ("Not soon," hope the Danes) have a new tenant: It has recently been restored to house the tomb of the current queen, **Margrethe II,** and her husband Henrik. She teamed up with an artist to design her own tomb (there is likely a model on display). Her body will reside in the stepped area at the bottom, upon which stand three columns representing the far-flung Danish holdings: one made of basalt from the Faroe Islands, another of marble from Greenland, and the third of stone from Denmark proper. Topping the columns are elephants (symbols of Danish royalty) and a semitransparent glass tomb, symbolizing the unpredictability of life.

The next chapel, of St. Andrew, is a modern addition to the church, with a glittering mosaic over the altar. Standing in front of this chapel, look across the nave to see the gorgeous 16th-century Baroque organ.

The next, larger chapel (up the stairs behind the small wooden organ) dates from the era of **Christian IV,** the larger-than-life 17th-century king who created modern Denmark. Christian also left his mark on Roskilde Cathedral, building the altarpiece, pulpit, distinctive twin towers...and this chapel. In here you'll see a fine statue of the king, by Bertel Thorvaldsen; a large 3-D painting with Christian IV wearing his trademark eye patch, after losing his eye in battle; and his rather austere tomb (black with silver trim, surrounded by several others).

Head into the nave and climb up the stairs into the choir area, taking in the gorgeous gilded altarpiece and finely carved stalls.

Behind the altar is the ornately decorated tomb of **Margrethe I,** the Danish queen who added Norway to her holdings by marrying Norwegian King Håkon VI in 1363. Buried in a nearby column are the supposed remains of Harold (read the Latin: *Haraldus*) Bluetooth, who ruled more than a millennium ago (r. 958-985 or 986), made Roskilde the capital of his realm, and converted his subjects to Christianity.

Go down the stairs and through the little door, and circle around the apse (area behind the altar), noticing more fine tombs behind Margrethe's. Hooking back around toward the front, dip into the many more chapels you'll pass, including the grand, textbook-Neoclassical tomb of Frederik V (with white pillars, gold trim, and mourning maidens in ancient Greek gowns); and the room housing elaborate, canopied Baroque tombs. Imagine: Each king or queen commissioned a tomb that suited his or her time—so different, yet all so grand.

▲▲▲Viking Ship Museum (Vikingeskibsmuseet)

Vik literally means "shallow inlet," and "Vikings" were the people who lived along those inlets. Roskilde—and this award-winning museum—are strategically located along one such inlet. (They call it

a "fjord," but it's surrounded by much flatter terrain than the Norwegian fjords.) Centuries before Europe's Age of Exploration, Viking sailors navigated their sleek, sturdy ships as far away as the Mediterranean, the Black Sea, the Persian Gulf, and the Americas. This museum displays five different Viking ships, which were discovered in the Roskilde fjord and painstakingly excavated, preserved, and pieced back together beginning in the 1960s. The ships aren't as intact or as ornate as those in Oslo (see page 262), but this museum does a better job of explaining shipbuilding. The outdoor area (on "Museum Island") continues the experience, with a chance to see modern-day Vikings creating replica ships, chat with an old-time ropemaker, and learn more about the excavation. The English descriptions are excellent—it's the kind of museum where you want to read everything.

Cost and Hours: 100 kr, price drops to 70 kr Oct-April when many outdoor exhibits are closed, open daily late June-Aug 10:00-17:00, Sept-late June 10:00-16:00, tel. 46 30 02 00, www.vikingeskibsmuseet.dk.

Tours: Free 45-minute tours in English run late June-Aug daily at 12:00 and 15:00; May-late June and Sept Sat-Sun at 12:00; none off-season.

Boat Ride: The museum's workshop has re-created working replicas of all five of the ships on display here, plus others. For an extra 80 kr, you can go for a fun hour-long sail around Roskilde's harbor in one of these replica Viking vessels (frequent departures—up to 7/day—in summer, fewer off-season, ask about schedule when you arrive or call ahead).

Eating: The "summer café" on Museum Island has 25-40-kr cakes and sandwiches; the bigger restaurant, in the large modern building, has 45-kr lunch sandwiches and 175-225-kr dinners.

Getting There: It's on the harbor at Vindeboder 12. From the train station, catch bus #216 or #607 toward Boserup (hourly, 7-minute ride). From the cathedral, it's a 10-minute downhill walk.

Visiting the Museum: The museum has two parts: the Viking Ship Hall, with the remains of the five ships; and, across the drawbridge, Museum Island with workshops, replica ships, and more exhibits.

As you enter the **Viking Ship Hall,** check the board for the day's activities and demonstrations (including shipbuilding, weaving, blacksmithing, and minting). Consider buying the 20-kr guidebook, and request the 14-minute English movie introduction.

The core of the exhibit is the remains of those five ships. These vessels were deliberately sunk a thousand years ago to block an easy channel into this harbor (leaving open only the most challenging approach—virtually impossible for anyone but a local to navigate). The ships, which are named for the place where they were found (Skuldelev), represent an impressively wide range of Viking shipbuilding technology. *Skuldelev 1* is a big, sail-powered ocean-going trade ship, with a crew of six to eight men and lots of cargo; it's like the ship Leif Eriksson took to America 1,000 years ago. *Skuldelev 2* is a 100-foot-long, 60-oar longship; loaded with 65 or 70 bloodthirsty warriors, it struck fear into the hearts of foes. It's similar to the ones depicted in the Bayeux Tapestry in Normandy, France. *Skuldelev 3* is a modest coastal trader that stayed closer to home (wind-powered with oar backup, similar to #1 in design). *Skuldelev 5* is a smaller longship—carrying about 30 men, it's the little sibling of #2. And *Skuldelev 6* is a small fishing vessel—a row/sail hybrid that was used for whaling and hunting seals. (There's no #4 because they originally thought #2 was two different ships...and the original names stuck.)

Exhibits in the surrounding rooms show the 25-year process of excavating and preserving the ships, explain a step-by-step attack and defense of the harbor, and give you a chance to climb aboard a couple of replica ships for a fun photo op. You'll also see displays describing the re-creation of the *Sea Stallion,* a replica of the big longship (#2) constructed by modern shipbuilders using ancient techniques. A crew of 65 rowed this to Dublin, Ireland, in 2007, and then back to Roskilde in the summer of 2008. You can watch a 20-minute film of their odyssey.

Leaving the hall, cross the drawbridge to **Museum Island.** Replicas of all five ships—and others—bob in the harbor; you can

actually climb on board the largest, the *Sea Stallion.* At the boatyard, watch modern craftsmen re-create millennium-old ships using the original methods and materials. Poke into the various workshops, with exhibits on tools and methods. The little square called *Tunet* ("Gathering Place") is ringed by traditional craft shops—basketmaker, ropemaker, blacksmith, woodcarver—which are sometimes staffed by workers doing demonstrations. In the archaeological workshop, exhibits explain how they excavated and preserved the precious timbers of those five ships.

Frederiksborg Castle

Frederiksborg Castle, rated ▲▲, sits on an island in the middle of a lake in the cute town of Hillerød. This grandest castle in

Scandinavia is often called the "Danish Versailles." Built from 1602 to 1620, Frederiksborg was the castle of Denmark's King Christian IV. Much of it was reconstructed after an 1859 fire, with the normal Victorian over-the-top flair, by the brewer J. C. Jacobsen and his Carlsberg Foundation.

You'll still enjoy some of the magnificent spaces of the castle's heyday: The breathtaking grounds and courtyards, the sumptuous chapel, and the regalia-laden Great Hall. But most of the place was turned into a fine museum in 1878. Today it's the Museum of National History, taking you on a chronological walk through the story of Denmark from 1500 until today (the third/top floor covers modern times). The countless musty paintings are a fascinating scrapbook of Danish history—it's a veritable national portrait gallery, with images of great Danes from each historical period of the last half-millennium.

A fine path leads around the lake, with ever-changing views of the castle. The traffic-free center of Hillerød is also worth a wander (just outside the gates of the castle, toward train station).

Tourist Information: Hillerød's **TI,** with a good town map and brochures for the entire North Zealand region, is in the free-standing white house next to the castle parking lot (to the left as you face the main castle gate; Mon-Fri 9:30-16:00, closed Sat-Sun except open Sat in July 9:30-13:30, likely closed Oct-April, Frederiksværksgade 2A, tel. 48 24 26 26, www.visitnordsjaelland .com). Because the TI is inside an art gallery, if the TI is "closed" while the gallery is open, you can still slip inside and pick up a town map and brochures.

Getting There: From Copenhagen, take the S-tog to Hillerød (line E, 6/hour, 40 minutes). From the Hillerød station, you can enjoy a pleasant 20-minute walk to the castle (see next page), or catch bus #301 or #302 (free with S-tog ticket or Copenhagen Card, buses are to the right as you exit station, ride three stops to Frederiksborg Slot bus stop). Drivers will find easy parking at the castle.

When you're exiting the station, bear left down the busy road

(Jernbanegade) until the first big intersection, where you'll turn right. After a couple of blocks, where the road curves to the left, keep going straight; from here, bear left and downhill to the pleasant square Torvet, with great views of the castle and a café pavilion. At this square, turn left and walk through the pedestrianized shopping zone directly to the castle gate.

After your visit, if you'd like to continue directly to Helsingør (with Kronborg Castle), hop on the regional train (departs from track 16 at Hillerød station, Mon-Fri 2/hour, Sat-Sun 1/hour, 30 minutes). From Helsingør, it's a quick trip on the S-tog to Humlebæk and Louisiana Art Museum.

Cost and Hours: 75 kr, daily April-Oct 10:00-17:00, Nov-March 11:00-15:00. Take advantage of the free, extensive, informative (if fairly dry) iPod audioguide; ask for it when you buy your ticket. My tour, below, zooms in on the highlights, but the audioguide is more extensive. There are also posted explanations and/or borrowable English descriptions in many rooms, but—like the audioguide—these tend to be quite dry (tel. 48 26 04 39, www .dnm.dk).

Eating: You can picnic in the castle's moat park or enjoy the elegant **Spisestedet Leonora** at the moat's edge (65-90-kr *smørrebrød* and sandwiches, 90-kr salads, 105-125-kr hot dishes, 148-kr brunch buffet Sun until 13:00, open daily 10:00-17:00, slow service, tel. 48 26 75 16).

● Self-Guided Tour: From the entrance of the castle complex, it's an appropriately regal approach to the king's residence. You can almost hear the clopping of royal hooves as you walk over the moat and through the first island (which housed the stables and small businesses needed to support a royal residence). Then walk down the winding (and therefore easy-to-defend) lane to the second island, which was home to the domestic and foreign ministries. Finally, cross over the last moat to the main palace, where the king lived.

Main Courtyard: Survey the castle exterior from the Fountain of Neptune in the main courtyard. Christian IV imported Dutch architects to create this "Christian IV style," which you'll see all over Copenhagen. The brickwork and sandstone are products of the local clay and sandy soil. The building, with its horizontal lines, triangles, and squares, is generally in Renaissance style, but notice how this is interrupted by a few token Gothic elements on the church's facade. Some say this homey touch was to let the villagers know the king was "one of them."

Go in the door in the middle of the courtyard to buy your ticket, pick up your free audioguide, and put your bag in a locker (mandatory, 20-kr coin required and will be refunded). Be sure to pick up a free floor plan; room numbers will help orient you on this tour. You'll enter the Knights' Parlor, also called The Rose, a long room decorated as it was during the palace's peak of power. Go up the stairs on the left side of this hall to the...

Royal Chapel: Christian IV wanted to have the grandest royal chapel in Europe. For 200 years the coronation place of

Danish kings, this chapel is still used for royal weddings (and is extremely popular for commoner weddings—book long in advance). The chapel is nearly all original, dating back to 1620. As you walk around the upper level, notice the graffiti scratched on the windowpanes by the diamond rings of royal kids visiting for the summer back in the 1600s. Most of the coats of arms show off noble lineage—with a few exceptions we'll get to soon. At the far end of the chapel, the wooden organ is from 1620, with its original hand-powered bellows. (If you like music, listen for hymns on the old carillon at the top of each hour.)

Scan the hundreds of coats-of-arms lining the walls. These belong to people who have received royal orders from the Danish crown (similar to Britain's knighthoods). While most are obscure princesses and dukes, a few interesting (and more familiar) names show up just past the organ. In the first window bay after the organ, look for the distinctive red, blue, black, and green shield of South Africa—marking Nelson Mandela's coat of arms. (Notice he was awarded the highly prestigious Order of the Elephant, usually reserved for royalty.) Around the side of the same column (facing the chapel interior), find the

coats of arms for Dwight D. Eisenhower (with the blue anvil and the motto "Peace through understanding"), Winston Churchill (who already came from a noble line), and Field Marshal Bernard "Monty" Montgomery. Around the far side of this column is the coat of arms for France's wartime leader, Charles de Gaulle.

Leaving the chapel, you step into the king's oratory, with evocative Romantic paintings (restored after a fire) from the mid-19th century.

You'll emerge from the chapel into the museum collection. But before seeing that, pay a visit to the Audience Room: Go through the door in the left corner marked *Audienssalen,* and proceed through the little room to the long passageway (easy to miss).

Audience Room: Here, where formal meetings took place, a grand painting shows the king as a Roman emperor firmly in command (with his two sons prominent for extra political stability). This family is flanked by Christian IV (on the left) and Frederik III (on the right). Christian's military victories line the walls, and the four great continents—Europe, North America, Asia, and Africa—circle the false cupola (notice it's just an attic). Look for the odd trapdoor in one corner with a plush chair on it. This was where they could majestically lower the king to the exit.

Now go back to the museum section, and proceed through the numbered rooms. Spanning three floors and five centuries, this exhaustive (or, for some, exhausting) collection juxtaposes portraits, paintings of historical events, furniture, and other objects from the same time period, all combining to paint a picture of a moment in Danish history. While fascinating, a little goes a long way, so I've selected only the most interesting items to linger over.

First Floor: Proceed to **Room 26,** which is focused on the Reformation. The case in the middle of the room holds the first Bible translated into Danish (from 1550—access to the word of God was a big part of the Reformation). Over the door to the next room is the image of a monk, Hans Tausen, invited by the king to preach the new thinking of the Reformation...sort of the "Danish Martin Luther." Also note the effort noble families put into legitimizing themselves with family trees and family seals.

Pass through Rooms 27, 28, and 29, and into **Room 30**—with paintings telling the story of Christian IV (for more on this dynamic Renaissance king, who built this castle and so much

more, see page 98). Directly across from the door you entered is a painting of the chancellor on his deathbed, handing over the keys to the kingdom to a still-wet-behind-the-ears young Christian IV—the beginning of a long and fruitful career. On the right wall is a painting of Christian's coronation (the bearded gentleman looking out the window in the upper-left corner is Carlsberg brewer and castle benefactor J. C. Jacobsen—who, some 300 years before his birth, was probably not actually in attendance). Room 31 covers the royal family of Charles IV, while the smaller, darkened corner Room 32 displays the various Danish orders; find the most prestigious, the Order of the Elephant.

Hook back through Room 30, go outside on the little passage, and climb up the stairs.

Second Floor: Go to the corner **Room 39,** which has a fascinating golden globe designed to illustrate Polish astronomer

Nicolaus Copernicus' bold new heliocentric theory (that the sun, not the earth, was the center of our world). Look past the constellations to see the tiny model of the solar system at the very center, with a brass ball for the sun and little figures holding up symbols for each of the planets. The mechanical gears could actually make this model move to make the illustration more vivid.

Continue into one of the castle's most jaw-dropping rooms, the **Great Hall** (Room 38). The walls are lined with tapestries and royal portraits (including some modern ones, near the door). The remark-

able wood-carved ceilings include panels illustrating various industries. The elevated platform on the left was a gallery where musicians could play without getting in the way of the revelry.

Head back out and walk back along the left side of the hall. You can go quickly through the rooms numbered in the 40s and 50s (though pause partway down the long hallway; on the left, find the optical-illusion portrait that shows King Frederik V when viewed from one angle, and his wife when viewed from another). At the far end of this section, Room 57 has a portrait of Hans Christian Andersen. Notice that fashion styles have gotten much more modern...suits and ties instead of tights and powdered wigs. It's time to head into the modern world.

Find the modern spiral staircase nearby. Downstairs are late-19th-century exhibits—which are skippable. Instead, head up to the top floor.

Third Floor: This staircase puts you (confusingly) right in the middle of the modern collection. To keep our chronological focus, find your way to Room 70. From here, the museum's focus shifts, focusing more on the art and less on the history. For example, in Room 70, *The Art Critics* shows four past-their-prime, once-rambunctious artists themselves, now leaning back to critique a younger artist's work...happily entrenched in the art institution. Proceed through the collection. Room 73 focuses on Denmark's far-flung Greenland, with a porcelain polar bear and portraits of explorers. Room 74 has a distinctive Impressionist/Post-Impressionist flavor, with a Danish spin. In Room 77, *Ninth of April, 1940* shows the (ultimately unsuccessful) Danish defense against Nazi invaders on that fateful date. Room 82 focuses on the royal family, with a life-size, photorealistic portrait of the beloved Queen Margrethe II. Facing her is her daughter-in-law, Mary Donaldson—who, in this portrait at least, bears a striking resemblance to another young European royal.

Rounding out the collection is one of its most recent works, Peter Carlsen's *Denmark 2009*—a brilliant parody of Eugène Delacroix's famous painting *Liberty Leading the People* (a copy of the inspiration is on the facing wall). Carlsen has replaced the stirring imagery of the original with some dubious markers of contemporary Danish life: football flags, beer gut, shopping bags, tabloids, bikini babes, even a

Christiania flag. It's a delightfully offbeat (and oh-so-Danish) note to end our visit to this seriously impressive palace.

Louisiana

This is Scandinavia's most-raved-about modern-art museum. Located in the town of Humlebæk, beautifully situated on the coast 18 miles north of Copenhagen, Louisiana is a holistic place that masterfully mixes its art, architecture, and landscape.

Cost and Hours: 95 kr, included in a special 176-kr round-trip tour ticket from

Copenhagen—ask at any train station, open Tue-Fri 11:00-22:00, Sat-Sun 11:00-18:00, closed Mon, Gammel Strandvej 13, tel. 49 19 07 19, www.louisiana.dk.

Getting There: Take the train from **Copenhagen** toward Helsingør, and get off at Humlebæk (4/hour, 36 minutes). It's a pleasant 10-minute walk (partly through a forest) to the museum: Exit the station and immediately go left onto Hejreskor Allé, a residential street; when the road curves right, continue straight along the narrow footpath through the trees. After you exit the trail, the museum is just ahead and across the street.

If you're arriving by train from **Helsingør,** take the pedestrian underpass beneath the tracks, then follow the directions above. Louisiana is also connected to Helsingør by bus #388 (runs hourly, stops right at Louisiana as well as at Humlebæk).

If you're coming from **Frederiksborg Castle,** you have two options: You can catch the Lille Nord train from Hillerød to Helsingør, then change there to a regional train heading south to Humlebæk (2/hour, 45 minutes). Alternately, you can take the S-tog toward Copenhagen and Køge, get off at Hellerup, then catch a regional train north toward Helsingør to reach Humlebæk (4/hour, about 1 hour, longer but runs more frequently).

Eating: The cafeteria, with indoor and outdoor seating, is reasonable and welcomes picnickers who buy a drink (80-kr sandwiches at lunch, 120-kr lunch buffet, 150-kr dinner buffet, 30-40-kr cakes).

Visiting the Museum: Wander from famous Chagalls and Picassos to more obscure art (everything is post-1945). Poets spend days here nourishing their creative souls with new angles, ideas, and perspectives. Even those who don't think they're art-lovers can get sucked into a thought-provoking exhibit and lose track of time. There's no permanent exhibit; they constantly organize their substantial collection into ever-changing arrangements, augmented with borrowed and special exhibits (check www .louisiana.dk for the latest)—so that Andy Warhol *Marilyn Monroe* you see on one visit may not be there the next. (One favorite item, French sculptor César's *The Big Thumb*— which is simply a six-foot-tall bronze thumb— isn't going anywhere, since anytime they move it, patrons complain.) There's no audioguide, but everything is labeled in English.

Outside, a delightful sculpture garden sprawls through the grounds, downhill toward the sea. The views over the Øresund, one of the busiest passages in the nautical world, are nearly as inspiring as the art. The museum's floor plan is a big loop, and the seaward side is underground—so as not to block the grand views. It's fun to explore the grounds, peppered with sculptures and made accessible by bridges and steps. The sculptures include items by Alexander Calder, Jean Dubuffet, Joan Miró, and others.

Taken as a whole, the museum is a joy to explore. What you see from the inside draws you out, and what you see from the outside draws you in. The place can't be rushed. Linger and enjoy.

Karen Blixen Museum

Danish writer Karen Blixen, a.k.a. Isak Dinesen of *Out of Africa* fame, lived most of her life in Rungstedlund—her family house in Rungsted, on the Øresund coast. The house, one of the area's finest mansions, is now a museum about her life and writing. For fans of Blixen's works, the house is a ▲▲ sight, though Blixen's dramatic life story and the house's beautiful setting are enough to make a visit enjoyable even for those who've never heard of *Out of Africa.*

Unlike many houses-turned-museums that file you past roped-off doorways, you'll don slippers to pad through the house, mostly unchanged from the time of Blixen's life. Over headphones, listen to Blixen read selections from her own stories as you look out at the same views she enjoyed. She wrote her best-known books (including *Babette's Feast*) in this house, surrounded by mementos of her 17 years in Kenya. Her simple grave is a short walk away through the mansion's backyard gardens.

Cost and Hours: 60 kr; May-Sept Tue-Sun 10:00-17:00, closed Mon; Oct-April Wed-Fri 13:00-16:00, Sat-Sun 11:00-16:00, closed Mon-Tue; tel. 45 57 10 57, www.karen-blixen.dk.

Getting There: From Copenhagen, take the train 30 minutes to Rungsted Kyst (3/hour). From the station, take bus #388, or simply walk 15-20 minutes (follow signs to the house). Rungsted is a short hop away from Humlebæk (7 minutes by train) and Helsingør (20 minutes).

NEAR COPENHAGEN

Kronborg Castle

Kronborg Castle is located in Helsingør, a pleasant, salty Danish seaside town that's often confused with its Swedish sister, Helsingborg, just two miles across the channel. Kronborg Castle (also called Elsinore, the Anglicized version of Helsingør) is a ▲▲ sight famous for its tenuous (but profitable) ties to Shakespeare. Most of the "Hamlet" castle you'll see today—a dar-

ling of every big-bus tour and travelogue—was built long after the historical Hamlet died (more than a thousand years ago), and Shakespeare never saw the place. But this Renaissance castle existed when a troupe of English actors performed here in Shakespeare's time (Shakespeare may have known them). These days, various Shakespearean companies from around the world perform *Hamlet* in Kronborg's courtyard each August. Among the actors who've donned the tights here in the title role are Laurence Olivier, Christopher Plummer, Kenneth Branagh, and Jude Law.

To see or not to see? The castle is most impressive from the outside. The free grounds between the walls and sea are great for picnics, with a close-up view of the strait between Denmark and Sweden. If you're heading to Sweden, Kalmar Castle (described in the Southeast Sweden chapter) is a better medieval castle. And in Denmark, Frederiksborg (described earlier), which was built as an upgrade to this one, is far more opulent inside. But if Kronborg is handy to your itinerary—or you never met a castle you didn't like—it's worth a visit...even if just for a short romp across the ramparts (no ticket required). Many big-bus tours in the region stop both here and at Frederiksborg (you'll recognize some of the same fellow tourists at both places)—not a bad plan if you're a castle completist.

The town of Helsingør has a **TI** (late June-early Aug Mon-Fri 10:00-17:00, Sat-Sun 10:00-14:00; early Aug-late Sept Mon-Fri 10:00-16:00, Sat 10:00-13:00, closed Sun; rest of year Mon-Fri 10:00-16:00, closed Sat-Sun; tel. 49 21 13 33, www.visithelsingor .dk), a medieval center, the ferry to Sweden, and lots of Swedes who come over for the lower-priced alcohol.

Getting There: Helsingør is a 50-minute train ride from Copenhagen (3/hour). Exit the station out the front door: The TI is on the little square to your left, and the castle is dead ahead along the coast (about a 15-minute walk). Between the station and the castle, you'll pass through a recently renovated harborfront zone with the town's new cultural center and the new home of the maritime museum.

Cost: The wonderful grounds are free, but you'll need a ticket to enter the main building: 75 kr covers the royal apartments and the casements, add the tower/maritime museum for 95 kr; also possible to visit only the casements (30 kr) or only the tower/maritime museum (50 kr). Unless you're a fan of nautical sights, I'd skip the maritime museum and just do the apartments and casements.

Hours: The whole complex is open June-Aug daily 10:00-17:30; April-May and Sept-Oct daily 11:00-16:00; Nov-March Tue-Sun 11:00-16:00, closed Mon; tel. 33 95 42 00, www.kronborgcastle.com.

Tours: Free **tours** in English are offered of the casements (daily at 11:00 and 13:00) and of the royal apartments (daily at 11:30 and 13:30). You can use your mobile device to access a free **audioguide** at the castle, but it takes some tech savvy to make it work; unfortunately, the audioguide isn't available any other way. Dry English descriptions are posted throughout the castle. The equally arid 20-kr printed **guide** (sold at the ticket counter) tries to inject some life into the rooms.

Visiting the Castle: Approaching the castle, pretend you're an old foe of the king, kept away by many layers of earthen ramparts and moats—just when you think you're actually at the castle, you'll find there's another gateway or waterway to pass. On the way in, you'll pass a small model of the complex to help get your bearings. On a sunny day, you could have an enjoyable visit to Kronborg just walking around these grounds and playing "king of the castle," without buying a ticket. Many do.

Finally you'll enter the innermost courtyard of the castle complex. Follow the signs into the ticket desk, buy your ticket, stick your bag in a locker (insert a 20-kr coin, which will be returned), and head upstairs. You'll pop out at the beginning of both the royal apartments and the maritime museum/tower.

Maritime Museum and Tower: I'd give the museum a miss, but if you're a sailor at heart or want to climb the tower, here's the scoop: You'll pass through a seemingly endless series of rooms detailing the salty history of this seafaring nation, with sailor's bric-a-brac, paintings and models of ships and captains, and a few particularly interesting sections (such as the collection of mastheads in the large room, or the small exhibit on Inuit boats of Greenland). Halfway through, you'll pass through a tight, stone spiral staircase leading up to the top of one of the castle's corner towers, with a fine view of the prickly spires, the town of Helsingør, and the Øresund strait. It's easy to imagine why this was such a strategic point for a fortress—with Sweden so close and the strait so narrow, this passage could be easily monitored from here. Note that the maritime collection will be moved to its brand-new home just around the harbor from the castle, likely by mid-summer of 2013. (When that happens, there's speculation that this space will be filled by an exhibit on Hamlet—a topic that's otherwise in surprisingly short supply in the castle exhibits, given its touristic currency.)

Royal Apartments: Visitors are able to walk through one and a half floors of the complex. The first few rooms are filled with high-tech exhibits, using touchscreens and projected videos to explain the history of the place. You'll learn how, in the 1420s, Danish King Eric of Pomerania built a fortress here to allow for the collection of "Sound Dues," levied on any passing ship hoping to enter the sound of Øresund. This proved hugely lucrative, eventually providing up to two-thirds of Denmark's entire income. By the time of Shakespeare, Kronborg was well-known both for its profitable ability to levy these dues, and for its famously lavish banquets—what better setting for a tale of a royal family unraveling?

Continuing into the apartments themselves, you'll find that the interior is a shadow of its former self; while the structure was rebuilt by Christian IV after a 1629 fire, its rooms were never returned to their former grandeur, making it feel like something of an empty shell. And yet, there are still some fine pieces of furniture and art to see. Frederik II ruled Denmark from the king's chamber in the 1570s; a model shows how it

likely looked back in its heyday. After passing through two smaller rooms, you come to the queen's chamber; from there, stairs lead up to the queen's gallery, custom-built for Queen Sophie to be able to quickly walk directly from her chambers to the ballroom or chapel. Follow her footsteps into the ballroom, a vast hall of epic proportions decorated by a series of paintings commissioned by Christian IV (explained by the board near the entry). At the far end, a model (enlivened by seemingly holographic figures) illustrates how this incredible space must have looked in all its original finery. Beyond the ballroom, the "Little Hall" is decorated with a fine series of

Øresund Region

When the Øresund (UH-ra-soond) Bridge, which connects Denmark and Sweden, opened in July of 2000, it created a dynamic new metropolitan area. Almost overnight, the link forged an economic power with the 12th-largest gross domestic product in Europe. The Øresund region has surpassed Stockholm as the largest metro area in Scandinavia. Now 3.5 million Danes and Swedes—a highly trained and highly technical workforce—are within a quick commute of each other.

The bridge opens up new questions of borders. Historically, southern Sweden (the area across from Copenhagen, called Skåne) had Danish blood. It was Danish for a thousand years before Sweden took it in 1658. Notice how Copenhagen is the capital on the fringe of its realm—at one time it was in the center.

The 10-mile-long link, which has a motorway for cars (the toll is about 300 kr) and a two-track train line, ties together the main islands of Denmark with Europe and Sweden. The $4 billion project consisted of a 2.5-mile-long tunnel, an artificial island called Peberholm, and a 5-mile-long bridge. With speedy connecting trains, Malmö in Sweden is now an easy half-day side-trip from Copenhagen (78 kr each way, 3/hour, 35 minutes). The train drops you at the "Malmö C" (central) station right in the heart of Malmö, and all the important sights are within a short walk. The *Malmö This Week* publication (free from Copenhagen TI) has everything you need for a well-organized visit.

tapestries depicting Danish monarchs. Then wind through several more royal halls, chambers, and bedrooms on your way back down into the courtyard. Once there, go straight across and enter the chapel. The enclosed gallery at the upper-left was the private pew of the royal family.

Casements: You'll enter the underground part of the castle

through a door on the main courtyard (diagonally across from the chapel). While not particularly tight, these passages are very dark and intentionally not very well-lit; a vending machine at the entrance sells 20-kr flashlights (bring yours—or, at least, a bright mobile phone). This extensive network of dank cellars is a double-decker substructure that teemed with activity. The upper level, which you'll see first, was used as servants' quarters, a stable, and a storehouse. The lower level was used to train and barrack soldiers during wartime (an efficient use of so much prime, fortified space). As you explore this creepy, labyrinthine, nearly pitch-black zone (just follow the arrows), imagine the miserably claustrophobic conditions the soldiers lived in, waiting to see some action.

The most famous "resident" of the Kronborg casements was Holger Danske ("Ogier the Dane"), a mythical Viking hero  revered by Danish children. The story goes that if the nation is ever in danger, this Danish superman will awaken and restore peace and security to the land (like King Arthur to the English, Barbarossa to the Germans, and Wenceslas to the Czechs). While this legend has been around for many centuries, Holger's connection to Kronborg was cemented by a Hans Christian Andersen tale, so now everybody just assumes he lives here. In one of the first rooms, you'll see a famous, giant statue of this sleeping Viking...just waiting for things to get *really* bad.

Near Copenhagen Connections

Route Tips for Drivers

Copenhagen to Hillerød (45 minutes) to Helsingør (30 minutes) to Kalmar (4 hours): Just follow the town-name signs. Leave Copenhagen following signs for *E-4* and *Helsingør*. The freeway is great. *Hillerød* signs lead to the Frederiksborg Castle (not to be confused with the nearby Fredensborg Palace) in the pleasant town of Hillerød. Follow signs to *Hillerød C* (for "center"), then *slot* (for "castle"). Though the E-4 freeway is the fastest, the Strandvejen coastal road (152) is pleasant, passing some of Denmark's grandest mansions (including that of Karen Blixen, described earlier).

The 10-mile Øresund Bridge linking Denmark with Sweden (€40 toll, or about 300 kr) lets drivers and train travelers skip non-stop from one country to the next.

If you're nostalgic for the pre-bridge days, the Helsingør-Helsingborg ferry still putters across the Øresund Channel twice hourly (follow the signs to *Helsingborg, Sweden*—freeway leads to dock). Buy your ticket as you roll on board (320 kr one-way for car, driver, and up to nine passengers, increases to 345 kr in summer). Reservations are free but not usually necessary, as ferries depart every 30 minutes (tel. 33 15 15 15, or book online at www.scandlines.dk; also see www.hhferries.se). If you arrive early, you can probably drive onto any ferry. The 20-minute Helsingør-

Helsingborg ferry ride gives you just enough time to enjoy the view of the Kronborg "Hamlet" castle, be impressed by the narrowness of this very strategic channel, and exchange any leftover Danish kroner into Swedish kronor (the ferry exchange desk's rate is decent).

In Helsingborg, follow signs for *E4* and *Stockholm*. The road is good, traffic is light, and towns are all clearly signposted. At Ljungby, road 25 takes you to Växjö and Kalmar. Entering Växjö, skip the first Växjö exit and follow the freeway into *Centrum*, where it ends. It takes about four hours total to drive from Copenhagen to Kalmar.

CENTRAL DENMARK

Ærø • Odense

The sleepy isle of Ærø is the cuddle after the climax. It's the perfect time-passed world in which to wind down, enjoy the seagulls, and take a day off. Wander the unadulterated cobbled lanes of Denmark's best-preserved 18th-century town. Get Ærø-dynamic and pedal a rented bike into the essence of Denmark. Settle into a world of sailors, who, after the invention of steam-driven boat propellers, decided that building ships in bottles was more their style.

Between Ærø and Copenhagen, drop by bustling Odense, home of Hans Christian Andersen. Its Hans Christian Andersen House is excellent, and with more time, you can also enjoy its other museums (art, town history, trains, folk) and stroll the car-free streets of its downtown.

Planning Your Time

Allow four hours to get from Copenhagen to Ærø (not counting a possible stopover in Odense). All trains stop in Roskilde (with its Viking Ship Museum—see previous chapter) and bustling Odense (see the end of this chapter). On a quick trip, you can leave Copenhagen in the morning and do justice to both towns en route to Ærø. (With just one day, Odense and Roskilde together make a long but doable day trip from Copenhagen.)

While out of the way, Ærø is worth the journey. Once there, you'll want two

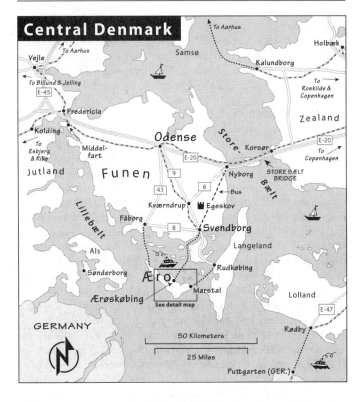

nights and a day to properly enjoy it (for details, see "Planning Your Time" for Ærøskøbing, page 161).

Ærø

This small (22 by 6 miles) island on the south edge of Denmark is as salty and sleepy as can be. A typical tombstone reads: "Here lies Christian Hansen at anchor with his wife. He'll not weigh until he stands before God." It's the kind of island where baskets of strawberries sit in front of houses—for sale on the honor system.

Ærø statistics: 7,000 residents, 500,000 visitors and 80,000 boaters annually, 350 deer, seven priests, no crosswalks, and three police officers. The three big industries are farming (wheat and dairy), shipping, and tourism—in that order. Twenty percent of the Danish fleet still resides on Ærø, in the town of Marstal. But jobs are scarce, the population is slowly dropping, and family farms are consolidating into larger units.

Ærø, home to several windmills and one of the world's largest solar power plants, is going "green." They hope to become completely wind- and solar-powered. Currently, nearly half the island's heat and electricity is provided by renewable sources, and most of its produce is organically grown. New technology is expected to bring Ærø closer to its goal within the next few years.

Getting Around Ærø

On a short visit, you won't need to leave Ærøskøbing, except for a countryside bike ride—everything is within walking or pedaling distance. But if you have more time or want to explore the rest of the island, you can take advantage of Ærø's **bus** network. Buses leave from a stop just above the ferry dock (leaving the ferry, walk up about a block and look right). Ærø recently made its main bus line, #790, free for visitors (Mon-Fri hourly until about 19:00; Sat 4/day; Sun 3-4/day). There are two different branches—one going to Marstal at the east end of the island, and the other to Søby in the west (look for the town name under the bus number). The main reason to take the bus is to go to Marstal on a rainy day to visit its maritime museum (see page 173).

You can also take a subsidized **taxi** ride to points around the island—but it requires some planning ahead. To use this "Telebus" system, you have to make the trip between 5:00 and 22:00 (from 7:00 on Sat-Sun). At least two hours in advance, call FynBus at 63 11 22 55 to reserve; a ride to anywhere on Ærø costs just 40 kr per person.

Ærøskøbing

Ærøskøbing is Ærø's village in a bottle. It's small enough to be cute, but just big enough to feel real. The government, recognizing the value of this amazingly preserved little town, prohibits modern building anywhere in the center. It's the only town in Denmark protected in this way. Drop into the 1680s, when Ærøskøbing was the wealthy home port of a hundred windjammers. The many Danes and Germans who come here for the tranquility—washing up the cobbled main drag in waves with the landing of each boat—call it the fairy-tale town. The Danish word for "cozy," *hyggelig*, describes Ærøskøbing perfectly.

Ærøskøbing is simply a pleasant place to wander. Stubby little porthole-type houses, with their birth dates displayed in proud decorative rebar, lean on each other like drunk, sleeping sailors. Wander under flickering old-time lamps. Snoop around town. It's OK. Peek into living rooms (if people want privacy, they shut their drapes). Notice the many "snooping mirrors" on the houses—antique locals are following your every move. The harbor now caters to holiday yachts, and on midnight low tides you can almost hear the crabs playing cards.

The town economy, once rich with the windjammer trade, hit the rocks in modern times. Kids 15 to 18 years old go to a boarding school in Svendborg; many don't return. It's an interesting discussion: Should the island folk pickle their culture in tourism, or forget about the cuteness and get modern?

Planning Your Time

You'll regret not setting aside a minimum of two nights for your Ærøskøbing visit. In a busy day you can "do" everything you like—except relax. If ever a place was right for recreating, this is it. I'd arrive in time for an evening stroll, dinner, and the Night Watchman's tour (21:00 nightly in summer). The next morning, do the island bike tour, returning by midafternoon. You can see the town's three museums in less than two hours (but note that they all close by 17:00 in summer, even earlier off-season), then browse the rest of your daylight away. Your second evening is filled with options: Stroll out to the summer huts for sunset, watch the classic sailing ships come in to moor for the evening (mostly Dutch and German boats crewed by vacationers), watch a movie in the pint-sized town cinema, go bowling with local teens, or check out live music in the pub.

Note that during the off-season (basically Sept-May), the town is quite dead and may not be worth a visit. Several shops and restaurants are closed, the Night Watchman's tour stops running, and bad weather can make a bike ride unpleasant.

Orientation to Ærøskøbing

Ærøskøbing is tiny. Everything's just a few cobbles from the ferry landing.

Tourist Information

The TI, which faces the ferry landing, is a clearinghouse for brochures promoting sights and activities on the island, has info on other Danish destinations, can help book rooms, rents small electric cars (300 kr/half-day, 500 kr/day, reserve a day or two in advance, available June-Aug only), and offers Internet access and Wi-Fi (late-June-mid-Aug Mon-Fri 9:00-18:00, Sat 10:00-18:00, Sun 10:00-15:00; off-season Mon-Fri 10:00-16:00, closed Sat-Sun; tel. 62 52 13 00, www.aeroe.dk).

Helpful Hints

Money: The town's only ATM is on Torvet Square.

Internet Access: Try the TI (steady hours) or the library on Torvet Square (sketchy hours).

Laundry: Ærøskøbing's self-service launderette (on Gyden) is looking for a new owner; in the meantime, most of its machines are out of order. You might be able to do laundry, but don't count on it.

Ferries: See "Ærøskøbing Connections" on page 178.

Bike Rental: Pilebækkens Cykler rents bikes year-round at the gas station at the top of the town. Manager Janne loans read-

ers of this book the 25-kr island *cykel* map so they won't get lost (three-speed bikes-55 kr/24 hours, seven-speed bikes-75 kr/24 hours; Mon-Fri 9:00-16:30, Sat 9:00-12:00, closed Sun except in July—when it's open 10:00-13:00; from Torvet Square, go through green door at Søndergade end of square, past garden to next road, in the gas station at Pilebækken 7; tel. 62 52 11 10). **Hotel Ærøhus** rents seven-speed bikes (75 kr/24 hours, 200-kr deposit, open very long hours). The campground also rent bikes (see "Sleeping in Ærøskøbing," later). Most people on Ærø don't bother locking up their bikes—if your rental doesn't have a lock, don't fret.

Shopping: The town is speckled with cute little shops, including a funky flea market shop next to the bakery. Each July, local artisans show their creations in a warehouse facing the ferry landing.

Self-Guided Walk

▲▲▲Welcome to Ærøskøbing

Ideally, take this stroll with the sun low, the shadows long, and the colors rich. Start at the harbor.

Harbor: Loiter around the harbor a bit first. German and Dutch vacationers on grand old sailboats come into port each evening. Because Ærø is only nine miles across the water from Germany, the island is popular with Germans who regularly return to this peaceful retreat.

• *From the harbor and TI, walk up the main street a block and go left on...*

Smedegade: This is the poorest street in town, with the most architectural and higgledy-piggledy charm. Have a close look at

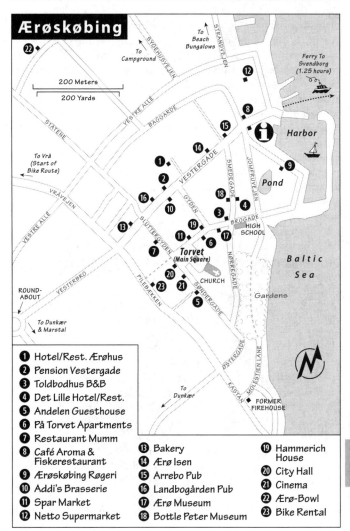

Ærøskøbing

200 Meters
200 Yards

To Beach Bungalows
To Campground
Ferry To Svendborg (1.25 hours)

STRANDVEJEN
SYGEHUSVEJEN
VESTRE ALLÉ
BAGGÅRDE
STÅTENE
Harbor
Pond
Baltic Sea
Gardens
To Vrå (Start of Bike Route)
VRÅVEJEN
VESTRE ALLÉ
VESTERBRO
VESTERGADE
SLUTTERGYDEN
GYDEN
SMEDEGADE
JOMFRUVEJEN
BROGADE
NØRREGADE
PILEBÆKKEN
SØNDERGADE
ØSTERGADE
KASTAN
MOLESTIEN LANE
ROUND-ABOUT
To Dunkær & Marstal
Torvet (Main Square)
CHURCH
HIGH SCHOOL
To Dunkær
FORMER FIREHOUSE

1. Hotel/Rest. Ærøhus
2. Pension Vestergade
3. Toldbodhus B&B
4. Det Lille Hotel/Rest.
5. Andelen Guesthouse
6. På Torvet Apartments
7. Restaurant Mumm
8. Café Aroma & Fiskerestaurant
9. Ærøskøbing Røgeri
10. Addi's Brasserie
11. Spar Market
12. Netto Supermarket
13. Bakery
14. Ærø Isen
15. Arrebo Pub
16. Landbogården Pub
17. Ærø Museum
18. Bottle Peter Museum
19. Hammerich House
20. City Hall
21. Cinema
22. Ærø-Bowl
23. Bike Rental

the "street spies" on the houses—clever mirrors letting old women inside keep an eye on what's going on outside. The ship-in-a-bottle Bottle Peter Museum is on the right (described later, under "Sights in Ærøskøbing"). Notice the gutters—some protect only the doorway. Locals find the rounded modern drainpipes less charming than the old-school ones with hard angles. Appreciate the finely carved old doors. Each is proudly unique—try to find two the same. Number 37 (on the left, after Det Lille Hotel), from the 18th century, is Ærøskøbing's cutest house. Its tiny dormer is from some old ship's poop deck. The plants above the door have a traditional purpose—to keep this part of the house damp and slow to burn in case of fire.

Smedegade ends at the Folkehøjskole (folks' high school). Inspired by the Danish philosopher Nikolaj Gruntvig—who wanted people to be able to say "I am good at being me"—it offers people of any age the benefit of government-subsidized cultural education (music, art, theater, and so on).

• *Jog left, then turn right after the school, and stroll along the peaceful, harborside...*

Molestien Lane: This gravel path is lined with gardens, a quiet beach, and a row of small-is-beautiful houses—beginning

with humble and progressing to captain's class. These fine buildings are a reminder that through the centuries, Ærøskøbing has been the last town in Germany, independent, the first town in Denmark...and always into trade—legal and illegal. (The smuggling spirit survives in residents' blood even today. When someone returns from a trip, friends eagerly ask, "And what did you bring back?") Each garden is cleverly and lovingly designed. The harborfront path, nicknamed "Virgin's Lane," was where teens could court within view of their parents.

The dreamy-looking island immediately across the way is a nature preserve and a resting spot for birds making their long journey from the north to the Mediterranean. There's one lucky bull here (farmers raft over their heifers, who return as cows). Rainbows often end on this island—where plague victims were once buried. In the winter, when the water freezes (about once a decade), locals slip and slide over for a visit. The white building you can see at the end of the town's pier was the cooking house, where visiting sailors (who tried to avoid working with open flame on flammable ships) could do their baking.

At the end of the lane stands the former firehouse (with the tall brick tower, now a place for the high school garage band to practice). Twenty yards before the firehouse, a trail cuts left about 100 yards along the shore to a place the town provides for fishermen to launch and store their boats and tidy up their nets. A bench is strategically placed to enjoy the view.

• *Follow the rutted lane inland, back past the firehouse. Turn right and walk a block toward town. At the first intersection, take a right onto...*

Østergade: This was Ærøskøbing's east gate. In the days of German control, all island trade was legal only within the town. All who passed this point would pay various duties and taxes at a tollbooth that once stood here.

As you walk past the traditional houses, peer into living rooms. Catch snatches of Danish life. (After the bend, you can see right through the windows to the sea.) Ponder the beauty of a society with such a keen sense of civic responsibility that fishing permits entrust you "to catch only what you need." You're welcome to pick berries where you like...but "no more than what would fit in your hat."

The wood on these old houses prefers organic coverings to modern paint. Tar painted on beams as a preservative blisters in the sun. An old-fashioned paint of chalk, lime, and clay lets old houses breathe and feel more alive. (It gets darker with the rain and leaves a little color on your fingers.) Modern chemical paint has much less personality.

The first square (actually a triangle, at #55) was the old goose market. Ærøskøbing—born in the 13th century, burned in the 17th, and rebuilt in the 18th—claims (believably) to be the best-preserved town from that era in Denmark. The original plan, with 12 streets laid out by its founder, survives.

• *Leaving the square, stay left on...*

Søndergade: Look for wrought-iron girders on the walls, added to hold together bulging houses. (On the first corner, at

#55, notice the nuts that could be tightened like a corset to keep the house from sagging.) Ærøskøbing's oldest houses (check out the dates)—the only ones that survived a fire during a war with Sweden—are #36 and #32. At #32, the hatch upstairs was where masts and sails were stored for the winter. These houses also have some of the finest doors in town (and in Ærøskøbing, that's really saying something). The red on #32's door is the original paint job—ox blood, which, when combined with the tannin in the wood, really lasts. The courtyard behind #18 was a parking lot in pre-car days.

Farmers, in town for their shopping chores, would leave their horses here. Even today, the wide-open fields are just beyond.

• *Wander down to Ærøskøbing's main square...*

Torvet (Main Square): Notice the two pumps. Until 1951, townspeople came here for their water. The linden tree is the town

symbol. The rocks around it celebrate the reunion of a big chunk of southern Denmark (including this island), which was ruled by Germany from 1864 to 1920. See the town seal featuring a linden tree, over the door of the old City Hall (now the library, with Internet stations in former prison cells). Read the Danish on the wall: "With law shall man a country build."

• *Our walk is over. Continue straight (popping into recommended Restaurant Mumm, the best place in town, to make a reservation for dinner). You'll return to the main street (Vestergade) and—just when you need it—the town bakery. If you're ready to launch right into a bike ride, go through the green door right of the City Hall to reach the town's bike-rental place (listed earlier, under "Helpful Hints").*

Sights in Ærøskøbing

Museums

Ærøskøbing's three tiny museums cluster within a few doors of each other just off the main square (if visiting all three, buy the 85-kr combo-ticket; tel. 62 52 29 50, www.arremus.dk). In July, they organize daily chatty tours. While quirky and fun (and with sketchy English handouts), these museums would be much more interesting and worthwhile if they translated their Danish descriptions for the rare person on this planet who doesn't speak *Dansk*. (Your gentle encouragement might help get results.)

Ærø Museum (Ærøskøbing Bymuseum)—This museum fills two floors of an old house with the island's local history, from seafaring to farming. On the ground floor, you'll see household objects (such as pottery, kitchenware, and tools), paintings, a loom from 1683, and a fun diorama showing an aerial view of Ærøskøbing in 1862—notice the big gardens behind nearly every house. (This museum

carries on the tradition with its own garden out back—be sure to go out and explore it before you leave.) Upstairs are 19th-century outfits, lots more paintings, an 18th-century peasant's living room with colorful furniture, and the gear from a 100-year-old pharmacy.

Cost and Hours: 30 kr; late June-Aug Mon-Fri 11:00-16:00, Sat-Sun 11:00-15:00; Sept-late Oct and April-late June daily 11:00-15:00; shorter hours off-season and closed Sat-Sun; Brogade 3-5, www.arremus.dk.

▲**Bottle Peter Museum (Flaske-Peter Samling)**—This fascinating house has 750 different bottled ships. Old Peter Jacobsen,

 who made his first bottle at 16 and his last at 85, created some 1,700 total ships-in-bottles in his lifetime. He bragged that he drank the contents of each bottle...except those containing milk. This museum opened in 1943, when the mayor of Ærøskøbing offered Peter and his wife a humble home in exchange for the right to display his works. Bottle Peter died in 1960 (and is most likely buried in a glass bottle), leaving a lifetime of tedious little creations for visitors to squint and marvel at.

Cost and Hours: 40 kr; late June-early Aug daily 10:00-17:00; April-late June and early Aug-late Oct daily 10:00-16:00; shorter hours off-season and closed Sat-Sun; Smedegade 22.

Visiting the Museum: In two buildings facing each other across a cobbled courtyard, you'll see rack after rack of painstaking models in bottles and cigar boxes. Some are "right-handed" and some are "left-handed" (referring to the direction the bottle faced, and therefore which hand the model-maker relied on to execute the fine details)—Bottle Peter could do it all.

In the entrance building, you'll see Peter's "American collection," which he sold to a Danish-American collector so he could have funds to retire. One of Peter's favorites was the "diver-bottle"—an extra-wide bottle with two separate ship models inside: One shipwreck on the "ocean floor" at the bottom of the bottle, and, above that, a second one floating on the "surface." A video shows the artist at work, and nearby you can see some of his tools.

In the second building, you can read some English panels about Peter's life (including his mischievous wit, which caused his friends great anxiety when he had an audience with the king) and see the headstone he designed for his own grave: A cross embedded with seven ships-in-bottles, representing the seven seas he explored in his youth as a seaman.

Hammerich House (Hammerichs Hus)—These 12 funky rooms in three houses are filled with 200- to 300-year-old junk.

Cost and Hours: 30 kr, late May-late Aug daily 12:00-16:00, closed off-season, Gyden 22.

CENTRAL DENMARK

Ærø Island Bike Ride (or Car Tour)

This 15-mile trip shows you the best of this windmill-covered island's charms. The highest point on the island is only 180 feet above sea level, but the wind can be strong and the hills seem long and surprisingly steep. If you'd rather drive the route, you can rent an electric car at the TI (summer only, see page 161).

As a bike ride, it's good exercise, though it may be more exhausting than fun if you've done only light, recreational cycling at home. You'll pay more for seven gears instead of five, but it's worth it.

Rent your bike in town (see "Helpful Hints," page 162), and while my map and instructions work, a local cycle map is helpful (free loaner maps if you rent from Pilebækkens Cykler, or buy one at the TI). Bring along plenty of water, as there are few opportunities to fill up (your first good chance is at the WC at the Bregninge church; there are no real shops until downtown Bregninge).

• *Leave Ærøskøbing to the west on the road to Vrå (Vråvejen, signed* Bike Route #90*). From downtown, pedal up the main street (Vestergade) and turn right on Vråvejen; from the bike-rental place on Pilebækken, just turn right and pedal straight ahead—it turns into Vråvejen.*

Leaving Ærøskøbing: You'll see the first of many U-shaped farms, typical of Denmark. The three sides block the wind and store cows, hay, and people. *Gård* (farm) shows up in many local surnames.

At Øsemarksvej, bike along the coast in the protection of the dike built in 1856 to make the once-salty swampland to your left farmable. While the weak soil is good for hay and little else, they get the most out of it. Each winter, certain grazing areas flood with seawater. (Some locals claim this makes their cows produce fatter milk and meat.) As you roll along the dike, the land on your left is about eight feet below sea level. The little white pump house—alone in the field—is busy each spring and summer.

• *At the T-junction, go right (over the dike) toward...*

Borgnæs: The traditional old "straw house" (50 yards down, on left) is a café and shop selling fresh farm products. Just past that, a few roadside tables sell farm goodies on the honor system. Borgnæs is a cluster of modern summer houses. In spite of huge demand, a weak economy, and an aging population, development like this is no longer allowed.

• *Keep to the right (passing lots of wheat fields); at the next T-junction, turn right, following signs for Ø. Bregningemark (don't turn off for Vindeballe). After a secluded beach, head inland (direction: Ø. Bregninge). Pass the island's only water mill, and climb uphill over the island's 2,700-inch-high summit toward Bregninge. The tallest point on Ærø is called Synneshøj (probably means "Seems High" and it sure*

Ærø Island Bike Ride

To Svendborg

To Søby

Urehoved

BEACH
BUNGALOWS

Borgnæs

Drejø

Ommels-
hoved

CHURCH

CAMPING

Bregninge

Synneshøj

DIKE

Vrå

Ærøskøbing
(start & end bike ride)

VINDEBALLE KRO

SHORTCUTS BACK
TO ÆRØSKØBING

Lilleø

Vindeballe

Stokkeby

Tranderup

Olde

Lille
Rise

Kragnæs

Vodrup
Klint
(Cliffs)

TINGSTEDET
DOLMEN

Store
Rise

BREWERY

Dunkær

To Marstal
& Maritime
Museum

Baltic Sea

3 Kilometers

2 Miles

Vejnæs Nakke

100 KM
50 MI

DENMARK

Odense Cope.

Ærø

GER.

N

does—if you're even a bit out of shape, you'll feel every one of those inches).

Gammelgård: Take a right turn marked only by a *Bike Route #90* sign. The road deteriorates (turns to gravel—and can be slushy

if there's been heavy rain, so be careful). You'll wind scenically and sometimes steeply through "Ærø's Alps," past classic thatched-roofed "old farms" (hence the name of the lane—Gammelgård).

• *At the modern road, turn left (leaving Bike Route #90) and bike to the big village church. Before turning left to roll through Bregninge, visit the church.*

Bregninge Church: The interior of the 12th-century Bregninge church is still painted as a Gothic church would have been. Find the painter's self-portrait (behind the pulpit, right of front pew). Tradition says that if the painter wasn't happy with his pay, he'd paint a fool's head in the church (above third pew on left). Note how the fool's mouth—the hole for a rope tied to the bell—has been worn wider and wider by centuries of ringing. (During services, the ringing bell would call those who were ill and too contagious to be allowed into the church to come for communion—distributed through the square hatches flanking the altar.)

The altarpiece—gold leaf on carved oak—is from 1528, six years before the Reformation came to Denmark. The cra-

nium carved into the bottom indicates it's a genuine masterpiece by Claus Berg (from Lübeck, Germany). This Crucifixion scene is such a commotion, it seems to cause Christ's robe to billow up. The soldiers who traditionally gambled for Christ's robe have traded their dice for knives. Even the three wise men (lower right; each perhaps a Danish king) made it to this Crucifixion. Notice the escaping souls of the two thieves— the one who converted on the cross being carried happily to heaven, and the other, with its grim-winged escort, heading straight to hell. The scene at lower left—a disciple with a bare-breasted, dark-skinned woman feeding her child—symbolizes the Great Commission: "Go ye to all the world." Since this is a Catholic altarpiece, a roll call of saints lines the wings. During the restoration, the identity of the two women on the lower right was unknown, so the lettering—even in Latin—is clearly gibberish. Take a moment to study the 16th-century art on the ceiling (for example, the crucified feet ascending, leaving only footprints on earth). In the narthex, a list of pastors goes back to 1505. The current pastor (Agnes) is the first woman on the list.

• *Now's the time for a bathroom break (public WC in the churchyard). Then roll downhill through...*

Bregninge: As you bike through what is supposedly Denmark's "second-longest village," you'll pass many more U-shaped *gårds*. Notice how the town is in a gully. Imagine pirates trolling along the coast, looking for church spires marking unfortified villages. Ærø's 16 villages are all invisible from the sea—their church spires carefully designed not to be viewable from sea level.

• *About a mile down the main road is Vindeballe. Just before the main part of the village (soon after you pass the official* Vindeballe *sign and the* din fart *sign—which tells you "your speed"), take the* Vodrup Klint *turnoff to the right.*

Vodrup Klint: A road leads downhill (with a well-signed jog to the right) to dead-end at a rugged bluff called Vodrup Klint (WC, picnic benches). If I were a pagan, I'd worship here—the sea, the wind, and the chilling view. Notice how the land steps in sloppy slabs down to the sea. When saturated with water, the slabs of clay that make up the land here get slick, and entire chunks can slide.

Hike down to the foamy beach (where you can pick up some flint, chalk, and wild thyme). While the wind at the top could drag a kite-flyer, the beach below can be ideal for sunbathing. Because Ærø is warmer and drier than the rest of Denmark, this island is home to plants and animals found nowhere else in the country. This southern exposure is the warmest area. Germany is dead ahead.

• *Backtrack 200 yards and follow the signs to* Tranderup. *On the way, you'll pass a lovely pond famous for its bell frogs and happy little duck houses.*

*Popping out in Tranderup, you can backtrack (left) about 300 yards to get to the traditional **Vindeballe Kro**—a handy inn for a stop if you're hungry or thirsty (30-45-kr lunches served daily July–mid-Aug 12:00-14:00, 150-200-kr dinners served daily year-round 18:00-21:00, tel. 62 52 16 13).*

If you're tired or if the weather is turning bad, you can shortcut from here back to Ærøskøbing: Go down the lane across the street from the Vindeballe Kro, and you'll zip quickly downhill across the island to the dike just east of Borgnæs; turn right and retrace your steps back into town.

But there's much more to see. To continue our pedal, head on into...

Tranderup: Still following signs for *Tranderup*, stay on Tranderupgade parallel to the big road through town. You'll pass a lovely farm and a potato stand. At the main road, turn right. At the Ærøskøbing turnoff (another chance to bail out and head home), side-trip 100 yards left to the big stone (commemorating the return of the island to Denmark from Germany in 1750) and a grand island panorama. Seattleites might find Claus Clausen's rock interesting (in the picnic area, next to WC). It's a memorial to an extremely obscure pioneer from the state of Washington.

• *Return to the big road (continuing in direction: Marstal), pass through Olde, pedal past FAF (the local wheat farmers' co-op facility), and head toward Store Rise (STOH-reh REE-zuh), the next church spire in the distance. Think of medieval travelers using spires as navigational aids.*

Store Rise Prehistoric Tomb, Church, and Brewery: Thirty yards after the Stokkeby turnoff, follow the rough, tree-lined path on the right to the Langdysse (Long Dolmen) Tingstedet, just behind the church spire. This is a 6,000-year-old **dolmen,** an early

Neolithic burial place. Though Ærø once had more than 200 of these prehistoric tombs, only 13 survive. The site is a raised mound the shape and length (about 100 feet) of a Viking ship, and archaeologists have found evidence that indicates a Viking ship may indeed have been burned and buried here.

Ting means assembly spot. Imagine a thousand years ago: Viking chiefs representing the island's various communities gathering here around their ancestors' tombs. For 6,000 years, this has been a holy spot. The stones were considered fertility stones. For centuries, locals in need of virility chipped off bits and took them home (the nicks in the rock nearest the information post are mine).

Tuck away your chip and carry on down the lane to the Store Rise **church.** Inside you'll find little ships hanging in the nave, a fine 12th-century altarpiece, a stick with offering bag and a ting-a-ling bell to wake those nodding off (right of altar), double seats (so worshippers can flip to face the pulpit during sermons), and Martin Luther in the stern keeping his Protestant hand on the rudder. The list in the church allows today's pastors to trace their pastoral lineage back to Doctor Luther himself. (The current pastor, Janet, is the first woman on the list.) The churchyard is circular—a reminder of how churchyards provided a last refuge for humble communities under attack. Can you find anyone buried in the graveyard whose name doesn't end in "-sen"?

The buzz lately in Ærø is its **brewery,** located in a historic brewery 400 yards beyond the Store Rise church. Follow the smell of the hops (or the *Rise Bryggeri* signs). It welcomes visitors with free samples of its various beers. The Ærø traditional brews are available in pilsner (including the popular walnut pilsner), light ale, dark ale, and a typical dark Irish-style stout. The Rise organic brews come in light ale, dark ale, and walnut (mid-June-mid-Sept daily 10:00-14:00; mid-Sept-mid-June Wed-Fri 10:00-14:00, closed Sat-Tue; tel. 62 52 11 32, www.risebryggeri.dk).

• *From here, climb back to the main road and continue (direction: Marstal) on your way back home to Ærøskøbing. The three 330-foot-high modern windmills on your right are communally owned and, as they are a nonpolluting source of energy, state-subsidized. At Dunkær (3 miles from Ærøskøbing), take the small road, signed* Lille Rise, *past the topless windmill. Except for the Lille Rise, it's all downhill from here, as you coast past great sea views back home to Ærøskøbing.*

Huts at the Sunset Beach: Still rolling? Bike past the campground along the Urehoved beach (*strand* in Danish) for a look at the coziest little beach houses you'll never see back in the "big is beautiful" US. This is Europe, where small is beautiful, and the concept of sustainability is neither new nor subversive. (For more details, see "Beach Bungalow Sunset Stroll," later.)

Rainy-Day Options

Ærø is disappointing but not unworkable in bad weather. In addition to the museums listed earlier, you could rent a car (such as the TI's electric cars) to cruise the island. Also, many of the evening options under "Nightlife in Ærøskøbing" (next) are good in bad weather.

If you want to find out more about the island's seafaring history, hop on the free bus #790 to the dreary town of Marstal to visit its fine **Marstal Maritime Museum** (Marstal Søfartsmuseum). Ride the bus all the way to the harbor (about a 20-minute trip), where you'll find the museum. You'll see plenty of model ships, nautical paintings (including several scenes by acclaimed painter Carl Rasmussen), an original ship's galley, a re-created wheelhouse (with steering and navigation equipment), a collection of exotic goods brought back from faraway lands, and a children's area with a climbable mast. Designed by and for sailors, the museum presents a warts-and-all view of the hardships of the seafaring life, rather than romanticizing it (55 kr; July-Aug daily 9:00-18:00; June daily 9:00-17:00; May and Sept-Oct daily 10:00-16:00; Nov-April Mon-Fri 10:00-16:00, Sat 11:00-15:00, closed Sun; Prinsensgade 1, tel. 62 53 23 31, www.marmus.dk).

Nightlife in Ærøskøbing

These activities are best done in the evening, after a day of biking around the island.

▲**Town Walk with Night Watchman**—Each evening in summer, Mr. Jan Pedersen becomes the old night watchman and leads

visitors through town. The hour-long walk is likely in Danish and English—and often in German, too—so you'll hang around a lot. But it's a fine time to be out, meet other travelers, and be charmed by gentle Jan (25 kr, daily late June-late Aug, no tours off-season, meet on Torvet near the church at 21:00, Jan also available as private guide, mobile 40 40 60 13, www.aeroe-turguide.dk, jan.leby @mail.dk).

▲▲Beach Bungalow Sunset Stroll—At sunset, stroll to Ærøskøbing's sand beach. Facing the ferry dock, go left, following the harbor. Upon leaving the town, you'll pass the Netto supermarket (convenient for picking up snacks, beer, or wine), a mini-golf course, and a children's playground. In the rosy distance, past a wavy wheat field, is Vestre Strandvejen—a row of tiny, Monopoly-like huts facing the sunset. These tiny beach escapes  are privately owned on land rented from the town (no overnight use, WCs at each end). Each is different, but all are stained with merry memories of locals enjoying themselves Danish-style. Bring a beverage or picnic. It's perfectly acceptable—and very Danish—to borrow a porch for your sunset sit. From here, it's a fine walk out to the end of Urehoved (as this spit of land is called).

Cinema—The cute little 30-seat Andelen Theater (a former grain warehouse near Torvet Square) plays movies in their original language (Danish subtitles, closed Mon and in July—when it hosts a jazz festival, new titles begin every Tue). It's run in a charming community-service kind of way. The management has installed heat, so tickets no longer come with a blanket.

Bowling—Ærø-Bowl is a six-lane alley in a modern athletic club at the edge of town. In this old-fashioned town, where no modern construction is allowed in the higgledy-piggledy center, this hip facility is a magnet for young people. One local told me, "I've never seen anyone come out of there without a smile" (hot dogs, junk food, arcade games, kids on dates; Tue-Thu 16:00-22:00, later on Fri-Sat, closed Sun-Mon, Søndergade 28, tel. 62 52 23 06, www.arrebowl.dk).

Pubs—Ærøskøbing's two bars are at the top and bottom of Vestergade. **Arrebo Pub,** near the ferry landing, attracts a young crowd and is *the* place for live music (but no food). The low-key **Landbogården** was recently taken over by a Sri Lankan family who have made it non-smoking and have started serving food—both Indian and Danish dishes (daily for 45-75-kr lunches and 100-160-kr dinners, near the top of Vestergade).

Sleeping in Ærøskøbing

The accommodations scene here is boom or bust. Summer weekends and all of July are packed (book long in advance). It's absolutely dead in the winter. These places come with family-run personality, and each is an easy stroll from the ferry landing.

Sleep Code

(6 kr = about $1, country code: 45)
S = Single, **D** = Double/Twin, **T** = Triple, **Q** = Quad, **b** = bathroom,
s = shower. Credit cards are accepted (with a 4 percent surcharge), staff speak English, and breakfast is included unless otherwise noted.

To help you sort easily through these listings, I've divided the accommodations into three categories, based on the price for a standard double room with bath during high season:

$$$ Higher Priced—Most rooms 1,000 kr or more.
$$ Moderately Priced—Most rooms between 450-1,000 kr.
$ Lower Priced—Most rooms 450 kr or less.

Prices can change without notice; verify the hotel's current rates online or by email.

In Ærøskøbing

$$$ Hotel Ærøhus is big and sprawling, with 33 uninspired rooms. Although it is less personal and cozy than some of the other listings here, it's the closest thing to a grand hotel in this capital of quaint (S-600 kr, Sb-990 kr, D-800 kr, Db-1,250 kr, free Internet access and Wi-Fi, bike rentals-75 kr/day, possible noise from large dinner parties—ask for a quiet room, tel. 62 52 10 03, fax 62 52 31 68, www.aeroehus.dk, mail@aeroehus.dk, Ole Jensen and family). Their modern holiday apartments nearby are used as overflow accommodations and can be a fine value for groups and families (details on their website).

$$ Pension Vestergade is your best home away from home in Ærøskøbing. It's lovingly run by Susanna Greve and her daughters,

Henrietta and Celia. Susanna, who's fun to talk with and is always ready with a cup of tea, has a wealth of knowledge about the town's history and takes good care of her guests. Built in 1784 for a sea captain's daughter, this creaky, sagging, and venerable eight-room place—with each room named for its particular color scheme—is on the main street in the town center. Picnic in the back garden and get to know Tillie, the live-in dog. Reserve well in advance (singles-600 kr year-round; doubles fluctuate, July: D-990 kr; spring and fall: D-890 kr; winter: D-790 kr; cash only, cuddly hot-water bottles, shared bathrooms, free Internet access

CENTRAL DENMARK

and Wi-Fi, Vestergade 44, tel. 62 52 22 98, www.vestergade44
.com, pensionvestergade44@post.tele.dk).

$$ Toldbodhus B&B, a tollhouse from 1770 to 1906, now
rents four delightful rooms. Three rooms share two bathrooms
in the main house, and a small garden house has a double room
with a detached bathroom. Owners Karin and John Steenberg
have named and decorated each room after cities they've lived
in: Amsterdam, København, London, and Hong Kong. They
may be closing after the summer 2013 season (April-Sept: S-750
kr, Db-890 kr; Oct-March: S-650 kr, Db-790 kr; cash only, free
Wi-Fi, near harbor on corner of Smedegade at Brogade 8, tel. 62
52 18 11, www.toldbodhus.com, toldbodhus@mail.dk).

$$ Det Lille Hotel is a former 19th-century captain's home
with six tidy but well-worn rooms (June-Sept: S/D-950 kr; Oct-
May: S/D-850 kr; extra bed-265 kr, free Wi-Fi, Smedegade 33,
tel. & fax 62 52 23 00, www.det-lille-hotel.dk, mail@det-lille
-hotel.dk).

$$ Andelen Guesthouse, brimming with nautical charm,
is in an old warehouse that's been converted into a hotel. The five
guest rooms share two bathrooms (S-500 kr, D-600 kr, break-
fast-75 kr, free Wi-Fi, Søndergade 28A, tel. 61 60 75 11, www
.andelenguesthouse.com, andelenguesthouse@hotmail.com).

$$ På Torvet rents eight newly renovated apartments—each
with private kitchen and bathroom—on the main square (Db-750
kr, 200-kr linen and cleaning fee, free Wi-Fi, Torvet 7, tel. 62 52
40 50, www.paatorvet.dk, info@paatorvet.dk).

Outside of Ærøskøbing

$$ Vindeballe Kro, about three miles from Ærøskøbing, is a tra-
ditional inn in Vindeballe at the island's central crossroads. Maria
and Steen rent 10 straightforward, well-kept rooms (S-450 kr,
D-650 kr, tel. 62 52 16 13, www.vindeballekro.dk, mail@vinde
ballekro.dk; see page 171 for details on their restaurant).

$ Ærø Campground is set on a fine beach a few minutes'
walk out of town. This three-star campground offers a lodge with a
fireplace, campsites, cabins, and bike rental (camping-75 kr/person,
4- to 6-bed cabins-150-300 kr plus per-person fee, bedding-75 kr/
person, open May-Sept; facing the water, follow waterfront to the
left; tel. 62 52 18 54, www.aeroecamp.dk, info@aeroecamp.dk).

Eating in Ærøskøbing

Ærøskøbing has a handful of charming and hardworking little
eateries. Business is so light that chefs and owners come and go
constantly, making it tough to predict the best value for the com-
ing year. As each place has a distinct flavor, I'd spend 20 minutes

enjoying the warm evening light and do a strolling survey before making your choice. While there are several simple burger-type joints, I've listed only the serious kitchens. Note that everything closes by 21:00—don't wait too late to eat (if you'll be taking a later ferry from Svendborg to Ærø, either eat before your boat trip or call ahead to reserve a place...otherwise you're out of luck). The only places in town serving food daily during the winter are Addi's Brasserie, Det Lille Hotel, Hotel Ærøhus, and the Landbogården bar (see "Nightlife in Ærøskøbing," earlier).

Restaurant Mumm is where visiting yachters go for a good and classy meal. Portions are huge, and on balmy days their garden terrace out back is a hit. Call ahead to reserve (180-kr daily specials, 80-kr starters, 140-220-kr main courses, daily 16:30-21:00, closed Sun-Mon off-season, near Torvet Square, tel. 62 52 12 12, Peter Sorensen).

Café Aroma, an inexpensive Danish café that feels like a rustic old diner, has a big front porch filled with tables and good, reasonably priced entrées, sandwiches, and burgers for 60-175 kr. Ask about the daily special, which will save you money and is not listed on the confusing menu. Order at the bar (May-Aug daily 11:00-21:00, closed Sept-April, on Vestergade). They also run a high-quality, pricey fish restaurant (aptly named **Fiskerestaurant**) next door.

Ærøskøbing Røgeri serves wonderful smoked fish meals on paper plates and picnic tables. Facing the harbor, it's great for a light meal (50-75 kr for fish with potato salad and bread). Eat there or find a pleasant picnic site at the beach or at the park behind the fish house. A smoked fish dinner and a couple of cold Carlsbergs are a well-earned reward after a long bike ride (May-Sept daily 11:00-18:00, in summer until 20:00, Havnen 15, tel. 62 52 40 07).

Addi's Brasserie is a rare place that's open all year, serving fresh seafood and meat dishes. Eat in the main dining room among portraits of Danish royalty, or in the larger side room (daily lunch and dinner specials, lunch main courses-48-85 kr, dinner main courses-180 kr, daily 12:00-15:00 & 18:00-21:00, across street from Pension Vestergade, Vestergade 39, tel. 62 52 21 43).

Hotel Restaurants: Two hotels in town have dining rooms with good but expensive food; I'd eat at the restaurants I've listed above, unless they're closed. But in a pinch, try these: **Det Lille Hotel** serves meals in an inviting dining room or garden (200-kr daily specials, 70-100-kr starters, 190-240-kr main dishes, daily 12:00-21:00, dinner only off-season—but at least they're open year-round, Smedegade 33, tel. 62 52 23 00, Klaus cooks with attitude). **Hotel Ærøhus** is a last resort, serving creative but pricey French-inspired modern fare in a sprawling complex of dining rooms, big and small (115-kr starters, 225-300-kr main dishes, open daily, on

Vestergade, tel. 62 52 10 03).

Grocery: Buy picnic fixings plus wine and beer at the **Spar Market** (Mon-Fri 9:00-18:00, Sat 9:00-14:00, Sun 10:00-15:00, on Torvet Square) or the bigger **Netto** supermarket (chilled beer and wine—handy for walks to the little huts on the beach at sunset, Mon-Fri 9:00-19:00, Sat 8:00-17:00, closed Sun, kitty-corner from ferry dock).

Bakery: Ærøskøbing's old-school little bakery sells homemade bread, cheese, yogurt, and tasty pastries (Tue-Fri 7:00-17:00, Sat-Sun 7:00-14:00, closed Mon, top of Vestergade).

Ice Cream: Halfway up the main drag (Vestergade), you'll smell fresh-baked waffles and see benches filled with happy ice-cream lickers. **Ærø Isen** serves good ice cream in fresh waffle cones, with whipped cream and jam topping. Their "Ærø-Isen Special" (walnut-maple syrup ice cream topped with whipped cream and maple syrup) is 9 kr more than the other flavors (daily  11:00-21:00). Be sure to check out the gallery behind the shop to see paintings and sculptures featuring local artists.

Ærøskøbing Connections

Ærø-Svendborg Ferry

The ferry ride between **Svendborg,** with connections to Copenhagen, and **Ærøskøbing,** on the island of Ærø, is a relaxing 75-minute crossing. Just get on, and the crew will come to you for your payment. While they accept Danish credit cards, American ones don't work—so be sure to bring enough cash (189 kr round-trip per person, 418 kr round-trip per car—not including driver/passengers, you'll save a little money with round-trip tickets, you can leave the island via any of the three different Ærø ferry routes, ferry not covered by or discounted with railpass).

The ferry always has room for walk-ons, but drivers should reserve a spot in advance, especially on weekends and in summer. During these busy times, reserve as far ahead as you can—ideally at least a week in advance. Car reservations by phone or email are free and easy—simply give your name and license-plate number. If you don't know your license number (i.e., you're reserving from home and haven't yet picked up your rental car), try asking nicely if they're willing to just take your name. They may want you to call them with the number when you pick up your car, but if that's not practical, you can usually just tell the attendant your name before you drive onto the boat (office open Mon-Fri 8:00-16:00, Sat-Sun 9:00-15:30, tel. 62 52 40 00, www.aeroe-ferry.dk, info@aeroe -ferry.dk).

Ferries depart Svendborg daily at 10:15, 13:15, 16:15, 19:15, and 22:30 (plus a 7:15 departure Mon-Fri). Ferries depart Ærøskøbing daily at 8:45, 11:45, 14:45, 17:45, and 20:45 (plus a 5:45 departure Mon-Fri). Drivers with reservations just drive on (be sure to get into the *med* reservations line). If you won't use your car in Ærø, park it in Svendborg (big, safe lot two blocks in from ferry landing, or at the far end of the harbor near the Bendix fish shop). On Ærø, parking is free.

Trains Connecting with Ærø-Svendborg Ferry

The train from **Odense** dead-ends at the Svendborg harbor (2/hour Mon-Sat, 1/hour Sun, 45 minutes; don't get off at the "Svendborg Vest" station—wait until you get to the end of the line, called simply "Svendborg"). Train departures and arrivals are coordinated with the ferry schedule.

Arriving in Svendborg: The ferry leaves Svendborg about five minutes after your train arrives. If you know where you're going, it takes about that long to walk briskly from the station to the dock. Don't dawdle—the boat leaves stubbornly on time, even if the train is a minute or two late. Since trains run every half-hour during summer (except on Sundays), I recommend leaving Odense on an earlier train, so you have a little more time to absorb delays and find your way (in other words, take the train that arrives in Svendborg 35 minutes before your boat). If you're cutting it close, be ready to hop off the train and follow these directions:

To get from the Svendborg train station to the dock, turn left after exiting the train, following the sidewalk between the tracks and the station, then take a left (across the tracks) at the first street, Brogade. Head a block downhill to the harbor, make a right, and the ferry dock is ahead, across from Hotel Ærø. If you arrive early, you can head to the waiting room in the little blue building across the street from the hotel. There are several carry-out restaurants along Brogade, and a few hotels overlooking the ferry line have restaurants.

Departing from Svendborg: All Svendborg trains go to Odense (where you can connect to Copenhagen or Aarhus). Trains leave shortly after the ferry arrives (tight connections for hurried commuters). To reach the train from the Svendborg ferry dock, pass Hotel Ærø and continue a block along the waiting lane for the ferry, turn left and go up Brogade one block, then take a right and follow the sidewalk between the tracks and the train station. A train signed *Odense* should be waiting on the single track (departs at :20 or :50 past each hour).

Odense

Founded in A.D. 988 and named after Odin (the Nordic Zeus),

Odense is the main city of the big island of Funen (Fyn in Danish) and the birthplace of storyteller Hans Christian Andersen (whom the Danes call simply H. C., pronounced "hoe see"). Although the author was born here in poverty and left at the tender age of 14 to pursue a career in the theater scene of Copenhagen, H. C. is Odense's favorite son—you'll find his name and image all over town. He once said, "Perhaps Odense will one day become famous because of me." Today, Odense (OH-then-za) is one of Denmark's most popular tourist destinations.

Orientation to Odense

As Denmark's third-largest city, with 166,000 people, Odense is big and industrial. But its old center, tidy and neatly urbanized, retains some pockets of the

fairy-tale charm it had in the days of H. C. Everything is within easy walking distance, except for the open-air folk museum.

The train station sits at the north end of the town center. A few blocks south runs the main pedestrian shopping boulevard, Vestergade. Near the eastern end of this drag, and a couple of blocks up, is a tight tangle of atmospheric old lanes, where you'll find the Hans Christian Andersen House and town history museum.

Tourist Information

The TI is in the Town Hall (Rådhuset), the big brick palace overlooking the square at the east end of the Vestergade pedestrian street (July-Aug Mon-Fri 9:30-18:00, Sat 10:00-15:00, Sun 11:00-14:00; Sept-June Mon-Fri 9:30-16:30, Sat 10:00-13:00, closed Sun; tel. 63 75 75 20, www.visitodense.com). For all the information

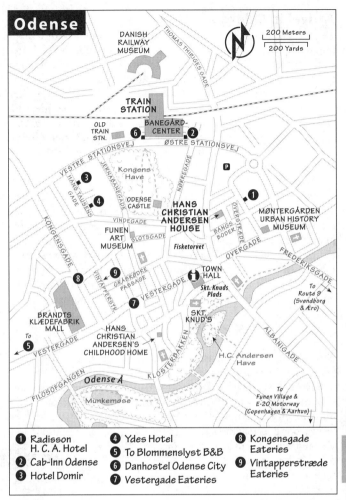

Odense

DANISH
RAILWAY
MUSEUM

THOMAS THRIGES GADE

200 Meters
200 Yards

TRAIN
STATION

OLD
TRAIN
STN.

BANEGÅRD-
CENTER

6 **2**

ØSTRE STATIONSVEJ

VESTRE STATIONSVEJ

JERNBANEGADE

H.C. ANDERSENS GADE

NØRREGADE

Kongens
Have

3

ODENSE
CASTLE

4

VINDEGADE

SLOTSGADE

FUNEN
ART
MUSEUM

1

MØNTERGÅRDEN
URBAN HISTORY
MUSEUM

HANS
CHRISTIAN
ANDERSEN
HOUSE

BANGS
BODER

OVERGADE

OVERSTRÆDE

FREDERIKSGADE

Fisketorvet

KONGENSGADE

VINTAPPERSTR.

9

GRÅBRØDRE
PASSAGE

8

TOWN
HALL

7

VESTERGADE

*Skt. Knuds
Plads*

SKT.
KNUD'S

To
Route 9
(Svendborg
& Ærø)

ALBANIGADE

BRANDTS
KLÆDEFABRIK
MALL

To
5

VESTERGADE

HANS
CHRISTIAN
ANDERSEN'S
CHILDHOOD HOME

KLOSTERBAKKEN

H.C. Andersen
Have

FILOSOFGANGEN

Odense Å

Munkemose

To
Funen Village &
E-20 Motorway
(Copenhagen & Aarhus)

1 Radisson
H. C. A. Hotel

2 Cab-Inn Odense

3 Hotel Domir

4 Ydes Hotel

5 To Blommenslyst B&B

6 Danhostel Odense City

7 Vestergade Eateries

8 Kongensgade
Eateries

9 Vintapperstræde
Eateries

needed for a longer stop, pick
up their excellent and free *Go
Odense* guide. If you plan to
visit multiple sights, consider
the **Odense Pass,** which
fully covers the museum at
H. C.'s birthplace, city history museum, art museum,
railway museum, and open-

air folk museum. It saves you money if you visit at least three sights
(159 kr, buy at TI).

Arrival in Odense

The train station is located in the Bånegard Center, a large shopping complex, which also holds the bus station, library (with free Internet access), Galaxy Internet café, shops, eateries, and a movie theater. For a quick visit, check your luggage at the train station (20/40-kr lockers in corridor next to DSB Resjebureau office), pick up a free town map inside the ticket office, jot down the time your train departs, and hit the town (follow signs to *Odense Centrum*).

To make a beeline to the **Hans Christian Andersen House,** turn left out of the station and walk to the corner (at the Cab-Inn). Turn right across the busy street and head one block down Nørregade, then turn left (at the Super Spar market) down Skulkenborg. After one short block, turn right and walk along the highway to the crosswalk by the yellow Oluf Bagers Gård; crossing here will put you at the start of a cute cobbled zone with the Hans Christian Andersen House on your right.

To get to the **TI,** turn right out of the station, cross the busy road, then cut through the Kongens Have (King's Garden) park and head down Jernabanegade. When you come to Vestergade, take a left and follow this fine pedestrian street 100 yards to the TI.

Sights in Odense

Note that some of Odense's museums charge higher admission (about 15-20 kr extra) during school holidays.

▲▲▲**Hans Christian Andersen House**—To celebrate Hans Christian Andersen's 100th birthday in 1904, the city founded this museum in the house where he was born. Today the humble (and rebuilt) house is the corner of an expansive, high-tech museum packed with mementos from the writer's life—and hordes of children and tourists. You could spend several delightful hours here getting into his life story and work. It's fun if you like the man and his tales.

Cost and Hours: 70 kr (30 percent discount if you have a ticket for Fyrtøjet or **Møntergården**—see next two listings), free for kids under 18, daily 10:00-16:00, July-late-Aug until 17:00, Bangs Boder 29, tel. 65 51 46 01, www.museum.odense.dk.

Information: Everything is well described in English. The 50-kr guidebook is unnecessary, but makes a nice souvenir. For more on the author, see the sidebars on pages 66 and 81.

Performances: The garden fairy-tale theater—with pleas-

CENTRAL DENMARK

ing vignettes—thrills kids daily in July and early August in the museum garden at 11:00, 13:00, and 15:00, weather permitting (30-minute show in Danish, but fun regardless of language).

Eating: The café next door offers seating indoors and out with sandwiches, burgers, and pancakes (80-120 kr).

Visiting the Museum: At the ticket desk, pick up the floor plan and follow the one-way route through the collection. Touchscreens invite you to delve deeper into specific topics, and headsets and benches throughout let you to listen to a selection of fairy tales.

You'll kick things off with **"The Age"** exhibit, which considers the era in which Andersen lived (1805-1875), putting the author in his historical context—the time of Abraham Lincoln, Charles Darwin, and Karl Marx. "The Man" paints a portrait of this quirky individual, who was extremely tall and gangly, with a big nose...an ugly duckling, indeed. He spent hours in the mirror perfecting an expression of wry cleverness for photographic portraits (several of which are displayed). You'll learn how bad teeth caused H. C. a lifetime of pain, and how this deeply sensitive, introspective fellow worried about his family history of mental illness even as he astounded the world with his exuberant creativity. "The Art" demonstrates that H. C. was as talented with visual arts as the written word; this darkened room shows off intricate paper cutouts he created (some of which illustrated his tales) and sketches from his travels.

"The Life" is a circular exhibit (turn left and proceed counterclockwise, following the footprints) with a step-by-step biography of the writer, accompanied by artifacts from his life. This is arranged around a central Memorial Hall slathered with eight frescoes depicting scenes from H. C.'s past, under a dome filled with natural light. Notice that as the story of his life—starting with a tearful hug to his mother on his departure from Odense at age 14—progresses, the scenes change from daylight to sunset to evening. Under the dome are items relating to H. C.'s fervent crush on the opera singer Jenny Lind: a love letter that he wrote to her, and the champagne glass she used to toast him as her "brother" (a painful rebuff that broke H. C.'s heart—he kept the glass his entire life as a reminder).

Continuing around the biographical section, you'll pass a movie theater with a 13-minute introductory **film** about

CENTRAL DENMARK

H. C. (plays every 15 minutes, alternates between Danish and English).

Don't miss the stairs down into the basement, where you'll find the **"Cabinet of Curiosities"**—several items that belonged to H. C. While some are ordinary (his top hat, pocket watch, pen, shaving kit, lock of hair, vest, and so on), other items have fascinating stories to tell. The 30-foot length of rope was an essential bit of travel gear for H. C., who went around the world; the phobic author kept it in his hotel room so that he could escape in case of fire. Displayed next to his actual bed is an eight-panel screen decorated with impressively detailed sketches by H. C. himself of his travels and his friends (executed while he was stuck in his apartment recovering from illness).

Near the top of the steps, you can enter H. C.'s **birth house,** with descriptions of the people his family lived with and repli-

cas of the type of furniture that likely filled these humble rooms. Later on, the author was highly ashamed of having been born in such a modest house in a very poor neighborhood—the theme of poverty turns up frequently in his works.

Near the end of the exhibit is a recreation of H. C.'s **study** from his apartment in Nyhavn, Copenhagen. You'll exit through "The Works," a library of Andersen's books from around the world (his tales have been translated into nearly 150 languages). The museum gift shop is full of mobiles, cut-paper models, and English versions of Andersen's fairy tales.

Another H. C. House: The writer's childhood home (with a small exhibit of its own) is a few blocks southwest of here, but it's skippable because the main museum here is so excellent and comprehensive.

Fyrtøjet ("Tinderbox")—Next door to the H. C. Andersen House is this privately run, modern, and fun hands-on center for children based on works by H. C. The centerpiece is Fairytale Land, with giant props and sets inspired by the author's tales. Kids can dress up in costumes and get their faces painted at the "magical wardrobe," act out a fairy tale, and do arts and crafts in the "atelier." Ask about performances (generally daily at 12:00 and 14:00; some are in Danish only, but others are done without dialogue).

Cost and Hours: 80 kr for ages 3-69 (free to other ages), 30 percent discount if you have a ticket for the H. C. Andersen House or **Møntergården;** July-mid-Aug daily 10:00-17:00; off-season Fri-Sun 10:00-16:00, closed Mon-Thu; Hans Jensens Stræde 21, tel. 66 14 44 11, www.fyrtoejet.com. On school holidays, there are more activities, the museum is open later (until 17:00), and you'll pay 15 kr extra.

▲**Møntergården (Urban History Museum)**—This well-presented museum, three short blocks from the H. C. Andersen House, fills several medieval buildings with exhibits on the history of Odense. You'll time-travel from prehistoric times (lots of arrow, spear, and ax heads) through to 1660, when the king stripped the town of its independent status. The main exhibit, "Life of the City," fills a stately 17th-century, red house (Falk Gøyes Gård) with a high-tech, well-presented exhibit about Odense in medieval and Renaissance times, covering historical events as well as glimpses of everyday life. Wedged along the side of this building is a surviving medieval lane; at the far end are four miniscule houses which the city used to house widows and orphaned students who couldn't afford to provide for themselves. It's fascinating to squeeze into these humble interiors and imagine that people lived in these almshouses through 1955 (open only in summer, but at other times you can ask at the ticket desk to have them unlocked). A new museum building with expanded exhibits may be open by the time you visit.

Cost and Hours: 50 kr, 30 percent discount if you have a ticket for the H. C. Andersen House or **Fyrtøjet;** Tue-Sun 10:00-16:00, closed Mon; Overgade 48, tel. 65 51 46 01, www.museum .odense.dk.

▲**Danish Railway Museum (Danmarks Jernbanemuseum)**— Conveniently (and appropriately) located directly behind the train

station, this is an ideal place to kill time while waiting for a train—and is worth a look for anyone who enjoys seeing old locomotives and train cars. Here at Denmark's biggest (and only official) rail museum, the huge round-house is filled with classic trains, while upstairs you'll walk past long display cases of model trains and enjoy good views down onto the trains. The information is in English, and there are lots of children's activities.

Cost and Hours: 60 kr, daily 10:00-16:00; Dannebrogsgade 24—just exit behind the station, near track 7/8, and cross the street; tel. 66 13 66 30, www.railmuseum.dk.

Funen Art Museum (Fyns Kunstmuseum)—This small, pleasant museum displays Danish art from 1750 to the present. The chronological exhibit starts on the first floor, where you'll see everything from Danish Romanticism (portraits, landscapes, and slice-of-life scenes) to the earliest inklings of Modernism. Down on the ground floor, the collection gets very abstract. Abstraction seems to suit the Danes, skilled as they are with clean, eye-pleasing design. The large central courtyard is filled with temporary exhibits.

Cost and Hours: 50 kr, Tue-Sun 10:00-16:00, closed Mon, Jernbanegade 13, tel. 65 51 46 01, www.museum.odense.dk.

▲**Funen Village/Den Fynske Landsby Open-Air Museum**— The sleepy gathering of 26 old buildings located about two miles out of town preserves the 18th-century culture of this region. There are no explanations in the buildings, because many school groups who visit play guessing games. Buy the guidebook to make your visit meaningful.

Cost and Hours: 80 kr in summer, 60 kr off-season; July-mid-Aug daily 10:00-18:00; April-June and mid-Aug-late Oct Tue-Sun 10:00-17:00, closed Mon; closed late Oct-March except grounds—but not buildings—open Sun only; bus #110 or #111 from Odense station, or take train to Fruens Bøge station and walk 15 minutes, tel. 65 51 46 01, www.museum.odense.dk.

Sleeping in Odense

(6 kr = about $1, country code: 45)

The demand (and prices) are higher in Odense on weekdays and in winter; in summer and on weekends, you can often get a better deal.

$$$ Radisson H. C. A. Hotel is big, comfortable, and impersonal, with 145 rooms a block from the Hans Christian Andersen House. It's older but nicely updated, and offers great rates every day through the summer (Sb-1,445 kr, Db-1,595 kr, elevator, free Internet access and Wi-Fi, Claus Bergs Gade 7, tel. 66 14 78 00, fax 66 14 78 90, www.radissonblu.com/hotel-odense, hcandersen @radissonblu.com).

$$ Cab-Inn Odense brings its no-frills minimalist economy to town, with 201 simple, comfy, and modern rooms (economy Sb-495 kr, Db-625 kr; standard Sb-545 kr, Db-675 kr; larger "Commodore" Sb-575 kr, Db-705 kr; biggest "Captains Class" Sb-675 kr, Db-805 kr; breakfast-70 kr, elevator, free Internet and Wi-Fi, parking for small cars only-80 kr/day, next to the station at Østre Stationsvej 7-9, tel. 63 14 57 00, www.cabinn.com, odense @cabinn.com). For more about this chain, see page 118.

$$ Hotel Domir, recently remodeled with new bathrooms, has 35 tidy, basic, stylish little rooms along its tiny halls. It's located on a quiet side-street just a few minutes from the train station and features extra soundproofing (Sb-575-695 kr, twin Db-650-745 kr, double bed for 100 kr more, Tb-800-845 kr, price depends on demand, elevator, free Internet access and Wi-Fi, limited parking-50-100 kr/day, free loaner bikes, Hans Tausensgade 19, tel. 66 12 14 27, fax 66 12 14 13, www.domir.dk, booking@domir.dk). They also run **Ydes Hotel,** just down the street, with industrial and metallic simplicity (about 50-70 kr cheaper).

$$ Blommenslyst B&B rents four rooms in two private guesthouses just outside Odense (S-330 kr, D-460 kr, breakfast-70 kr, 10-minute drive from town center, Ravnebjerggyden 31, tel. 65 96 81 88, www.blommenslyst.dk, ingvartsen-speth@post.tele.dk, Marethe and Poul Erik Speth).

Hostel: **$ Danhostel Odense City** is a huge, efficient hostel towering above the train station, with 140 beds in 4- and 6-bed rooms with baths, plus private rooms. "Better" rooms have "better beds and a TV"; the room prices listed here reflect standard/better rooms (dorm bed-250 kr, Sb-450/500 kr, Db-620/670 kr, sheets-60 kr, breakfast-65 kr—it can add up, elevator, pay Internet access, free Wi-Fi, laundry, reception open 8:00-12:00 & 16:00-20:00 but self-service check-in kiosk at other times, Østre Stationsvej 31, tel. 63 11 04 25, odensedanhostel.dk, info@cityhostel.dk).

Eating in Odense

If you are in town for just a short stopover to visit the Hans Christian Andersen House, consider the café at the museum for lunch. Otherwise, Odense's main pedestrian shopping streets, **Vestergade** and **Kongensgade,** offer the best atmosphere and most options for lunch and dinner.

Vintapperstræde is an alleyway full of restaurants just off Vestergade (look for the ornamental entryway). Choose from Danish, Mexican, Italian, and more. Study the menus posted outside each restaurant to decide, then grab a table inside or join the locals at an outdoor table.

Odense Connections

From Odense by Train to: Copenhagen (3/hour, 1.75 hours, some go direct to the airport), **Aarhus** (2/hour, 1.5 hours), **Billund/Legoland** (2/hour, 50-minute train to Vejle; transfer to bus #43, #143, #166, or #179; allow 2 hours total), **Svendborg/Ærø ferry** (2/hour on Mon-Sat, hourly on Sun, 45 minutes, to Svendborg dock—Ærø ferry runs 5-6/day, 75-minute crossing), **Roskilde** (2/hour, 70 minutes).

Route Tips for Drivers

Aarhus or Billund to Ærø: Figure about two hours to drive from Billund (or 2.5 hours from Aarhus) to Svendborg. The freeway takes you over a bridge to the island of Funen (or *Fyn* in Danish); from Odense, take the highway south to Svendborg.

Leave your car in Svendborg (at the convenient long-term parking lot two blocks from the ferry dock or at the far end of the harbor near the Bendix fish shop) and sail for Ærø. It's an easy 75-minute crossing; note there are only five or six boats a day (see page 178). Cars need reservations but walk-on passengers don't.

Ærø to Copenhagen via Odense: From Svendborg, drive north following signs to *Fëborg*, past Egeskov Castle, and on to Odense. For the open-air folk museum (Den Fynske Landsby), leave Route 9 just south of town at Højby, turning left toward Dalum and the Odense campground (on Odensevej). Look for *Den Fynske Landsby* signs (near the train tracks, south edge of town). If you're going directly to the Hans Christian Andersen House, follow the signs.

Continuing toward Copenhagen, you'll take the world's third-longest suspension bridge (Storebælt Bridge, 220-kr toll, 12.5 miles long). Follow signs marked *København* (Copenhagen). If you're following my three-week itinerary by car: When you get to Ringsted, signs point you to Roskilde—aim toward the twin church spires and follow signs for *Vikingskibene* (Viking ships). Otherwise, if you're heading to Copenhagen or the airport, stay on the freeway, following signs to *København C* or to *Dragør/Kastrup Airport.*

JUTLAND

Aarhus • Legoland • Jelling

Jutland (Jylland—pronounced "YEW-lan"—in Danish) is the part of Denmark that juts up from Germany. It's a land of windswept sandy beaches, inviting lakes, Lego toys, moated manor houses, and fortified old towns. In Aarhus, the lively and student-filled capital of Jutland, you can ogle the artwork in one of Denmark's best art museums, experience centuries-old Danish town life in its open-air folk museum, and meet a boggy prehistoric man. After you wander the pedestrian street, settle in to nurse a drink along the canalside people zone. This region is particularly family-friendly. Make a pilgrimage to the most famous land in all of Jutland: the pint-sized kids' paradise, Legoland. The nearby village of Jelling is worth a quick stop to see the ancient rune stones known as "Denmark's birth certificate."

Planning Your Time

Aarhus makes a natural stop for drivers connecting Kristiansand, Norway and Hirtshals, Denmark by ferry. Trains also link Aarhus to Hirtshals, as well as to points south, such as Odense and Copenhagen. Allow one day and an overnight to enjoy this busy port town.

Families will likely want a whole day at Legoland (near the town of Billund), while historians might consider a brief detour to Jelling, just 10 minutes off the main Billund-Vejle road. Both are best by car but are doable by public transportation.

Aarhus

Aarhus (OAR-hoos, sometimes spelled Århus), Denmark's second-largest city, has a population of 243,000 and calls itself the "World's Smallest Big City." I'd
argue it's more like the world's biggest little town: easy to handle and easy to like. Aarhus is Jutland's capital and cultural hub. Its Viking founders settled here—where a river hit the sea— in the eighth century, calling their town Aros. Today, modern Aarhus bustles with an important university, an inviting café-lined canal, a bursting-with-life pedestrian boulevard (Strøget), a collection of top-notch museums (modern art, open-air folk, and prehistory), and an adorable "Latin Quarter" filled with people living very, very well. Aarhus, a pleasant three-hour train ride from Copenhagen, is well worth a stop.

Orientation to Aarhus

Aarhus lines up along its tranquil canal—formerly a busy highway—called Åboulevarden, which runs through the middle of town. The cathedral and lively Latin Quarter are directly north of the canal, while the train station is about five blocks to the south (along the main pedestrianized shopping street—the Strøget). The main museums are scattered far and wide: The ARoS Art Museum is at the western edge of downtown, the Den Gamle By open-air folk museum is a bit farther to the northwest, and the Moesgård Museum (prehistory—and closed for renovation until 2014) is in the countryside far to the south.

Tourist Information

The Aarhus TI has become entirely virtual (www.visitaarhus.com). There's no office and no telephone number; to fill the gap, the local tourist board has installed computer kiosks that access the TI website in various hotel lobbies around town. But if you have a question, try asking your hotelier or other helpful locals. Hotels sell the **Aarhus Card,** which provides small discounts on major sights and free entry to some minor sights, and includes public transportation. This can be a money-saver for busy sightseers (129 kr/1 day, 179 kr/2 days).

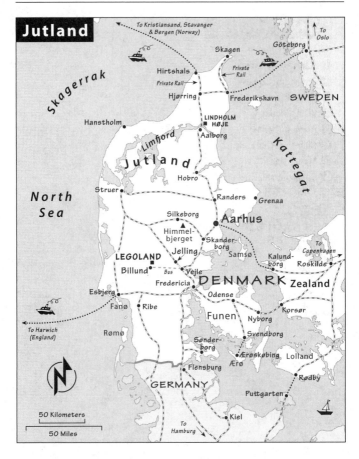

Arrival in Aarhus

At Aarhus' user-friendly train station, all tracks feed into a con-course, with ticket offices *(billetsalg)* and a waiting room between tracks 2-3 and 4-5. One direction (marked *Bruun's Galleri*), takes you directly into a shopping mall; the other direction (under the clock), leads into the blocky main terminal hall, with lockers (20-40 kr), fast food, and automated ticket machines. Near the main doors, notice electronic screens showing departure times for upcoming city and regional buses.

To get into town, it's a pleasant 10-minute walk: Exit straight ahead, cross the street, and proceed up the wide, traffic-free shop-ping street known as the Strøget, which takes you directly to the canal, cathedral, and start of my self-guided walk.

Aarhus Center

Self-Guided Walk
1. Aarhus Cathedral
2. Cathedral Square
3. Hotel Royal
4. Viking Museum
5. Aarhus Theater
6. Church of Our Lady
7. Møllestien
8. Canal (Åboulevarden)

200 Meters
200 Yards

Botanical Gardens

DEN GAMLE BY FOLK MUSEUM

MAIN ENTRANCE

Canal

Mølleparken

ARoS ART MUSEUM

GODSBANEGÅRD

CONCERT HALL

JUTLAND

Rådhuspladsen

TOWN HALL

Bus #4A, #11, #15 & #19

Bus #18 & #16

Banegårds-pladsen

To 25

Hotels, Restaurants & Services
9. Villa Provence
10. Hotel Guldsmeden
11. Best Western Hotel Ritz
12. Scandic Plaza Aarhus Hotel
13. Cab-Inn
14. To Danhostel Aarhus
15. City Sleep In
16. Lecoq Restaurant
17. Den Rustikke Brasserie
18. Pilhkjær Restaurant
19. Jacob's Pita Bar
20. Sota Sushi
21. Carlton Brasserie
22. Åboulevarden Canal Eateries
23. Bryggeriet Sct. Clemens
24. Teater Bodega
25. To Launderette

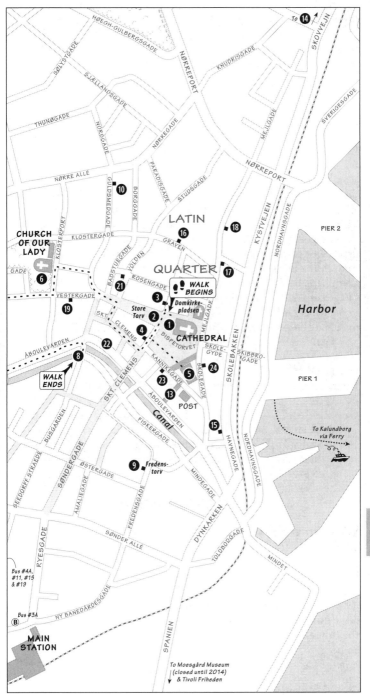

Getting Around Aarhus

The sights mentioned in my self-guided walk and the ARoS Art Museum are all within a 15-minute walk; the Den Gamle By open-air folk museum is a few minutes farther, but still walkable. The Moesgård Museum (prehistory; closed until 2014) and Tivoli Friheden (amusement park) are best reached by bus.

You can buy bus tickets from the coin-op machines on board the bus (a 20-kr, 2-zone ticket covers any of my recommended sights, and is good for 2 hours). Bus drivers are friendly and speak English.

A few local buses leave from in front of the train station, but most depart around the corner, along Park Allé in front of the Town Hall. Bus #3A to the Den Gamle By open-air folk museum leaves from a stop across the street from the station. Other buses leave from in front of the Town Hall, about two blocks away: Cross the street in front of the station, turn left and walk to the first major corner, then turn right up Park Allé; the stops are in front of the blocky Town Hall (with the boxy tower, on the left). From here, buses #4A, #11, #15, and #19 go to Den Gamle By; bus #16 goes to the Tivoli Friheden amusement park; and bus #18 goes to the Moesgård Museum. To help you find your bus stop, look for the handy bus-stop diagram at the start of the Strøget.

Taxis are easy to flag down but pricey (30-kr drop fee).

Helpful Hints

Internet Access: Many hotels, cafés, and restaurants offer free Wi-Fi.

Laundry: An unstaffed, coin-op launderette *(mønt-vask)* is four short blocks south of the train station, on the square in front of St. Paul's Church (daily 7:30-21:00, bring lots of coins—30 kr to wash, about 25 kr to dry, 5 kr for soap, M.P. Bruuns-gade 64).

Self-Guided Walk

Welcome to Aarhus

This quick little walk acquaints you with the historic center, covering everything of sightseeing importance except the three big museums (modern art, prehistory, and open-air folk). You'll begin at the cathedral, check out the modest sights in its vicinity, wander the cute Latin Quarter, take a stroll down the "most beautiful street" in Aarhus, and end at the canal. After touring the impressive cathedral, the rest of the walk should take about an hour.

• *Start by touring Aarhus Cathedral.*

▲▲Aarhus Cathedral (Domkirke)

While Scandinavia's biggest church (330 feet long and tall) is typically stark-white inside, it also comes with some vivid decorations dating from before the Reformation.

Cost and Hours: Free entry; May-Sept Mon and Wed-Sat 9:30-16:00, Tue 10:30-16:00; Oct-April Mon and Wed-Sat 10:00-15:00, Tue 10:30-15:00; closed Sun except for services at 12:00 and 17:00; www.aarhus -domkirke.dk.

Visiting the Cathedral: The cathedral was finished in 1520 in all its Catholic glory. Imagine it with 55 side chapels, each dedicated to a different saint and wallpapered with colorful frescos. Bad timing. Just 16 years later, in 1536, the Reformation hit and Protestants cleaned out the church—side altars gone, paintings whitewashed over—and added a pulpit mid-nave so parishioners could hear the sermon. The front pews were even turned away from the altar to face the pulpit (a problem for weddings today).

Ironically, that Lutheran whitewash protected the fine 16th-century Catholic art. When it was peeled back in the 1920s, the fres-

coes were found perfectly preserved. In 1998, the surrounding whitewash was redone, making the old original paintings, which have never been restored, pop. Noble tombs that once lined the floor (worn smooth by years of traffic) now decorate the walls. The fancy text-filled wall medallions are epitaphs, originally paired with tombs. Ships hang from the ceilings of many Danish churches (you'll find a fine example in the left transept)—in this nation of seafarers, there were invariably women praying for the safe return of their sailors.

Step into the enclosed choir area at the front of the church. The main altarpiece, dating from 1479, features the 12 apostles flanking St. Clement (the patron saint of Aarhus and sailors—his symbol is the anchor), St. Anne, and John the Baptist. On top, Jesus is crowning Mary in heaven.

Head down the stairs to the apse area behind the altar. Find the model of the altarpiece, which demonstrates how the polyptych (many-paneled altarpiece) you just saw can be flipped to different scenes throughout the church year.

Also in this area, look for the fresco in the aisle (right of altar, facing windows) that shows a three-part universe: heaven, earth (at Mass), and—under the thick black line—purgatory...an ugly land with angels and devils fighting over souls. The kid on the gallows illustrates how the medieval Church threatened even little children with ugly damnation. Notice the angels trying desperately to save the damned. Just a little more money to the Church and...I...think...we...can...pull...Grandpa...OUT.

An earlier Romanesque church—just as huge—once stood on this spot. As you exit, notice the tiny, pointy-topped window in the back-right. It survives with its circa-1320 fresco from that earlier church. Even back then—when the city had a population of 1,000—the church seated 1,200. Imagine the entire community (and their dogs) assembled here to pray and worship their way through the darkness and uncertainty of medieval life.

• *Then, standing at the cathedral door, survey the...*

Cathedral Square

The long, triangular square is roughly the shape of the original Viking town from A.D. 770. Aarhus is the Viking word for "mouth of river." The river flows to your left to the beach, which—before modern land reclamation—was just behind the church. The green spire peeking over the buildings dead ahead is the Church of Our Lady (which we'll visit later on this walk). Fifty yards to the right, the nubile caryatids by local artist Hans Krull decorate the entry to the **Hotel Royal** and town casino. (Krull's wildly decorated bar is just beyond, down the stairs at the corner.)

• *Fifty yards to the left of the church (as you face the square), in the basement of the Nordea Bank, is the tiny...*

Viking Museum

When excavating the site for the bank building in 1960, remains of Viking Aarhus were uncovered. Today you can ride an escalator down to the little bank-sponsored museum showing a surviving bit of the town's original boardwalk *in situ* (where it was found), Viking artifacts, and a murder victim (missing his head)—all well-described in English.

Cost and Hours: Free, open bank hours: Mon-Fri 10:00-16:00, Thu until 17:30, closed Sat-Sun.
• *Leaving the bank, walk straight ahead along the substantial length of the cathedral (brides have plenty of time to reconsider things during their procession) to the fancy building opposite.*

Aarhus Theater

This ornate facade, with its flowery stained glass, is Danish Art Nouveau from around 1900. Under the tiny balcony is the town

seal, featuring towers, the river, St. Clement with his anchor, and St. Paul with his sword. High above, on the roofline, crouches the devil. The local bishop made a stink when this "house of sin" was allowed to be built facing the cathedral. The theater build-ers had the last say, finishing their structure with this smart-aleck devil triumphing (this was a hit with the secular, modern locals).
• *Return to the square in front of the cathedral.*

Latin Quarter

The higgledy-piggledy old town encompasses the six or eight square blocks in front of the cathedral and to the right. Latin was

never spoken here—the area was named in the 1960s after the cute, boutique-ish, and similarly touristy zone in Paris. Though Aarhus' canal strip is the new trendy spot, the Latin Quarter is still great for shopping, cafés, and strolling. Explore

these streets: Volden (named for the rampart), Graven (moat), and Badstuegade ("Bath Street"). In the days when fires routinely deci-mated towns, bathhouses—with their open fires necessary to heat the water—were located outside the walls. Back in the 15th cen-tury, finer people bathed monthly, while everyday riff-raff took their "Christmas bath" once a year.
• *Back at the far end of the cathedral square, side-trip away from the cathedral to the green spire of the...*

Church of Our Lady (Vor Frue Kirke)

The smart brick building you see today is in the Dutch Renaissance style from the 15th century, but this local "Notre-Dame" is the

oldest church in town. After Christianity came to Viking Denmark in 965, a tiny wooden church was built here. The crypt of its 11th-century stone rebuild was discovered in 1955. Four rune stones were also discovered on this site. Enter the church around the back, and climb below the main altar into an evocative arcaded space (c. 1060). Like the Aarhus Cathedral, the church's whitewashed walls are covered with fine epitaph medallions with family portraits. Step through the low door behind the rear pew (on the right with your back to the altar) into the peaceful cloister. With the Reformation, this became a hospital. Today, it's a retirement home for lucky seniors.

Cost and Hours: Free; May-Aug Mon-Fri 10:00-16:00, Sat 10:00-14:00; Sept-April Mon-Fri 10:00-14:00, Sat 10:00-12:00; closed Sun year-round, www.aarhusvorfrue.dk.

• *Walk west on Vestergade to the next street, Grønnegade. Turn left, then take the next right onto...*

Møllestien

Locals call this quiet little cobbled lane the "most beautiful street in Aarhus." The small, pastel cottages—draped in climbing roses and hollyhock in summer—date from the 18th century. Notice the small mirrors on some of the windows. Known as "street spies," they allow people inside to inconspicuously watch what's going on outside.

• *At the end of the lane, head left toward the canal. The park on your right, Mølleparken, is a good spot for a picnic. The big, boxy building with the rainbow ring on top is the ARoS Art Museum (described later, under "Sights in Aarhus")—consider visiting it now, or backtrack here when the walk is over.*

When you reach the canal, turn left and walk until you get to the concrete bridge. Stand with the Mølleparken toward your right.

Canal (Åboulevarden)

You're standing on the site of the original Viking bridge. The open sea was to the left. A protective harbor was to the right. When attacked, the bridge on this spot was raised, ships were tucked safely away, and townsmen stood here to defend their fleet. Given the choice, they'd let the town burn and save their ships.

In the 1930s, the Aarhus River was covered over to make a new road—an event marked by much celebration. In the 1980s, locals reconsidered the change, deciding that the road cut a boring, people-mean swath through the center of their town. They removed the road, artfully canalized the river, and created a trendy new people zone—the town's place to see and be seen. This strip of modern restaurants ensures the street stays as lively as possible even after the short summer.

• *Your walk is over. Following the canal to the right takes you to **ARoS Art Museum**, then to the **Den Gamle By** open-air folk museum. Following it to the left takes you past the best of the Aarhus canal zone. Crossing the canal and going straight (with a one-block jog left) gets you to the Strøget pedestrian boulevard, which leads all the way to the train station (where you can catch a bus—either at the station or the Town Hall nearby—to Tivoli Friheden amusement park, the Den Gamle By open-air folk museum, or the Moesgård Museum). All of these sights are described in the next section.*

Sights in Aarhus

▲▲**ARoS**—The Aarhus Art Museum is a must-see sight, both for the building's architecture and for its knack for making cutting-edge art accessible and fun. Everything is described in English. Square and unassuming from the outside, the bright white interior—with its spiral staircase winding up the museum's eight floors— is surprising. The building has two sections, one for the exhibits and one for administration. The halves are divided by a vast atrium, which is free to enter if you just want to peek at the building itself (or to visit the gift shop or café). But to see any of the items described below, you'll have to buy a ticket. In  addition to the permanent collections that I've described, the museum displays an impressive range of temporary exhibits—be sure to find out what's on during your visit.

Cost and Hours: 100 kr; Tue-Sun 10:00-17:00, Wed-Thu until 22:00; closed Mon, ARoS Allé 2, tel. 87 30 66 00, www.aros .dk.

Eating: The lunch café on the museum's ground floor serves 60-125-kr light meals, while the fancier restaurant on the top floor serves 190-kr lunch specials.

Visiting the Museum: After entering at the fourth-floor

lobby, buy your ticket, pick up a museum floor plan, and walk two floors down the spiral staircase (to Floor 2) to find one of the museum's prized pieces: the squatting sculpture called *Boy* (by Australian artist Ron Mueck)—15 feet high, yet astonishingly realistic, from the wrinkly skin on his elbows to the stitching on his shorts.

Next, head down to the lowest level. Here, amid black walls, artists from around the world (including Bill Viola and James Turrell) exhibit their immersive works of light and sound in each of nine spaces *(De 9 Rum)*. In this unique space, you're plunged into the imagination of the artist.

Now ride the elevator all the way to the top floor (Floor 8), then climb up the stairs (or ride a different elevator) to the rooftop.

Here you can enjoy the museum's newest icon: Olafur Eliasson's *Your Rainbow Panorama,* a 150-yard-long, 52-yard-diameter circular walkway enclosed in glass that gradually incorporates all the different colors of the spectrum. The piece provides 360-degree views over the city, while you're immersed in mind-bending, highly saturated hues. (It's "your" panorama because you are experiencing the colors.) This recent addition is a striking contrast to the mostly dark and claustrophobic works you've just seen in the nine spaces down below—yet, like those, it's all about playing with light. It's also practical—from a distance, it can be used by locals throughout the city as a giant compass (provided they know which color corresponds with which direction).

Back on Floor 8, stroll through the manageable permanent collection of works from 1770 to 1930. Paintings dating from the **Danish Golden Age** (1800-1850) are evocative of the dewy-eyed Romanticism that swept Europe during that era: pastoral scenes of flat Danish countryside and seascapes, slices of peasant life, aristocratic portraits, "postcards" from travels to the Mediterranean world, and poignant scenes of departures and arrivals at Danish seaports. The **Danish Modernist** section, next, mostly feels derivative of big-name artists (you'll see the Danish answers to Picasso, Matisse, Modigliani, and others).

Continue down the spiral staircase, past various temporary exhibits. On Floor 5, take a spin through the **contemporary art**

gallery, featuring art (including many multimedia installations) since 1980. Like the rest of this museum, these high-concept, navel-gazing works are well-presented and very accessible.

▲▲**Den Gamle By**—"The Old Town" open-air folk museum has 75 half-timbered houses and craft shops. Unlike other

Scandinavian open-air museums that focus on rural folk life, Den Gamle By is designed to give you the best possible look at Danish urban life in centuries past. A fine botanical garden is next door.

Cost: Because peak-season days offer more activities, the cost depends on the time of year. July–mid-Sept: 125 kr, April–June and mid-Sept–mid-Nov: 100 kr; Jan–March: 50 kr; mid-Nov–Dec: special Christmas-themed events and prices.

Hours: Daily July–mid-Sept 10:00-18:00; shorter hours off-season. After hours, the buildings of the open-air museum are locked, but the peaceful park is open (tel. 86 12 31 88, www.den gamleby.dk).

Getting There: Stroll 20 minutes up the canal from down-town, or catch a bus from near the train station: Bus #3A departs directly across the street from the station, while others (#4A, #11, #15, and #19) depart across the street from the Town Hall, on Park Allé.

Eating: This is a perfect place to enjoy a picnic lunch (bring your own, or order a lunch packet at the reception desk by the ticket booth)—outdoor and indoor tables are scattered around the grounds. The only eatery in the park open year-round is the cheery indoor/outdoor Simonsens Have, an inviting cafeteria serving affordable light meals (30-kr sandwiches, three *smørrebrød* for 60 kr). In peak season, you'll have many other options, including *pølse* and other snack stands, a café next to the ticket kiosk, and Wineke's Cellar, an 18th-century public house serving beer, wine, and sandwiches (in the basement of the Mintmaster's Mansion).

Visiting the Museum: At the ticket desk, pick up the free map of the grounds; also pick up the flier listing what's on (and plan your time around taking advantage of those options). Though each building is described with a plaque, and there are maps throughout the park, the 50-kr guidebooklet is a worthwhile investment and a nice souvenir.

The grounds reward an adventurous spirit. They're designed to be explored, so don't be too shy to open doors or poke into seemingly abandoned courtyards—you may find a chatty docent inside, telling their story, answering questions, or demonstrating an

old-timey handicraft. Follow sounds and smells to discover a whole world beyond the main streets.

The main part of the exhibit focuses on the 18th and 19th centuries. You'll start by heading up Navnløs, then hanging a right at Vestergade (passing a row house and a flower garden with samples for sale) to the canal. Head straight over the bridge and hike up the cute street lined with market stalls, shops, and a bakery until you pop out on the main square, Torvet. The building on the left side of Torvet, the Mayor's House (from 1597), contains a museum upstairs featuring home interiors from 1600 to 1850, including many with gorgeously painted walls. At the top of Torvet is the Mintmaster's Mansion, the residence of a Copenhagen noble (from 1683). Enter around back to tour the boldly colorful, 18th-century Baroque rooms. Under the heavy timbers of the attic is an exhibit about the history of this recently restored building.

Continuing out the far end of Torvet on Søndergade, you enter the 20th century. The streets and shops here evoke the year 1927, including a hardware store and (down Havbogade) a brewery where you can often buy samples (in the courtyard behind). At the end of Søndergade (on the left) is the Legetoj toy museum, with two floors of long hallways crammed with nostalgic playthings.

Walking into the next zone, you come to a street scene from 1974, including a hi-fi record shop and the Udstillinger building, which houses the Danish Poster Museum (a delightful collection of retro posters) and the Gallery of Decorative Arts (porcelain, clocks, and silverware).

The area under construction on the right is where they are re-creating a harborfront area from the 1970s (due to open in 2014). Continue down along the construction zone, cross the canal, and turn right (back toward the entrance). You'll pass idyllic pond scenery and the Simonsens Have cafeteria, before winding up at the bridge you crossed earlier.

Moesgård Museum—The museum is closed until 2014, when its brand-new, state-of-the art building is due to open south of town. Billed as "cultural history in a new setting," the sloping build-

JUTLAND

ing will emerge from the
fields, with grass growing
on the roof; in addition to
the existing prehistory collection, plans call for new
exhibits on ethnography
and the Arabian Gulf, plus
space for temporary exhib-

its (tel. 89 42 11 00, www.moesmus.dk).

Tivoli Friheden Amusement Park—The local Tivoli, about a
mile south of the train station, offers great fun for the family.

Cost and Hours: 80 kr for entry only, 215 kr includes rides;
daily early July-early Aug 11:00-22:00, May-early July and early
Aug-Sept weekends only and shorter hours, closed Oct-April
except special events; bus #16 from Park Allé near Town Hall, tel.
86 14 73 00, www.friheden.dk.

Sleeping in Aarhus

My recommendations include the following: two tired business
hotels facing the train station with rates that flex with demand (a
good value if booked in advance and arriving on a weekend or in
the summer); two charming hotels with personality; a stripped-
down, functional, Motel 6-type place; and two backpacker/
student-friendly hostels.

$$$ Villa Provence, named for owners Steen and Annette's
favorite vacation destination, is a *petit* taste of France in the center
of Aarhus, and makes a very cozy and convenient home base. Its
40 fun-yet-tasteful rooms, decorated with antique furniture and
old French movie posters, surround a quiet courtyard. Prices vary
depending on the size and elegance of the room (Sb-1,095-2,300
kr, Db-1,295-2,900 kr, free Wi-Fi, parking-125 kr/day, 10-minute
walk from station, near Åboulevarden at the end of Fredensgade,
Fredens Torv 12, tel. 86 18 24 00, fax 86 18 24 03, www.villa
provence.dk, hotel@villaprovence.dk).

$$$ Hotel Guldsmeden ("Dragonfly") is a small, welcoming,
and clean hotel with 27 rooms, fluffy comforters, a delightful stay-
awhile garden, and a young, disarmingly friendly staff. A steep
staircase takes you to the best rooms (Sb-1,195 kr, Db-1,325 kr),
while the cheaper rooms (five rooms sharing two bathrooms) are in
a ground-floor annex behind the garden (S-745 kr, D-945 kr; extra
bed-250 kr, 10 percent off rooms with private bath with this book
based on availability, free Wi-Fi, 15-minute walk or 70-kr taxi
from the station, in Aarhus' quiet Latin Quarter at Guldsmedgade
40, tel. 86 13 45 50, fax 86 13 76 76, www.hotelguldsmeden.com,
aarhus@hotelguldsmeden.com).

JUTLAND

Sleep Code

(6 kr = about $1, country code: 45)

S = Single, **D** = Double/Twin, **T** = Triple, **Q** = Quad, **b** = bathroom, **s** = shower. You can assume credit cards are accepted and breakfast is included unless otherwise noted.

To help you sort easily through these listings, I've divided the accommodations into three categories based on the price for a standard double room with bath during high season:

$$$ Higher Priced—Most rooms 1,000 kr or more.
  $$ Moderately Priced—Most rooms between 500-1,000 kr.
   $ Lower Priced—Most rooms 500 kr or less.

Prices can change without notice; verify the hotel's current rates online or by email.

$$$ Best Western Hotel Ritz, also across the street from the station, has 67 older but clean rooms. It's a bit less welcoming than my other listings (tiny budget Sb-765 kr, Sb-850-1,200 kr, Db-1,000-1,400 kr, bigger "superior" Db-1,300-1,600 kr, higher rates are for weekdays while lower rates are for weekends and summer, elevator, free Internet access and Wi-Fi, Banegårdspladsen 12, tel. 86 13 44 44, fax 86 13 45 87, www.hotelritz.dk, mail@hotel ritz.dk).

$$ Scandic Plaza Aarhus Hotel rents 162 sleek, well-furnished, business-class rooms 100 yards from the station (weekends and summer: Db-800-1,140 kr; weekdays: Db-1,240-1,915 kr; check website for best deals, kids under age 13 free, elevator, free Internet access and Wi-Fi, gym, Banegårdspladsen 14, tel. 87 32 01 00, fax 87 32 01 99, www.scandichotels.com, plaza.aarhus @scandichotels.com). They offer a 12-20 percent discount for pre-paid, nonrefundable "early rate" online bookings.

$$ Cab-Inn, overlooking the atmospheric Åboulevarden canal, is extremely practical. Its 197 simple, minimalist-yet-comfy little rooms each come with a single bed that expands into a twin and one or two fold-down bunks on the walls. The service, like the rooms, is no-nonsense (Sb-495 kr, Db-625-805 kr, Tb-805 kr, Qb-935 kr, breakfast-70 kr, free Wi-Fi, easy parking-80 kr—reserve ahead, rooms overlook boisterous canal or quieter courtyard, Kannikegade 14, tel. 86 75 70 00, fax 86 75 71 00, www.cabinn.dk, aarhus@cabinn.dk). For more on this chain, see page 118.

$ Danhostel Aarhus, an official HI hostel with six-bed dorms and plenty of two- and four-bed rooms, is near the water two miles out of town (dorm bed-200 kr, S/D-380-506 kr, Sb/Db-570-670 kr, price depends on season, nonmembers-35 kr/night extra, sheets-45 kr, towels-10 kr, adult breakfast-59 kr, kids break-fast-29 kr, pay Wi-Fi, laundry, served by several buses from the train station—see website for details, Marienlundsvej 10, tel. 86 21 21 20, www.aarhus-danhostel.dk, info@aarhus-danhostel.dk).

$ City Sleep In, a creative independent hostel, has a shared kitchen, fun living and games room, laundry service, and lockers. It's on a busy road facing the harbor (with thin windows—expect some street noise), a 15-minute hike from the station. It's pretty grungy, but is the only centrally located budget option in town (170 kr/bunk in 4- to 6-bed dorms, D-440 kr, Db-500 kr, extra bed-120 kr, sheets-50 kr, towel-20 kr, breakfast-65 kr, elevator, free Internet access and Wi-Fi; no curfew; reception open daily 8:00-11:00 & 16:00-19:00 & 19:30-21:00, Fri-Sat until 23:00; Havnegade 20, tel. 86 19 20 55, fax 86 19 18 11, www.citysleep-in .dk, sleep-in@citysleep-in.dk).

Eating in Aarhus

Affluent Aarhus has plenty of great little restaurants. All of these are in the old town, within a few minutes' stroll from the cathedral.

In the Latin Quarter

The streets of the Latin Quarter are teeming with hardworking and popular eateries. The street called Mejlgade, along the western edge of downtown, has a smattering of youthful, trendy restaurants that are just far enough off the tourist trail to feel local.

Lecoq is a pricey favorite. Chef/owner Troels Thomsen and his youthful gang (proud alums from a prestigious Danish cooking school) serve up a fresh twist on traditional French cuisine in a single Paris-pleasant yet unassuming 10-table room. They pride themselves on their finely crafted presentation. Reservations are smart (300-kr three-course meals, 200-kr main dishes, 100-kr starters, Thu 16:00-24:00, Fri 15:00-24:00, Sat-Wed 17:00-24:00, Graven 16, tel. 86 19 50 74). The attached bar, with outdoor seating, serves drinks only.

Den Rustikke is a French-style brasserie offering affordable, mostly French dishes, either in the rollicking interior or outside, under a cozy colonnade (45-85-kr lunches, 165-kr three-course dinners, daily 11:30-15:00 & 17:00-late, Mejlgade 20, tel. 86 12 00 95).

Pilhkjær is a bit more sedate, filling a cellar with elegantly casual atmosphere. The menu changes daily and is available only as a 300-kr, three-course meal—no à la carte (Tue-Thu 17:30-22:30, Fri-Sat 17:30-23:30, closed Sun-Mon, at the end of a long courtyard at Mejlgade 28, tel. 86 18 23 30).

Cheap Eats: **Jacob's Pita Bar** is a popular spot for pita sandwiches that are a cut above the average *shawarma*. Choose from grilled beef, chicken, lamb, ground beef, or turkey and melted cheese, plus your choice of a wide selection of sauces. These sandwiches are great for an inexpensive, quick meal: Sit at the counter, or get your order to go and find a spot to sit on the nearby square, along the canal, or Møllerparken (46-kr pita sandwiches, "menu" with fries and a drink-78 kr, Mon-Thu 11:00-21:00, Fri-Sat 11:00 until late, Sun 17:00-21:00, Vestergade 3, tel. 87 32 24 20). The pita bar is part of the adjacent, decent but overpriced steak house, Jacob's BarBQ (nightly until the wee hours).

Sushi: A few short blocks farther from the action (past the Church of Our Lady), **Sota** is a local favorite for sushi. This split-level sushi bar, in a half-timbered old house, is a sleek Tokyo-Scandinavian hybrid (50-90-kr rolls, 120-190-kr combo meals, pricier splurges available, Mon-Thu 16:00-22:00, Fri-Sat 16:00-23:00, closed Sun, Vestergade 47, tel. 86 47 47 88).

Carlton Brasserie, facing a pretty square, is a solid bet for good Danish and international food in classy (verging on stuffy) surroundings. The restaurant has tables on the square, with more formal seating in back (inviting menu, 135-235-kr plates, 380-kr formal three-course dinner, closed Sun, Rosensgade 23, tel. 86 20 21 22).

Along Åboulevarden Canal

The canal running through town is lined with trendy eateries—all overpriced unless you value making the scene with the locals (and all open daily until late). They have indoor and canalside seating with heaters and blankets, so diners can eat outdoors even when it's cold. Before settling in, cruise the entire strip, giving special consideration to **Cross Café** (with red awnings, right at main bridge) and **Ziggy,** both of which are popular for salads, sandwiches, burgers, and drinks; and **Grappa,** a classy Italian place with 95-135-kr pastas and pizzas, as well as pricier plates. Several places along here serve basic 25-45-kr breakfast buffets, which are popular with students for brunch.

Near the Cathedral

These places, while a bit past their prime and touristy, are convenient and central.

Bryggeriet Sct. Clemens (St. Clement's Brewery), facing the cathedral, is a bright, convivial, fun-loving, and woody land of happy eaters and drinkers. Choose from a hearty menu and eat amid shiny copper vats. If you're dropping by for just a beer, they have enticing 40-80-kr beer snacks—including little *Nürnberger* bratwurst (80-105-kr lunch and light meals; 175-270-kr hearty dinners such as steak, ribs, and fish; Mon-Sat 11:30-24:00, closed Sun, Kannikegade 10-12, tel. 86 13 80 00).

Teater Bodega is the venerable best bet for traditional Danish—where local men go for "food their wives won't cook." While a bit tired and old-fashioned for Aarhus' trendy young student population, it's a sentimental favorite for old-timers. Facing the theater and cathedral, it's dressy and draped in theater memorabilia (130-230-kr main dishes, 60-110-kr open-face sandwiches at lunch only, Mon-Sat 11:30-22:30, closed Sun, Skolegade 7, tel. 86 12 19 17).

Aarhus Connections

From Aarhus by Train to: Odense (2/hour, 1.5 hours), **Copenhagen** (1-2/hour, 3 hours), Ærøskøbing (5-6/day, transfer to ferry in Svendborg, total trip-4.25 hours, sample schedules: 10:27-14:45 or 13:27-17:45), **Hamburg, Germany** (2 direct/day, more with transfers, 5 hours), **Hirtshals/Ferry to Kristiansand, Norway** (hourly, 2.5-3 hours; to meet the Color Line ferry, transfer at Hjørring and continue to Hirtshals Havn; note that railpasses don't cover the Hjørring-Hirtshals train—www.rejseplanen.com—but do give a 50 percent discount; buy your ticket in Hjørring or on board; for the latest ferry schedule, see www.colorline.com).

Route Tips for Drivers
From the Ferry Dock at Hirtshals to Jutland Destinations: From the dock in Hirtshals, drive south (signs to *Hjørring, Ålborg*). It's about 2.5 hours to Aarhus. (To skip Aarhus, skirt the center and follow E45 south.) To get to downtown **Aarhus,** follow signs to the center, then *Domkirke.* Park in the pay lot across from the cathedral. Signs all over town direct you to Den Gamle By open-air folk museum. From Aarhus, it's 60 miles to Billund/Legoland (go south on Skanderborg Road and get on E45; follow signs to *Vejle, Kolding*). For **Jelling,** take the *Vejle N* exit and follow signs to *Vejle,* then veer right on the ring road (following signs to *Skovgade*), then follow Route 442 north. For **Legoland,** take the *Vejle S* exit for Billund (after *Vejle N*—it's the first exit after the dramatic Vejlefjord bridge).

Legoland

Legoland is Scandinavia's top kids' sight. If you have a child (or are a child at heart), it's a fun stop. This huge park is a happy com-

bination of rides, restaurants, trees, smiles, and 33 million Lego bricks creatively arranged into such wonders as Mount Rushmore, the Parthenon, "Mad" King Ludwig's castle, and the Statue of Liberty. It's a Lego world here, as everything is cleverly related to this popu-

lar toy. If your time in Denmark is short, or if your family has already visited a similar Legoland park in California, England, or Germany, consider skipping the trip. But if you're in the neighborhood, a visit to the mothership of all things Lego will be a hit with kids ages two through the pre-teens.

Cost: 299 kr entry includes all rides (279 kr for kids ages 3-12 and over 65). Legoland generally doesn't charge in the evening (free after 19:30 in July and late Aug, otherwise after 17:30). Tel. 75 33 13 33, www.legoland.dk.

Hours: Generally April-Oct daily 10:00-18:00, until 20:00 Sat-Sun and most of Aug, until 21:00 daily early July-early Aug, closed Nov-March and Wed-Thu in Sept-mid-Oct. Activities close an hour before the park, but it's basically the same place after dinner as during the day, with fewer tour groups.

Crowd-Beating Tips: Legoland is crowded during the Danish summer school vacation, from early July through mid-August. To bypass the ticket line, purchase tickets in advance (simply scan them at the entry turnstile). Advance tickets are sold online at www.legoland.dk (reduced-price family tickets also available), and at many Danish locations (at stores, hotels, and TIs), including the Dagli' Brugsen store in Vandel, just west of Billund. Advance tickets include a 30-kr food-and-drink coupon and a 40-kr coupon for certain special activities.

Money-Saving Deals: If a one-day visit is not enough, you can pay an extra 99 kr (once at the park) to cover the following day's admission. If you hate waiting in lines, consider shelling out for the Express Pass add-on, which allows holders to skip to the front of the (often long) lines for up to eight rides. The cost is based on the user's height—59 kr for kids 100-119 cm tall (3'3"-3'11"), and 99 kr for those 120 cm (3'11") and taller.

Getting There: Legoland, located in the town of Billund, is easiest to visit by car (see "Route Tips for Drivers" on page 207), but doable by public transportation. The nearest train station to Billund is Vejle. Trains arrive at Vejle from **Copenhagen** (hourly, 2.25 hours), **Odense** (2/hour, 50 minutes), and **Aarhus** (3/hour, 45 minutes). At Vejle, catch the bus (generally #43, #143, #166, or #179) to travel the remaining 25 miles to Billund (30-45 minutes). For train and bus details, see www.rejseplanen.dk.

Eating: Surprisingly, the park's restaurants don't serve Lego-lamb, but there are plenty of other food choices. Prices are high, so consider bringing a picnic to enjoy at one of the several spots set aside for bring-it-yourselfers.

Background: Lego began in 1932 in the workshop of a local carpenter who named his wooden toys after the Danish phrase *leg godt* ("play well"). In 1949, the company started making the plastic interlocking building bricks for which they are world famous. Since then, Lego has continued to expand its lineup and now produces everything from Ninjago ninja warriors to motorized models, Clikits jewelry, board games, and video games—many based on popular movies (*Lego Star Wars, Lego Harry Potter,* etc.)—making kids drool in languages all around the world. According to the company, each person on this planet has, on average, 62 Lego blocks.

Self-Guided Tour

Legoland is divided into eight different "worlds" with fun themes such as Adventure Land, Pirate Land, and Knight's Kingdom.

Pick up a brochure at the entrance and make a plan using the colorful 3-D map. You can see it all in a day, but you'll be exhausted. The Legoredo section (filled with Wild West clichés Europeans will enjoy more than Americans) merits just a quick look, though your five-year-old might enjoy roasting a biscuit-on-a-stick around the fire with a tall, blond park employee wearing a Native American headdress.

A highlight for young and old alike is Miniland (near the entrance), where landscaped gardens are filled with carefully constructed Lego landscapes and cityscapes. Anyone who has ever picked up a Lego block will marvel at seeing representations of the world's famous sights, including Danish monuments, Dutch windmills, German castles, and an amazing representation of the Norwegian harbor of Bergen. Children joyfully watch as tiny Lego boats ply the waters and Lego trains chug merrily along the tracks.

Nearby, kids can go on mellow rides in child-size cars, trains, and boats. A highlight of Miniland is the Traffic School, where young drivers (ages 7-13) learn the rules of the road and get a souvenir license. (If interested in this popular attraction, make a reservation upon arrival.)

More rides are scattered throughout the park. While the rides aren't thrilling by Disneyland standards, most kids will find something to enjoy (parents should check the brochure for strictly enforced height restrictions). The Falck Fire Brigade ride in Lego City invites family participation as you team up to put out a (fake) fire. The Temple is an Indiana Jones-esque Egyptian-themed treasure hunt/shoot-'em-up, and the Dragon roller coaster takes you in and around a medieval castle. Note that on a few rides (including the Pirate Splash Battle), you'll definitely get wet. Special walk-in, human-sized dryers help you warm up and dry off.

The indoor museum features company history, high-tech Lego creations, a great doll collection, and a toy exhibit full of mechanical wonders from the early 1900s, many ready to jump into action with the push of a button. A Lego playroom encourages hands-on fun, and a campground is across the street if your kids refuse to move on.

Nearby: Those looking for water fun with a tropical theme can check out the Aquadome (one of Europe's largest water parks), located outside Legoland in Billund at the family resort of Lalandia (www.lalandia.dk).

Sleeping near Legoland

(6 kr = about $1, country code: 45)
$$$ Legoland Hotel adjoins Legoland (Sb-1,600 kr, Db-1,900 kr, special family deals: 3,000 kr for room big enough for 2 adults and 2 kids, some room prices include 2-day admission to park, prices slightly lower Sept-May or for 2 or more nights, free Wi-Fi, tel. 75 33 12 44, fax 75 35 38 10, www.hotellegoland.dk, hotel@lego land.dk).

JUTLAND

$$$ **Hotel Svanen** is close by, in Billund (standard Sb-1,095 kr, standard Db-1,195 kr, fancier rooms cost more, extra child's bed-100 kr, free Wi-Fi, Nordmarksvej 8, tel. 75 33 28 33, fax 75 35 35 15, www.hotelsvanen.dk, info@hotelsvanen.dk).

$$ **Legoland Village** is a family hostel-type place offering inexpensive rooms that sleep one to five people (Db-585-985 kr, Tb-895-1,045 kr, Qb-975-1,135 kr, Quint/b-860-1,265 kr, higher prices are for mid-May-late Sept, sheets and towels-70 kr/person, Ellehammers Allé 2, tel. 75 33 27 77, fax 75 33 28 77, www.lego land-village.dk, info@legoland-village.dk).

Private Rooms: Private rooms are key to a budget visit here. In a forest just outside of Billund, Erik and Mary Sort run $ **Gregersminde,** with a great setup: six double rooms, plus a cottage that sleeps up to six people. Their guests enjoy a huge living room, a kitchen, lots of Lego toys, and a kid-friendly yard (S-200-300 kr, Sb-260-390 kr, D-320-350 kr, Db-380-450 kr, cottage-660-750 kr—towels and sheets extra, higher prices are for June-Sept, breakfast-50-60 kr, cash only, 10 percent cheaper for 2 nights or more, free Internet access, rental bikes-15 kr, cash only, leave Billund on Grindsted Road, turn right on Stilbjergvej, go a half-mile to Stilbjergvej 4B, tel. 61 27 33 23, www.gregersminde .dk, info@gregersminde.dk).

Jelling

On your way to or from Legoland, consider a short side-trip to the tiny village of Jelling (pronounced "YELL-ing"), a place of

immense importance in Danish history. Here you'll find two rune stones, set next to a 900-year-old church that's flanked by two enormous, man-made burial mounds. The two stones are often called "Denmark's birth certificate"—the first written record of Denmark's status as a nation-state. An excellent (and free) museum lies just across the street.

Two hours is ample for a visit. If pressed for time, an hour is enough to see the stones and take a quick look at the museum. Note that the museum is closed on Monday.

Jelling is too small for a TI, but the museum staff can answer most questions. If you're here around lunchtime, Jelling is a great

JUTLAND

spot for a picnic. There are several central eateries and a café and WC inside the museum, and another WC in the parking lot near the North Mound.

Getting There: Drivers can easily find Jelling, just 10 minutes off the main Vejle-Billund road (see "Route Tips for Drivers" on page 207). Train travelers coming from Copenhagen or Aarhus must change in Vejle, which is connected to Jelling by hourly trains (direction: Herning) and bus #211.

Self-Guided Walk

Denmark is proud of being Europe's oldest monarchy and of the fact that Queen Margrethe II, the country's current ruler, can trace her lineage back 1,300 years to this sacred place.

• *Begin your visit at the...*

Kongernes Jelling Museum: Inside this modern, light-filled building you'll find informative exhibits, historical models of the area, and replicas of the rune stones. Kids will love the room in the back on the ground level where they can write their name in the runic alphabet—and the gift shop bristling with wooden swords and Viking garb (free, June-Aug Tue-Sun 10:00-17:00, Sept-May Tue-Sun 12:00-16:00, closed between Christmas and New Year's and on Mon year-round, café, tel. 75 87 23 50, www.kongernes jelling.dk).

• *Cross the street and walk through the graveyard to examine the actual...*

Rune Stones: The stones stand just south of the church. The modern bronze-and-glass structure is designed to protect the stones from the elements while allowing easy viewing.

The smaller stone was erected by King Gorm the Old (a.k.a. Gorm the Sleepy), who ruled Denmark for 40 years in the ninth century. You probably don't read runic so I'll translate: *"King Gorm made this monument in memory of Thyra, his wife, Denmark's salvation."* These are the oldest recorded words of a Danish king, and the first time that the name Denmark is used to describe a country and not just the region.

The **larger stone** was erected by Gorm's son, Harald Bluetooth, to honor his parents, commemorate the conquering of Denmark and Norway, and mark the conversion of the Danes to Christianity. (Bluetooth technology—which transmits electronic data wirelessly—takes its name from Harald, who created the decidedly non-wireless connection between the Danish and Norwegian peoples.)

Harald was a shrewd politician who had practical reasons for being baptized. He knew that if he declared Denmark to be a Christian land, he could save it from possible attack by the preda-

JUTLAND

tory German bishops to the south. The inscription reads: *"King Harald ordered this monument made in memory of Gorm, his father, and in memory of Thyra, his mother; that Harald who won for himself all of Denmark and Norway and made the Danes Christian."*

This large stone has three sides. One side reveals an image of Jesus and a cross, while the other has a serpent wrapped around a lion. This is important imagery that speaks to the transition from Nordic paganism to Christianity. These designs carved into  the rock were once brightly painted.

• *Go around the back of the church and climb the steps to the 35-foot-high, grass-covered...*

North Mound: According to tradition, Gorm was buried in a chamber inside this mound, with his queen Thyra interred in the smaller mound to the south. But excavations in the 1940s turned up no royal remains in either mound. (In the 1970s, what is believed to be Gorm's body was discovered below the church.) Scan the horizon and mentally remove the trees. Imagine the commanding view this site had in the past. Look north to stones that trace the outline of a ship. Below you lies a graveyard with typically Danish well-manicured plots.

• *Now descend the stairs to the...*

Church: Within the sparse interior, note the ship model hanging from the ceiling, a holdover from a pre-Christian tradition seeking a safe journey for ship and crew. The church, which dates from around 1100, is decorated with restored frescoes. A zig-zag motif is repeated in the modern windows and the inlaid floor. The metal "Z" in the floor marks the spot where Gorm's body lies.

More Jutland Sights

Himmelbjerget and Silkeborg—If you're connecting the Billund and Jelling area with Aarhus, consider this slower but more scenic route north through the idyllic Danish Lake District. (With less time, return to Vejle and take the E45 motorway.)

Himmelbjerget, best seen by car, lies in the middle of Jutland near the town of Silkeborg. Both are about an hour north of Billund (22 miles west of Aarhus). Silkeborg is accessible by train from Aarhus with a change in Skanderborg.

Denmark's landscape is vertically challenged when compared to its mountainous neighbors Norway and Sweden. If you have a hankering to ascend to one of the country's highest points, consider a visit to the 482-foot-tall **Himmelbjerget,** which translates loftily as "The Heaven Mountain." That may be overstating it, but by Danish standards the view's not bad. One can literally drive to the top, where a short trail leads to an 80-foot-tall brick tower. Climb the **tower** (small admission fee, April-Oct daily 10:00-17:00, longer hours July-mid-Sept) for a commanding view. Clouds roll by above a patchwork of green and gold fields while boats ply the blue waters of the lake below. You may see the vintage paddle steamers make the hour-long trip between Himmelbjerget and Silkeborg in season (the dock is accessed by a short hike from the tower down to the lake).

Silkeborg, in the center of the Danish Lake District, has an excellent freshwater aquarium/exhibit/nature park called **AQUA** that's worth a visit, especially if you're traveling with kids (adults-140 kr, kids 3-11-75 kr, free for kids 3 and under; Mon-Fri 10:00-16:00, Sat-Sun 10:00-17:00, longer hours in summer, closed most of Dec; tel. 89 21 21 89, www.ferskvandscentret.dk). Also in Silkeborg, modern-art lovers will enjoy the **Museum Jorn Silkeborg,** featuring colorful abstract works by Asger Jorn—a prominent member of the 1960s' COBRA movement—plus other Danish and foreign art (70 kr, free for kids 18 and under, April-Oct Tue-Sun 10:00-17:00, closed Mon, shorter hours off-season, tel. 86 82 53 88, www.museumjorn.dk).

▲**Ribe**—A Viking port 1,000 years ago, Ribe, located about 30 miles southwest of Billund, is the oldest, and possibly loveliest, town in Denmark. It's an entertaining mix of cobbled lanes and leaning medieval houses, with a fine **cathedral** with modern paintings under Romanesque arches (free entry, tower-10 kr). The **TI** can find accommodations for a booking fee (Torvet 3, tel. 75 42 15 00, www.visitribe.dk), or try **$$ Weis Stue,** a smoky, low-ceilinged, atmospheric inn, which rents primitive rooms and serves good meals (S-395 kr, D-495 kr, no breakfast, across from church, tel. 75 42 07 00, www.weis-stue.dk). Take the free **Night Watchman** tour (daily May-mid-Oct at 22:00, additional tour at 20:00 June-Aug).

NORWAY

NORWAY

Norge

Norway is stacked with superlatives—it's the most mountainous, most scenic, and most prosperous of all the Scandinavian countries. Perhaps above all, Norway is a land of intense natural beauty, its famously steep mountains and deep fjords carved out and shaped by an ancient ice age.

Norway is also a land of rich harvests—timber, oil, and fish. In fact, its wealth of resources is a major reason why Norwegians have voted *"nei"* to membership in the European Union. They don't want to be forced to share fishing rights with EU countries.

The country's relatively recent independence (in 1905, from Sweden) makes Norwegians notably patriotic and proud of their traditions and history.

Norway's Viking past (c. A.D. 800-1050) can still be seen today in the country's 28 remaining stave churches—with their decorative nods to Viking ship prows—and the artifacts housed in Oslo's Viking Ship Museum.

The Vikings, who also lived in present-day Denmark and Sweden, were great traders, shipbuilders, and explorers. However, they are probably best known for their infamous invasions, which terrorized much of Europe. The sight of their dragon-prowed ships on the horizon struck fear into the hearts of people from Ireland to the Black Sea.

Named for the Norse word *vik*, which means fjord or inlet, the Vikings sailed their sleek, seaworthy ships on extensive voyages, laden with amber and furs for trading—and weapons for fighting. They traveled up the Seine and deep into Russia, through the Mediterranean east to Constantinople, and across the Atlantic to Greenland and even "Vinland" (Canada). In fact, they touched the soil of the Americas centuries before Columbus, causing proud "ya sure ya betcha" Scandinavian immigrants in the US to display bumper stickers that boast, "Columbus used a Viking map!"

Both history and Hollywood have painted a picture of the Vikings as fierce barbarians, an image reinforced by the colorful names of leaders like Sven Forkbeard, Erik Bloodaxe, and Harald Bluetooth. Unless you're handy with an axe, these don't sound like

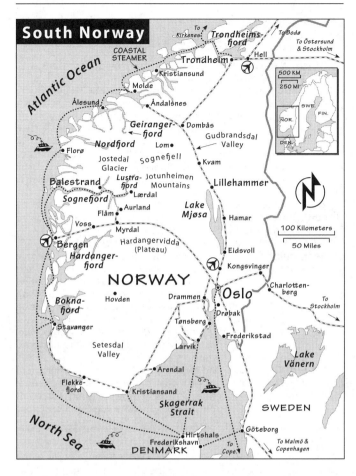

the kind of men you want to hoist a tankard of mead with. They kept slaves and were all-around cruel (though there is no evidence that they forced their subjects to eat lutefisk). But the Vikings also had a gentle side. Many were farmers, fishermen, and craftsmen who created delicate works with wood and metal. Faced with a growing population constrained by a lack of arable land, they traveled south not just to rape, pillage, and plunder, but in search of greener pastures. Sometimes they stayed and colonized, as in northeast England, which was called the "Danelaw," or in northwest France, which became known as Normandy ("Land of the North-men").

The Vikings worshipped many gods and had a rich tradition of mythology. Epic sagas were verbally passed down through generations or written in angular runic writing. The sagas told the heroic tales of the gods, who lived in Valhalla, the Viking heaven,

NORWAY

Norway Almanac

Official Name: Kongeriket Norge—"The Kingdom of Norway"— or simply Norge (Norway).

Population: Norway's 4.7 million people (about 39 per square mile) are mainly of Nordic and Germanic heritage, with a small population of indigenous Sami people in the north. The rapidly growing immigrant population is primarily from Pakistan, Sweden, Denmark, Iraq, Vietnam, and Somalia. Most Norwegians speak one of two official forms of Norwegian (Bokmål and Nynorsk), and the majority speak English as a second language. While church attendance is way down, the vast majority of Norwegian Christians consider themselves Lutheran.

Latitude and Longitude: 62°N and 10°E, similar latitude to Canada's Northwest Territories.

Area: 148,900 square miles, slightly larger than Montana.

Geography: Sharing the Scandinavian Peninsula with Sweden, Norway also has short northern borders with Finland and Russia. Its 51,575-mile coastline extends from the Barents Sea in the Arctic Ocean to the Norwegian Sea and North Sea in the North Atlantic. Shaped by glaciers, Norway has a rugged landscape of mountains, plateaus, and deep fjords. In the part of Norway that extends north of the Arctic Circle, the sun never sets at the height of summer, and never comes up in the deep of winter.

Biggest Cities: Norway's capital city, Oslo, has a population of 575,000; more than a million live in its metropolitan area.

Economy: The Norwegian economy grows around 4 percent each year, contributing to a healthy $269 billion Gross

presided over by Odin, the god of both wisdom and war. Like the Egyptians, the Vikings believed in life after death, and chieftains were often buried in their ships within burial mounds, along with prized possessions such as jewelry, cooking pots, food, and Hagar the Horrible cartoons.

Like the Greeks and Etruscans before them, the Vikings never organized on a large national scale and eventually faded away due to bigger, better-organized enemies and the powerful influence of Christianity. By 1150, the Vikings had become Christianized and assimilated into European society. But their memory lives on in Norway.

Beginning in the 14th century, Norway came under Danish rule for more than 400 years, until the Danes took the wrong side in the Napoleonic Wars. The Treaty of Kiel forced Denmark to cede Norway to Sweden in 1814. Sweden's rule of Norway lasted until 1905, when Norway voted to dissolve the union. Like many European countries, Norway was taken over by Germany during

NORWAY

Domestic Product and a per capita GDP of $54,200. Its primary export is oil—Norway ranks behind only Saudi Arabia and Russia in the amount of oil exported, making it one of the world's richest countries. Thanks to this oil wealth, and the country's generally prudent approach to debt, the recent economic crisis has been relatively easy on Norway.

Currency: 6 Norwegian kroner (kr, officially NOK) = about $1.

Government: As the leader of Norway's constitutional monarchy, King Harald V has largely ceremonial powers. Since October 2005 the government has been led by Prime Minister Jens Stoltenberg, who narrowly won re-election in 2009. The legislative body is the Stortinget, with 169 members elected for four-year terms. The Labor Party currently holds 64 seats, followed by the Progress Party with 41, the Conservative Party with 30, and the Socialist Left Party with 11. The remaining seats are divided among smaller political parties.

Flag: The Norwegian flag is red with a blue Scandinavian cross outlined in white.

The Average Norwegian: He or she is 40 years old, has 1.77 children, and will live to be 80. One in three Norwegians is employed in the service sector, one in four in industry, and only 3 percent in agriculture.

World War II. April 1940 marked the start of five years of Nazi occupation, during which a strong resistance movement developed, hindering some of the Nazi war efforts.

Each year on May 17, Norwegians celebrate their ill-fated but idealistic 1814 constitution with fervor and plenty of flag-waving. Men and women wear folk costumes *(bunads),* each specific to a region of Norway. Parades are held throughout the country. The parade in Oslo marches past the Royal Palace, where the royal family waves to the populace from their balcony. While the king holds almost zero political power (Norway has a parliament chaired by a prime minister), the royal family is still highly revered and respected.

Several holidays in spring and early summer disrupt transportation schedules: the aforementioned Constitution Day (May 17), Ascension Day (May 9 in 2013, May 29 in 2014), and Whitsunday and Whitmonday (a.k.a. Pentecost and the following day, May 19-20 in 2013, June 8-9 in 2014).

High taxes contribute to Norway's high standard of living. Norwegians receive cradle-to-grave social care: university education, health care, nearly yearlong paternity leave, and an annual six weeks of vacation. Norwegians feel there is no better place than home. Norway regularly shows up in first place on the annual UN Human Development Index.

Visitors enjoy the agreeable demeanor of the Norwegian people—friendly but not overbearing, organized but not uptight, and with a lust for adventure befitting their gorgeous landscape. Known for their ability to suffer any misfortune with an accepting (if a bit pessimistic) attitude, Norwegians are easy to get along with.

Despite being looked down upon as less sophisticated by their Scandinavian neighbors, Norwegians are proud of their rich folk traditions—from handmade sweaters and folk costumes to the small farms that produce a sweet cheese called *geitost*. Less than 7 percent of the country's land is arable, resulting in numerous small farms. The government recognizes the value of farming, especially in the remote reaches of the country, and provides rich subsidies to keep this tradition alive. These subsidies would not be allowed if Norway joined the European Union—yet another reason the country remains an EU holdout.

Appropriate for a land with countless fjords and waterfalls, Norway is known for its pristine water. Norwegian-bottled artisanal water has an international reputation for its crisp, clean taste. Although the designer Voss water—the H2O of choice for Hollywood celebrities—comes with a high price tag, the blue-collar Olden is just as good. (The tap water is actually wonderful, too—and much cheaper.)

While the Norwegian people speak a collection of mutually understandable dialects, the Norwegian language has two official forms: *bokmål* (book language) and *nynorsk* (New Norse). During the centuries of Danish rule, people in Norway's cities and upper classes adopted a Danish-influenced style of speech and writing (called Dano-Norwegian), while rural language remained closer to the Old Norse. After independence, Dano-Norwegian was renamed *bokmål,* and the rural dialects were formalized as *nynorsk,* as part of a nationalistic drive for a more purely Norwegian language. Despite later efforts to combine the two forms, *bokmål* remains the most commonly used, especially in urban areas, books, newspapers, and government agencies. Students learn both.

The majority of the population under 70 years of age also speaks English, but a few words in Norwegian will serve you well. For starters, see the Norwegian survival phrases on page 690. If you visit a Norwegian home, be sure to leave your shoes at the door; indoors is usually meant for stocking-feet only. At the end

NORWAY

of a meal, it's polite to say "Thanks for the food"—*"Takk for maten"* (tahk for MAH-ten). Norwegians rarely feel their guests have eaten enough food, so be prepared to say *"Nei, takk"* (nigh tahk; "No, thanks"). You can always try *"Jeg er met"* (yigh ehr met; "I am full"), but be careful not to say *"Jeg er full"*—"I am drunk."

Stave Churches

Norway's most distinctive architecture is the stave church. These medieval houses of worship—tall, skinny, wooden pagodas with

dragon's-head gargoyles— are distinctly Norwegian and palpably historic, trans- porting you right back to the Viking days. On your visit, make it a point to visit at least one stave church.

Stave churches are the finest architecture to come out of medieval Norway. Wood was plentiful and cheap, and locals had an expertise with woodworking (from all that boat-building). In 1300, there were as many as 1,000 stave churches in Norway. After a 14th-century plague, Norway's population dropped, and many churches fell into disuse or burned down. By the 19th cen- tury, only a few dozen stave churches survived. Fortunately, they became recognized as part of the national heritage and were pro- tected. Virtually all of Norway's surviving stave churches have been rebuilt or renovated, with painstaking attention to the origi- nal details.

A distinguishing feature of the "stave" design is its frame of tall, stout vertical staves (Norwegian *stav*, or "staff"). The churches typically sit on stone foundations, to keep the wooden structure away from the damp ground (otherwise it would rot). Most stave churches were made of specially grown pine, carefully prepared before being felled for construction. As the trees grew, the tips and most of the branches were cut off, leaving the trunks just barely alive to stand in the woods for about a decade. This allowed the sap to penetrate the wood and lock in the resin, strengthening the wood while keeping it elastic. Once built, a stave church was slath- ered with black tar to protect it from the elements.

Stave churches are notable for their resilience and flexibility. Just as old houses creak and settle over the years, wooden stave churches can flex to withstand fierce winds and the march of time. When the wind shifts with the seasons, stave churches groan and moan for a couple of weeks...until they've adjusted to the new influences, and settle in.

Even after the Vikings stopped raiding, they ornamented

the exteriors of their churches with warlike, evil spirit-fighting dragons reminiscent of their ships. Inside, a stave church's structure makes you feel like you're huddled under an overturned ship. The churches are dark, with almost no windows (aside from a few small "portholes" high up). Typical decorations include carved, X-shaped crossbeams; these symbolize the cross of St. Andrew (who was crucified on such a cross). Round, Romanesque arches near the tops of the staves were made from the "knees" of a tree, where the roots bend to meet the trunk (typically the hardest wood in a tree). Overall, these churches are extremely vertical: the beams inside and the roofline outside both lead the eye up, up, up to the heavens.

Most surviving stave churches were renovated during the Reformation (16th and 17th centuries), when they acquired more horizontal elements such as pews, balconies, pulpits, altars, and other decorations to draw attention to the front of the church. In some (such as the churches in Lom and Urnes), the additions make the church feel almost cluttered. But the most authentic (including Hopperstad near Vik) feel truly medieval. These time-machine churches take visitors back to early Christian days: no pews (worshippers stood through the  service), no pulpit, and a barrier between the congregation and the priest, to symbolically separate the physical world from the spiritual one. Incense filled the church, and the priest and congregation chanted the service back and forth to each other, creating an otherworldly atmosphere that likely made worshippers feel close to God. (If you've traveled in Greece, Russia, or the Balkans, Norway's stave churches might remind you of Orthodox churches, which reflect the way all Christians once worshipped.)

When traveling through Norway, you'll be encouraged to see stave church after stave church. Sure, they're interesting, but there's no point in spending time seeing more than a few of them. Of Norway's 28 remaining stave churches, seven are described in this book. The easiest to see are the ones that have been moved to open-air museums in Oslo and Lillehammer. But I prefer to appreciate a stave church in its original fjords-and-rolling-hills setting. My two favorites are both near Sognefjord: Borgund and Hopperstad. They are each delightfully situated, uncluttered by more recent additions, and evocative as can be. Borgund is in a pristine wooded valley, while Hopperstad is situated on a fjord. Borgund comes with the only good adjacent stave church museum.

(Most stave churches on the Sognefjord are operated by the same preservation society; for more details, see www.stavechurch.com.)

Other noteworthy stave churches include the one in Lom, near the Jotunheimen Mountains, which is one of Norway's biggest, and is indeed quite impressive. The Urnes church, across from Solvorn, is technically the oldest of them all—but it's been thoroughly renovated in later ages (it is still worth considering, however, if only for its exquisite carvings and the fun excursion to get to it; see the More on the Sognefjord chapter). The Fantoft church, just outside Bergen, burned down in 1992, and the replica built to replace it has none of the original's magic. The stave church in Undredal (see the Norway in a Nutshell chapter) advertises itself as the smallest. I think it's also the dullest.

OSLO

While Oslo is the smallest of the Scandinavian capitals, this brisk little city offers more sightseeing thrills than you might expect. As an added bonus, you'll be inspired by a city that simply has its act together.

Sights of the Viking spirit—past and present—tell an exciting story. Prowl through the remains of ancient Viking ships, and marvel at more peaceful but equally gutsy modern boats (the *Kon-Tiki, Ra,* and *Fram*). Dive into the traditional folk culture at the Norwegian open-air folk museum, and get stirred up by the country's heroic spirit at the Norwegian Resistance Museum.

For a look at modern Oslo, tour the striking City Hall, take a peek at sculptor Gustav Vigeland's people-pillars, climb the newly rebuilt Holmenkollen Ski Jump, walk all over the Opera House, and then celebrate the world's greatest peacemakers at the Nobel Peace Center.

Situated at the head of a 60-mile-long fjord, surrounded by forests, and populated by more than a half-million people, Oslo is Norway's cultural hub. For 300 years (1624-1924), the city was called Christiania, after Danish King Christian IV. With independence, it reverted to the Old Norse name of Oslo. As an important port facing the Continent, Oslo has been one of Norway's main cities for a thousand years and the de facto capital since around 1300. Still, Oslo has always been small by European standards; in 1800, Oslo had 10,000 people, while cities such as Paris and London had 50 times as many.

Today the city sprawls out from its historic core to encompass over a million people in its metropolitan area, about one in five Norwegians. Oslo's port hums with international shipping

and a sizeable cruise industry. Its waterfront, once traffic-congested and slummy, has undergone a huge change: Cars and trucks now travel in underground tunnels, upscale condos and restaurants are taking over, and the neighborhood has a splashy Opera House. Though it's always been a great city, Oslo seems to be constantly improving its infrastructure and redeveloping slummy old quarters along the waterfront into cutting-edge residential zones. Oslo feels as if it's rushing to prepare for an Olympics-like deadline. But it isn't—it just wants to be the best city it can be.

Oslo is full of rich Norwegians and is, understandably, expensive. Its streets are a mix of grand Neoclassical facades and boxy 60s-style modernism. But overall, the feel of this major capital is green and pastoral—spread out, dotted with parks and lakes, and surrounded by hills and forests. For the visitor, Oslo is an all-you-can-see *smörgåsbord* of historic sights, trees, art, and Nordic fun.

Planning Your Time

Oslo offers an exciting two-day slate of sightseeing thrills. Ideally, spend two days, and leave on the night boat to Copenhagen or on the scenic "Norway in a Nutshell" train to Bergen the third morning. Spend the two days like this:

Day 1: Take my self-guided introductory walk. Tour the Akershus Fortress and the Norwegian Resistance Museum. Catch the City Hall tour. Spend the afternoon at the National Gallery and at the Holmenkollen Ski Jump and museum.

Day 2: Ferry across the harbor to Bygdøy and tour the *Fram, Kon-Tiki,* and Viking Ship museums. Spend the afternoon at the Norwegian Folk Museum. Finish the day at Frogner Park, enjoying the Vigeland statues (two recommended restaurants are nearby).

Keep in mind that the National Gallery and the Vigeland Museum (at Frogner Park) are always closed on Monday. The Nobel Peace Center and the Edvard Munch Museum are closed on Mondays in the off-season.

Orientation to Oslo

Oslo is easy to manage. Its sights cluster around the main boulevard, Karl Johans Gate (with the Royal Palace at one end and the train station at the other), and in the Bygdøy (big-doy) district, a 10-minute ferry ride across the harbor. The city's other main sight,

Frogner Park (with Gustav Vigeland's statues), is about a mile behind the palace.

The monumental, homogenous city center contains most of the sights, but head out of the core to see the more colorful neighborhoods. Choose from Majorstuen and Frogner (chic boutiques, trendy restaurants), Grünerløkka (bohemian cafés, hipsters), and Grønland (multiethnic immigrants' zone).

Tourist Information

Oslo has two centrally located TIs: The **Oslo Tourist Information Center** faces City Hall (June-Aug Mon-Fri 9:00-19:00, Sat-Sun 9:00-18:00, shorter hours and closed Sat-Sun off-season, Fridtjof Nansens Plass 5, enter from Roald Amundsens Gate, www.visit oslo.com). Another TI is in front of the **train station** (Mon-Fri 7:00-20:00; Sat-Sun 8:00-18:00). Go early or late to avoid lines; otherwise, grab a number as you enter and wait. They answer the phone only on weekdays from 9:00 to 16:00 (tel. 81 53 05 55). Also, a **TI kiosk** at the port opens when cruise ships arrive (Akerhusstranda 15, tel. 81 53 05 55).

At any TI, pick up these freebies: an Oslo map, the helpful public-transit map, the annual *Oslo Guide* (with plenty of details on sightseeing, shopping, and eating), the *What's On in Oslo* monthly (for the most accurate listing of museum hours and special events), and *Streetwise* magazine (an insightful, worthwhile student guide that's fun to read and full of offbeat ideas). If you're traveling on, pick up the *Bergen Guide* and information for the rest of Norway, including the useful, annual *Fjord Norway Travel Guide*. Consider buying the Oslo Pass (described below), unless you get the Oslo Package, which includes your hotel accommodation and an Oslo Pass (described under "Sleeping in Oslo," page 274).

Use It, a hardworking information center, is officially geared for those under age 26 but is generally happy to offer anyone its solid, money-saving, experience-enhancing advice (Mon-Fri 11:00-17:00, Sat 12:00-17:00, longer hours in Aug, closed Sun; Møllergata 3, look for *Ungdomsinformasjonen* sign, tel. 24 14 98 20, www.use-it.no). They can find you the cheapest beds in town (no booking fee), and offer free Internet access (30-minute limit, may have to wait for a computer). Their free *Streetwise* magazine—packed with articles on Norwegian culture, ideas on eating and sleeping cheap, good nightspots, the best beaches, and so on—is a must for young travelers and worthwhile for anyone curious about probing the Oslo scene.

Oslo Pass: This pass covers the city's public transit, ferry boats, and entry to nearly every major sight—all described in a useful handbook (270 kr/24 hours, 395 kr/48 hours, 495 kr/72

OSLO

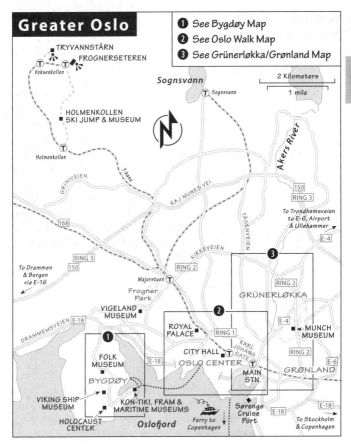

Greater Oslo

❶ See Bygdøy Map
❷ See Oslo Walk Map
❸ See Grünerløkka/Grønland Map

TRYVANNSTÅRN
FROGNERSETEREN
Voksenkollen
Sognsvann
Sognsvann
2 Kilometers
1 mile
HOLMENKOLLEN
SKI JUMP & MUSEUM
Holmenkollen
Akers River
GRINIVEIEN
T-bane
KAJ MUNKS VEI
TÅSENVEIEN
150
RING 3
To Trondhemsveien
to E-6, Airport
& Lillehammer
E-4
RING 2
KIRKEVEIEN
To Drammen
& Bergen
via E-16
RING 3
150
RING 2
Majorstuen
GRÜNERLØKKA
RING 2
Frogner
Park
E-4
VIGELAND
MUSEUM
E-18
ROYAL
PALACE
RING 1
MUNCH
MUSEUM
DRAMMENSVEIEN
E-18
CITY HALL
OSLO CENTER
KARL JOHANS GATE
RING 2
E-6
FOLK
MUSEUM
E-18
MAIN
STN.
GRØNLAND
BYGDØY
VIKING SHIP
MUSEUM
KON-TIKI, FRAM &
MARITIME MUSEUMS
Sørenge
Cruise
Port
E-18
To Stockholm
& Copenhagen
HOLOCAUST
CENTER
Oslofjord
Ferry to
Copenhagen

hours; big discounts for kids ages 4-15 and seniors age 67 and over, www.visitoslo.com/en/activities-and-attractions/oslo-pass/). Do the math before buying; add up the individual costs of the sights you want to see to determine whether an Oslo Pass will save you money. (Here are some sample charges: 8-ride transit pass-216 kr, Nobel Peace Center-80 kr, three boat museums at Bygdøy-210 kr, National Gallery-50 kr. These costs alone, which total 556 kr, more than justify buying a 48-hour pass.) Students with an ISIC card may be better off without the Oslo Pass. The TI's Oslo Package (see "Sleeping in Oslo," later) includes an Oslo Pass with your discounted hotel room.

Entertainment Listings: The periodical *What's On in Oslo* has an extensive listing of happenings every day. Pick it up free at the TI, and review the busy lineup of special events, tours, and concerts. *Streetwise* magazine is also good.

Arrival in Oslo
By Train
The central train station (Oslo Sentralstasjon, or "Oslo S" for short) is slick and helpful. You'll find Internet cafés, ATMs, and two Forex exchange desks. The station is plugged into a lively modern shopping mall called Byporten (Mon-Fri 10:00-21:00, Sat 10:00-20:00, closed Sun). You'll also find a Bit sandwich shop with seating for a cheap meal, an ICA supermarket (near west exit—follow *West Exit* signs; Mon-Fri 6:00-21:00, Sat 8:00-19:00, Sun 10:00-18:00), and a Vinmonopolet liquor store (Oslo's most central place to buy wine or liquor, sold only at Vinmonopolet stores). The TI is across the square in front of the station.

For tickets and train info, you can go to the station's ticket office located between tracks 8 and 9 (Mon-Fri 6:30-23:00, Sat 10:00-18:00, Sun 12:00-23:00) or to the helpful train office at the National Theater railway and T-bane station, which can have shorter lines (Mon-Fri 7:00-20:00, Sat 11:00-18:00, closed Sun; Ruseløkkveien, southwest of National Theater). At either ticket office, you can buy domestic and Norway in a Nutshell tickets, and pick up leaflets on the Flåm and Bergen Railway, but only the station office sells international tickets. The TIs also sell domestic train tickets (same price, likely friendlier and faster).

By Plane
Oslo Airport
Oslo Lufthavn, also called Gardermoen, is about 30 miles north of the city center and has a helpful 24-hour information center (airport code: OSL, tel. 91 50 64 00, www.osl.no).

The speedy **Flytoget** train zips travelers between the airport and the central train station in 20-25 minutes (170 kr, less for students and seniors, 4/hour, runs roughly 5:00-24:00, not covered by railpasses; buy and validate ticket before boarding, keep it to exit; tel. 81 50 07 77, www.flytoget.no). Note that Flytoget trains alternate between those that go only to the central train station, and others that also continue on through Oslo, stopping at the National Theater station (which is closer to some recommended hotels and uses the same ticket).

Local trains cost less than Flytoget trains and take only a little longer (90 kr, hourly, 25 minutes, covered by railpasses, some also serve National Theater station). You'll save about 30 kr on this trip with an Oslo Pass because the pass covers transportation within Oslo; you only need to pay the fare for the stretch between the airport and the edge of town.

To reach the Flytoget and local train counters at the airport: After you leave customs, exit right and walk all the way to the far corner; you'll see two separate ticket counters (one for Flytoget,

NSB for the cheaper local trains) and separate TV screens show-ing the timetables for Flytoget and the "lokal-InterCity-fjerntog" trains.

Flybus airport buses stop directly outside the arrival hall and make several downtown stops, including the central train station (150 kr one-way, 3/hour, 40 minutes).

Taxis run to and from the airport (895-kr fixed rate until 17:00, 1,095-kr rate after 17:00, confirm price before you commit). **Oslo Taxi** is the most reliable (tel. 02323). I prefer the slick and faster Flytoget train, but the taxi can be a good value for families and those with lots of luggage.

Other Airports near Oslo

If you arrive at the Rygge or Sandefjord airports, catch a Flybus airport bus to downtown Oslo. If you're going from Oslo *to* either airport, note that buses depart Oslo's central bus terminal (next to the train station) about three hours before all flight departures.

Rygge Airport: Ryanair and Norwegian use this airport near the city of Moss, 40 miles south of Oslo—140 kr, buy Flybus ticket from bus driver, tel. 67 98 04 80, www.rygge-ekspressen.no (airport code: RYG, tel. 69 23 00 00, www.en.ryg.no).

Sandefjord Airport Torp: Ryanair, WizzAir, and other dis-count airlines use this airport, 70 miles south of Oslo—200 kr, buy Flybus ticket from driver, tel. 67 98 04 80, www.torpekspressen.no (airport code: TRF, tel. 33 42 70 00, www.torp.no).

By Boat

For details on arriving in Oslo by cruise ship, see the end of this chapter.

Helpful Hints

Pickpocket Alert: They're a problem in Oslo, particularly in crowds on the street and in subways and buses. Always wear your money belt. To call the police, dial 112.

Street People and Drug Addicts: Oslo's street population loiters around the train station. While a bit unnerving to some trav-elers, locals consider this rough-looking bunch harmless. The police have pretty much corralled them to the square called Christian Frederiks Plass, south of the station.

Currency Exchange: Banks in Norway don't change money. Use ATMs or Forex exchange offices (outlets near City Hall at Fridtjof Nansens Plass 6, at train station, and at Egertorget at the crest of Karl Johans Gate; hours vary by location but generally Mon-Fri 9:00-18:00, Sat 9:00-16:00, closed Sun).

Internet Access: You have two options at the train station. **Side-walk Express,** the budget choice, is near the Forex exchange office by the south exit—look for *South Exit* signs (29 kr/1.5 hours, open 24/7, coin-op). **@rctic Internet Café,** in the station's main hall and above track 13, is quieter but pricey (60 kr/hour, daily 8:00-23:00, sells international phone cards).

Post Office: It's in the train station.

Pharmacy: Jernbanetorgets Vitus Apotek is open 24 hours daily (across from train station on Jernbanetorget, tel. 23 35 81 00).

Laundry: Selva Laundromat is on the corner of Wessels Gate and Ullevålsveien at Ullevålsveien 15, a half-mile north of the train station (daily self-serve 8:00-21:00, full-serve 10:00-19:00, walk or catch bus #37 from station, tel. 41 64 08 33).

Bike Rental: Bikes are tough to rent in Oslo. A public system lets you grab simple, one-speed city bikes out of locked racks at various points around town (80 kr/24 hours; rent a card from TI that allows you to release bike from rack, leave credit-card number as deposit, and return the card to TI). A more expensive, conventional bike-rental company delivers bikes to your hotel (details at TI). To rent a bike in the countryside, see page 266.

Updates to This Book: For news about changes to this book's coverage since it was published, see www.ricksteves.com/update.

Getting Around Oslo

By Public Transit: Commit yourself to taking advantage of Oslo's excellent transit system, made up of buses, trams, ferries, and a subway (*Tunnelbane,* or T-bane for short). Use the TI's free public transit map to navigate. The system runs like clockwork, with schedules clearly posted and followed. Many stops have handy electronic reader boards showing the time remaining before the next tram arrives (usually less than 10 minutes). **Ruter,** the public-transit information center, faces the train station under the glass tower (same building as TI; Mon-Fri 7:00-22:00, Sat-Sun 8:00-22:00, tel. 177 or 81 50 01 76, www.ruter.no).

Individual **tickets** work on buses, trams, ferries, and the T-bane for one hour (30 kr if bought at a Narvesen kiosk/convenience store, or 50 kr if bought on board). Other options include the **Reisekort** smartcard (216 kr for 8 rides within zone 1; buy at Narvesen, 7-Eleven stores, or transit offices; the cost of a ride is automatically deducted from the smartcard balance, reload at machines, not shareable with others on same ride), the 24-hour **Dagskort Tourist Ticket** (75 kr, pays for itself in 3 rides), and the **Oslo Pass** (gives free run of entire system; described earlier). Validate your ticket or smartcard by holding it next to the card reader when you board.

By Taxi: Taxis come with a 150-kr drop charge that covers you for three or four kilometers—about two miles (more on eve-

OSLO

nings and weekends). To get a taxi, wave one down, find a taxi stand, or call 02323.

Tours in Oslo

By Boat, Bus, and Foot

Oslo Fjord Tours—A fascinating world of idyllic islands sprinkled with charming vacation cabins is minutes away from the Oslo harborfront. For locals, the fjord is a handy vacation getaway. Tourists can get a glimpse of this island world by public ferry or tour boat. Cheap ferries regularly connect the nearby islands with downtown (covered by Oslo Pass, transit tickets, and Reisekort smartcard).

Several tour boats leave regularly from pier 3 in front of City Hall. Båtservice has a relaxing and scenic 1.5-hour hop-on, hop-off service, with a live-but-boring multi-language commentary, which departs from the City Hall dock (175 kr, daily at 9:45, 11:15, 12:45, and 14:15; departs 30 minutes later from Opera House and one hour later from Bygdøy; tel. 23 35 68 90, www.boatsight seeing.com). They won't scream if you bring something to munch. They also offer two-hour fjord tours (250 kr, 3-4/day late March-Sept) and a "Summer Evening on the Fjord" dinner cruise (395 kr; joyride without narration that includes a "shrimp buffet"—just shrimp, bread, and butter; daily mid-June-Sept 19:00-22:00).

Bus Tours—Båtservice, which runs the harbor cruises (above), also offers four-hour **bus tours** of Oslo, with stops at the ski jump, Bygdøy museums, and Frogner Park (340 kr, 2/day late May-Aug, departs from ticket office on pier 3, longer tours also available, tel. 23 35 68 90, www.boatsightseeing.com). HMK also does daily city bus tours (200 kr/2 hours, 340 kr/4 hours, departs from TI across from City Hall, tel. 22 78 94 00, www.hmk.no).

Two different companies run **hop-on, hop-off bus tours:** CitySightseeing Oslo (150 kr/all day, 16 stops, www.citysight seeing.no) and Open Top/Oslo Sightseeing (220 kr/all day, 20 stops, www.opentopsightseeing.no; both run every 30 minutes, English headphone commentary, buy ticket from driver). While these tours help you get your bearings, most of Oslo's sightseeing is concentrated in a few discrete zones that are well-connected by the excellent public-transportation network—making pricey bus tours a lesser value.

Guided Walking Tour—The local guides' union offers 1.5-hour historic "Oslo Promenade" walks (150 kr, free with Oslo Pass; Mon, Wed, Fri at 17:30 in summer; leaves from sea side of City Hall, confirm departures at TI, tel. 22 42 70 20, www.guide service.no).

Local Guide—To hire a private guide, call the guides' association at tel. 22 42 70 20 (1,550 kr/2 hours, www.guideservice.no).
Another local guide bureau is at tel. 22 42 28 18.

Self-Guided Tram Tour

Tram #11/#12: A Hop-On, Hop-Off Introduction to Oslo

Tram #12, which becomes tram #11 halfway through its loop (at
Majorstuen), circles the city from the train station, lacing together
many of Oslo's main sights. Apart from the practical value of being
able to hop on and off as you sightsee your way around town (trams
come by at least every 10 minutes), this 40-minute trip gives you a
fine look at parts of the city you wouldn't otherwise see.

The route starts at the main train station, at the traffic-island
tram stop located immediately in front of the transit office tower.
The route makes almost a complete circle and finishes at Stortorvet
(the cathedral square), dropping you off a three-minute walk from
where you began the tour. You want tram #12 leaving from the second set of tracks, going toward Majorstuen. (Confirm with your
driver that the particular tram #12 you're boarding becomes tram
#11 and finishes at Stortorvet; some of these may turn into tram
#19 instead, which takes a different route. If yours becomes #19,
simply hop out at Majorstuen and wait for the next #11.) Here's
what you'll see and ideas on where you might want to hop out:

From the **station,** you'll go through the old grid streets of
16th-century Christiania, King Christian IV's planned Renaissance town. After the city's 17th fire, in 1624, the king finally got
fed up. He decreed that only brick and stone buildings would
be permitted in the city center, with wide streets to serve as fire
breaks.

You'll turn a corner at the **fortress** (Christiana Torv stop; get
off here for the fortress and Norwegian Resistance Museum), then
head for **City Hall** (Rådhus stop). Next comes the harbor and
upscale **Aker Brygge** waterfront neighborhood (jump off at the
Aker Brygge stop for the harbor and restaurant row). Passing the
harbor, you'll see on the left a few old shipyard buildings that still
survive. Then the tram goes uphill, past the **House of Oslo** (a mall
of 20 shops highlighting Scandinavian interior design; Vikatorvet
stop) and into a district of ugly 1960s buildings (when elegance was
replaced by "functionality"). The tram then heads onto the street
Norwegians renamed **Henrik Ibsens Gate** in 2006 to commemorate the centenary of Ibsen's death, honoring the man they claim is
the greatest playwright since Shakespeare.

After Henrik Ibsens Gate, the tram follows Frognerveien
through the chic **Frogner neighborhood.** Behind the fine

old facades are fancy shops and spendy condos. Here and there you'll see 19th-century mansions built by aristocratic families who wanted to live near the Royal Palace; today, many of these house foreign embassies. Turning the corner, you roll along the edge of **Frogner Park,** stopping at its grand gate (hop out at the Vigelandsparken stop for Frogner Park and Vigeland statues).

Ahead on the left, a statue of 1930s ice queen Sonja Henie marks the arena where she learned to skate. Turning onto Bogstadveien, the tram usually becomes #11 at the Majorstuen stop. **Bogstadveien** is lined with trendy shops, restaurants, and cafés—it's a fun place to stroll and window-shop. (You could get out here and walk along this street all the way to the Royal Palace park and the top of Karl Johans Gate.) The tram veers left before the palace, passing the **National Historical Museum** and stopping at the **National Gallery** (Tullinløkka stop). As you trundle along, you may notice that lots of roads are ripped up for construction. It's too cold to fix the streets in winter, so, when possible, the work is done in summer. Jump out at **Stortorvet** (a big square filled with flower stalls and fronted by the cathedral and the big GlasMagasinet department store). From here, you're a three-minute walk from the station, where this tour began.

Self-Guided Walk

▲▲Welcome to Oslo

This stroll covers the heart of Oslo—the zone where most tourists find themselves walking—from the train station, up the main drag, and past City Hall to the harborfront. It takes a brisk 30 minutes if done nonstop.

Train Station: Start at the plaza just outside the main entrance of Oslo's central train station (Oslo Sentralstasjon). The statue of the tiger prowling around out front commemorates the 1,000th birthday of Oslo's founding, celebrated in the year 2000. The statue alludes to the town's nickname of Tigerstaden ("Tiger Town"). In the 1800s, Oslo was considered an urban tiger, leaving its mark on the soul of simple country folk who ventured into the wild and crazy New York City of Norway. (These days, the presence of so many beggars, or *tigger,* has prompted the nickname "Tiggerstaden.")

With your back to the train station, look for the glass Ruter tower that marks the **public transit office** (and TI); from here, trams zip to City Hall (harbor, boat to Bygdøy), and the underground subway (T-bane, or *Tunnelbane*—look for the *T* sign to your right) goes to Frogner Park (Vigeland statues) and Holmenkollen. Tram #12—featured in the self-guided tram tour described earlier—leaves from directly across the street.

OSLO

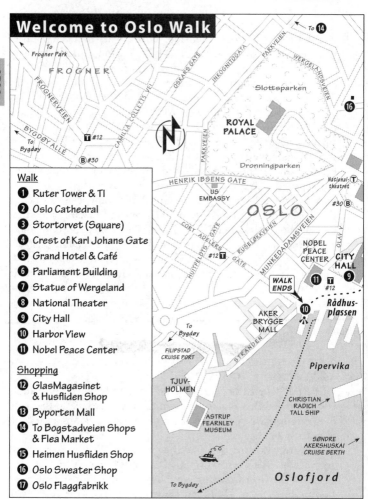

Welcome to Oslo Walk

Walk

1. Ruter Tower & TI
2. Oslo Cathedral
3. Stortorvet (Square)
4. Crest of Karl Johans Gate
5. Grand Hotel & Café
6. Parliament Building
7. Statue of Wergeland
8. National Theater
9. City Hall
10. Harbor View
11. Nobel Peace Center

Shopping

12. GlasMagasinet & Husfliden Shop
13. Byporten Mall
14. To Bogstadveien Shops & Flea Market
15. Heimen Husfliden Shop
16. Oslo Sweater Shop
17. Oslo Flaggfabrikk

The green building behind the Ruter tower is a shopping mall called **Byporten** (literally, "City Gate," see big sign on rooftop), built to greet those arriving from the airport on the shuttle train. Oslo's 37-floor pointed-glass **skyscraper,** the Radisson Blu Plaza Hotel, looms behind that. Its 34th-floor pub welcomes the public with air-conditioned views and pricey drinks (daily 16:00-24:00). The tower was built with reflective glass so that, from a distance, it almost disappears. The area behind the Radisson—the lively and colorful "Little Karachi," centered along a street called Grønland—is where most of Oslo's immigrant population settled. It's become a vibrant nightspot, offering a fun contrast to the predictable homogeneity of Norwegian cuisine and culture.

OSLO

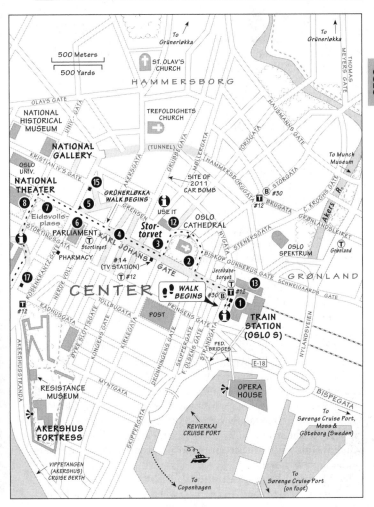

Oslo allows hard-drug addicts and prostitutes to mix and mingle in the station area. (While it's illegal to buy sex in Norway, those who sell it are not breaking the law.) Troubled young people come here from small towns in the countryside for anonymity and community. The two cameras near the top of the Ruter tower monitor drug deals. Signs warn that this is a "monitored area," but victimless crimes proceed while violence is minimized.

• *Turn your attention to Norway's main drag, called...*

Karl Johans Gate: This grand boulevard leads directly from the train station to the Royal Palace. The street is named for the French general Jean Baptiste Bernadotte, who was given a Swedish name, established the current Swedish dynasty, and ruled as a popular king (1818-1844) during the period after Sweden took Norway from Denmark.

Walk three blocks up Karl Johans Gate. This stretch is referred to as **"Desolation Row"** by locals because it has no soul, just shops greedily looking to devour tourist dollars and euros.

• *Hook right around the curved old brick structure of an old market and walk to the...*

Oslo Cathedral (Domkirke): This Lutheran church, from 1697, is where Norway commemorates its royal marriages and deaths. Seventy-seven deaths were mourned here following the tragic shootings and bombing of July 2011 (see sidebar, page 270). In the grass in front of the cathedral, you may see a semi-permanent memorial to the victims, consisting of a row of stones shaped like a heart.

Before going inside, stroll around to the right, behind the church. The **courtyard** is lined by a circa-1850 circular row of stalls from an old market. Rusty meat hooks now decorate the lamps of a peaceful café, which has quaint tables around a fountain. The atmospheric **Café Bacchus,** at the far left end of the arcade, serves food outside and in a classy café downstairs (light 150-kr meals, Mon-Fri 11:00-22:00, Sat 12:00-21:00, closed Sun, salads, good cakes, coffee, tel. 22 33 34 30).

Now go around the other side to face the cathedral's main door (under the tall tower). Look for the cathedral's cornerstone (right of entrance), a thousand-year-old carving from Oslo's first and long-gone cathedral showing how the forces of good and evil tug at each of us. Step inside beneath the red, blue, and gold seal of Oslo and under an equally colorful ceiling. The box above on the right is for the royal family. Back outside, notice the tiny square windows midway up the copper cupola—once the lookout quarters of the fire watchman.

• *The big square that faces the cathedral is called...*

Stortorvet: In the 17th century, when Oslo's wall was located about here, this was the point where farmers were allowed to enter and sell their goods. Today it's still lively as a flower and produce market (Mon-Fri). The statue shows Christian IV, the Danish king who ruled Norway around 1600, dramatically gesturing that-a-way. He named the city, rather immodestly, Christiania. (Oslo took back its old Norse name only in 1924.) Christian was serious about Norway. During his 60-year reign, he visited it 30 times (more than all other royal visits combined during 300 years of Danish rule). The big GlasMagasinet department store is a landmark on this square.

• *Return to Karl Johans Gate, and continue up the boulevard past street musicians, cafés, shops, and hordes of people. If you're here early in the morning (Mon-Fri) you may see a commotion at #14 (in the first block, on the left, look for the big 2 sign). This is the studio of a TV station (channel 2) where the Norwegian version of the* Today *show is taped, and as on Rockefeller Plaza, locals gather here, clamoring to get their mugs on TV.*

At the next corner, Kongens Gate leads left, past the 17th-century grid-plan town to the fortress. But we'll continue hiking straight up to the crest of the hill, enjoying some of the street musicians along the way. Pause at the wide spot in the street just before Akersgata to appreciate the...

Crest of Karl Johans Gate: Look back at the train station. A thousand years ago, the original (pre-1624) Oslo was located at the foot of the wooded hill behind the station. Now look ahead to the Royal Palace in the distance, which was built in the 1830s "with nature and God behind it and the people at its feet." If the flag flies atop the palace, the king is in the country. Karl Johans Gate is a parade ground from here to the palace—the axis of modern Oslo. Each May 17th, Norway's Independence Day, an annual children's parade turns this street into a sea of marching student bands and costumed young flag-wavers, while the royal family watches from the palace balcony. Since 1814, Norway has preferred peace. Rather than celebrating its military on the national holiday, it celebrates its children.

King Harald V and Queen Sonja moved back into the palace in 2001, after extensive (and costly) renovations. To quell the controversy caused by this expense, the public is now allowed inside to visit each summer with a pricey one-hour guided tour (95 kr, daily English tours late June-mid-Aug at 14:00 and 14:20, Mon-Thu and Sat also at 12:00, buy tickets in advance at any post office or convenience store, or by calling 81 53 31 33, www.kongehuset.no).

In the middle of the small square, the *T* sign marks a stop of the T-bane (Oslo's subway). Let W. B. Samson's bakery tempt you with its pastries (and short cafeteria line; WC in back). Next to that, David Andersen's jewelry store displays traditional silver art and fine enamel work. Inside, halfway down the wall on the right (next to the free water dispenser), is a display of Norwegian folk costumes *(bunader)* with traditional jewelry—worn on big family occasions and church holidays. From here, the street called Akersgata kicks off a worthwhile stroll past the site of the July 2011 bombing, the national cemetery, and through a park-like river gorge to the trendy Grünerløkka quarter (an hour-long walk, described on page 269).

People-watching is great along Karl Johans Gate, but remember that if it's summer, half of the city's regular population is gone—vacationing in their cabins or farther away—and the city center is filled mostly with visitors.

Hike two blocks down Karl Johans Gate, past the big brick

Parliament building (on the left). This section of sidewalk is heated during the frigid winter so it won't be icy. On the right, seated in the square, is a statue of the painter Christian Krohg. Farther down Karl Johans Gate, just past the Freia shop (Norway's oldest and best chocolate), the venerable **Grand Hotel** (Oslo's celebrity hotel—Nobel Peace Prize winners sleep here) overlooks the boulevard.

• *Ask the waiter at the Grand Café if you can pop inside for a little sightseeing (he'll generally let you).*

Grand Café: This historic café was for many years the meeting place of Oslo's intellectual and creative elite (the playwright Henrik Ibsen was a regular here). Notice the photos and knickknacks on the wall. At the back of the café, a mural shows Norway's literary and artistic clientele—from a century ago—enjoying this fine hangout. On the far left, find Ibsen, coming in as he did every day at 13:00. Edvard Munch is on the right, leaning against the window, looking pretty drugged. Names are on the sill beneath the mural.

• *For a cheap bite with prime boulevard seating, continue past the corner to Deli de Luca, a convenience store with a super selection of take-away food and a great people-watching perch. Across the street, a little park faces Norway's...*

Parliament Building (Stortinget): Norway's Parliament meets here (along with anyone participating in a peaceful protest outside). Built in 1866, the building seems to counter the Royal Palace at the other end of Karl Johans Gate. If the flag's flying, Parliament's in session. Today the king is a figurehead, and Norway is run by a unicameral Parliament and a prime minister. Guided tours of the Stortinget are offered for those interested in Norwegian government (free; mid-June-Aug Mon-Fri at 10:00, 11:30, and 13:00; enter on Karl Johans Gate side, tel. 23 31 35 96, www.stortinget.no).

• *Cross over into the park and stroll toward the palace, past the fountain. Pause at the...*

Statue of Wergeland: The poet Henrik Wergeland helped inspire the movement for Norwegian autonomy. In the winter, the pool here is frozen and covered with children happily ice-skating. Across the street behind Wergeland stands the **National Theater** and statues of Norway's favorite playwrights: Ibsen and Bjørnstjerne Bjørnson. Across Karl Johans Gate, the pale yellow building is the first university building in Norway, dating from 1854. A block behind that is the National Gallery, with Norway's best collection of paintings (self-guided tour on page 248).

• *Facing the theater, follow Roald Amundsens Gate left, to the towering brick...*

City Hall (Rådhuset): Built mostly in the 1930s with contri-

Browsing

Oslo's pulse is best felt by strolling. Three good areas are along and near the central Karl Johans Gate, which runs from the train station to the palace (follow my self-guided walk); in the trendy harborside Aker Brygge mall, a glass-and-chrome collection of sharp cafés, fine condos, and polished produce stalls (really lively at night, trams #10 and #12 from train station); and along Bogstadveien, a lively shopping street with no-nonsense modern commerce, lots of locals, and no tourists (T-bane to Majorstuen and follow this street back toward the palace and tourist zone). While most tourists never get out of the harbor/Karl Johans Gate district, the real, down-to-earth Oslo is better seen elsewhere, in places such as Bogstadveien. The bohemian, artsy Grünerløkka district, described on page 267, is good for a daytime wander.

butions from Norway's leading artists, City Hall is full of great art and is worth touring (see page 243). The mayor has his office here

(at the base of one of the two 200-foot towers), and every December 10, this building is where the Nobel Peace Prize is presented. For the best exterior art, circle the courtyard clockwise, studying the colorful woodcuts in the arcade. Each shows a scene from Norwegian mythology, well-explained in English: Thor with his billy-goat chariot, Ask and Embla (a kind of Norse Adam and Eve), Odin on his eight-legged horse guided by ravens, the swan maidens shedding their swan disguises, and so on. Circle to the right around City Hall, until you reach the front. The statues (especially the six laborers on the other side of the building, facing the harbor, who seem to guard the facade) celebrate the nobility of the working class.

• *Walk to the...*

Harbor: A decade ago, you would have dodged several lanes of busy traffic to get to Oslo's harborfront. But today, most cars cross underneath the city in tunnels. In addition, the city has made its town center relatively quiet and pedestrian-friendly by levying a traffic-discouraging 27-kr toll for every car entering town. (This system, like a similar one in London, subsidizes public transit and the city's infrastructure.)

At the water's edge, find the shiny metal plaque (just left of center) listing the contents of a sealed time capsule planted in 2000 out in the harbor in the little Kavringen lighthouse straight ahead

Oslo at a Glance

▲▲▲**City Hall** Oslo's artsy 20th-century government building, lined with huge, vibrant, municipal-themed murals, best visited with included tour. **Hours:** Daily 9:00-18:00; tours daily at 10:00, 12:00, and 14:00, tours run Wed only in winter. See page 243.

▲▲▲**National Gallery** Norway's cultural and natural essence, captured on canvas. **Hours:** Tue-Fri 10:00-18:00, Thu until 19:00, Sat-Sun 11:00-17:00, closed Mon. See page 247.

▲▲▲**Frogner Park** Sprawling park with works by Norway's greatest sculptor, Gustav Vigeland, and the studio where he created them (now a museum). **Hours:** Park—always open; Vigeland Museum—June-Aug Tue-Sun 10:00-17:00, Sept-May Tue-Sun 12:00-16:00, closed Mon year-round. See page 255.

▲▲▲**Norwegian Folk Museum** Norway condensed into 150 historic buildings in a large open-air park. **Hours:** Daily mid-May-mid-Sept 10:00-18:00, off-season park open Mon-Fri 11:00-15:00, Sat-Sun 11:00-16:00, but most historical buildings closed. See page 261.

▲▲**Norwegian Resistance Museum** Gripping look at Norway's tumultuous WWII experience. **Hours:** June-Aug Mon-Sat 10:00-17:00, Sun 11:00-17:00; Sept-May Mon-Fri 10:00-16:00, Sat-Sun 11:00-16:00. See page 246.

▲▲**Viking Ship Museum** An impressive trio of ninth-century Viking ships, with exhibits on the people who built them. **Hours:** Daily May-Sept 9:00-18:00, Oct-April 10:00-16:00. See page 262.

▲▲**Fram Museum** Captivating exhibit on the Arctic exploration ship. **Hours:** June-Aug daily 9:00-18:00; May and Sept daily 10:00-17:00; Oct and March-April daily 10:00-16:00; Nov-Feb Mon-Fri 10:00-15:00, Sat-Sun 10:00-16:00. See page 263.

▲▲**Kon-Tiki Museum** Adventures of primitive *Kon-Tiki* and *Ra II* ships built by Thor Heyerdahl. **Hours:** Daily June-Aug 9:00-18:00, March-May and Sept-Oct 10:00-17:00, Nov-Feb 10:00-16:00. See page 264.

▲▲**Holmenkollen Ski Jump and Ski Museum** Dizzying vista and a schuss through skiing history. **Hours:** Daily June-Aug 9:00-

20:00, May and Sept 10:00-17:00, Oct-April 10:00-16:00. See page 265.

▲**Nobel Peace Center** Exhibit celebrating the ideals of the Nobel Peace Prize and the lives of those who have won it. **Hours:** Mid-May-Aug daily 10:00-18:00; Sept-mid-May Tue-Sun 10:00-18:00, closed Mon. See page 244.

▲**Opera House** Stunning performance center that's helping revitalize the harborfront. **Hours:** Foyer and café/restaurant open Mon-Fri 10:00-23:00, Sat 11:00-23:00, Sun 12:00-22:00. See page 245.

▲**Akershus Fortress Complex and Tours** Historic military base and fortified old center, with guided tours, a ho-hum castle interior, and a couple of museums (including the excellent Norwegian Resistance Museum, listed above). **Hours:** Park generally open daily 6:00-21:00; 45-minute tours of the grounds generally offered May-mid-June Sat-Sun at 13:00; late June daily at 13:00 and 16:00; July-mid-Aug daily at 11:00, 13:00, 14:00, and 16:00; late Aug Sat-Sun at 15:00, no tours off-season. See page 245.

▲**Norwegian Holocaust Center** High-tech walk through rise of anti-Semitism, the Holocaust in Norway, and racism today. **Hours:** Daily mid-June-mid-Aug 10:00-18:00, mid-Aug-mid-June 11:00-16:00. See page 263.

▲**Norwegian Maritime Museum** Dusty cruise through Norway's rich seafaring heritage. **Hours:** Mid-May-Aug daily 10:00-18:00; Sept-mid-May Tue-Fri 10:00-15:00, Sat-Sun 10:00-16:00, closed Mon. See page 264.

▲**Edvard Munch Museum** Works of Norway's famous Expressionistic painter. **Hours:** June-Aug daily 10:00-17:00; Sept-May Tue-Sat 10:00-16:00, Sun 10:00-17:00, closed Mon. See page 265.

▲**Grünerløkka** Oslo's bohemian district, with bustling cafés and pubs. **Hours:** Always open. See page 267.

(to be opened in 1,000 years). Go to the end of the stubby pier (on the right). This is the ceremonial "enter the city" point for momentous occasions. One such instance was in 1905, when Norway gained its independence from Sweden and a Danish prince sailed in from Copenhagen to become the first modern king of Norway. Another milestone event occurred at the end of World War II, when the king returned to Norway after the country was liberated from the Nazis.

• *Stand at the harbor and give it a sweeping counterclockwise look.*

Harborfront Spin-Tour: Oslofjord is a huge playground, with 40 city-owned, park-like islands. Big white cruise ships— a large part of the local tourist economy—dock just under the Akershus Fortress on the left. Just past the fort's impressive 13th-century ramparts, a statue of FDR grabs the shade. He's here in gratitude for the safe refuge the US gave to members of the royal family (including the young prince who is now Norway's king) during World War II—while the king and his government-in-exile waged Norway's fight against the Nazis from London.

Enjoy the grand view of City Hall. The yellow building farther to the left was the old West Train Station; today it houses the **Nobel Peace Center,** which celebrates the work of Nobel Peace Prize winners (see page 244). The next pier is the launchpad for harbor boat tours and the shuttle boat to the Bygdøy museums. A fisherman often moors his boat here, selling shrimp from the back.

At the other end of the harbor, shipyard buildings (this was the former heart of Norway's once-important shipbuilding industry) have been transformed into **Aker Brygge**—Oslo's thriving restaurant/shopping/nightclub zone (see "Eating in Oslo").

Just past the end of Aker Brygge is a brand-new housing development, which you may see still under construction, called **Tjuvholmen.** It's anchored by the Astrup Fearnley Museum—an international modern art museum complex designed by renowned architect Renzo Piano (most famous for Paris' Pompidou Center; www.afmuseet.no). This zone is just one more reminder of Oslo's bold march toward becoming a city that is at once futuristic and people-friendly. An ambitious urban renewal project called Fjord City (Fjordbyen)—which kicked off years ago with Aker Brygge, and led to the construction of Oslo's dramatic new Opera House (see page 245)—is making remarkable progress in turning the formerly industrial waterfront into a thriving people zone.

• *From here, you can tour City Hall (cheap lunches Mon–Fri 12:30-13:30 only), visit the Nobel Peace Center, hike up to Akershus Fortress, take a harbor cruise (see "Tours in Oslo," earlier), or catch a boat across the harbor to the museums at Bygdøy (from pier 3). The sights just mentioned are described in detail in the following section.*

Sights in Oslo

Near the Harborfront

▲▲▲**City Hall (Rådhuset)**—In 1931, Oslo tore down a slum and began constructing its richly decorated City Hall. It was finally

finished—after a WWII delay—in 1950 to celebrate the city's 900th birthday. Norway's leading artists all contributed to the building, an avant-garde thrill in its day. City halls, rather than churches, are the dominant buildings in Scandinavian capitals. The prominence of this building on the harborfront makes sense in this most humanistic, yet least churchgoing, northern end of the Continent. Up here, people pay high taxes, have high expectations, and are generally satisfied with what their governments do with their money.

Cost and Hours: Free, daily 9:00-18:00, free 50-minute guided tours daily at 10:00, 12:00, and 14:00 in summer, tours run Wed only in winter, free WC, enter on Karl Johans Gate side, tel. 23 46 12 00.

Visiting City Hall: At Oslo's City Hall, the six statues facing the waterfront—dating from a period of Labor Party rule in Norway—celebrate the nobility of the working class. The art implies a classless society, showing everyone working together. The theme continues inside, with 20,000 square feet of bold and colorful Socialist Realist murals showing town folk, country folk, and people from all walks of life working harmoniously for a better society. The huge murals take you on a voyage through the collective psyche of Norway, from its simple rural beginnings through the scar tissue of the Nazi occupation and beyond. Filled with significance and symbolism—and well-described in English—the murals become even more meaningful with the excellent guided tours.

The main hall feels like a temple to good government, with its altar-like mural celebrating "work, play, and civic administration." The mural emphasizes Oslo's youth participating in community life—and rebuilding the country after Nazi occupation. Across the bottom, the slum that once cluttered up Oslo's harborfront is being cleared out to make way for this building. Above that, scenes show Norway's pride in its innovative health care and education systems. Left of center, near the top, Mother Norway rests on a church—reminding viewers that the Lutheran Church of Norway (the official state religion) provides a foundation for this society. On the right, four forms represent the arts; they illustrate how creativity springs from children. And in the center, the figure of Charity is surrounded by Culture, Philosophy, and Family.

The "Mural of the Occupation" lines the left side of the hall. It tells the story of Norway's WWII experience. Looking left to right, you'll see the following: The German blitzkrieg overwhelms the country. Men head for the mountains to organize a resistance movement. Women huddle around the water well, traditionally where news is passed, while Quislings (traitors named after the Norwegian fascist who ruled the country as a Nazi puppet) listen in. While Germans bomb and occupy Norway, a family gathers in their living room. As a boy clenches his fist (showing determination) and a child holds the beloved Norwegian flag, the Gestapo steps in. Columns lie on the ground, symbolizing how Germans shut down the culture by closing newspapers and the university. Two resistance soldiers are executed. A cell of resistance fighters (wearing masks and using nicknames so if tortured they can't reveal their compatriots' identities) plan a sabotage mission. Finally, prisoners are freed, the war is over, and Norway celebrates its happiest day: May 17, 1945—the first Independence Day after five years under Nazi control.

While gazing at these murals, keep in mind that the Nobel Peace Prize is awarded in this central hall each December (though the general Nobel Prize ceremony occurs in Stockholm's City Hall). You can see videos of the ceremony and acceptance speeches in the adjacent Nobel Peace Center (see next).

Eating: A wonderful budget-lunch cafeteria is downstairs, offering a simple hot meal and salad bar at a nonprofit price; it's primarily for the building's workers, but the public is welcome (Mon-Fri 12:30-13:30 only). Fans of the explorer Fridtjof Nansen might enjoy a coffee or beer across the street at Fridtjof, an atmospheric bar filled with memorabilia from Nansen's Arctic explorations (Mon-Sat 12:00 until late, Sun 14:00-22:00, Nansens Plass 7, near Forex, tel. 93 25 22 30).

▲**Nobel Peace Center (Nobels Fredssenter)**—This thoughtful and thought-provoking museum, housed in the former West Train Station (Vestbanen), poses the question, "What is the opposite of conflict?" It celebrates the 800-some past and present Nobel Peace Prize winners with engaging audio and video exhibits and high-tech gadgetry (all with good English explanations). Allow time for reading about past prizewinners and listening to acceptance speeches by recipients from President Carter to Mother Theresa. Check out the astonishing interactive book detailing the life and work of Alfred Nobel, the Swedish inventor of dynamite, who initiated the prizes—perhaps to assuage his conscience.

Cost and Hours: 80 kr; mid-May-Aug daily 10:00-18:00; Sept-mid-May Tue-Sun 10:00-18:00, closed Mon; included guided tours at 12:00, 14:00, and 15:00, fewer in winter; Brynjulfs Bulls Plass 1, tel. 48 30 10 00, www.nobelpeacecenter.org.

▲**Opera House**—Opened in 2008, Oslo's striking Opera House is the talk of the town and a huge hit. The Opera House rises

from the water on the city's eastern harbor, across the highway from the train station (use the sky-bridge). Its boxy, low-slung, glass center holds a state-of-the-art, 1,400-seat main theater. The jutting white marble planes of its roof double as a public plaza. When visiting, you feel a need to walk all over it. The Opera House is part of a larger harbor-redevelopment plan that includes rerouting traffic into tunnels and turning a once-derelict industrial zone into an urban park.

Cost and Hours: Foyer and café/restaurant open Mon-Fri 10:00-23:00, Sat 11:00-23:00, Sun 12:00-22:00.

Tours: In summer, the Opera House offers guided tours of

the auditorium and back-stage area (100 kr, daily usually at 14:00, time can vary) and sporadic foyer concerts (50 kr, generally at 13:00). For tours, reserve by email at omvisninger@operaen.no or online at www.operaen.no (tel. 21 42 21 00).

Getting There: The easiest way to get to the Opera House is from the train station. Just follow signs for *Exit South/Utgang Syd* (standing in the main hall with the tracks to your back, it's to the left). Exiting the station, proceed straight ahead onto the pedestrian bridge (marked *Velkommen til Operaen*), which takes you effortlessly above traffic congestion to your goal.

▲Akershus Fortress Complex

This park-like complex of sights scattered over Oslo's fortified old center is still a military base. But as you dodge patrol guards and vans filled with soldiers, you'll see the castle, a prison, war memorials, the Norwegian Resistance Museum, the Armed Forces Museum, and cannon-strewn ramparts affording fine harbor views and picnic perches. There's an unimpressive changing of the guard daily at 13:30 (at the parade ground, deep in the castle complex). The park is generally open daily 6:00-21:00, but because the military is in charge here, times can change without warning. Expect bumpy cobblestone lanes and steep hills. To get here from the harbor, follow the stairs (which lead past the FDR statue) to the park.

Fortress Visitors Center: Located immediately inside the gate, the information center has an interesting exhibit tracing the story of Oslo's fortifications from medieval times through the environmental struggles of today. Stop here to pick up a castle overview booklet, quickly browse through the museum, watch the quick video, and consider catching a tour (see next; museum entry free, mid-June-mid-Aug Mon-Fri 10:00-17:00, Sat-Sun 11:00-17:00, shorter hours off-season, tel. 23 09 39 17, www.mil.no /felles/ak).

▲**Fortress Tours**—The free 45-minute English walking tours of the grounds help you make sense of the most historic piece of real estate in Oslo (offered May-mid-June Sat-Sun at 13:00; late June daily at 13:00 and 16:00; July-mid-Aug daily at 11:00, 13:00, 14:00, and 16:00; late Aug Sat-Sun at 15:00; no tours off-season; depart from Fortress Visitors Center, call center at tel. 23 09 39 17 in advance to confirm times).

Akershus Castle—Although it's one of Oslo's oldest buildings (c. 1300), the castle overlooking the harbor is mediocre by European standards; the big, empty rooms recall Norway's medieval poverty. From the old kitchen, where the ticket desk and gift shop are located, you'll follow a one-way circuit of rooms open to the public. Descend through a secret passage to the dungeon, crypt, and royal tomb. Emerge behind  the altar in the chapel, then walk through echoing rooms including the Daredevil's Tower, Hall of Christian IV, and Hall of Olav I. There are terrific harbor views from the rampart just outside.

Cost and Hours: 70 kr, sparse English descriptions throughout; May-Aug Mon-Sat 10:00-16:00, Sun 12:30-16:00; Sept-April Sat-Sun 12:00-17:00 only, closed Mon-Fri; tel. 22 41 25 21.

▲▲**Norwegian Resistance Museum (Norges Hjemme-frontmuseum)**—This fascinating museum tells the story of Norway's WWII experience: appeasement, Nazi invasion (they made Akershus their headquarters), resistance, liberation, and, finally, the return of the king.

OSLO

Cost and Hours: 50 kr, 100-kr family ticket covers 2 adults plus up to 2 kids; June-Aug Mon-Sat 10:00-17:00, Sun 11:00-17:00; Sept-May Mon-Fri 10:00-16:00, Sat-Sun 11:00-16:00; next to castle, overlooking harbor, tel. 23 09 31 38, www.mil.no/felles/nhm.

Visiting the Museum: It's a one-way, chronological, can't-get-lost route—enter through the 1940 door.

You'll see propaganda posters attempting to get Norwegians to join the Nazi party, and the German ultimatum to which the king gave an emphatic "No." Various displays show secret radios, transmitters, underground newspapers, crude but effective home-made weapons, and the German machine that located clandestine radio stations. Exhibits explain how the country coped with 350,000 occupying troops; how airdrops equipped a home force of 40,000 ready to coordinate with the Allies when liberation was imminent; and the happy day when peace and freedom returned to Norway.

The museum is particularly poignant because many of the patriots featured inside were executed by the Germans right outside the museum's front door; a stone memorial marks the spot. (At war's end, the traitor Vidkun Quisling was also executed here.) With good English descriptions, this is an inspirational look at how the national spirit can endure total occupation by a malevolent force.

Armed Forces Museum (Forsvarsmuseet)—Across the fortress parade ground, a too-spacious museum traces Norwegian military history from Viking days to post-World War II. The early stuff is sketchy, but the WWII story is compelling.

Cost and Hours: Free, May-Aug Mon-Fri 10:00-17:00, Sat-Sun 11:00-17:00, shorter hours off-season, tel. 23 09 35 82.

▲▲▲National Gallery (Nasjonalgalleriet)

While there are many schools of painting and sculpture displayed in Norway's National Gallery, focus on what's uniquely Norwegian. Paintings come and go in this museum (pesky curators may have even removed some of the ones listed in the self-guided tour on the next page), but you're sure to see plenty that showcase the harsh beauty of Norway's landscape and people. A thoughtful visit here gives those heading into the mountains and fjord country a chance to pack along a little of Norway's cultural soul. Tuck these images carefully away with your goat cheese—they'll sweeten your explorations.

The gallery also has several Picassos, a noteworthy Impressionist collection, a Van Gogh self-portrait, and some Vigeland statues. Its many raving examples of Edvard Munch's work, including one of his famous *Scream* paintings, make a trip to the Munch Museum unnecessary for most (see page 265). It has about 50 Munch paintings in its collection, but only about a third are on display. Be prepared for changes, but don't worry—no matter what

the curators decide to show, you won't have to scream for Munch's masterpieces.

Cost and Hours: 50 kr, free on Sun, Tue-Fri 10:00-18:00, Thu until 19:00, Sat-Sun 11:00-17:00, closed Mon, chewing gum prohibited, Universitets Gata 13, tel. 22 20 04 04, www.national museum.no.

The museum's 20-kr audioguide covers 15 paintings, has a poetic narrative with quotes from artists, and forces you to linger at each work of art—but doesn't have much more information than my self-guided tour below.

Self-Guided Tour

This easy-to-handle museum gives an effortless tour back in time and through Norway's most beautiful valleys, mountains, and fjords, with the help of its Romantic painters (especially Johan Christian Dahl). The paintings are organized roughly chronologically, from 1814 through 1950.

• *Go up the stairs but before entering the first room, look to the right at the large canvas in the stairwell.*

❶ **Christian Krohg—***Albertine to See the Police Surgeon* **(c. 1885-1887):** Christian Krohg (1852-1925) is known as Edvard Munch's inspiration, but to Norwegians, he's famous in his own right for his artistry and giant personality. Krohg had a sharp interest in social justice. In this painting, Albertine, a sweet girl from the countryside, has fallen into the world of prostitution in the big city. She's the new kid on the red-light block in the 1880s, as Oslo's prostitutes are pulled into the police clinic for their regular checkup. Note her traditional dress and the disdain she gets from the more experienced girls. Krohg has buried his subject in this scene. His technique requires the viewer to find her, and that search helps humanize the prostitute.

• *We'll look at more stark Norwegian realism later. But for now, let's head somewhere more idyllic. Walk into Room Z, turn left, and enter Room L.*

National Gallery—Upper Floor

❶ KROHG — Albertine to See the Police Surgeon

❷ DAHL — View of Fortundalen

❸ DAHL — Hellefossen near Hokksund

❹ FEARNLEY — Labro Falls at Kongsberg

❺ TIDEMAND & GUDE — The Bridal Voyage

❻ TIDEMAND — Low Church Devotion

❼ PETERSSEN — Christian II

❽ KROHG — A Sick Girl

❾ SUNDT-HANSEN —Burial at Sea

❿ SOHLBERG — Winter Night in the Mountains

⓫ MUNCH — Self-Portrait with a Cigarette

⓬ MUNCH — Puberty

⓭ MUNCH — The Sick Child

⓮ MUNCH — Madonna

⓯ MUNCH — The Scream

⓰ MUNCH — Dance of Life

Landscape Paintings and Romanticism

Landscape painting has always played an important role in Norwegian art, perhaps because Norway provides such an awesome and varied landscape to inspire artists. The style reached its peak during the Romantic period in the mid-1800s, which stressed the beauty of unspoiled nature. (This passion for landscapes sets Norway apart from Denmark and Sweden.) After 400 years of Danish rule, the soul of the country was almost snuffed out. But with semi-independence and a constitution in the early 1800s, there was a national resurgence. Romantic paintings featuring the power of Norway's natural wonders and the toughness of its salt-of-the-earth folk came into vogue.

❷ **Johan Christian Dahl—*View of Fortundalen* (1836):** This painting epitomizes the Norwegian closeness to nature. It shows a view similar to the one that 21st-century travelers enjoy on their Norway in a Nutshell excursion (see page 290): mountains, rivers, and a waterfall. Painted in 1836, it's textbook Romantic style.

Nature rules—the background is as detailed as the foreground, and you are sucked in.

Johan Christian Dahl (1788-1857) is considered the father of Norwegian Romanticism. Romantics such as Dahl (and Turner, Beethoven, and Lord Byron) put emotion over rationality. They reveled in the power of nature—death and pessimism ripple through their work. The birch tree—standing boldly front and center—is a standard symbol for the politically downtrodden Norwegian people: hardy, cut down, but defiantly sprouting new branches. In the mid-19th century, Norwegians were awakening to their national identity. Throughout Europe, nationalism and Romanticism went hand in hand.

Find the typical Norse farm with its haystacks looking like rune stones. It reminds us that these farmers are hardworking, independent, small landowners. There was no feudalism in medieval Norway. People were poor...but they owned their own land. You can almost taste the *geitost.*

• *Look at the other works in Rooms L and M. Dahl's paintings and those by his Norwegian contemporaries, showing heavy clouds and glaciers, repeat these same themes—drama over rationalism, nature pounding humanity. Human figures are melancholy. Norwegians, so close to nature, are fascinated by those plush, magic hours of dawn and twilight. The dusk makes us wonder: What will the future bring?*

In particular, focus on the painting to the left of the door in Room L.

❸ **Dahl—***Hellefossen near Hokksund* **(1838):** Another typical Dahl setting: romantic nature and an idealized scene. A fisherman checks on wooden baskets designed to catch salmon migrating up the river. In the background, a water-powered sawmill slices trees into lumber. Note another Dahl birch tree at the left, a subtle celebration of the Norwegian people and their labor.

• *Now continue into Room M. At the far end is...*

❹ **Thomas Fearnley—***Labro Falls at Kongsberg* **(1837):** Man cannot control nature or his destiny. The landscape in this painting is devoid of people—the only sign of humanity is the jumble of sawn logs in the foreground. A wary eagle perched on one log seems to be saying, "While you can cut these trees, they'll always be mine."

• *Facing this painting, turn left into Room N.*

❺ **Adolph Tidemand and Hans Gude—***The Bridal Voyage* **(1848):** This famous painting shows the ultimate Norwegian scene: a wedding party with everyone decked out in traditional garb, heading for the stave church on the quintessential fjord (Hardanger). It's a studio work (not real) and a collaboration: Hans Gude painted the landscape, and Adolph Tidemand painted the people. Study their wedding finery. This work trumpets the greatness of both the landscape and Norwegian culture.

• Also in Room N are examples of...

OSLO

The Photographic Eye

At the end of the 19th century, Norwegian painters traded the emotions of Romanticism for more slice-of-life detail. This was the end of the Romantic period and the beginning of Realism. With the advent of photography, painters went beyond simple realism and into extreme realism.

❻ Tidemand—*Low Church Devotion* **(1848):** This scene shows a dissenting Lutheran church group (of which there were many in the 19th century) worshipping in a smokehouse. The light of God powers through the chimney, illuminating salt-of-the-earth people with strong faiths. Rather than accept the Norwegian king's "High Church," they worshipped in their homes in a more ascetic style. Later, many of these people emigrated to America for greater religious freedom.

• On the facing wall is...

❼ Eilif Peterssen—*Christian II* **(1875):** The Danish king signs the execution order for the man who'd killed the king's beloved mistress. With camera-like precision, the painter captures the whole story of murder, anguish, anger, and bitter revenge in the king's set jaw and steely eyes.

• Go through Rooms O and P and into Room Q. Take time to browse the paintings.

Vulnerability

Death, disease, and suffering were themes seen again and again in art from the late 1800s. The most serious disease during this period was tuberculosis (which killed Munch's mother and sister).

❽ Krohg—*A Sick Girl* **(1880):** This extremely realistic painting shows a child dying of tuberculosis, as so many did in Norway in the 19th century. The girl looks directly at you. You can almost feel the cloth, with its many shades of white.

❾ Carl Sundt-Hansen—*Burial at Sea* **(1890):** While Monet and the Impressionists were busy abandoning the realistic style, Norwegian artists continued to embrace it. In this painting, you're invited to participate. A dead man's funeral is attended by an ethnically diverse group of sailors and passengers, but only one is a woman—the widow. Your presence completes the half-circle at the on-deck ceremony. Notice how each person in the painting has his or her own way of confronting death. Their faces speak volumes about the life of toil here. A common thread in Norwegian art is the cycle—the tough cycle—of life. There's also an interest in everyday experiences. *Burial at Sea* may not always be on display. If it's not here, you may instead see a similar canvas, **Erik Werenskiold's *A Peasant Burial* (1885).**

Also in this room may be another Krohg painting, *I Leden* (1892), which is notable for non-artistic reasons: It was on loan to one of the Oslo buildings that was damaged in the July 2011 car bombing (see sidebar on page 270). The painting was badly damaged, but has since been repaired. You may see the painting, along with a small exhibit about how the canvas, shredded by a madman, has been lovingly repaired.

• *Continue through Room R and into Room S.*

Atmosphere

Landscape painters were often fascinated by the phenomena of nature, and the artwork in this room takes us back to this ideal from the Romantic Age. Painters were challenged by capturing atmospheric conditions at a specific moment, since it meant making quick sketches outdoors, before the weather changed yet again.

❿ **Harald Sohlberg—*Winter Night in the Mountains* (1914):**
Harald Sohlberg was inspired by this image while skiing in the mountains in the winter of 1899. Over the years, he attempted to re-create the scene that inspired this remark: "The mountains in winter reduce one to silence. One is overwhelmed, as in a mighty, vaulted church, only a thousand times more so."

• *Follow the crowds into Room T, the Munch room.*

Turmoil

Room T is filled with works by Norway's single most famous painter, Edvard Munch (see sidebar). Norway's long, dark winters and social isolation have produced many gloomy artists, but none gloomier than Munch. He infused his work with emotion and expression at the expense of realism. After viewing the paintings in general, take a look at these in particular (listed in clockwise order).

Edvard Munch
(1863-1944)

Edvard Munch (pronounced "moonk") is Norway's most famous and influential painter. His life was rich, complex, and sad. His father was a doctor who had a nervous breakdown. His mother and sister both died of tuberculosis. He knew suffering. And he gave us the enduring symbol of 20th-century pain, *The Scream.*

He was also Norway's most forward-thinking painter, a man who traveled extensively through Europe, soaking up the colors of the Post-Impressionists and the curves of Art Nouveau. He helped pioneer a new style—Expressionism—using lurid colors and wavy lines to "express" inner turmoil and the angst of the modern world.

After a nervous breakdown in late 1908, followed by eight months of rehab in a clinic, Munch emerged less troubled—but a less powerful painter. His late works were as a colorist: big, bright, less tormented...and less noticed.

❶ Edvard Munch—*Self Portrait with a Cigarette* (1895): In this self-portrait, Munch is spooked, haunted—an artist working, immersed in an oppressive world. Indefinable shadows inhabit the background. His hand shakes as he considers his uncertain future. (Ironic, considering he created his masterpieces during this depressed period.) After eight months in a Danish clinic, he found peace—and lost his painting power. Afterward, Munch never again painted another strong example of what we love most about his art.

❷ Munch—*Puberty* (1894-1895): One of the artist's most important non-*Scream* canvases reveals his ambivalence about women (see also his *Madonna*, below). This adolescent girl, grappling with her emerging sexuality, covers her nudity self-consciously. The looming shadow behind her—frighteningly too big and amorphous—threatens to take over the scene. The shadow's significance is open to interpretation—is it phallic, female genitalia, death, an embodiment of sexual anxiety...or Munch himself?

❸ Munch—*The Sick Child* (1896): The death of Munch's sister in 1877 due to tuberculosis likely inspired this painting. The girl's face melts into the pillow. She's becoming two-dimensional, halfway between life and death. Everything else is peripheral, even her despairing mother saying good-bye. You can see how Munch scraped and repainted the face until he got it right.

❹ **Munch—***Madonna* **(1894-1895):** Munch had a tortured relationship with women. He never married. He dreaded and struggled with love, writing that he feared if he loved too much, he'd lose his painting talent. This painting is a mystery: Is she standing or lying? Is that a red halo or some devilish accessory? Munch wrote that he would strive to capture his subjects at their holiest moment. His alternative name for this work: *Woman Making Love.* What's more holy than a woman at the moment of conception?

❺ **Munch—***The Scream* **(1893):**
Munch's most famous work shows a man
screaming, capturing the fright many feel
as the human "race" does just that. The
figure seems isolated from the people on
the bridge—locked up in himself, unable
to stifle his scream. Munch made four versions of this scene, which has become *the*
textbook example of Expressionism. On
one, he graffitied: "This painting is the
work of a madman." He explained that
the painting "shows today's society, rever-
berating within me...making me want to

scream." He's sharing his internal angst. In fact, this Expressionist
masterpiece is a breakthrough painting; it's angst personified.

❻ **Munch—***Dance of Life* **(1899-1900):** In this scene of five
dancing couples, we glimpse Munch's notion of femininity. To
him, women were a complex mix of Madonna and whore. We see
Munch's take on the cycle of women's lives: She's a virgin (discard-
ing the sweet flower of youth), a whore (a jaded temptress in red),
and a widow (having destroyed the man, she is finally alone, aging,
in black). With the phallic moon rising on the lake, Munch demon-
izes women as they turn men into green-faced, lusty monsters.

• *Our tour is over, but there's more to see in this fine collection. Take a
break from Nordic gloom and doom by visiting Rooms O and Y, with
works by Impressionist and Post-Impressionist artists...even Munch
got into the spirit with his Parisian painting, titled* Rue Lafayette.
*You'll see lesser known, but still beautiful, paintings by non-Norwegian
big names such as Picasso, Modigliani, Monet, Manet, Van Gogh,
Gauguin, and Cézanne.*

Near the National Gallery

National Historical Museum (Historisk Museum)—Directly
behind the National Gallery and just below the palace is a fine
Art Nouveau building offering an easy (if underwhelming) peek at
Norway's history.

Gustav Vigeland
(1869-1943)

As a young man, Vigeland studied sculpture in Oslo, then supplemented his education with trips abroad to Europe's art capitals. Back home, he carved out a successful, critically acclaimed career feeding newly independent Norway's hunger for homegrown art.

During his youthful trips abroad, Vigeland had frequented the studio of Auguste Rodin, admiring Rodin's naked, restless, intertwined statues. Like Rodin, Vigeland explored the yin/yang relationship of men and women. Also like Rodin, Vigeland did not personally carve or cast his statues. Rather, he formed them in clay or plaster, to be executed by a workshop of assistants. Vigeland's sturdy humans capture universal themes of the cycle of life—birth, childhood, romance, struggle, child-rearing, growing old, and death.

Cost and Hours: 50 kr, included 45-minute Viking tours daily at noon in the summer; mid-May-mid-Sept Tue-Sun 10:00-17:00, mid-Sept-mid-May Tue-Sun 11:00-16:00, closed Mon year-round; Frederiks Gate 2, tel. 22 85 99 12, www.khm.uio.no.

Visiting the Museum: The ground floor offers a walk through the local history from prehistoric times. It includes the country's top collection of Viking artifacts, displayed in low-tech, old-school exhibits with barely a word of English to give it meaning. There's also some medieval church art. The museum's highlight is upstairs: an exhibit (well-described in English) about life in the Arctic for the Sami people (previously known to outsiders as Laplanders). In this overview of the past, a few Egyptian mummies and Norwegian coins through the ages are tossed in for good measure.

▲▲▲Frogner Park

This 75-acre park contains a lifetime of work by Norway's greatest sculptor, Gustav Vigeland (see sidebar). In 1921, he made a deal with the city. In return for a great studio and state support, he'd spend his creative life beautifying Oslo with this sculpture garden. From 1924 to 1943 he worked on-site, designing 192 bronze and granite statue groupings—600 figures in all, each nude and unique. Vigeland even planned the landscaping. Today the park is loved and respected by the people of Oslo (no police, no fences—and no graffiti). The Frognerbadet swimming pool is also at Frogner Park.

Cost and Hours: The garden is always open and free. The park is safe (cameras monitor for safety) and lit in the evening.

Getting There: Tram #12—which leaves from the central

train station, Rådhusplassen in front of City Hall, Aker Brygge, and other points in town—drops you off right at the park gate (Vigelandsparken stop). Tram #19 (with stops along Karl Johans Gate) takes you to Majorstuen, a 10-minute walk to the gate (or you can change at Majorstuen to tram #12 and ride it one stop to Vigelandsparken).

Visiting the Park: Vigeland's park is more than great art: It's a city at play. Appreciate its urban Norwegian ambience. The park is huge, but this visit is a snap. Here's a quick, four-stop, straight-line, gate-to-monolith tour:

1. Enter the Park from Kirkeveien: For an illustrated guide and fine souvenir, pick up the 75-kr book in the Visitors Center (Besøkssenter) on your right as you enter. The modern cafeteria has sandwiches (indoor/outdoor seating, daily 9:00-20:30, shorter hours Sun and off-season), plus books, gifts, and WCs. Look at the statue of Gustav Vigeland (hammer and chisel in

hand, drenched in pigeon poop) and consider his messed-up life. He lived with his many models. His marriages failed. His children entangled his artistic agenda. He didn't age gracefully. He didn't name his statues, and refused to explain their meanings. While those who know his life story can read it clearly in the granite and bronze, I'd forget Gustav's troubles and see his art as observations on the bittersweet cycle of life in general—from a man who must have had a passion for living.

2. Bridge: The 300-foot-long bridge is bounded by four granite columns: Three show a man fighting a lizard, the fourth shows a woman submitting to the lizard's embrace. Hmmm. (Vigeland was familiar with medieval mythology, where dragons represent man's primal—and sinful—nature.) But enough lizard love; the 58 bronze statues along the bridge are a general study of the human body. Many deal with relationships between people. In the middle, on the right, find the circular statue of a man and woman going round and round—perhaps the eternal attraction and love between the sexes. But directly opposite, another circle feels like a prison—man against the world, with no refuge. From the man escaping, look down at the children's playground: eight bronze infants circling a head-down fetus.

On your left, see the famous *Sinnataggen,* the hot-headed little boy. It's said Vigeland gave him chocolate and then took it away to get this reaction. The statues capture the joys of life (and, on a sunny day, so do the Norwegians filling the park around you).

3. Fountain: Continue through a rose garden to the earliest sculpture unit in the park. Six giants hold a fountain, symbolically toiling with the burden of life, as water—the source of life—cascades steadily around them. Twenty tree-of-life groups surround the fountain. Four clumps of trees (on each corner) show humanity's relationship to nature and the seasons of life: childhood, young love, adulthood, and winter.

Take a quick swing through life, starting on the right with youth. In the branches you'll see a swarm of children (Vigeland

called them "geniuses"): A boy sits in a tree, boys actively climb while most girls stand by quietly, and a girl glides through the branches wide-eyed and ready for life...and love. Circle clockwise to the next stage: love scenes. In the third corner, life becomes more complicated: a sad woman in an animal-like tree, a lonely child, a couple plummeting downward (perhaps falling out of love), and finally an angry man driving away babies. The fourth corner completes the cycle, as death melts into the branches of the tree of life and you realize new geniuses will bloom.

The 60 bronze reliefs circling the basin develop the theme further, showing man mixing with nature and geniuses giving the carousel of life yet another spin. Speaking of another spin, circle again and follow these reliefs.

The sidewalk surrounding the basin is a maze—life's long and winding road with twists, dead ends, frustrations, and, ultimately, a way out. If you have about an hour to spare, enter the labyrinth (on the side nearest the park's entrance gate, there's a single break in the black border) and follow the white granite path until (on the monolith side) you finally get out. (Tracing this path occupies older kids, affording parents a peaceful break in the park.) Or you can go straight up the steps to the monolith.

4. Monolith: The centerpiece of the park—a teeming monolith of life surrounded by 36 granite groups—continues Vigeland's

cycle-of-life motif. The figures are hunched and clearly earthbound, while Vigeland explores a lifetime of human relationships. At the center, 121 figures carved out of a single block of stone rocket skyward. Three stone carvers worked daily for 14 years, cutting Vigeland's full-size plaster model into the final 180-ton, 50-foot-tall erection.

Circle the plaza, once to trace the stages of life in the 36 statue groups, and a second time to enjoy how Norwegian kids relate to the art. The statues—both young and old—seem to speak to children.

Vigeland lived barely long enough to see his monolith raised. Covered with bodies, it seems to pick up speed as it spirals skyward. Some people seem to naturally rise. Others struggle not to fall. Some help others. Although the granite groups around the monolith are easy to understand, Vigeland left the meaning of the monolith itself open. Like life, it can be interpreted many different ways.

From this summit of the park, look a hundred yards farther, where four children and three adults are intertwined and spinning in the Wheel of Life. Now, look back at the entrance. If the main gate is at 12 o'clock, the studio where Vigeland lived and worked—now the Vigeland Museum—is at 2 o'clock (see the green copper tower poking above the trees). His ashes sit in the top of the tower in clear view of the monolith. If you liked the park, visit the Vigeland Museum (described next), a delightful five-minute walk away, for an intimate look at the art and how it was made.

▲▲**Vigeland Museum**—Filled with original plaster casts and well-described exhibits on his work, this palatial city-provided studio was Vigeland's home and workplace. The high south-facing

windows provided just the right light.

Vigeland, who had a deeply religious upbringing, saw his art as an expression of his soul. He once said, "The road between feeling and execution should be as short as possible." Here, immersed in his work, Vigeland super-

vised his craftsmen like a father, from 1924 until his death in 1943.

Cost and Hours: 50 kr; June-Aug Tue-Sun 10:00-17:00, Sept-May Tue-Sun 12:00-16:00, closed Mon year-round; bus #20 or tram #12 to Frogner Plass, Nobels Gate 32, tel. 23 49 37 00, www .vigeland.museum.no.

Oslo City Museum (Oslo Bymuseum)—This hard-to-be-thrilled-about little museum tells the story of Oslo. For a quick overview of the city, watch the 15-minute English video.

Cost and Hours: Free, Tue-Sun 11:00-17:00, closed Mon, borrow English description sheet, located in Frogner Park at Frogner Manor Farm across street from Vigeland Museum, tel. 23 28 41 70, www.oslomuseum.no.

▲▲Oslo's Bygdøy Neighborhood

This thought-provoking and exciting cluster of sights is on a park-like peninsula just across the harbor from downtown. It provides a busy and rewarding half-day (at a minimum) of sightseeing. Here, within a short walk, are six important sights (listed in order of importance):

• **Norwegian Folk Museum,** an open-air park with traditional log buildings from all corners of the country.

• **Viking Ship Museum,** showing off the best-preserved Viking longboats in existence.

• **Fram Museum,** showcasing the modern Viking spirit with the ship of arctic-exploration fame.

• **Kon-Tiki Museum,** starring the *Kon-Tiki* and the *Ra II,* in which Norwegian explorer Thor Heyerdahl proved that early civilizations—with their existing technologies—could have crossed the oceans.

• **Norwegian Maritime Museum,** interesting mostly to old salts, has a wonderfully scenic movie of Norway.

• **Norwegian Holocaust Center,** a high-tech look at the Holocaust in Norway and contemporary racism.

Getting There: Sailing from downtown to Bygdøy is fun, and it gets you in a seafaring mood. Ride the Bygdøy ferry—marked *Public Ferry Bygdøy Museums*—from pier 3 in front of City Hall (50 kr one-way; covered by Oslo Pass, transit tickets, and Reisekort smartcard; May-Sept daily 8:45-20:45, usually 3/hour; doesn't run Oct-April). Boats generally leave from downtown and from the museum dock at :05, :25, and :45 past each hour. In summer, avoid the nearby (much more expensive) tour boats. For a less memorable

OSLO

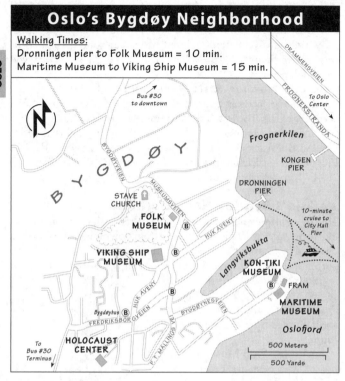

Oslo's Bygdøy Neighborhood

Walking Times:
Dronningen pier to Folk Museum = 10 min.
Maritime Museum to Viking Ship Museum = 15 min.

Bus #30
to downtown

To Oslo
Center

DRAMMENSVEIEN

FROGNERSTRANDA

Frognerkilen

KONGEN
PIER

BYGDØY

BYGDØYVEIEN

MUSEUMSVEIEN

DRONNINGEN
PIER

10-minute
cruise to
City Hall
Pier

STAVE
CHURCH

FOLK
MUSEUM

HUK AVENY

VIKING SHIP
MUSEUM

Langviksbukta

KON-TIKI
MUSEUM

HUK AVENY

BYGDØYNESVEIEN

FRAM

MARITIME
MUSEUM

Bygdøyhus

FREDRIKSBORGVEIEN

Oslofjord

To
Bus #30
Terminus

HOLOCAUST
CENTER

F.T. MALLINGS VEI

500 Meters

500 Yards

approach, you can take bus #30 (from train station or National Theater, direction: Bygdøy).

Getting Around Bygdøy: The Norwegian Folk and Viking Ship museums are a 10-minute walk from the ferry's first stop (Dronningen). The other boating museums (*Fram, Kon-Tiki,* and Maritime) are at the second ferry stop (Bygdøynes). The Holocaust Center is off Fredriksborgveien, about halfway between these two museum clusters. All Bygdøy sights are within a pleasant (when sunny) 15-minute walk of each other. The walk gives you a picturesque taste of small-town Norway.

City bus #30 connects the sights four times hourly in this order: Norwegian Folk Museum, Viking Ship Museum, *Kon-Tiki* Museum, Norwegian Holocaust Center. (For the Holocaust Center, you'll use the Bygdøyhus stop a long block away; tell the bus driver you want the stop for the "HL-Senteret"). The bus turns around at its final stop (Huk), then passes the sights in reverse order on its way back to the city center. If you take the bus within an hour of having taken the public ferry, your ticket is still good on the bus. Note that after 17:00, bus and boat departures are sparse. If returning to Oslo by ferry, get to the dock a little early—otherwise the boat is likely to be full, and you'll have to wait for the next sailing.

Eating at Bygdøy: Lunch options near the *Kon-Tiki* are a sandwich bar (relaxing picnic spots along the grassy shoreline) and a cafeteria (with tables overlooking the harbor). The Norwegian Folk Museum has a decent cafeteria inside and a fun little farmers' market stall across the street from the entrance. The Holocaust Center has a small café on its second floor.

▲▲▲**Norwegian Folk Museum (Norsk Folkemuseum)**—Brought from all corners of Norway, 150 buildings have been reassembled here on 35 acres. While Stockholm's Skansen was the first museum of this kind to open to the public (see page 450), this museum is a bit older, started in 1882 as the king's private collection (and the inspiration for Skansen).

Cost and Hours: 100 kr, daily mid-May-mid-Sept 10:00-18:00, off-season park open Mon-Fri 11:00-15:00, Sat-Sun 11:00-16:00 but most historical buildings closed, free lockers, Museumsveien 10, bus #30 stops immediately in front, tel. 22 12 37 00, www.norskfolkemuseum.no.

Visiting the Museum: Think of the visit in three parts: the park sprinkled with old buildings, the re-created old town, and the folk-art museum. In peak season, the park is lively, with craftspeople doing their traditional things and costumed guides all around. (They're paid to happily answer your questions—so ask many.) The evocative Gol stave church, at the top of a hill at the park's edge, is a must-see (built in 1212 in Hallingdal and painstakingly reconstructed here; for more on stave churches, see page 221). Across the park, the old town comes complete with apartments from various generations (including some reconstructions of actual people's homes) and offers an intimate look at lifestyles here in 1905, 1930, 1950, 1979, and even a modern-day Norwegian-Pakistani apartment.

The museum beautifully presents woody, colorfully painted folk art (ground floor), exquisite-in-a-peasant-kind-of-way folk costumes (upstairs), and temporary exhibits. Everything

is thoughtfully explained in English. Don't miss the best Sami culture exhibit I've seen in Scandinavia (across the courtyard in the green building, behind the toy exhibit).

Upon arrival, pick up the site map and review the list of activities, concerts, and guided tours on that day. In summer, guided tours go daily at 12:00 and 14:00;

the Telemark Farm hosts a small daily fiddle-and-dance show on the hour; and a folk music-and-dance show is held each Sunday at 14:00. The folk museum is lively only June through mid-August, when buildings are open and staffed. Otherwise, the indoor museum is fine, but the park is just a walk past lots of locked-up log cabins. If you don't take a tour, glean information from the 10-kr guidebook and the informative attendants stationed in buildings throughout the park.

▲▲▲Viking Ship Museum (Vikingskiphuset)—In this impressive museum, you'll gaze with admiration at two finely crafted,

majestic oak Viking ships dating from the 9th and 10th centuries. Along with the well-preserved ships, you'll see remarkable artifacts that may cause you to consider these notorious raiders in a different light. Over a thousand years ago, three things drove Vikings on their far-flung raids: hard economic times in their bleak homeland, the lure of prosperous and vulnerable communities to the south, and a mastery of the sea. There was a time when most frightened Europeans closed every prayer with, "And deliver us from the Vikings, Amen." Gazing up at the prow of one of these sleek, time-stained vessels, you can almost hear the screams and smell the armpits of those redheads on the rampage.

Cost and Hours: 60 kr, daily May-Sept 9:00-18:00, Oct-April 10:00-16:00, Huk Aveny 35, tel. 22 13 52 80, www.khm.uio.no.

Visiting the Museum: You'll see two ships, starting with the *Oseberg*, from A.D. 834. With its ornate carving and impressive rudder, it was likely a royal pleasure craft. It seems designed for sailing on calm inland waters during festivals, but not in the open ocean.

The *Gokstad*, from A.D. 950, is a practical working boat, capable of sailing the high seas. A ship like this brought settlers to the west of France (Normandy was named for the Norsemen). And in such a vessel, explorers such as Eric the Red hopscotched from Norway to Iceland to Greenland and on to what they called Vinland—today's Newfoundland in Canada. Imagine 30 men hauling on long oars out at sea for weeks and months at a time. In 1892, a replica of this ship sailed from Norway to America in 44 days to celebrate the 400th anniversary of Columbus *not* discovering America.

The ships tend to steal the show, but don't miss the hall displaying **jewelry and personal items** excavated along with the ships. The ships and related artifacts survived so well because they

OSLO

were buried in clay as part of a gravesite. Many of the finest items were not actually Viking art, but goodies they brought home after raiding more advanced (but less tough) people. Still, there are lots of actual Viking items, such as metal and leather goods, that give insight into their culture. Highlights are the cart and sleighs, ornately carved with scenes from Viking sagas.

The museum doesn't offer tours, but it's easy to eavesdrop on the many guides leading big groups through the museum. Everything is well-described in English. You probably don't need the little museum guidebook—it repeats exactly what's already posted on the exhibits.

▲**Norwegian Holocaust Center (HL-Senteret)**—Located in the stately former home of Nazi collaborator Vidkun Quisling, this museum and study center offers a high-tech look at the racist ideologies that fueled the Holocaust. To show the Holocaust in a Norwegian context, the first floor displays historical documents about the rise of anti-Semitism and personal effects from Holocaust victims. Downstairs, the names of 760 Norwegian Jews killed by the Nazis are listed in a bright, white room. The *Innocent Questions* glass-and-neon sculpture outside shows an old-fashioned punch card, reminding viewers of how the Norwegian puppet government collected seemingly innocuous information before deporting its Jews. The *Contemporary Reflections* video is a reminder that racism and genocide continue today.

Cost and Hours: 50 kr, ask for free English audioguide or catalog with translation of exhibit text, daily mid-June-mid-Aug 10:00-18:00, mid-Aug-mid-June 11:00-16:00, Huk Aveny 56—follow signs to *HL-Senteret*, tel. 22 84 21 00, www.hlsenteret.no.

▲▲**Fram Museum (Frammuseet)**—This museum holds

the 125-foot, steam- and sail-powered ship that took modern-day Vikings Roald Amundsen and Fridtjof Nansen deep into the Arctic and Antarctic, farther north and south than any vessel had gone before. For three years, the *Fram*—specially designed to survive the crushing pressures of a frozen-over sea—drifted, trapped in the Arctic ice. The exhibit is engrossing and newly improved.

Cost and Hours: 80 kr; June-Aug daily 9:00-18:00; May and Sept daily 10:00-17:00; Oct and March-April daily 10:00-16:00; Nov-Feb Mon-Fri 10:00-15:00, Sat-Sun 10:00-16:00; Bygdøynesveien 36, tel. 23 28 29 50, www.frammuseum.no.

Visiting the Museum: Read the ground-floor displays, check out the videos below the bow of the ship, then climb the steps to the third-floor gangway to explore the *Fram*'s claustrophobic but fascinating interior. Also featured are a tent like the one Amundsen used, reconstructed shelves from his Artic kitchen, models of the *Fram* and the motorized sled they used to traverse the ice and snow, and a "polar simulator" plunging visitors to a 15° Fahrenheit environment.

The museum also tells the chilling tales of other Arctic and Antarctic adventures undertaken beneath the Norwegian flag. The polar sloop *Gjøa*, dry-docked outside next to the ferry dock, is the ship that Amundsen and a crew of six used from 1903 to 1906 to "discover" the Northwest Passage.

▲▲Kon-Tiki Museum (Kon-Tiki Museet)—Next to the *Fram* is a museum housing the *Kon-Tiki* and the *Ra II*, the ships built by Thor Heyerdahl (1914-2002). In 1947, Heyerdahl and five crewmates constructed the *Kon-Tiki* raft out of balsa wood, using only pre-modern tools and techniques. They set sail from Peru on the tiny craft, surviving for 101 days on fish, coconuts, and sweet potatoes (which were native to Peru). About 4,300 miles later, they arrived in Polynesia. The point was to show that early South Americans could have settled Polynesia. (While Heyerdahl proved they could have, anthropologists doubt they did.) The *Kon-Tiki* story became a best-selling book and award-winning documentary (and helped spawn the "Tiki" culture craze in the US). In 1970, Heyerdahl's *Ra II* made a similar 3,000-mile journey from Morocco to Barbados to prove that Africans could have populated America. Both ships are well-displayed and described in English. Short clips from *Kon-Tiki*, the Oscar-winning 1950 documentary film, play in a small theater at the end of the exhibit.

Cost and Hours: 70 kr, daily June-Aug 9:00-18:00, March-May and Sept-Oct 10:00-17:00, Nov-Feb 10:00-16:00, Bygdøynesveien 36, tel. 23 08 67 67, www.kon-tiki.no.

▲Norwegian Maritime Museum (Norsk Sjøfartsmuseum)— If you like the sea, this museum is a salt lick, providing a wide-ranging look at Norway's maritime heritage. Its dusty collection includes the charred remains of Norway's oldest boat (2,200 years old), artifacts from the immigration days, and a case devoted to World War II. Don't miss the movie *The Ocean: A Way of Life*, included with your admission. It's a breathtaking widescreen film swooping you scenically over Norway's dramatic sea and fishing townscapes from here all the way to North Cape in a comfy theater (20 minutes, shown at the top and bottom of the hour, follow *Supervideografen* signs).

Cost and Hours: 60 kr, kids under 6 free; mid-May-Aug daily 10:00-18:00; Sept-mid-May Tue-Fri 10:00-15:00, Sat-Sun 10:00-16:00, closed Mon; Bygdøynesveien 37, tel. 24 11 41 50, www.marmuseum.no.

OSLO

Outer Oslo

▲▲**Holmenkollen Ski Jump and Ski Museum**—The site of one of the world's oldest ski jumps (from 1892), Holmenkollen has hosted many championships, including the 1952 Winter Olympics. To win the privilege of hosting the 2011 World Ski Jump Championship, Oslo built a bigger jump to match modern ones built elsewhere. This futuristic, cantilevered, Olympic-standard **ski jump** has a tilted elevator that you can ride to the top (on a sunny day, you may have to wait your turn for the elevator). Stand right at the starting gate, just like an athlete, and get a feel for this daredevil sport. The jump empties into a 50,000-seat amphitheater, and if you go when it's clear, you'll see one of the best possible views of Oslo.

The **ski museum,** a must for skiers, traces the evolution of the sport, from 4,000-year-old rock paintings to crude 1,500-year-old wooden sticks to the slick and quickly evolving skis of modern times, including a fun exhibit showing the royal family on skis. You'll see gear from Roald Amundsen's famous trek to the South Pole, including the stuffed remains of Obersten (the Colonel), one of his sled dogs.

Cost and Hours: 110-kr ticket includes museum and viewing platform at top of jump; daily June-Aug 9:00-20:00, May and Sept 10:00-17:00, Oct-April 10:00-16:00; tel. 22 92 32 64, www.holmenkollen.com or www.skiforeningen.no.

Simulator: To cap your Holmenkollen experience, step into the simulator and fly down the ski jump and ski in a virtual downhill race. My legs were exhausted after the five-minute terror. This simulator (or should I say stimulator?), at the lower level of the complex, costs 60 kr (if you pay for four tickets, try getting a fifth one free).

Getting There: T-bane line #1 gets you out of the city, through the hills, forests, and mansions that surround Oslo, and to the jump (direction: Frognerseteren; alternatively, you can take any westbound train—that's *tog mot vest*—to Majorstuen, then transfer to line #1). From the Holmenkollen station, you'll hike up the road 10 minutes to the ski jump.

For an easy downhill jaunt through the Norwegian forest, with a woodsy coffee or meal break in the middle, stay on the T-bane past Holmenkollen to the end of the line (Frognerseteren) and walk 10 minutes downhill to the recommended **Frognerseteren Hovedrestaurant,** a fine traditional eatery with a sod roof, reindeer meat on the griddle, and a city view. Continue on the same road another 20 minutes downhill to the ski jump, and then to the Holmenkollen T-bane stop.

▲**Edvard Munch Museum (Munch Museet)**—The only Norwegian painter to have had a serious impact on European art,

Munch (pronounced "moonk") is a surprise to many who visit this fine museum, located one mile east of Oslo's center. The emotional, disturbing, and powerfully Expressionistic work of this strange and perplexing man is arranged chronologically. You'll see an extensive collection of paintings, drawings, lithographs, and photographs. Note that Oslo's centrally located National Gallery, which also displays many Munch works, can be a good alternative if you find the Munch Museum too time-consuming to reach.

The Munch Museum was in the news in August of 2004, when two Munch paintings, *Madonna* and a version of his famous *Scream*, were brazenly stolen right off the walls in broad daylight. Two men in black hoods simply entered through the museum café, waved guns at the stunned guards and tourists, ripped the paintings off the wall, and sped off in a black Audi station wagon. Happily, in 2006, the thieves were caught and the stolen paintings recovered. Today they are on display again, behind glass and with heightened security.

Cost and Hours: 95 kr; June-Aug daily 10:00-17:00; Sept-May Tue-Sat 10:00-16:00, Sun 10:00-17:00, closed Mon; 25-kr audioguide, guided tours daily July-Aug at 13:00, T-bane or bus #20 to Tøyen, Tøyengata 53, tel. 23 49 35 00, www.munch .museum.no. For more on Munch, see page 253.

Forests, Lakes, and Beaches—Oslo is surrounded by a vast forest dotted with idyllic little lakes, huts, joggers, bikers, and sun-worshippers. Mountain-biking possibilities are endless (as you'll discover if you go exploring without a good map). Consider taking your bike on the T-bane (for the added cost of a child's ticket) to the end of line #1 (Frognerseteren, 30 minutes from National Theater) to gain the most altitude possible. Then follow the gravelly roads (mostly downhill but with some climbing) past several dreamy lakes to Sognsvann at the end of T-bane line #3. Farther east, from Maridalsvannet, a bike path follows the Akers River all the way back into town. (The TI has details.) While Oslo isn't much on bike rentals, you can rent them in summer at Skiservice, located at the Voksenkollen stop on T-bane line #1, at the high end of the woods (about 350 kr/day, tel. 22 13 95 00, www.skiservice .no). However, keep in mind that you'll need to bring your bike back here—via T-bane if you like.

For plenty of trees and none of the exercise, ride T-bane line #3 to its last stop, Sognsvann (with a beach towel rather than a bike), and join the lakeside scene. A pleasant trail leads around the lake.

Other popular beaches are located on islands in the harbor (such as Bygdøy Huk—direct boat from pier 3 in front of City Hall). The various island getaways are described in Use It's *Streetwise* magazine.

Tusenfryd—This giant amusement complex just out of town offers a world of family fun. It's sort of a combination Norwegian Disneyland/Viking Knott's Berry Farm, with more than 50 rides, plenty of entertainment, and restaurants.

Cost and Hours: Admission is based on your height: under 95 centimeters (3 feet)—free, under 1.2 meters (4 feet)—270 kr, over 1.2 meters (4 feet)—345 kr. Daily June-late Aug 10:30-19:00, closed in winter, tel. 64 97 66 99, www.tusenfryd.no.

Getting There: Bus #541 takes fun-seekers to the park from behind Oslo's train station (48 kr, 2/hour, 20-minute ride, departs Oslo 10:00-16:00, departs Tusenfryd 14:30-17:30).

Wet Fun—Oslo offers a variety of water play. In Frogner Park, the **Frognerbadet** has three outdoor pools, a waterslide, high dives, a cafeteria, and lots of young families (80 kr, students-59 kr, mid-May-late Aug Mon-Fri 7:00-19:00, Sat-Sun 10:00-18:00, last entry one hour before closing, closed late Aug-mid-May, Middelthunsgate 28, tel. 23 27 54 50).

Tøyenbadet, a modern indoor/outdoor pool complex with a 330-foot-long waterslide, also has a gym and sauna (80 kr, children-38 kr, Mon-Fri 7:00-19:30, Sat-Sun 9:00-15:00, sometimes closed mornings for school events, 10-minute walk from Edvard Munch Museum, Helgengate 90, tel. 23 30 44 70). Oslo's free botanical gardens are nearby.

From Akers River to the Grünerløkka District

Connect the dots by following the self-guided "Walk up the Akers River to Grünerløkka" (see page 269).

Akers River—This river, though only about five miles long, powered Oslo's early industry: flour mills in the 1300s, sawmills in the 1500s, and Norway's Industrial Revolution in the 1800s. A walk along the river not only spans Oslo's history, but also shows the contrast the city offers. The bottom of the river (where this walk doesn't go)—bordered by the high-rise Oslo Radisson Blu Plaza Hotel and the "Little Pakistan" neighborhood of Grønland—has its share of drunks and drugs, reflecting a new urban reality in Oslo. Farther up, the river valley becomes a park as it winds past decent-size waterfalls and red-brick factories. The source of the river (and Oslo's drinking water) is the pristine Lake Maridal, situated at the edge of the Nordmarka wilderness. The idyllic recreation scenes along Lake Maridal are a world apart from the rougher reality downstream.

▲**Grünerløkka**—The Grünerløkka district is the largest planned urban area in Oslo. It was built in the latter half of the 1800s to house the legions of workers employed at the factories powered by the Akers River. The first buildings were modeled on similar places built in Berlin. (German visitors observe that there's now more

OSLO

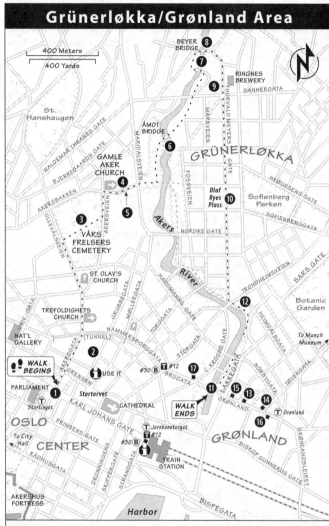

Grünerløkka/Grønland Area

400 Meters
400 Yards

BEYER BRIDGE **8**
7
RINGNES BREWERY
9
SANNERGATA

St. Hanshaugen

ÅMOT BRIDGE
6

HORVALD MEYERS GATE

MARKVEIEN

GRÜNERLØKKA

WALDEMAR THRANES GATE

BJERREGAARDS GATE

GAMLE AKER CHURCH
4

MARIDALSVEIEN

FOSSVEIEN

HEDGESENS GATE

Olaf Ryes Plass **10**
Sofienberg Parken

AKERSBAKKEN

ULLEVÅLSVEIEN

AKERSVEIEN

3
VÅRS FRELSERS CEMETERY

5

Akers

NØRDRE GATE

SOFIENBERGGATA

ST. OLAV'S CHURCH

River

TRONDHEIMSVEIEN

SARS GATE

Botanic Garden

UNIV. GATA

TREFOLDIGHETS CHURCH

GRUBBEGATA

MØLLERGATA

HAUSMANNS GATE

TORGGATA

12

HEIMDALSGATA

To Munch Museum

NAT'L GALLERY

HAMMERSBORGGATA
(TUNNEL)

2

USE IT

STORGATA

C. KROGHS GATE

TØYENGATA

AKERSGATA

GRENSEN

#30 B T #12
BRUGATA

17

11

15 **13**

NORBYGATA

GRØNANDSLEIRET

WALK BEGINS

PARLIAMENT
1

Stortorvet

KARL JOHANS GATE

CATHEDRAL

WALK ENDS

SKIPPERGATA

GRØNLAND

14

T Grønland

16

OSLO CENTER

PRINSENS GATE

DRONNINGENS

STRANDGATA

Jernbanetorget

T #12

#30 B

TRAIN STATION

GRØNLAND

BISKOP GUNNERUS GATE

To City Hall

Stortinget

RÅDHUSGATA

AKERSHUS FORTRESS

BISPEGATA

Harbor

Walk

1 Akersgata & Start of Walk
2 July 2011 Bombing Site
3 Vår Frelsers Cemetery
4 Gamle Aker Church
5 Telthusbakken Road
6 Åmotbrua (Bridge)
7 Big Waterfall
8 Fabrikkjentene Statue & Honse-Lovisas Hus
9 Thorvald Meyers Gate
10 Olaf Ryes Plass
11 Vaterlands Bridge & End of Walk

Eateries

12 Südøst Asian Crossover Rest.
13 Punjab Tandoori & Asylet Rest.
14 Alibaba Restaurant
15 Dattera Til Hagen Rest.
16 Olympen Brown Pub & Pigalle Rest.
17 Café Con Bar

turn-of-the-20th-century Berlin here than in present-day Berlin.) While slummy in the 1980s, today it's trendy. Locals sometimes refer to it as "Oslo's Greenwich Village." Although that's way over the mark, it is a bustling area with lots of cafés, good spots for a fun meal, and few tourists.

Getting There: Grünerløkka can be reached from the center of town by a short ride on tram #11, #12, or #13, or by taking the short but interesting walk described next.

▲**Walk up the Akers River to Grünerløkka**—While every tourist explores the harborfront and main drag of Oslo, few venture into this neighborhood that evokes the Industrial Revolution. Once housing poor workers, it now attracts hip professionals. A hike up the Akers River, finishing in the stylish Grünerløkka district, shines a truly different light on Oslo. Allow about an hour at a brisk pace, including a fair bit of up and down. Navigate with the TI's free city map and the map in this chapter. This walk is best during daylight hours.

Begin the walk by leaving Karl Johans Gate at the top of the hill, and head up **Akersgata**—Oslo's "Fleet Street" (lined with major newspaper companies). After two blocks, at Apotekergata, you may see the side street blocked off and construction work to the right. They're cleaning up from the horrific bombing of July 2011 (see sidebar); the car bomb went off just a block to the right of here, on Grubbegata. Posters around this area identify four buildings that suffered structural damage in the bombing. Continuing up Akersgata, the street name becomes Ullevålsveien as it passes those buildings. Norwegians are planning to build a memorial here in the near future.

Continuing past this somber site, you'll approach the massive brick Trefoldighets Church and St. Olav's Church before reaching the **Vår Frelsers (Our Savior's) Cemetery.** Enter the cemetery across from the Baby Shop store (where Ullevålsveien meets Wessels Gate).

Stop at the big metal map just inside the gate to chart your course through the cemetery: Go through the light-green Æreslunden section—with the biggest plots and highest elevation—and out the opposite end (#13 on the metal map) onto Akersveien.

En route, check out some of the tombstones of the illuminati and literati buried in the honorary Æreslunden section. They include Munch, Ibsen, Bjørnson, and many of the painters whose works you can see in the National Gallery (all marked on a map posted at the entrance).

OSLO

In Cold Blood

Norway likes to think of itself as a quiet, peaceful nation on the edge of Europe—after all, its legislators award the Nobel Peace Prize. So the events of July 22, 2011—when an anti-immigration fanatic named Anders Behring Breivik set off a car bomb in Oslo, killing eight, and then traveled to a Labor Party summer camp where he shot and killed 69 young people and counselors—have had a profound effect on the country's psyche.

Unlike the US, Britain, or Spain, Norway had escaped 21st-century terrorism until Breivik's attack. When the public found out that the man behind the bombing and gunfire was a native Norwegian—dressed in a policeman's uniform—who hunted down his victims in cold blood, it became a national nightmare.

Though Norwegians are often characterized as stoic, there was a huge outpouring of grief. Bouquets flooded the square in front of Oslo Cathedral. Permanent memorials will eventually be built at the sites of the tragedies.

Breivik, who was arrested after the shootings, was described by police as a gun-loving fundamentalist obsessed with what he saw as the "threat" of multiculturalism and immigration to Norwegian values. His targets

Exiting on the far side of the cemetery, walk left 100 yards up Akersveien to the church.

The Romanesque **Gamle Aker Church** (from the 1100s), the oldest building in Oslo, is worth a look inside (free, Mon-Thu 14:00-16:00, Fri 12:00-14:00). The church, which fell into ruins and has been impressively rebuilt, is pretty bare except for a pulpit and baptismal font from the 1700s.

From the church, backtrack 20 yards, head left at the playground, and go downhill on the steep **Telthusbakken Road** toward the huge, gray former grain silos (now student housing). The cute lane is lined with colorful old wooden houses: The people who constructed these homes were too poor to meet the no-wood fire-safety building codes within the city limits, so they built in what used to be suburbs. At the bottom of Telthusbakken, cross the busy Maridalsveien and walk directly through the park to the Akers River. The lively Grünerløkka district is straight across the river from here, but if you have 20 minutes and a little energy, detour upstream first and hook back down. Don't cross the river yet.

Walk along the riverside bike lane upstream through the river were the Norwegian government and politically active youths—some only 14 years old—and their counselors at an island summer camp sponsored by Norway's center-left party.

It's true that Norway has a big and growing immigrant community. More than 11 percent of today's Norwegians are not ethnic Norwegians, and a quarter of Oslo's residents are immigrants. These "new Norwegians" have provided a much-needed and generally appreciated labor force, filling jobs that wealthy Norwegians would rather not do.

But there is some resentment in a country that is disinclined to be a melting pot. There have been scuffles between Norwegian gangs and immigrant groups. Another source of friction is the tough love Norwegians feel they get from their government compared to the easy ride offered to needy immigrants: "They even get pocket money in jail!"

Horrified by Breivik's actions, many Norwegians are now going out of their way to make immigrants feel welcome. And the anti-immigrant Progress Party (which condemned the attacks) lost support in a round of local elections held shortly after the attack.

Norway seems determined not to let the July 22 massacre poison its peaceful soul. Calls for police to start carrying weapons or to reinstate the death penalty were quickly rejected. "Breivik wanted to change Norway," an Oslo resident told me. "We're determined to keep Norway the way it was."

gorge park. Just above the first waterfall, cross **Åmotbrua,** the big white springy suspension footbridge from 1852 (moved here in 1958). Keep hiking uphill along the river. At the base of the next big waterfall, cross over again to the large brick buildings, hiking up

the stairs to the Beyer bridge (above the falls) with *Fabrikkjentene,* a statue of four women laborers. They're pondering the textile factory where they and 700 like them toiled long and hard. This gorge was once lined with the water mills that powered Oslo through its 19th-century Industrial Age boom. The tiny red house next to the bridge—the **Honse-Lovisas Hus**

cultural center—makes a good rest-stop (Tue-Sun 11:00-18:00, closed Mon, coffee and cake). Cross over to the red-brick Ringnes Brewery and follow **Thorvald Meyers Gate** downhill directly into the heart of Grünerløkka. The main square, called **Olaf Ryes Plass,** is a happening place to grab a meal or drink. Trams take you from here back to the center.

• To continue exploring, you could keep going straight and continue walking until you reach a T-intersection with a busy road (Trondheimsveien). From there (passing the recommended Südøst Asian Crossover Restaurant), you can catch a tram back to the center, or drop down to the riverside path and follow it downstream to Vaterlands bridge in the Grønland district. From here the train station is a five-minute walk down Stenersgata. (The last section, around Grønland, is a bit seedy and best done in daylight.)

Near Oslo

▲**Eidsvoll Manor**—During the Napoleonic period, control of Norway changed from Denmark to Sweden. This ruffled the patriotic feathers of Norway's Thomas Jeffersons and Ben Franklins, and on May 17, 1814, Norway's constitution was written and signed in this stately mansion (in the town of Eidsvoll Verk, north of Oslo). While Sweden still ruled, Norway had more autonomy than ever.

To get ready for the bicentennial of Norway's constitution, the manor itself is undergoing restoration and will be closed until February of 2014. However, a brand-new visitors center in the nearby Wergeland House tells the history of Norway's march to independence with 21st-century high-tech touches.

Cost and Hours: Wergeland House—75 kr, includes guided tour; May-Aug daily 10:00-17:00; April and Sept Tue-Fri 10:00-15:00, Sat-Sun 12:00-17:00, closed Mon; Oct-March Wed-Fri 10:00-15:00, Sat-Sun 12:00-17:00, closed Mon-Tue; tel. 63 92 22 10, www.eidsvoll1814.no.

Getting There: Eidsvoll is 45 minutes from Oslo by car (take road E-6 toward Trondheim, turn right at *Eidsvolls Bygningen* sign, free parking) or bus (direct bus #854 runs hourly from Oslo Airport). You can also take the train to Eidsvoll (hourly, 45 minutes plus 15-minute walk). If you're driving from Oslo to Lillehammer and the Gudbrandsdal Valley, it's right on the way and worth a stop.

Drøbak—This delightful fjord town is just an hour from Oslo by bus (95 kr one-way, 2/hour, bus #541 or #542 from behind the train station) or ferry (70 kr one-way, sporadic departures usually Wed and Fri-Sun, check at pier 1 or ask at Oslo TI). Consider taking the 1.25-hour boat trip down, exploring the town, having dinner, and taking the bus back.

For holiday cheer year-round, stop into **Tregaarden's Julehuset** Christmas shop, right off Drøbak's main square (generally Mon-Fri 10:00-17:00, Sat 10:00-15:00, variable hours on Sun, longer hours in Dec, closed Jan-Feb, tel. 64 93 41 78, www.julehus .no). Then wander out past the church and cemetery on the north side of town to a pleasant park. Looking out into the fjord, you can see the old **Oscarsborg Fortress,** where Norwegian troops fired their cannons to sink Hitler's battleship, *Blücher.* The attack bought enough time for Norway's king and Parliament to escape capture and eventually set up a government-in-exile in London during the Nazi occupation of Norway (1940-1945). Nearby, a monument is dedicated to the commander of the fortress, and the *Blücher*'s anchor rests aground. (A 70-kr round-trip summer ferry shuttles visitors from the town harbor.)

If you want to spend the night, the **TI** can recommend accommodations (June-Aug Mon-Fri 8:30-17:00, Sat-Sun 9:30-16:00; Sept-May Mon-Fri 8:30-16:00, closed Sat-Sun; tel. 64 93 50 87, www.visitdrobak.no). **Restaurant Skipperstuen** is a good option for dinner, with outdoor seating that overlooks the fjord and all the Oslo-bound boat traffic (entrées from 300 kr, Mon-Sat 11:00-21:00, closed Sun, tel. 64 93 07 03).

Shopping in Oslo

Shops in Oslo are generally open 10:00-18:00. Many close early on Saturday and all day Sunday. Shopping centers are open Monday through Friday 10:00-21:00, Saturday 9:00-18:00, and are closed Sunday. Remember, when you make a purchase of 315 kr or more, you can get the 25 percent tax refunded when you leave the country if you hang on to the paperwork (see page 18).

Oslo's fanciest department store is **GlasMagasinet** (top end, near the cathedral on Stortorvet, good souvenir shop). The big, splashy **Byporten** mall, adjoining the central train station, is more youthful and hip (Mon-Fri 10:00-21:00, Sat 10:00-20:00, closed Sun). The trendiest boutiques and chic, high-quality shops lie along the street named **Bogstadveien** (running from behind the Royal Palace to Frogner Park). And on Saturday mornings, you can browse the **flea market** at Vestkanttorvet (March-Nov only, two blocks east of Frogner Park at the corner of Professor Dahl's Gate and Neubergsgate).

Sweaters and colorful Norwegian folk crafts are on many visitors' shopping lists. The **Husfliden shop,** in the basement of the GlasMagasinet department store, is much appreciated for its traditional yarn and Norsk folk items (Mon-Fri 10:00-18:00, Thu until 19:00, Sat 10:00-16:00, closed Sun, tel. 22 42 10 75). For a superb selection of sweaters and other Norwegian crafts (top quality at high prices), visit **Heimen Husfliden** (Mon-Fri 10:00-18:00, Sat 10:00-15:00, closed Sun, Rosenkrantz Gate 8, tel. 22 41 40 50). The **Oslo Sweater Shop** has good prices for sweaters (Mon-Fri 10:00-18:00, Sat 10:00-15:00, closed Sun, in Radisson Blu Scandinavia Hotel at Tullinsgate 5, tel. 22 11 29 22). For flags (a long, skinny *vimple* dresses up a boat or cabin wonderfully), pop into **Oslo Flaggfabrikk** (Mon-Fri 9:00-17:00, Sat 10:00-15:00, closed Sun, near City Hall at Hieronymus Heyerdahlsgate 1, tel. 22 40 50 60).

Vinmonopolet stores are the only place where you can buy wine and spirits in Norway. The most convenient location is at the central train station (Mon-Thu 10:00-18:00, Fri 9:00-18:00, Sat 9:00-15:00, closed Sun). The bottles used to be kept behind the counter, but now you can actually touch the merchandise. Locals say it went from being a "jewelry store" to a "grocery store."

Sleeping in Oslo

In Oslo, the season and type of hotel dictate the best deals. The basic formula: In midsummer and on weekends, discounted business-class hotels offer the best value; otherwise, consider a cheap hotel or a hostel.

Like those in its sister Scandinavian capitals, Oslo's hotels are mostly designed for business travelers; they're expensive during the tourists' off-season (autumn through spring), full in May and June for conventions, and wide open otherwise. From July through mid-August—and weekends (Fri-Sat but not Sun) year-round—fancy business-class hotels deeply discount their rooms. At half-price (about 1,000 kr for a double), you get a huge breakfast and a lot of extra comfort for little more than the cost of a cheap hotel or hostel.

During business days (Sun-Thu) outside of summer, business hotels hold out for their inflated "rack rates," and budget travelers opt for Oslo's dumpy-for-Scandinavia (but still nice by European standards) cheapie options: doubles for about 800 kr in central "cheap" hotels, or 800 kr in private homes on the outskirts of the city. For a meet-the-Norwegians experience—but not convenience—go for a private home. For convenience and modern comfort, I like the Thon Budget Hotels.

If you arrive without a reservation, the TI can try to sort through all of the confusing hotel specials and get you the best deal going on fancy hotel rooms on the push list. With the uncertain economy and "dynamic pricing," it's tough to get a hotel to give a firm rate. If booking on your own and on a budget, check hotel websites far in advance to see who's willing to offer the most aggressive discount.

The most predictable special is the TI's **Oslo Package,** which offers business-class rooms plus an Oslo Pass for 500-800 kr per person (based on double occupancy); prices vary depending on the hotel you choose. The Oslo Package is offered daily year-round. It's a good deal for couples and ideal for families with young children. Two kids under 16 sleep free, breakfast is included, and up to four

Sleep Code

(6 kr = about $1, country code: 47)

S = Single, **D** = Double/Twin, **T** = Triple, **Q** = Quad, **b** = bathroom, **s** = shower. You can assume credit cards are accepted and breakfast is included unless otherwise noted. Everyone speaks English.

To help you sort through these listings easily, I've divided the accommodations into three categories, based on the price for a standard double room with bath during high season:

$$$ Higher Priced—Most rooms 1,100 kr or more.
$$ Moderately Priced—Most rooms between 600-1,100 kr.
$ Lower Priced—Most rooms 600 kr or less.

Prices can change without notice; verify the hotel's current rates online or by email.

family members get free Oslo Passes, covering admission to sights and all public transportation (see page 226). These passes are valid for four days, even if you only stay one night at the hotel (allowing you to squeeze two days of sightseeing out of a one-night stay—for example, if you take an overnight train or boat out of town on your second evening). Buy the Oslo Package through your travel agent at home, ScanAm World Tours in the US (US tel. 800-545-2204), or upon arrival in Oslo at the TI. Even if you show up late in the day when prices may be deeply discounted, you still get the Oslo Pass along with your room. For details on the Oslo Package, see www.visitoslo.com.

Near the Train Station and Karl Johans Gate

These accommodations are within a 15-minute walk of the station. While evidence of an earlier, shadier time survives nearest the station, the hotels feel secure and comfortable. Parking in a central garage will run you about 250-300 kr per day.

Thon Hotels

This chain of business-class hotels (found in big cities throughout Norway) knows which comforts are worth paying for and which are not. They offer little character, but provide maximum comfort per krone in big, modern, conveniently located buildings. Each hotel has a cheery staff and lobby, tight but well-designed rooms, non-smoking floors, free Wi-Fi, and a big buffet breakfast.

Thon Hotels come in categories: Their "City Hotels" are a cut above their "Budget Hotels." While City Hotels are much more expensive during business times (weekdays outside of summer),

OSLO

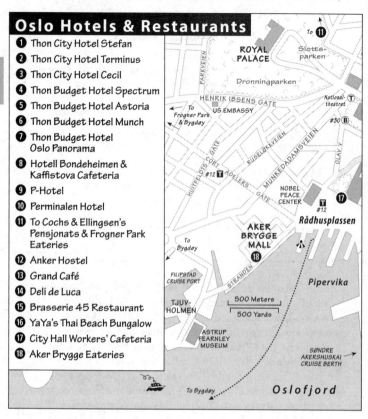

Oslo Hotels & Restaurants

1. Thon City Hotel Stefan
2. Thon City Hotel Terminus
3. Thon City Hotel Cecil
4. Thon Budget Hotel Spectrum
5. Thon Budget Hotel Astoria
6. Thon Budget Hotel Munch
7. Thon Budget Hotel Oslo Panorama
8. Hotell Bondeheimen & Kaffistova Cafeteria
9. P-Hotel
10. Perminalen Hotel
11. To Cochs & Ellingsen's Pensjonats & Frogner Park Eateries
12. Anker Hostel
13. Grand Café
14. Deli de Luca
15. Brasserie 45 Restaurant
16. YaYa's Thai Beach Bungalow
17. City Hall Workers' Cafeteria
18. Aker Brygge Eateries

Budget Hotels have lower rates all year. That means City Hotels can be a better value in low season when they often are discounted. City Hotels generally offer free juice and coffee all day. In Budget Hotels (which have no phones or mini-fridges in the rooms), rooms with double beds are a bit bigger than twin-bedded rooms for the same price.

Thon Hotels base their prices on demand. Rates vary wildly, so the following prices are roughly the midpoint of a huge range: **Thon City Hotels**—Sb-1,525, Db-1,825 kr; **Thon Budget Hotels**—Sb-750 kr, Db-1,075 kr, higher in winter. Extra beds are 300 kr for an adult and 150 kr for a child under 17 (kids under 6 stow away for free). Book by phone or online (central booking tel. 23 08 02 00, www.thonhotels.no).

Thon Hotels generally offer a 10 percent discount for those who prepay via their website with no option to change or cancel their booking. The free Thon Membership Card offers a 10 percent discount if you stay five nights in one year (doesn't apply to summer/weekend rates). My price ratings for Thon Hotels are based

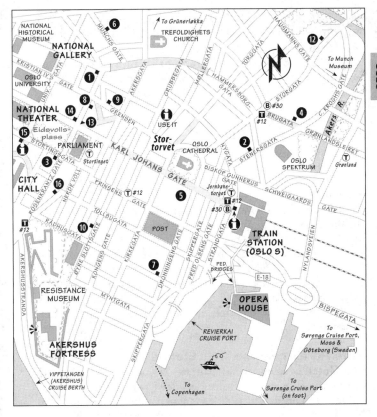

on their average summer/weekend rates. Of the 14 Thon Hotels in Oslo, I find the following most convenient:

$$$ Thon City Hotel Stefan, in a classy and central location two blocks off Karl Johans Gate, is a cut above its sisters in comfort and charm. If you want to splurge, this is the place to do it (Rosenkrantz Gate 1, entrance on Kristian Augusts Gate side, tel. 23 31 55 00, fax 23 31 55 55, www.thonhotels.no/stefan, stefan @thonhotels.no).

$$$ Thon City Hotel Terminus is similar but closer to the station (Steners Gate 10, tel. 22 05 60 00, fax 22 17 08 98, www .thonhotels.no/terminus, terminus@thonhotels.no).

$$$ Thon City Hotel Cecil is near the Parliament building a block below Karl Johans Gate (Stortingsgata 8, tel. 23 31 48 00, fax 23 31 48 50, www.thonhotels.no/cecil, cecil@thonhotels.no).

$$ Thon Budget Hotel Spectrum is four blocks from the station near the Grønland Torg shopping street. A quarter of its rooms are plagued by disco noise on weekends (leave station out north entrance toward bus terminal, go across footbridge toward tall glass Radisson Blu Plaza Hotel, and pass through Grønland Torg, Brugata 7; tel. 23 36 27 00, fax 23 36 27 50, www.thonhotels .no/spectrum, spectrum@thonhotels.no).

$$ Thon Budget Hotel Astoria has the least charm of my recommended Thon Hotels, but it's well-located and perfectly serviceable (3 blocks in front of station, 50 yards off Karl Johans Gate, Dronningens Gate 21, tel. 24 14 55 50, fax 22 42 57 65, www.thon hotels.no/astoria, astoria@thonhotels.no).

$$ Thon Budget Hotel Munch, a few blocks from the National Gallery, is like its sisters. Of all the Thon Budget hotels listed, this one has the most upscale location (Munchs Gate 5, tel. 23 21 96 00, fax 23 21 96 01, www.thonhotels.no/munch, munch @thonhotels.no).

$$ Thon Budget Hotel Oslo Panorama is a 15-story attempt at a downtown condominium building (the condos didn't work so now it's a budget hotel). While higher rooms are more expensive, even those reserving a cheap room often get bumped up. If you request anything higher than the fourth floor, you'll likely enjoy a bigger room, perhaps with a balcony (just off Dronningens Gate at Rådhusgata 7, about 6 blocks from station, tel. 23 31 08 00, fax 23 31 08 10, www.thonhotels.no/oslopanorama, oslopanorama @thonhotels.no).

More Hotels near the Train Station

$$$ Hotell Bondeheimen ("Farmer's Home") is a historic hotel run by the farmers' youth league, *Bondeungdomslaget*. It once housed the children of rural farmers attending school in Oslo. Now a Best Western, its 127 rooms have all the comforts of a modern hotel (July Db-850 kr, Aug Db-1,990 kr; higher off-season, you generally save money by booking on their website; nonsmoking rooms, elevator, Rosenkrantz Gate 8, tel. 23 21 41 00, www.bondeheimen.com, bookingoffice@bondeheimen.com). This almost-100-year-old building is also home to the Kaffistova cafeteria (see "Eating in Oslo") and the Heimen Husflid shop (see "Shopping in Oslo").

$$$ P-Hotel rents 92 comfortable rooms—some with hardwood-slick floors—for the same price every day of the year. You get a boxed breakfast delivered each morning, as well as free Internet access and Wi-Fi. Avoid late-night street noise by requesting a room high up or in the back (Sb-895 kr, Db-1,250 kr, bigger rooms add 200 kr per person up to five, some sixth-floor rooms have balconies, pay by credit card—no cash accepted, Grensen 19, T-bane: Storting, tel. 23 31 80 00, www.p-hotels.com, oslo@p -hotels.no).

$$ Perminalen Hotel, a place for military personnel on leave, is perfectly central, spartan, inexpensive, and welcoming to civvies.

They have the same fair prices all year. Spliced invisibly into a giant office block on a quiet street, it has sleek woody furniture and a no-nonsense reception desk (Sb-620 kr, twin Db-860 kr, some seventh-floor rooms have balconies, entirely non-smoking, elevator, pay Internet access, free Wi-Fi in lobby, tram #12 from station to Øvre Slotts Gate 2, tel. 23 09 30 81, fax 23 41 18 58, www.perminalen.com, post.perminalen@iss.no). Single beds in shared quads segregated by sexes (with lockers and breakfast) rent for 380 kr each. Its cheap mess hall is open all day.

The West End

$$ Cochs Pensjonat has 88 characteristic rooms (20 remodeled doubles), many with kitchenettes. It's on the far side of the Royal Palace (S-500 kr, Sb-600-650 kr, D-720 kr, Db-820-880 kr, Q-1,140 kr, Qb-1,300 kr, breakfast-69 kr at nearby café, non-smoking rooms, elevator; T-bane to National Theater, exit to Parkveien, and 10-minute walk through park; or more-convenient trams #11, #17, or #18 to Welhavens Gate; Parkveien 25; tel. 23 33 24 00, fax 23 33 24 10, www.cochspensjonat.no, booking@cochs.no, three generations of the Skram family).

$$ Ellingsen's Pensjonat rents 18 clean, bright rooms with fluffy down comforters. It's in a residential neighborhood four blocks behind the Royal Palace (S-400 kr, Sb-480 kr, D-610 kr, Db-670 kr, extra bed-150 kr, breakfast-69 kr at nearby café, cash only, non-smoking, back rooms have less street noise, tram #19 from central station to Uranienborgveien, near Uranienborg church at Holtegata 25, tel. 22 60 03 59, fax 22 60 99 21, www.ellingsenspensjonat.no, post@ellingsenspensjonat.no).

Private Homes

The central station TI can find you an 800-kr double for a 55-kr fee (minimum two-night stay, breakfast not included, likely a tram ride out of the center).

Hostels

$ Anker Hostel, a huge student dorm open to travelers of any age, offers 250 of Oslo's best cheap doubles. Though it comes with the ambience of a bomb shelter, each of its rooms is spacious, simple, and clean. There are kitchens and elevators (bed in 6-bed room-230-250 kr, bed in quad-260-280 kr, Db-600-620 kr, Tb-800-820 kr, higher prices are weekend rates, sheets-50 kr, towel-20 kr, breakfast-55 kr, self-serve laundry, parking-175 kr/day; tram #12 or #13, or bus #30 or #31 from central station, bus and tram stop: Hausmannsgate; or 10-minute walk from station; Storgata 55, tel. 22 99 72 00, fax 22 99 72 20, www.ankerhostel.no, hostel@anker.oslo.no).

$ **Haraldsheim Youth Hostel (IYHF)**, a huge, modern hostel open all year, comes with a grand view, laundry, self-service kitchen, 270 beds...and a long commute (2.5 miles out of town). Beds in the fancy quads with private showers and toilets are 270 kr per person (bed in simple quad with bathroom down the hall-245 kr). They also offer private rooms (S-415 kr, Sb-470 kr, bunk-bed D-540 kr, Db-625 kr; all include breakfast, members get 10 percent off, sheets-50 kr, catch bus #31 or tram #17 or T-bane lines #4 or #6 from Oslo's central train station to Sinsenkrysset, then 5-minute uphill hike to Haraldsheimveien 4, tel. 22 22 29 65, fax 22 22 10 25, www.haraldsheim.no, oslo.haraldsheim@hihostels .no). Eurailers can train to the hostel with their railpass (2/hour, to Grefsen and walk 10 minutes).

Sleeping on the Train or Boat

Norway's trains and ferries offer ways to travel while sleeping. The eight-hour night train between Bergen and Oslo leaves at about 23:00 in each direction (nightly except Sat). Eurail hobos sleep cheap, if not well, for the cost of a 50-kr train reservation (sleep on a train ride out, cross platform, and sleep back). Overnight trains connect Oslo with Copenhagen June-August only (leaves nightly at 20:30, arrives at Malmö Central Station at 6:42 the next morning, easy transfers to Copenhagen). The overnight cruise between these Nordic capitals is a clever way to avoid a night in a hotel and to travel while you sleep, saving a day in your itinerary (see "Oslo Connections," later).

Eating in Oslo

Eating Cheaply

How do the Norwegians afford their high-priced restaurants? They don't eat out much. This is one city in which you might just settle for simple or ethnic meals—you'll save a lot and miss little. Many menus list small and large plates. Because portions tend to be large, choosing a small plate or splitting a large one makes some otherwise pricey options reasonable. You'll notice many locals just drink free tap water, even in fine restaurants. For a description of Oslo's classic  (and expensive) restaurants, see the TI's *Oslo Guide* booklet.

Splurge for a hotel that includes breakfast, or pay for it if it's optional. At 75 kr, a Norwegian breakfast fit for a Viking is a good deal. Picnic for lunch or dinner. Basements of big department

Oslo's One-Time Grills

Norwegians are experts at completely avoiding costly restaurants. "One-time grills," or *engangsgrill*, are the rage for locals  on a budget. For about 20 kr, you get a disposable outdoor cooker consisting of an aluminum tray, easy-to-light charcoal, and a flimsy metal grill. All that's required is a sunny evening, a grassy park, and a group of friends. During balmy summer evenings, the air in Oslo's city parks is thick with the smell of disposable (and not terribly eco-friendly) grills. It's fun to see how prices for this kind of "dining" aren't that bad in the supermarket: Norwegian beer-12 kr/bottle, potato salad-20 kr/tub, cooked shrimp-75 kr/half kilo, "ready for grill" steak-two for 110 kr, *grill pølse* hot dogs-60 kr per dozen, *lomper* (Norwegian tortillas for wrapping hot dogs)-15 kr per stack, and the actual grill itself.

Bars are also too expensive for the average Norwegian. Young night owls drink at home before *(forspiel)* and after *(nachspiel)* an evening on the town, with a couple of hours, generally around midnight, when they go out for a single drink in a public setting. A beer in a bar costs about $8-10 (compared to $6 in Ireland and $2 in the Czech Republic), while they can get an entire six-pack for that price in a grocery store.

stores have huge, first-class supermarkets with lots of alternatives to sandwiches for picnic dinners. The little yogurt tubs with cereal come with collapsible spoons. Wasa crackers and meat, shrimp, or cheese spread in a tube are cheap and pack well. The central station has an ICA supermarket with long hours (Mon-Fri 6:00-21:00, Sat 8:00-19:00, Sun 10:00-18:00). Many supermarkets have take-out food that is discounted just before closing—showing up just before 20:00 to buy some roast chicken could be your cheapest meal in Oslo.

You'll save 12 percent by getting take-away food from a restaurant rather than eating inside. (The VAT on take-away food is 12 percent; restaurant food is 24 percent.) Fast-food restaurants ask if you want to take away or not before they ring up your order on the cash register. Even McDonald's has a two-tiered price list.

Oslo is awash with little budget eateries (modern, ethnic, fast food, pizza, department-store cafeterias, and so on). **Deli de Luca,** a cheery convenience store chain, notorious for having a store on every key corner in Oslo, is a step up from the similarly ubiquitous

Norwegian Cuisine

Traditionally Norwegian cuisine doesn't rank very high in terms of excitement value. But the typical diet of meat, fish, and potatoes is now evolving to incorporate more diverse products, and the food here is steadily improving. Fresh produce, colorful markets, and efficient supermarkets abound in Europe's most expensive corner.

In this land of farmers and fishermen, you'll find raw ingredients like potatoes, salmon, or beef in traditional recipes. Norway's national dish is *Fårikål*, a lamb or mutton stew with cabbage, peppercorns, and potatoes. It's served with lingonberry jam and *lefse*—a soft flatbread made from potatoes, milk, and flour. This dish is so popular that the last Thursday in September is *Fårikål* day in Norway. Norwegian grandmothers prepare this hearty stew by throwing together the basic ingredients with whatever leftovers are lying around the kitchen. There's really no need for a recipe, so every stew turns out differently—and every grandma claims hers is the best.

Because of its long, cold winters, Norway relies heavily on the harvesting and preservation of fish. Smoked salmon, called *laks*, is prepared by salt-curing the fish and cold-smoking it, ensuring the temperature never rises above 85°F. This makes the texture smooth and almost raw. *Bacalao* is another favorite: salted and dried cod that is soaked in water before cooking. You'll often find *bacalao* served with tomatoes and olives.

Some Norwegians serve lutefisk around Christmas time, but you'll rarely see this salty, pungent dish on the menu. Instead, try the more pleasant *fiskekake*, small white fish cakes made with cream, eggs, milk, and flour. You can find these patties year-round. For a break from the abundance of seafood, try local specialties such as reindeer meatballs, or pork-and-ground beef meat cakes called *kjøttkaker*. True to Scandinavian cuisine, *kjøttkaker* are usually slathered in a heavy cream sauce.

Dessert and coffee after a meal are essential. *Bløtkake*, a popular delight on Norway's Constitution Day (May 17), is a layered cake drizzled with strawberry juice, covered in whipped cream, and decorated with fresh strawberries. The cloudberry, which grows in the Scandinavian tundra, makes a unique jelly that tastes delicious on vanilla ice cream, or even whipped into a rich cream topping for heart-shaped waffles. Norwegians are proud of their breads and pastries, and you'll never be too far from a bakery that sells an almond-flavored *kringle* or a cone-shaped *krumkake* cookie filled with whipped cream.

7-Elevens. Most are open 24/7, selling sandwiches, pastries, sushi, and to-go boxes of warm pasta or Asian noodle dishes. You can fill your belly here for about 75 kr. Some outlets (such as the one at the corner of Karl Johans Gate and Rosenkrantz Gate) have seating on the street or upstairs. Beware: Because this is still a *convenience* store, not everything is well-priced. Convenience stores—while convenient—charge double what supermarkets do.

Eating on or near Karl Johans Gate

Consider the restaurants and eateries listed below. They're grouped by those that are from Karl Johans Gate and slightly to the north (between this main boulevard and the National Gallery) and to the south (between Karl Johans Gate and City Hall).

Strangely, **Karl Johans Gate** itself—the most Norwegian of boulevards—is lined with a strip of good-time American chain eateries where you can get ribs, burgers, and pizza, including T.G.I. Fridays and the Hard Rock Cafe. Egon Pizza offers a daily 100-kr all-you-can-eat pizza deal (available Tue-Sat 11:00-18:00, Sun-Mon all day). Each place comes with great sidewalk seating and essentially the same prices.

Grand Café is perhaps the most venerable place in town. At lunchtime, they set up a sandwich buffet (110-kr single-sandwich, 310-kr all-you-like). Lunch plates are 150 kr, and dinner plates run about 250-300 kr. Reserve a window, and if you hit a time when there's no tour group, you're suddenly a posh Norwegian (daily 11:00-23:00, Karl Johans Gate 31, tel. 23 21 20 18).

Deli de Luca, just across from the Grand Café, offers good-value food and handy seats on Karl Johans Gate. For a fast meal with the best people-watching view in town, you may find your-self dropping by here repeatedly (daily 11:00-23:00, slightly shorter hours Sat-Sun, Karl Johans Gate 33, tel. 22 33 35 22).

Kaffistova is where my thrifty Norwegian grandparents always took me. After remaining unchanged for 30 years, it got a facelift in 2007. This alcohol-free cafeteria still serves simple, hearty, and typically Norwegian (read: bland) meals for a good price (Mon-Fri 10:00-21:00, Sat-Sun 11:00-19:00; Rosenkrantz Gate 8, tel. 23 21 42 10).

Brasserie 45, overlooking Stortingsgata and the National Theater from its second-floor perch, is a modern eatery offering decent Continental cuisine with energetic service. While larger entrées go for about 200 kr, their "wok chicken" goes for 140 kr. It's worth calling ahead to reserve a window seat with a view of Karl Johans Gate (Mon-Thu 15:00-23:00, Fri-Sat 14:00-24:00, Sun 14:00-22:00, always a veggie option, Stortingsgata 20, tel. 22 41 34 00).

YaYa's Thai Beach Bungalow is a welcome change from Norwegian bland. The tiki-bar decor is infectious, and the food is surprisingly authentic—I slurped up every morsel of my green curry pork. Don't be surprised if your dinner is accompanied by the sounds and lights of an hourly tropical thunderstorm (starters-80 kr, main dishes-150 kr, vegetarian options, daily 16:00-22:00, Fri-Sat until 23:00, between the Parliament building and City Hall at Øvre Vollgate 13, tel. 22 83 71 10).

City Hall workers' cafeteria, just steps off the harborfront, welcomes the public with the cheapest lunch I've found in Oslo. It has soup, an inexpensive salad bar measured by weight (35 kr for a meal-sized bowl), and a daily hot dish for around 50 kr (Mon-Fri 12:30-13:30 only). While City Hall workers get access to the place before 12:30 and the food can be pretty picked over, it's still a fine, handy value. From the grand harbor entrance, it's up one flight of stairs above the city info desk and WC. From the tour entrance on its inland courtyard, it's just downstairs.

Harborside Dining in Aker Brygge

The **Aker Brygge** harborfront mall is popular with businesspeople and tourists. While it isn't cheap, its inviting cafés and restaurants with outdoor, harborview tables make for a memorable waterfront meal. Before deciding where to eat, you might want to walk the entire lane (including the back side), considering both the regular places (some with second-floor view seating) and the various floating options. Nearly all are open for lunch and dinner.

Druen, the first restaurant on the strip—while not a particularly good food value—is best for people-watching. I like the balcony seats upstairs, under outside heaters and with a harbor view. They serve international dishes—spicy Asian, French, and seafood—in small plates for 175 kr, hearty salads for 155 kr, and big meals for 220-260 kr (daily from 11:00, Stranden 1, Aker Brygge, tel. 23 11 54 60).

Lekter'n, right on the water, offers the best harbor view (rather than views of strolling people). This trendy bar has a floating dining area open only when the weather is warm. It serves hamburgers, pizza, and shrimp buckets. Budget eaters can split a 160-kr pizza (all outdoors, Stranden 3, tel. 22 83 76 46).

Rorbua, the "Fisherman's Cabin," is a lively yet cozy eatery tucked into this mostly modern stretch of restaurants. Inside, it's extremely woody with a rustic charm and candlelit picnic tables surrounded by harpoons and old B&W photos. Grab a stool at one of the wooden tables, and choose from a menu of meat-and-potato dishes (150-200 kr) and seafood offerings (200-250 kr). A hearty daily special with coffee for 145 kr is one of the best restaurant deals in the city (daily 12:30-23:00, Stranden 71, tel. 22 83 53 86).

Lofoten Fiskerestaurant serves fish amid a dressy yacht-club atmosphere at the end of the strip. While it's beyond the people-watching action, it's comfortable even in cold and blustery weather because of its heated atrium, which makes a meal here practically outdoor dining. Reservations are a must, especially if you want a harborside window table (lunch-150-225 kr, dinner from 275 kr, open daily, Stranden 75, tel. 22 83 08 08).

Budget Tips: If you're on a budget, get a take-out meal from the fast-food stands and grab a bench along the boardwalk. The **ICA "Gourmet"** grocery store—in the middle of the mall a few steps behind all the fancy restaurants—has salads, warm take-away dishes, and more (turn in about midway down the board-walk, Mon-Fri 9:00-22:00, Sat 9:00-20:00, closed Sun).

Dining near Frogner Park

Lofotstua Restaurant feels transplanted from the far northern islands it's named for. Kjell Jenssen and his son, Jan Hugo, proudly serve up fish Lofoten-style. Evangelical about fish, they will patiently explain to you the fine differences between all the local varieties, with the help of a photo-filled chart. They serve only the freshest catch, perfectly—if simply—prepared. If you want meat, they've got it—whale or seal (170-290-kr plates, Mon-Fri 15:00-22:00, generally closed in July, 5-minute walk from gate of Vigeland statue garden, tram #12, in Majorstuen at Kirkeveien 40, tel. 22 46 93 96). This place is packed daily in winter for their famous lutefisk.

Curry and Ketchup Indian Restaurant is filled with in-the-know locals enjoying tasty and hearty meals for about 100 kr. This happening place requires no reservations and feels like an Indian market. If you want a reasonable Indian meal in Oslo, this is hard to beat (daily 14:00-23:00, cash only, a 5-minute walk from gate of Vigeland statue garden, tram #12, in Majorstuen at Kirkeveien 51, tel. 22 69 05 22).

Trendy Dining at the Bottom of Grünerløkka

Südøst Asian Crossover Restaurant, once a big bank, now fills its vault with wine (which makes sense, given Norwegian alcohol prices). Today it's popular with young Norwegian professionals as a place to see and be seen. It's a fine mix of Norwegian-chic woody ambience inside with a trendy menu, and a big riverside terrace outdoors with a more casual menu. Diners enjoy its chic setting,

OSLO

smart service, and Asian fusion cuisine (Mon-Fri 16:00-1:00 in the morning, Sat 13:00-3:00 in the morning, Sun 13:00-22:00, also serves lunch in summer, at bottom of Grünerløkka, tram #17 to Trondheimsveien 5, tel. 23 35 30 70).

Eating Cheap and Spicy in Grønland

The street called Grønland leads through this colorful immigrant neighborhood (a short walk behind the train station or T-bane: Grønland). After the cleanliness and orderliness of the rest of the city, the rough edges and diversity of people here can feel like a breath of fresh air. Whether you eat here or not, the street is fun to explore. In Grønland, backpackers and immigrants munch street food for dinner. Cheap and tasty *börek* (feta, spinach, mushroom) is sold hot and greasy to go for 25 kr.

Punjab Tandoori is friendly and serves hearty meals (lamb and chicken curry, tandoori specials) for 70 kr. They're open late when other places aren't. I like eating outside here with a view of the street scene (daily 11:00-23:00, Grønland 24).

Alibaba Restaurant is clean, simple, and cheap for Turkish food. They have good indoor or outdoor seating (99-kr fixed-price meal Mon-Thu only, open daily 12:30-22:30, corner of Grønlandsleiret and Tøyengata at Tøyengata 2, tel. 22 17 22 22). The 99-kr special is much cheaper than the menu items, but isn't advertised very clearly; you may need to request it.

Asylet is more expensive and feels like it was here long before Norway ever saw a Pakistani. This big, traditional eatery—like a Norwegian beer garden—has a rustic, cozy interior and a gravelly backyard filled with picnic tables (150-200-kr plates and hearty dinner salads, daily 11:00-24:00, Grønland 28, tel. 22 17 09 39).

Dattera Til Hagen feels like a college party. It's a lively scene filling a courtyard with picnic tables and benches under strings of colored lights. If it's too cold, hang out inside. Locals like it for the tapas, burgers, and salads (150-kr plates, pricey beers, Grønland 10, tel. 22 17 18 61). On weekends after 22:00, it becomes a disco.

Olympen Brown Pub is a dressy dining hall that's a blast from the past. You'll eat in a spacious, woody saloon with big dark furniture, faded paintings of circa-1920 Oslo lining the walls, and huge chandeliers. It's good for solo travelers, because sharing the long dinner tables is standard practice. They serve hearty 200-kr plates and offer a huge selection of beers. The grill restaurant upstairs, called **Pigalle,** comes with music and can be more fun (daily 11:00-2:00 in the morning, Grønlandsleiret 15, tel. 22 17 28 08).

Café Con Bar is a trendy yuppie eatery on the downtown edge of Grønland. Locals consider it to have the best burgers in town (150 kr). While the tight interior seating is very noisy, the sidewalk tables are great for people-watching (open daily, kitchen closes at 23:00, bar closes late; where Grønland hits Brugata).

Roasted Rudolph Under a Thatched Roof High on the Mountain

Frognerseteren Hovedrestaurant, nestled high above Oslo (and 1,400 feet above sea level), is a classy, sod-roofed old restaurant. Its terrace, offering a commanding view of the city, is a popular stop for famous apple cake and coffee. The café is casual and less expensive, with indoor and outdoor seating (90-kr sandwiches and cold dishes, 125-kr entrées, Mon-Sat 11:00-22:00, Sun 11:00-21:00, reservations unnecessary). The elegant view restaurant is pricier (275-365-kr plates, Mon-Fri 12:00-22:00, Sat 13:00-22:00, Sun 13:00-21:00, reindeer specials, reserve for evening dining, tel. 22 92 40 40).

You can combine a trip into the forested hills surrounding the city with lunch or dinner and get a chance to see the famous Holmenkollen Ski Jump up close (see page 265).

Oslo Connections

By Train, Bus, or Car

For train information, call 81 50 08 88 and press 4 for English. For international trains, dial 81 56 81 00. Even if you have a rail-pass, reservations are required for long rides (e.g., a reservation to Stockholm in first class costs 140 kr, second class for 50 kr). First class often comes with a hot meal, fruit bowl, and unlimited juice and coffee.

Be warned that international connections from Oslo are often in flux. Schedules can vary depending on the day of the week, so carefully confirm the specific train you need and purchase any required reservations in advance. Aside from the occasional direct train to Stockholm, most trips from Oslo to Copenhagen or Stockholm require a change in Sweden. From June through August only, direct night trains run from Oslo to Stockholm and to Malmö, Sweden (which is very close to Copenhagen).

From Oslo by Train to Bergen: Oslo and Bergen are linked by a spectacularly scenic train ride (3-5/day, 7 hours, overnight possible daily except Sat). Many travelers take it as part of the **Norway in a Nutshell** route, which combines train, ferry, and bus travel in an unforgettably beautiful trip. For information on times and prices, see the next chapter.

By Train to: Lillehammer (almost hourly, 2.5 hours), **Kristiansand** (4/day, 4.5 hours), **Stavanger** (4/day, 8-8.5 hours, overnight possible), **Copenhagen** (2/day, 8 hours, transfer at Göteborg; for night train—which runs in summer only—sleep on the direct train to Malmö, Sweden, easy transfer for 35-minute ride to Copenhagen, www.sj.se), **Stockholm** (2/day direct InterCity trains, 6 hours; 2/day with change in Kristinehamn, 6 hours; plus a direct 9-hour night train in summer only).

By Bus to Stockholm: Taking the bus to Stockholm is cheaper but slower than the train (3/day, 8 hours, www.swebus.se).

By Car to the Jotunheimen Mountains: See "Route Tips for Drivers" on page 357.

By Cruise Ship

Oslo has four cruise ports, described below. For more in-depth cruising information, pick up my *Rick Steves' Northern European Cruise Ports* guidebook.

Getting Downtown: To varying degrees, all of Oslo's cruise ports are within walking distance of the city center—but from the farther-flung ports (Filipstad and Sørenge), your best option is probably to take advantage of your cruise line's shuttle bus, even if you have to pay for it (most drop off by the Nobel Peace Center, near City Hall on the harborfront). No public transit serves the ports, but two different companies operate hop-on, hop-off bus tours from your cruise ship dock (pricey but convenient; see page 231). A taxi into town from any of the ports costs a hefty 150 kr.

Once you arrive at the City Hall/harbor area, you can simply walk up the street behind City Hall to find the TI, Karl Johans Gate, and the National Gallery; hop on tram #12 (ride it toward Majorstuen to reach Frogner Park—use the Vigelandsparken stop; or ride it toward Disen to reach the train station—use the Jernbanetorget stop); or take the shuttle boat across the harbor to the museums at Bygdøy.

Port Details: Akershus, right on the harbor below Akershus Fortress, has two berths: **Søndre Akershuskai,** a bit closer to town, and **Vippetangen,** a bit farther out (at the tip of the peninsula). Both are within an easy 10-minute walk of City Hall (just stroll with the harbor on your left). Søndre Akershuskai has a terminal building with a handy TI inside.

Revierkai, around the east side of the Akershus Fortress peninsula, faces Oslo's can't-miss-it, cutting-edge Opera House. From the Opera House, a pedestrian overpass takes you directly to the train station and the start of my self-guided "Welcome to Oslo" walk, or you can head up the street called Rådhusgata to City Hall.

Filipstad is just west of downtown, next to the brand-new Tjuvholmen development (around the far side of Aker Brygge from City Hall). From here, it's a dull 20-minute walk into town: Walk out of the port, turn right at the roundabout, then head to the busy highway and follow it to the right. As construction at

Tjuvholmen concludes, you may be able to take a scenic short-cut through that housing development to reach Aker Brygge and the main harbor zone (visually scout your options from your ship's top deck before disembarking). Given the long slog, I'd opt for a cruise-line shuttle bus instead.

Sørenge, farthest afield, is around the east side of the bay that Oslo's Opera House sits on. It's a long 20-minute walk to the Opera House (save time by cutting through the new Sørenge housing development, then taking the footbridge across the bay). From the Opera House, you're still 10 minutes from the train station or City Hall. I'd opt for a cruise shuttle bus to save time and sweat.

By Overnight Boat to Copenhagen

Consider connecting Oslo and Copenhagen by cruise ship. The boat leaves daily from Oslo at 17:00 (arrives in Copenhagen at 9:30 the following morning; going the other way, it departs Copenhagen at 17:00 and arrives in Oslo at 9:30; about 16 hours sailing each way). The boat leaves Oslo from the far (non-City Hall) side of the Akershus Fortress peninsula (get there via bus #60 from the train station, 2-3/hour, get off at Vippetangen stop and follow signs to DFDS ticket office). Boarding is from 15:30 to 16:00. From Oslo, you'll sail through the Oslofjord—not as dramatic as Norway's western fjords, but impressive if you're not going to Bergen. On board are three gourmet restaurants, dinner and breakfast buffets, cafés, nightclubs, shops, a sauna, hot tub, and swimming pool. This is fun and convenient, but more expensive and not as swanky as the Stockholm-Helsinki cruise (see the Helsinki chapter).

You can take this cruise one-way or do a round-trip from either city. Book online or by phone (from Norway, call DFDS Seaways' Denmark office at 00-45-33 42 30 10, Mon-Fri 8:30-17:00, closed Sat-Sun, www.dfdsseaways.us; in the US, call 800-533-3755, www.dfdsseawaysusa.com). Book in advance for the best prices. For more specifics and sample prices, see "By Overnight Boat to Oslo" on page 133.

NORWAY in a NUTSHELL

A Scenic Journey to the Sognefjord

While Oslo and Bergen are the big draws for tourists, Norway is first and foremost a place of unforgettable natural beauty. There's a certain mystique about the "land of the midnight sun," but you'll get the most scenic travel thrills per mile, minute, and dollar by going west from Oslo rather than north.

Norway's greatest claims to scenic fame are her deep, lush fjords. Three million years ago, an ice age made this land as inhabitable as the center of Greenland. As the glaciers advanced and cut their way to the sea, they gouged out long grooves—today's fjords.

The entire west coast is slashed by stunning fjords, and the Sognefjord—Norway's longest (120 miles) and deepest (1 mile)—is tops. Anything but the Sognefjord is, at best, foreplay. The seductive Sognefjord has tiny but tough ferries, towering canyons, and isolated farms and villages marinated in the mist of countless waterfalls.

A series of well-organized and spectacular bus, train, and ferry connections—appropriately nicknamed "Norway in a Nutshell"—lays Norway's beautiful fjord country before you on a scenic platter. With the Nutshell, you'll delve into two offshoots of the Sognefjord, which make an upside-down "U" route: the Aurlandsfjord and the Nærøyfjord. You'll link the ferry ride to the rest of Norway with two trains and a bus: The main train is an express route that takes you through stark polar scenery above the tree line. To get from the express train down to the ferry, you'll catch an old-fashioned slow train one way (passing waterfalls and forests) and a bus the other way (offering fjord views and more waterfalls). All connections are designed for tourists, explained in English, convenient, and easy. At the start of the fjord, you'll go

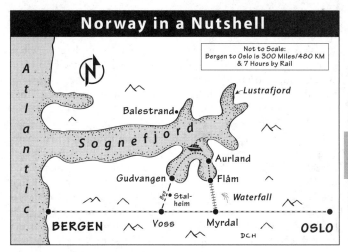

through the town of Flåm (a transit hub), then pass briefly by the workaday town of Aurland and the hamlet of Undredal (by taking the Nutshell trip segments at your own pace, you can visit the latter two fjord towns on your own; all are described in this chapter).

This region enjoys mild weather for its latitude, thanks to the warm Gulf Stream. (When it rains in Bergen, it just drizzles here.) But if the weather is bad—don't fret. I've often arrived to gloomy weather, only to enjoy sporadic splashes of brilliant sunshine all day long.

Recently the popularity of the Nutshell route has skyrocketed. And the 2005 completion of the longest car tunnel in the world (15 miles between Flåm and Lærdal) rerouted the main E-16 road between Bergen and Oslo through this idyllic fjord corner. All of this means that July and August come with a crush of crowds, dampening some of the area's magic. Unfortunately, many tourists are overcome by Nutshell tunnel-vision, and spend so much energy scurrying between boats, trains, and buses that they forget to simply enjoy the fjords. Relax—you're on vacation.

Planning Your Time

Even the blitz tourist needs a day for the Norway in a Nutshell trip. With more time, sleep in a town along the fjord, and customize your fjord experience to include sights outside the Nutshell.

Day 1: The Nutshell works well as a single day (one-way between Oslo and Bergen in either direction, or as a long day trip from either city). Those with a car and only one day should leave the car in Oslo and do the Nutshell by train, bus, and boat. If you're using public transportation and want to make efficient use of your time, organize your trip so that it ends in Bergen, or return to Oslo on a night train (sleeping through all the scenery you saw westbound).

Day 2: If you have enough time, spend the night somewhere on the Sognefjord—either along the Nutshell route itself (in Flåm or Aurland; accommodations listed later), or in another, even more appealing fjordside town (such as Balestrand or Solvorn, both described in the next chapter).

With More Time: The Sognefjord deserves more than a day. If you can spare the time, venture off the Nutshell route. You can easily connect to some non-Nutshell towns (such as Balestrand) via the handy express boat. Drivers can improve on the Nutshell by taking a northern route: From Oslo, drive through the Gudbrandsdal Valley, go over the Jotunheimen Mountains, then along Lustrafjord to Balestrand; from there, you can cross the Sognefjord on a car ferry (such as Kaupanger-Gudvangen) and drive the Nutshell route on to Bergen. (Most of these sights, and the car ferry connection, are covered in the next two chapters.) For more tips, see the "Beyond the Nutshell" sidebar.

Orientation to the Nutshell

The most exciting single-day trip you could make from Oslo or Bergen is this circular train/boat/bus/train jaunt through fjord

country. Everybody does this famous trip...and if you're looking for a delicious slice of Norway's scenic grandeur, so should you.

Local TIs (listed throughout this chapter) are well-informed about your options, and they sell tickets for various segments of the trip. At TIs, train stations, and hotels, look for souvenir-worthy brochures with photos, descriptions, and exact times (a sidebar later in this chapter has sample schedules).

Route Overview: The basic idea is this: Take a train halfway across the mountainous spine of Norway, make your way down to the Sognefjord for a boat cruise, then climb back up out of the fjord to rejoin the main train line. Each of these steps is explained in the self-guided tour, below. Transportation along the Nutshell route is carefully coordinated. If any segment of the journey is delayed, your transportation for the next segment will wait (because everyone on board is catching the same connection).

The route works round-trip from Oslo or Bergen, or one-way

Beyond the Nutshell

The Sognefjord is the ultimate natural thrill Norway has to offer, and there's no doubt that the Nutshell route outlined in this chapter is the most efficient way to see it quickly. Unfortunately, its trains, buses, and boats are thronged with other visitors who have the same idea. Those who stick with the Nutshell crowd enjoy it, but—as they spend the day jostling with a United Nations of tourists for the best photo—can't shake that lemming feeling.

Travelers with a bit more time, and the willingness to chart their own course, often have a more rewarding Sognefjord experience. It's surprisingly easy to break out of the Nutshell and hit the northern part of the Sognefjord (for example, using the Bergen-Vik-Balestrand-Aurland-Flåm express boat, described on page 330).

In the next chapter, you'll find some tempting stopovers on the north bank of the Sognefjord, including adorable fjordside villages (such as Balestrand and Solvorn), evocative stave churches (including Hopperstad and Urnes), and a chance to get up close to a glacier (at the Nigard Glacier).

Read up on your options, then be adventurous about mixing and matching the fjordside attractions that appeal to you most. Use the Nutshell as a springboard for diving into the Back Door fjords of your travel dreams.

between those two cities (going in either direction). Doing the Nutshell one-way between Bergen and Oslo is most satisfying—you'll see the whole shebang, and it's extremely efficient if you're connecting the two cities anyway. Doing the Nutshell as a round-trip from Bergen is cheaper, but it doesn't include the majestic train ride between Myrdal and Oslo. Conversely, even though the round-trip from Oslo doesn't go all the way to Bergen, it still includes all the must-sees (the Voss-Bergen leg is the least thrilling anyway).

When to Go: The Nutshell trip is possible all year. In the summer (late June-late Aug), the connections are most convenient, the weather is most likely to be good...and the route is at its most crowded. Outside of this time, sights close and schedules become more challenging. Some say the Nutshell is most beautiful in winter, though schedules are severely reduced (and you can't do it as a day trip from Oslo). It's easy to confirm schedules, connections, and prices locally or online (latest info posted each May on www .ruteinfo.net).

Express Boat to Balestrand and Bergen: If you don't want to do the entire Nutshell route, take note of the very handy and

Sample Norway in a Nutshell Schedules

Here are several one-day options for doing the Nutshell in the summer (late June-late Aug). Confirm specific times before your trip (www.ruteinfo.net).

Oslo-Bergen: Train departs Oslo-8:05, arrives Myrdal-12:44; Flåmsbana train departs Myrdal-13:27, arrives Flåm-14:25; boat departs Flåm-15:10, arrives Gudvangen-17:30; bus departs Gudvangen-17:45, arrives Voss-19:00; train departs Voss-19:37, arrives Bergen-20:54.

Bergen-Oslo: Train departs Bergen-8:40, arrives Voss-9:54; bus departs Voss-10:00, arrives Gudvangen-11:10; boat departs Gudvangen-11:45, arrives Flåm-14:10; Flåmsbana train departs Flåm-16:05, arrives Myrdal-17:03; train departs Myrdal-17:53, arrives Oslo-22:45.

Day Trip from Oslo: Train departs Oslo-6:43, arrives Myrdal-12:01; Flåmsbana train departs Myrdal-12:11, arrives Flåm-13:05; boat departs Flåm-13:20, arrives Gudvangen-15:30; bus departs Gudvangen-15:40, arrives Voss-16:55; train departs Voss-17:08, arrives Oslo-22:45.

Day Trip from Bergen: Train departs Bergen-8:40, arrives Voss-9:55; bus departs Voss-10:00, arrives Gudvangen-11:00; boat departs Gudvangen-11:45, arrives Flåm-14:10; Flåmsbana train departs Flåm-14:40, arrives Myrdal-15:30; train departs Myrdal-17:01, arrives Bergen-19:05.

Variations: If you spend a night (or more) on the fjords, you have many options other than the speedy itineraries outlined above. One popular variation is to take the express boat from Bergen to Balestrand for an overnight, then plunge into the Nutshell the next day (or vice versa—do the Nutshell partway, then boat to Bergen; for express boat information, see page 330).

speedy express boat connecting this area (Aurland and Flåm) with two other worthwhile destinations: Balestrand (on the Sognefjord's northern bank) and Bergen. While this boat misses the best fjord (Nærøyfjord), many travelers use it to craft their own itinerary that escapes the Nutshell rut. For more on this boat, see page 330.

Eating: Options along the route aren't great—on the Nutshell I'd consider food just as a source of nutrition and forget about fine dining. You can buy some food on the fjord cruises (50-75-kr hot dogs, burgers, and pizza) and the Oslo-Bergen train (50-100-kr

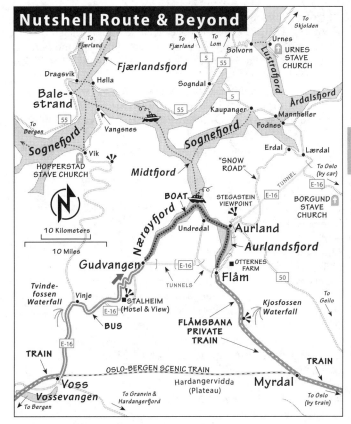

NORWAY IN A NUTSHELL

hot meals, 150-kr daily specials). Depending on the timing of your layovers, Myrdal, Voss, or Flåm are your best lunch-stop options (the Myrdal and Flåm train stations have decent cafeterias, and other eateries surround the Flåm and Voss stations)—although you won't have a lot of time there if you're making the journey all in one day. Your best bet is to pack a picnic lunch. While some hotels sell a sack lunch assembled from their breakfast buffet, many will let you snag a sandwich for free if you ask politely. Or you can plan ahead and buy picnic fixings at a grocery store to bring along.

With a Package Deal or On Your Own?

The Fjord Tours package deals are easy to book—they'll save you time as well as a little money. If you have a railpass, or if you're a student or a senior (and therefore eligible for discounts), you'll save money doing the Nutshell on your own—if you don't mind the hassle (described on the next page).

Package Deals

Fjord Tours sells the Nutshell package and other package trips at all Norwegian State Railways stations, including Oslo and Bergen, or through their customer-service line in Norway (tel. 81 56 82 22, www.fjordtours.no).

The costs of the Nutshell packages are as follows:
• One-way from Bergen or Oslo-1,480 kr
• Round-trip from Oslo via Voss (but not Bergen)-2,030 kr
• Round-trip from Oslo via Bergen-2,310 kr
• Round-trip from Bergen via Myrdal (but not Oslo)-1,090 kr
• Round-trip from Flåm-740 kr

They also sell a "Sognefjord in a Nutshell" tour, which takes an express boat from Bergen to Flåm, then picks up the Nutshell route from there (round-trip back to Bergen-1,305 kr; one-way to Oslo-1,690 kr; runs only May-Sept).

On Your Own

Unless you have a railpass or are eligible for student or senior discounts, you'll pay roughly the same to do the Nutshell on your own as you would with a package tour (see prices above).

Railpass Discounts: If you have any railpass that includes Norway, the Oslo-Bergen train is covered (except a 50-kr reservation fee for second class; free for first-class passholders); you also get a 30 percent discount on the Myrdal-Flåm Flåmsbana train (195 kr). You still have to pay full fare for the boat cruise (285 kr) and the Gudvangen-Voss bus (98 kr). Your total one-way cost between Oslo and Bergen: about 578 kr with a first-class pass, 628 kr with a second-class pass.

Buying Tickets: You can get Nutshell train tickets at the train station in Oslo or Bergen. In summer, it's smart to reserve the Oslo-Myrdal segment in advance (see below). Get your Flåmsbana ticket at the first Flåmsbana station you come to (either in Flåm or in Myrdal); purchase your fjord-cruise ticket on the boat or from the TI in Flåm (or reserve ahead in peak season; see below); and buy the tickets for the Gudvangen bus on board from the driver. If you're a student or senior, always ask about discounts.

Reservations: At peak season (July-Aug), the **Oslo-Bergen train**—especially the segment between Oslo and Myrdal—can fill up well in advance: It's very important to reserve a seat at least a week ahead: Dial 81 50 08 88 or 23 15 15 15 (from the US, call 011-47-81-50-08-88 or 011-47-23-15-15-15), and press 9 for English. It can be difficult to get through to this number in peak season—keep trying. Once connected, you can make a seat reservation (works for railpass holders, too). After booking your seat, you'll be given a reservation number to use to pick up and pay for your ticket at the train station in Norway. It's also possible to obtain a seat reservation by sending an email to help@nsb.no with specifics about the ticket you need. Unfortunately, at this time, tickets cannot be purchased online from the US. Be sure to ask about cancellation policies before you book.

The **Flåmsbana train** is tricky: If several big cruise liners come into Flåm, a few departures of this train can sell out—but likely not the ones you'll need for a Nutshell connection. You can only buy Flåmsbana tickets for a specific departure at one of the Flåmsbana train stations (i.e., in Flam or Myrdal). The only exception is for those buying the Nutshell package, which includes a Flåmsbana ticket for the departure you'll need. (For details, see page 300.)

It's smart to reserve ahead for the **Flåm-Gudvangen fjord** boat trip (see page 301). You don't need a reservation for the **Gudvangen-Voss bus.**

Tips for Cruise-Ship Passengers Arriving in Flåm

Tiny Flåm—in the heart of Nutshell country—is an increasingly popular destination for huge cruise ships. If your cruise is stopping in Flåm, you can do the middle part of the Nutshell loop in a day, but it helps to know a few pointers:

• Plan your day in advance (using this chapter), disembark as early as possible, and head straight for the train station (a short walk from the dock). Many ships arrive around 8:00; Flåm's TI and train-station ticket office both open at 8:15; and the first Nutshell fjord boat sets sail at 9:00—leaving you a narrow window of time to confirm schedules and book tickets. Stragglers may get stuck in long lines and (literally) miss the boat.

• The Nutshell loop is practical for cruisers only if done counterclockwise: Flåm-Gudvangen boat, 9:00-11:25; Gudvangen-Voss bus, 11:40-12:55; Voss-Myrdal train, 13:10-14:00; Flåmsbana train from Myrdal to Flåm, 14:43-15:27 (these are 2013 times; confirm locally). The opposite direction (Flåm-Myrdal-Voss-Gudvangen-Flåm) returns to Flåm too late for most cruise ships.

• The same "package vs. on your own" considerations, explained earlier, apply to cruisers. Unless you're eligible for student, senior, or railpass discounts, book the Flåm round-trip package (at the Flåm TI).

• If you'd rather not do the full Nutshell on your day in port, you could do one or two legs: For example, cruise to Gudvangen, then bus back to Flåm; or simply go for a round-trip ride on the Flåmsbana to Myrdal and back (this popular-with-cruisers option often sells out—get your tickets as quickly as possible on arrival in Flåm). For other ideas of what to do in Flåm, see page 305.

Self-Guided Tour

▲▲▲Norway in a Nutshell

If you only have one day for this region, it'll be a thrilling day. The following segments of the Nutshell route are narrated from Oslo to Bergen. If you're going the other way, hold the book upside down.

▲▲Oslo-Bergen Train

This is simply the most spectacular train ride in northern Europe. The scenery crescendos as you climb over Norway's mountainous spine. After a mild three hours of deep woods and lakes, you're into the barren, windswept heaths and glaciers. These tracks were begun in 1894 to link Stockholm and Bergen, but Norway won its independence from Sweden in 1905, so the line served to link the two main cities in the new country—Oslo and Bergen. The entire railway, an amazing engineering feat completed in 1909, is 300 miles long; peaks at 4,266 feet, which, at this Alaskan latitude, is far above the tree line; goes under 18 miles of snow sheds; trundles over 300 bridges; and passes through 200 tunnels in just under seven hours.

Here's what you'll see traveling westward from Oslo: Leaving Oslo, you pass through a six-mile-long tunnel and stop in Drammen, Norway's fifth-largest town. The scenery stays low-key and woodsy up Hallingdal Valley until you reach Geilo, a popular ski resort. Then you enter a land of big views and tough little cabins. Finse, at about 4,000 feet, is the highest stop on the line. From here, you enter the longest high-mountain stretch of railway in Europe. Much of the line is protected by snow tunnels. The scenery gets more dramatic as you approach Myrdal (MEER-doll). Just before Myrdal, look to the right and down into the Flåm Valley, where the Flåmsbana branch line winds its way down to the fjord. Nutshell travelers get off at Myrdal.

Cost: Note that the Nutshell route includes only part of this train ride (as a day trip from Oslo, for instance, you take the Oslo-Myrdal and Voss-Oslo segments). Here are the one-way fares for various segments: Oslo-Bergen-815 kr, Oslo-Myrdal-650 kr, Myrdal-Voss-113 kr, Myrdal-Bergen-278 kr, Voss-Bergen-184 kr. You can save money on these fares if you book in advance at www .nsb.no.

Remember, second-class railpass-holders pay just 50 kr to reserve, and first-class passholders pay nothing. If you have a second-class railpass or ticket, you can pay 90 kr to upgrade to "Komfort" class, with more legroom, reclining seats, free coffee and tea, and an electrical socket for your laptop (reserve ahead or ask the conductor when you board; free for first class).

NORWAY IN A NUTSHELL

The Facts on Fjords

The process that created the majestic Sognefjord began during an ice age about three million years ago. A glacier up to 6,500 feet thick slid downhill at an inch an hour, following a former river valley on its way to the sea. Rocks embedded in the glacier gouged out a steep, U-shaped valley, displacing enough rock material to form a mountain 13 miles high. When the climate warmed up, the ice age came to an end. The melting glaciers retreated and the sea level rose nearly 300 feet, flooding the valley now known as the Sognefjord. The fjord is more than a mile deep, flanked by 3,000-foot mountains—for a total relief of 9,300 feet. Waterfalls spill down the cliffs, fed by runoff from today's glaciers. Powdery sediment tinges the fjords a cloudy green, the distinct color of glacier melt.

Why are there fjords on the west coast of Norway, but not, for instance, on the east coast of Sweden? The creation of a fjord requires a setting of coastal mountains, a good source of moisture, and a climate cold enough for glaciers to form and advance. Due to the earth's rotation, the prevailing winds in higher latitudes blow from west to east, so chances of glaciation are ideal where there is an ocean to the west of land with coastal mountains. When the winds blow east over the water, they pick up a lot of moisture, then bump up against the coastal mountain range, and dump their moisture in the form of snow—which feeds the glaciers that carve valleys down to the sea.

You can find fjords along the northwest coast of Europe—including western Norway and Sweden, Denmark's Faroe Islands, Scotland's Shetland Islands, Iceland, and Greenland; the northwest coast of North America (from Puget Sound in Washington state north to Alaska); the southwest coast of South America (Chile); the west coast of New Zealand's South Island; and on the continent of Antarctica.

As you travel through Scandinavia, bear in mind that, while we English-speakers use the word "fjord" to mean only glacier-cut inlets, Scandinavians often use it in a more general sense to include bays, lakes, and lagoons that weren't formed by glacial action.

Schedule: This train runs three to five times per day (overnight possible daily except Sat). The segment from Oslo to Myrdal takes 4.75-5.5 hours; going all the way to Bergen takes 7-7.5 hours.

Reservations: In peak season, get reservations for this train at least a week in advance (see page 296).

▲▲Myrdal-Flåm Train (Flåmsbana)

The little 12-mile spur line leaves the Oslo-Bergen line at Myrdal (2,800 feet), which is nothing but a scenic high-altitude train junction with a decent cafeteria. From Myrdal, the train winds down to Flåm (sea level) through 20 tunnels (more than three miles' worth) in 55 thrilling minutes. It's party time on board, and the engineer even stops the train for photos at the best waterfall, Kjosfossen. According to a Norwegian legend, a temptress lives behind these falls and tries to lure men to the rocks with her singing...look out for her.

The train line is an even more impressive feat of engineering when you realize it's not a cogwheel train—it's held to the tracks only by steel wheels, though it does have five separate braking systems. Before boarding, pick up the free, multilingual souvenir pamphlet with lots of info on the trip (or see www.flaamsbana.no). Video screens onboard and sporadic English commentary on the loudspeakers explain points of interest, but there's not much to say—it's all about the scenery.

While the grass is always greener on the other side of the train, if you're choosing seats, you'll enjoy slightly more scenery if you sit on the west-facing side of the train (on the left going down, on the right going up).

Cost: 280 kr one-way (railpass holders pay 195 kr), 380 kr round-trip. You can buy tickets only at the Flåmsbana stations in Myrdal or Flåm (not at other train ticket offices in Norway—though if you book the whole package in Oslo or Bergen, you can reserve a specific train). If you're in a rush to make a tight connection, you can try to buy them on board (but if the train is sold out, the ticket-takers may send you back to the ticket office).

Schedule: The train departs in each direction nearly hourly.

Reservations: This train can get jammed with travelers, particularly when multiple cruise ships are in Flåm. On trains going from Myrdal down to Flåm, you can always squeeze in, even if it's standing-room only. However, trains ascending from Flåm to Myrdal can sell out. You can buy advance tickets for a particular train (though not reserve a specific seat) at the Flåmsbana ticket office in either Flåm or Myrdal, or—if you're booking the full Nutshell—at the train stations in Oslo or Bergen. In practice, this is a concern only for those wanting to leave Flåm to Myrdal in the morning; if possible, buy your ticket the night before to avoid the possibility of sold-out trains—or get to the ticket office early in the morning (it opens at 8:15).

▲▲▲Flåm-Gudvangen Fjord Cruise

The Flåmsbana train deposits you at **Flåm,** a scenic, functional transit hub at the far end of the Aurlandsfjord. If you're doing

the Nutshell route nonstop, follow the crowds and hop on the sightseeing boat that'll take you to **Gudvangen.** With minimal English narration, the boat takes you close to the goats, sheep, waterfalls, and awesome cliffs.

You'll cruise up the lovely **Aurlandsfjord,** motoring by the

town of **Aurland** (a good home base, but your boat may not stop here unless you ask), pass **Undredal,** and hang a left at the stunning **Nærøyfjord** ("Narrow Fjord"). The cruise ends at the apex of the Nærøyfjord, in **Gudvangen.**

The trip is breathtaking in any weather. For the last hour, as you sail down the Nærøyfjord, camera-clicking tourists scurry around the drool-stained deck like nervous

roosters, scratching fitfully for a photo that will catch the magic. Waterfalls turn the black cliffs into bridal veils, and you can nearly reach out and touch the cliffs of the Nærøyfjord. It's the world's narrowest fjord: six miles long and as little as 820 feet wide and 40 feet deep. On a sunny day, the ride is one of those fine times—like when you're high on the tip of an Alp—when a warm camaraderie spontaneously combusts between the strangers who've come together for the experience.

Cost: For the whole route (Flåm-Gudvangen), you'll pay 285 kr one-way (143 kr for students with ISIC cards; 390 kr round-trip).

Schedule: In summer (May-Sept), boats run four to five times each day in both directions. Specific departure times can vary, but generally boats leave Flåm at 9:00, 13:20, 15:10, and 18:00 (with an additional 11:00 departure from late June to late August); and leave Gudvangen at 10:30, 11:45, 15:45, and 17:40 (with an additional

13:30 departure from late June to late August). Frequency drops off-season. The trip takes about two hours and 15 minutes.

Reservations: If your itinerary hinges on a specific departure, it's smart to reserve the boat trip in advance: You can email booking @fjord1.no, book online at www.fjord1.no, or call 55 90 70 70 by 14:00 one business day before.

Other Ways to Cruise Nærøyfjord: While most visitors thunder onto the state-run ferry described above, consider taking a trip on a Sognefjorden Cruise ship, or a thrilling ride on little inflatable FjordSafari speedboats (both described later, under "Sights in and near Flåm"; see page 305).

▲Gudvangen-Voss Bus

Nutshellers get off the boat at Gudvangen and take the bus to Voss. Gudvangen is little more than a boat dock and giant tourist kiosk. If you want, you can browse through the grass-roofed souvenir stores and walk onto a wooden footbridge—then catch your bus. Buses meet each ferry, or will show up soon. (It's smart to confirm this in advance if you plan to take the last boat of the day, which arrives in Gudvangen at about 17:20—the ferry crew can call ahead to be sure the bus waits for you). While some buses—designed for commuters rather than sightseers—take the direct route to Voss, buses tied to the Nutshell schedule take a super-scenic detour via Stalheim (described below). If you're a waterfall junkie, sit on the left.

First the bus takes you up the **Nærøydal** and plunges you into a couple of long tunnels. Then you'll  take a turnoff to drive past the landmark **Stalheim Hotel** for the first of many spectacular views back into fjord country. While some buses stop at the hotel for a photo op, others drive right past. Though the hotel dates from 1885, there's been an inn here since about 1700, where the royal mailmen would change horses. The hotel is geared for tour groups (genuine trolls sew the pewter buttons on the sweaters), but the priceless view from the backyard is free. If your bus pauses here, snap your classic photo, then stop in the living room to survey the art showing this perch in the 19th century.

Leaving the hotel, the bus wends its way down a road called **Stalheimkleiva,** with a corkscrew series of switchbacks flanked by a pair of dramatic waterfalls. With its 18 percent grade, it's the steepest road in Norway.

After winding your way down into the valley, you're back

on the same highway. The bus goes through those same tunnels again, then continues straight on the main road through pastoral countryside to Voss. You'll pass a huge lake, then follow a crystal-clear, surging river. Just before Voss, look to the right for the wide **Tvindefossen waterfall,** tumbling down its terraced cliff. Drivers will find the grassy meadow and flat rocks at its base ideal for letting the mist fog their glasses and enjoying a drink or snack (be discreet, as "picnics are forbidden").

Cost: 98 kr, pay on board, no railpass discounts.

Reservations: Not necessary.

Voss

The Nutshell bus from Gudvangen drops you at the Voss train station, which is on the Oslo-Bergen train line. Nutshellers should catch the next train out. A plain town in a lovely lake-and-mountain setting, Voss lacks the striking fjordside scenery of Flåm, Aurland, or Undredal, and is basically a home base for summer or winter sports (Norway's Winter Olympics teams often practice here). Voss surrounds its fine, 13th-century church with workaday streets—busy with both local shops and souvenir stores—stretching in several directions. Fans of American football may want to see the humble monument to player and coach Knute Rockne, who was born in Voss in 1888; look for the metal memorial plaque on a rock near the train station.

Voss' helpful **TI** is a five-minute walk from the train station—just head toward the church (June-Aug Mon-Fri 8:00-19:00, Sat 9:00-19:00, Sun 12:00-19:00; Sept-May Mon-Fri 8:30-17:00, Sat 9:00-15:00, closed Sun; facing the church in the center of town at Vangsgatan 20, mobile 40 61 77 00, www.visitvoss.no).

Drivers should zip right through Voss, but two miles outside town, you can stop at the **Mølstertunet Folk Museum,** which has 16 buildings showing off farm life in the 17th and 18th centuries (60 kr; mid-May-Aug daily 10:00-17:00; Sept-mid-May Mon-Fri 10:00-15:00, Sun 12:00-15:00, closed Sat; Mølstervegen 143, tel. 56 51 15 11, www.vossfolkemuseum.no).

▲Voss-Bergen Train

The least exciting segment of the trip—but still pleasantly scenic—this train chugs along the valley between the midsize town of Voss (described above) and Bergen. For the best scenery, sit on the right side of the train if coming from Oslo/Voss, or the left side if coming from Bergen. Between Voss and Dale, you'll pass several scenic lakes; near Bergen, you'll go along the Veafjord.

Cost: The train costs 184 kr between Voss and Bergen and is fully covered by railpasses that include Norway.

Schedule and Reservations: Unlike the long-distance

Oslo-Bergen journey, this line is also served by more frequent commuter trains (about hourly, 1-1.25 hours), and reservations aren't necessary.

Voss-Oslo Train: Note that if you're doing the Nutshell round-trip from Oslo, you should catch the train from Voss (rather than Bergen) back to Oslo. The return trip takes 5.5-6 hours and costs 735 kr; reservations are strongly recommended in peak season.

Flåm

Flåm (sometimes spelled Flaam, pronounced "flome")—where the boat and Flåmsbana train meet, at the head of the Aurlandsfjord—feels more like a transit junction than a village. But its striking setting, easy transportation connections, and touristy bustle make it appealing as a home base for exploring the nearby area.

Orientation to Flåm

Most of Flåm's services are inside the train station, including the TI (see below), train ticket desk, pay Wi-Fi, public WC, cafeteria, and souvenir shops hawking overpriced reindeer pelts (cheaper in Bergen). Just outside the station, the little red shed at the head of the tracks serves as a left-luggage desk (25 kr, daily 8:00-19:45, on your right as you depart the train, ring bell if nobody's there), and displays a chart of the services you'll find in the station. The boat dock for fjord cruises is just beyond the end of the tracks. Surrounding the station are a Co-op Marked grocery store (with a basic pharmacy and post office inside, Mon-Fri 9:00-20:00, Sat 9:00-18:00, shorter hours off-season, closed Sun year-round) and a smattering of hotels, travel agencies, and touristy restaurants. Aside from a few scattered farmhouses and some homes lining the road, there's not much of a town here. (The extremely sleepy old town center—where tourists rarely venture, and which you'll pass on the Flåmsbana train—is a few miles up the river, in the valley.)

Tourist Information

At the TI inside the train station, you can purchase your boat tickets and load up on handy brochures (daily May and late Sept 8:15-16:00, June-mid-Sept 8:15-20:00, closed Oct-April, tel. 57 63 21 06, www.visitflam.com or www.alr.no, very helpful Vladimir). The TI hands out a variety of useful items: an excellent flyer with a good map and up-to-date schedules for public transit options; a diagram of the train-station area, identifying services available in each building; and a map of Flåm and the surrounding area, marked with suggested walks and hikes. Answers to most of your questions can be found posted on the walls and from staff at the counter. Bus schedules, boat and train timetables, maps, and more are photocopied and available for your convenience. To get online, buy a Wi-Fi voucher at the TI counter (20 kr/1 hour, 40 kr/3 hours, 50 kr/day).

Sights in and near Flåm

Along the Waterfront

Flåm's village activities are all along or near the pier.

The **Flåm Railway Museum** (Flåmsbana Museet), sprawling through the long old train station building alongside the tracks, has surprisingly good exhibits about the history of the train that connects Flåm to the main line up above. You'll find good English explanations, artifacts, recreations of historic interiors (such as the humble schoolhouse up at Myrdal), and an actual train car. It's the only real museum in town and a good place to kill time while waiting for your boat or train (free, daily 9:00-17:00).

The Torget Café is attached to a **fjord "panorama" movie** (55 kr, 23 minutes).

I'd skip the pointless and overpriced **tourist train** that does a 45-minute loop around Flåm (95 kr).

The pleasantly woody **Ægir Bryggeri,** a microbrewery designed to resemble an old Viking longhouse, offers tastes of its five beers (125 kr; also pub grub in the evening).

The TI hands out a map suggesting several **walks and hikes** in the area, starting from right in town.

If you want to linger, consider renting a **boat** to go out on the usually calm, peaceful waters of the fjord. You can paddle near the walls of the fjord and really get a sense of the immensity of these mountains. You can rent rowboats, motorboats, and paddleboats at the little marina across the harbor. If you'd rather have a kayak, Njord does kayak tours, but won't rent you one unless you're certified (tel. 91 32 66 28, www.njord.as).

But the main reason people come to Flåm is to leave it—see some options below. Because Aurland and Flåm are close together (10 minutes away by car or bus, or 20 minutes by boat), I've also listed attractions near Aurland, below.

▲▲▲Cruising Nærøyfjord

The most scenic fjord I've seen anywhere in Norway is about an hour from Flåm (basically the last half of the 2-hour Flåm-Gudvangen trip). There are several ways to cruise it: You can take the state-run ferry, described earlier as part of the Norway in a Nutshell trip (4.5-hour round-trips departing Flåm in peak season at 9:00, 11:00, and 13:20, 390 kr; these should also stop in Aurland—make sure the crew knows if you want to get off, and that the cruise ends in Gudvangen). Or you can consider two other Flåm-based options:

Sognefjorden Sightseeing & Tours—This private company runs trips from Flåm to Gudvangen and back to Flåm, using their own boats and buses (rather than the public ones on the "official" Nutshell route). If the Nutshell departures don't work for you, consider these trips as an alternative. Their main offering, the World Heritage Cruise, is a boat trip up the Nærøyfjord with a return by bus (335 kr, 2.5-3 hours, multiple departures daily mid-May-mid-Sept). They also do a variation on this trip with a 45-minute stop in the village of Undredal for lunch and a goat-cheese tasting (630 kr, June-Aug only); a bus trip up to the Stalheim Hotel for the view (290 kr, or combined with return from Gudvangen by boat for 510 kr); a bus ride up to the thrilling Stegastein viewpoint (otherwise impossible to reach without a car, 190 kr, mid-May-mid-Sept); and more. For details, drop by their office inside the Flåm train station, call 57 66 00 55, or visit www.visitflam.com/sognefjorden.

▲▲FjordSafari to Nærøyfjord—FjordSafari takes little groups out onto the fjord in small, open Zodiac-type boats with an English-speaking guide. Participants wear full-body weather suits, furry hats, and spacey goggles (making everyone on the boat look like crash-test dummies). As the boat rockets across the water, you'll be thankful for the gear, no matter what the weather. You'll get the same scant information and stops as on the slow ferry, except that Safari boats stop right under a towering rock cliff—a magnificent experience. Their two-hour Flåm-Gudvangen-Flåm tour focuses on the Nærøyfjord, and gets you all the fjord magnificence you can imagine (590 kr). Their three-hour tour (700 kr) is the same as the two-hour tour, except that it includes a stop in Undredal, where you can see goat cheese being made, taste the finished product, and wander that sleepy village. They run several departures daily from June through August (fewer off-season, kids get discounts, tel. 99 09 08 60, www.fjordsafari.no, Maylene). They also offer a 1.5-hour "mini" tour that costs 490 kr and just barely touches on the Nærøyfjord...so what's the point?

▲Flåm Valley Bike Ride or Hike

For the best single-day, non-fjord activity from Flåm, take the Flåmsbana train to Myrdal, then hike or mountain-bike along the road (part gravel but mostly paved) back down to Flåm (2-3 hours by bike, gorgeous waterfalls, great mountain scenery, and a cute church with an evocative graveyard, but no fjord views). The Flåm TI rents mountain bikes (50 kr/hour, 250 kr/day) as does the local youth hostel. It costs 90 kr to take a bike to Myrdal on the train.

You can hike just the best two hours from Myrdal to Berekvam, where you can catch the train into the valley. Pick up the helpful map with this and other hiking options (easy to strenuous) at the Flåm TI.

▲▲Otternes Farms

This humble but magical cluster of four centuries-old farms, real-istically accessible only to drivers, is perched high on a ridge, up  a twisty gravel road midway between Flåm and Aurland. Laila Kvellestad runs this low-key sight, valiantly working to save and share traditional life as it was back when butter was the farmers' gold. (That was before emigration decimated the workforce, coinage replaced barter, and industrial-ized margarine became more popular than butter—all of which left farmers to eke out a living relying only on their goats and the cheese they produce.) Until 1919 the only road between Aurland and Flåm passed between this huddle of 27 buildings, high above the fjord. First settled in 1522, farmers lived here until the 1990s. Laila gives 45-minute English tours through several time-warp houses and barns at 10:00, 12:00, 14:00, and 16:00 (50-kr entry plus 30 kr for guided tour, June-mid-Sept daily 10:00-17:00, tel. 48 12 51 38, www.otternes.no). It's wise to call first to confirm tour times and that it's open. For an additional 65 kr, Laila serves a tra-ditional snack with your tour (pancakes with coffee or tea), but you must book in advance.

Over (or Under) the Mountains, to Lærdal and Borgund

To reach these sights, you'll first head along the fjord to Aurland (described on page 311). Of the sights below, the Lærdal Tunnel, Stegastein viewpoint, and Aurlandsvegen "Snow Road" are best for drivers. The Borgund Stave Church can be reached by car, or by bus from Flåm or Aurland.

For more specifics on driving through the Lærdal Tunnel or on the Aurlandsvegen "Snow Road," see next page.

Lærdal Tunnel

Drivers find that this tunnel makes connecting Flåm and Lærdal a snap. It's the world's longest road-vehicle tunnel, stretching 15 miles between Aurland and Lærdal as part of the E-16 highway. It also makes the wonderful Borgund Stave Church (described on the next page) less than an hour's drive from Aurland. The downside to the tunnel is that it goes beneath my favorite scenic drive in Norway (the Aurlandsvegen "Snow Road," described next). But with about two hours, you can drive through the tunnel to Lærdal and then return via the "Snow Road," with the Stegastein viewpoint as a finale, before dropping back into Aurland.

▲▲Stegastein Viewpoint and Aurlandsvegen "Snow Road"

With a car and clear weather, consider twisting up the mountain behind Aurland on route 243 for about 20 minutes for a fine view

over the Aurlandsfjord. A new viewpoint called Stegastein—which looks like a giant, wooden, inverted number "7"—provides a platform from which you can enjoy stunning views across the fjords. Immediately beyond the viewpoint, you leave the fjord views and enter the mountaintop world of the Aurlandsvegen "Snow Road." When you finally hit civilization on the other side, you're a mile from the Lærdal tunnel entrance and about 30 minutes from the fine Borgund Stave Church.

▲▲Borgund Stave Church

About 16 miles east of Lærdal, in the village of Borgund, is Norway's most-visited and one of its best-preserved stave churches.

Borgund's church comes with one of this country's best stave-church history museums, which beautifully explains these icons

of medieval Norway. Dating from around 1180, the interior features only a few later additions, including a 16th-century pulpit, 17th-century stone altar, painted decorations, and cross-beam reinforcements.

The oldest and most authentic item in the church is the stone baptismal font. In medieval times, priests conducting baptisms would go outside to shoo away the evil spirits from an infant before bringing it inside the church for the ritual. (If infants died before being baptized, they couldn't be buried in the churchyard, so parents would put their bodies in little coffins and hide them under the church's floorboards to get them as close as possible to God.)

Explore the dimly lit interior, illuminated only by the original, small, circular windows up high. Notice the X-shaped crosses of St. Andrew (the church's patron), carvings of dragons, and medieval runes.

Cost and Hours: 75 kr, buy tickets in museum across street, daily mid-June–mid-Aug 8:00-20:00, May–mid-June and mid-Aug–Sept 10:00-17:00, closed Oct-April. The museum has a shop and a fine little cafeteria serving filling and tasty lunches (70-kr soup with bread, tel. 57 66 81 09, www.stavechurch.com).

Getting There: It's about a 30-minute **drive** east of Lærdal, on E-16 (the road to Oslo—if coming from Aurland or Flåm, consider taking the scenic route via the Stegastein viewpoint, described above). There's also a convenient **bus** connection: The bus departs Flåm and Aurland around midday (direction: Lillehammer) and heads for the church, with a return bus departing Borgund in mid-afternoon (240-kr round-trip, get ticket from driver, about 1 hour each way with about 1 hour at the church, bus runs daily May-Sept, tell driver you want to get off at the church).

Sleeping in Flåm

My recommended accommodations are away from the tacky train-station bustle, but a close enough walk to be convenient. The first two places are located along the waterfront a quarter-mile from the station: Walk around the little harbor (with the water on your left) for about 10 minutes. It's more enjoyable to follow the level, waterfront dock than to hike up the main road.

$$$ Flåm Marina and Apartments, perched right on the fjord, is ideal for families and longer stays. They offer 10 new-feeling, self-catering apartments that sleep 2-5 people each. All units offer views of the fjord with a balcony, kitchenette, and small dining area (Db-1,195 kr June–mid-Sept, less off-season, 320 kr more for each additional adult, check online or ask about specials for longer stays, no breakfast, café open during high season, boat rental, laundry facilities, next to the guest harbor just below Heimly Pensjonat—see next, tel. 57 63 35 55, www.flammarina.no, booking@flammarina.no).

$$ Heimly Pensjonat, with 23 straightforward rooms, is clean, efficient, and the best small hotel in town. Sit on the porch with new friends and watch the clouds roll down the fjord (Sb-895 kr, Db-1,045 kr, view Db costs 100 kr more in summer, extra bed-325 kr for adult or 225 kr for child, includes breakfast, cheaper Oct-May, Db rooms are mostly twins, try to reserve a room with a view at the standard price, bike and car rental, tel. 57 63 23 00, fax 57 63 23 40, www.heimly.no, post@heimly.no). The budget annex out back has more rooms that share bathrooms (D-510 kr, sheets and towels-100 kr/person, breakfast-95 kr).

Sleep Code

(6 kr = about $1, country code: 47)
S = Single, **D** = Double/Twin, **T** = Triple, **Q** = Quad, **b** = bathroom,
s = shower. You can assume that staff speak English, break-
fast is included, and credit cards are accepted unless otherwise noted.

To help you sort easily through these listings, I've divided
the accommodations into three categories, based on the price
for a standard double room with bath during high season:

$$$ Higher Priced—Most rooms 1,100 kr or more.
$$ Moderately Priced—Most rooms between 600-1,100 kr.
$ Lower Priced—Most rooms 600 kr or less.

Note that the season is boom or bust here. It can be dead
in June and packed in July and August. Prices can change
without notice; verify the hotel's current rates online or by
email.

$-$$ Flåm Youth Hostel and Camping Bungalows, voted
Scandinavia's most beautiful campground, is run by the friendly
Håland family, who rent the cheapest beds in the area (hostel:
bunk in 4-bed room-210 kr, S-340 kr, D-550-580 kr; newer, fancier
building: bunk in 4-bed room-275 kr, Db-755 kr; cabins-700-1,100
kr; sheets and towels-60 kr, showers-10 kr, 10 percent discount for
members, no meals but kitchen access, laundry, apple grove, tel. 57
63 21 21, www.flaam-camping.no, camping@flaam-camping.no).
It's a five-minute walk toward the valley from the train station:
Cross the bridge and turn left up the main road; then look for the
hostel on the right.

Eating in Flåm

Dining options beyond your hotel's dining room or kitchenette
are expensive and touristy. Don't aim for high cuisine here—go
practical. Almost all eateries are clustered near the train station
complex. Hours can be unpredictable, flexing with the season, but
you can expect these to be open daily in high season. Places here
tend to close pretty early (especially in shoulder season)—don't
wait too long for dinner.

The **Flåmsbrygga** complex, sprawling through a long building toward the fjord from the station, includes a hotel, the affordable **Furukroa Café** (cafeteria with 50-65-kr cold sandwiches,
100-150-kr fast-food meals, and 200-225-kr pizzas), and the pricey
Flåmstova Restaurant (235-kr lunch buffet, 325-kr dinner buffet,

plus other menu options at dinner). Next door is their fun, Viking-longhouse-shaped brewpub, Ægir Bryggeri (145-165-kr pub grub after 16:00). **Torget Café,** with seating in old train cars, is under new management that prides itself on using as many locally sourced and organic ingredients as possible (65-75-kr sandwiches, 160-195-kr main dishes).

NORWAY IN A NUTSHELL

Aurland

A few miles north of Flåm, Aurland is more of a real town and less of a tourist depot. While it's nothing exciting (Balestrand is

more lively and appealing, and Solvorn is cuter—see next chapter), it's a good, easy-going fjordside home base. And thanks to its location—on the main road and boat lines, near Flåm—it's relatively handy for those taking public transportation.

Getting There: Aurland is an easy 10-minute drive or bus trip from Flåm. If you want to stay overnight in Aurland, note that every train (except the late-night one) arriving in Flåm connects with a bus or boat to Aurland. Eleven buses and at least four ferries link the towns daily in summer (bus-33 kr, 10 minutes; boat-85 kr, 20 minutes). The Flåm-Gudvangen boat doesn't have a scheduled stop at Aurland, but they're usually willing to stop there if you ask—so it's possible to continue the Nutshell route from Aurland without backtracking to Flåm. Boat tickets bought at the Aurland TI come with a reservation (helpful on the busiest days in July and August, when the boats can fill up in Flåm). The Bergen-Balestrand-Flåm express boat stops in Aurland (for details, see page 330).

Orientation to Aurland

From Aurland's dingy boat dock area, walk one block up the paved street into the heart of town. On your right are the Rimi and Spar supermarkets (handy for picnic supplies) and Aurlandskafeen, the best restaurant in town (at the bridge). To your left is the Vangsgården Guest House and, behind it, Aurland Fjordhotel. To reach the TI, go straight ahead and bear right, then look behind the white church (800 years old and worth a peek). The bus stop, with buses to Flåm, is in front of the TI. For attractions near Aurland, see page 305.

Tourist Information

The TI stocks English-language brochures about hikes and day trips from the area, offers free Internet terminals, and hosts a small history exhibit (June-Aug Mon-Fri 8:30-17:00, Sept-May Mon-Fri 8:30-15:30, closed Sat-Sun year-round; behind the white church—look for green-and-white *i* sign; tel. 57 63 33 13, www.alr.no).

Sleeping in Aurland

(6 kr = about $1, country code: 47)

$$$ **Aurland Fjordhotel** is big, modern, and centrally located. While it has a business-hotel vibe, most of its 30 rooms come with gorgeous fjord-view balconies (Sb-995 kr, Db-1,490 kr, Tb-1,785, prices lower off-season, check website for deals, includes breakfast, free Wi-Fi, tel. 57 63 35 05, fax 57 63 36 22, www.aurland-fjord hotel.com, post@aurland-fjordhotel.com, Steinar Kjerstein).

$$ **Vangsgården Guest House,** closest to the boat landing, is a complex of old buildings dominating the old center of Aurland and run from one reception desk (free Wi-Fi in main building, tel. 57 63 35 80, www.vangsgaarden.no, vangsgaarden@alb.no, open all year, Astrid). The main building is a simple, old guesthouse offering basic rooms and a fine old-timey living room (Sb-600 kr, Db-1,050 kr). Their old-fashioned **Aabelheim Pension** is Aurland's best *koselig* (cozy)-like-a-farmhouse place (same prices). And lining the waterfront are their six adorable, recently renovated, wood cabins, each with a kitchen, bathroom, and two bedrooms (1,250 kr for 2-6 people, sheets-65 kr/person, book 2 months in advance). The optional 80-kr breakfast is served in a delightfully homey dining room. The owners also run the Duehuset Pub (see "Eating in Aurland," later) and rent bikes for 200 kr/day.

Near Aurland

$$ **Skahjem Gard** is an active farm run by Aurland's former deputy mayor, Nils Tore. He's converted his old sheep barn into seven spick-and-span family apartments with private bathrooms and kitchenettes, each sleeping up to four people (700 kr for studio, 800 kr with separate bedroom; sheets and towels-70 kr/person, free Wi-Fi, two miles up the valley—road #50, follow *Hol* signs, tel. 57 63 33 29, mobile 95 17 25 67, www.skahjemgard.com, nskahjem@online.no). It's a 25-minute walk from town, but Nils will pick up and drop off travelers at the ferry. This is best for families and foursomes with cars.

$ **Winjum Huts,** about a half-mile from Aurland's dock, rents 14 basic cabins on a peaceful perch overlooking the majestic fjord. The washhouse/kitchen is where you'll find the toilets and showers. Follow the road uphill past the Aurland Fjordhotel; the huts are after the first hairpin curve (350-500 kr for up to 4 people, 2-bed apartment-900-1,200 kr, sheets-50 kr/person, showers-10 kr/5 minutes, no food available—just beer, tel. 57 63 34 61 or 41 47 47 51).

Eating in Aurland

Aurlandskafeen is a basic little café/diner serving the best-value food in town from its inviting cafeteria line. It's a block from the main square, at the bridge over the river. Sit upstairs or on its riverside terrace (95-kr daily plates, open daily 10:00-21:00—provided there are customers, shorter hours off-season, tel. 57 63 36 66).

Duehuset Pub ("The Dove's House"), run by Vangsgården Guest House, serves up decent food in the center of town (190-240-kr pizzas big enough for four, 155-240-kr main dishes; June-Sept daily 15:00-23:00; Oct-May Fri-Sun 18:00-23:00, closed Mon-Thu).

The **Aurland Fjordhotel** is your only alternative for splurges (195-kr main dishes, 65-kr starters, 240-295-kr dinner buffet, daily 19:00-22:00, shorter hours off-season, bar open later, tel. 57 63 35 05).

For cheap eats on dockside benches, gather a picnic at the **Spar** or **Rimi** supermarkets (both open Mon-Fri 9:00-20:00, Sat 9:00-18:00, closed Sun).

Undredal

This almost impossibly remote community is home to about 75 people (and 400 goats). A huge percentage of the town's former

population (300 people) emigrated to the US between 1850 and 1925. Undredal was accessible only by boat until 1988, when the road from Flåm opened. There's not much in the town, which is famous for its church and its goat cheese, but I'll never forget the picnic I had on the ferry wharf. While appealing, Undredal is quiet (some say better from the boat) and difficult to reach—you'll have to be patient to connect to other towns. For more information on the town, see www.undredal.no.

Undredal has Norway's smallest still-used **church,** seating 40 people for services every fourth Sunday. The original church was built in 1147 (look for the four original stave pillars inside). It was later expanded, pews added, and the interior painted in the 16th century in a way that resembles the traditional Norwegian *rosemaling* style (which came later). You can get in only with an overpriced 15-minute tour (60 kr, mid-June–mid-Aug daily 9:30–18:30, less in shoulder season, closed Oct–April, tel. 95 29 76 68).

Undredal's farms exist to produce cheese. The beloved local cheese comes in two versions: brown and white. The brown version is unaged and slightly sweet, while the white cheese has been aged and is mild and a bit salty. For samples, visit the Undredalsbui grocery store at the harbor (Mon–Fri 9:00–17:00, Sat 9:00–15:00, Sun 12:00–16:00, shorter hours and closed Sun off-season).

The 15-minute drive from Flåm is mostly through a tunnel. By sea, you'll sail past Undredal on the Flåm-Gudvangen boat (you can request a stop). To get the ferry to pick you up in Undredal, turn on the blinking light (though some express boats will not stop).

This sleepy town can accommodate about eight visitors a night. **$$ Undredal Overnatting** rents four modern, woody, comfortable rooms and two apartments. The reception is at the café on the harbor, while the accommodations are at the top of town (Db-740 kr, apartments start at 990 kr, sheets-60 kr/person, breakfast-90 kr, tel. 57 63 30 80 or 57 63 31 00, www.visitundredal.no, visit@undredal.no).

MORE on the SOGNEFJORD

Balestrand • The Lustrafjord • Scenic Drives

Norway's world of fjords is decorated with medieval stave churches, fishing boats, cascading waterfalls, dramatic glaciers, and brightly painted shiplap villages. Travelers in a hurry zip through the fjords on the Norway in a Nutshell route (see previous chapter). Their heads spin from all the scenery, and most wish they had more time on the Sognefjord. If you can linger in fjord country, this chapter is for you.

Snuggle into the fjordside village of Balestrand, which has a variety of walking and biking options and a fun local arts scene. Balestrand is also a handy jumping-off spot for adventures great and small, including a day trip up the Fjærlandsfjord to gaze at a receding tongue of the Jostedal Glacier, or across the Sognefjord to the truly medieval-feeling Hopperstad Stave Church. Farther east is the Lustrafjord, a tranquil branch of the Sognefjord offering drivers an appealing concentration of visit-worthy sights. On the Lustrafjord, you'll enjoy enchanting hamlets with pristine fjord views (such as Solvorn), historic churches (including Norway's oldest stave church at Urnes and the humble village Dale Church in Luster), an opportunity to touch and even hike on a glacier (the Nigard), and more stunning fjord views.

This region is important to the people of Norway. After four centuries under Danish rule, the soul of the country was nearly lost. With semi-independence and a constitution in the early 1800s, the country experienced a resurgence of national pride. Urban Norwegians headed for the fjord country here in the west. Norway's first Romantic painters and writers were drawn to Balestrand, inspired by the unusual light and dramatic views of mountains plunging into the fjords. The Sognefjord, with its many

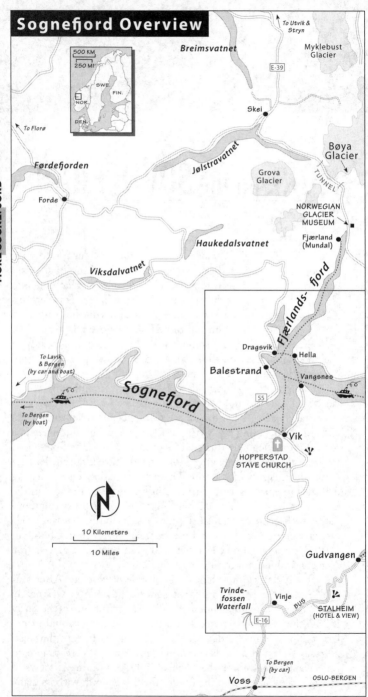

Sognefjord Overview

500 KM
250 MI

SWE.
FIN.
NOR.
DEN.

To Florø

To Utvik &
Stryn

Breimsvatnet

Myklebust
Glacier

E-39

Skei

Førdefjorden

Jølstravatnet

Grova
Glacier

Bøya
Glacier

TUNNEL

Forde

NORWEGIAN
GLACIER
MUSEUM

Fjærland
(Mundal)

Haukedalsvatnet

Viksdalvatnet

Fjærlands-
fjord

To Lavik
& Bergen
(by car and boat)

Dragsvik

Hella

Balestrand

Vangsnes

Sognefjord

55

To Bergen
(by boat)

Vik

HOPPERSTAD
STAVE CHURCH

N

10 Kilometers

10 Miles

Gudvangen

Tvinde-
fossen
Waterfall

Vinje

BUS

STALHEIM
(HOTEL & VIEW)

E-16

To Bergen
(by car)

Voss

OSLO-BERGEN

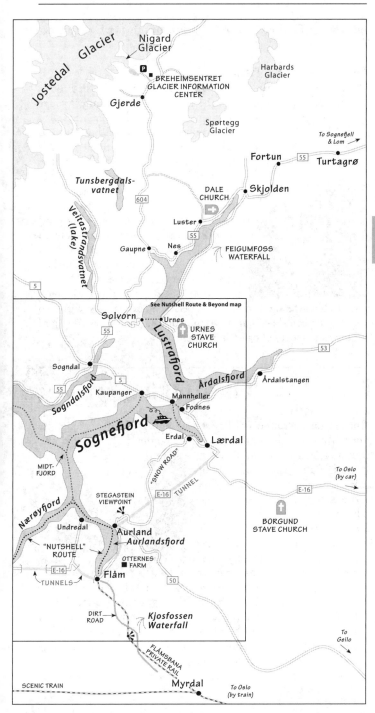

branches, is featured in more Romantic paintings than any other fjord.

Planning Your Time

If you can spare a day or two off the Norway in a Nutshell route, spend it here. Balestrand is the best home base, especially if you're

relying on public transportation (it's well-connected by express boat both to the Nutshell scene and to Bergen). If you have a car, consider staying in the heart of the Lustrafjord region in sweet little Solvorn (easy ferry connection to the Urnes Stave Church and a short drive to the Nigard Glacier). As fjord home bases go, Balestrand and Solvorn are both better—but less convenient—than Flåm or Aurland on the Nutshell route (see previous chapter).

With one night in this area, you'll have to blitz the sights on the way between destinations; with two nights, you can slow your pace (and your pulse) to enjoy the fjord scenery and plenty of day-trip possibilities.

Balestrand

The pleasant fjord town of Balestrand (pop. 2,000) has a long history of hosting tourists, thanks to its landmark Kviknes Hotel.

But it also feels real and lived-in, making Balestrand a nice mix of cuteness and convenience. The town is near, but not *too* near, the Nutshell bustle across the fjord— and yet it's an easy express-boat trip away if you'd like to dive into the Nuttiness. In short, consider Balestrand a worthwhile detour

from the typical fjord visit—allowing you to dig deeper into the Sognefjord, just like the glaciers did during the last ice age.

With two nights, you can relax and consider some day trips: Cruise up the nearby Fjærlandsfjord for a peek at a distant tongue of the ever-less-mighty Jostedal Glacier, or head across the Sognefjord to the beautiful Hopperstad Stave Church in Vik. Balestrand also has outdoor activities for everyone, from dreamy

MORE SOGNEFJORD

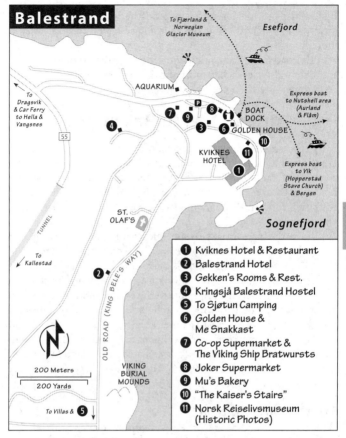

Balestrand

To Fjærland &
Norwegian
Glacier Museum

Esefjord

AQUARIUM

To
Dragsvik
& Car Ferry
to Hella &
Vangsnes

55

Express boat
to Nutshell area
(Aurland
& Flåm)

P

BOAT
DOCK

GOLDEN HOUSE

KVIKNES
HOTEL

Express boat
to Vik
(Hopperstad
Stave Church)
& Bergen

ST.
OLAF'S

Sognefjord

TUNNEL

To
Kallestad

OLD ROAD (KING BELE'S WAY)

N

200 Meters

200 Yards

VIKING
BURIAL
MOUNDS

To Villas & ❺

① Kviknes Hotel & Restaurant
② Balestrand Hotel
③ Gekken's Rooms & Rest.
④ Kringsjå Balestrand Hostel
⑤ To Sjøtun Camping
⑥ Golden House &
   Me Snakkast
⑦ Co-op Supermarket &
   The Viking Ship Bratwursts
⑧ Joker Supermarket
⑨ Mu's Bakery
⑩ "The Kaiser's Stairs"
⑪ Norsk Reiselivsmuseum
   (Historic Photos)

MORE SOGNEFJORD

fjordside strolls and strenuous mountain hikes to wildly scenic bike rides. For dinner, splurge on the memorable *smörgåsbord*-style *store koldt bord* dinner in the Kviknes Hotel dining room, then sip coffee from its balcony as you watch the sun set (or not) over the fjord.

Planning Your Time

Balestrand's key advantage is its easy express-boat connection to Bergen, offering an alternative route to the fjord from the typical Nutshell train-bus combo. Consider zipping here on the Bergen boat, then continuing on via the Nutshell route.

One night is enough to get a taste of Balestrand. But two nights buy you some time for day trips. Note that the first flurry of day trips departs early, around 7:30-8:05 (includes the boat to Vik/Hopperstad Stave Church or the full-day Fjærlandsfjord glacier excursion), and the next batch departs around noon (the half-day

Fjærlandsfjord glacier excursion and the boat to Flåm). If you wait until after 12:00 to make your choice, you'll miss the boat... literally.

Balestrand pretty much shuts down from mid-September through mid-May—when most of the activities, sights, hotels, and restaurants listed here are likely closed.

Orientation to Balestrand

Most travelers arrive in Balestrand on the express boat from Bergen or Flåm. The tidy harbor area has a TI, two grocery stores, a couple of galleries, a town history museum, and a small aquarium devoted to marine life found in the fjord. The historic wooden Kviknes Hotel and its ugly modern annex dominate Balestrand's waterfront.

Even during tourist season, Balestrand is quiet. How quiet? The police station closes on weekends. And it's tiny—from the harbor to the Balestrand Hotel is a five-minute stroll, and you can walk from the aquarium to the Kviknes Hotel in less than that.

Balestrand became accessible to the wider world in 1858 when an activist minister (from the church you see across the fjord from town) brought in the first steamer service. That put Balestrand on the Grand Tour map of the Romantic Age. Even the German *Kaiser* chose to summer here. Today, people from around the world come here to feel the grandeur of the fjord country and connect with the essence of Norway.

Tourist Information

At the TI, located next to the Joker supermarket at the harbor, pick up the free, helpful *Outdoor Activities in Balestrand* brochure. If you're planning on a longer hike, consider buying the good 70-kr hiking map. The TI has numerous brochures about the Sognefjord area and detailed information on the more challenging hikes. It offers terminals with Internet access (1 kr/minute) and pay Wi-Fi, rents bikes (50 kr/hour, 250 kr/day), sells day-trip excursions to the glacier, and more (late June-late Aug Mon-Sat 7:30-18:00, Sun 10:00-17:30, shorter hours in spring and fall, closed Oct-April, tel. 57 69 12 55—answered all year).

Local Guide: Bjørg Bjøberg, who runs the Golden House art gallery, knows the town well and is happy to show visitors around (500 kr/1.5 hours, mobile 91 56 28 42).

Car Rental: The Kviknes Hotel can arrange a one-day car rental for you (tel. 57 69 42 00), or contact the Balholm Car Rental agency (tel. 41 24 82 53, post@rentacarbalholm.com, www.renta carbalholm.com).

Sights in Balestrand

Balestrand Harborfront Stroll—The tiny harbor stretches from the aquarium to the big, old Kviknes Hotel. Stroll its length, starting at the aquarium (described later) and little marina. Across the street, at The Viking Ship shack, a German woman named Carola sells German sausages with an evangelical zeal (see "Eating in Balestrand," later). Next door, the Spindelvev ("Spider's Web") shop sells handicrafts made by people with physical and mental disabilities. A local home for the disabled was closed in the 1980s, but many of its former residents stayed in Balestrand because the government gave them pensions and houses in town.

Then, in the ugly modern strip mall, you'll find the TI, supermarket, and a community bulletin board with the schedule for the summer cinema (the little theater, 800 yards away, runs films nightly in their original language). On the corner is the Golden House art gallery and museum (described later). Just beyond that is the dock where the big Bergen-Sognefjord express catamaran ties up.

Across the street is a cute white house (at #8), which used to stand at the harborfront until the big Joker supermarket and Kviknes Hotel, with its modern annex, partnered to ruin the town center. This little house was considered historic enough to be airlifted 100 yards to this new spot. It's flanked by two other historic buildings, which house a gallery and an artisans' workshop.

Farther along, find the rust-red building that was the waiting room for the 19th-century steamer that first brought tourism to town. Today it houses the Norsk Reiselivsmuseum (Norwegian Travel Museum). It's filled with historic photos, described in English, that show this part of Norway over the last 150 years (free and open daily). In a few years Balestrand is hoping to build a much larger museum and visitors center; it may be under construction during your visit.

Walk a few steps farther, and stop at the tall stone monument erected to celebrate the North Bergen Steamship Company. Its boats first connected Balestrand to the rest of the world in 1858. In front of the monument, some nondescript concrete steps lead into the water. These are "The Kaiser's Stairs," built for the German emperor, Kaiser Wilhelm II, who made his first summer visit (complete with navy convoy) in 1899 and kept returning until the outbreak of World War I.

Behind the monument stands one of the largest old wooden buildings in Norway, the Kviknes Hotel. It was built in the 1870s and faces the rare little island in the fjord, which helped give the town its name: "Balestrand" means the strand or promenade in front of an island. (The island is now connected to the hotel's front yard and is part of a playground for its guests.) Hike up the black driveway that leads from the monument to the hotel's modern lobby. Go inside and find (to your left) the plush old lounge, a virtual painting gallery. All the pieces are by artists from this area, celebrating the natural wonder of the fjord country—part of the trend that helped 19th-century Norway reconnect with its heritage. (While you're here, consider making a reservation and choosing a table for a *smörgåsbord* dinner tonight.) Leave the hotel lobby (from the door opposite to the one you entered), and head up to St. Olaf's Church (300 yards, described next). To continue this stroll, take King Bele's Way (described later) up the fjord.

St. Olaf's Church—This distinctive wooden church was built in 1897. Construction was started by Margaret Sophia Kvikne, the

wife of Knut Kvikne (of the Kviknes Hotel family; her portrait is in the rear of the nave), but she died in 1894, before the church was finished. This devout Englishwoman wanted a church in Balestrand where English services were held...and to this day, bells ring to announce services by British clergy. St. Olaf, who brought Christianity to Norway in the 11th century, was the country's patron saint in Catholic times. The church was built in a "Neo-stave" style, with lots of light from its windows and an altar painting inspired by the famous *Risen Christ* statue in Copenhagen's Cathedral of Our Lady. Here, Christ is flanked by fields of daisies (called "priests' collars" in Norwegian) and peace lilies. From the door of the church, enjoy a good view of the island in the fjord.

Cost and Hours: Free, open daily, services in English every Sun from late May through August.

Golden House (Det Gylne Hus)—This golden-colored house facing the ferry landing was built as a general store in 1928. Today it houses an art gallery and a quirky museum created by local watercolorist and historian Bjørg Bjøberg, and her Scottish husband, Arthur Adamson.

On the ground floor, you'll find Bjørg's gallery, with her watercolors celebrating the beauty of Norway, and Arthur's paintings, celebrating the beauty of women. Upstairs is a free exhibit of historical knickknacks, contributed by locals wanting to preserve treasures from their own families' past. You'll see a medicine cabinet stocked with old-fashioned pills, an antiquated tourist map, lots of skis, and WWII-era mementos. A wheel in the wall once powered a crane that could winch up goods from the fjord below (before today's embankment was built, when this store was right on the waterfront). While there are no written English explanations, Bjørg is happy to explain things.

Unable to contain her creative spirit, Bjørg has paired an eccentric wonderland experience with her private tour of the Golden House's hidden rooms. The tour includes a 30-minute movie, either about her art and local nature, or about Balestrand in winter. Bjørg and Arthur also run the recommended on-site café, Me Snakkast.

Cost and Hours: Free entry; optional private one-hour tour-50/kr person, 100-kr minimum, 200-kr maximum; May-Aug daily 10:00-22:00, shorter hours late April and Sept, mobile 91 56 28 42, www.detgylnehus.no.

Strolling King Bele's Way up the Fjord—For a delightful walk (or bike ride), head west out of town up the "old road"—once the

main road from the harbor—for about a mile. It follows the fjord's edge, passing numerous "villas" from the late 1800s. At the time, this Swiss style was popular with some locals, who hoped to introduce a dose of Romanticism into Norwegian architecture. Look for the dragons' heads (copied from Viking-age stave churches) decorating the gables. Along the walk, you'll pass a swimming area, a campground, and two burial mounds from the Viking age, marked by a ponderous statue of the Viking King Bele. Check out the wooden shelters for the mailboxes; some give the elevation (*m.o.h.* stands for "meters over *havet*"—the sea)—not too high, are they? The walk is described in the *Outdoor Activities in Balestrand* brochure (free at the TI or your hotel).

Aquarium—The tiny aquarium gives you a good look at marine life in the Sognefjord. For descriptions, borrow the English booklet at the front desk. While not thrilling, the well-explained place is a decent rainy-day option. A 15-minute slide show starts at the top and bottom of each hour. The last room is filled with wood carvings depicting traditional everyday life in the fjordside village of Munken. The fish-filled tanks on the dock outside are also worth a look.

Cost and Hours: 70 kr, June-Aug daily 9:00-19:00, closed Sept-May, tel. 57 69 13 03.

Biking—You can cycle around town, or go farther by circling the scenic Esefjord (north of town, en route to the ferry landing at Dragsvik—about 6 miles each way). Or pedal scenically west up Sognefjord along King Bele's Way (described above). The roads here are relatively flat. Rental bikes are available at the TI.

Near Balestrand

These two side-trips are possible only if you've got the better part of a day in Balestrand. With a car, you can see Hopperstad Stave Church on the drive to Bergen.

▲▲Hopperstad Stave Church (Hopperstad Stavkyrkje) in Vik

The most accessible stave church in the area—and perhaps the most scenically situated in all Norway—is located just a

15-minute express-boat ride across the Sognefjord, in the town of Vik. Hopperstad Stave Church boasts a breathtaking exterior, with several tiers of dragon heads overlooking rolling fields between fjord cliffs. The interior is notable for its emptiness. Instead of being crammed full of later additions, the church is blissfully uncluttered, as it was when built in the mid-12th century. (For more on stave churches, see page 221.)

Cost and Hours: 60 kr, good 30-kr color booklet in English, daily mid-May-mid-Sept 10:00-17:00, mid-June-mid-Aug until 18:00, closed mid-Sept-mid-May, tel. 57 69 52 70, www.stave church.com.

Tours: The attendant will give you a free tour at your request, provided she's not too busy. (Ask where the medieval graffiti is, and she'll grab her flashlight and show you.)

Location: The church is a 20-minute walk up the valley from Vik's harbor. From the boat landing, walk up the main street from the harbor about 200 yards (past the TI, a grocery store, and hotel). Take a right at the sign for *Hopperstad Stavkyrkje*, walk 10 minutes, and you'll see the church perched on a small hill in the distance.

Getting There: Pedestrians can ride the express passenger boat between Balestrand and Vik (72 kr each way, 15 minutes). The only way to get to the church and back in one day (only possible Mon-Sat) is to take the 7:50 departure from Balestrand, then return on the 11:30 departure from Vik, arriving back in Balestrand at 11:50—just in time to join a 12:00 glacier excursion (described below). Because schedules can change, be sure to double-check these times at the TI or www.norled.no. Since cars can't go on this express boat, **drivers** must go around the small Esefjord to the town of Dragsvik, then catch the ferry across the Sognefjord to Vangsnes (a 20-minute drive from Vik and the church).

Visiting the Church: Originally built around 1140 and retaining most of its original wood, Hopperstad was thoroughly

restored and taken back to basics in the 1880s by renowned architect Peter Blix. Unlike the famous stave church at Urnes (described later), whose interior has been rejiggered by centuries of engineers and filled with altars and pews, the Hopperstad church looks close to the way it did when it was

built. You'll see only a few non-original features, including the beautifully painted canopy that once covered a side altar (probably dating from around 1300), and a tombstone from 1738. There are only a few colorful illustrations and some very scant medieval "graffiti" carvings and runic inscriptions. Notice the intact chancel screen (the only one surviving in Norway), which separates the altar area from the congregation. As with the iconostasis (panel of icons) in today's Orthodox faith, this screen gave priests privacy to do the spiritual heavy lifting. Because Hopperstad's interior lacks the typical adornments, you can really grasp the fundamentally vertical nature of stave church architecture, leading your gaze to the heavens. Follow that impulse and look up to appreciate the Viking-ship rafters. Imagine the comfort this ceiling brought the church's original parishioners, whose seafaring ancestors had once sought refuge under overturned boats. For a unique angle on this graceful structure, lay your camera on the floor and shoot the ceiling.

▲Excursion to Fjærland and the Jostedal Glacier

From Balestrand, cruise up the Fjærlandsfjord to visit the Norwegian Glacier Museum in Fjærland and to see a receding tongue of the Jostedal Glacier (Jostedalbreen). Half-day and full-day (660 kr for either tour) excursions are sold by Balestrand's TI or on board the boat. Reservations are smart (tours offered daily May-Sept only, tel. 57 63 32 00, www.visitflam.com/sognefjorden and follow links for "Fjærlandsfjord").

While the museum and the glacier's tongue are underwhelming, it's a pleasant excursion with a dreamy fjord cruise (80 minutes each way). To take the all-day trip, catch the 8:05 ferry; for the shorter trip, hop on the 11:50 boat. They both return on the same boat, getting you back in Balestrand at 16:50 (in time to catch the fast boat back to Bergen). Both tours offer the same fjord ride, museum visit, and trip to the glacier. The all-day version, however, gives you a second glacier viewing point and 2.5 hours to hang out in the town of Fjærland. (This sleepy village, famous for its secondhand book shops, is about as exciting as Walter Mondale, the US vice president whose ancestors came from here.)

The ferry ride (no stops, no narration) is just a scenic glide with the gulls. Bring a picnic, as there's almost no food sold on board, and some bread to toss to the gulls (they do acrobatics to catch whatever you loft into the air). You'll be met at the ferry dock (labeled *Mundal*) by a bus—and your guide, who reads a script about the glacier as you drive up the valley for about 15 minutes. You'll stop for an hour at the **Norwegian Glacier Museum** (Norsk Bremuseum). After watching an 18-minute aerial tour of the dramatic Jostedal Glacier in the theater, you'll learn how glaciers were formed, experiment with your own hunk of glacier, weigh evidence of the woolly mammoth's existence in Norway, and learn about the effect of global climate change on the fjords (way overpriced at 120 kr, included in excursion price, daily June-Aug 9:00-19:00, April-May and Sept-Oct 10:00-16:00, closed Nov-March, tel. 57 69 32 88, www.bre.museum.no). From the museum, the bus runs you up to a café near a lake, at a spot that gives you a good look at the Boyabreen, a tongue of the Jostedal Glacier. Marvel at how far the glacier has retreated—10 years ago, the visit was more dramatic. With global warming, glacier excursions like this become more sad than majestic. I wonder how long they'll even be able to bill this as a "glacier visit."

Considering that the fjord trip is the highlight of this journey, you could save time and money by just riding the ferry up and back (8:05-11:30). At 380 kr for the round-trip boat ride, it's much cheaper than the 660-kr tour.

Note that if you're into glaciers, a nearby arm of the Jostedal, called the **Nigard Glacier,** is a more dramatic and boots-on experience (see page 333). It's easy for drivers to reach; see page 320 for car-rental info.

Sleeping in Balestrand

$$$ Kviknes Hotel is the classy grande dame of Balestrand, dominating the town and packed with tour groups. The picturesque wooden hotel—and five generations of the Kvikne family—have welcomed tourists to Balestrand since the late 19th century. The hotel has two parts: a new wing, and the historic wooden section, with 17 older, classic rooms, and no elevator. All rooms come with balconies. The elegant Old World public spaces in the old

Sleep Code

(6 kr = about $1, country code: 47)

S = Single, **D** = Double/Twin, **T** = Triple, **Q** = Quad, **b** = bathroom, **s** = shower. Unless otherwise noted, these accommodations accept credit cards.

To help you sort easily through these listings, I've divided the accommodations into three categories, based on the price for a standard double room with bath during high season:

$$$ Higher Priced—Most rooms 1,100 kr or more.
$$ Moderately Priced—Most rooms between 500-1,100 kr.
$ Lower Priced—Most rooms 500 kr or less.

Prices can change without notice; verify the hotel's current rates online or by email.

section make you want to just sit there and sip tea all afternoon (Db-1,660 kr in new building, Db-2,210 kr in old building, about

400 kr more with view, includes breakfast, mostly non-smoking, pay Wi-Fi, family rooms available, closed Oct-April, tel. 57 69 42 00, fax 57 69 42 01, www .kviknes.no, booking@kviknes .no). Part of the Kviknes ritual is gorging on the *store koldt bord* buffet dinner—open to non-guests, and a nice way to soak in the hotel's old-time elegance without splurging on an overnight (see "Eating in Balestrand," later; cheaper if you stay at the hotel for 2 or more nights).

$$ Balestrand Hotel, family-run by Unni-Marie Kvikne, her California-born husband Eric Palmer, and their three children, is your best fjordside home. Open mid-May through early September, this cozy, welcoming place has 30 well-appointed, comfortable, quiet rooms; a large, modern common area with lots of English paperbacks; laundry service, free Wi-Fi, balconies (in some rooms), and outdoor benches for soaking in the scenery. The waterfront yard has inviting lounge chairs and a mesmerizing view. When reserving, let them know your arrival time, and they'll pick you up at the harborfront (non-view Sb-700 kr, view Sb-850 kr, non-view Db-1,040 kr, view Db-1,340 kr, includes breakfast, 5-minute walk from dock, past St. Olaf's Church—or free pick-up, tel. 57 69 11 38, www.balestrand.com, info@balestrand.com).

$$ At Gekken's Rooms, Geir rents four homey rooms above his restaurant in the town center (D-600 kr, small D-450 kr, extra bed-150 kr, shared kitchen and WC, open May-Aug only, tel. 57 69 14 14, mobile 97 51 29 26, baleson2004@yahoo.com).

$-$$ Kringsjå Balestrand Hostel, a camp school for sixth-graders, rents beds and rooms to budget travelers from mid-June to mid-August. Half of their 58 beds are in doubles. All the four-bed rooms have private bathrooms and view balconies (bunk in 4-bed dorm-265 kr, Sb-600 kr, Db-820 kr, extra bed-100 kr, includes breakfast, discount for hostel members, sheets/towels-50 kr/person, free Wi-Fi, tel. 57 69 13 03, www.kringsja.no, kringsja @kringsja.no).

$ Sjøtun Camping rents the cheapest beds around, in rustic huts (4-person hut-300 kr, sheets-50 kr/person, no breakfast, a mile west of town, mobile 95 06 72 61, www.sjotun.com).

Eating in Balestrand

Balestrand's dining options are limited, but good.

Kviknes Hotel offers a splendid, spendy *store koldt bord* buffet dinner in a massive yet stately old dining room. For a memorable fjordside *smörgåsbord* experience, it doesn't get any better than this. Don't rush. Consider taking a preview tour—surveying the reindeer meat, lingonberries, and fjord-caught seafood—before you dive in, so you can budget your stomach space. Get a new plate with each course and save room for dessert. Each dish is labeled in English (500 kr/person, May-Sept daily 19:00-21:00, closed Oct-April). After dinner, head into the rich lounge to pick up your cup of coffee or tea (included), which you'll sip sitting on classy old-fashioned furniture and basking in fjord views. For tips on enjoying this feast, see page 30.

Me Snakkast ("Let's Talk"), inside the Golden House at the harbor, dishes up Norwegian home cooking and a variety of salads. Sit outside or inside, in a dining area built to resemble a traditional Norwegian kitchen. The restaurant upstairs shows off part of owner Bjørg's antique collection. They serve 100-130-kr lunches and pricier meals for dinner, such as 150-220-kr meat and fish dishes (May-Sept daily 14:00-21:30, closed Oct-April, mobile 91 56 28 42).

Gekken's is an informal summer restaurant serving good-value meat, fish, and vegetarian dishes, along with burgers, fish-and-chips, and other fried fare. Sit in the simply decorated interior, or out on the shaded little terrace. Geir Arne "Gekken" Bale can trace his family's roots back 400 years in Balestrand. He has filled his walls with fascinating historic photos and paintings, making his dining hall an art gallery of sorts (light dishes-60-100 kr, daily dinner plates-100-150 kr, May-Aug daily 12:00-22:00, closed Sept-April, above and behind the TI from the harbor, tel. 57 69 14 14).

The Viking Ship, the hot-dog stand facing the harbor, is proudly run by Carola. A bratwurst missionary from Germany, she claims it took her years to get Norwegians to accept the tastier bratwurst over their beloved *pølser* weenies. Eat at her picnic tables or across the street on the harbor park (fine sausages, fish-and-chips, May-Sept daily 11:00-20:00, closed Oct-April).

Picnic: The delightful waterfront park next to the aquarium has benches and million-dollar fjord views. The Co-op and Joker **supermarkets** at the harbor have basic grocery supplies, including bread, meats, cheeses, and drinks. Co-op is bigger and has a wider selection (both open Mon-Fri 9:00-18:00—until 20:00 in summer, Sat 9:00-15:00, closed Sun). **Mu's Bakery** heats up baked goodies trucked here all the way from Germany (Mon-Sat 9:30-18:00, Sun 9:30-15:00, closed mid-Sept-early May, between Co-op and Joker supermarkets).

Balestrand Connections

Because Balestrand is separated from the Lustrafjord by the long Fjærlandsfjord, most Balestrand connections involve a boat trip.

By Express Passenger Boat

The easiest way to reach Balestrand is on the handy express boat, which connects to **Bergen, Vik** (near Hopperstad Stave Church), **Aurland,** and **Flåm** (see sidebar on next page for schedules). Note that you can also use this boat to join the Nutshell trip in Flåm. From here, continue on the Nutshell boat down the Nærøyfjord to Gudvangen, where you'll join the crowd onward to Voss, then Bergen or Oslo. As you're making schedule and sightseeing decisions, consider that the Balestrand-Flåm boat skips the Nærøyfjord, the most dramatic arm of the Sognefjord.

By Car Ferry

Balestrand's main car-ferry dock is at the village of **Dragsvik,** a six-mile, 15-minute drive around the adorable little Eselfjord. From Dragsvik, a car ferry makes the short crossing east to **Hella** (a 30-minute drive from Sogndal and the Lustrafjord), then crosses the Sognefjord south to **Vangsnes** (a 20-minute drive to

Express Boat Between Bergen and the Sognefjord

The made-for-tourists express boat makes it a snap to connect Bergen with Balestrand and other Sognefjord towns (for foot passengers only—no cars). In summer, the boat links Bergen, Vik, Balestrand, Aurland, and Flåm. You can also use this boat to connect towns on the Sognefjord, such as zipping from quiet Balestrand to busy Flåm, in the heart of the Nutshell action (reservations are smart—call 51 86 87 00 or visit www.norled.no; discounts for students and seniors, tickets also sold on boat and at TI). The following times were good for 2012—confirm them locally.

Between Bergen and the Sognefjord: The boat trip between Bergen and **Balestrand** takes four hours (515 kr, departs Bergen May-Sept daily at 8:00, also Mon-Fri at 16:30, Sat at 14:15, some Sun at 16:30—but not mid-June-late Aug; Oct-April Mon-Fri at 8:00, Sun-Fri at 16:30, Sat at 14:15; departs Balestrand May-Sept daily at 16:55, Mon-Sat also at 7:50, some Sun at 11:30—but not mid-June-late Aug; Oct-April Mon-Sat at 7:50, Sun at 15:55).  In summer, the 8:00 boat from Bergen continues to **Flåm**.

Between Flåm and Balestrand: Going by boat between Flåm and Balestrand takes about 1.5 hours (230 kr, departs Flåm May-Sept daily at 15:30, stops at Aurland, arrives in Balestrand at 16:55; departs Balestrand daily at 11:50 arriving Flåm at 13:25; no express boats between Flåm and Balestrand Oct-April).

From Oslo to Balestrand via the Nutshell: This variation on the standard Norway in a Nutshell route is called "Sognefjord in a Nutshell" (Oslo-Myrdal-Flåm-Balestrand-Bergen). From **Oslo,** you can take an early train to Flåm (no later than the 8:05 train as part of the Norway in a Nutshell route—see previous chapter), then catch the 15:30 express boat to Balestrand. After your visit, you can continue on the express boat to Bergen, or return to the Nutshell route by taking the express boat to Flåm, and transferring to the next boat to Gudvangen.

Hopperstad Stave Church and onward to Bergen). The ferry goes at least once per hour (2/hour in peak times, fewer boats Sun, 79 kr for car and driver).

Note that you can also drive through Sogndal to catch the **Kaupanger-Gudvangen** or **Mannheller-Fodnes** ferries (described under "Lustrafjord Connections," near the end of this chapter).

By Bus
A local bus links Balestrand to **Sogndal** (Mon-Fri 3/day, none Sat-Sun, 1.25 hours, includes ride on Dragsvik-Hella ferry, get details at TI).

The Lustrafjord

This arm of the Sognefjord is rugged country—only 2 percent of the land is fit to build or farm on. The Lustrafjord is ringed with tiny villages where farmers sell cherries and giant raspberries. A few interesting attractions lie along the Lustrafjord: the village Dale Church at Luster; the impressive Nigard Glacier (a 45-minute drive up a valley); the postcard-pretty village of Solvorn; and, across the fjord, Norway's oldest stave church at Urnes. While a bit trickier to explore by public transportation, this beautiful region is easy by car, but still feels remote. There are no ATMs between Lom and Gaupne—that's how remote this region is.

Suggested Route for Drivers
The Lustrafjord can be seen either coming from the north (over the Sognefjell pass from the Jotunheimen region—see next chapter) or from the south (from Balestrand or the Norway in a Nutshell route—see previous chapter). Note that public buses between Lom and Sogndal follow this same route (see "Lustrafjord Connections," later).

Here's what you'll see if you're driving from the north (if you're coming from the south, read this section backwards): Descending from Sognefjell, you'll hit the fjord at the village of Skjolden (decent TI in big community center, mobile 97 60 04 43). Follow Route 55 along the west bank of the fjord. In the town of Luster, consider visiting the beautifully decorated Dale Church (described next). Farther along, near the hamlet of Nes, you'll have views across the fjord of the towering Feigumfoss waterfall. Drops and dribbles come from miles around for this 650-foot tumble. Soon Route 55 veers along an inlet to the town of Gaupne, where you can choose to detour about an hour to the Nigard Glacier (up Route 604; described under "Sights on the Lustrafjord," next). After Gaupne, Route 55 enters a tunnel and cuts inland, emerging at a long, fjord-like lake at the town of Hafslo. Just beyond is the turnoff for Solvorn, a fine home-base town with the ferry across to Urnes and its stave church (Solvorn and Urnes Stave Church both described under "Sights on the Lustrafjord," next). Route 55 continues to Sogndal, where you can choose to turn off for the Kaupanger and Mannheller ferries across the Sognefjord, or continue on Route 55 to Hella and the boat across to either Dragsvik (near Balestrand) or Vangsnes (across the Sognefjord, near Vik and Hopperstad Stave Church).

Route Timings: If you're approaching from Lom in the Gudbrandsdal Valley, figure about 1.5 hours over Sognefjell to the start of the Lustrafjord at Skjolden, then another 30 minutes to Gaupne (with the optional glacier detour: 2 hours to see it, 4 hours to hike on it). From Gaupne, figure 30 minutes to Solvorn or 40 minutes to Sogndal. Solvorn to Sogndal is about 30 minutes. Sogndal to Hella, and its boat to Balestrand, takes about 40 minutes. These estimated times are conservative, but they don't include photo stops.

Sights on the Lustrafjord

These attractions are listed as you'll reach them driving from north to south along the fjordside Route 55. If you're sleeping in this area, you could visit all four sights in a single day (but it'd be a busy, somewhat rushed day). If you're passing through, Dale Church and Solvorn are easy, but the other two involve major detours—choose one or skip them both.

▲Dale Church (Dale Kyrkje) in Luster

The namesake town of Luster, on the west bank of the Lustrafjord, boasts a unique 13th-century Gothic church. In a land of wooden stave churches, this stone church, with its richly decorated interior, is worth a quick stop as you pass through town.

Cost and Hours: Free entry but donation requested, daily 10:00-20:00 but often closed for services and off-season, good posted English info inside, 5-kr English brochure, just off the main road—look for red steeple, WC in graveyard, fresh goodies at bakery across the street.

Visiting the Church: The soapstone core of the church dates from about 1250, but the wooden bell tower and entry porch were likely built around 1600. As you enter, on the left you'll see a tall, elevated platform with seating, surrounded by a wooden grill. Nicknamed a "birdcage" for the feathery fashions worn by the ladies of the time, this high-profile pew—three steps higher than the pulpit—was built in the late-17th century by a wealthy parishioner. The beautifully painted pulpit, decorated with faded images of the four evangelists, dates from the 13th century. In the chancel (altar area), restorers have uncovered

frescoes from three different time periods: the 14th, 16th, and 17th centuries. Most of the ones you see here were likely created around the year 1500. The crucifix high over the pews, carved around 1200, predates the church, as does the old bench (with lots of runic carvings)—making them more than eight centuries old.

▲▲Jostedal's Nigard Glacier

The Nigard Glacier (Nigardsbreen) is the most accessible branch of mainland Europe's largest glacier (the Jostedalsbreen, 185

square miles). Hiking to or on the Nigard offers Norway's best easy opportunity for a hands-on glacier experience. It's a 45-minute detour from the Lustrafjord up Jostedal Valley. Visiting a glacier is a quintessential Norwegian experience, bringing you face-to-face with the majesty of nature. If you can spare the time, it's worth the detour (even if you don't do a guided hike). But if glaciers don't give you tingles and you're feeling pressed, skip it.

Getting There: It's straightforward for **drivers**. When the main Route 55 along the Lustrafjord reaches Gaupne, turn onto Route 604, which you'll follow for 25 miles up the Jostedal Valley to the Breheimsenteret Glacier Information Center. Access to the glacier itself is down the toll road past the information center (all described next).

In July and August, a **Glacier Bus** connects the Nigard

Glacier to various home-base towns around the region (leaves Sogndal at 8:45, passes through Solvorn en route, arrives at the glacier around 10:00; departs glacier at 17:00, arrives back in Sogndal around 18:35; buses or boats from other towns—including Flåm and Aurland—coordinate to meet this bus in Sogndal; combo-tickets include various glacier visits and hikes; no bus Sept-June; for complete timetable, see www.jostedal.com). While handy, the bus is designed for those spending the entire day at the glacier.

Breheimsenteret Glacier Information Center—The national park's information center (with an info desk/gift shop and WCs) burned down in 2011, but a new center should be open by the time you visit. It's worth dropping by just to confirm your glacier plans—likely with Peter, who runs the place. The center's highlights include a relaxing 20-minute film with highlights of the glacier and region, and a gallery of glacier-related exhibits that use models and illustrations to explain these giant, slow-moving walls of ice (daily mid-June-mid-Aug 9:30-17:30, May-mid-June and mid-Aug-Sept 10:00-17:00, closed Oct-April, tel. 57 68 32 50, www.jostedal.com).

Visiting the Glacier—The best quick visit is to walk to, but not on, the glacier. (If you want to walk *on* it, see "Hikes on the Glacier," next.) From the information center, a 30-kr toll road continues two miles to a lake facing the actual tongue of the glacier. About 75 years ago, the glacier reached all the way to today's parking lot. (It's named for the ninth farm—*ni gard*—where it finally stopped, after crushing eight farms higher up the valley.) From the lot, you can hike all the way to the edge of today's glacier (about 45 minutes each way); or, to save about 20 minutes of walking, take a special boat to a spot that's a 20-minute hike from the glacier (20 kr each way, 10-minute boat trip, 4/hour, mid-June-mid-Sept 10:00-17:00).

The walk is uneven but well-marked—follow the red *T*'s and take your time. You'll hike on stone polished smooth by the glacier, and scramble over and around boulders big and small that were deposited by it. The path takes you right up to the face of the Nigardsbreen. Respect the glacier. It's a powerful river of ice, and fatal accidents do happen. If you want to walk on the glacier, read the next listing first.

Hikes on the Glacier—If you want to actually walk on top of the glacier, don't attempt it by yourself. The Breheimsenteret Glacier Information Center offers guided family-friendly walks that include about one hour on the ice (250 kr, 100 kr for kids, cash only, minimum age 6, I'd rate the walks PG-13 myself, about 4/day, generally between 11:30-15:00, no need to reserve—just call glacier center to find out time and show up). Leave the information center one hour before your tour, then meet the group on the ice,

where you'll pay and receive your clamp-on crampons. One hour roped up with your group gives you the essential experience. You'll find yourself marveling at how well your strap-on crampons work on the 5,000-year-old-ice. Even if it's hot, wear long pants, a jacket, and your sturdiest shoes. (Think ahead. It's awkward to empty your bladder after you're roped up.)

Longer, more challenging, and much more expensive hikes get you higher views, more exercise, and real crampons (starting at 445 kr, includes boots, mid-May-mid-Sept daily at 11:45, also July-Aug daily at 13:00, 4 hours including 2 hours on the ice, book by phone the day before—tel. 57 68 32 50, arrive at the information center 45 minutes early to pay for tickets and pick up your gear). If you're adventurous, ask about even longer hikes and glacier kayaking. While it's legal to go on the glacier on your own, it's dangerous and crazy to do so without crampons.

▲▲Solvorn

On the west bank of the Lustrafjord, 10 miles northeast of Sogndal, idyllic Solvorn is a sleepy little Victorian town with colorful wooden sheds lining its waterfront. My favorite town on the Lustrafjord is tidy and quaint, well away from the bustle of the Nutshell action. Its tiny ferry crosses the fjord regularly to Urnes and its famous stave church

(next). While not worth going far out of your way for, Solvorn is a mellow and surprisingly appealing place to kill some time waiting for the ferry...or just munching a picnic while looking across the fjord. A pensive stroll or photo shoot through the village's back lanes is a joy (look for plaques that explain historic buildings in English). Best of all, Solvorn also has a pair of excellent accommodations: a splurge (Hotel Walaker) and a budget place (Eplet Bed & Apple), described later under "Sleeping on the Lustrafjord."

Getting There: Solvorn is a steep five-minute **drive** down a switchback road from the main Route 55. The main road into town leads right to the Urnes ferry (see next) and dead-ends into a handy parking lot (free, 2-hour posted—but unmonitored—

limit). It's a 30-minute drive or bus trip into Sogndal, where you can transfer to other **buses** (2-3 buses/day between Solvorn and Sogndal, including the Glacier Bus to the Nigard Glacier—described earlier).

▲▲Urnes Stave Church

The hamlet of Urnes (sometimes spelled "Ornes") has Norway's oldest surviving stave church, dating from 1129. While not easy to reach (it's across the Lustrafjord from other attractions), it's worth the scenic ferry ride. The exterior is smaller and simpler than most stave churches, but its interior—modified in fits and starts over the centuries—is uniquely eclectic. For more on stave churches, see page 221. If you want to pack along a bike (rentable in Solvorn), see "Bring a Bike?" at the end of this listing.

Cost and Hours: 80 kr, includes 25-minute English tour (departs at :40 past most hours, to coincide with ferry arrival—described below); mid-May-mid-Sept daily 10:30-17:30, closed off-season, tel. 57 68 39 45, www.stavechurch.com.

Services: A little café/restaurant is at the farm called Urnes Gard, across from the church (same hours as church, homemade apple cakes, tel. 57 68 39 44).

Getting There: Urnes is perched on the east bank of the Lustrafjord (across the fjord from Route 55 and Solvorn). Ferries running between Solvorn and Urnes depart Solvorn at the top of most hours and Urnes at the bottom of most hours (32 kr one-way passenger fare, 87 kr one-way for car and driver, no round-trip discount, 15-minute ride, mobile 91 79 42 11, www.urnesferry.com). You can either drive or walk onto the boat—but, since you can't drive all the way up to the church, you might as well leave your car in Solvorn. Once across, it's about a five-minute uphill walk to the main road and parking lot (where drivers must leave their cars; parking lot at the church only for disabled visitors). From here, it's a steep 15-minute walk up a switchback road to the church (follow signs for *Urnes*).

Planning Your Time: Don't dawdle on your way up to the church, as the tour is scheduled to depart at :40 past most hours, about 25 minutes after the ferry arrives (giving most visitors just enough time to make it up the hill to the church). The first boat of the day departs Solvorn at 10:00; the last boat departs Solvorn at 16:00 (last tour at 16:40); and the last boat back to Solvorn departs

Urnes at 18:00. Confirm the "last boat" time, and keep an eye on your watch to avoid getting stranded in Urnes.

Visiting the Church: Most visitors to the church take the included 25-minute tour (scheduled to begin soon after the ferry arrives—described earlier). Here are some highlights:

Buy your ticket in the white house across from the church. Visit the little museum here after you see the church, so you don't miss the tour.

Many changes were made to the exterior to modernize the church after the Reformation (the colonnaded gallery was

replaced, the bell tower was added, and modern square windows were cut into the walls). Go around the left side of the church, toward the cemetery. This is the third church on this spot, but the carved doorway embedded in the wall here was inherited from the second church. Notice the two mysterious beasts— a warm-blooded predator (standing) and a cold-blooded dragon—weaving and twisting around each other, one entwining the other. Yet, as they bite each other on the neck, it's impossible to tell which one is "winning"... perhaps symbolizing the everlasting struggle of human existence. The door you see in the middle, however, has a very different message: the harmony of symmetrical figure-eights, an appropriately calming theme for those entering the church.

Now go around to the real entry door (with a wrought-iron lock and handle probably dating from the first church) and head inside. While it feels ancient and creaky, a lot of what you see in here is actually "new" compared to the 12th-century core of the church. The exquisitely carved, voluptuous, column-topping capitals are remarkably well-preserved originals. The interior initially was stark (no pews) and dark—lit not by windows (which were added much later), but by candles laid on the floor in the shape of a cross. Looking straight ahead, you see a cross with Mary on the left (where the women stood) and John the Baptist on the right (with the men). When they finally added seating, they kept things segregated: Notice the pews carved with hearts for women, crowns for men.

When a 17th-century wealthy family wanted to build a special pew for themselves, they simply sawed off some of the pinecone-topped columns to make way for it. When the church began to lean, it was reinforced with the clumsy, off-center X-shaped supports. Churchgoers learned their lesson, and never cut anything again.

The ceiling, added in the late 17th century, prevents visitors from enjoying the Viking-ship roof beams. But all of these additions have stories to tell. Experts can read various cultural influences into the church decorations, including Irish (some of the carvings) and Romanesque (the rounded arches).

Bring a Bike? To give your Lustrafjord excursion an added dimension, take a bike on the ferry to Urnes (free passage, rentable for 150 kr/day with helmets from Eplet Bed & Apple hostel in Solvorn, where you can park your car for free). From the stave church, bike the super-scenic fjordside road (4.5 miles—with almost no traffic—to big Feigumfossen waterfall and back).

Sleeping on the Lustrafjord

(6 kr = about $1, country code: 47)
These accommodations are along the Lustrafjord, listed from north to south.

In Nes
$$ Nes Gard Farmhouse B&B rents 15 homey rooms, offering lots of comfort in a grand 19th-century farmhouse for a good price (D-410 kr, Db-490 kr, rooms in main building more traditional, family apartment, tel. 57 68 39 43, mobile 95 23 26 94, www.nesgard.no, post@nesgard.no, Manum family). Mari and Asbjorn serve a three-course dinner for 300 kr.

$ Viki Fjord Camping has great fjordside huts—many directly on the water, with fjord views and balconies—located directly across from the Feigumfossen waterfall (250 kr without a private bathroom, 340-850 kr with bathroom, price depends on size and season, sheets-70 kr, tel. 57 68 64 20, mobile 99 53 97 30, www.vikicamping.no, post@vikicamping.no, Berit and Svein).

In Solvorn
For more on this delightful little fjordside town—my favorite home base on the Lustrafjord—see the description earlier in this chapter. While it lacks the handy boat connections of Flåm, Aurland, or Balestrand, that's part of Solvorn's charm.

$$$ Walaker Hotel, a former inn and coach station, has been run by the Walaker family since 1690 (that's a lot of pressure on ninth-generation owner Ole Henrik). The hotel, set right on the Lustrafjord (with a garden perfect for relaxing and, if necessary, even convalescing), is open May through September. In the main house, the halls and living rooms are filled with tradition. Notice the patriotic hymns on the piano. The 22 rooms are divided into two types: nicely appointed standard rooms in the modern annex (big Sb-1,450 kr, Db-1,750 kr); or recently renovated "historic" rooms with all the modern conveniences in two different old buildings: rooms with Old World elegance in the main house, and brightly painted rooms with countryside charm in the Tingstova house next door (Sb-1,950 kr, Db-2,250 kr, 500 kr more for larger room #20 or room #23; all prices include breakfast, non-smoking, free Wi-Fi, sea kayak rental, tel. 57 68 20 80, fax 57 68 20 81, www .walaker.com, hotel@walaker.com). They serve excellent four-course dinners (575 kr plus drinks, nightly at 19:30, savor your dessert with fjordside setting on the balcony). Their impressive gallery of Norwegian art is in a restored, historic farmhouse out back (free for guests; Ole Henrik leads one-hour tours of the collection, peppered with some family history, nightly after dinner).

$-$$ Eplet Bed & Apple is my kind of hostel: innovative and friendly. It's creatively run by Trond, whose entrepreneurial spirit and positive attitude attract enjoyable guests. With welcoming public spaces and 22 beds in seven rooms (all with views, some with decks), this place is worth considering even if you don't normally sleep at hostels (open May-Sept only; camping space-100 kr, bunk in 7-bed dorm-200 kr, S-500 kr, D-600 kr, T-800 kr, S/D/T cost 50 kr less for 2 nights or more, laundry-50 kr, kitchen, free Internet access and Wi-Fi, free loaner bikes for guests, tel. 41 64 94 69, www.eplet.net, trondhenrik@eplet.net). It's about 300 yards uphill from the boat dock—look for the white house with a giant red apple painted on it. It's surrounded by a raspberry and apple farm (they make and sell tasty juices from both). The hostel rents bikes and helmets to non-guests for 150 kr/day. If you plan to bike along the fjord from Urnes, consider that if you stay at the hostel, the free bikes will save you 300 kr (for two people).

Eating in Solvorn: Sleepy Solvorn is blessed with the cheery **Linahagen Kafé,** next door to Walaker Hotel, where delightful Signe and her family serve up good meals (120-kr dinner salads, 140-kr dinner plates, June-Aug daily 12:30-19:30, closed Sept-May, tel. 57 68 18 00).

In Sogndal

Sogndal is the only sizeable town in this region. While it lacks the charm of Solvorn and Balestrand, it's big enough to have a busy shopping street and a helpful **TI** (mid-June-mid-Aug Mon-Fri 9:00-18:00, Sat 10:00-16:00, closed Sun; shorter hours in May and Sept, closed in winter; in the Kulturhus at Hovevegen 2, mobile 97 60 04 43).

$$ Loftesnes Pensjonat, with 13 rooms, houses travelers mid-June through mid-August, and mostly students—reserving four rooms for travelers—during the school year (S-400 kr, Sb-420 kr, D-600 kr, Db-650 kr, no breakfast, kitchen, above a Chinese restaurant near the water, tel. & fax 57 67 15 77, mobile 90

93 51 71, loftesnes.pensjonat@gmail.com).

$-$$ Sogndal Youth Hostel rents good, cheap beds (bunk in 4-bed room-225 kr, S-310 kr, D-520 kr, Db-725 kr, 10 percent less for members, includes breakfast, sheets-70 kr, towel-40 kr, fully equipped members' kitchen, mid-June-mid-Aug only, closed 10:00-17:00, at fork in the road as you enter town, tel. 57 62 75 75, mobile 90 93 51 71, fax 57 62 75 70, www.vandrerhjem.no, sogndal@hihostels.no).

Lustrafjord Connections

Sogndal is the transit hub for the Lustrafjord region.

From Sogndal by Bus

Buses go to **Lom** over the Sognefjell pass (2/day late June-Aug only, road closed off-season, 3.25 hours), **Solvorn** (4/day in summer, 2/day in winter, fewer Sat-Sun, 30 minutes), **Balestrand** (3/Mon-Fri, none Sat-Sun, 1.25 hours, includes ride on Hella-Dragsvik ferry), **Nigard Glacier** via the Glacier Bus (1/day, 1.5 hours, departs Sogndal daily at 8:45, returns to Sogndal in the afternoon, also stops at Solvorn in each direction, July-Aug only). Most buses run less (or not at all) on weekends—check the latest at www.ruteinfo.net.

By Boat

Car ferries cost roughly $5 per hour for walk-ons and $20 per hour for a car and driver. Reservations are generally not necessary, and on many short rides, aren't even possible (for info and free and easy reservations for longer rides, call 55 90 70 70). Confirm schedules at www.ruteinfo.net. From near Sogndal, various boats fan out to towns around the Sognefjord. Most leave from two towns at the southern end of the Lustrafjord: **Kaupanger** (a 15-minute drive from Sogndal) and **Mannheller** (a 5-minute drive beyond Kaupanger, 20 min from Sogndal).

From Kaupanger: While Kaupanger is little more than a ferry landing, the small stave-type church at the edge of town merits a look. Boats go from Kaupanger all the way down the gorgeous Nærøyfjord to **Gudvangen,** which is on the Norway in a Nutshell route (where you catch the bus to Voss). Taking this boat allows you to see the best part of the Nutshell fjord scenery (the Nærøyfjord), but misses the other half of that cruise (Aurlandsfjord). The boat leaves Kaupanger daily in summer at 9:30, 12:00, 14:40, and 16:00 for the two-hour trip (these times are for June-Aug, only goes 1/day in May and Aug-mid-Sept departing Kaupanger at 9:30 and Gudvangen at 12:00, none mid-Sept-April; car and driver-625 kr, adult passenger-250 kr; reserve at least one day in advance—or longer in July-Aug, especially for the popular 12:00 departure; tel. 55 90 70 70, www.fjord1.no). Prices are high because this route is mainly taken by tourists, not locals. Boats also connect Kaupanger to **Lærdal,** but the crossing from Mannheller to Fodnes is easier (described next).

From Mannheller: Ferries frequently make the speedy 15-minute crossing to **Fodnes** (67 kr for a car and driver, 3/hour, no reservations possible). From Fodnes, drive through the five-mile-long tunnel to Lærdal and the main E-16 highway (near Borgund Stave Church, the long tunnel to Aurland, and the scenic overland road to the Stegastein fjord viewpoint—all described in the previous chapter).

To Balestrand: To reach Balestrand from the Lustrafjord, you'll take a short ferry trip (Hella-Dragsvik). For information on the car ferries to and from Balestrand, see "Balestrand Connections," earlier.

Scenic Drives from the Sognefjord

If you'll be doing a lot of driving, pick up a good local map. The 1:335,000-scale *Sør-Norge nord* map by Cappelens Kart is excellent (about 100 kr, available at local TIs and bookstores).

▲▲From the Lustrafjord to Aurland

The drive to the pleasant fjordside town of Aurland (see previous chapter) takes you either through the world's longest car tunnel,

or over an incredible mountain pass. If you aren't going as far as Lom and Jotunheimen, consider taking the pass, as the scenery here rivals the famous Sognefjell pass drive.

From Sogndal, drive 20 minutes to the Mannheller-Fodnes ferry (described under "Lustrafjord Connections," earlier), float across the Sognefjord, then drive from Fodnes to Lærdal. From Lærdal, you have two options to Aurland: The speedy route is on E-16 through the new 15-mile-long **tunnel** from Lærdal, or the Aurlandsvegen **"Snow Road"** over the pass.

The tunnel (described on page 307) is free, and impressively nonchalant—it's signed as if it were just another of Norway's countless tunnels. But driving it is a bizarre experience: A few miles in, as you find yourself trying not to be hypnotized by the monotony, it suddenly dawns on you what it means to be driving under a mountain for 15 miles. To keep people awake, three rest chambers, each illuminated by a differently colored light, break up the drive visually. Stop and get out—if no cars are coming, test the acoustics from the center.

The second, immeasurably more scenic, route is a breathtaking one-hour, 30-mile drive that winds over a pass into Aurland, cresting at over 4,000 feet and offering classic aerial fjord views (it's worth the messy pants). From the Mannheller-Fodnes ferry, take the first road to the right (to Erdal), then leave E-68 at Erdal (just west of Lærdal) for the Aurlandsvegen. This road, while well-maintained, is open only in summer, and narrow and dangerous during snowstorms (which can hit with a moment's notice, even in warm weather). You'll enjoy vast and terrifying views of lakes, snowfields, and remote mountain huts and farmsteads on what feels like the top of Norway. As you begin the 12-hairpin zigzag descent to Aurland, you'll reach the new "7"-shaped **Stegastein viewpoint**—well worth a stop. The "Snow Road" and viewpoint are both described on page 308.

▲From the Lustrafjord to Bergen, via Nærøyfjord and Gudvangen

Car ferries take tourists between Kaupanger and the Nutshell town of Gudvangen through an arm and elbow of the Sognefjord, including the staggering Nærøyfjord (for details on the ferry, see "Lustrafjord Connections," earlier). From Gudvangen, it's a 90-mile drive to Bergen, via Voss (figure about one hour to Voss, then another two hours into Bergen). This follows essentially the same route as the Norway in a Nutshell (Gudvangen-Voss bus, Voss-Bergen train). For additional commentary on the journey, see page 302.

Get off the ferry in Gudvangen and drive up the Nærøy valley past a river. You'll see the two giant falls and then go uphill through a tunnel. After the tunnel, look for a sign marked *Stalheim* and turn right. Stop for a break at the touristy Stalheim Hotel (described on page 302). Then follow signs marked *Stalheimskleiva*. This incredible road doggedly worms its way downhill back into the depths of the valley. My brakes started overheating in a few minutes. Take it easy. As you wind down, you can view the falls from several turnouts.

The road rejoins E-16. You retrace your route through the tunnel and then continue into a mellower beauty, past lakes and farms, toward Voss. Soon before you reach Voss itself, watch the right side of the road for Tvindefossen, a waterfall with a handy campground/WC/kiosk picnic area that's worth a stop. Highway E-16 takes you through Voss and into Bergen. If you plan to visit Edvard Grieg's Home and the nearby Fantoft Stave Church, now is the ideal time, since you'll be driving near them—and they're a headache to reach from downtown. Both are worth a detour if you're not rushed, and open until 18:00 in summer (see pages 381 and 382 of the Bergen chapter).

▲▲From Balestrand to Bergen, via Vik

If you're based in Balestrand and driving to Bergen, you have two options: Take the Dragsvik-Hella ferry, drive an hour to Kaupanger (via Sogndal), and drive the route just described; or, take the following slower, twistier, more remote, and more scenic route, with a stop at the beautiful Hopperstad Stave Church. This route is slightly longer, with more time on mountain roads and less time on the boat. Figure 20 minutes from Vangsnes to Vik, then about 1.5 hours to Voss, then another 2 hours into Bergen.

From Vagsnes, head into Vik on the main Route 13. In Vik, follow signs from the main road to Hopperstad Stave Church

(described earlier in this chapter). Then backtrack to Route 13 and follow it south, to Voss. You'll soon begin a series of switchbacks that wind you up and out of the valley. The best views are from the Storesvingen Fjellstove restaurant (on the left). Soon after, you'll crest the ridge, go through a tunnel, and find yourself on top of the world, in a desolate and harshly scenic landscape of scrubby mountain-tops, snow banks, lakes, and no trees, scattered with vacation cabins. After cruising atop the plateau for a while, the road twists its way down (next to a waterfall) into a very steep valley, which it meanders through the rest of the way to Voss. This is an hour-long, middle-of-nowhere journey, with few road signs—you might feel lost, but keep driving toward Voss. When Route 13 dead-ends into E-16, turn right (toward Voss and Bergen) and re-enter civilization. From here, the route follows the same roads as in the Lustrafjord-Bergen drive described earlier (including the Tvindefossen waterfall).

GUDBRANDSDAL VALLEY and JOTUNHEIMEN MOUNTAINS

Norway in a Nutshell is a great day trip, but with more time and a car, consider a scenic meander from Oslo to Bergen. You'll arc up the Gudbrandsdal Valley and over the Jotunheimen Mountains, then travel along the Lustrafjord (see previous chapter).

After an introductory stop in Lillehammer, with its fine folk museum, you might spend the night in a log-and-sod farmstead-turned-hotel, tucked in a quiet valley under Norway's highest peaks. Next, Norway's highest pass takes you on an exhilarating roller-coaster ride through the heart of the myth-inspiring Jotunheimen, bristling with Norway's biggest mountains. Then the road hairpins down into fjord country (see previous chapter).

Planning Your Time

While you could spend five or six days in this area on a three-week Scandinavian rampage, this slice of the region is worth three days. By car, I'd spend them like this:

Day 1: Leave Oslo early, and spend midday at Lillehammer's Maihaugen Open-Air Folk Museum for a tour and picnic. Drive up the Gudbrandsdal Valley, stopping at the stave church in Lom. Stay overnight in the Jotunheimen countryside.

Day 2: Drive the Sogne-

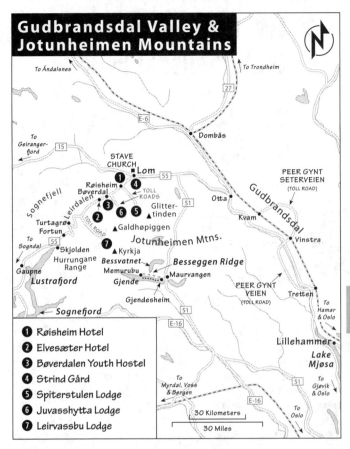

Gudbrandsdal Valley & Jotunheimen Mountains

To Åndalsnes
To Trondheim
27
E-6
Dombås
To Geiranger-fjord
15
STAVE CHURCH
Lom
55
❶ Røisheim
❹
Bøverdal
TOLL ROADS
51
Otta
❸
❻ ❺
Glittertinden
Turtagrø
Fortun
❷
▲Galdhøpiggen
Kvam
To Sogndal
55
TOLL ROAD
Jotunheimen Mtns.
Vinstra
Skjolden
❼ ▲Kyrkja
Hurrungane Range
Bessvatnet
Bessegen Ridge
Gaupne
Memurubu
Maurvangen
Lustrafjord
Gjende
PEER GYNT VEIEN (TOLL ROAD)
Tretten
Gjendesheim
51
To Hamar & Oslo
— *Sognefjord*
E-16
Lillehammer
Lake Mjøsa
❶ Røisheim Hotel
❷ Elvesæter Hotel
❸ Bøverdalen Youth Hostel
❹ Strind Gård
❺ Spiterstulen Lodge
❻ Juvasshytta Lodge
❼ Leirvassbu Lodge
To Myrdal, Voss & Bergen
E-16
To Gjøvik & Oslo
To Oslo
30 Kilometers
30 Miles

PEER GYNT SETERVEIEN (TOLL ROAD)

Gudbrandsdal

GUDBRANDSDAL

fjell road over the mountains, then down along the Lustrafjord, stopping to visit the Dale Church and the Nigard Glacier (see previous chapter). Sleep in your choice of fjord towns, described in previous chapters (such as Solvorn—see page 338, Balestrand—see page 326, or Aurland—see page 312).

Day 3: Cruise the Aurland and/or Nærøy fjords and try to visit another stave church or two (such as Urnes—see page 336, Hopperstad—see page 324, or Borgund—see page 308) before carrying on to Bergen.

This plan can be condensed into two days if you skip the Nigard Glacier side-trip.

Lillehammer and the Gudbrandsdal Valley

The Gudbrandsdal Valley is the tradition-steeped country of Peer Gynt, the Norwegian Huck Finn. This romantic valley of time-worn hills, log cabins, and velvet farms has connected northern and southern Norway since ancient times. While not as striking as other parts of the Norwegian countryside, Gudbrandsdal offers a suitable first taste of the natural wonders that crescendo farther north and west (in Jotunheimen and the Sognefjord). Throughout this region, the government subsidizes small farms to keep the countryside populated and healthy. (These subsidies would not be permitted if Norway were a member of the European Union.)

Orientation to Lillehammer

The de facto capital of Gudbrandsdal, Lillehammer, is a pleasant winter and summer resort town of 25,000. While famous for its brush with Olympic greatness (as host of the 1994 Winter Olympiad), Lillehammer is a bit disappointing—worthwhile only for its excellent Maihaugen Open-Air Folk Museum, or to break up the long drive between Oslo and the Jotunheimen region. If you do wind up here, Lillehammer has happy, old, woody pedestrian zones (Gågata and Storgata).

Tourist Information
Lillehammer's TI is inside the train station (mid-June-mid-Aug Mon-Fri 8:00-18:00, Sat-Sun 10:00-16:00; mid-Aug-mid-June Mon-Fri 8:00-16:00, Sat 10:00-14:00, closed Sun; Jernbanetorget 2, tel. 61 28 98 00, www.lillehammer.com).

Sights in Lillehammer

Lillehammer's two most worthwhile sights are up the hill behind the center of town. It's a fairly steep 15-minute walk from the train station to either sight and a 10-minute, mostly level walk between the two (follow the busy main road that connects them). Because the walk from the station is uphill (and not very well-signed), consider catching the bus from in front of the train station (bus #003 to Olympics Museum, 2/hour; bus #006 to Maihaugen, 1/hour; 30 kr one-way for either bus).

▲▲**Maihaugen Open-Air Folk Museum (Maihaugen Friluftsmuseet)**—This idyllic park, full of old farmhouses and

pickled slices of folk culture, provides a good introduction to what you'll see as you drive through the Gudbrandsdal Valley. Anders Sandvig, a "visionary dentist," started the collection in 1887. You'll divide your time between the fine indoor museum at the entrance and the sprawling exterior exhibits.

Upon arrival, ask about special events, crafts, or musical performances. A TV monitor shows what's going on in the park. Summer is busy with crafts in action and people re-enacting life in the past, à la Colonial Williamsburg. There are no tours, so it's up to you to initiate conversations with the "residents." Off-season it's pretty dead, with no live crafts and most buildings locked up.

Cost and Hours: 150 kr in summer, 110 kr off-season; 25 percent off when combined with Olympics Museum; June-Aug daily 10:00–17:00; Sept-May Tue-Sun 11:00–16:00, closed Mon; paid parking.

Information: Because English descriptions are scant, the 95-kr English guidebook is worth considering; tel. 61 28 89 00, www.maihaugen.no.

Visiting the Museum: The outdoor section, with 200 buildings from the Gudbrandsdal region, is divided into three areas:

the "Rural Collection," with old sod-roof log houses and a stave church; the "Town Collection," with reconstructed bits of old-time Lillehammer; and the "Residential Area," with 20th-century houses that look like most homes in today's Norway. The time trip can be jarring: In the 1980s house, a bubble-gum-chewing girl enthused about her new, "wireless" TV remote and played ABBA tunes from a cassette-tape player.

The museum's excellent "We Won the Land" exhibit (at the entry) sweeps you through Norwegian history from the Ice Age to the Space Age. The Gudbrandsdal art section shows village life at its best. And you can walk through Dr. Sandvig's old dental office and the original shops of various crafts- and tradespeople.

Though the museum welcomes picnickers and has a simple cafeteria, Lillehammer's town center (a 15-minute walk below the museum), with lots of fun eateries, is better for lunch (see "Eating

GUDBRANDSDAL

in the Gudbrandsdal Valley," later).

Norwegian Olympics Museum (Norges Olympiske Museum)—This cute museum is housed in the huge Olympic ice-hockey arena, Håkon Hall. With brief English explanations, an emphasis on Norwegians and Swedes, and an endearingly gung-ho Olympic spirit, it's worth a visit on a rainy day or for sports fans. The ground-floor exhibit traces the ancient history of the Olympics, then devotes one wall panel to each of the summer and winter Olympiads of the modern era (with special treatment for the 1952 Oslo games). Upstairs, walk the entire concourse, circling the arena seating while reviewing the highlights (and lowlights) of the 1994 games (remember Tonya Harding?). While you're up there, check out the gallery of great Norwegian athletes and the giant egg used in the Lillehammer opening ceremony. With more time, see the 13-minute film on the 1994 Lillehammer Olympiad (included in museum ticket, 2/hour, usually in English, near ticket desk).

Cost and Hours: 110 kr, 25 percent off when combined with Maihaugen Museum; June-Aug daily 10:00-17:00; Sept-May Tue-Sun 11:00-16:00, closed Mon; tel. 61 25 21 00, www.maihaugen.no.

Nearby: On the hillside above Håkon Hall (a 30-minute hike or quick drive) are two ski jumps that host more Olympics sights, including a ski lift, the ski jump tower, and a bobsled ride (www.olympiaparken.no). In the summer, ski jumpers practice on the ski jumps, which are sprayed with water.

In the Gudbrandsdal Valley

If you're driving from Oslo to the Gudbrandsdal Valley, you'll go right past the historic Eidsvoll Manor (described on page 272).

Scenic Drives—The main E-6 road north of Lillehammer (en route to Otta and Lom) passes through a bucolic valley with fine but unremarkable scenery. Along this road, a pair of toll-road side-trips (Gynt Veien and Peer Gynt Seterveien) loop off the E-6 road. While they sound romantic, they're basically windy, curvy dirt roads over high, desolate heath and scrub-brush plateaus with fine mountain  views. They're scenic, but pale in comparison to the Sognefjell road between Lom and the Lustrafjord (described later in this chapter).

Sleeping in the Gudbrandsdal Valley

I prefer sleeping in the more scenic and Norwegian-feeling Jotunheimen area (described later). But if you're sleeping here, Lillehammer and the surrounding valley offer several good options. My choices for Lillehammer are near the train station; the accommodations in Kvam provide a convenient stopping point in the valley.

In Lillehammer

$$$ **Mølla Hotell,** true to its name, is situated in an old mill along the little stream running through Lillehammer. The 58 rooms blend Old World charm with modern touches. It's more cutesy-cozy and less businesslike than other Lillehammer hotels in this price range (Db-1,000-1,450 kr depending on demand, elevator, free Internet access and Wi-Fi, a block below Gågata at Elvegata 12, tel. 61 05 70 80, fax 61 05 70 81, www.mollahotell.no, post@mollahotell.no).

$$$ **First Hotel Breiseth** is a business-class hotel with 89 rooms in a handy location directly across from the train station (Sb-880-1,100 kr, Db-1,320 kr, free Wi-Fi, free parking, Jernbanegaten 1-5, tel. 61 24 77 77, www.firsthotels.no/breiseth, breiseth@firsthotels.no).

$ **Vandrerhjem Stasjonen,** Lillehammer's youth hostel, is actually upstairs inside the train station. With 100 beds in 34 institutional but new-feeling rooms—including 18 almost hotel-like doubles—it's a winner (340-kr bunk in a 3- to 4-bed dorm, Sb-700 kr, Db-890 kr, 15 percent cheaper for members, includes sheets

GUDBRANDSDAL

Sleep Code

(6 kr = about $1, country code: 47)
S = Single, **D** = Double/Twin, **T** = Triple, **Q** = Quad, **b** = bathroom, **s** = shower. You can assume staff speak English, breakfast is included, and credit cards are accepted unless otherwise noted.

To help you sort easily through these listings, I've divided the accommodations into three categories, based on the price for a standard double room with bath during high season:

$$$ **Higher Priced**—Most rooms 1,000 kr or more.
$$ **Moderately Priced**—Most rooms between 500-1,000 kr.
$ **Lower Priced**—Most rooms 500 kr or less.

Prices can change without notice; verify the hotel's current rates online or by email.

and breakfast, elevator, free Wi-Fi, Jernbanetorget 2, tel. 61 26 00 24, www.stasjonen.no, post@stasjonen.no).

In Kvam

This is a popular vacation valley for Norwegians, and you'll find loads of reasonable small hotels and campgrounds with huts for those who aren't quite campers (*hytter* means "bungalows," *rom* is "private room," and *ledig* means "vacancy"). These huts normally cost about 400-600 kr, depending on size and amenities, and can hold from four to six people. Although they are simple, you'll have a kitchenette and access to a good WC and shower. When available, sheets rent for around 60 kr per person. Here are a couple of listings in the town of Kvam, located midway between Lillehammer and Lom.

$$$ Vertshuset Sinclair has a quirky Scottish-Norwegian ambience. The 15 fine rooms are in old-fashioned motel wings, while the main building houses an inexpensive cafeteria, described below (Sb-890 kr, Db-1,090 kr, family deals, free Internet access and Wi-Fi, tel. 61 29 54 50, fax 61 29 54 51, www.vertshuset -sinclair.no, post@vertshuset-sinclair.no). The motel was named after a Scotsman who led a band of adventurers into this valley, attempting to set up their own Scottish kingdom. They failed. All were kilt.

$-$$ Kirketeigen Ungdomssenter ("Church Youth Center"), behind the town church, welcomes travelers year-round (camping spots-120 kr/tent; small cabins without water-400 kr; cabins with kitchen and bath-800 kr, sleeps up to 5 people; simple 4-bed rooms in the main building-450 kr for 2-4 people with sheets; sheets and blankets-100 kr, Wi-Fi, tel. 61 21 60 90, www.kirketeigen.no, post@kirketeigen.no).

Eating in the Gudbrandsdal Valley

In Lillehammer: Good restaurants are scattered around the city center, but for the widest selection, head to where the main pedestrian drag (Gågata) crosses the little stream running downhill through town. Poke a block or two up and down **Elvegata,** which stretches along the river and hosts a wide range of tempting eateries—from pubs (both rowdy and upscale) to pizza and cheap sandwich stands.

In the Valley: Vertshuset Sinclair, described above, has a cafeteria handy for a quick and filling bite on the road between Lillehammer and Lom (50-70-kr sandwiches, 100-180-kr meals, daily 7:00-2:30 in the morning).

Jotunheimen Mountains

Norway's Jotunheimen Mountains ("Giants' Home") feature the country's highest peaks and some of its best hikes and drives. This national park stretches from the fjords to the glaciers. You can play roller-coaster with mountain passes, take rugged hikes, wind up scenic toll roads, get up close to a giant stave church...and sleep in a time-passed rural valley. The gateway to the mountains is the unassuming town of Lom.

Lom

Pleasant Lom—the main town between Lillehammer and Sogndal—feels like a modern ski resort village. It's home to one of Norway's most impressive stave churches. While Lom has little else to offer, the church causes the closest thing to a tour-bus traffic jam this neck of the Norwegian woods will ever see.

Orientation to Lom

Park by the stave church—you'll see its dark spire just over the bridge. The church shares a parking lot with a gift shop/church museum and some public WCs. Across the street is the TI. If you're heading over the mountains, Lom's bank (at the Kommune building) has the last ATM until Gaupne.

Tourist Information

Lom's TI is an excellent source of information for hikes and drives in the Jotunheimen Mountains (mid-June-mid-Aug Mon-Fri 9:00-19:00, Sat-Sun 10:00-19:00; shorter hours off-season, closed Sat-Sun Oct-April; in the sod-roofed building across the busy road from the stave church parking lot, tel. 61 21 29 90, www.visit jotunheimen.com).

The TI also serves as a national park office and hosts a worthwhile **Mountain Museum** (Norsk Fjellmuseum), tracing the history of the people who have lived off the land in Jotunheimen from the Stone Age to today. This is one of the better exhibits in fjord country. Its theater shows a 10-minute montage of images backed by Kenny G-type music, and the displays are well-presented, with plenty of actual historic artifacts (50 kr, same hours as TI). The museum also has a computer with free Internet access for travelers.

GUDBRANDSDAL

Sights in Lom

▲▲Lom Stave Church (Lom Stavkyrkje)

Despite extensive renovations, Lom's church (from 1158) remains a striking example of a Nordic stave church. For more on these distinctive medieval churches, see page 221.

Cost and Hours: Church—55 kr, daily mid-June-mid-Aug 9:00-19:00, May-mid-June 10:00-17:00, mid-Aug-Sept 9:00-17:00, closed in winter and during funerals, fine 15-kr leaflet; museum—15 kr, mid-July-mid-Aug daily 9:00-20:00, progressively shorter hours in shoulder season, in winter Mon-Sat 10:00-15:00, closed Sun; tel. 61 21 73 00.

Tours: Try to tag along with a guided tour of the church—or, if it's not too busy, a docent can give you a quick private tour (included in ticket). Even outside of opening times—including winter—small groups can arrange a tour (45 kr/person, 300-kr minimum, call 97 07 53 97 in summer or 61 21 73 00 in winter).

Visiting the Church: Buy your ticket and go inside to take in the humble **interior** (still used by locals for services—notice the posted hymnal numbers). Men sat on the right, women on the left, and prisoners sat with the sheriff in the caged area in the rear. Standing in the middle of the nave, look overhead to see the earliest surviving parts of the church, such as the circle of X-shaped St. Andrew crosses and the Romanesque arches above them. High above the door (impossible to see without a flashlight—ask a docent to show you) is an old painting of a dragon- or lion-like creature—likely an old Viking symbol, possibly drawn here to smooth the forced conversion local pagans made to Christianity. When King Olav II (later to become St. Olav) swept through this valley in 1021, he gave locals an option: convert or be burned out of house and home.

On the white town flag, notice the spoon—a symbol of Lom. Because of its position nestled in the mountains, Lom gets less rainfall than other towns, so large spoons were traditionally used to spread water over the fields. The apse (behind the altar) was added in 1240, when trendy new Gothic cathedrals made an apse a must-have accessory for churches across Europe. Lepers came to the grilled window in the apse for a blessing. When the Reformation hit in 1536, the old paintings were whitewashed over. The church has changed over the years: Transepts, pews, and windows were added in the 17th century. And the circa-1720 paintings were done by a local priest's son.

Drop into the **gift shop/church museum** in the big black building in the parking lot. Its one-room exhibit celebrates 1,000 years of the stave church—interesting if you follow the loaner English descriptions. Inside you'll find a pair of beautiful model churches, headstones and other artifacts, and the only surviving stave-church dragon-head "steeple." In the display case near the early-1900s organ, find the little pencil-size stick carved with runes, dating from around 1350. It's actually a love letter from a would-be suitor. The woman rejected him, but she saved them both from embarrassment by hiding the stick under the church floorboards beneath a pew...where it was found in 1973. (Docents inside the church like to show off a replica of this stick.)

Before or after your church visit, explore the tidy, thought-provoking **graveyard** surrounding the church. Also, check out the precarious-looking little footbridge over the waterfall (the best view is from the modern road bridge into town).

Sleeping near Lom

Lom itself has a handful of hotels, but the most appealing way to overnight in this area is at a rural rest stop in the countryside. All of these are on Route 55 south of Lom, toward Sognefjord—first is Strind Gård, then Bøverdalen, Røisheim, and finally Elvesæter (all within 20 minutes of Lom).

$$$ Røisheim, in a marvelously remote mountain setting, is an extremely expensive storybook hotel composed of a cluster of centuries-old, sod-roofed log farmhouses. Its posh and generous living rooms are filled with antiques. Each of the 20 rooms (in eight different buildings) is rustic but elegant, with fun "barrel bathtubs" and four-poster or canopy beds. Some rooms are in old, wooden farm buildings—*stabburs*—with low ceilings and heavy beams. The deluxe rooms are larger, with king beds and fireplaces. Call ahead so they'll be prepared for your arrival (open May-Sept; standard Db-3,600 kr, deluxe Db-3,950 kr; includes breakfast, packed lunch, and an over-the-top four-course traditional dinner served at 19:30; non-smoking, free Wi-Fi, 10 miles south of Lom on Route 55, tel. 61 21 20 31, fax 61 21 21 51, www.dvgl.no, booking @roisheim.no).

$$$ Elvesæter Hotel has its own share of Old World romance, but is bigger, cheaper, and more modest. Delightful public spaces bunny-hop through its traditional shell, while its 200 beds sprawl through nine buildings. The Elvesæter family has done a great job of retaining the historic character of their medieval farm, even though the place is big enough to handle large tour groups. The renovated "superior" rooms are new-feeling, but have sterile modern furniture; the older, cheaper "standard" rooms are well-worn but more characteristic (open May-Sept, standard Db-1,150 kr, superior Db-1,550 kr, extra bed-450 kr, family deals, includes breakfast, good 325-kr three-course dinners, strictly non-smoking, free Wi-Fi, swimming pool, farther up Route 55, just past Bøverdal, tel. 61 21 99 00, fax 61 21 99 01, www.topof norway.no, elveseter@topofnorway.no). Even if you're not staying here, stop by to wander through the public spaces and pick up a flier explaining the towering Sagasøyla (Saga Column). It was started in 1926 to celebrate the Norwegian constitution, and was to stand in front of Oslo's Parliament Building—but the project stalled after World War II (thanks to the artist's affinity for things German and membership in Norway's fascist party). It was eventually finished and erected here in 1992.

$ **Bøverdalen Youth Hostel** offers 32 cheap-but-comfortable beds and a far more rugged clientele—real hikers rather than car hikers. While a bit institutional, it's well-priced and well-run (open late May-Sept, bunk in 4- to 6-bed room-180 kr, D-480 kr, 4-person cabins-700 kr, sheets-65 kr, breakfast-80 kr, free Wi-Fi, kitchen, hot meals, self-serve café, tel. & fax 61 21 20 64, www .hihostels.no, boverdalen@hihostels.no, Anna Berit). It's in the center of the little community of Bøverdal (store, campground, and toll road up to Galdhøpiggen area).

$ **Strind Gård** is your very rustic option if you can't spring for Røisheim or Elvesæter, but still want the countryside-farm experience. This 150-year-old farmhouse, situated by a soothing waterfall, rents two rooms and one apartment, plus four sod-roofed log huts. The catch: Many of the buildings have no running water, so you'll use the shared facilities at the main building. While not everyone's cup of tea, this place will appeal to romantics who always wanted to sleep in a humble log cabin in the Norwegian mountains—it's downright idyllic for those who like to rough it (2-person huts: without bathroom-300-500 kr depending on size, beautiful private hut with bathroom-700 kr; rooms in main house: D-400-500 kr depending on size, apartment for 4-6 with private bath-700 kr; sheets and towels-70 kr, no breakfast, free Wi-Fi, low ceilings, farm smells, valley views, 2 miles south of Lom on Route 55, tel. 61 21 12 37, www.strind-gard.no, post@strind-gard .no, Anne Jorunn and Trond Dalsegg).

Drives and Hikes in the Jotunheimen Mountains

Route 55, which runs between Lom and the Sognefjord to the south, is the sightseeing spine of this region. From this main (and already scenic) drag, other roads spin upwards into the mountains—offering even better views and exciting drives and hikes. Many of these get you up close to Norway's highest mountain, Galdhøpiggen (8,100 feet). I've listed these attractions from north to south, as you'll reach them driving from Lom to the Sognefjord; except for the first, they all branch off from Route 55. Another great high-mountain experience nearby—the hike to the Nigard Glacier near Lustrafjord—is covered on page 333.

Remember that the TI in Lom acts as a national park office, offering excellent maps and advice for drivers and hikers—a stop here is obligatory if you're planning a jaunt into the mountains (see "Orientation to Lom," earlier). For locations, see the map on page 345.

GUDBRANDSDAL

Besseggen

This trail offers an incredible opportunity to walk between two lakes separated by a narrow ridge and a 1,000-foot cliff. It's one of Norway's most beloved hikes, which can make it crowded in the summer. To get to the trailhead, drivers detour down Route 51 after Otta south to Maurvangen. Turn right to Gjendesheim to park your car. From Gjendesheim, catch the boat to Memurubu, where the path starts at the boat dock. Hike along the ridge—with a blue lake (Bessvatnet) on one side and a green lake (Gjende) on the other—and keep your balance. The six-hour trail loops back to Gjendesheim. Because the boat runs sporadically, time your visit to catch one (120 kr for 20-minute ride, 3 morning departures daily, latest schedules at www.gjende.no, tel. 61 23 85 09). This is a thrilling but potentially hazardous hike, and it's a major detour: Gjendesheim is about 1.5 hours and 50 miles from Lom.

Spiterstulen

From Røisheim, this 11-mile toll road (50 kr) takes you from Route 55 to the Spiterstulen mountain hotel/lodge in about 30 minutes (3,600 feet). This is the best destination for serious all-day hikes to Norway's two mightiest mountains, Glittertinden and Galdhøpiggen (a 5-hour hike up and a 3-hour hike down, doable without a guide). Or consider a guided, two-hour glacier walk (tel. 61 21 94 00, www.spiterstulen.no).

Juvasshytta

This toll road takes you (in about 40 minutes) to the highest you can drive and the closest you can get to Galdhøpiggen (6,050 feet) by car. The road starts in Bøverdal, and costs 85 kr; at the end of it, daily, guided, six-hour hikes go across the glacier to the summit and back (200 kr, late June-late Sept daily at 10:00, July-mid-Aug also daily at 11:30, check in 30 minutes before, strict age limit—no kids under age 7, 4 miles each way, easy ascent but very dangerous without a guide, hiking boots required—possible to rent from nearby ski resort). You can sleep in the newly updated **$$$ Juvasshytta lodge** (Db-1,100 kr with sheets, D without sheets-860 kr, sheets-100 kr, includes breakfast, dinner-330 kr, open June-Sept, tel. 61 21 15 50, www.juvasshytta.no).

Leirvassbu

This 11-mile, 50-kr toll road (about 30 minutes one-way from Bøverkinnhalsen, south of Elvesæter) is most scenic for car hikers. It takes you to a lodge at 4,600 feet with great views and easy walks. A serious (5-hour round-trip) hike goes to the lone peak, Kyrkja—"The Cathedral," which looms like a sanded-down mini-Matterhorn on the horizon (6,660 feet).

▲▲Sognefjell Drive to the Sognefjord

Norway's highest pass (at 4,600 feet, the highest road in northern Europe) is a thrilling drive through a cancan line of mountains, from Jotunheimen's Bøverdal Valley to the Lustrafjord (an arm of the Sognefjord—see previous chapter). Centuries ago, the farmers of Gudbrandsdal took their horse caravans over this difficult mountain pass on treks to Bergen. Today, the road (Route 55) is still narrow, windy, and

otherworldly (and usually closed mid-Oct-May).

As you begin to ascend just beyond Elvesæter, notice the viewpoint on the left for the Leirdalen Valley—capped at the end with the Kyrkja peak (described earlier). Then you'll twist up into a lake-filled valley, then through a mild canyon with grand waterfalls. Before long, as you corkscrew up more switchbacks, you're above the tree line, enjoying a "top of the world" feeling. The best views (to the south) are of the cut-glass range called Hurrungane ("Noisy Children"). The 10 hairpin turns between Turtagrø and Fortun are exciting. Be sure to stop, get out, look around, and enjoy the lavish views. Treat each turn as if it were your last.

Just before you descend to the fjord, the terrain changes, and you reach a pullout on the right, next to a hilltop viewpoint—offering your first glimpse of the fjord. The Lustrafjord village of Skjolden is just around the bend (and down several more switchbacks). Entering Skjolden, continue following Route 55, which now traces the west bank of the Lustrafjord. For more on the sights from here on out, turn to page 332.

Gudbrandsdal and Jotunheimen Connections

Cars are better, but if you're without wheels: **Oslo to Lillehammer** (trains almost hourly, 2.5 hours, just 2 hours from Oslo airport), **Lillehammer to Otta** (6 trains/day, 1.5 hours); a bus meets some trains (confirm schedule at the train station in Oslo) for travelers heading on to **Lom** (2 buses/day, 1 hour) and onward from **Lom to Sogndal** (2 buses/day late June-Aug only, road closed off-season, 3.25 hours).

Route Tips for Drivers

Use low gears and lots of patience both up (to keep the engine cool) and down (to save your brakes). Uphill traffic gets the right-of-way, but drivers, up or down, dive for the nearest fat part of the road whenever they meet. Ask backseat drivers not to scream until you've actually been hit or have left the road.

From Oslo to Jotunheimen: It's 2.5 hours from Oslo to Lillehammer and 3 hours after that to Lom. Wind out of Oslo following signs for *E-6* (not to *Drammen*, but for *Stockholm* and then to *Trondheim*). In a few minutes, you're in the wide-open pastoral countryside of eastern Norway. Norway's Constitution Hall—Eidsvoll Manor—is a five-minute detour off E-6, several miles south of Eidsvoll in Eidsvoll Verk (described on page 272; follow the signs to *Eidsvoll Bygningen*). Then E-6 takes you along Norway's largest lake (Mjøsa), through the town of Hamar, and past more lake scenery into Lillehammer. Signs direct you uphill from downtown Lillehammer to the Maihaugen Open-Air Folk Museum. From Lillehammer, signs to *E-6/Trondheim* take you up the valley of Gudbrandsdal. At Otta, exit for Lom. Halfway to Lom, on the left, look for the long suspension bridge spanning the milky-blue river—a good opportunity to stretch your legs, and a scenic spot to enjoy a picnic.

BERGEN

Bergen is permanently salted with robust cobbles and a rich sea-trading heritage. Norway's
capital in the 12th and 13th centuries, Bergen's
wealth and importance came thanks to its
membership in the heavyweight medieval
trading club of merchant cities called the
Hanseatic League. Bergen still wears her
rich maritime heritage proudly—nowhere more scenically than
the colorful wooden warehouses that make up the picture-perfect
Bryggen district along the harbor.

Protected from the open sea by a lone sheltering island,
Bergen is a place of refuge from heavy winds for the giant working
boats that serve the North Sea oil rigs. (Much of Norway's current affluence is funded by the oil it drills just offshore.) Bergen is
also one of the most popular cruise-ship ports in northern Europe,
hosting hundreds of ships a year and up to seven ships a day in
peak season. Each morning is rush hour, as cruisers hike past the
fortress and into town.

Bergen gets an average of 80 inches of rain annually (compared to 30 inches in Oslo). A good year has 60 days of sunshine.
The natives aren't apologetic about their famously lousy weather. In
fact, they seem to wear it as a badge of pride. "Well, that's Bergen,"
they'll say matter-of-factly as they wring out their raincoats. When
I complained about an all-day downpour, one resident cheerfully
informed me, "There's no such thing as bad weather—just inappropriate clothing"...a local mantra that rhymes in Norwegian.

With 250,000 people, Bergen has big-city parking problems and high prices, but visitors sticking to the old center find
it charming. Enjoy Bergen's salty market, then stroll the easy-on-
foot old quarter, with cute lanes of delicate old wooden houses.

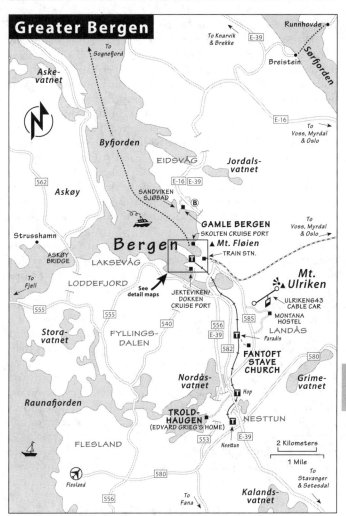

From downtown Bergen, a funicular zips you up a little mountain for a bird's-eye view of this sailors' town. A short foray into the countryside takes you to a variety of nearby experiences: a dramatic cable-car ride to a mountaintop perch (Ulriken643); a scenic stave church (Fantoft); and the home of Norway's most beloved composer, Edvard Grieg, at Troldhaugen.

Planning Your Time

Bergen can be enjoyed even on the tail end of a day's scenic train ride from Oslo before returning on the overnight train. But that teasing taste will make you wish you had more time. On a three-week tour of Scandinavia, Bergen is worth a whole day.

While Bergen's sights are visually underwhelming and pricey, nearly all come with thoughtful tours in English. If you dedicate the time to take advantage of these tours, otherwise barren attractions (such as Håkon's Hall and Rosenkrantz Tower, the Bryggen quarter, the Leprosy Museum, and Gamle Bergen) become surprisingly interesting. For a busy day, you could do this (enjoying tours at all but the last): 9:00—Stroll through the Fish Market; 10:00—Visit Håkon's Hall and Rosenkrantz Tower (joining a guided tour); 12:00—Take the Bryggen Walking Tour (June-Aug only); 14:00—Take a harbor cruise or check out the Leprosy Museum and cathedral; 16:00—Enjoy some free time in town (consider returning to the Bryggens Museum using your tour ticket), or catch the bus out to Gamle Bergen; 18:00—Ride up the Fløibanen funicular.

Although Bergen has plenty of attractions and charms of its own, it's most famous as the "Gateway to the Fjords." If you plan to use Bergen as a springboard for fjord country, you have three options: Pick up a rental car here (fjord wonder is a three-hour drive away); take the express boat down the Sognefjord (about four hours to Balestrand and Flåm/Aurland); or do the "Norway in a Nutshell" as a scenic loop from Bergen. The "Nutshell" option also works well as a detour midway between Bergen and Oslo (hop the train from either city to Voss or Myrdal, then take a bus or spur train into the best of the Sognefjord; scenic ferry rides depart from there). While there are a million ways to enjoy the fjords, first-timers should start with this region (covered thoroughly in the Norway in a Nutshell and More on the Sognefjord chapters).

Also note that Bergen, a geographic dead-end, is actually an efficient place to begin or end your Scandinavian tour. Consider flying into Bergen and out of another city, such as Helsinki (or vice versa).

Orientation to Bergen

Bergen clusters around its harbor—nearly everything listed in this
chapter is within a few minutes'
walk. The busy Torget (the square
with the Fish Market) is at the
head of the harbor. As you face
the sea from here, Bergen's TI is
at the left end of the Fish Market.
The town's historic Hanseatic
Quarter, Bryggen (BREW-gun),
lines the harbor on the right.
Express boats to the Sognefjord

(Balestrand and Flåm) and Stavanger dock at the harbor on the left.

Charming cobbled streets surround the harbor and climb the encircling hills. Bergen's popular Fløibanen funicular climbs high above the city to the top of Mount Fløyen for the best view of the town. Surveying the surrounding islands and inlets, it's clear why this city is known as the "Gateway to the Fjords."

Tourist Information

The centrally located TI is upstairs in the long, skinny, modern, yellow-and-red-striped Torghallen market building, which runs alongside the harbor next to the Fish Market (June-Aug daily 8:30-22:00; May and Sept daily 9:00-20:00; Oct-April Mon-Sat 9:00-16:00, closed Sun; tel. 55 55 20 00, www.visitbergen.com). The TI covers Bergen and western Norway, provides information and tickets for tours, has a fjord information desk, books rooms, and maintains a very handy events board listing today's and tomorrow's slate of tours, concerts, and other events. Pick up this year's edition of the free *Bergen Guide* (also likely at your hotel), which has a fine map and lists all sights, hours, and special events. This booklet can answer most of your questions. If you need assistance and there's a line, take a number. They also have free Wi-Fi: Look for the password posted on the wall.

Bergen Card: You have to work hard to make this greedy little card pay off (200 kr/24 hours, 260 kr/48 hours, sold at TI and Montana Family & Youth Hostel). It gives you free use of the city buses, half off the Mount Fløyen funicular, free admission to most museums (but not the Hanseatic Museum; aquarium included only in winter), and discounts on some events and sights—such as a discount on Edvard Grieg's Home.

Arrival in Bergen

By Train or Bus: Bergen's train and bus stations are on Strømgaten, facing a park-rimmed lake. The small, manageable train station has an office open long hours for booking all your travel in Norway—get your Nutshell reservations here if you haven't already (Mon-Fri 6:45-19:30, Sat 7:30-16:10, Sun 7:30-19:30). There are luggage lockers (30 kr/day, daily 6:30-23:30), pay toilets, a newsstand, sandwich shop, and coffee shop. (To get to the bus station, follow the covered walkway behind the Narvesen newsstand via the Storcenter shopping mall.) Taxis wait to the right (with the tracks at your back). From the train station, it's a 10-minute walk to the TI: Cross the street (Strømgaten) in front of the station and take Marken, a cobbled street that eventually turns into a modern retail street. Continue walking in the same direction until you reach the water.

By Plane: Bergen's cute little Flesland Airport is 12 miles south of the city center (airport code: BGO, tel. 67 03 15 55, www .avinor.no/bergen). The airport bus runs between the airport and downtown Bergen, stopping at the Radisson Blu Royal Hotel in Bryggen, the harborfront area near the TI (if you ask), the SAS Hotel Norge (in the modern part of town at Ole Bulls Plass), and the bus station (about 95 kr, pay driver, 4/hour at peak times, less in slow times, 30-minute ride). Two different companies run this bus, but the cost and frequency is about the same—just take the first one that shows up. Taxis take up to four people and cost about 400 kr for the 20-minute ride (depending on the time of day).

By Car: Driving is a headache in Bergen—avoid it if you can. Approaching town on E-16 (from Voss and the Sognefjord area), follow signs for *Sentrum*, which spits you out near the big, modern bus station and parking garage. Parking is difficult and costly— ask at your hotel for tips. Note that all drivers entering Bergen must pay a 15-kr toll, but there are no toll-collection gates (since the system is automated). Assuming they bill you, it'll just show up on your credit card (which they access through your rental-car company). For details, ask your rental company or see www.auto pass.no.

By Cruise Ship: Bergen is easy for cruise passengers, regard- less of which of the city's two ports your ship uses.

The **Skolten** cruise port is just past the fortress on the main harborfront road. Arriving here, simply walk into town (stroll with the harbor on your right, figure about 10 minutes to Bryggen, plus five more minutes to the Fish Market and TI). After about five minutes, you'll pass the fortress—the starting point for my self- guided walk. A taxi into downtown costs about 50-60 kr; hop-on, hop-off buses pick up passengers at the port (though in this com- pact town, I'd just walk).

The **Jekteviken/Dokken** cruise port is in an industrial zone to the south, a bit farther out (about a 20-minute walk). To dis- courage passengers from walking through all the containers, the port operates a convenient and free **shuttle bus** that zips you into town. It drops you off along Rasmus Meyers Allé right in front of the Bergen Art Museum, facing the cute manmade lake called Lungegårdsvann. From here, it's an easy 10-minute walk to the TI and Fish Market: Walk with the lake on your right, pass through the park (with the pavilion) and head up the pedestrian mall called Ole Bulls Plass, and turn left (at the bluish slab) up the broad square called Torgallmenningen. Note that my self-guided walk conveniently ends right near the shuttle bus stop. A taxi from the cruise port into downtown runs about 100 kr.

For more in-depth cruising information, pick up my *Rick Steves' Northern European Cruise Ports* guidebook.

Helpful Hints

Museum Tours: Many of Bergen's sights are hard to appreciate without a guide. Fortunately, several include a wonderful and intimate guided tour with admission. Make the most of the following sights by taking advantage of their included tours: Håkon's Hall and Rosenkrantz Tower, Bryggens Museum, Hanseatic Museum, Leprosy Museum, Gamle Bergen, and Edvard Grieg's Home.

Crowd Control: In high season, cruise-ship passengers mob the waterfront between 10:00 and 15:00; to avoid the crush, consider visiting an outlying sight during this time, such as Gamle Bergen or Edvard Grieg's Home.

Internet Access: The **TI** offers free, fast Wi-Fi (look for the password posted on the wall), but no terminals. **Kanel** in the Galleriet Shopping Mall is a convenient Internet café (2 kr/minute, 20-kr minimum, Mon-Fri 7:30-21:00, Sat 9:00-18:00, closed Sun, located on ground floor next to Body Shop, tel. 40 62 22 27). The **Bergen Public Library,** next door to the train station, has free terminals in their downstairs café (30-minute limit, Mon-Thu 8:30-20:00, Fri 8:30-16:30, Sat 10:00-16:00, closed Sun, Strømgaten 6, tel. 55 56 85 60).

Laundry: If you drop your laundry off at **Hygienisk Vask & Rens,** you can pick it up clean the next day (70 kr/kilo, no self-service, Mon-Fri 8:30-16:30, closed Sat-Sun, Halfdan Kjerulfsgate 8, tel. 55 31 77 41).

Updates to This Book: For news about changes to this book's coverage since it was published, see www.ricksteves.com/update.

Getting Around Bergen

Most in-town sights can easily be reached by foot; only the aquarium and Gamle Bergen (and farther-flung sights such as the Fantoft Stave Church, Edvard Grieg's Home at Troldhaugen, and the Ulriken643 cable car) are more than a 10-minute walk from the TI.

By Bus: City buses cost 27 kr per ride (pay driver). The best buses for a Bergen joyride are #20 (north along the coast) and #11 (into the hills).

By Tram: Bergen's recently built light-rail line (Bybanen) is a convenient way to visit Edvard Grieg's Home or the Fantoft Stave Church. The tram begins next to Byparken (on Kaigaten, between Bergen's little lake and Ole Bulls Plass), then heads to the train station and continues south. Buy your 27-kr ticket from the machine prior to boarding (to use a US credit card, you'll need to know your PIN code). You'll get both a paper ticket and a gray *minikort* pass. Validate the pass when you board by holding it next to the card reader (watch how other passengers do it). Ride it about

Bergen

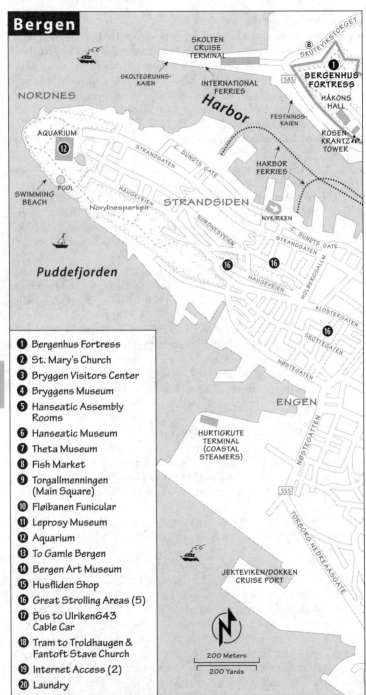

NORDNES

SKOLTEGRUNNS-
KAIEN

SKOLTEN
CRUISE
TERMINAL

INTERNATIONAL
FERRIES

Harbor

SKUTEVIKSTORGET

585

B

1 BERGENHUS
FORTRESS

HÅKONS
HALL

FESTNINGS-
KAIEN

ROSEN-
KRANTZ
TOWER

AQUARIUM

12

POOL

SWIMMING
BEACH

Nordnesparken

HAUGEVEIEN

STRANDGATEN

C. SUNDTS GATE

STRANDSIDEN

NORDNESVEIEN

HARBOR
FERRIES

NYKIRKEN

C. SUNDTS GATE

STRANDGATEN

Puddefjorden

16

16

HAUGEVEIEN

HOLBERGSALLM.

KLOSTERGATEN

16

SKOTTEGATEN

NØSTEGATEN

ENGEN

NØSTEGATTEN

HURTIGRUTE
TERMINAL
(COASTAL
STEAMERS)

555

TORBORG NEDREAASGATE

JEKTEVIKEN/DOKKEN
CRUISE PORT

1 Bergenhus Fortress
2 St. Mary's Church
3 Bryggen Visitors Center
4 Bryggens Museum
5 Hanseatic Assembly Rooms
6 Hanseatic Museum
7 Theta Museum
8 Fish Market
9 Torgallmenningen (Main Square)
10 Fløibanen Funicular
11 Leprosy Museum
12 Aquarium
13 To Gamle Bergen
14 Bergen Art Museum
15 Husfliden Shop
16 Great Strolling Areas (5)
17 Bus to Ulriken643 Cable Car
18 Tram to Troldhaugen & Fantoft Stave Church
19 Internet Access (2)
20 Laundry

N

200 Meters
200 Yards

BERGEN

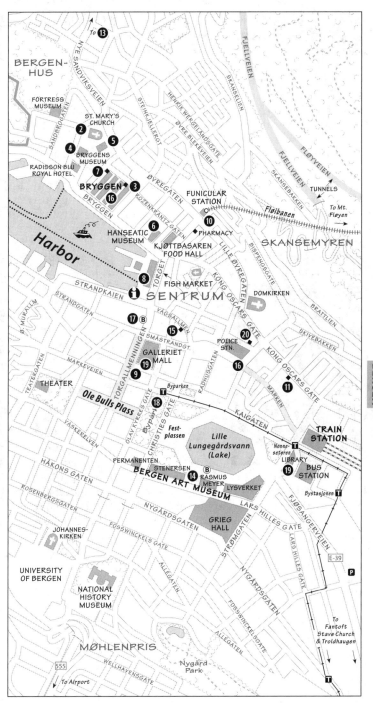

BERGEN

20 minutes to the Paradis stop for Fantoft Stave Church (don't get off at the "Fantoft" stop, which is farther from the church); or continue to the next stop, Hop, to hike to Troldhaugen.

By Ferry: The *Beffen*, a little orange ferry, chugs across the harbor every half-hour, from the dock a block south of the Bryggens Museum to the dock—directly opposite the fortress—a block from the Nykirken church (20 kr, Mon-Fri 7:30-16:00, plus Sat only in July 11:00-16:00, never on Sun, 3-minute ride). The *Vågen* ferry runs from the Fish Market every half-hour to a dock near the aquarium (45 kr, June-Aug 10:00-18:00, 10 minutes). These short "poor man's cruises" have good harbor views.

By Taxi: For a taxi, call 07000 or 08000 (not as expensive as you might expect).

Tours in Bergen

▲▲▲**Bryggen Walking Tour**—This tour of the historic Hanseatic district is one of Bergen's best activities. Local guides

take visitors on an excellent 1.5-hour walk through 900 years of Bergen history via the old Hanseatic town (20 minutes in Bryggens Museum, 20-minute visit to the medieval Hanseatic Assembly Rooms, 20-minute walk through Bryggen, and 20 minutes in Hanseatic Museum). Tours leave from the Bryggens Museum (next to the Radisson Blu Royal Hotel). When you consider that the price includes entry tickets to all three sights, the tour more than pays for itself (120 kr, June-Aug daily at 11:00 and 12:00, none Sept-May, tel. 55 58 80 10, bryggens.museum@bymuseet.no). While the museum visits are a bit rushed, your tour ticket allows you to re-enter the museums for the rest of the day. The 11:00 tour can sell out, especially in July; to be safe, you can call, email, or drop by ahead to reserve.

Local Guides—**Sue Lindelid** and **Jim Paton** are British expats who have spent more than 25 years showing visitors around Bergen (600 kr for 1.5-hour group tour, 700 kr for 2 hours, mobile 90 78 59 52, suelin@hotmail.no).

▲**Bus Tours**—The TI sells tickets for various bus tours, including a three-hour tour that goes to Edvard Grieg's Home at Troldhaugen—a handy way to reach that distant sight (350 kr, May-Sept daily at 10:00, departs from curb across from Fish Market). Buses are comfy, with big views and a fine recorded commentary. There are also several full-day tour options from Bergen, including bus/boat tours to nearby Hardanger and Sogne fjords. The TI is packed with brochures describing all the excursions.

Hop-On, Hop-Off Bus—City Sightseeing's hop-on, hop-off bus links most of Bergen's major sights and also stops at the Skolten cruise port. Buy tickets on board or at the TI (155 kr/24 hours, late May-Aug 9:00-16:30, 2/hour, also stops right in front of Fish Market, mobile 97 78 18 88, www.citysightseeing-bergen.net).

▲**Harbor Tours**—The *White Lady* leaves from the Fish Market daily in summer at 14:30 for a 50-minute cruise. The ride is both scenic and informative, with a relaxing sun deck and good—if scant—recorded narration (130 kr, mid-May-Aug). A four-hour fjord trip is also available (480 kr, May-mid-Sept daily at 10:00, July-late Aug also daily at 15:30, tel. 55 25 90 00, www.white lady.no).

Tourist Train—The tacky little "Bergen Express" train departs from in front of the Hanseatic Museum for a 55-minute loop around town (150 kr, 2/hour in peak season, otherwise hourly; runs daily May 10:00-16:00, June-Aug 10:00-19:00, Sept 10:00-15:00; headphone English commentary).

Self-Guided Walk

Welcome to Bergen

For a quick orientation stroll through Bergen, follow this walk from the city's fortress, through its old wooden Hanseatic Quarter and smelly Fish Market, to the modern center of town. This walk is also a handy sightseeing spine, passing most of Bergen's best museums; ideally, you'll get sidetracked and take advantage of their excellent tours (included with admission). I've pointed out the museums you'll pass en route—all of them are described in greater detail later, under "Sights in Bergen."

• *Begin where Bergen did, at the historic fortress. From the harborfront road, enter the sprawling complex, then walk up into the courtyard at the heart of the place (through the gate marked 1728).*

Bergenhus Fortress: In the 13th century, Bergen became the Kingdom of Norway's first capital. (Prior to the 13th century, kings would circulate, staying on royal farms.) This fortress—built in the 1240s—was a garrison, with a tower for the king's residence (**Rosenkrantz Tower**) and a large hall for his banquets (**Håkon's Hall,** the stepped-gabled building facing the port). Today the fortress grounds are used for big events (Bruce Springsteen filled it in 2009). Visitors can go inside the tower and the hall; while they feel empty and a bit dull on your own, the guided tour (included in admission) brings them to life.

• *Head back out to the main road and continue with the harbor on*

BERGEN

Bryggen's History

Pretty as Bryggen is today, it has a rough-and-tumble history. A horrific plague decimated the population and economy of Norway in 1350, killing about half of its people. A decade later, German merchants arrived and established a Hanseatic trading post, bringing order to that rustic society. For the next four centuries, the port of Bergen was German territory.

Bergen's old German trading center was called "the German wharf" until World War II (and is now just called "the wharf," or "Bryggen"). From 1370 to 1754, German merchants controlled Bergen's trade. In 1550, it was a Germanic city of 1,000 workaholic merchants—surrounded and supported by some 5,000 Norwegians.

The German merchants were very strict and lived in a harsh, all-male world (except for Norwegian prostitutes). This wasn't a military occupation, but a mutually beneficial economic partnership. The Norwegian cod fishermen of the far north shipped their dried cod to Bergen, where the Hanseatic merchants marketed it to Europe. Norwegian cod provided much of Europe with food (a source of easy-to-preserve protein) and cod oil (which lit the lamps until about 1850).

While the city dates from 1070, little survives from before the last big fire in 1702. In its earlier heyday, Bergen was one of the largest wooden cities in Europe. Congested wooden buildings, combined with lots of small fires (to provide heat and light in this cold and dark corner of Europe), spelled disaster for Bergen. Over the centuries, the city suffered countless fires, including 10 devastating blazes. Each time the warehouses burned, the merchants would toss the refuse into the bay and rebuild. Gradually, the land crept out, and so did the buildings. (Looking at the Hanseatic Quarter from the harborfront, you can see how the buildings have settled. The foundations, composed of debris from the many fires, settle as they rot.)

your right. After a block, history buffs could follow Bergenhus *signs (up the street to the left, Sandbrogaten) to reach the* **Fortress Museum**—*though its collection of Norwegian military history (focusing on World War II) isn't worth the detour for most.*

Proceed one more block along the harbor until you reach the open, parklike space on your left. Standing at the top of this area is...

St. Mary's Church (Mariakirken): Dating from the 12th century, this is Bergen's oldest building. It's closed through 2015 while a 100-million-kroner renova-

After 1702, the city rebuilt using more stone and brick, and suffered fewer fires. But this one small wooden quarter was built after the fire, in the early 1700s. To prevent future blazes, the Germans forbade all fires and candles for light or warmth except in isolated and carefully guarded communal houses behind each tenement. It was in these communal houses that apprentices studied, people dried out their soggy clothes, hot food was cooked, and the men drank and partied. One of these medieval Hanseatic Assembly Rooms is preserved and open to the public (the Schøtstuene—separate entrance behind St. Mary's Church, included in Bryggen Walking Tour, difficult to appreciate without a guide).

Flash forward to the 20th century. One of the biggest explosions of World War II occurred in Bergen's harbor on April 20, 1944. An ammunition ship loaded with 120 tons of dynamite blew up just in front of the fortress. The blast leveled entire neighborhoods on either side of the harbor (notice the ugly 1950s construction opposite the fortress) and did serious damage to Håkon's Hall and Rosenkrantz Tower. How big was the blast? There's a hut called "the anchor cabin" a couple of miles away in the mountains. That's where the ship's anchor landed. The blast is considered to be accidental, despite the fact that April 20 happened to be Hitler's birthday and the ship blew up about 100 yards away from the Nazi commander's headquarters (in the fortress).

After World War II, Bryggen was again slated for destruction. Most of the locals wanted it gone—it reminded them of the Germans who had occupied Norway for the miserable war years. Then excavators discovered rune stones indicating that the area predated the Germans. This boosted Bryggen's approval rating, and the quarter was saved. Today this picturesque and historic zone is the undisputed tourist highlight of Bergen.

BERGEN

tion is underway. This stately church of the Hanseatic merchants has a dour stone interior, enlivened by a colorful, highly decorated pulpit.

• *In front of the church, the boxy, modern building houses the excellent* **Bryggens Museum,** *which provides helpful historical context for the Hanseatic Quarter we're about to visit. The museum's outstanding* **Bryggen Walking Tour** *is your best bet for seeing this area (see "Tours in Bergen," earlier.)*

Behind the church is the back wall of the Hanseatic Quarter and the entrance to the communal **Hanseatic Assembly Rooms** *(Schøtstuene)— not worth visiting on your own, but well explained by the Bryggen Walking Tour. The red house straight ahead marks the corner of the...*

Bergen Hanseatic Quarter (Bryggen): Bergen's fragile

wooden old town is its iconic
front door. The long "tenements"
(rows of warehouses) hide atmospheric lanes that creak and
groan with history.

• *To get your bearings, first read the
"Bryggen's History" sidebar; if it's
nice out, stand in the people zone in
front of all the colorful buildings, or*
*cross the street to the wharf and look back for a fine overview of this
area. But let me guess—it's raining, right? In that case, huddle under
an awning.*

Remember that while we think of Bergen as "Norwegian,"
Bryggen was German—the territory of *Deutsch*-speaking merchants and traders. From the front of Bryggen, look down at the
Rosenkrantz Tower. The little red holes at its top mark where
cannons were once pointed at the German quarter by Norwegian
royalty. The threat was never taken seriously, however, because
everyone knew that without German grain, the Norwegians would
starve.

Now enter the woody guts of Bryggen. You can't get inside
the lanes in the first stretch of houses, so proceed to the second
stretch and explore some alleys. Strolling through Bryggen, you
feel swallowed up by history. Long rows of planky buildings
(medieval-style double tenements) lean haphazardly across narrow alleys. The last Hanseatic merchant moved out centuries ago,
but this is still a place of (touristy) commerce. You'll find artists'
galleries, massage parlors, T-shirt boutiques, leather workshops,
atmospheric but overpriced restaurants, fishing tackle shops, and
sweaters, sweaters, sweaters...plus trolls.

The area is flanked by two worthwhile museums within a five-
minute walk of each other (the Bryggens Museum and Hanseatic
Museum). Right in the middle of Bryggen is the tiny, often-closed
Theta Museum, giving a glimpse into the WWII resistance
movement.

Up Bellgården (at the far-right end as you face wooden
Bryggen—it's the lane under the golden deer head) is the little
"visitors center," which is more of a gift shop in disguise. Here
you'll find a video and a few photos illustrating how they are trying to rebuild the tenement houses using the original methods and
materials (good 80-kr Bryggen guidebook, daily June-Aug 9:00-
17:00, May and Sept 10:00-16:00, closed Oct-April).

The visitors center faces a wooden tenement that is currently
undergoing restoration. If this preservation work is still going on
during your visit, it's a fascinating chance to see modern people
wrestling with old technology in the name of history.

BERGEN

Just past the visitors center, you'll pop out into a small square with a wishing well and a giant, grotesque wooden sculpture of a **dried cod**—the unlikely resource that put this town on the map. As you may have noticed, around Bergen, cod is as revered as, well, God.

• *When you're done exploring the bowels of Bryggen, head back out to the main road and continue strolling with the harbor on your right.*

Half of Bryggen (the brick-and-stone stretch between the old wooden facades and the head of the bay) was torn down around 1900. Today these stately buildings—far less atmospheric than Bryggen's original wooden core—are filled with tacky trinket shops and touristy splurge restaurants.

Head to the lone wooden red house at the end of the row, which today houses the **Hanseatic Museum.** The man who owned this building recognized the value of the city's heritage and kept his house as it was. Considered a nutcase back then, today he's celebrated as a visionary, as his decision has left visitors with a fine example of an old merchant house that they can tour. This highly recommended museum is your best chance to get a peek inside one of those old wooden tenements.

• *Directly across the street from the Hanseatic Museum—past the Narvesen kiosk—is the...*

Fish Market (Fisketorget): A fish market has thrived here since the 1500s, when fishermen rowed in with their catch and

haggled with hungry residents. While it's now become a food circus of eateries selling fishy treats to tourists—no local would come here to actually buy fish—this famous market still offers lots of smelly photo fun and free morsels to taste. Many stands sell pre-made smoked-salmon (laks) sandwiches, fish soup, and other

snacks ideal for a light lunch (confirm prices before ordering—it can get pricey). To try Norwegian jerky, pick up a bag of dried cod snacks (torsk). The red meat is minke whale, caught off the coast of northern Norway. You'll also find local fruit in season and hand-knit sweaters (June-Aug daily 7:00-19:00, less lively on Sun; Sept-May Mon-Sat 7:00-16:00, closed Sun). Watch your wallet: If you're going to get pickpocketed in Bergen, it'll likely be here.

• *When you're done exploring, stand with your back to the market and harbor to get oriented.*

The streets heading straight away from the market are worth exploring; within a few blocks, you'll find the **Leprosy Museum** and Bergen's **cathedral**.

BERGEN

The Hanseatic League, Blessed by Cod

Middlemen in trade, the clever German merchants of the Hanseatic League ruled the waves of northern Europe for 500 years (c. 1250-1750). These sea-traders first banded together in a *Hanse*, or merchant guild, to defend themselves against pirates. As they spread out from Germany, they established trading posts in foreign lands, cut deals with local leaders for trading rights, built boats and wharves, and organized armies to protect ships and ports.

By the 15th century, these merchants had organized more than a hundred cities into the Hanseatic League, a free-trade zone that stretched from London to Russia. The League ran a profitable triangle of trade: Fish from Scandinavia was exchanged for grain from the eastern Baltic and luxury goods from England and Flanders. Everyone benefited, and the German merchants—the middlemen—reaped the profits.

At its peak in the 15th century, the Hanseatic League was the dominant force—economic, military, and political—in northern Europe. This was an age when much of Europe was fragmented into petty kingdoms and dukedoms. Revenue-hungry kings and robber-baron lords levied chaotic and extortionist tolls and duties. Pirates plagued shipments. It was the Hanseatic League, rather than national governments, that brought the stability that allowed trade to flourish.

Bergen's place in this Baltic economy was all about cod—a form of protein that could be dried, preserved, and shipped anywhere. Though cursed by a lack of natural resources, the city

*Two short blocks up the street to the left (Vetrlidsallmenningen, past the red-brick market hall with frilly white trim) is the bottom station of the **Fløibanen funicular**, which zips you up to fine views from Mount Fløyen.*

But to continue our walk into the modern part of town, turn right and walk one block up to the wide square. Pause at the blocky monument.

Seafarers' Monument: Nicknamed "the cube of goat cheese" for its shape, this monument dates from about 1950. It celebrates Bergen's contact with the sea and remembers those who worked on it and died in it. Study the faces: All social classes are represented. The statues relate to the scenes depicted in the reliefs above. Each side represents a century (start with the Vikings and work clockwise): 10th century—Vikings, with a totem pole in the panel above recalling the pre-Columbian Norwegian discovery of America; 18th century—equipping Europe's ships; 19th century—whaling; 20th century—shipping and war. For the 21st century, see the real people—a cross-section of today's Norway—sitting at the statue's base. Major department stores (Galleriet, Xhibition, was blessed with a good harbor conveniently located between the rich fishing spots of northern Norway and the markets of Europe. Bergen's port shipped dried cod and fish oil southward and imported grain, cloth, beer, wine, and ceramics.

Bryggen was one of four principal Hanseatic trading posts (*Kontors*), along with London, Bruges, and Novgorod. It was the last *Kontor* opened (c. 1360), the least profitable, and the final one to close. Bryggen had warehouses, offices, and living quarters. Ships docked here were unloaded by counterpoise cranes. At its peak, as many as a thousand merchants, journeymen, and apprentices lived and worked here.

Bryggen was a self-contained German enclave within the city. The merchants came from Germany, worked a few years here, and retired back in the home country. They spoke German, wore German clothes, and attended their own churches. By law, they were forbidden to intermarry or fraternize with the Bergeners, except on business.

The Hanseatic League peaked around 1500, then slowly declined. Rising nation-states were jealous of the Germans merchants' power and wealth. The Reformation tore apart old alliances. Dutch and English traders broke the Hanseatic monopoly. Cities withdrew from the League and *Kontors* closed. In 1754, Bergen's *Kontor* was taken over by the Norwegians. When it closed its doors on December 31, 1899, a sea-trading era was over, but the city of Bergen had become rich...by the grace of cod.

BERGEN

and Telegrafen) are all nearby.

• *The monument marks the start of Bergen's main square...*

Torgallmenningen: Allmenningen means "for all the people." Torg means "square." And, while this is the city's main gathering place, it was actually created as a fire break. The residents of this wood-built city knew fires were inevitable. The street plan was designed with breaks, or open spaces like this square, to help contain the destruction. In 1916, it succeeded in stopping a fire, which is why it has a more modern feel today.

• *Walk along the square to the angled slab. This "blue stone," a popular meeting point at the far end of the square, marks the center of a park-like swath known as...*

Ole Bulls Plass: This drag leads from the National Theater (above on right) to a little lake (below on left).

Detour a few steps up for a better look at the **National Theater,** built in Art Nouveau style in 1909. Founded by violinist Ole Bull in 1850, this was the first theater to host plays in the Norwegian language. After 450 years of Danish and Swedish rule, 19th-century Norway enjoyed a cultural awakening, and Bergen became an artistic power. Ole Bull (a pop idol and heartthrob in his day—women fainted when they heard him play his violin) collaborated with the playwright Henrik Ibsen. Ibsen commissioned Edvard Grieg to write the music for his *Peer Gynt*. These three lions of Norwegian culture all lived and worked right here in Bergen.

The park that spills downhill from the theater has a pleasantly bustling urban ambience. It leads past a popular fountain of Ole Bull (under the trees) to a cast-iron pavilion given to the city by Germans in 1889, and on to the little manmade lake (Lille Lungegårdsvann), which is circled by an enjoyable path. This green zone is considered a park and is cared for by the local parks department.

• *If you're up for a lakeside stroll, now's your chance. Also notice that alongside the lake (to the right as you face it from here) is a row of buildings housing the enjoyable **Bergen Art Museum**. And to the left of the lake are some fine residential streets (including the picturesque, cobbled Marken); within a few minutes' walk are the **Leprosy Museum** and the **cathedral**.*

Sights in Bergen

Several museums listed here—including the Bryggens Museum, Håkon's Hall, Rosenkrantz Tower, Leprosy Museum, and Gamle Bergen—are part of the Bergen City Museum (Bymuseet) organization. If you buy a ticket to any of them, you can pay half-price at any of the others simply by showing your ticket.

▲Bergenhus Fortress: Håkon's Hall and Rosenkrantz Tower—The tower and hall, sitting boldly out of place on the harbor just beyond Bryggen, are reminders of Bergen's importance as the first permanent capital of Norway. Both sights feel vacant and don't really speak for themselves; the included guided tours, which provide a serious introduction to Bergen's history, are essential for grasping their significance.

Cost and Hours: Hall and tower—60 kr each, includes guided tour; mid-May-Aug—both open daily 10:00-16:00; Sept-mid-May—hall open daily 12:00-15:00, Thu until 18:00, tower open Sun only 12:00-15:00; tel. 55 31 60 67.

Visiting the Hall and Tower: While each sight is covered by a separate ticket and tour, it's best to consider them as one and start at Håkon's Hall (mid-May-Aug tours leave daily at the top of the hour; Sept-mid-May full tour runs on Sat, Sun Håkon's Hall tour only, no tours Mon-Fri). Stick with your guide, as the Rosenkrantz Tower is part two of the tour.

Håkon's Hall, dating from the 13th century, is the largest

secular medieval building in Norway. It's essentially a giant, grand reception hall (used today for banquets) under a ceiling that feels like an upturned Viking boat. While recently rebuilt, the ceiling's design is modeled after grand wooden roofs of that era. Beneath the hall is a whitewashed cellar. Banquets were a men-only affair. The raised seats gave royal, church, and military dignitaries the appropriate elevation.

Rosenkrantz Tower, the keep of a 13th-century castle, has a jumbled design, thanks to a Renaissance addition. The tour brings it to life. There's a good history exhibit on the top floors and a fine view from the rooftop.

Fortress Museum (Bergenhus Festningmuseum)—This humble museum, set back a couple of blocks from the fortress, may interest historians with its thoughtful exhibits about military history, especially Bergen's WWII experience. You'll learn about the resistance movement in Bergen (including its underground newspapers), the role of women in the Norwegian military, and Norwegian troops who have served with UN forces in overseas conflicts. Some exhibits are in English, while others are in Norwegian only.

Cost and Hours: Free, Tue-Sun 11:00-17:00, closed Mon, just behind Thon Hotel Bergen Brygge at Koengen, tel. 55 54 63 87.

▲▲**Bryggens Museum**—This modern museum explains the 1950s archaeological dig to uncover the earliest bits of Bergen (1050-1500). Brief English explanations are posted. From September through May, when there is no tour, consider buying the good museum guidebook (25 kr).

Cost and Hours: 60 kr; in summer, entry included with Bryggen Walking Tour described earlier; mid-May-Aug daily 10:00-16:00; Sept-mid-May Mon-Fri 11:00-15:00, Sat 12:00-15:00, Sun 12:00-16:00; inexpensive cafeteria with soup-and-bread specials; in big, modern building just beyond the end of Bryggen and the Radisson Blu Royal Hotel, tel. 55 58 80 10, www.bymuseet.no.

Visiting the Museum: The manageable, well-presented permanent exhibit occupies the ground floor. First up are the foundations from original wooden tenements dating back to the 12th century (displayed right where they were excavated) and a giant chunk of the hull of a 100-foot-long, 13th-century ship that was found here. Next, an exhibit (roughly shaped like the long, wooden double-tenements outside) shows off artifacts and explains lifestyles from medieval Bryggen. Behind that is a display of items you might have bought at the medieval market. You'll finish with exhibits about the church in Bergen, the town's role as a royal capital, and its status as a cultural capital. Upstairs are two floors of temporary exhibits.

▲▲**Hanseatic Museum (Hanseatiske Museum)**—This little museum was founded in the late 1900s to preserve a tenement interior. Today it offers the best possible

look inside the wooden houses that are Bergen's trademark. Its creaky old rooms—with hundred-year-old cod hanging from the ceiling—offer a time-tunnel experience back to Bryggen's glory days. It's located in an atmospheric old merchant house furnished with dried fish, antique ropes, an old oxtail (used for wringing spilled cod-liver oil back into the bucket), sagging steps, and cupboard beds from the early 1700s—one with a medieval pinup girl. You'll explore two upstairs levels, fully furnished and with funhouse floors. The place still feels eerily lived-in; neatly sorted desks with tidy ledgers seem to be waiting for the next workday to begin.

Cost and Hours: 60 kr; in summer, entry included with Bryggen Walking Tour; daily mid-May-mid-Sept 9:00-17:00; mid-Sept-mid-May Tue-Sat 11:00-14:00, Sun 11:00-16:00, closed Mon; Finnegården 7a, tel. 55 54 46 96, www.museumvest.no.

Tours: There are English explanations, but it's much better if you take the good, included 45-minute guided tour (3/day in English, mid-May-mid-Sept only, times displayed just inside door). Even if you tour the museum with the Bryggen Walking Tour, you're welcome to revisit (using the same ticket) and take this longer tour.

Theta Museum—This small museum highlights Norway's resistance movement (specifically, a 10-person local group called Theta) during the Nazi occupation in World War II. It's housed in Theta's former headquarters—a small room in a wooden Bryggen building.

Cost and Hours: 30 kr, June-Aug Tue and Sat-Sun 14:00-16:00, closed Mon, Wed-Fri, and off-season, Enhjørningsgården, tel. 55 31 53 93.

▲▲**Fløibanen Funicular**—Bergen's popular funicular climbs 1,000 feet in seven minutes to the top of Mount Fløyen for the

best view of the town, surrounding islands, and fjords all the way to the west coast. The top is a popular picnic or pizza-to-go dinner spot (Peppe's Pizza is tucked behind the Hanseatic Museum, a block away from the base of the lift). The recommended Fløien Folkerestaurant, at the top of the funicular, offers affordable self-service food all day and fancier dinners in the evenings (both restaurant and cafeteria open daily in summer; off-season only the cafeteria is open and only on weekends). Sunsets are great here. The top is also the starting point for many peaceful hikes (ask for the *Fløyen Hiking Map* at the Fløibanen ticket window at the base). It's a pleasant but steep walk back down into Bergen. To save your knees, get off at the Promsgate stop halfway down and then wander through the delightful cobbled and shiplap lanes (note that only the :00 and :30 departures stop at Promsgate). This funicular is regularly used by locals commuting into and out of downtown.

Cost and Hours: 80 kr round-trip, Mon-Fri 7:30-23:00, Sat-Sun 8:00-23:00, departures generally 4/hour—on the quarter-hour most of the day, runs continuously if busy, tel. 55 33 68 00, www .floibanen.no.

Cathedral (Domkirke)—Bergen's main church, dedicated to St. Olav (the patron saint of Norway), dates from 1301. As it's just a couple of blocks off the harbor, if you're nearby (for example, on way to the Leprosy Museum), drop in to enjoy its stoic, plain interior with stuccoed stone walls and giant wooden pulpit. Like so many old Norwegian structures, its roof makes you feel like you're huddled under an overturned Viking ship. The church is oddly lopsided, with just one side aisle. Before leaving, look up to see the gorgeous wood-carved organ over the main entrance. In the entryway, you'll see portraits of each bishop dating all the way back to the Reformation.

Cost and Hours: Free but donations appreciated; mid-June-mid-Aug Mon-Fri 10:00-16:00, Sun 9:30-13:00, closed Sat; off-season Tue-Fri 11:00-12:30, closed Sun-Mon except for worship; tel. 55 59 32 70, www.bergendomkirke.no.

Leprosy Museum (Lepramuseet)—Leprosy is also known as "Hansen's Disease" because in the 1870s a Bergen man named Armauer Hansen did groundbreaking work in understanding the ailment. This unique museum is in St. Jørgens Hospital, a

BERGEN

leprosarium that dates back to about 1700. Up until the 19th century, as much as 3 percent of Norway's population had leprosy. This hospital—once called "a graveyard for the living" (its last patient died in 1946)—has a meager exhibit in a thought-provoking shell attached to a 300-year-old church. It's really only worth your time and money if you stick around for one of the free tours, which generally leave at the top of the hour or by request.

Cost and Hours: 50 kr, mid-May-Aug daily 11:00-15:00, closed Sept-mid-May, between train station and Bryggen at Kong Oscars Gate 59, tel. 55 96 11 55, www.bymuseet.no.

▲Bergen Art Museum (Bergen Kunstmuseum)—If you need to get out of the rain (and you enjoyed the National Gallery in Oslo), check out this collection of collections in four neighboring buildings facing the lake along Rasmus Meyers Allé. The Lysverket building has an eclectic cross section of both international and Norwegian artists. The Rasmus Meyer branch specializes in Norwegian artists (with an especially good Munch exhibit). The Stenersen building has installations of contemporary art (and a recommended café), while the Permanenten building has decorative arts. Small description sheets in English are in each room.

Cost and Hours: 100 kr, daily 11:00-17:00, closed Mon mid-Sept-mid-May, Rasmus Meyers Allé 3, tel. 55 56 80 00, www.kunstmuseene.no.

Visiting the Museum: Many visitors focus on the **Lysverket** ("Lighthouse"), featuring an easily digestible collection. Here are some of its highlights: The ground floor includes an extensive collection of works by Nikolai Astrup (1880-1928), who depicts Norway's fjords with bright colors and Expressionistic flair. Up on the first floor is a great collection of J. C. Dahl and his students, who captured the majesty of Norway's natural wonders (look for Adelsteen Normann's impressive, photorealistic view of Romsdalfjord). "Norwegian Art 1840-1900" includes works by Christian Krohg, as well as some portraits by Harriet Backer. Also on this floor are icons and various European Old Masters.

Up on the second floor, things get modern. The Tower Hall (Tårnsalen) features Norwegian modernism and an extensive exhibit of Bergen's avant-garde art (1966-1985), kicked off by "Group 66." The International Modernism section has four stars: Pablo Picasso (sketches, etchings, collages, and a few Cubist paintings), Paul Klee (the Swiss childlike painter), and the dynamic

Norwegian duo of Edvard Munch and Ludvig Karisten. Rounding it out are a smattering of Surrealist, Abstract Expressionist, and Op Art pieces.

▲**Aquarium (Akvariet)**—Small but fun, this aquarium claims to be the second-most-visited sight in Bergen. It's wonderfully laid out and explained in English. Check out the informative exhibit downstairs on Norway's fish-farming industry.

Cost and Hours: 200 kr, kids-150 kr, cheaper off-season, daily May-Aug 9:00-19:00, Sept-April 10:00-18:00, feeding times at the top of most hours in summer, cheery cafeteria with light sandwiches, Nordnesbakken 4, tel. 55 55 71 71, www.akvariet.no.

Getting There: It's at the tip of the peninsula on the south end of the harbor—about a 20-minute walk or short ride on bus #11 from the city center. Or hop on the handy little *Vågen* "Akvariet" ferry that sails from the Fish Market to near the aquarium (45 kr one-way, 70 kr round-trip, 2/hour, daily May-Aug 10:00-18:00).

Nearby: The lovely park behind the aquarium has views of the sea and a popular swimming beach (described later, under "Activities in Bergen"). The totem pole erected here was a gift from Bergen's sister city in the US—Seattle.

▲**Gamle Bergen (Old Bergen)**—This Disney-cute gathering of 50-some 18th- and 19th-century shops was founded in 1934 to save old buildings from destruction as Bergen modernized. Each of the houses was moved from elsewhere in Bergen and reconstructed here. Together, they create a virtual town that offers a cobbled look at the old life. It's free to wander through the town and park to enjoy the facades of the historic buildings, but to get into the 20 or so museum buildings, you'll have to join a tour (departing on the hour 10:00-16:00).

Cost and Hours: Free entry, 70-kr tour (in English) required for access to buildings, mid-May-early Sept Mon-Sat 11:00-15:00, Sun 10:00-16:00, closed off-season, tel. 55 39 43 04, www.gamle bergen.museum.no.

Getting There: Take any bus heading west from Bryggen (such as #20, direction: Lonborg) to Gamle Bergen (first stop after the tunnel). You'll get off at a freeway pullout and walk 200 yards, following signs to the museum. Any bus heading back into town takes you to the center (buses come by every few minutes). With the easy bus connection, there's no reason to taxi.

Activities in Bergen

▲**Strolling**—Bergen is a great town for wandering. The harborfront is a fine place to kick back and watch the pigeons mate. Other good areas to explore are over the hill past Klostergaten, Knosesmauet, and Ytre Markevei; near Marken; and the area behind Bryggen.

Shopping in Bergen—Most shops, including Husfliden (described below), are open Mon-Fri 9:00-17:00, Thu until 19:00, Sat 9:00-15:00, and closed Sunday. Many of the tourist shops at the harborfront strip along Bryggen are open daily—even during holidays—until 20:00 or 21:00.

Bryggen is bursting with sweaters, pewter, and trolls. The **Husfliden** shop is popular for its handmade Norwegian sweaters and goodies (fine variety and quality but expensive, just off Torget, the market square, at Vågsallmenninge 3, tel. 55 54 47 40).

The **Galleriet** shopping center on Torgallmenningen has six floors of shops, cafés, and restaurants. You'll find a pharmacy, photo shops, clothing, sporting goods, bookstores, mobile-phone shops, an Internet café, and a basement grocery store (Mon-Fri 9:00-20:00, Sat 9:00-18:00, closed Sun).

Swimming—Bergen has two seaside public swimming areas: one at the aquarium and the other in Gamle Bergen. Each is a great

local scene on a hot sunny day. **Nordnes Sjøbad,** near the aquarium, offers swimmers an outdoor heated pool and a protected area of the sea (40 kr, kids-20 kr, mid-May-Aug Mon-Fri 7:00-19:00, Sat 7:00-14:00, Sun 10:00-14:00, Sat-Sun until 19:00 in good weather, closed off-season, Nordnesparken 30, tel. 55 90 21 70). **Sandviken Sjobad,** at Gamle Bergen, is free. It comes with changing rooms, a roped-off bit of the bay (no pool), a high dive, and lots of sunbathing space.

Sights near Bergen

▲Ulriken643 Cable Car—It's amazingly quick and easy to zip to the 643-meter-high (that's 2,110 feet) summit of Ulriken, the tallest mountain near Bergen.

Stepping out of the cable car, you enter a different world, with views stretching to the ocean. A chart clearly shows the many well-marked and easy hikes that fan out over the vast rocky and grassy plateau above the tree line (circular walks of various lengths, a 40-minute hike down, and a 4-hour hike to the top of the Fløibanen funicular). For less exercise, you can simply sunbathe, crack open a picnic, or enjoy the Ulriken restaurant.

Getting There: To get from downtown Bergen to the cable

car, you can take a blue Bergen Sightseeing hop-on, hop-off bus (245 kr includes cable-car ride, ticket valid 24 hours, May-Sept daily 10:00-17:30, 2/hour, departs Fish Market and Bryggen, also stops at aquarium, buy ticket on board or at TI). The cable-car ride takes five minutes (prices without bus ride: 145 kr round-trip, 80 kr one-way, 8/hour, daily 9:00-21:00, off-season until 17:00, tel. 53 64 36 43, www.ulriken643.no).

▲▲**Edvard Grieg's Home, Troldhaugen**—Norway's greatest composer spent his last 22 summers here (1885-1907), soaking up inspirational fjord beauty and composing many of his greatest works. Grieg fused simple Norwegian folk tunes with the bombast of Europe's Romantic style. In a dreamy Victorian setting, Grieg's "Hill of the Trolls" is pleasant for anyone and essential for Grieg fans. You can visit his house on your own, but it's more enjoyable if you take  the included 20-minute tour. The house and adjacent museum are full of memories and artifacts, including the composer's Steinway. The walls are festooned with photos of the musical and literary superstars of his generation. When the hugely popular Grieg died in 1907, 40,000 mourners attended his funeral. His little studio hut near the water makes you want to sit down and modulate.

Cost and Hours: 80 kr, includes guided tour in English, daily May-Sept 9:00-18:00, Oct-April 10:00-16:00, tel. 55 92 29 92, www.troldhaugen.com.

Concerts: Ask at the TI about piano performances in the concert hall at Grieg's home—a gorgeous venue with the fjord  stretching out behind the big black grand piano (220 kr, concerts roughly mid-June-late Aug Sun and Wed at 18:00, free shuttle bus from TI if you show concert ticket). Delightful 30-minute lunch piano concerts are offered daily at 13:00 in peak season (20 kr plus entry ticket, daily June-Aug, Mon-Sat in Sept).

Getting to Troldhaugen: Bergen's slick **tram** drops you a long 20-minute walk from Troldhaugen. Catch the tram in the city center at its terminus near Byparken (between the lake and Ole Bulls Plass), ride it for about 25 minutes, and get off at the stop called Hop. Walk in the direction of Bergen (about 25 yards), cross at the crosswalk, and follow signs to Troldhaugen. Part of the way is on a pedestrian/bike path; you're halfway there when the path crosses over a busy highway. If you want to make the 13:00 lunch-time concert, leave Bergen at 12:00.

To avoid the long walk from the tram stop, consider the three-hour city bus tour promoted by the TI, which comes with infor-mative recorded narration, gets you to within a five-minute walk of Troldhaugen, and includes a brief tour of the house (300 kr, May-Sept daily at 11:00). If you're driving into Bergen from the east (such as from the Sognefjord), you'll drive right by Troldhaugen on your way into town.

Fantoft Stave Church—This huge, preserved-in-tar stave church burned down in 1992. It was rebuilt and reopened in 1997, but it will never be the same (for more on stave churches, see page 221). Situated in a quiet forest next to a mysterious stone cross, this replica of a 12th-century wooden church is bigger, though no better, than others covered in this book. But it's worth a look if you're in the neighborhood, even after-hours, for its atmospheric setting.

Cost and Hours: 44 kr, mid-May-mid-Sept daily 10:30-18:00, interior closed off-season, no English information, tel. 55 28 07 10, www.fantoftstavkirke.com.

Getting There: The church is located three miles south of Bergen on E-39 in Paradis. Take the tram (from Byparken, between the lake and Ole Bulls Plass) or bus #83 (from Torget, by the Fish Market) to the Paradis stop (not the "Fantoft" stop). From Paradis, walk uphill to the parking lot on the left, and find the steep footpath to the church.

Sleeping in Bergen

Busy with business travelers and increasingly popular with tour-ists, Bergen can be jammed any time of year. Even with this crush, proud and pricey hotels may be willing to make deals. You might save a bundle by emailing the bigger hotels and asking for their best price. Otherwise, Bergen has some fine budget alternatives to normal hotels that can save you a bundle.

Hotels

$$$ Hotel Havnekontoret, with the best location in town, fills a grand old shipping headquarters dating from the 1920s. It's an

---

Sleep Code

(6 kr = about $1, country code: 47)
S = Single, **D** = Double/Twin, **T** = Triple, **Q** = Quad, **b** = bathroom, **s** = shower. You can assume that staff speak English, break-fast is included, and credit cards are accepted unless other-wise noted.

To help you sort easily through these listings, I've divided the accommodations into three categories, based on the price for a standard double room with bath during high season:

$$$ Higher Priced—Most rooms 1,400 kr or more.
$$ Moderately Priced—Most rooms between 900-1,400 kr.
$ Lower Priced—Most rooms 900 kr or less.

Prices can change without notice; verify the hotel's current rates online or by email.

---

especially fine value on weekends and in the summer, for those who eat the included dinner. While part of a chain, it has a friendly spirit. Guests are welcome to climb its historic tower (with a magnificent view) or enjoy its free sauna and exercise room downstairs. The hotel's 116 rooms are expensive during the week, and half-price on weekends and through most of the summer. If you aren't interested in fancy dining, the room price includes virtually all your food—a fine breakfast, self-service waffles and pancakes in the afternoon, fruit and coffee all day, and a light dinner buffet each evening. If you take advantage of them, these edible extras are easily worth 600 kr per day per couple, making the cost of this fancy hotel little more than a hostel (Db during business peak-2,300 kr, Db Fri-Sun and most of summer-about 1,700 kr, extra bed-300 kr, book online to save, free Wi-Fi, facing the harbor across the street from the Radisson Blu Royal Hotel at Slottsgaten 1, tel. 55 60 11 00, www.choicehotels.no, cc.havnekontoret@choice.no).

$$$ Hotel Park Bergen is classy, comfortable, and in a fine residential neighborhood a 15-minute uphill walk from the town center (10 minutes from the train station). It's tinseled in Old World, lived-in charm, yet comes with all of today's amenities. The 35 rooms are split between two buildings, with 22 in the classy old-fashioned hotel and 13 in the modern annex across the street (Sb-1,110 kr, Db-1,500 kr, extra bed-350 kr, winter weekend discounts, free Wi-Fi, Harald Hårfagres Gate 35, tel. 55 54 44 00, fax 55 54 44 44, www.hotelpark.no, booking@hotelpark.no).

$$$ Thon Hotel Rosenkrantz, with 129 rooms, is one block behind Bryggen, between the Bryggens Museum and the Fløibanen funicular station—right in the heart of Bergen's

BERGEN

Bergen Hotels & Restaurants

SKOLTEN CRUISE TERMINAL

SKOLTEGRUNNS-KAIEN

INTERNATIONAL FERRIES

SKUTEVIKSTORGET

B

585

BERGENHUS FORTRESS

HÅKONS HALL

NORDNES

Harbor

FESTNINGS-KAIEN

ROSEN-KRANTZ TOWER

AQUARIUM

STRANDGATEN

C. SUNDTS GATE

HARBOR FERRIES

POOL

HAUGEVEIEN

Nordnesparken

STRANDSIDEN

NYKIRKEN

SWIMMING BEACH

NORDNESVEIEN

C. SUNDTS GATE

STRANDGATEN

Puddefjorden

HOLBERGSALLM.

HAUGEVEIEN

KLOSTERGATEN

SKOTTEGATEN

NØSTEGATEN

24

ENGEN

① Hotel Havnekontoret
② Hotel Park Bergen
③ Thon Hotel Rosenkrantz
④ P-Hotel
⑤ Thon Hotel Bergen Brygge
⑥ Basic Hotel Victoria
⑦ Citybox
⑧ Guest House Skiven
⑨ Skansen Pensjonat
⑩ Marken Gjestehus
⑪ Bergen YMCA Hostel
⑫ To Montana Family & Youth Hostel
⑬ Enhjørningen & Restaurant To Kokker
⑭ Bryggeloftet & Stuene
⑮ Pingvinen Pub
⑯ Naboen Pub
⑰ Zupperia Café
⑱ Café Opera
⑲ Dickens Restaurant
⑳ To Fløien Folkerestaurant
㉑ Lido Cafeteria
㉒ Peppe's Pizza (2)
㉓ Baker Brun
㉔ Bon Appétit
㉕ Deli de Luca (3)
㉖ Fish Market
㉗ Trekroneren Hot-Dog Stand
㉘ Kjøttbasaren Food Hall
㉙ Marken Street Eateries

HURTIGRUTE TERMINAL (COASTAL STEAMERS)

NØSTEGATTEN

555

TORBORG NEDREAASGATE

JEKTEVIKEN/DOKKEN CRUISE PORT

N

200 Meters

200 Yards

BERGEN

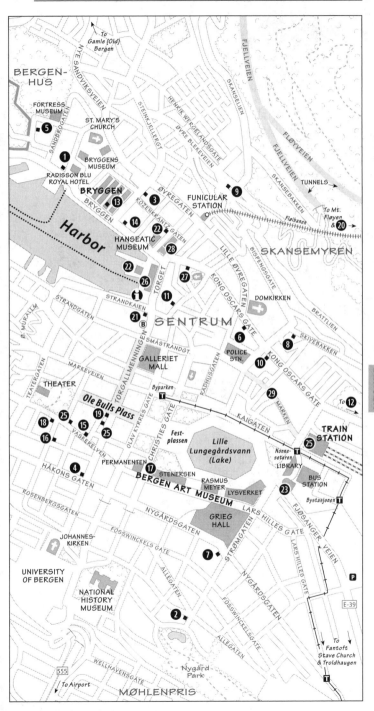

BERGEN

appealing old quarter. However, the next-door nightclub is noisy on Friday and Saturday nights—be sure to request a quiet room (average rates: Sb-1,295 kr, Db-1,695 kr, elevator, free Internet access and Wi-Fi, Rosenkrantzgate 7, tel. 55 30 14 00, www.thon hotels.no/rosenkrantz, rosenkrantz@thonhotels.no).

$$ P-Hotel has 43 basic rooms just up from Ole Bulls Plass. While it's not particularly charming and some rooms come with street noise, it's got a prime location. Ask for a room facing the courtyard in the renovated wing (Sb-950 kr, Db-1,250 kr, credit card only—no cash, box breakfast in your room, elevator, free Wi-Fi, Vestre Torggate 9, tel. 80 04 68 35, www.p-hotels.no, bergen@p-hotels.no).

$$ Thon Hotel Bergen Brygge, beyond Bryggen near Håkon's Hall, is part of Thon's cheaper "Budget" chain. However, the 229 spartan rooms can be just about as nice as those in its sister hotels. Because of its relatively good prices and great location, it fills up quickly—book ahead. Light sleepers, beware: Many rooms face the fortress grounds, which sometimes host summer evening concerts. Ask for a room on the quiet side, bring earplugs, or go elsewhere (Db-1,100-1,400 kr, discounts unlikely but you save if you book online, elevator, free Internet access and Wi-Fi, Bradbenken 3, tel. 55 30 87 00, fax 55 32 94 14, www.thonhotels .com/bergenbrygge, bergen.brygge@thonhotels.no).

$$ Basic Hotel Victoria is an old hotel turned into a college dorm that becomes a utilitarian, minimalist budget hotel each summer. There are no public spaces, the tiny reception is open only 9:00-23:00, and you won't get your towels changed. But its 43 modern, bright, simple rooms are plenty comfortable for the price (open June-Aug only, Sb-895 kr, Db-995 kr, Tb-1,395 kr, free Wi-Fi, Kong Oscarsgate 29, tel. 55 31 44 04, www.basichotels.no, victoria@basichotels.no).

$ Citybox is a unique, no-nonsense hotel concept: plain, white, clean, and practical. It rents 55 rooms online and provides you with a confirmation number. Check-in is automated—just punch in your number and get your ticket. The reception is staffed daily 9:00-16:30, except May-Oct until 23:00 (S-400 kr, Sb-500 kr, D-600 kr, Db-700 kr, extra bed-150 kr, family room for up to four-1,200 kr, no breakfast, elevator, just away from the bustle in a mostly residential part of town at Nygårdsgaten 31, tel. 55 31 25 00, www.citybox.no, post@citybox.no).

Private Homes and Pensions

If you're looking for local character and don't mind sharing a shower, these accommodations—far more quiet, homey, and convenient than hostel beds—might just be the best values in town. Both require guests to climb outdoor stairways, which may be tough for those not packing light.

$ Guest House Skiven is a humble little place beautifully situated on a steep, traffic-free cobbled lane called "the most painted street in Bergen." Alf and Elizabeth Heskja (who live upstairs) rent four non-smoking doubles that share a shower, two WCs, and a kitchen (D-600 kr for Rick Steves readers, no breakfast, free Wi-Fi, 4 blocks from station at Skivebakken 17, tel. 55 31 30 30, mobile 90 05 30 30, www.skiven.no, rs@skiven.no). From the train station, go down Kong Oscars Gate, uphill on D. Krohns Gate, and up the stairs at the end of the block on the left.

$ Skansen Pensjonat (not to be confused with the nearby Skansen Apartments) is situated 100 yards directly behind the entrance to the Fløibanen funicular. Jannicke Alvær rents seven tastefully decorated rooms with views over town (small non-view S-450 kr, larger S-500 kr, D-800 kr, fancy D on corner with view and balcony-900 kr, apartment-1,000 kr, includes breakfast, 2 showers on ground floor, 2 WCs, sinks in rooms, family room with TV; all non-smoking, free Wi-Fi, Vetrlidsalmenning 29, tel. 55 31 90 80, www.skansen-pensjonat.no, post@skansen-pensjonat.no). Follow the switchback road behind the Fløibanen funicular station to the paved plateau with benches, and look for the sign.

Dorms and Hostels

$ Marken Gjestehus is a quiet, tidy, and conveniently positioned 100-bed place between the station and the harborfront. Its rooms, while spartan, are modern and cheery. Prices can rise with demand (dorm bed in 8-bed room-195 kr, in 4-bed room-225 kr, S-495 kr, D-570 kr, extra bed-135 kr, sheets-65 kr one-time fee, towels-15 kr, breakfast voucher-90 kr, free Wi-Fi, elevator, kitchen, laundry, open all year but with limited reception hours, fourth floor at Kong Oscars Gate 45, tel. 55 31 44 04, fax 55 31 60 22, www.marken-gjestehus.com, post@marken-gjestehus.com).

$ Bergen YMCA Hostel, located two blocks from the Fish Market, is the best location for the price, and its rooms are nicely maintained (bunk in 12- to 32-bed dorm with shared shower and kitchen-190 kr, bunk in 4-6-bed family room with private bathroom and kitchen-280-320 kr, Db with kitchen-900 kr, includes sheets, breakfast-65 kr, pay Internet access, free Wi-Fi, roof terrace, fully open June-Aug, no dorm beds off-season, Nedre Korskirkeallmenningen 4, tel. 55 60 60 55, www.bergenhostel.com, booking@bergenhostel.com).

Away from the Center: **$ Montana Family & Youth Hostel (IYHF),** while one of Europe's best, is high-priced for a hostel and way out of town. Still, the bus connections (#31, 20 minutes from the center) and the facilities—modern rooms, classy living room, no curfew, huge free parking lot, and members' kitchen—are

BERGEN

excellent (dorm bed in 20-bed room-215 kr—cheaper off-season, bed in Q-280 kr, Sb-660 kr, Db-830 kr, 10 percent cheaper for members, sheets-70 kr, includes breakfast, 30 Johan Blytts Vei, tel. 55 20 80 70, www.montana.no, bergen.montana@hihostels.no).

Eating in Bergen

Bergen has numerous choices: restaurants with rustic, woody atmosphere, candlelight, and steep prices (main dishes around 300 kr); trendy pubs and cafés that offer good-value meals (100-190 kr); cafeterias, chain restaurants, and ethnic eateries with less ambience where you can get quality food at lower prices (100-150 kr); and take-away sandwich shops, bakeries, and cafés for a light bite (50-100 kr).

You can always get a glass or pitcher of water at no charge, and fancy places give you free seconds on potatoes—just ask. Remember, if you get your food to go, it's taxed at a lower rate and you'll save 12 percent.

Splurges in Bryggen

You'll pay a premium to eat at these three restaurants, but you'll have a memorable meal in a pleasant set-

ting. If they appear to be beyond your budget, remember that you can fill up on potatoes and drink tap water to dine for exactly the price of the dinner plate.

Enhjørningen Restaurant ("The Unicorn") is *the* place in Bergen for fish. With thickly painted walls and no right angles, this dressy-yet-old-time wooden interior wins my "Bryggen Atmosphere" award. The dishes, while not hearty, are close to gourmet and beautifully presented (300-330-kr main dishes, 530-600-kr multi-course meals, nightly 16:00-22:30, #29 on Bryggen harborfront—look for anatomically correct unicorn on the old wharf facade and dip into the alley and up the stairs, tel. 55 30 69 50).

Restaurant To Kokker, down the alley from Enhjørningen (and with the same owners), serves more meat and game. The prices and quality are equivalent, but even though it's also in an elegant old wooden building, I like The Unicorn's atmosphere much better (most main dishes around 350 kr, 600-685-kr multi-course meals, Mon-Sat 17:00-23:00, closed Sun, tel. 55 30 69 55).

Bryggeloftet & Stuene Restaurant, in a brick building just before the wooden stretch of Bryggen, is a vast eatery serving seafood, vegetarian, and traditional meals. To dine memorably yet affordably, this is your best Bryggen bet. Upstairs feels more elegant and less touristy than the main floor—if there's a line downstairs, just head on up (145-165-kr lunches, 200-350-kr dinners, Mon-Sat 11:00-23:30, Sun 13:00-23:30, #11 on Bryggen harborfront, try reserving a view window upstairs, tel. 55 30 20 70).

Deals near Ole Bulls Plass

Bergen's "in" cafés are stylish, cozy, small, and open very late—a great opportunity to experience its yuppie scene. Around the cinema on Neumannsgate, there are numerous ethnic restaurants, including Italian, Middle Eastern, and Chinese.

Pingvinen Pub ("The Penguin") is a homey place in a charming neighborhood, serving traditional Norwegian home cooking to an enthusiastic local clientele. The pub has only indoor seating, with a long row of stools at the bar and five charming, living-room-cozy tables—a great setup for solo diners. After the kitchen closes, the place stays open very late as a pub. For unpretentious Norwegian cooking in a completely untouristy atmosphere, this is one of your best budget choices (140-190-kr main dishes, Sun-Thu 14:00-12:45, Fri-Sat 12:00-20:45, Vaskerelven 14 near the National Theater, tel. 55 60 46 46).

Naboen ("Neighbor") is another good deal, but only if you skip the tableclothed main-floor dining room and go straight downstairs to the popular pub. The bar menu features Swedish specialties for 100-160 kr—the plank steak with potatoes and veggies is a bargain. The draft beers *(Fatøl)* are also relatively inexpensive—for Norway (daily 16:00-23:00 except Sun until 22:00, bar open much later, Sigurdsgate 4, tel. 55 90 02 90).

Zupperia, a café in the basement of the Bergen Art Museum's Stenersen wing, has cool ambience and even cooler prices. The cuisine has a slight Asian twist (the Thai soup is a local favorite), but you can also find burgers, salads, and Norwegian standards (75-150 kr). The 109-kr lasagna special (includes bread and salad) is a steal in this high-price city. If you're not very hungry, you can order off the lunch menu any time of day (Sun-Thu 12:00-22:00, Fri-Sat until 22:30; facing the museum, go to the entrance on the ground level at the right, Nordahl Bruns Gate 9, tel. 55 55 81 14).

Café Opera, with a playful-slacker vibe, is the hip budget choice for its loyal, youthful following. With two floors of seating and tables out front across from the theater, it's a winner (light 30-40-kr sandwiches until 16:00, 100-150-kr dinners, daily 10:00-24:00, occasional live music, live locals nightly, English newspapers in summer, chess, around the left side of the theater at Engen 18, tel. 55 23 03 15).

Dickens is a lively, checkerboard, turn-of-the-century-feeling place serving fish, chicken, and steak. The window tables in the atrium are great for people-watching, as is the fine outdoor terrace, but you'll pay higher prices for the view. To save money, go for lunch and skip the view (150-kr lunches, 250-300-kr dinners, Mon-Sat 11:00-23:00, later on Fri and Sat, Sun 13:00-23:00, reservations smart, Kong Olav V's Plass 4, tel. 55 36 31 30).

Atop Mount Fløyen, at the Top of the Funicular

Fløien Folkerestaurant offers meals with a panoramic view. The cheaper cafeteria section has a light menu, with coffee, cake, and sandwiches for around 60 kr and a 139-kr soup buffet (May-Aug daily 10:00-22:00, Sept-April Sat-Sun only 12:00-17:00). The restaurant section has decent but expensive dinners with an emphasis on locally caught fish for about 300-350 kr (150-200-kr lighter dishes, May-Aug daily 17:00-23:00, restaurant closed Sept-April, tel. 55 33 69 99).

Cafeteria Overlooking the Fish Market

Lido offers basic, affordable food with great harbor and market views, better ambience than most self-serve places, and a museum's worth of old town photos on the walls. For cold items (such as open-face sandwiches and desserts, 50-80 kr), grab what you want, pay the cashier, and find a table. For hot dishes (120-170-kr Norwegian standards, including one daily special discounted to 109 kr), grab a table, order and pay at the cashier, and they'll bring your food to you (June-Aug Mon-Fri 10:00-22:00, Sat-Sun 13:00-22:00; Sept-May Mon-Sat 10:00-19:00, Sun 13:00-19:00; second floor at Torgallmenningen 1a, tel. 55 32 59 12).

Good Chain Restaurants

You'll find these tasty chain restaurants in Bergen and throughout Norway. All of these are open long hours daily (shorter off-season). In good weather, enjoy a take-out meal with sun-worshipping locals in Bergen's parks.

Peppe's Pizza has cold beer and good pizzas (medium size for 1-2 people-175-200 kr, large for 2-3 people-200-250 kr, take-out possible; consider the Moby Dick, with curried shrimp, leeks, and bell peppers). There are six Peppe's in Bergen, including one behind the Hanseatic Museum near the Fløibanen funicular station and another inside the Zachariasbryggen harborfront complex, next to the Fish Market (with views over the harbor).

Baker Brun makes 50-70-kr sandwiches, including wonderful shrimp baguettes and pastries such as *skillingsbolle*—cinnamon rolls—warm out of the oven (open from 9:00, seating inside or take-away; several locations including Bryggen and the Storsenter shopping mall next to the bus station).

Bon Appétit sells 60-kr baguette sandwiches and wraps, plus ice cream (locations include Baneveien 15 and Bryggen). Restaurant desserts run 100 kr; strolling with an ice-cream cone can save plenty.

Deli de Luca is a cut above other take-away joints, adding sushi and calzones to the normal lineup of sandwiches. While a bit more expensive than the others, the variety and quality are appealing (open 24/7; branches in train station and near Ole Bulls Plass at Torggaten 5, branch with indoor seating on corner of Engen and Vaskerelven, tel. 55 23 11 47).

Budget Bets

The **Fish Market** has lots of stalls bursting with salmon sandwiches, fresh shrimp, fish-and-chips, and fish cakes. For a tasty, memorable, and inexpensive Bergen meal, assemble a seafood picnic here (ask for prices first; June-Aug daily 7:00-19:00, less lively on Sun; Sept-May Mon-Sat 7:00-16:00, closed Sun).

Trekroneren, your classic hot-dog stand, sells a wide variety of sausages (various sizes and flavors—including reindeer). The well-described English menu makes it easy to order your choice of artery-clogging guilty pleasures (20-kr tiny weenie, 50-kr medium-size weenie, 75-kr jumbo, open daily 11:00-5:00 in the morning, you'll see the little hot-dog shack a block up Kong Oscar Gate from the harbor, Kenneht is the boss).

Kjøttbasaren, the restored meat market of 1887, is a genteel-feeling food hall with stalls selling groceries such as meat, cheese, bread, and olives—a great opportunity to assemble a bang-up picnic (Mon-Fri 10:00-17:00, Thu until 18:00, Sat 9:00-16:00, closed Sun).

Marken Pedestrian Street Eateries

This cobbled lane, leading from the train station to the harbor, is lined with creative little restaurants and trendy cafés. Strolling along here, you can choose among cheap chicken and burgers, the elegant **Bambus Marken** for Vietnamese (daily 14:00-23:00, seating indoors and out, Marken 33, tel. 55 56 00 60), the **Taste of Indian** (69-kr daily special, daily 13:00-24:00, Marken 12, tel. 55 31 11 55), and the **Aura Café** for classy sandwiches and salads (Mon-Sat until 22:00, Sun until 19:00, indoors and out, Marken 9).

Bergen Connections

Bergen is conveniently connected to **Oslo** by plane and train (trains depart Bergen daily at 7:58, 10:28, 15:58, 16:10, and 22:58—but no night train on Sat, arrive at Oslo seven scenic hours later, additional departures in summer and fall, confirm times at station,

392 Rick Steves' Scandinavia

50-kr seat reservation required—but free with first-class railpass, book well in advance if traveling mid-July-Aug). From Bergen, you can take the Norway in a Nutshell train/bus/ferry route; for information, see the Norway in a Nutshell chapter. Train info: tel. 81 50 08 88, www.nsb.no.

To get to **Stockholm** or **Copenhagen,** you'll go via Oslo (see "Oslo Connections" on page 287). Before buying a ticket for a long train trip from Bergen, look into cheap flights.

By Express Boat to Balestrand and Flåm (on Sognefjord): A handy express boat links Bergen with Balestrand (4 hours) and Flåm (5.5 hours). For details, see page 330.

By Bus to Kristiansand: If you're heading to Denmark on the ferry from Kristiansand, catch the Haukeli express bus (departing Bergen daily at 7:30). After a nearly two-hour layover in Haukeli, take the bus at 14:40, arriving at 18:55 in Kristiansand in time for the evening ferry to Denmark (for boat details, see page 410).

By Boat to Stavanger: Flaggruten catamarans sail to Stavanger (1-2/day, 4.5 hours, 770 kr one-way, 990 kr round-trip; nearly half-price for students and railpass-holders; tel. 55 23 87 00 or 05505, www.tide.no). From Stavanger, trains run to Kristiansand and Oslo, and ships sail to Denmark (for Stavanger's transportation connections, see page 404).

By Boat to Denmark: Fjordline runs a boat from Bergen to Hirtshals, Denmark (17 hours; departs Mon and Wed at 13:00, Fri generally at 11:00; boat from Hirtshals runs Sun, Tue, and Thu; seat in reclining chair-around 1,500 kr, tel. 81 53 35 00, www .fjordline.com).

By Boat to the Arctic: Hurtigruten coastal steamers depart nearly daily (mid-April-mid-Sept at 20:00, mid-Sept-mid-April at 22:30) for the seven-day trip  north up the scenic west coast to Kirkenes on the Russian border. This route was started in 1893 as a postal and cargo delivery service along the west coast of Norway. Although no longer delivering mail, their ships still fly the Norwegian postal flag by special permission and deliver people, cars, and cargo from Bergen to Kirkenes. A lifeline for remote areas, the ships call at 34 fishing villages and cities.

For the seven-day trip to Kirkenes, allow from $1,599 and up per person based on double occupancy (includes three meals per day, taxes, and port charges). Prices vary greatly depending on the season (highest June-July), cabin, and type of ship. Their fleet includes those with a bit of brass built in the 1960s, but the majority of the ships were built in the mid-1990s and later. Shorter voyages are possible (including even just a day trip to one of the villages along the route). Cabins should be booked well in advance. Ship services include a 24-hour cafeteria, a launderette on newer ships, and optional port excursions. Check online for senior and off-season (Oct-March) specials at www.hurtigruten.com.

Call Hurtigruten in New York (US tel. 866-552-0371) or in Norway (tel. 81 00 30 30). For most travelers, the ride makes a great one-way trip, but a flight back south is a logical last leg (rather than returning to Bergen by boat—a 12-day round-trip).

SOUTH NORWAY

Stavanger • Setesdal Valley • Kristiansand

South Norway is not about must-see sights or jaw-dropping scenery—it's simply pleasant and pretty. Spend a day in the harborside town of Stavanger. Delve into your Scandinavian roots at the Norwegian Emigration Center or into the oil industry at the surprisingly interesting Norwegian Petroleum Museum. Window-shop in the old town, cruise the harbor, or hoof it up Pulpit Rock for a fine view.

A series of time-forgotten towns stretch across the Setesdal Valley, with sod-roofed cottages and locals who practice fiddles and harmonicas, rose painting, whittling, and gold- and silver-work. The famous Setesdal filigree echoes the rhythmical designs of the Viking era and Middle Ages. Each town has a weekly rotating series of hikes and activities for the regular, stay-put-for-a-week visitor. The upper valley is dead in the summer but enjoys a bustling winter.

In Kristiansand, Norway's answer to a seaside resort, promenade along the strand, sample a Scandinavian zoo, or set sail to Denmark.

Planning Your Time

Even on a busy itinerary, Stavanger warrants a day. If you are an avid genealogist, consider two. The port town is connected by boat to Bergen (and Hirtshals, Denmark) and by train to Kristiansand.

Frankly, without a car, the Setesdal Valley is not worth the trouble. There are no trains in the valley, bus schedules are as sparse as the population, and the sights are best for joyriding. If you're in Bergen with a car, and want to get to Denmark, this route is more interesting than repeating Oslo. On a three-week Scandinavian trip, I'd do it in one long day, as follows: 7:00—Leave Bergen; 9:00—Catch Kvanndal ferry to Utne; 10:00—Say good-bye to the last fjord at Odda; 13:00—Lunch in Hovden at the top of Setesdal Valley; 14:00—Frolic south with a few short stops in the valley; 16:30—Arrive in Kristiansand for dinner. Spend the night and catch the 9:00 boat to Denmark the next morning.

Kristiansand is not a destination town, but rather a place to pass through, conveniently connecting Norway to Denmark by ferry.

Stavanger

This burg of about 117,000 is a mildly charming (if unspectacular) waterfront city whose streets are lined with unpretentious shiplap cottages that echo its perennial ties to the sea. Stavanger feels more cosmopolitan than most small Norwegian cities, thanks in part to its oil industry—which brings multinational workers (and their money) into the city. Known as Norway's festival city, Stavanger hosts several lively events, including jazz in May (www.maijazz .no), Scandinavia's biggest food festival in July (www.gladmat.no), and chamber music in August (www.icmf.no). With all of this culture, it's no surprise that Stavanger was named a European Capital of Culture for 2008.

From a sightseeing perspective, Stavanger barely has enough to fill a day: The Norwegian Petroleum Museum is the only big-time sight in town, while the Norwegian Emigration Center thrills only those with family ties here. The city's fine cathedral is worth a peek, but beyond those options, the chief activity is dodging the thousands of cruise passengers routinely dumped here throughout the summer season. For most visitors, the main reason to come to Stavanger is to use it as a launch pad for side-tripping to Lysefjord and/or the famous, iconic Pulpit Rock: an eerily flat-topped peak thrusting up from the fjord, offering perfect, point-blank views deep into the Lysefjord.

Orientation to Stavanger

The most scenic and interesting parts of Stavanger surround its harbor. Here you'll find the Norwegian Emigration Center, lots of shops and restaurants (particularly around the market plaza and along Kirkegata, which connects the cathedral to the Petroleum Museum), the indoor fish market, and a produce market (Mon-Fri 9:00-16:00, Sat 9:00-15:00, closed Sun). The artificial Lake Breiavatnet—bordered by Kongsgaten on the east and Olav V's

SOUTH NORWAY

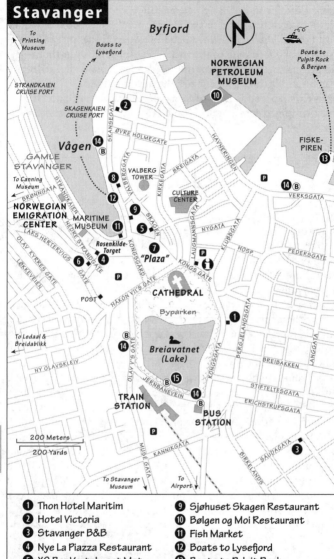

Stavanger

Byfjord

To Printing Museum

Boats to Lysefjord

STRANDKAIEN CRUISE PORT

SKAGENKAIEN CRUISE PORT

NORWEGIAN PETROLEUM MUSEUM

Boats to Pulpit Rock & Bergen

Vågen

GAMLE STAVANGER

To Canning Museum

NORWEGIAN EMIGRATION CENTER

MARITIME MUSEUM

Rosenkilde-Torget

"Plaza"

VALBERG TOWER

CULTURE CENTER

FISKE-PIREN

CATHEDRAL

POST

Byparken

To Ledaal & Breidablikk

Breiavatnet (Lake)

TRAIN STATION

BUS STATION

To Stavanger Museum

To Airport

200 Meters
200 Yards

SOUTH NORWAY

1 Thon Hotel Maritim
2 Hotel Victoria
3 Stavanger B&B
4 Nye La Piazza Restaurant
5 XO Bar Vertshuset Mat & Vin Restaurant
6 Meny Supermarket
7 Market Plaza Eateries
8 N. B. Sorensen's Dampskibsexpedition Pub & Restaurant

9 Sjøhuset Skagen Restaurant
10 Bølgen og Moi Restaurant
11 Fish Market
12 Boats to Lysefjord
13 Boats to Pulpit Rock & Bergen
14 Flybussen Stops (4)
15 Bus to Fjordline Terminal (Ferries to Hirtshals, Denmark)

Gate on the west—separates the train and bus stations from the harbor.

Tourist Information

The helpful staff at the TI can help you plan your time in Stavanger, and can also give you hiking tips and day trip information. Pick up a free city guide and map (June-Aug daily 9:00-20:00; Sept-May Mon-Fri 9:00-16:00, Sat 9:00-14:00, closed Sun; Domkirkeplassen 3, tel. 51 85 92 00, www.regionstavanger.com).

Arrival in Stavanger

By Boat: Express boats from Bergen dock at Fiskepiren, just east of the city-center peninsula and near the Petroleum Museum. From here, it's about a 10-minute walk to the center of town (turn right onto the busy road, Verksgata, then left on Klubbgata straight to the cathedral) or to the train station. A taxi to a downtown hotel costs about 100 kr (tel. 51 90 90 90 or 51 90 90 50). The more central Vågen harbor is used only by cruise ships and excursion boats to Lysefjord.

By Cruise Ship: Conveniently, cruise liners dock right at the Vågen harbor in the very center of town. Some tie up on the west side of the harbor (called **Strandkaien**), and others put in along the east side (called **Skagenkaien**)—but both are an easy five- to fifteen-minute walk to the central market plaza (depending on how far out the ship is docked).

By Train and Bus: Stavanger's train and bus stations are a five-minute walk around Lake Breiavatnet to the inner harbor, cathedral, and TI (train ticket and reservation office Mon-Fri 7:00-17:30, Sat 9:00-16:30, Sun 10:00-16:15). Luggage lockers and Norway-wide train timetables are available at the train station.

By Plane: Stavanger's Sola Airport is about nine miles outside the city (airport code: SVG, tel. 67 03 10 00, www.avinor.no). It's connected to downtown by the Flybussen (100 kr, buy ticket on bus, Mon-Fri 7:45-24:15, 3-4/hour, less Sat-Sun, 30 minutes, tel. 51 59 90 60, www.flybussen.no). This airport bus shuttles travelers to the bus station (Byterminalen) and train station (next to each other), the Atlantic Hotel near the city center, and the boat terminal (Fiskepiren). To get to the airport from the city center, catch the shuttle at any of these stops.

Sights in Stavanger

▲**Stavanger Cathedral (Domkirke)**—While it's hardly the most impressive cathedral in Scandinavia, Stavanger's top church—which overlooks the town center on a small ridge—has a harmonious interior and a few intriguing details worth lingering

SOUTH NORWAY

over. Good English information throughout the church brings meaning to the place.

Cost and Hours: 30 kr, free weekdays after 16:00, open May-mid-Sept Mon-Fri 8:30-14:00 & 16:00-19:00, Sat 9:00-13:00, Sun 13:00-19:00, free and open shorter hours off-season, tel. 51 84 04 00, www.kirken.stavanger.no.

Visiting the Church: St. Swithun's Cathedral (its official name) was originally built in 1125 in a Norman style, with basket-handle Romanesque arches. After a fire badly damaged the church in the 13th century, a new chancel was added in the pointy-arched Gothic style. You can't miss where the architecture changes about three-quarters of the way up the aisle. On the left, behind the baptismal font, notice the ivy-lined railing on the stone staircase; this pattern is part of the city's coat of arms. And nearby, appreciate the colorful, richly detailed "gristle Baroque"-style pulpit (from 1658). Notice that the whole thing is resting on Samson's stoic shoulders—even as he faces down a lion.

Stroll the church, perusing its several fine "epitaphs" (tomb markers), which are paintings in ornately decorated frames. Go on a scavenger hunt for two unique features; both are on the second columns from the back of the church. On the right, at the top facing away from the nave, notice the stone carvings of Norse mythological figures: Odin on the left, and a wolf-like beast on the right. Although the medieval Norwegians were Christians, they weren't ready to entirely abandon all of their pagan traditions. On the opposite column, circle around the base and look at ankle level, facing away from the altar. Here you see a grotesque sculpture that looks like a fish head with human hands. Notice that its head has been worn down. One interpretation is that early worshippers would ritualistically put their foot on top of it, as if to push the evil back to the underworld. Mysteriously, both of these features are one-offs—you won't find anything like them on any other column in the church.

▲▲Norwegian Petroleum Museum (Norsk Oljemuseum)—

This entertaining, informative museum—dedicated to the discovery of oil in Norway's North Sea in 1969 and the industry built

up around it—offers an unapologetic look at the country's biggest moneymaker. With half of Western Europe's oil reserves, Norway is the Arabia of the North. Since the discovery of oil here in 1969, the formerly poor agricultural nation has been transformed into a world-class player. It's ranked third among the world's top oil exporters, producing 1.6 million barrels a day.

Cost and Hours: 100 kr; June-Aug daily 10:00-19:00; Sept-May Mon-Sat 10:00-16:00, Sun 10:00-18:00; tel. 51 93 93 00, www.norskolje.museum.no. The small museum shop sells various petroleum-based products. The museum's Bølgen og Moi restaurant, which has an inviting terrace over the water, serves lunch and dinner (see listing under "Eating in Stavanger," later).

Visiting the Museum: The exhibit describes how oil was formed, how it's found and produced, and what it's used for. You'll see models of oil rigs, actual drill bits, see-through cylinders that you can rotate to investigate different types of crude, and lots of explanations (in English) about various aspects of oil. Interactive exhibits cover everything from the "History of the Earth" (4.5 billion years displayed on a large overhead globe, showing how our planet has changed—stay for the blast that killed the dinosaurs), to day-to-day life on an offshore platform, to petroleum products in our lives (though the peanut-butter-and-petroleum-jelly sandwich is a bit much). Kids enjoy climbing on the model drilling platform, trying out the emergency escape chute at the platform outside, and playing with many other hands-on exhibits.

Several included movies delve into specific aspects of oil: The kid-oriented "Petropolis" 3-D film is primitive but entertaining and informative, tracing the story of oil from creation to extraction. Other movies (in the cylindrical structures outside) highlight intrepid North Sea divers and the construction of an oil platform. Each film is 12 minutes long, and runs in English at least twice hourly.

Even the museum's architecture was designed to echo the foundations of the oil industry—bedrock (the stone building), slate and chalk deposits in the sea (slate floor of the main hall), and the rigs (cylindrical platforms). While the museum has its fair share of propaganda, it also has several good exhibits on the environmental toll of drilling and consuming oil.

Norwegian Emigration Center (Det Norske Utvandrersenteret Ble)—This fine facility, in an old warehouse near the wharf where the first boats sailed with emigrants to "Amerika" in 1825, is worth ▲▲▲ for anyone seeking his or her Norwegian roots.

Cost and Hours: Library—free, museum—20 kr, Mon-Fri 9:00-15:00, closed Sat-Sun, Strandkaien 31, enter through the door just to the left of the tacky souvenir shop, tel. 51 53 88 60, www.emigrationcenter.com.

Visiting the Center: On the first floor up, the modest but nicely presented **People on the Move exhibit** traces the Norwegian emigrant experience. It tells the story of the first emigrants who left for America—why they left, the journey, and what life was like in the New World. You'll learn how the Norwegian population boom in the early to mid-19th century (from 882,000 people in 1810, to 1.7 m‌‍ ‌‍n in 1865) led to a critical shortage of basic resources. Whil‌ ‍ 78,000 Norwegians emigrated before 1865, the number le‌ 677,000 in the steamship era (1865-1915). Once in Nort‌ ca, Norwegians (unique among immigrant groups) tende‌ ‍ in rural farmlands rather than cities.

On the se‌ ‍r, you'll find a **study center and library.** It's free to use the‌ ers, microfilm viewers, and historic record books to look ‌ elatives. The staff can help answer questions and steer you ‌ ‍ght direction at no charge, or you can pay them to do a st‌ tep consultation (see next).

Researchi‌ r Roots: The Emigration Center is a great resource for tho‌ ping to trace their ancestors' trail from the Old Country. B‌ to get the most out of the experience, do some homework ahead of time. Many of the resources used by the center are digitized and available free online. Most helpful is the official national archive at www.arkivverket.no/digitalarkivet (free, English menus); the center also uses www.ancestry.com (fee) and www.norwayheritage.com (most useful for earlier emigrations). See what you can find on these sites, then use the center to fill in the rest. Their library has many resources not available online; it's lined with shelves of *bygdebøker*—books from farm districts all over Norway, documenting the history of landowners and local families. When looking up relatives, it helps to know at least two or three of the following: family surname, farm name, birth year, and emigration year. (If your family records show two different surnames for the same person, it's likely the one ending in -son or -sen is the surname, and the other one is the farm name.)

Or you can pay them to do all the work for you. They charge 500 kr per hour of research time, and estimate that most cases take about two hours of work. If you'd like to do this, it's smart to contact them before your trip to let them know you're coming. You can fill out the form on their website and pay by credit card. You don't need to actually be in Stavanger to use this service, but searching for your roots in the place where your ancestors likely took their last steps on Norwegian soil has a certain romantic appeal.

Gamle Stavanger—Stavanger's "old town" centers on Øvre Strandgate, on the west side of the harbor. Wander the narrow, winding, cobbled back lanes, with tidy wooden houses, oasis gardens, and flower-bedecked entranceways. Peek into a workshop or gallery to find ceramics, glass, jewelry, and more. Many shops are open roughly daily 10:00-17:00, coinciding with the arrival of cruise ships (which loom ominously right next to this otherwise tranquil zone).

Museum Stavanger (M.U.S.T.)—This "museum" is actually 10 different museums scattered around town. The various branches include the **Stavanger Museum,** featuring the history of the city and a zoological exhibit (Muségate 16); the **Maritime Museum** (Sjøfartsmuseum), right next to the cruise dock on Strandkaien (Nedre Strandgate 17-19); the **Norwegian Canning Museum** (Norsk Hermetikkmuseum; the *brisling*—herring—is smoked mid-June-mid-Aug Tue and Thu, Øvre Strandgate 88A); the **Printing Museum** (24 Sandvigå); **Ledaal,** a royal residence and manor house (Eiganesveien 45); and **Breidablikk,** a wooden villa from the late 1800s (Eiganesveien 40A).

Cost: You can buy one 100-kr ticket to cover all of them, or you can pay 60 kr for any individual museum (if doing at least two, the combo-ticket is obviously the better value). Note that a single 60-kr ticket gets you into the Maritime Museum, Canning Museum, and Printing Museum, which are a three-for-one sight. You can get details and buy tickets at any of the museums; handiest is the Maritime Museum right along the harbor.

Hours: Museum hours vary but generally open mid-June-mid-Aug daily 10:00 or 11:00-16:00; off-season Tue-Sun 11:00-16:00, closed Mon, except Ledaal, Breidablikk, and Printing Museum—these are open Sun only in winter; www.museum stavanger.no.

Day Trips to Lysefjord and Pulpit Rock

The nearby Lysefjord is an easy day trip. Those with more time (and strong legs) can hike to the top of the 1,800-foot-high Pulpit Rock (Preikestolen). The dramatic 270-square-foot plateau atop the rock gives you a fantastic view of the fjord and surrounding mountains. The TI has brochures for several boat tour companies and sells tickets.

Boat Tour of Lysefjord—**Rødne Clipper Fjord Sightseeing** offers three-hour round-trip excursions from Stavanger to Lysefjord (including a view of Pulpit Rock—but no stops). Conveniently, their boats depart from the main Vågen harbor in the heart of town (east side of the harbor, in front of Skansegata, along Skagenkaien; 400 kr; July-Aug daily at 10:00 and 14:00, Thu-Sat also at 12:00; June daily at 10:00 and 14:00; May and Sept daily at 12:00; Oct-April Wed-Sun only at 12:00; tel. 51 89 52 70, www.rodne.no). A different company, **Norled,** also runs similar trips, as well as slower journeys up the Lysefjord on a "tourist car ferry" (www.norled.no).

Ferry and Bus to Pulpit Rock—Hiking up to the top of Pulpit Rock is a popular outing that will take the better part of a day; plan on at least four hours of hiking (two hours up, two hours down), plus time to linger at the top for photos, plus round-trip travel from Stavanger (about an hour each way by a ferry-and-bus combination)—eight hours minimum should do it. The trailhead is easily reached in summer by public transit or tour package. Then comes the hard part: the hike to the top. The total distance is 4.5 miles and the elevation gain is roughly 1,000 feet. Pack a lunch and plenty of water, and wear good shoes.

Two different companies sell ferry-and-bus packages to the trailhead from Stavanger. Ferries leave from the Fiskepiren boat terminal to Tau; buses meet the incoming ferries and head to Pulpit Rock cabin or to Preikestolen Fjellstue, the local youth hostel. Be sure to time your hike so that you can catch the last bus leaving Pulpit Rock cabin for the ferry (confirm time when booking your ticket). These trips generally go daily from mid-May through mid-September; weekends only in April, early May, and late September; and not at all from October to March (when the ferry stops running). As the details tend to change from year to year, confirm all schedule details with the TI or the individual companies: **Tide Reiser** (240 kr, best options for an all-day round-trip are departures at 8:00 or 9:30, last return bus from trailhead to ferry leaves at 18:15, mobile 97 04 74 19, www.tidereiser.com) and **Boreal** (140 kr for the bus plus 88 kr for the ferry—you'll buy the ferry ticket separately, best options depart at 8:30 or 9:00, last return bus from trailhead to ferry leaves at 19:55, tel. 51 74 02 40, www.pulpitrock.no).

Rødne Clipper Fjord Sightseeing (listed earlier) may run a handy trip in July and August that begins with a scenic Lysefjord cruise, then drops you off at Oarnes to catch the bus to the Pulpit Rock hut trailhead; afterwards, you can catch the bus to Tau for the ferry return to Stavanger. It's similar to the options described above, but adds a scenic fjord cruise at the start. To confirm this is still going and get details, contact Rødne (650 kr plus 44 kr for return ferry to Stavanger, tel. 51 89 52 70, www.rodne.no).

Sleeping in Stavanger

$$$ Thon Hotel Maritim, with 177 rooms, is two blocks from the train station near the artificial Lake Breiavatnet. It can be a good deal for a big-business class hotel (flexible rates: Db-1,850-2,225 kr on weekdays, likely 1,095 on weekends, almost as cheap in July, Sb is always 200 kr less, elevator, free Wi-Fi, Kongsgaten 32, tel. 51 85 05 00, fax 51 85 05 01, www.thonhotels.no/maritim, maritim@thon hotels.no).

$$$ Hotel Victoria has 107 business-class rooms over a stately, high-ceilinged lobby facing the Skagenkaien embankment right on the harbor (in summer and weekends: Sb-890 kr, Db-1,140

Sleep Code

(6 kr = about $1, country code: 47)

S = Single, **D** = Double/Twin, **T** = Triple, **Q** = Quad, **b** = bathroom,
s = shower. You can assume that staff speak English, break-
fast is included, and credit cards are accepted unless otherwise noted.

To help you sort easily through these listings, I've divided
the accommodations into three categories, based on the price
for a standard double room with bath during high season:

$$$ Higher Priced—Most rooms 1,000 kr or more.

$$ Moderately Priced—Most rooms between 600-1,000 kr.

$ Lower Priced—Most rooms 600 kr or less.

Prices can change without notice; verify the hotel's
current rates online or by email.

---

kr; weekdays outside of summer: Sb-1,790 kr, Db-2,060 kr; elevator, free Wi-Fi, Skansegata 1, tel. 51 86 70 00, www.victoria
-hotel.no, victoria@victoria-hotel.no).

$$ Stavanger B&B is Stavanger's best budget option. This
large red house among a sea of white houses has tidy, tiny rooms.
The lodgings are basic, verging on institutional—not cozy or
doily—but they're affordable and friendly. The shared toilet is
down the hall; 13 rooms have their own showers, while eight share
showers on the hall. Waffles, coffee, and friendly chatter are served
up every evening at 21:00 (Ss-790 kr, Ds-890 kr, Ts-990 kr, 100 kr
less per room for shared shower, extra bed-150 kr, free Internet
access and Wi-Fi, 10-minute uphill walk behind train station in
residential neighborhood, Vikedalsgate 1A, tel. 51 56 25 00, fax 51
56 25 01, www.stavangerbedandbreakfast.no, post@sbb.no). If you
let them know in advance, they may be able to pick you up or drop
you off at the boat dock or train station.

Eating in Stavanger

Casual Dining

Nye La Piazza, just off the harbor, has an assortment of pasta and
other Italian dishes, including pizza, for 145-200 kr (100-kr lunch
special, 275-320-kr meat options, Mon 13:00-24:00, Tue-Sat 12:00-
24:00, Sun 12:00-22:00, Rosenkildettorget 1, tel. 51 52 02 52).

XO Bar Vertshuset Mat & Vin, in an elegant setting, serves
up big portions of traditional Norwegian food and pricier contem-
porary fare (280-350 kr, light meals-180-190 kr, open daily 11:00-
22:30, a block behind main drag along harbor at Skagen 10 ved

SOUTH NORWAY

Prostbakken, tel. 51 89 51 12).

Meny is a large supermarket with a good selection and a fine deli for super-picnic shopping (Mon-Fri 9:00-20:00, Sat until 18:00, closed Sun, in Straen Senteret shopping mall, Lars Hertervigs Gate 6, tel. 51 50 50 10).

Market Plaza Eateries: The busy square between the cathedral and the harbor is packed with reliable Norwegian chain restaurants. If you're a fan of **Deli de Luca, Peppe's Pizza,** or **Dickens Pub,** you'll find all of them within a few steps of here.

Dining Along the Harbor with a View

The harborside street of Skansegata is lined with lively restaurants and pubs, and most serve food. Here are a couple options:

N. B. Sorensen's Dampskibsexpedition consists of a lively pub on the first floor (245-365 kr for pasta, fish, meat, and vegetarian dishes; Mon-Sat 11:00-24:00, Sun 13:00-24:00) and a fine-dining restaurant on the second floor, with tablecloths, view tables overlooking the harbor, and entrées from 300 kr (Mon-Sat 18:00-23:00, closed Sun, Skagenkaien 26, tel. 51 84 38 20). The restaurant is named after an 1800s company that shipped from this building, among other things, Norwegians heading to the US. Passengers and cargo waited on the first floor, and the manager's office was upstairs. The place is filled with emigrant-era memorabilia.

Sjøhuset Skagen, with a woodsy interior, invites diners to its historic building for lunch or dinner. The building, from the late 1700s, housed a trading company. Today, you can choose from local seafood specialties with an ethnic flair, as well as plenty of meat options (160-180-kr lunches, 230-390-kr dinners, Mon-Sat 11:30-23:00, Sun 13:00-21:30, Skagenkaien 16, tel. 51 89 51 80).

Bølgen og Moi, the restaurant at the Petroleum Museum, has fantastic views over the harbor (lunch: 170-kr lunch special, 150-200-kr main dishes, served daily 11:00-17:00; dinner: 250-kr main dishes, 500 kr three-course meal, served Tue-Sat 18:00-24:00—reservations recommended; Kjeringholmen 748, tel. 51 93 93 53).

Stavanger Connections

From Stavanger by Train to: Kristiansand (4-7/day, 3.5 hours), **Oslo** (4/day, 8-8.5 hours, overnight possible).

By Boat to Bergen: Flaggruten catamarans sail between Bergen and Stavanger (1-2/day, 4.5 hours, 770 kr one-way, 990 kr round-trip; nearly half-price for students and railpass-holders; tel. 55 23 87 00, www.tide.no).

By Boat to Hirtshals, Denmark: For details on this boat, see the "Sailing Between Norway and Denmark" sidebar.

The Setesdal Valley

Welcome to the remote, and therefore very traditional, Setesdal Valley. Probably Norway's most authentic cranny, the valley is a

mellow montage of sod-roofed water mills, ancient churches, derelict farmhouses, yellowed recipes, and gentle scenery.

The Setesdal Valley joined the modern age with the construction of the valley highway in the 1950s. All along the valley you'll see the unique two-story storage sheds called *stabburs* (the top floor was used for storing clothes; the bottom, food) and many sod roofs. Even the bus stops have rooftops the local goats love to munch.

In the high country, just over the Sessvatn summit (3,000 feet), you'll see herds of goats and summer farms. If you see an *ekte geitost* sign, that means genuine, homemade goat cheese is for sale. (It's sold cheaper and in more manageable sizes in grocery stores.) To some, it looks like a decade's accumulation of earwax. I think it's delicious. Remember, *ekte* means all-goat—really strong. The more popular and easier-to-eat version is a mix of cow and goat cheese.

For more information on the Setesdal Valley, see www.setesdal.com.

From Odda to Hovden

Attractions from here to Kristiansand are listed roughly from north to south.

Odda—At the end of the Hardanger Fjord, just past the huge zinc and copper industrial plant, you'll hit the industrial town of Odda (well-stocked **TI** for whole region and beyond; in summer Mon-Fri 9:00-19:00, Sat-Sun 11:00-17:00; off-season Mon-Fri 9:00-15:00, closed Sat-Sun; on market square at Torget 2-4, tel. 53 65 40 05, www.visitodda.com). Odda brags that Kaiser Wilhelm came here a lot, but he's dead and I'd drive right through. If you want to visit the tongue of a glacier, drive to Buar and hike an hour to Buarbreen. From Odda, drive into the land of boulders. The many mighty waterfalls that line the road seem to have hurled huge rocks (with rooted trees) into the rivers and fields. Stop at the giant double waterfall (on the left, pullout on the right, drive slowly through it if you need a car wash).

Setesdal Valley

SOUTH NORWAY

Røldal—Continue over Røldalsfjellet and into the valley below, where the old town of Røldal is trying to develop some tourism. Drive on by. Its old church isn't worth the time or money. Lakes are like frosted mirrors, making desolate huts come in pairs. Haukeliseter, a group of sod-roofed buildings filled with cultural clichés and tour groups, offers pastries, sandwiches, and reasonable hot meals (from 100 kr) in a lakeside setting. Try the traditional *rømmegrøt* porridge.

Haukeligrend—Haukeligrend is a bus/traffic junction, with daily bus service to/from Bergen and to/from Kristiansand (TI inside the café, open daily all year 10:00-19:00, brochures available all the time, TI staff available periodically, Internet access, tel. 35 07 03 67).

Hovden

A ski resort at the top of the Setesdal Valley (2,500 feet), Hovden is barren in the summer and painfully in need of charm. Still, it makes a good home base if you want to explore the area for a couple of days. Locals come here to walk and relax for a week.

Tourist Information: The TI is open all year (Mon-Fri 9:00-16:00, summer Sat 10:00-15:00, July also Sun 10:00-15:00, otherwise closed Sat-Sun, tel. 37 93 93 70, www.hovden.com, post @hovden.com).

Sights and Activities in Hovden

Boat Rental—Hegni Center, on the lake at the south edge of town, rents rowboats, canoes, and kayaks (240-350 kr/day, 140-200 kr/half-day, hourly rentals also possible, cash only, mid-June-mid-Aug daily 10:00-20:00, mid-Aug-mid-Sept daily 11:00-18:00, mid-Sept-mid-Oct Sat-Sun only 11:00-16:00, closed mid-Oct-mid-June, tel. 37 93 93 70).

Hikes and Mountain Biking near Hovden—Good walks offer you a chance to see reindeer, moose, arctic fox, and wabbits—so they say. The TI and most hotels stock brochures, maps, and other information about moderate to strenuous hikes in the area as well as biking options. Berry picking is popular in late August, when small, sweet blueberries are in season. A chairlift sometimes takes sightseers to the top of a nearby peak, with great views in clear weather. Bikers can ride the trails downhill (90 kr, 100 kr to bring a bike, June-July daily 11:00-14:00, Aug-mid-Oct Wed and Sat-Sun only). Hunting season starts in late August for reindeer (only in higher elevations) and later in the fall for grouse and moose.

Moose Safari—Per Johanson offers a 2.5-hour *Elg Safari* (that's Norwegian for "moose"). Learn more about this "king of the forest" during a late-night drive through Setesdal's back roads with a stop for moose-meat soup (370 kr, June-Aug only; generally Tue, Fri, and Sun at 22:00—other days on request; 50 percent money-back guarantee if you don't see a moose, tel. 37 93 93 70, post @hovden.com).

Museum of Iron Production (Jernvinnemuseum)—Learn about iron production from the late Iron Age (about 1,000 years ago) with the aid of drawings, exhibits, and recorded narration from a "Viking" (available in English). The museum is about 100 yards behind the Hegni Center (look for the sign from the road to *Jernvinnemuseum*).

Cost and Hours: Free, mid-June-mid-Aug daily 11:00-17:00, otherwise ask for the key at the TI or Hegni Center.

Swimming Pool—A super indoor spa/pool complex, the Hovden Badeland, provides a much-needed way to spend an otherwise dreary and drizzly early evening here.

Cost and Hours: 135-150 kr for 3 hours or more, cheaper for shorter visits, daily 10:00-19:00 in summer, shorter hours off-season, tel. 37 93 93 93, www.badeland.com.

Sleeping and Eating in Hovden

$$ Hovden Fjellstoge is a big, old ski chalet renting Hovden's only cheap beds. Even if you're just passing through, their café is a good choice for lunch or an early dinner. Check out the mural in the balcony overlooking the lobby—an artistic rendition of this area's history. Behind the mural is a frightening taxidermy collection (hotel: Sb-750 kr, bunk-bed Db-990 kr, includes breakfast; cabins: from 650 kr for 2-4 people with bathroom and kitchen; dorms: dorm bed-200 kr, D-500 kr, 25 kr extra if you're not a hostel member, breakfast-70 kr, sheets-100 kr, towel-20 kr; tel. 37 93 95 43, www.hovdenfjellstoge.no, post@hovdenfjellstoge.no).

From Hovden to Kristiansand

▲**Dammar Vatnedalsvatn**—Nine miles south of Hovden is a two-mile side-trip to a 400-foot-high rock-pile dam (look for the *Dammar* signs). Enjoy the great view and impressive rockery. This is one of the highest dams in northern Europe. Read the chart. Sit out of the wind a few rows down the rock pile and ponder the vastness of Norwegian wood.

▲**Bykle**—The most interesting folk museum and church in Setesdal are in the teeny town of Bykle. The 17th-century church has two balconies—one for men and one for women (free, late June-mid-Aug daily 11:00-17:00, closed off-season; tel. 37 93 85 00, www.setesdalsmuseet.no). Drivers should note that the Bykle tollbooth accepts only exact change.

Grasbrokke—On the east side of the main road (at the *Grasbrokke* sign) is an old water mill (1630). A few minutes farther south, at the sign for *Sanden Såre Camping*, exit onto a little road to stretch your legs at another old water mill with a fragile, rotten-log sluice.

Flateland—The **Setesdal Museum** (Rygnestadtunet) offers more of what you saw at Bykle (30 kr, two buildings; late June-Aug daily 11:00-17:00; closed off-season; 1 mile east of the road, tel. 37 93 63 03, www.setesdalsmuseet.no). Unless you're a glutton for culture, I wouldn't do both.

Honneevje—Past Flateland is a nice picnic and WC stop, with a dock along the water for swimming...for hot-weather days or polar bears.

▲**Valle**—This is Setesdal's prettiest village (but don't tell Bykle). In the center, you'll find fine silver- and gold-work, homemade crafts next to the TI, and old-fashioned *lefse* cooking demonstrations (in the small log house by the Valle Motell). The fine suspension bridge attracts kids of any age (b-b-b-b-bounce), and anyone interested in a great view over the river to strange mountains that look like polished, petrified mudslides. European rock climbers, tired of the over-climbed Alps, often entertain spectators with their sport. Is anyone climbing? (TI tel. 37 93 75 27.)

Sleeping in Valle: **$$ Valle Motell** rents basic rooms (Sb-625 kr, Db-790 kr, includes breakfast, cabins with kitchen and bath but no breakfast-725-875 kr, tel. 37 93 77 00, www.valle-motell.no, post@valle-motell.no).

Nomeland—The Sylvartun silversmith shop sells Setesdal silver in a 17th-century log cabin (May-Sept daily 10:00-17:00, closed Oct-April, tel. 37 93 63 06).

Grendi—The Ardal Church (1827) has a rune stone in its yard. Three hundred yards south of the church is a 900-year-old oak tree.

Evje—A huge town by Setesdal standards (3,500 people), Evje is famous for its gems and mines. Fancy stones fill the shops here. Rock hounds find the nearby mines fun; for a small fee, you can hunt for gems. The TI is by Route 9 in the center of Evje (daily 10:00-15:00; tel. 37 93 14 00). The **Setesdal Mineral Park** is on the main road, two miles south of town (110 kr; July-mid-Aug daily 10:00-18:00, mid-Aug-mid-Oct Mon-Sat 10:00-16:00, Sun 10:00-17:00; May-June Mon-Sat 10:00-16:00, Sun 10:00-17:00, closed mid-Oct-April; tel. 37 93 13 10, www.mineralparken.no).

Kristiansand

This "capital of the south" has 80,000 inhabitants, a pleasant Renaissance grid-plan layout (Posebyen), a famous zoo with Norway's biggest amusement park (6 miles toward Oslo on the main road), a daily bus to Bergen, and lots of big boats going to Denmark. It's the closest thing to a beach resort in Norway. Markensgate is the bustling pedestrian market street—a pleasant place for good browsing, shopping, eating, and people-watching. Stroll along the Strand Promenaden (marina) to Christiansholm Fortress.

Orientation to Kristiansand

The TI is at Rådhusgata 6, a few blocks from the boat, bus, and train station (mid-June-mid-Aug Mon-Fri 9:00-18:00, Sat 10:00-18:00, Sun 12:00-16:00; mid-Aug-mid-June Mon-Fri 9:00-16:00, closed Sat-Sun; tel. 38 12 13 14, www.visitkrs.no). The bank at the Color Line terminal opens for each arrival and departure (even the midnight ones). The Fønix Kino cinema complex is within two blocks of the ferry and TI (70-100 kr, seven screens, movies shown in English, schedules at the entrance, tel. 38 10 42 00).

Sailing Between Norway and Denmark

Two companies sail between the tips of Norway and Denmark. **Color Line** and **Fjordline** sail fast boats between Kristiansand, Norway, and Hirtshals, Denmark (2.25-3.25 hours). In addition, Fjordline boats connect Stavanger, Norway, and Hirtshals (11.5 hours, covered below). They also link Bergen with Hirtshals, though at 19.5 hours, it's a long haul. (For information on an Oslo-Copenhagen cruise—run by a different company—see page 289.)

Both Color Line and Fjordline offer car packages (covering up to 5 people and the car) and have various on-board amenities such as restaurants, coffee bars, duty-free shops, and several classes of travel. I've listed prices in euros, as they appear on the companies' websites.

Sailing Between Kristiansand and Hirtshals, Denmark: Color Line ships generally sail twice daily, all year, with a few more sailings added during summer, but mysteriously they sail only once a day in mid-April. Sailing from Norway to Denmark, Color Line boats usually leave Kristiansand at 8:00 and 16:30, arriving in Hirtshals at 11:15 and 19:45. Going from Denmark to Norway, the boats leave Hirtshals at 12:15 and 20:45, arriving in Kristiansand at 15:30 and midnight. Fares vary with day of week and season (cheaper weekdays and off-season). During the summer, one-way passenger fares start at €20/person mid-week, €40/person on weekends; car packages start at €77 mid-week and €102 on weekends.

Fjordline's seasonal ferry makes the crossing two times a day from late June to mid-August in a speedy 2.25 hours. The schedule is cut back in late spring and early fall, with no ferries from September to mid-May. In high season, sailing from Norway to Denmark, Fjordline boats leave Kristiansand at 8:30

Sleeping and Eating in Kristiansand

(6 kr = about $1, country code: 47)
Kristiansand hotels are expensive and nondescript. The otherwise uninteresting harbor area has a cluster of wooden buildings called **Fiskebasaren** ("Fish Bazaar"). The indoor fish market is only open during the day, but numerous restaurants (serving fish, among other dishes) provide a nice atmosphere for dinner. Follow Vester Strandgate past the Fønix movie theater to Østre Strandgate, take a right, and follow the signs to Fiskebrygga.

and 15:00, arriving in Hirtshals at 10:45 and 17:15. Going from Denmark to Norway, the boats leave Hirtshals at 11:45 and 18:00, arriving in Kristiansand at 14:00 and 20:15. One-way passenger fares start at €21/person mid-week; car packages start at €55 mid-week.

Sailing Between Stavanger and Hirtshals, Denmark: Fjordline ships sailing from Norway to Denmark travel overnight, which can save you the cost of a hotel. Enjoy an evening in Stavanger, then sleep (or vomit) as you sail to Denmark. The boat generally sails four times a week (usually Mon, Wed, Fri, and Sat; departing Stavanger at either 19:00 or 21:00; arriving in Hirtshals at either 7:00 or 9:00 the next day). Ships sailing from Denmark to Norway leave Hirtshals in the morning or afternoon, arriving in Stavanger at night, not as desirable an option. These boats also sail four days a week (typically Tue, Thu, Sat, and Sun; departing Hirtshals at either 8:30, 12:30, 13:00 or 15:00; arriving in Stavanger at either 20:00, 00:15, 00:45, or 02:30 in the morning).

Fares vary, depending on how far in advance you book, the time of year, the day of the week, and the type of accommodation you want. Basic one-way fares range from €13 to €102, plus the cost of meals (€17 breakfast, €38 dinner) and accommodations (an airline-type seat or cabin). A seat, referred to as a "sleeperette," starts at €9. But if you're efficient enough to spend a night traveling, you owe yourself the comfort of a private room. Cabins start at €68 for a basic, two-berth, inside cabin, and go up to €149 for a "Fjord Class" cabin with a double bed and ocean view. Car packages range from €52 to €438.

Reservations: To get the best fare, book online and early—as soon as you can commit to a firm date (http://fjordline.no and www.colorline.com). This is especially true for Fjordline. Many cheaper fares are non-refundable and non-changeable, so be sure to check the details carefully when you book. Days of the week and departure/arrival times can vary—confirm specific schedules when you make your reservations.

SOUTH NORWAY

$$$ Rica Hotel Norge is a modern option (Sb-1,395 kr, Db-1,595 kr, prices are averaged—rates vary with demand, Dronningensgate 5, tel. 38 17 40 00, fax 38 17 40 01, www.hotel -norge.no, firmapost@hotel-norge.no).

$$$ Thon Hotel Wergeland is inviting for a large chain hotel. It's within earshot of the church bells and busy Kirkegate—ask for a quieter room away from the street (Sb-1,395 kr, Db-1,695 kr, prices are averaged—rates vary with demand, includes breakfast, non-smoking rooms, no elevator, Internet access and Wi-Fi, Kirkegate 15, tel. 38 17 20 40, fax 38 02 73 21, www.thonhotels.no /wergeland, wergeland@thonhotels.no).

Kristiansand Connections

From Kristiansand by Train to: Stavanger (4-7/day, 3.5 hours), **Oslo** (4/day, 4.5 hours).

By Boat to Hirtshals, Denmark: For details on this boat, see the "Sailing Between Norway and Denmark" sidebar.

Route Tips for Drivers

Bergen to Kristiansand via the Setesdal Valley (10 hours): Your first key connection is the Kvanndal-Utne ferry (departures hourly 6:00-23:00, fewer on weekends, reservations not possible or even necessary if you get there 20 minutes early, breakfast in cafeteria, www.tide.no). If you make the 9:00, your day will be more relaxed. Driving comfortably, with no mistakes or traffic, it's two hours from your Bergen hotel to the ferry dock. Leaving Bergen is a bit confusing. Pretend you're going to Oslo on the road to Voss (Route E-16, signs for *Nestune, Landås, Nattland*). About a half-hour out of town, after a long tunnel, leave the Voss road and take Route 7 heading for Norheimsund, and then Kvanndal. This road, treacherous for the famed beauty of the Hardanger Fjord it hugs as well as for its skinniness, is faster and safer if you beat the traffic (which you will with this plan).

The ferry drops you in Utne, where a lovely road takes you to Odda and up into the mountains. From Haukeligrend, turn south and wind up to Sessvatn at 3,000 feet. Enter the Setesdal Valley. Follow the Otra River downhill for 140 miles south to the major port town of Kristiansand. Skip the secondary routes. South of Valle, you'll have to pass a 30-kr tollbooth. The most scenic stretch is between Hovden and Valle. South of Valle, there is a lot more logging (and therefore less scenic). As you enter Kristiansand, pay a 21-kr toll and follow signs for Denmark.

SWEDEN

SWEDEN

Sverige

Scandinavia's heartland, Sweden is far bigger than Denmark and far flatter than Norway. This family-friendly land is home to Ikea, Volvo, WikiLeaks, ABBA, and long summer vacations at red-painted, white-trimmed summer cottages. Its capital, Stockholm, is Scandinavia's grandest city.

Once the capital of blond, Sweden is now home to a huge immigrant population. Sweden is committed to its peoples' safety and security, and proud of its success in creating a society with the lowest poverty rate in the world. Yet Sweden has thrown in its lot with the European Union, and locals debate whether to open their economy even further.

Swedes are often stereotyped as sex-crazed, which could not be further from the truth. Several steamy films and film stars from the 1950s and 1960s stuck Sweden with the sexpot stereotype, which still reverberates among male tourists. Italians continue to travel up to Sweden looking for those bra-less, loose, and lascivious blondes...but the real story is that Sweden simply relaxed film censorship

"Do you see the world as the world sees you?"

earlier than other European countries. Like other Scandinavians, Swedes are frank and open about sexuality. Sex education in schools is routine, living together before marriage is the norm (and has been common for centuries), and teenagers have easy access to condoms. But Swedes, who are the most unmarried people in the world, choose their partners carefully.

Before the year 2000, Sweden was a Lutheran state, with the Church of Sweden as its official religion. Until 1996, Swedes automatically became members of the Lutheran Church at birth if one parent was Lutheran. Now you need to choose to join the church, and although the culture is nominally Lutheran, few people attend

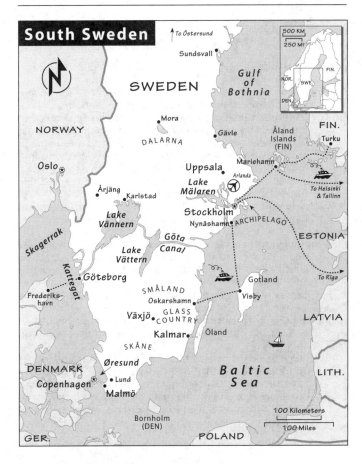

South Sweden

↑ To Östersund

Sundsvall

SWEDEN

Gulf
of
Bothnia

NORWAY

Mora

DALARNA

Gävle

Åland
Islands
(FIN)

FIN.

Turku

Oslo

Uppsala

Mariehamn

Arlanda

To Helsinki
& Tallinn

Årjäng   Karlstad

Lake
Mälaren

Stockholm

Lake
Vännern

Nynäshamn ARCHIPELAGO

ESTONIA

Skagerrak

Göta
Canal

Lake
Vättern

To Riga

Göteborg

SMÅLAND

Gotland

Frederiks-
havn

Kattegat

Oskarshamn

Visby

Växjö GLASS
COUNTRY

LATVIA

Kalmar   Öland

SKÅNE

Øresund

DENMARK

Lund

Baltic
Sea

LITH.

Copenhagen

Malmö

Bornholm
(DEN)

100 Kilometers

100 Miles

GER.

POLAND

500 KM

250 MI

NOR.   SWE.   FIN.

DEN.

services regularly. While church is handy for Christmas, Easter, marriages, and burials, most Swedes are more likely to find religion in nature, hiking in the vast forests or fishing in one of the thousands of lakes or rivers.

Sweden is almost 80 percent wilderness, and modern legislation incorporates an ancient common law called *allemans rätt*, which guarantees people the right to move freely through Sweden's natural scenery without asking the landowner for permission, as long as they behave responsibly. In summer, Swedes take advantage of the long days and warm evenings for festivals such as Midsummer (in late June) and for crayfish parties in August. Many Swedes have a summer cottage—or know someone who has one—where they spend countless hours swimming, soaking up the sun, and devouring boxes of juicy strawberries.

While Denmark and Norway look westward to Britain and the Atlantic, Sweden has always faced east, across the Baltic

Sweden Almanac

Official Name: Konungariket Sverige—the Kingdom of Sweden—
or simply Sweden.

Population: Sweden's 9.5 million people (about 57 per square
mile) are mostly ethnically Swedish. Foreign-born and first-
generation immigrants account for about 12 percent of
the population and are primarily from Finland, the former
Yugoslavia, and the Middle East. Sweden is also home to
about 17,000 indigenous Sami people. Swedish is the dominant language, with most speaking English as well. While
immigrants bring their various religions with them, ethnic
Swedes who go to church tend to be Lutheran.

Latitude and Longitude: 62°N and 15°E, similar latitude to
Canada's Northwest Territories.

Area: 174,000 square miles (a little bigger than California).

Geography: A chain of mountains divides Sweden from Norway
on the Scandinavian Peninsula. Sweden's mostly forested
landscape is flanked to the east by the Baltic Sea, which
contributes to the temperate climate. Sweden also encompasses several islands, of which Gotland and Öland are the
largest.

Biggest City: Sweden's capital city, Stockholm, has a population
of 870,000; more than two million live in the metropolitan
area.

Economy: Sweden has a $386 billion Gross Domestic Product
and a per capita GDP of $40,900—similar to Canada's.
Manufacturing, telecommunications, automobiles, and
pharmaceuticals rank among its top industries, along with
timber, hydropower, and iron ore. The Swedish economy
emerged from the recent financial crisis as one of the stron-

Sea. As Vikings, Norwegians went west to Iceland, Greenland,
and America; Danes headed south to England, France, and the
Mediterranean; and the Swedes went east into Russia. (The word
"Russia" has Viking roots.) In the early Middle Ages, Swedes
founded the Russian cities of Nizhny Novgorod and Kiev, and
even served as royal guards in Constantinople (modern-day
Istanbul). During the later Middle Ages, German settlers and
traders strongly influenced Sweden's culture and language. By
the 17th century, Sweden was a major European power, with one
of the largest naval fleets in Europe and an empire extending
around the Baltic, including Finland, Estonia, Latvia, and parts
of Poland, Russia, and Germany. But by the early 19th century,
Sweden's war-weary empire had shrunk. The country's current
borders date from 1809.

During a massive wave of emigration from the 1860s to World
War II, about a quarter of Sweden's people left for the Promised

gest in Europe, helped by its competitive high-tech businesses—and by the government's generally conservative fiscal policies. Eighty percent of Swedish workers belong to a labor union.

Currency: 7 Swedish kronor (kr, officially SEK) = about $1.

Government: King Carl XVI Gustav is the ceremonial head of Sweden's constitutional monarchy. Elected every four years, the 349-member Swedish Parliament (Riksdag) is currently led by Prime Minister Fredrik Reinfeldt of the conservative Moderate Party (elected in October 2006). *The Economist* magazine—which considered factors such as participation, impact of people on their government, and transparency—ranked Sweden by far the world's most democratic country (followed by the other Scandinavian countries and the Netherlands, with North Korea coming in last.)

Flag: The Swedish flag is blue with a yellow Scandinavian cross. The colors are derived from the Swedish coat of arms, with yellow symbolizing the generosity of the people and blue representing vigilance, truth, loyalty, perseverance, and justice.

The Average Swede: He or she is 42 years old, has 1.67 children, and will live to be 81.

Land—America. Many emigrants were farmers from the southern region of Småland. The museum in Växjö tells their story (see the Southeast Sweden chapter), as do the movies *The Emigrants* and *The New Land*, based on the series of books by Vilhelm Moberg.

The 20th century was good to Sweden. While other European countries were embroiled in the two World Wars, neutral Sweden grew stronger, finding a balance between the extremes of communism and the free market. After a recession hit in the early 1990s, and the collapse of Soviet communism reshaped the European political scene, some started to criticize Sweden's "middle way" as extreme and unworkable. But during the late 1990s and early 2000s, Sweden's economy improved, buoyed by a strong lineup of successful multinational companies. Volvo, Scania (trucks and machinery), Ikea, and Ericsson (the telecommunications giant) are leading the way in manufacturing, design, and technology. The recent economic downturn, however, has had its impact on

Sweden's export-driven economy—its Saab car manufacturer filed for bankruptcy protection in the fall of 2011.

Sweden has come a long way when it comes to accepting immigrants. Less than a century ago, only Swedes who traveled overseas were likely to ever see people of different ethnicities. In 1927 a black man worked in a Stockholm gas station, and people journeyed from great distances to fill up their car there...just to get a look. (Business boomed and his job was secure.)

Since the 1960s, however, Sweden (like Denmark and Norway) has accepted many immigrants and refugees from southeastern Europe, the Middle East, and elsewhere. This praiseworthy humanitarian policy has dramatically—and sometimes painfully—diversified a formerly homogenous country. The suburbs of Rinkeby, Tensta, and Botkyrka are Stockholm's ethnic neighborhoods, and are worth visiting. Many of the service-industry workers you will meet have come to Sweden from elsewhere.

For great electronic fact sheets on everything in Swedish society from health care to its Sami people, see www.sweden.se.

Most Swedes speak English, but a few Swedish words are helpful. "Hello" is *"Hej"* (hey) and "Good-bye" is *"Hej då"* (hey doh). "Thank you" is *"Tack"* (tack), which can also double for "Please." For a longer list of Swedish survival phrases, see page 691.

STOCKHOLM

If I had to call one European city home, it might be Stockholm. One-third water, one-third parks, one-third city, on the sea, surrounded by woods, bubbling with energy and history, Sweden's stunning capital is green, clean, and underrated.

The city is built on an archipelago of islands connected by bridges. Its location midway along the Baltic Sea made it a natural port, vital to the economy and security of the Swedish peninsula. In the 1500s, Stockholm became a political center when Gustav Vasa established the monarchy (1523). A century later, the expansionist King Gustavus Adolphus made it an influential European capital. The Industrial Revolution brought factories and a flood of farmers from the countryside. In the 20th century, the fuming smokestacks were replaced with steel-and-glass Modernist buildings housing high-tech workers and an expanding service sector.

Today, with more than two million people in the greater metropolitan area (one in five Swedes), Stockholm is Sweden's largest city, as well as its cultural, educational, and media center. It's also the country's most ethnically diverse city. Despite its size, Stockholm is committed to limiting its environmental footprint. Development is strictly monitored, and pollution-belching cars must pay a toll to enter the city.

For the visitor, Stockholm offers both old and new. Crawl through Europe's best-preserved old warship and relax on a scenic harbor boat tour. Browse the cobbles and antique shops of the lantern-lit Old Town. Take a trip back in time at Skansen, Europe's first and best open-air folk museum. Marvel at Stockholm's glittering City Hall, slick shopping malls, and art museums.

While progressive and sleek, Stockholm respects its heritage. In summer, military bands parade daily through the heart of town to the Royal Palace, announcing the Changing of the Guard and turning even the most dignified tourist into a scampering kid.

Planning Your Time

On a two- to three-week trip through Scandinavia, Stockholm is worth two days. For the busiest and best two- to three-day plan, I'd suggest this:

Day 1: 10:00—See the *Vasa* warship (starting with video and tour); 12:00—Visit Nordic Museum; 13:00—Tour Skansen open-air museum and grab lunch there; 16:00—Ride boat to Nybroplan (summer only) and follow my self-guided walk through the modern city from Kungsträdgården; 18:30—Take Royal Canal boat tour (confirm last sailing time, no boats Jan-March).

Day 2: 10:00—Catch 1.25-hour bus tour from the Royal Opera House, or take the City Hall tour; 12:15—Catch the Changing of the Guard at the palace (13:15 on Sun); 13:00—Lunch on Stortorget; 14:00—Tour Royal Palace Museums and Armory and follow my Old Town self-guided walk; 18:30—Free evening (could take a harbor dinner cruise).

Day 3: With an extra day, add a cruise through the scenic island archipelago (easy to do from Stockholm), visit the royal palace at Drottningholm, take a side-trip to charming Uppsala, or spend more time in Stockholm (there's plenty left to do and experience).

Orientation to Stockholm

Greater Stockholm's two million residents live on 14 islands woven together by 54 bridges. Visitors need only concern themselves with these districts, most of which are islands:

• **Norrmalm** is downtown, with most of the hotels and shopping areas, and the combined train and bus station. **Östermalm**, to the east, is more residential.

• **Kungsholmen,** the island across from Norrmalm, is home to City Hall and several inviting lakefront eateries.

• **Gamla Stan** is the Old Town island of winding, lantern-lit streets, antiques shops, and classy cafés clustered around the Royal Palace.

• **Skeppsholmen** is the small, central, traffic-free park/island with the Museum of Modern Art and two fine youth hostels.

• **Djurgården** is the park island—Stockholm's wonderful green playground, with many of the city's top sights (bike rentals just over bridge as you enter island).

• **Södermalm,** just south of the other districts, is sometimes

Stockholm: City of Islands

To Sigtuna,
Arlanda
Airport
& Uppsala

Lilla
Värtan
(sea)

2 Kilometers

1 Mile

277 MILLESGÅRDEN

E-4

LIDINGÖ

VÅRTAHAMNEN
(TALLINK SILJA
TERMINALS)

E-20

Gärdet

See detail maps

FRIHAMNEN
CRUISE PORT

NORRMALM

To
Helsinki
& Tallinn

ÖSTERMALM

KAKNÄS
TV TOWER

GÄRDET

To
Drottningholm
Palace

CENTRAL
STATION

KUNGSHOLMEN

CITY
HALL

SKEPPS-
HOLMEN

SKANSEN

Lake Mälaren

GAMLA
STAN

DJURGÅRDEN

To
Archipelago

LÅNGHOLMEN

VIKING
TERMINAL

Baltic
Sea

SLUSSEN
(LOCKS)

BERTH 160

BERTH 165/167

To
Helsinki

E-20

STADSGÅRDEN
CRUISE PORT

222

SÖDERMALM

To Malmö
& Oslo

To
Nynäshamn

called "Stockholm's Brooklyn" and is the primary setting for Stieg Larsson's Millennium novels (see sidebar on page 449). Its "SoFo" quarter (south of Folkungagatan) is young, creative, and trendy. Apart from its fine views and some good eateries, this residential island may be of less interest to those on a quick visit.

Tourist Information

Stockholm's official **TI** is across the street from the main entrance to the train station. The efficient staff provides free city maps, pamphlets on everything, Stockholm Cards (see below), transportation passes, day-trip and bus-tour information and tickets, and a room-booking service (75-kr fee for hotels, 25-kr/person fee for hostels). Avoid lines at the counter by looking up sightseeing details on one of the 10 user-friendly computer terminals (some with Internet access, 1 kr/minute; free Wi-Fi also available). Check out their helpful "today's events" board and grab a copy of *What's On Stockholm*, a free monthly magazine with hours and directions for most sights, special event listings, and details on public transportation (Mon-Fri 9:00-19:00—until 18:00 in winter, Sat 9:00-16:00, Sun 10:00-16:00, Vasagatan 14, T-bana: T-Centralen, tel. 08/5082-8508, www.visitstockholm.com). The tourist booth in the Gallerian shopping mall is not an official TI.

The **Airport Visitor Information Center,** a branch of the TI, is in Arlanda Airport's Terminal 5, where most international flights arrive. It offers many of the same services as the main TI (staffed daily 6:00-24:00, brochures available 24 hours, tel. 08/797-6000).

The Stockholm Card, a 24-hour pass for 450 kr, includes all public transit, free entry to almost every sight (75 attractions), some free or discounted tours, and a handy sightseeing handbook. An added bonus is the substantial pleasure of doing everything without considering the cost (many of Stockholm's sights are worth the time but not the money). The card pays for itself if you use public transportation and see Skansen, the Vasa Museum, and Drottningholm Palace. You can stretch it by entering Skansen on your 24th hour. A child's pass (age 7-17) costs about 60 percent less. The Stockholm Card also comes in 48-hour (625 kr), 72-hour (750 kr), and 120-hour (950 kr) versions. Cards are sold at the main TI, airport TI, many hotels, hostels, larger subway stations, Pressbyrån newsstands, and at www.visitstockholm.com.

Arrival in Stockholm

By Train or Bus

Stockholm's adjacent train (Centralstation) and bus (City-terminalen) stations, at the southwestern edge of Norrmalm, are a hive of services, shops, exchange desks, and people on the move. From the train station, the bus station is up the escalators from the main hall and across the street. Underground is the T-Centralen subway (T-bana) station, and taxi stands are outside. Those sailing to Finland or Estonia will find cruise-ship offices in the bus terminal, and can catch a shuttle bus to the port from here. The best way to connect the city and its airport is via the Arlanda Express shuttle train, which leaves from here (see below).

Stockholm is building a new commuter rail line right beneath the T-Centralen station—expect lots of construction until at least 2014.

By Plane

Arlanda Airport: Stockholm's Arlanda Airport is 28 miles north of town (airport code: ARN, tel. 08/797-6000, www.arlanda.se). The airport TI (described earlier) can advise you on getting into Stockholm and on your sightseeing plans.

The **airport shuttle train,** the Arlanda Express, is the fastest way to zip between the airport and the central train station—but it's not cheap (260 kr one-way, 490 kr round-trip, kids under 17 free with adult, covered by railpass; generally 4/hour—departing at :05, :20, :35, and :50 past the hour in each direction; even more frequent midday, 20-minute trip, has its own dedicated train station platform—follow signs to *Arlanda*, toll-free tel. 020-222-224, www.arlandaexpress.com). Buy your ticket either at the window near the track or from a ticket-vending machine, or pay an extra 50 kr to buy it on board. In summer and on weekends, a special fare lets two people travel for nearly half-price (two for 280 kr one-way, available daily mid-June-Aug, Sat-Sun year-round).

Airport shuttle buses (Flygbussarna) run between the airport and Stockholm's train/bus stations (99 kr, 6/hour, 40 minutes, may take longer at rush hour, buy tickets from station kiosks or at airport TI, www.flygbussarna.se).

Taxis between the airport and the city center take about 30-40 minutes (about 500 kr, depends on company, look for price printed on side of cab). Establish the price first. Reputable taxis accept credit cards.

The **cheapest airport connection** is to take bus #583 from the airport to Märsta, then switch to the *pendeltåg* (suburban train, 4/hour), which goes to Stockholm's central train station (72 kr, 1 hour total journey time, covered by Stockholm Card).

Skavsta Airport: Some discount airlines use Skavsta Airport, about 60 miles south of Stockholm (airport code: NYO, www.skavsta.se). Flygbussarna shuttle buses connect to the city (149 kr, timed to meet arriving flights, 80 minutes, www.flygbussarna.se).

By Boat

For details on arriving in Stockholm by cruise ship, see page 478. For information on Stockholm's ferry terminals, see page 602 for boats to Tallinn, or page 552 for boats to Helsinki.

By Car

Only a Swedish meatball would drive a car in Stockholm. Park it and use public transit instead. The TI has a *Parking in Stockholm* brochure. Those sailing to Finland or Estonia should ask about long-term parking at the terminal when reserving tickets; to minimize the risk of theft and vandalism, pay extra for the most secure parking garage.

Helpful Hints

Theft Alert: Even in Stockholm, when there are crowds, there are pickpockets (such as at the Royal Palace during the Changing of the Guard). Too-young-to-arrest teens—many from Eastern Europe—are hard for local police to control.

Emergency Assistance: In case of an emergency, dial 112.

Medical Help: For around-the-clock medical advice, call 08/320-100, then press 2 to get into the queue. The **C. W. Scheele**

24-hour pharmacy is near the train station at Klarabergsgatan 64 (tel. 08/454-8130).

Telephone Calls: For operator assistance, call 118-118. Numbers starting with 020 are toll-free. Numbers beginning with 070 and 073 are mobile phones—about triple the cost of a regular call. Some kiosks sell cheap international phone cards; look for shops serving Sweden's immigrant population (1 kr/minute calls to the US).

Internet Access: Some **7-Eleven** stores and **Pressbyrån** newsstands host "Sidewalk Express" Internet terminals. These are the best deal going. Just buy a card (29 kr/1.5 hours), remember your password, and you can pop into participating branches to log on. The card is shareable (but only one person at a time can use it) and valid for three days from your first log-in (branches open daily until late). There's a Sidewalk Express nook at the T-Centralen subway station and at the airport departure lounge (good if you have time to kill and an unexpired card).

English Bookstore: The aptly named **English Bookshop,** in Gamla Stan, sells a variety of reading materials (including Swedish-interest books) in English (Mon-Fri 10:00-18:30, Sat 10:00-16:00, Sun 12:00-15:00, Lilla Nygatan 11, tel. 08/790-5510).

Laundry: Tvättomaten is a rare find—the only independent launderette in Stockholm (self-service-100-120 kr/load, 48-hour full-service-200 kr/load—bring it in early and you can get it back at the end of the day; open Mon-Fri 8:30-18:30, Sat 9:30-15:00, closed Sun; across from Gustav Vasa church, Västmannagatan 61 on Odenplan, T-bana: Odenplan, tel. 08/346-480, www.tvattomaten.com).

Bike Rental: You can rent bikes and boats at **Djurgårdsbrons Sjöcafe,** next to Djurgårdsbron bridge near the Vasa Museum (bikes-80 kr/hour, 275 kr/day; canoes-150 kr/hour, kayaks-125 kr/hour, handy city cycle maps, May-Oct daily 8:00-21:00, closed off-season and in bad weather, tel. 08/660-5757). It's ideally situated as a springboard for a pleasant bike ride around the park-like Djurgården island.

Stockholm's **City Bikes** program, similar to those in several other European cities, is another option for seeing this bike-friendly town. Purchase a 165-kr, three-day City Bike card at the TI, at the SL Center (Stockholm Transport) office at Sergels Torg, or at many hotels and hostels. The card allows you to grab a bike from one of the more than 90 City Bike racks around the city. You must return it within three hours (to any rack), but if you want to keep riding, just check out another bike. You can do this over and over for three days (available April-Oct only, www.citybikes.se).

Updates to This Book: For news about changes to this book's coverage since it was published, see www.ricksteves.com/update.

Getting Around Stockholm

By Subway, Bus, and Tram: Stockholm's fine public transport network (officially Storstockholms Lokaltrafik—but signed as *SL*)

includes subway (Tunnelbana—universally called "T-bana") and bus systems, and a tram to the sights at Djurgården. Special passes take the bite out of the cost. It's a spread-out city, so most visitors will need public transport at some point (transit info tel. 08/600-1000, press * for English, www.sl.se/english). The subway is easy to figure out, but many sights are better served by bus. The main lines are listed on the map in *What's On Stockholm*. A more detailed system map is posted around town and available free from subway ticket windows and SL info desks in main stations. Check out the modern public art in the subway (such as at Kungsträdgården station). Because of rail construction near the main train station, some T-bana stops in the vicinity may be temporarily closed: Look for orange information signs or ask the helpful staff.

The subway and buses are covered by three different tickets: simple **paper tickets** (36 kr for a single ride); **travelcards** good for 24 hours (115 kr) or 72 hours (250 kr)—these are issued as reloadable smartcards, so you'll pay an additional 20 kr for the card itself; and presold **strip tickets** called *Förköpsremsa* (you pay 200 kr for a strip of 16 "coupons"; each ride costs 2 coupons, so the per-ride cost is 25 kr—but if you don't use all the rides, you're out of luck). Buy tickets from machines (US credit cards OK if you know your PIN; strip tickets may not be available) or ticket booths (cash only) in underground stations, or at the Pressbyrån newsstands scattered throughout the city and inside almost every T-bana station. All SL ticket-sellers are clearly marked with a blue flag with the SL logo. Tickets are not sold on buses—buy one before you board.

By Harbor Shuttle Ferry: In summer, ferries let you make a fun, practical, and scenic shortcut across the harbor to Djurgården

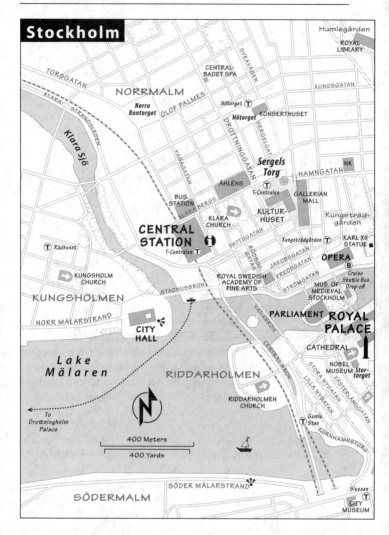

island. Boats leave from Slussen (at the south end of Gamla Stan) every 10-20 minutes, docking near the Gröna Lund amusement park on Djurgården (May-mid-Sept only, 10-minute trip, 45 kr, tel. 08/679-5830, www.waxholmsbolaget.se). There's also a ferry that stops near the Museum of Modern Art on Skeppsholmen Island. The Nybro ferry makes the five-minute journey from Nybroplan to Djurgården, landing next to the Vasa Museum (3/hour, June-Aug daily 10:00-20:00, check with TI for off-season schedule, 45 kr, tel. 08/1200-4000, www.stromma.se). The hop-on, hop-off boat tour (see page 428) also connects many of these stops. While buses and trams run between the same points more

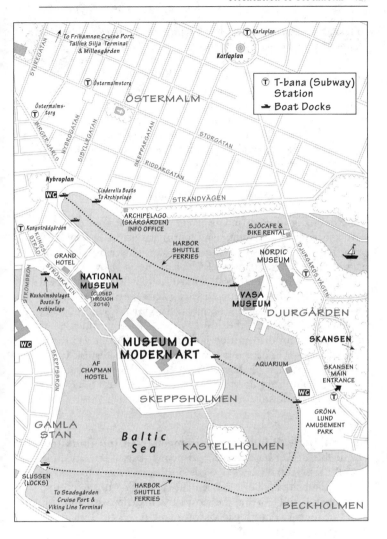

frequently, the ferry option gets you out onto the water and can be faster than overland connections.

By Taxi: Stockholm is a good taxi town—provided you find a reputable cab that charges fair rates. Taxis are unregulated, so companies can charge whatever they like. Before hopping in a taxi, look carefully at the big yellow label in the back window, which lists various fares. On the left, you'll see the per-kilometer fares for weekdays, evenings and weekends, and holidays. The largest number, on the right, shows their "highest comparison price" *(högsta järnförpriset)* for a specified ride; this number should be between 290 and 390—if it's higher, move on. (Legally, you're not obligated to take the first cab in line—feel free to compare fares.) Most cabs charge a drop fee of about 45 kr. Taxis with inflated rates tend to congregate at touristy places like the Vasa Museum or in Gamla Stan. I've been ripped off enough by cabs here to know: take only "Taxi Stockholm" cabs with the phone number (08/150-000) printed on the door. (Other companies that are reportedly honest include Taxi Kurir, tel. 08/300-000, and Taxi 020, tel. 08/850-400 or 020-20-20-20.) Your hotel, restaurant, or museum can call a cab, which will generally arrive within minutes (you'll pay no extra charge—the meter starts when you hop in).

Tours in Stockholm

Stockholm Sightseeing and its parent company Strömma seem to have a lock on all city sightseeing tours, whether by bus, by boat, or on foot. Their website (www.stockholmsightseeing.com) covers the entire program, many of which are listed below. For more information on their tours, call 08/1200-4000. Tours can be paid for in advance online, or simply as you board. The Stockholm Card provides the following discounts on Strömma's tours: hop-on, hop-off bus—60 kr off the 260-kr price; 1.25-hour quickie bus tour—50 percent discount on late afternoon departures; Royal Canal Tour—40 kr off the 150-kr price; 50-minute Historic Canal boat tour—free; hop-on, hop-off boat—free in May and Sept only. The Stockholm Card does not cover the Under the Bridges boat tour or Old Town walk.

By Bus

Hop-on, Hop-off Bus Tour—Strömma/Open Top Tours' topless double-decker buses make a 1.5-hour circuit of the city, linking all the essential places (the combo-ticket covers a total of 25 stops). The bus provides a convenient connection to sights from Skansen to City Hall, and the recorded commentary is good. The blue line tours the north part of town (and serves the Frihamnen cruise port); the yellow line covers the south end (and stops at the Stadsgården cruise port). A combo-ticket allows you to switch between lines (260 kr/24-hour combo-ticket; May-Sept 2/hour daily 10:00-16:00, fewer in off-season, none mid-Jan-mid-Feb, www.stromma.se). **Stockholm Red Buses** offers a similar hop-on, hop-off itinerary for the same price (only one route, 19 stops, also serves both cruise ports, 3/hour, www.redbuses.se).

Quickie Orientation Bus Tour—Several different city bus tours leave from the Royal Opera House on Gustav Adolfs Torg. Strömma/Stockholm Sightseeing's Stockholm Panorama tour provides a good overview (260 kr, 1.25 hours; daily at 10:00, 12:00, and 14:00; more frequent in summer).

By Boat

▲**City Boat Tours**—For a good floating look at Stockholm and a pleasant break, consider a sightseeing cruise. The handi-

est are the Strömma/Stockholm Sightseeing boats, which leave from Strömkajen, in front of the Grand Hotel, and from Nybroplan (each with recorded commentary). The **Royal Canal Tour** is short and informative (160 kr, 50 minutes, departs at :30 past each hour, generally daily May-Aug 10:30-18:30 but often as late as 19:30, April and Sept 10:30-16:30, Oct-Dec 10:30-13:30, none Jan-March). The nearly two-hour **Under the Bridges Tour** goes through two locks and under 15 bridges (210 kr, May-mid-Sept daily 10:00-16:00, June-Aug until 19:00, departures on the hour). A third option, the **Historic Canal Tour,** leaves from the Stadshusbron dock at City Hall (160 kr, 50 minutes, daily June-Aug 10:30-16:30, departs at :30 past each hour). You'll circle Kungsholmen island while learning about Stockholm's history from the early Industrial Age to modern times. To venture farther into Stockholm's archipelago, see the next chapter.

Hop-on, Hop-off Boat Tour—Stockholm is a city surrounded by water, making this boat option enjoyable and practical. Two different companies (Strömma/Stockholm Sightseeing and Royal Sightseeing) offer the same small loop, stopping at key spots such as Djurgården (Skansen and Vasa Museum), Gamla Stan (near Slussen and again near Royal Palace), the Viking Line dock next to the cruise terminal at Stadsgården, and Nybroplan. Use the boat strictly as transport from Point A to Point B, or make the whole 50-minute, eight-stop loop and enjoy the recorded commentary (100-kr ticket good 24 hours, runs May-mid-Sept daily 2-3/hour roughly 10:00-17:00, pick up map for locations of boat stops, www .stromma.se or www.royalsightseeing.com).

By Foot

Old Town Walk—Strömma/Stockholm Sightseeing offers a 1.25-hour Old Town walk (150 kr; daily July-Aug at 11:30, 13:30, and 15:30; leaves from Gustav Adolfs Torg, near the Royal Opera House).

Local Guides—**Marita Bergman** is a teacher and a licensed guide who enjoys taking around visitors during her school breaks (1,500 kr/half-day tour, mobile 073-511-9154, maritabergman@bred band.net). **Håkan Fränden** is another excellent guide who brings Stockholm to life (mobile 070-531-3379, hakan.franden@hotmail .com). You can also hire a private guide by calling 08/5082-8508

STOCKHOLM

(Mon-Fri 9:00-17:00, closed Sat-Sun) or visiting www.guidestock holm.com. The standard rate is about 1,500 kr for up to a three-hour tour.

Self-Guided Walks

This section includes two different walks to introduce you to Stockholm, both old (Gamla Stan) and new (the modern city).

▲▲Stockholm's Old Town (Gamla Stan) Walk

Stockholm's historic island core is charming, photogenic, and full of antiques shops, street lanterns, painted ceilings, and surprises. Until the 1600s, all of Stockholm fit on Gamla Stan. Stockholm traded with other northern ports such as Amsterdam, Lübeck, and Tallinn. German culture influenced art, building styles, and even the language, turning Old Norse into modern Swedish. With its narrow alleys and stairways, Gamla Stan mixes poorly with cars and modern economies. Today, it's been given over to the Royal Palace and to the tourists—sometimes seemingly unaware that most of Stockholm's best attractions are elsewhere—who throng Gamla Stan's main drag, Västerlånggatan. While you could just happily wander, this quick walk gives meaning to Stockholm's Old Town.

• Start at the base of Slottsbacken (the Palace Hill esplanade) leading up to the...

Royal Palace: Check out the ❶ statue of King Gustav III gazing at the palace, which was built on the site of Stockholm's first castle (described later, under "Sights in Stockholm"). Gustav turned Stockholm from a dowdy Scandinavian port into a sophisticated European capital, modeled on buildings he'd seen in Paris, Vienna, and Berlin. Gustav loved the arts, and he founded the Royal Dramatic Theater and the Royal Opera in Stockholm. Ironically, he was assassinated at a masquerade ball at the Royal Opera House in 1792, inspiring Verdi's opera *Un Ballo in Maschera*.

Walk up the broad, cobbled boulevard. Partway up the hill, stop and scan the harbor. The grand building across the water is the National Museum, which is often mistaken for the palace. Beyond that, in the distance, is the fine row of buildings on Strandvägen street. Until the 1850s, this area was home to peasant shacks, but as Stockholm entered its grand stage, it was cleaned up and replaced by fine apartments, including some of the city's smartest addresses. (Tiger Woods shared a home here with his Swedish wife during their now-defunct marriage.) The TV tower—a major attraction back in the 1970s—stands tall in the distance. Turn to the palace facade on your left (finished in 1754, replacing one that burned in 1697). The niches are filled with Swedish bigwigs (literally) from

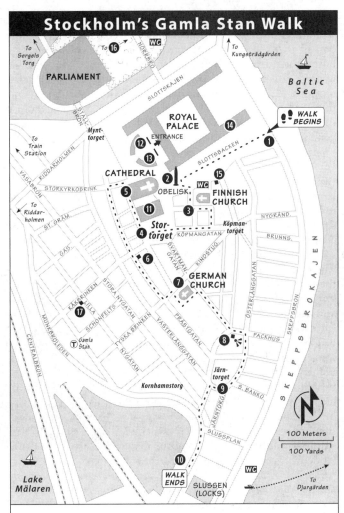

Stockholm's Gamla Stan Walk

To Sergels Torg

To **16**

WC

NORRBRO

To Kungsträdgården

PARLAMENT

Baltic Sea

SLOTTSKAJEN

ROYAL PALACE

14

WALK BEGINS

1

Mynt-torget

To Train Station

ENTRANCE

12

13

SLOTTSBACKEN

RIDDARHOLMEN

VASABRON

CATHEDRAL

STORKYRKOBRINK

2

OBELISK

WC

15

FINNISH CHURCH

NYGRÄND

5

To Riddar-holmen

ST. GRÄN.

GÅS.

11

3

Köpman-torget

BRUNNS.

4

Stor-torget

KÖPMANGATAN

SVARTMAN-GATAN

KINDSTUG.

ÖSTERLÅNGGATAN

SKEPPSBRON

6

7

GERMAN CHURCH

PRÄSTGATAN

SKEPPSBROKAJEN

KÅKBRINKEN

STORA NYGATAN

LILLA

SCHÖNFELTS

TYSKA BRINKEN

VÄSTERLÅNGGATAN

PACKHUS

8

17

MUNKBROLEDEN

Gamla Stan

NYGATAN

CENTRALBRON

Järn-torget

9

S. BANKO

Kornhamnstorg

JÄRNTORG.

N

100 Meters

100 Yards

10

WALK ENDS

SLUSSEN (LOCKS)

WC

To Djurgården

Lake Mälaren

Self-Guided Walk

1 King Gustav III Statue
2 Obelisk
3 Iron Boy Statue
4 Stortorget
5 Cathedral
6 Rune Stone
7 German Church
8 Viewpoint
9 Järntorget
10 Bridge & Lock

Additional Sights

11 Nobel Museum
12 Changing of the Guard
13 Palace Info Booth
14 Royal Armory
15 Royal Coin Cabinet & Swedish Economic Museum
16 To Museum of Medieval Stockholm
17 The English Bookshop

STOCKHOLM

the mid-18th century.

The ❷ obelisk honors Stockholm's merchant class for its support in a 1788 war against Russia. In front of the obelisk are tour buses (their drivers worried about parking cops) and a sand pit used for *boules*. The royal family took a liking to the French game during a Mediterranean vacation, and it's quite popular around town today. Behind the obelisk stands Storkyrkan, Stockholm's cathedral (which we'll visit later in this walk). From this angle, you see its Baroque facade, added to fit with the newer palace. Opposite the palace (orange building on left) is the Finnish church (Finska Kyrkan), which originated as the royal tennis hall. When the Protestant Reformation hit in 1527, church services could at last be said in the peoples' languages rather than Latin. Suddenly, each merchant community needed its own church. Finns worshipped here, the Germans built their church (coming up on this walk), and the Swedes got the cathedral.

Stroll behind the Finnish church into the shady churchyard where you'll find the fist-sized ❸ *Iron Boy,* the tiniest public statue (out of about 600 statues) in Stockholm. Swedish grannies knit caps for him in the winter. Local legend says the statue honors the orphans who had to transfer cargo from sea ships to lake ships before Stockholm's locks were built. Some people rub his head for good luck (which the orphans didn't have). Others, likely needy when it comes to this gift, rub his head for wisdom. The artist says it's simply a self-portrait of himself as a child, sitting on his bed and gazing at the moon

(notice the moonbeam-projecting light on the top of a pipe).

• *Continue through the yard, cross Trädgårdsgatan, go down the tiny lane to Köpmangatan (the medieval merchants' street, now popular with antiques dealers), turn right, and head for Stortorget, the old square.*

❹ **Stortorget, Stockholm's Oldest Square:** Colorful old buildings topped with gables line this square, which was the heart of medieval Stockholm (pop. 6,000 in 1400). This was where the many tangled lanes intersected, becoming the natural center for shopping and the town well. Today Stortorget is home to tourists, concerts, occasional demonstrators, and—in winter—Christmas shoppers at an outdoor market.

The grand building on the right is the **Stock Exchange.** It now houses the noble Nobel Museum (described later, under "Sights in Stockholm"). On the immediate left is the social-services agency **Stockholms Stadsmission** (offering the cheapest and best lunch around at the recommended Grillska Huset). If you peek into one wing of the café, you'll get a fine look at the richly decorated ceilings characteristic of Gamla Stan in the 17th century. The exotic flowers and animals implied that the people who lived or worked here were worldly. Stockholms Stadsmission's trendy secondhand shop is just across the square at Trångsund 8. The town well is still a popular meeting point. Scan the fine old facades.

The site of the **Stockholm Bloodbath** of 1520, this square has a notorious history. During a Danish power grab, many of Stockholm's movers and shakers who had challenged Danish rule—Swedish aristocracy, leading merchants, and priests—were rounded up, brought here, and beheaded. Rivers of blood were said to have flowed through the streets. Legend holds that the 80 or so white stones in the fine red facade across the square symbolize the victims. (One victim's son escaped, went into hiding, and resurfaced to lead a Swedish revolt against the Danish rulers. Three years later, the Swedes elected that rebel, Gustav Vasa, as their first king. He went on to usher in a great period in Swedish history—the Swedish Renaissance.) This square long held the town's pillory.

• *At the far end of the square (under the finest gables), turn right and follow Trångsund toward the cathedral.*

❺ **Cathedral (Storkyrkan):** Just before the church, you'll see my personal phone booth (Rikstelefon) and the gate to the church-

yard—guarded by statues of Caution and Hope. Enter the yellow-brick church—Stockholm's oldest, from the 13th century (40 kr, free on Sun; open daily mid-May–mid-Sept 9:00-18:00, until 16:00 off-season; worthwhile included English-language flier describes the interior). Signs explain events (busy with tours and services in summer).

The interior is cobbled with centuries-old **tombstones.** At one time, more than a thousand people were buried under the church. The tombstone of the Swedish reformer Olaus Petri is appropriately simple and appropriately located—under the pulpit. A witness to the Stockholm Bloodbath, Petri was nearly executed himself. He went on to befriend Gustav Vasa and guide him in Lutheranizing Sweden (and turning this cathedral from Catholic to Protestant).

Opposite the pulpit, find the **bronze plaque.** It recalls the 1925 Swedish-led ecumenical meeting of all Christian leaders—except the pope—that encouraged the Church to speak out against the type of evil that resulted in World War I's horrific death toll.

The **royal boxes** (between the pulpit and the altar) date from 1684. In front (on the left), *Saint George and the Dragon* (1489) is carved of oak and elk horn. To some, this symbolizes the Swedes' overcoming the evil Danes. In a broader sense, it's an inspiration to take up the struggle against even non-Danish evil. Regardless, it must be the gnarliest dragon's head in all of Europe.

Near the exit, a **painting** depicts Stockholm in the early 1500s, showing a walled city filling only today's Gamla Stan. It's a 1630 copy of the 1535 original. The strange sun and sky predicted big changes in Sweden—and as a matter of fact, that's what happened. Gustav Vasa brought on huge reforms in religion and beyond. (The copies show you the same painting, minus the glare.)

In June of 2010, this church hosted a royal wedding (Crown Princess Victoria, heir to the throne, married Daniel Westling, her personal trainer.) Imagine the pomp and circumstance as the nation's attention was drawn to this spot.

The plain door on the right leads to a free WC. The exit door next to the painting takes you into the kid-friendly churchyard (which was once the cemetery).

• *With your back to the church's front door, turn right and continue down Trångsund. At the next corner, go downhill on Storkyrkobrinken and take the first left on...*

Prästgatan Lane: Enjoy a quiet wander down this peaceful "Priests' Lane." (Västerlånggatan, the touristy drag, parallels this

lane one block over—you can walk back up on it later.) As you stroll this 15th-century lane, look for hoists (merchants used these to lift goods into their attics), tie bolts (iron bars necessary to bind the timber beams of tall buildings together), small coal or wood hatches (for fuel delivery back in the good old days), and flaming gold phoenixes under red-crown medallions (telling firefighters which houses paid insurance and could be saved in case of fire—for example, #46). Like other Scandinavian cities, Stockholm was plagued by fire until it was finally decreed that only stone, stucco, and brick construction (like you see here) would be allowed in the town center.

After a few blocks (at Kåkbrinken), a cannon barrel on the corner (look down) guards a Viking-age ❻ **rune stone.** In case you can't read the old Nordic script, it says: "Torsten and Frogun erected this stone in memory of their son."

Continue farther down Prästgatan to Tyska Brinken and turn left. You will see the powerful brick steeple of the ❼ **German**

Church (Tyska Kyrkan, free, Mon-Sat 11:00-17:00, closed Sun except for services). Its carillon has played four times a day since 1666. Think of the days when German merchants worked here. Today, Germans come to Sweden not to run the economy, but to enjoy its pristine nature (which is progressively harder to find in their own crowded homeland). Sweden formally became a Lutheran country even before the northern part of Germany—making this the first German Lutheran church.
• *Wander through the churchyard and out the back. Exit right onto Svartmangatan and follow it to the right, ending at an iron railing overlooking Österlånggatan.*

❽ **Viewpoint:** From this perch, survey the street below to the left and right. Notice how it curves. This marks the old shoreline. In medieval times, piers stretched out like fingers into the harbor. Gradually, as land was reclaimed and developed, these piers were extended, becoming lanes leading to piers farther away. Behind you is a cute shop where elves can actually be seen making elves.

Walk right along Österlånggatan to ❾ **Järntorget**—a customs square in medieval times, and home of Sweden's first bank back in 1680 (the yellow building with the bars on the windows). A nearby Co-op Nära supermarket offers picnic fixings. From here, Västerlånggatan—the eating, shopping, and commercial pedestrian mall of Gamla Stan—leads back across the island. You'll be there in a minute, but first finish this walk by continuing out of the square (opposite where you entered) down Järntorgsgatan.

Walk out into the traffic hell and stop on the ❿ **bridge** above the canal. This area is called Slussen, named for the locks between the salt water of the Baltic Sea (to your left) and the fresh water of the huge Lake Mälaren (to your right). In fact, Stockholm exists because this is where Lake Mälaren meets the sea. Traders would sail their goods from far inland to this point, where they'd meet merchants who would ship the goods south to Europe. In the 13th century, the new Kingdom of Sweden needed revenue, and began levying duty taxes on all the iron, copper, and furs shipped through here. From the bridge, you may notice a current in the water, indicating that the weir has been lowered and water is spilling from Lake Mälaren (about two feet above sea level) into the sea. Today, the locks are nicknamed "the divorce lock" because this is where captains and first mates learn to communicate under pressure and in the public eye.

Survey the view. Opposite Gamla Stan is the island of **Södermalm**—bohemian, youthful, artsy, and casual—with its popular Katarina viewing platform (see "Orientation Views," page 447). Moored on the saltwater side are the cruise ships, which bring thousands of visitors into town each day during the season. Many of these boats are bound for Finland. The old steamer *Patricia* (see its two white masts, 200 or so yards toward Södermalm) is a local favorite for raucous dining and dancing (described on page 474). The towering white syringe is the Gröna Lund amusement park's free-fall ride. The revolving *Djurgården Färjan* sign marks the ferry that zips from here directly to Gröna Lund and Djurgården. The equestrian statue is Jean-Baptiste Bernadotte, the French noble-man invited to establish the current Swedish royal dynasty in the early 1800s.

You could catch bus #2, which heads back downtown (the stop is just beyond Bernadotte, next to the waterfront). But better yet, linger longer in Gamla Stan—day or night, it's a lively place to enjoy. Västerlånggatan, Gamla Stan's main commercial drag, is a festival of distractions that keeps most visitors from seeing the historic charms of Old Town—which you just did. Now you can window-shop and eat (see "Eating in Stockholm"). Or, if it's late, find some live music (see "Nightlife in Stockholm").

• *For more sightseeing, consider the other sights in Gamla Stan or at the Royal Palace (all described later, under "Sights in Stockholm"). If you continue back up Västerlånggatan (always going straight), you'll reach the Parliament building and cross the water back over onto Norrmalm (where the street becomes Drottninggatan). This pedestrian street leads back into Stockholm's modern, vibrant new town.*

From here it's also a 10-minute walk to Kungsträdgården, the starting point of my Modern City self-guided walk (described next). On the way there, you'll walk past the Royal Opera House and Gustav Adolfs Torg, with its imposing statue of Gustavus Adolphus. He was the king who established the Swedish empire. Considered by many to be the father of modern warfare for his innovative tactics, he was a Protestant hero of the Thirty Years' War.

Stockholm's Modern City Walk

On this walk, we'll use the park called Kungsträdgården as a springboard to explore the modern center of Stockholm—a commercial zone designed to put the focus not on old kings and mementos of superpower days, but on shopping.

• *Find the statue of King Karl XII at the harbor end of the park.*

Kungsträdgården: Centuries ago, this "King's Garden" was the private kitchen garden of the king, where he grew his cabbage salad. Today, this downtown people-watching center, worth ▲, is considered Stockholm's living room, symbolizing the Swedes' freedom-loving spirit. While the English info board (near the harbor, 20 yards to the statue king's immediate right) describes the garden as a private royal domain, the nearby giant clump of elm trees reminds locals that it's the people who rule now. In the 1970s, demonstrators chained themselves to these trees to stop the building of an underground train station here. They prevailed, and today, locals enjoy the peaceful, breezy ambience of a teahouse instead. Watch the life-size game of chess and enjoy a summer concert at the bandstand. There's always something going on.

Kungsträdgården—surrounded by the harborfront and tour boats, the Royal Opera House, and, on the far side, a welcoming Volvo showroom (showing off the latest in Swedish car design), and the NK department store—is *the* place to feel Stockholm's pulse (but always ask first: *"Kan jag kanna på din puls?"*).

Kungsträdgården also throws huge parties. The Taste of Stockholm festival runs for a week in early June, when restaurateurs show off and bands entertain all day. Beer flows liberally—a rare public spectacle in Sweden.

The nearby Kungsträdgården T-bana station (on the side street called Arsenalsgaten) is famous for having the best art of any station in town. The man at the turnstile is generally friendly to tourists who ask *snälla rara* (snel-lah rar-rah; pretty please) for permission to nip down the escalator to see the far-out design, proving to the gullible that Stockholm sits upon a grand, ancient civilization.

• *Walk back to the park and stroll through Kungsträdgården up to Hamngatan street. Go left, and look for the...*

Gallerian Mall: Among this two-story world of shops, you'll find plenty of affordable little lunch bars, classy cafés for your *fika* (traditional Swedish coffee-and-bun break), and even a spa providing an oasis of relaxation for stressed-out shoppers.

• *Just beyond this huge mall, Hamngatan street leads to...*

Sergels Torg: This square, worth ▲, dominates the heart of modern Stockholm with its stark 1960s-era functionalist architec-

ture. The glassy tower in the middle of the fountain plaza is ugly in daylight but glows at night, symbolic of Sweden's haunting northern lights. The big, boxy, and glassy building overlooking the square is Stockholm's "culture center," the **Kulturhuset.** Inside, just past the welcoming info desk, you'll find a big model of the city. There's a library, Internet café, chessboards, fun shops, fine art cinema, art exhibits, a venue for new bands, and a rooftop café with foreign newspapers and a grand view (Tue-Fri 9:00-19:00, Sat-Sun 11:00-17:00, closed Mon but retail shops stay open; tel. 08/5083-1508, www.kulturhuset.stockholm.se).

Stand in front of the Kulturhuset (across from the fountain) and survey the expansive square nicknamed "Plattan" (the platter). Everything around you dates from the 1960s and 1970s, when this formerly run-down area was reinvented as an urban "space of the future." In the 1970s, with no nearby residences, the desolate Plattan became the domain of junkies. Now the city is actively revitalizing it, and the Plattan is becoming a people-friendly heart of the commercial town. Designtorget (on the lower level) is a place for independent Swedish designers to market and sell their clever products. Perhaps you need a banana case?

Nearby are the major boutiques and department stores: Nordiska Kompaniet (NK), H&M, and Åhléns. The thriving pedestrian street **Sergelgatan** leads past the five uniform white towers you see beyond the fountain. These office towers, so modern in the 1960s, have gone from seeming hopelessly out-of-date to being considered "retro," and are now quite popular with young professionals.

• *Walk up Sergelgatan past the towers, enjoying the public art and people-watching, to the market at Hötorget.*

Hötorget: "Hötorget" means "Hay Market," but today its stalls feed people rather than horses. The adjacent indoor market, Hötorgshallen, is fun and fragrant. It dates from 1914 when, for hygienic reasons, the city forbade selling fish and meat outdoors. Carl Milles' statue of *Orpheus Emerging from the Underworld* (with seven sad muses) stands in front of the city concert hall (which hosts the annual Nobel Prize award ceremony). The concert house, from 1926, is Swedish Art Deco (a.k.a. "Swedish Grace").

The lobby (open through most of summer, 70-kr tours) still evokes Stockholm's Roaring Twenties.

Popping into the Hötorget T-bana station provides a fun glimpse at local urban design. Stockholm's subway system was inaugurated in the 1950s, and many stations are modern art installations in themselves.

• *Our walk ends here. For more shopping and an enjoyable pedestrian boulevard leading back into the Old Town, cut down a block to Drottninggatan and turn left. This busy drag leads straight out of the commercial district, passes the Parliament, then becomes the main street of Gamla Stan.*

Sights in Stockholm

Gamla Stan

The best of Gamla Stan is covered in my self-guided walk, earlier. But here are a few ways to extend your time in the Old Town.

▲**Nobel Museum (Nobelmuseet)**—Opened in 2001 for the 100-year anniversary of the Nobel Prize, this wonderful little museum tells the story of the world's most prestigious prize.

Cost and Hours: 80 kr, audioguide-20 kr; open June-mid-Sept daily 10:00-18:00, Tue and Fri until 20:00; mid-Sept-May Wed-Sun 11:00-17:00, Tue 11:00-20:00; closed Mon year-round; free guided tours in English in summer daily at 10:15, 11:15, 15:00, and 16:00, fewer off-season; on Stortorget in the center of Gamla Stan a block from the Royal Palace, tel. 08/5348-1800, www.nobelmuseum.se.

Visiting the Museum: Stockholm-born Alfred Nobel was a great inventor, with more than 300 patents. His most famous

invention: dynamite. Living in the late 1800s, Nobel was a man of his age. It was a time of great optimism, wild ideas, and grand projects. His dynamite enabled entire nations to blast their way into the modern age with canals, railroads, and tunnels. It made warfare much more destructive. And it also made Alfred Nobel a very wealthy man. Wanting to leave a legacy that celebrated and supported people with great ideas, Alfred used his fortune to fund the Nobel Prize. Every year since 1901, laureates have been honored in the fields of physics, chemistry, medicine, literature, and peacemaking.

Inside, portraits of all 700-plus prizewinners hang from the ceiling—shuffling around the room like shirts at the dry cleaner's (miss your favorite, and he or she will come around again in three hours). Two video rooms run a continuous montage of quick programs (three-minute bios of various winners in one program, five-minute films celebrating various intellectual environments—from Cambridge to Parisian cafés—in the other). The Viennese-style Bistro Nobel is the place to get creative with your coffee...and sample the famous Nobel ice cream. All Nobel laureates who visit the museum are asked to sign the bottom of a chair in the café. Turn yours over and see who warmed your chair. And don't miss the lockable hangers, to protect your fancy, furry winter coat. The Swedish Academy, which awards the Nobel Prize for literature each year, is upstairs.

Parliament (Riksdaghuset)—For a firsthand look at Sweden's government, tour the Parliament buildings. It's also possible to watch the Parliament in session.

Cost and Hours: Free one-hour tours in English late June-Aug; usually Mon-Fri at 12:00, 13:00, 14:00, and 15:00; enter at Riksgatan 3a, call 08/786-4862 to confirm times, www.riksdagen.se.

Museum of Medieval Stockholm (Medeltidsmuseet)—This museum, recently renovated, provides a good look at medieval Stockholm. When the government was digging a parking garage near the Parliament building in the 1970s, workers uncovered a major archaeological find: parts of the town wall that King Gustav Vasa built in the 1530s, as well as a churchyard. This underground museum preserves these discoveries and explains how Stockholm grew from a medieval village to a major city.

Cost and Hours: 70 kr; July-Aug daily 12:00-17:00, Wed until 19:00; Sept-June Tue-Sun 12:00-17:00, Wed until 19:00, closed Mon; English audioguide, enter museum from park in front of Parliament, tel. 08/5083-1790, www.medeltidsmuseet .stockholm.se.

Nearby: The museum sits in **Strömparterren** park. With its café and Carl Milles statue of the *Sun Singer* greeting the day, it's a pleasant place for a sightseeing break (pay WC in park, free WC in museum).

Royal Palace (Kungliga Slottet)

Although the royal family beds down at Drottningholm, this complex in Gamla Stan is still the official royal residence. The palace, designed in Italian Baroque style, was completed in 1754 after a fire wiped out the previous palace. Today its exterior is undergoing a 20-year renovation—don't be surprised if parts are covered in scaffolding.

The Changing of the Guard and the awesome, can't-miss Royal Armory are the palace's highlights. The Royal Treasury is worth a look; the chapel is nice but no big deal; the Apartments of State are not much as far as palace rooms go; and you can skip Gustav III's Museum of Antiquities and the Museum of Three Crowns. The information booth in the semicircular courtyard (at the top, where the guard changes) gives out an explanatory brochure with a map marking the different entrances (main entrance is on the west side—away from the water—but the Royal Armory has a separate entrance. They also  have a list of today's guided tours. In peak season, there are up to three different English tours a day (included in the admission)—allowing you to systematically cover nearly the entire complex. Since the palace is used for state functions, it is sometimes closed to tourists.

▲▲Military Parade and Changing of the Guard—Starting two blocks from Nybroplan (in front of the Army

Museum at Riddargatan 13), Stockholm's marches over Norrbro bridge and up to the courtyard, where the band plays and the guar

The performance is fresh and spirited, are visiting Stockholm just like you—and it'

soldiers from ... over Sweden in every branch of the service to show their stuff in the big city. Pick your place at the palace courtyard, where the band arrives at about 12:15 (13:15 on Sun). The best spot to stand is along the wall in the inner courtyard, near the palace information and ticket office. There are columns with wide pedestals for easy perching, as well as benches that people stand on to view the ceremony (arrive early). Generally, after the barking and goose-stepping formalities, the band shows off for an impressive 30-minute marching concert. Though the royal family now lives out of town at Drottningholm, the palace guards are for real. If the guard by the cannon in the semicircular courtyard looks a little lax, try wandering discreetly behind him.

Cost and Hours: Free; mid-May-mid-Sept Mon-Sat parade begins at 11:45 (reaches palace at 12:15), Sun at 12:45 (palace at 13:15); April-mid-May and mid-Sept-Oct Wed and Sat at 11:45 (palace at 12:15), Sun at 12:45 (palace at 13:15); Nov-March starts at palace Wed and Sat at 12:15, Sun at 13:15. Royal appointments can disrupt the schedule; confirm times at TI. In summer, you might also catch the mounted guards (but they do not appear on a regular schedule).

▲▲**Royal Armory (Livrustkammaren)**—The oldest museum in Sweden is more than an armory and less than an armory. It displays impressive ceremonial royal armor (never used in battle), but there's a lot more to see. Everything is beautifully lit and displayed, and well-described in English and by the museum's evocative audioguide.

Cost and Hours: 80 kr; May-June daily 11:00-17:00; July-Aug daily 10:00-18:00; Sept-April Tue-Sun 11:00-17:00, Thu until 20:00, closed Mon; 20-kr audioguide is excellent—romantic couples can share it if they crank up the volume, information sheets in English available in most rooms; entrance at bottom of Slottsbacken at base of palace, tel. 08/5195-5546, www.livrust kammaren.se.

Visiting the Museum: The first room is almost a shrine for Swedish visitors. It contains the clothes Gustavus Adolphus wore, and even the horse he was riding, when he was killed in the Thirty

Stockholm at a Glance

▲▲▲**Skansen** Europe's first and best open-air folk museum, with more than 150 old homes, churches, shops, and schools. **Hours:** Park—daily May-mid-June 10:00-19:00, mid-June-Aug 10:00-22:00, Sept 10:00-18:00, Oct and March-April 10:00-16:00, Nov-Feb 10:00-15:00; historical buildings—generally 11:00-15:00, June-Aug some until 19:00, most closed in winter. See page 450.

▲▲▲*Vasa* **Museum** Ill-fated 17th-century warship dredged from the sea floor, now the showpiece of an interesting museum. **Hours:** June-Aug daily 8:30-18:00; Sept-May daily 10:00-17:00, Wed until 20:00. See page 452.

▲▲▲**Archipelago** Mostly half-day cruises to Vaxholm and many other small island destinations. **Hours:** Several options per day in summer, some including a meal on board. See the next chapter.

▲▲**Military Parade and Changing of the Guard** Punchy daily pomp starting near Nybroplan and finishing at Royal Palace outer courtyard. **Hours:** Mid-May-mid-Sept Mon-Sat parade begins at 11:45 (reaches palace at 12:15), Sun at 12:45 (palace at 13:15); April-mid-May and mid-Sept-Oct Wed and Sat at 11:45 (palace at 12:15), Sun at 12:45 (palace at 13:15); Nov-March starts at palace Wed and Sat at 12:15, Sun at 13:15. See page 440.

▲▲**Royal Armory** A fine collection of ceremonial medieval royal armor, historic and modern royal garments, and carriages, in the Royal Palace. **Hours:** May-June daily 11:00-17:00; July-Aug daily 10:00-18:00; Sept-April Tue-Sun 11:00-17:00, Thu until 20:00, closed Mon. See page 441.

▲▲**City Hall** Gilt mosaic architectural jewel of Stockholm and site of Nobel Prize banquet, with tower offering the city's best views. **Hours:** Required tours daily generally June-Aug every 30 minutes 9:30-16:00, off-season hourly 10:00-15:00. See page 445.

▲▲**Nordic Museum** Danish Renaissance palace design and five fascinating centuries of traditional Swedish lifestyles. **Hours:** Daily 10:00-17:00, Wed until 20:00 Sept-May. See page 454.

▲▲**Drottningholm Palace** Resplendent 17th-century royal residence with a Baroque theater. **Hours:** May-Aug daily 10:00-16:30,

Sept daily 11:00-15:30, Oct and April Fri-Sun only 11:00-15:30, Nov-Dec and mid-Jan-March Sat-Sun only 12:00-15:30, closed last two weeks of Dec. See page 456.

▲**Nobel Museum** Star-studded tribute to some of the world's most accomplished scientists, artists, economists, and politicians. **Hours:** June-mid-Sept daily 10:00-18:00, Tue and Fri until 20:00; mid-Sept-May Wed-Sun 11:00-17:00, Tue 11:00-20:00; closed Mon year-round. See page 438.

▲**Royal Palace Museums** Complex of Swedish royal museums, the two best of which are the Royal Apartments and Royal Treasury. **Hours:** Mid-May-mid-Sept daily 10:00-17:00; mid-Sept-mid-May Tue-Sun 12:00-16:00, closed Mon. See page 440.

▲**Royal Coin Cabinet and Swedish Economic Museum** Europe's best look at the history of money, with a sweep through the evolution of the Swedish economy to boot. **Hours:** Daily 10:00-16:00. See page 445.

▲**Kungsträdgården** Stockholm's lively central square, with life-size chess games, concerts, and perpetual action. **Hours:** Always open. See page 436.

▲**Sergels Torg** Modern square with underground mall. **Hours:** Always open. See page 437.

▲**National Museum of Fine Arts** Closes for renovation in mid-2013, but part of the collection—which features works by locals Larsson and Zorn, along with Rembrandt, Rubens, and Impressionists—will be on display at the Royal Swedish Academy of Fine Arts. **Hours:** Inquire locally. See page 447.

▲**Thielska Galleriet** Enchanting waterside mansion with works of local artists Larsson, Zorn, and Munch. **Hours:** Tue-Sun 12:00-17:00, Thu until 20:00, closed Mon. See page 455.

▲**Millesgården** Dramatic cliffside museum and grounds featuring works of Sweden's greatest sculptor, Carl Milles. **Hours:** May-Sept daily 11:00-17:00; Oct-April Tue-Sun 11:00-17:00, closed Mon. See page 455.

STOCKHOLM

Years' War. The exquisite workmanship on the **ceremonial armor** in this room is a fine example of weaponry as an art form. The next room shows royal suits and gowns through the ages. The 1766 wedding dress of Queen Sofia is designed to cleverly show off its fabulously rich fabric (the dress seems even wider when compared to her 20-inch corseted waist). There are some modern royal dresses here as well. The royal children get a section for themselves, featuring a cradle that has rocked heirs to the throne since the 1650s; eventually it will leave the armory to rock the next royal offspring as well. It's fun to imagine little princes romping around their 600-room home with these toys. A century ago, one prince treasured his boxcar and loved playing cowboys and Indians.

The basement is a royal garage filled with **lavish coaches.** The highlight: a plush coronation coach made in France in about 1700 and shipped to Stockholm, ready to be assembled Ikea-style. It last rolled a king to his big day—with its eight fine horses and what was then the latest in suspension gear—in the mid-1800s. A display of royal luggage over the centuries makes it obvious that Swedish royalty didn't know how to pack light.

▲**Other Royal Palace Museums**—The four museums below can be accessed through the main entrance. Stockholm Card-holders can go straight into each museum, bypassing the ticket office.

Cost and Hours: 150-kr combo-ticket, generally includes guided tour; mid-May–mid-Sept daily 10:00–17:00; mid-Sept–mid-May Tue–Sun 12:00–16:00, closed Mon; tel. 08/402-6130, www.royalcourt.se.

Royal Apartments: The stately palace exterior encloses 608 rooms (one more than Britain's Buckingham Palace) of glittering 18th-century Baroque and Rococo decor. Clearly the palace of Scandinavia's superpower, it's steeped in royal history. You'll walk the long halls through four sections: the Hall of State (with an exhibit of fancy state awards), the lavish Bernadotte Apartments (some fine Rococo interiors and portraits of the Bernadotte dynasty), the State Apartments (with rooms dating to the 1690s), and the Guest Apartments, where visiting heads of state still crash. Guided tours in English run daily in summer at 11:00 and 14:00 (45 minutes, off-season at 14:00 and 15:00).

Royal Treasury (Skattkammaren): Climbing down into the super-secure vault, you'll see 12 cases filled with fancy crowns, scepters, jeweled robes, and plenty of glittering gold. Nothing is explained, so pay for the flier or take the guided tour in English (May–Sept daily at 13:00, Oct–April Tue–Sun at 13:00).

Gustav III's Museum of Antiquities (Gustav III's Antik-museum): In the 1700s, Gustav III traveled through Italy and brought home an impressive gallery of classical Roman statues. These are displayed exactly as they were in the 1790s. This was a huge deal for those who had never been out of Sweden (closed mid-Sept-mid-May).

Museum of Three Crowns (Museum Tre Kronor): This museum shows off bits of the palace from before a devastating 1697 fire. It's basically just more old stuff, interesting only to real history buffs (guided tours in English at 15:00 in summer).

▲**Royal Coin-Cabinet (Kungliga Myntkabinettet) at the Swedish Economic Museum (Sveriges Ekonomiska Museum)**—More than your typical royal coin collection, this is the best money museum I've seen in Europe. A fine exhibit tells the story of money from crude wampum to credit cards, and traces the development of the modern Swedish economy. Unfortunately, there aren't many English translations, which makes the included audioguide critical.

Cost and Hours: 70 kr, free on Mon, open daily 10:00-16:00, Slottsbacken 6, tel. 08/5195-5304, www.myntkabinettet.se.

Downtown Stockholm

Waterside Walk—Enjoy Stockholm's ever-expanding shoreline promenades. Tracing the downtown shoreline while dodging in-line skaters and ice-cream trolleys (rather than cars and buses), you can walk from Slussen across Gamla Stan, all the way to the good ship *Vasa* in Djurgården. Perhaps the best stretch is along waterfront Strandvägen street (from Nybroplan past weather-beaten old boats and fancy facades to Djurgården). As you stroll, keep in mind that there's free fishing in central Stockholm, and the harbor waters are restocked every spring with thousands of new fish. Locals tell of one lucky lad who pulled in an 80-pound salmon.

▲▲**City Hall (Stadshuset)**—The Stadshuset is an impressive mix of eight million red bricks, 19 million chips of gilt mosaic, and

lots of Stockholm pride. While churches dominate cities in southern Europe, in Scandinavian capitals, city halls seem to be the most impressive buildings, celebrating humanism and the ideal of people working together in community. Built in 1923, this is still a functioning city hall. The members of the city council—101 people (mostly women) representing the 850,000 people of Stockholm—are hobby legislators with regular day jobs. That's why they meet in the evening. One of Europe's finest public buildings, the site of the annual Nobel Prize banquet, and a favorite spot for weddings (they do two per hour on Saturday afternoons), City Hall is particularly enjoyable and worthwhile for its entertaining and required 50-minute tour.

Cost and Hours: 100 kr; English-only tours offered daily, generally June-Aug every 30 minutes 9:30-16:00, off-season hourly 10:00-15:00; call to confirm, 300 yards behind the central train station—about a 15-minute walk from either the station or Gamla Stan, bus #3 or #62, tel. 08/5082-9059, www.stockholm.se/city hall. City Hall's cafeteria, which you enter from the courtyard, serves complete lunches for 95 kr (Mon-Fri 11:00-14:00, closed Sat-Sun).

Visiting City Hall: On the tour, you'll see the building's sumptuous National Romantic style interior (similar to Britain's Arts and Crafts style), celebrating Swedish architecture and craftwork, and created almost entirely with Swedish materials. Highlights include the so-called Blue Hall (the Italian piazza-inspired, loggia-lined courtyard that was originally intended to be open air—hence the name—where the 1,300-plate Nobel banquet takes place); the City Council Chamber (with a gorgeously painted wood-beamed ceiling that resembles a Viking longhouse—or maybe an overturned Viking boat); the Gallery of the Prince (lined with frescoes executed by Prince Eugene of Sweden); and the glittering, gilded, Neo-Byzantine-style, and aptly named Golden Hall, where the Nobel recipients cut a rug after the banquet. In this over-the-top space, a glimmering mosaic Queen of Lake Mälaren oversees the proceedings with a welcoming but watchful eye, as East (see Istanbul's Hagia Sophia and the elephant, on the right) and West (notice the skyscrapers with the American flag, on the left) meet here in Stockholm. Above the door across the hall is Sweden's patron saint, Erik, who seems to have lost his head (due to some sloppy mosaic planning). On the tour, you'll find out exactly how many centimeters each Nobel banquet attendee gets at the table, why the building's plans were altered at the last minute to make the tower exactly one meter taller, where the prince got the inspiration for his scenic frescoes, and how the Swedes reacted when they first saw that Golden Hall (hint: they weren't pleased).

▲City Hall Tower—This 348-foot-tall tower (an elevator takes you halfway up, leaving you 350 steps to mount) rewards those who make the climb with a grand city view. As you huff your way up, you'll come upon models of busts and statues that adorn City Hall and a huge, 25-foot-tall statue of St. Erik. Erik, the patron saint of Stockholm, was originally intended to be hoisted by cranes up through the middle of the tower to stand at its top. But plans

changed, big Erik is forever parked halfway up the structure, and the tower's top is open for visitors to gather and enjoy the view. At the roof terrace, you'll find smaller statues of Erik, Klara, Maria Magdalena, and Nikolaus: patron saints facing their respective parishes. Finally, you'll find yourself in the company of the tower's nine bells, with Stockholm spreading out all around you.

Cost and Hours: 40 kr, daily June-Aug 9:15-17:15, May and Sept 9:15-16:00, closed Oct-April. As only 30 people at a time are allowed up into the tower, there's often a very long wait. If there's a long line, I'd skip it.

▲**Orientation Views**—For a bird's-eye perspective on this wonderful urban mix of water, parks, concrete, and people, consider these three viewpoints: **City Hall Tower** (described above; view from tower pictured opposite); **Kaknäs Tower** (at 500 feet, once the tallest building in Scandinavia—45 kr; June-Aug daily 9:00-22:00; Sept-May Mon-Sat 10:00-21:00, Sun 10:00-18:00; restaurant on 28th floor, east of downtown—bus #69 from Nybroplan or Sergels Torg, tel. 08/667-2105); and the **Katarina** viewing platform in Södermalm, near the Slussen T-bana stop. (The Katarina elevator is no longer working, but you can get to the platform via a pedestrian bridge from Mosebacke Torg, to the south.)

▲**National Museum of Fine Arts (Nationalmuseum) at the Royal Swedish Academy of Fine Arts (Kungliga Akademien för de Fria Konsterna)**—Stockholm's 200-year-old art museum (on the Blasieholmen peninsula) is finally getting a facelift, as

its home closes from mid-2013 through 2016 for an extensive renovation. Beginning in the fall of 2013, part of the collection will be on display at the Royal Swedish Academy of Fine Arts.

Cost and Hours: Inquire locally about cost, hours, and other specifics of the National Museum's exhibition at the Royal Swedish Academy of Fine Arts; the academy is between the train station and the palace at Fredsgatan 12, tel. 08/232-925, www .konstakademien.se.

Visiting the Collection: Though mediocre by European standards, the National Museum owns a few good pieces. Highlights include several canvases by Rembrandt and Rubens, a fine group of Impressionist works, and a sizeable collection of Russian icons. Seek out the exquisite paintings by the Swedish artists Anders Zorn and Carl Larsson. It's unclear exactly which items will be on display at the Royal Swedish Academy of Fine Arts; if you visit, look for the following:

The Stockholm-born **Carl Larsson** (1853-1919) became very popular as the Swedish Norman Rockwell, chronicling the everyday family life of his own wife and brood of kids. If his two vast, 900-square-foot murals celebrating Swedish history are on display, they're worth a close look. *The Return of the King* shows Gustav Vasa astride a white horse. After escaping the Stockholm Bloodbath and leading Sweden's revolt, he drove out the Danes and was elected Sweden's first king (1523). Now he marches his victorious troops across a drawbridge, as Stockholm's burghers bow and welcome him home. In *The Midwinter Sacrifice,* it's solstice eve, and Vikings are gathered at the pagan temple at Gamla Uppsala. Musicians blow the *lur* horns, a priest in white raises the ceremonial hammer of Thor, and another priest in red (with his back to us) holds a sacrificial knife. The Viking king arrives on his golden sled, rises from his throne, strips naked, gazes to the heavens, and prepares to sacrifice himself to the gods of winter, so that spring will return to feed his starving people.

The museum also has an excellent collection that walks you through the evolution of modern Swedish design: gracefully engraved glass from the 1920s, works from the Stockholm Exhibition of 1930, industrial design of the 1940s, Scandinavian Design movement of the 1950s, plastic chairs from the 1960s, modern furniture from the 1980s, and the Swedish new simplicity from the 1990s.

Museum of Modern Art (Moderna Museet)—This bright, cheery gallery on Skeppsholmen island is as far out as can be, with Picasso, Braque, Dalí, Matisse, and lots of goofy Dada art (such as *Urinal*), as well as more contemporary stuff. Don't miss the beloved *Goat with Tire.* The excellent and included audioguide makes modern art meaningful to visitors who wouldn't otherwise appreciate it.

Cost and Hours: 100 kr, Tue 10:00-20:00, Wed-Sun 10:00-18:00, closed Mon, fine bookstore, harborview café, T-bana: Kungsträdgården plus 10-minute walk, or take bus #65, tel. 08/5195-5200, www.modernamuseet.se.

▲**Swedish Massage, Spa, and Sauna**—To treat yourself to a Swedish spa experience—maybe with an authentic "Swedish massage"—head for the elegant circa-1900 **CentralBadet Spa.** Admission includes entry to an extensive gym, "bubblepool," sauna, steam room, and an elegant Art Nouveau pool. A classic massage (50 minutes) costs 650 kr—you don't have to pay the entry fee if that's all you want. Reservations are smart. If you won't make it to Finland, enjoy a sauna here (for more on saunas, see page 578). There are two saunas—one mixed, one not. Bring your towel into the sauna—not for modesty, but for hygiene (to separate your body from the bench). The steam room is mixed; bring two towels (one

Once in a Millennium:
Stieg Larsson's Stockholm

With more than 65 million copies of Stieg Larsson's Millennium trilogy of novels in circulation—and both Swedish and Hollywood film adaptations thrilling moviegoers worldwide—Stockholm has a new breed of tourist. Fans of Larsson's punked-out computer hacker heroine Lisbeth Salander and jaded journalist hero Mikael Blomkvist are stalking the city's neighborhoods, particularly Södermalm, just south of the Old Town.

Stockholm's geography is key to Larsson's crime thrillers: Most of the good guys live and work in the formerly working-class Södermalm, while many of the villains hail from tony neighborhoods near Parliament and City Hall, across the water.

If you come looking for Lisbeth or Mikael, the best place to start is the **City of Stockholm Museum** in Södermalm, near the Slussen T-bana stop (70 kr, Tue-Sun 11:00-17:00, Thu until 20:00, closed Mon, Ryssgården, tel. 08/5083-1620, www.stadsmuseum.stockholm.se). The museum hosts a display of Larsson artifacts, including a reconstruction of Mikael Blomkvist's office at *Millennium* magazine, and offers Millennium walking tours in English (120 kr, Wed at 18:00, Sat at 11:30) and a Millennium sights map (40 kr).

A few blocks from the museum is the site of the fictional *Millennium* offices, above the Greenpeace headquarters at the corner of Götgatan and Hökens Gata (really it's just apartments). Two real businesses in Södermalm figure prominently in the trilogy: **Kvarnen**, an old-style pub where Lisbeth hangs out with an all-girl punk band (Tjärhovsgatan 4, near the Medborgarplasten T-bana stop; see "Eating in Stockholm," later); and the **Mellqvist café** (Hornsgatan 78, near the Hornstull T-bana stop), where the love-struck Lisbeth sees Mikael kiss his mistress.

for modesty and the other to sit on). The pool is more for floating than for jumping and splashing. The leafy courtyard restaurant is a relaxing place to enjoy affordable, healthy, and light meals.

Cost and Hours: 220 kr, increases to 320 kr on Sat, towels and robes available for rent; open Mon-Fri 7:00-21:00, Sat 9:00-21:00, Sun 9:00-18:00, last entry one hour before closing, ages 18 and up, Drottninggatan 88, 10 minutes up from Sergels Torg, tel. 08/5452-1300, tel. 08/5452-1313, www.centralbadet.se.

Djurgården

Four hundred years ago, Djurgården was the king's hunting ground. Now this entire lush island is Stockholm's fun center,

STOCKHOLM

Stockholm's Djurgården

protected as a national park. It still has a smattering of animal life among its biking paths, picnicking local families, art galleries, and various amusements. Of the three great sights on the island, the Vasa and Nordic museums are neighbors, and Skansen is a 10-minute walk away (or hop on any bus—they come every couple of minutes). To get around more easily, consider renting a bike as you enter the island (see page 424).

Getting There: Take tram #7 from Sergels Torg (the stop is right under the highway overpass) and get off at the Nordic Museum (also for the Vasa Museum), or continue on to the Skansen stop. In summer, you can take a ferry from Nybroplan or Slussen (see "Getting Around Stockholm," earlier). Walkers can enjoy the harborside Strandvägen promenade, which leads from Nybroplan directly to the island.

▲▲▲Skansen

This is Europe's original open-air folk museum, founded in 1891. It's a huge park gathering more than 150 historic buildings (homes, churches, shops, and school-houses) transplanted from all corners of Sweden.

Cost and Hours: 150 kr, kids-

STOCKHOLM

60 kr, less off-season; park open daily May-mid-June 10:00-19:00, mid-June-Aug 10:00-22:00, Sept 10:00-18:00, Oct and March-April 10:00-16:00, Nov-Feb 10:00-15:00; historical buildings generally open 11:00-15:00, June-Aug some until 19:00, most closed in winter. Check their excellent website for "What's Happening at Skansen" during your visit (www.skansen.se) or call 08/442-8000 (press 1 for a live operator). Gröna Lund, Stockholm's amusement park, is across the street (described later).

Music: Skansen does great music in summer. There's fiddling (30-minute performances June-Aug Tue-Fri at 18:15), folk-dancing (June-Aug Tue-Fri at 19:00, also Sat-Sun at 16:00), and public dancing to live bands (Mon-Sat from 20:00, call for that evening's theme—big band, modern, ballroom, folk).

Aquarium: Admission to the aquarium is the only thing not covered on your Skansen ticket, but it is covered by the Stockholm Card (100 kr; June-Aug daily 10:00-20:00; Sept-May Tue-Sun 10:00-16:30, closed Mon; tel. 08/660-1082, www.skansen-akvariet.se).

Visiting Skansen: Skansen was the first in what became a Europe-wide movement to preserve traditional architecture in open-air museums. Other languages have even borrowed the Swedish term "Skansen" (which originally meant "the Fort") to describe an "open-air museum." Today, tourists still explore this Swedish-culture-on-a-lazy-Susan, seeing folk crafts in action and wonderfully furnished old interiors. While it's lively June through August before about 17:00, at other times of the year it can seem pretty dead; consider skipping it if you're here off-season.

In "Old Stockholm" (top of the escalator), shoemakers, potters, and glassblowers are busy doing their traditional thing (daily 10:00-17:00) in a re-created Old World Stockholm. The rest of Sweden spreads out from Old Stockholm. Northern Swedish culture and architecture is in the north (top of park map), and southern Sweden's in the south (bottom of map).

Take advantage of the free map, and consider the 50-kr museum guidebook. With the book, you'll understand each building you duck into and even learn about the Nordic animals awaiting you in the zoo. Check the live crafts schedule at the information stand by the main entrance beneath the escalator to make a smart Skansen plan. Guides throughout the park are happy to answer your questions—but only if you ask them. The old houses come alive when you take the initiative to get information.

Kids love Skansen, where they can ride a life-size wooden *Dala*-horse and stare down a hedgehog, visit Lill' Skansen (a children's zoo), and take a mini-train or pony ride.

Eating at Skansen: The most memorable meals are at the small folk food court on the main square, **Bollnastorget.** Here, among the duck-filled lakes, frolicking families, and peacenik local toddlers who don't bump on the bumper cars, kiosks dish up "Sami slow food" (smoked reindeer), waffles, hot dogs, and more. There are lots of picnic benches—Skansen encourages **picnicking.** (A small grocery store is tucked away across the street and a bit to the left of the main entrance.) For a sit-down meal, three eateries share a building just up the hill inside the main entrance: Skansen's primary restaurant, **Solliden,** serves a big *smörgåsbord* lunch in a grand blue-and-white room (310 kr, June-Aug daily 12:00-16:00); **Tre Byttor Taverne** captures 18th-century pub ambience with an à la carte menu (June-Aug daily 12:00-21:00, shorter hours off-season); and the **Skansen Terrassen** cafeteria offers less-expensive self-service lunches with a view (90-kr daily specials; mid-June-mid-Aug daily 11:00-19:00, shorter hours off-season). Nearby, the old-time **Stora Gungan Krog,** right at the top of the escalator, is a cozy inn; their freshly baked cakes will tempt you (80-160-kr indoor or outdoor lunches—meat, fish, or veggie—with a salad-and-cracker bar, daily 10:00-22:00, until 15:00 in winter).

▲▲▲*Vasa* Museum (Vasamuseet)

Stockholm turned a titanic flop into one of Europe's great sightseeing attractions. The glamorous but unseaworthy warship *Vasa*—

top-heavy with an extra cannon deck—sank 40 minutes into her 1628 maiden voyage when a breeze caught the sails and blew her over. After 333 years at the bottom of Stockholm's harbor, she rose again from the deep with the help of marine archaeologists. Rediscovered in 1956 and raised in 1961, this Edsel of the sea is today the best-preserved ship of its age anywhere—housed since 1990 in a brilliant museum. The masts perched atop the roof—best seen from a distance—show the actual height of the ship.

Cost and Hours: 110 kr, includes video and tour; June-Aug daily 8:30-18:00; Sept-May daily 10:00-17:00, Wed until 20:00; Galärvarvet, Djurgården, tel. 08/5195-4800, www.vasamuseet.se.

Getting There: The *Vasa* is on the waterfront immediately behind the stately brick Nordic Museum (described later), a 10-minute walk from Skansen. Or you can take tram #7 from downtown. The museum also has a good café inside. To get from the Nordic Museum to the *Vasa* Museum, face the Nordic Museum and walk around to the right (going left takes you into a big dead-end parking lot).

Crowd-Beating Tips: The museum can have very long lines. But don't panic, as the lines generally move quickly. You likely won't wait more than 15-20 minutes, but extremely busy times can cause 30-minute delays (if it hits capacity, they have to stop admitting people for a while). If crowds are a concern, do your best to get here either right when it opens, or after about 16:00.

Planning Your Time: For a thorough visit, plan on spending at least an hour and a half: Watch the 17-minute video (which explains the modern-day excavation and preservation of the ship), take the free 25-minute tour (which generally focuses on the *Vasa*'s history)—in either order—then explore the boat and wander through the various exhibits. The **video** generally runs three times per hour; almost all showings are either in English or with English subtitles (check at the info desk). In summer, English **tours** run on the hour and at :30 past the hour; listen for the loudspeaker announcement, or check at the info desk; off-season (Sept-May), tours go only at :30 past each hour beginning at 9:30 (last tour departs at 16:30). Because each guide is given license to cover whatever he or she likes, no two tours are alike—if you're fascinated by the place, consider taking two different tours to pick up new details.

Background: The *Vasa*, while not quite the biggest ship in the world, had the most firepower, with two fearsome decks of cannons. The 500 carved wooden statues draping the ship—once painted in bright colors—are all symbolic of the king's power. The 10-foot lion on the magnificent prow is a reminder that Europe considered the Swedish King Gustavus Adolphus the "Lion from the North." With this great ship, Sweden was preparing to establish its empire and become more engaged in European power politics. Specifically, the Swedes (who already controlled much of today's Finland and Estonia) wanted to push south to dominate the whole of the Baltic Sea, in order to challenge their powerful rival, Poland.

Designed by a Dutch shipbuilder, the *Vasa* had 72 guns of the same size and type (a rarity on mix-and-match warships of the age), allowing maximum efficiency in reloading—since there was no need to keep track of different ammunition. Unfortunately, the king's unbending demands to build it high (172 feet tall) but skinny (less than 16 feet wide) made it extremely unstable; no amount of ballast could weigh the ship down enough to prevent it from tipping.

Visiting the Museum: Exhibits are situated on six levels around the grand hall, circling the ship itself. Most exhibits are on the entrance level (4). The lowest level (2) has displays on the shipyards where the *Vasa* was built; upstairs on level 5, you can walk through replicas of ship interiors (handy, since you can't enter the actual ship). All displays are well described in English. You'll learn about the ship's rules (bread can't be older than eight years), why it sank (heavy bread?), how it's preserved (the ship, not the bread), and so on. Best of all is the chance to do slow laps around the magnificent vessel at different levels. Now painstakingly restored, 95 percent of the *Vasa*'s wood is original (modern bits are the brighter and smoother planks).

▲▲Nordic Museum (Nordiska Museet)

Built to look like a Danish Renaissance palace, this museum offers a fascinating peek at 500 years of traditional Swedish lifestyles. It's arguably more informative than Skansen. Take time to let the excellent, included audioguide enliven the exhibits. Carl Milles' huge painted-wood statue of Gustav Vasa, father of modern Sweden, overlooks the main gallery.

Highlights are on the top two floors. The middle floor (level 3) holds the *Traditions* exhibit (showing and describing each old-time celebration of the Swedish year) and a section of exquisite table settings, and fancy fashions from the 18th through the 20th centuries. The top floor (level 4) has an extensive Sami (Lapp) collection, old furniture, and an exhibit showing Swedish living rooms over the last century; it provides an insightful look at today's Swedes, including an intimate peek at modern bedrooms (match photos of the owners with the various rooms).

Cost and Hours: 90 kr, free Wed after 17:00 Sept-May; daily 10:00-17:00, Wed until 20:00 Sept-May; Djurgårdsvägen 6-16, at Djurgårdsbron, tram #7 from downtown, tel. 08/5195-6000, www.nordiskamuseet.se.

Other Djurgården Sights

The long-rumored ABBA museum, backed by one of the former band members, is expected to open in 2013 on Djurgården. For the latest details, check www.abbathemuseum.com.

Gröna Lund—Stockholm's venerable and lowbrow Tivoli-type amusement park still packs in the local families and teens on cheap dates. It's a busy venue for local pop concerts.

Cost and Hours: 95 kr, May-Sept daily 12:00-23:00, closed off-season, www.gronalund.com.

▲**Thielska Galleriet**—If you liked the Larsson and Zorn art in the National Gallery, and/or if you're a Munch fan, this charming mansion on the water at the far end of the Djurgården park is worth the trip.

Cost and Hours: 100 kr, Tue-Sun 12:00-17:00, Thu until 20:00, closed Mon, bus #69—not #69K—from downtown, tel. 08/662-5884, www.thielska-galleriet.se.

▲**Biking the Garden Island**—In all of Stockholm, Djurgården is the natural place to enjoy a bike ride. There's a good and reasonably priced bike-rental place just over the bridge as you enter the island (see "Bike Rental" on page 424), and a world of park-like paths and lanes with harbor vistas to enjoy. Ask for a free map and route tips when you rent your bike. Figure about an hour to pedal around Djurgården's waterfront perimeter; it's mostly flat, though the stretches that take you up and over the middle of the island can be temporarily steep. A garden café at the eastern tip of the island offers a scenic break midway through your pedal. For a longer ride, you can cross the canal to the Ladugårdsgärdet peninsula ("Gärdet" for short), a swanky, wooded residential district just to the north.

Outer Stockholm

▲**Millesgården**—The villa and garden of Carl Milles is a veritable forest of statues by Sweden's greatest sculptor. Millesgården is dramatically situated on a bluff overlooking the harbor in Stockholm's upper-class suburb of Lidingö. While the art is engaging and enjoyable, even the curators have little to say about it from an interpretation point of view—so your visit is basically without guidance. But in Milles' house, which dates from the 1920s, you can see his north-lit studio and get a sense of his creative genius.

Carl Milles spent much of his career living in Michigan. But he's buried here at his villa, where he lived and worked for 20 years, lovingly designing this sculpture garden for the public. Milles wanted his art to be displayed on pedestals...to be seen "as if silhouettes against the sky." His subjects—often Greek mythological figures such as Pegasus or Poseidon—stand out as if the sky was a blank paper. Yet unlike silhouettes, Milles' images can be enjoyed from many angles. And

Milles liked to enliven his sculptures by incorporating water features into his figures. *Hand of God,* perhaps his most famous work, gives insight into Milles' belief that when the artist created, he was—in a way—divinely inspired.

Cost and Hours: 100 kr, 30-kr or 75-kr English booklet explains the art; May-Sept daily 11:00-17:00; Oct-April Tue-Sun 11:00-17:00, closed Mon; restaurant and café, tel. 08/446-7590, www.millesgarden.se.

Getting There: Catch the T-bana to Ropsten, then take bus #207 to within a five-minute walk of the museum (allow about 45 minutes total each way).

▲▲Drottningholm Palace (Drottningholms Slott)—The queen's 17th-century summer castle and current royal residence has been called "Sweden's

Versailles." Touring the palace, you'll see art that makes the point that Sweden's royalty is divine and belongs with the gods. You can walk the two floors on your own, but with no explanations or audioguides, it makes sense to take the included guided tour.

Cost and Hours: 100 kr, May-Aug daily 10:00-16:30, Sept daily 11:00-15:30, Oct and April Fri-Sun only 11:00-15:30, Nov-Dec and mid-Jan-March Sat-Sun only 12:00-15:30, closed last two weeks of Dec; free-with-admission palace tours in English are offered June-Aug usually at 10:00, 12:00, 14:00, and 16:00; fewer tours off-season; tel. 08/402-6280, www.royalcourt.se.

Services: There is no WC in the palace. The closest WC is a three-minute walk from the entrance, near the café and boat dock. The café serves light meals, and taxis usually wait nearby.

Getting There: Reach the palace via a relaxing one-hour boat ride (120 kr one-way, 175 kr round-trip, 130 kr round-trip with Stockholm Card, departs from Stadhusbron across from City Hall on the hour through the day, tel. 08/1200-4000), or take the

T-bana to Brommaplan, where you can catch any #300-series bus to Drottningholm (54 kr one-way, allow 30-45 minutes from city center). Consider approaching by water (as the royals traditionally did) and then returning by bus and T-bana (as a commoner).

Visiting the Palace: You'll see two floors of lavish rooms, where Sweden's royalty did their best to live in the style of Europe's divine monarchs. While rarely absolute rulers, Sweden's royals long struggled with stubborn parliaments. Perhaps this made the propaganda value of the palace decor even more important. Portraits and busts legitimize the royal family by connecting the Swedish blue bloods with Roman emperors, medieval kings, and Europe's great royal families. The portraits you'll see of France's Louis XVI and Russia's Catherine the Great are reminders that Sweden's royalty was related to or tightly networked with the European dynasties.

The king's bedroom looks like (and was) more of a theater than a place for sleeping. In the style of the French monarchs, this is where the ceremonial tucking-in and dressing of the king would take place. The Room of War—with kings, generals, battle scenes, and bugle-like candleholders—is from the time when Sweden was a superpower (1600-1750). The murals commemorate a victory over the Danes: It's said Swedish kings enjoyed taking the Danish ambassador here.

Of course, today's monarchs are figureheads ruled by a constitution. The royal family makes a point to be as accessible and as "normal" as royalty can be. King Carl XVI Gustaf (b. 1946)—whose main job is handing out Nobel Prizes once a year—is a car nut who talks openly about his dyslexia. He was the first Swedish king not to be crowned "by the grace of God." The popular Queen Silvia is a businessman's daughter. At their 1976 wedding festivities, ABBA serenaded her with "Dancing Queen." Their daughter and heir to the throne, Crown Princess Victoria, studied political science at Yale and interned with Sweden's European Union delegation. In 2010 she married gym owner Daniel Westling—the first royal wedding in Sweden since her parents' marriage. Victoria and Daniel's first child, Princess Estelle, was born on February 23, 2012—and instantly became the next heir to the throne.

Drottningholm Court Theater (Drottningholms Slottsteater): This 18th-century theater somehow survived the ages—complete with its instruments, sound-effects machines, and stage sets. It's one of two such theaters remaining in Europe (the other is in Český Krumlov, Czech Republic). Visit it on a 30-minute guided tour, offered at the top of the hour (90 kr, May-Aug 10:00-17:00, Sept 11:00-15:30, no tours off-season, tel. 08/759-0406), or check their schedule for the rare opportunity to see perfectly authentic operas (about 25 performances each summer). Tickets for this popular time-travel musical and theatrical experience cost 275-895 kr and go on sale each March; purchase online or by phone or fax (see www.dtm.se).

Sigtuna—This town, an old-time lakeside jumble of wooden houses and waffle shops, presents a fluffy, stereotyped version of Sweden as it was in the olden days. You'll see a medieval lane lined with colorful tourist boutiques, cafés, a romantic park, waterfront promenade, old town hall, and rune stones. The TI can help you get oriented (tel. 08/5948-0650, http://sal.sigtuna.se/turism). If traveling by car to Uppsala (described on page 481) or Oslo (see the Oslo chapter), Sigtuna is a short detour, good for a browse and an ice-cream cone, but little more. By public transport, it's probably not worth the tedious one-hour trip out (take the *pendeltåg* suburban train from Stockholm to Märsta and then change to bus #570).

▲▲▲**Archipelago (Skärgården)**—Some of Europe's most scenic islands (thousands of them) stretch 80 miles from Stockholm out to the open Baltic Sea. If you cruise to Finland, you'll get a good dose of this island beauty.  Otherwise, consider one of many half- or full-day trips from downtown Stockholm to the archipelago. Hopping the local ferries to visit an island or two and see the lazy comings and goings of the island vacationers makes for a great day. For all the details, see the next chapter.

Shopping in Stockholm

Sweden offers a world of shopping temptations. **Nordiska Kompaniet** (NK, short for "no kronor left"), Stockholm's top-end department store, is located in an elegant early 20th-century building that dominates the far end of Kungsträdgården. If it feels like an old-time American department store, that's because its architect was inspired by grand stores he'd seen in the US (circa 1910). The Swedish design section (downstairs) and the kitchenware section are particularly impressive.

The classy **Gallerian** mall is just up the street from NK and stretches seductively nearly to Sergels Torg. The **Åhléns** store, nearby at Sergels Torg, is less expensive than NK and has two cafeterias and a supermarket. Fashion-forward **H&M** is right across the street. Drottninggatan is a long pedestrian boulevard lined with shops.

Designtorget, a store dedicated to contemporary Swedish design, receives a commission for selling the unique works of local designers (Mon-Fri 10:00-19:00, Sat 10:00-18:00, Sun 11:00-17:00, underneath Sergels Torg—enter from basement level of Kulturhuset, tel. 08/219-150, www.designtorget.se).

For more on Swedish design, pick up the *Design Guide* flier at the TI (listing smaller stores throughout town with a flair for design). The trendy and exclusive shops (including Orrefors and Kosta) line Biblioteksgatan just off Stureplan.

Traditionally, stores are open weekdays 10:00-18:00, Saturdays until 17:00, and Sundays 11:00-16:00. Some of the bigger stores (such as NK, H&M, and Åhléns) are open later on Saturdays and Sundays.

When Swedes want the latest fashions by local designers, they skip the downtown malls and head for funky Södermalm. The main drag that leads from Slussen up to this neighborhood, **Götgatan,** is a particularly good choice, with shop after shop of Swedish (not international) designers. Local boutiques along here include Weekday jeans, Filippa K, J.Lindeberg, Tiogruppen, and others. For more on this area, see page 473 in "Eating in Stockholm."

For a *smörgåsbord* of Scanjunk, visit the **Loppmarknaden,** northern Europe's biggest flea market, at the planned suburb of Skärholmen (free entry weekdays and Sat-Sun after 15:00, 15 kr on weekends—when it's busiest; open Mon-Fri 11:00-18:00, Sat 10:00-16:00, Sun 11:00-16:00; T-bana: Varberg—on line #13—is just steps from the shopping action, tel. 08/710-0060, www.lopp marknaden.se). Hötorget, the produce market, also hosts a Sunday flea market in summer (see page 475).

Stockholms Stadsmission's secondhand shop in Gamla Stan is a great place to pick up an unusual gift and contribute to this worthwhile charity (near Stortorget at Trångsund 8, Mon-Fri 10:00-18:00, Sat 11:00-16:00, Sun 12:00-16:00, tel. 08/787-8682, www.stadsmissionen.se/secondhand).

Systembolaget is Sweden's state-run liquor store chain. A sample of each bottle of wine or liquor sits in a display case. A card in front explains how it tastes and suggests menu pairings. Look for the item number and order at the counter. There's a branch in Gamla Stan at Lilla Nygatan 18, in Hötorget underneath the movie theater complex, and in Norrmalm at Vasagatan 21 (Mon-Wed 10:00-18:00, Thu-Fri 10:00-19:00, Sat 10:00-15:00, closed Sun, www.systembolaget.se).

Nightlife in Stockholm

Bars and Music in Gamla Stan—The street called Stora Nygatan, with several lively bars, has perhaps the most accessible and reliable place for good jazz in town: Stampen.

Stampen Jazz & Rhythm 'n' Blues Pub has two venues: a stone-vaulted cellar below and a fun-loving saloon-like bar upstairs (check out the old instruments and antiques hanging from the ceiling). From Monday through Thursday, there's live music only in the saloon. On Friday and Saturday, bands alternate sets in both the saloon and the cellar (160-kr cover Fri-Sat only, 58-kr beers, open Mon-Sat 20:00-1:00 in the morning, even later Fri-Sat, free blues Mon-Thu, special free jam session Sat 14:00-18:00, closed Sun, Stora Nygatan 5, tel. 08/205-793, www.stampen.se). For the location, see the map on page 470.

Several other lively spots are within a couple of blocks of Stampen on Stora Nygatan, including **Wirströms Pub** (live blues bands play in crowded cellar Tue-Sat 21:00-24:00, no cover, 62-kr beers, open daily 11:00-1:00 in the morning, Stora Nygatan 13, www.wirstromspub.se), **O'Connells Irish Pub** (a lively expat sports bar with music downstairs, daily 12:00-1:00 in the morning, Stora Nygatan 21, www.oconnells.se), and **The Liffey** (classic Irish pub with 160-200-kr pub grub, live music nightly at 21:30, daily in summer 11:00-late, off-season 16:00-late, Stora Nygatan 40-42, www.theliffey.se). Just beyond Gamla Stan, the good ship *Patricia* rocks with live music and well-lubricated locals most nights (no cover, often live music, described on page 475). Another pub with music is a few doors down.

Icebar Stockholm—If you just want to put on a heavy coat and gloves and drink a fancy vodka in a modern-day igloo, consider the fun, if touristy, Icebar Stockholm. Everything's ice—shipped down from Sweden's far north.  The bar, the glasses, even the tip jar are made of ice. You get your choice of vodka drinks and 45 minutes to enjoy the scene (online booking-180 kr, drop-in after 21:45-195 kr, additional drinks-95 kr, reservations smart; daily June-Aug 11:15-24:00, Sept-May 15:00-24:00; last entry 45 minutes before closing, in the Nordic Sea Hotel adjacent to the main train station at Vasaplan 4, tel. 08/5056-3124, www .icebar.se). People are let in all at once every 45 minutes. That means there's a long line for drinks, and the place goes from being very crowded to almost empty as people gradually melt away. At first everyone's just snapping photos. While there are ice bars all over Europe now, this is the second one (after the Ice Hotel in Lapland). And it really is pretty cool...a steady 23°F.

Cinema—In Sweden, international movies are shown in their original language with Swedish subtitles. Swedish theaters sometimes charge more for longer films (95-135 kr, movies longer than 2 hours are usually the higher price), and tickets come with assigned seats (drop by to choose seats and buy a ticket, box offices generally open 11:00-22:00 daily). The Hötorget and Drottninggatan neighborhoods have many theaters.

Sleeping in Stockholm

Peak season for Stockholm's hotels—weeknights outside of summer vacation time—is dictated by business travelers. Rates drop by 30-50 percent in the summer (mid-June-mid-Aug) and on Friday and Saturday nights year-round. Because many hotels set prices based on demand, rates listed in this section can have a wide range. If you ask for discounts and comparison-shop, you're likely to save plenty. For more booking tips, see page 24.

Plenty of people offer private accommodations (600-800-kr doubles). Stockholm's hostels are among Europe's best, offering good beds in simple but interesting places for about 300 kr per night. Each has helpful English-speaking staff, pleasant family rooms, and good facilities. Hosteling is cheapest when you're a member, provide your own sheets, and buy your own food for breakfast.

A program called **Destination Stockholm** is, for many (especially families), the best way to book a big hotel on weekends or during the summer. When you reserve a hotel room through this service, a **Stockholm à la Carte** card is thrown in for free. It covers public transportation, most major sights, and lots of tours—and is even better than the Stockholm Card. Kids sleep and get cards for free, too. The card is valid every day of your stay, including arrival and departure days. Reserve by phone or online; be sure

---

Sleep Code

(7 kr = about $1, country code: 46, area code: 08)
S = Single, **D** = Double/Twin, **T** = Triple, **Q** = Quad, **b** = bathroom, **s** = shower. Unless otherwise noted, all of my listings have non-smoking rooms and elevators, accept credit cards, and include big breakfast buffets. Everyone speaks English.

To help you sort easily through these listings, I've divided the accommodations into three categories, based on the price for a standard double room with bath during high season:

$$$ Higher Priced—Most rooms 1,700 kr or more.
$$ Moderately Priced—Most rooms between 800-1,700 kr.
$ Lower Priced—Most rooms 800 kr or less.

Prices can change without notice; verify the hotel's current rates online or by email.

STOCKHOLM

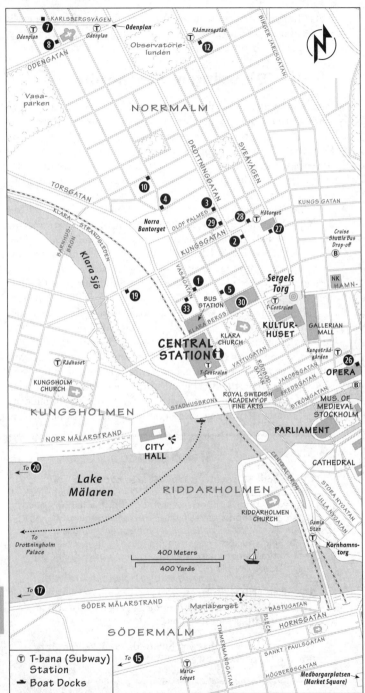

KARLSBERGSVÄGEN

Odenplan

⑦

Odenplan ← Odenplan

⑧ Odenplan

Rådmansgatan

ODENGATAN

Observatorie-lunden

Rådmansgatan ⑫

Vasa-parken

NORRMALM

DROTTNINGGATAN

SVEAVÄGEN

BIRGER JARLSGATAN

TORSGATAN

KUNGS GATAN

⑩

④

③

OLOF PALMES

Norra Bantorget

㉙

㉘

Hötorget

Ⓣ

㉗

KLARA STRANDLEDEN

KUNGSGATAN

② Cruise Shuttle Bus Drop-off Ⓑ

BARNHUS BRON

Klara Sjö

VASAGATAN

① ⑤

⑲

㉝

BUS STATION

㉚

Sergels Torg

Ⓣ T-Centralen

NK HAMN-

KLARABERGS-

KULTUR-HUSET

GALLERIAN MALL

Ⓣ Rådhuset

CENTRAL STATION ❶

KLARA CHURCH

Kungsträd-gården Ⓣ

㉖

KUNGSHOLM CHURCH

VATTUGATAN

RÖDBO GATAN

JAKOBSGATAN

OPERA

Ⓣ T-Centralen

ROYAL SWEDISH ACADEMY OF FINE ARTS

FREDSGATAN

STRÖMGATAN

MUS. OF MEDIEVAL STOCKHOLM

Ⓑ

KUNGSHOLMEN

STADHUSBRON

PARLIAMENT

NORR MÄLARSTRAND

CITY HALL

CATHEDRAL

To ⑳

Lake Mälaren

RIDDARHOLMEN

CENTRALBRON

STORA NYGATAN

LILLA NYGATAN

RIDDARHOLMEN CHURCH

Gamla Stan

To Drottningholm Palace

Kornhamns-torg

400 Meters

400 Yards

To ⑰

SÖDER MÄLARSTRAND

Mariaberget

BÄSTUGATAN

BLECK

HORNSGATAN

SÖDERMALM

TIMMERMANSGATAN

To ⑮

SANKT PAULSGATAN

Maria-torget

HÖGBERGSGATAN

Medborgarplatsen (Market Square)

Ⓣ T-bana (Subway) Station

Boat Docks

STOCKHOLM

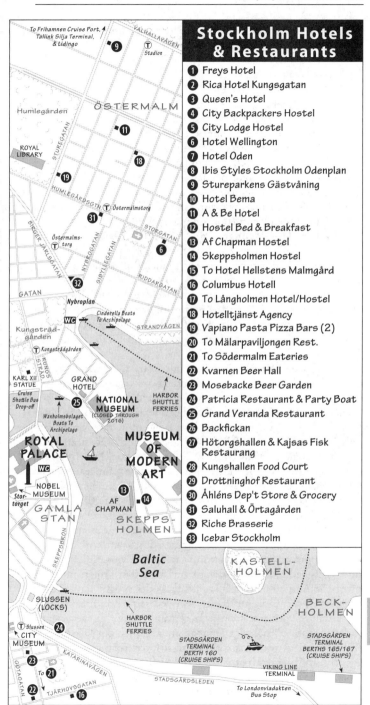

Stockholm Hotels & Restaurants

1. Freys Hotel
2. Rica Hotel Kungsgatan
3. Queen's Hotel
4. City Backpackers Hostel
5. City Lodge Hostel
6. Hotel Wellington
7. Hotel Oden
8. Ibis Styles Stockholm Odenplan
9. Stureparkens Gästvåning
10. Hotel Bema
11. A & Be Hotel
12. Hostel Bed & Breakfast
13. Af Chapman Hostel
14. Skeppsholmen Hostel
15. To Hotel Hellstens Malmgård
16. Columbus Hotell
17. To Långholmen Hotel/Hostel
18. Hotelltjänst Agency
19. Vapiano Pasta Pizza Bars (2)
20. To Mälarpaviljongen Rest.
21. To Södermalm Eateries
22. Kvarnen Beer Hall
23. Mosebacke Beer Garden
24. Patricia Restaurant & Party Boat
25. Grand Veranda Restaurant
26. Backfickan
27. Hötorgshallen & Kajsas Fisk Restaurang
28. Kungshallen Food Court
29. Drottninghof Restaurant
30. Åhléns Dep't Store & Grocery
31. Saluhall & Örtagården
32. Riche Brasserie
33. Icebar Stockholm

STOCKHOLM

to review the cancellation policy before you commit (tel. 08/663-0080, www.destination-stockholm.com).

In Downtown Norrmalm, near the Train Station

$$$ **Freys Hotel** is a Scan-mod, four-star place, with 124 compact, smartly designed rooms on a quiet pedestrian street. While big, it works hard to be friendly and welcoming. It's well-situated, located on a dead-end street across from the central train station. Its cool, candlelit breakfast room becomes a bar in the evening, popular for its selection of Belgian microbrews (Sb-1,050-1,750 kr, Db-1,550-2,050 kr, Internet access, Bryggargatan 12, tel. 08/5062-1300, fax 08/5062-1313, www.freyshotels.com, freys@freyshotels.com). Check their website for summer specials.

$$ **Rica Hotel Kungsgatan,** central but characterless, fills the top floors of a downsized department store with 270 rooms. If the Starship *Enterprise* had a low-end hotel, this would be it. Save 150-400 kr by taking a room with no windows—the same size as other rooms, extremely quiet, and well-ventilated. This is the rare hotel where you'll get the best price by booking online with a travel website—calling direct will get you a more expensive rate (Db-1,195-1,895 kr, Kungsgatan 47, tel. 08/723-7220, fax 08/723-7299, www.rica.se, rica@rica.no).

$$ **Queen's Hotel** enjoys a great location at the quiet top end of Stockholm's main pedestrian shopping street (about a 10-minute walk from the train station or Gamla Stan). The 52 well-priced rooms feel old-fashioned but have been renovated, and the plush Old World lounge is inviting. Three types of double rooms vary only in size (Sb-1,020-1,220 kr, "small standard" Db-1,120-1,320 kr, "large standard" Db-1,220-1,520 kr, "superior" Db with pull-out sofa bed-1,320-1,620 kr, 10 percent discount for readers who book direct—be sure to ask for it, extra bed-250 kr, elevator, free Internet access and Wi-Fi, Drottninggatan 71A, tel. 08/249-460, fax 08/217-620, www.queenshotel.se, info@queenshotel.se).

$ **City Backpackers** is central—a quarter-mile from the station—and open year-round. It's enthusiastically run, with 140 beds and plenty of creativity (bunk in 8- to 12-bed room-190 kr, bunk in 4- or 6-bed room-280 kr, bunk-bed D-650 kr, 6-person apartment-1,760 kr, 40 percent more for Fri- or Sat-night stay without weeknight, sheets-50 kr, free cook-it-yourself pasta, breakfast-40 kr, laundry-50 kr, free Internet access and Wi-Fi, movies, sauna, lockers, shoes-off policy, Upplandsgatan 2A, tel. 08/206-920, fax 08/100-464, www.citybackpackers.se, info@citybackpackers.se).

$ **City Lodge Hostel,** new and well-run, is just a block in front of the central train station on a quiet side street. It has a convivial lounge, kitchen, free Internet access, laundry, and no curfew. It's a good value for backpackers in Stockholm (65 beds, bunk in 18-bed dorm-220 kr, in 6-bed dorm-270 kr, in quad-315 kr, a few tiny bunk-bed doubles-640 kr, cheaper outside of summer, sheets-50 kr, 60-kr breakfast available, Klara Norra Kyrkogata 15, tel. 08/226-630, www.citylodge.se, info@citylodge.se).

In Norrmalm and Östermalm, in Quieter Residential Areas

These options are in stately, elegant neighborhoods of five- and six-story turn-of-the-century apartment buildings. All are too far to walk from the station with luggage, but still in easy reach of downtown sights and close to T-bana stops.

$$$ **Hotel Wellington,** two blocks off Östermalmstorg square, is in a less handy but charming part of town. It's modern and bright, with hardwood floors, 60 rooms, and a friendly welcome. While it may seem pricey, it's a cut above in comfort and its great amenities—such as a very generous buffet breakfast, free coffee all day long, and free buffet dinner in the evening—add up to a good value (prices range widely, but in summer generally Sb-1,220 kr, Db-1,420-1,620 kr, smaller Db for 200 kr less, fill out their Choice Card and save 5 percent, mention this book when reserving and you might save a little more, free Internet access and Wi-Fi, free sauna, old-fashioned English bar, garden terrace bar, T-bana: Östermalmstorg, exit to Storgatan and walk toward big church to Storgatan 6; tel. 08/667-0910, fax 08/667-1254, www.wellington .se, cc.wellington@choice.se).

$$ **Hotel Oden,** a recently renovated 140-room place with all the comforts, is three T-bana stops from the train station (Sb-960-1,410 kr, Db-1,240-1,750 kr, extra bed-160-190 kr, sauna, free Internet access and Wi-Fi, free coffee and tea in the evening; T-bana: Odenplan, exit in direction of Västmannagatan, Karlbergsvägen 24; tel. 08/457-9700, fax 08/457-9710, www .hoteloden.se). Some rooms come with a kitchenette for the same price (just request one).

$$ **Ibis Styles Stockholm Odenplan,** a half-block from Hotel Oden, rents 76 rooms on several floors of a late-19th-century apartment building (S-from 950 kr, Db-from 1,150 kr, lower in summer if you book two months in advance, T-bana: Odenplan, Västmannagatan 61, tel. 08/1209-0000, fax 08/307-372, www.ibis styles.se, odenplan@uniquehotels.se).

$$ **Stureparkens Gästvåning,** carefully run by Challe, an Iraqi-Swede, is one floor of an apartment building converted into nine bright, clean, quiet, and thoughtfully appointed rooms. Only two rooms have private bathrooms (S-850 kr, D-895-990 kr, Tb-1,495 kr, sprawling Db apartment-2,250 kr, kitchen, guest laundry facility, free Internet access; T-bana: Stadion, across from

Stureparken at Sturegatan 58, take elevator to fourth floor; tel. 08/662-7230, fax 08/661-5713, www.hotelstureparken.se, info @hotelstureparken.se).

$$ Hotel Bema is a humble place that rents out 12 fine rooms for some of the best prices in town (S-550-900 kr, Db-800-1,100 kr, extra person-250 kr, breakfast served in room, bus #65 from station to Upplandsgatan 13, tel. 08/232-675, www.hotelbema.se, hotell.bema@stockholm.mail.telia.com).

$$ A & Be Hotel, with 12 homey rooms, fills the first floor of a grand old building in a residential area (S-540 kr, Sb-840 kr, D-690 kr, Db-990 kr, breakfast-50 kr, free Wi-Fi, T-bana: Stadion, Grev Turegatan 50, tel. 08/660-2100, fax 08/660-5987, www.abehotel.com, info@abehotel.com).

$ Hostel Bed and Breakfast is a tiny, woody, and easygoing independent hostel renting 36 cheap beds in various dorm-style rooms. Many families stay here (bed in 4-bed room-320 kr, Sb-550 kr, Db-780 kr, sheets-50 kr, kitchen, laundry, across the street from T-bana: Rådmansgatan, just off Sveavägen at Rehnsgatan 21, tel. & fax 08/152-838, www.hostelbedandbreakfast.com).

On Gamla Stan and Skeppsholmen

These options are in the midst of sightseeing, a short bus or taxi ride from the train station. For the first two hotels, see the map on page 470. For the rest, see page 463.

$$$ Rica Hotel Gamla Stan offers Old World elegance in the heart of Gamla Stan (a 5-minute walk from Gamla Stan T-bana station). Its 51 small rooms are filled with chandeliers and hardwood floors (Sb-900-1,800 kr, Db-1,200-2,200 kr, 200 kr extra for larger room, Lilla Nygatan 25, tel. 08/723-7250, fax 08/723-7259, www.rica.se, info.gamlastan@rica.se).

$$$ Lady Hamilton Hotel, expensive and lavishly furnished, is shoehorned into Gamla Stan on a quiet street a block below the cathedral and Royal Palace. The centuries-old building has 34 small, plush rooms and is filled with antiques and thoughtful touches (Db-1,450-3,200 kr, free Internet access, Storkyrkobrinken 5, tel. 08/5064-0100, fax 08/5064-0110, www .ladyhamiltonhotel.se, info@ladyhamiltonhotel.se).

$ Af Chapman Hostel, a permanently moored 100-year-old schooner, is Europe's most famous youth hostel and has provided a berth for the backpacking crowd for years. Renovated from keel to stern, the old salt offers 120 bunks in four- to six-bed rooms (bunk-375 kr, D-830 kr, 50 kr/night discount for members, free Wi-Fi). Reception and breakfast are at Skeppsholmen Hostel (next).

$ Skeppsholmen Hostel, just ashore from the *Af Chapman*, has 160 beds (bunk in 17-bed dorm-265 kr, bunk in 3- to 6-bed room-310 kr, D-690 kr, 50 kr less for hostel members, sheets-70 kr, breakfast-80 kr, laundry service, no lockout, free Wi-Fi, bus #65 from train station or walk about 20 minutes, tel. 08/463-2266, www.stfchapman.com, chapman@stfturist.se).

On or near Södermalm

Södermalm is residential and hip, with Stockholm's best café and bar scene. You'll need to take the bus or T-bana to get here from the train station.

$$ Hotel Hellstens Malmgård is an eclectic collage of 50 rooms crammed with antiques in a circa-1770 mansion. No two rooms are alike, but all have modern baths and quirky touches such as porcelain stoves or four-poster beds. Unwind in its secluded cobblestone courtyard, and you may forget what century you're in (Sb-690-1,290 kr, Db-890-1,490 kr, elevator, free Wi-Fi; T-bana: Zinkensdamm, then a 5-minute walk to Brännkyrkagatan 110; tel. 08/4650-5800, fax 08/4650-5801, www.hellstensmalmgard.se, hotel@hellstensmalmgard.se).

$$ Columbus Hotell—located in a 19th-century building that formerly housed a brewery, a jail, and a hospital—has 69 quiet rooms in the heart of Södermalm. Half of its rooms (first and second floors) have private facilities. Third-floor rooms have facilities down the hall (S-845 kr, Sb-995-1,350 kr, D-995 kr, Db-1,350-1,650 kr, T-1,250 kr, no elevator; T-bana: Medborgarplatsen or bus #53 from train station to Tjärhovsplan, then a 5-minute walk to Tjärhovsgatan 11; tel. 08/5031-1200, fax 08/5031-1201, www.columbushotell.se, info@columbushotell.se).

$$ Långholmen Hotel/Hostel is on Långholmen, a small island off Södermalm that was transformed in the 1980s from Stockholm's main prison into a lovely park. Rooms are converted cells in the old prison building. You can choose between hostel- and hotel-standard rooms at many different price levels (hostel rooms: dorm bed-270 kr, D-650 kr, Tb-900 kr, Q-1,080 kr, 50-kr discount for hostel members, sheets-60 kr, breakfast-95 kr; hotel rooms: Db-1,700-1,890 kr, extra bed-250 kr, includes breakfast; free Wi-Fi, laundry room, kitchen, cafeteria, free parking, on-site swimming; T-bana: Hornstull, walk 10 minutes down and cross small bridge to Långholmen island, follow hotel signs 5 minutes farther; tel. 08/720-8500, fax 08/720-8575, www.langholmen.com, hotel@langholmen.com).

Rooms in Private Homes

Stockholm's private rooms can be a deal in high season if you want to have an at-home experience. During hotels' weekend/summer discount periods, private rooms don't save you much over a hotel. Be sure to get the front-door security code when you call, in case there's no intercom. Contact **Hotelltjänst,** a private-room booking

STOCKHOLM

agency (S-600 kr, D-750 kr, cash only, no breakfast, 2-night minimum; fully furnished apartments also available: Sb-800 kr, Db-1,200 kr; rates vary based on demand, Nybrogatan 44, tel. 08/104-437, fax 08/213-716, www.hotelltjanst.com, caretaker @hotelltjanst.com).

Eating in Stockholm

To save money, eat your main meal at lunch, when cafés and restaurants have 95-kr daily special plates called *dagens rätt* (generally Mon-Fri only). Most museums have handy cafés (with lots of turnover and therefore fresh food, 100-kr lunch deals, and often with fine views). Convenience stores serve gas station-style food (and often have seats). As anywhere, department stores and malls are eager to feed shoppers and can be a good, efficient choice. If you want culturally appropriate fast food, stop by a local hot dog stand. Picnics are a great option—especially for dinner, when restaurant prices are highest. There are plenty of park-like, harborside spots to give your cheap picnic some class.

In Gamla Stan

Most restaurants in Gamla Stan serve the 95-kr weekday lunch special mentioned above, which comes with a main dish, small salad,

bread, and free tap water. Choose from Swedish, Asian, or Italian cuisine. Several popular places are right on the main square (Stortorget) and near the cathedral. Järntorget, at the far end, is another fun tables-in-the-square scene and has a small Co-op Nära supermarket for picnic shopping. The Munkbrohallen supermarket downstairs in the Gamla Stan T-bana station is very picnic-friendly (daily 7:00-22:00). Touristy places line Västerlånggatan. You'll find more romantic spots hiding on side lanes. I've listed my favorites below (for locations, see the map on page 470).

Grillska Huset is a cheap and handy cafeteria run by Stockholms Stadsmission, a charitable organization helping the poor. It's grandly situated right on the old square, with indoor and outdoor seating (tranquil garden up the stairs and out back), fine daily specials, a hearty salad bar, and a staff committed to helping others. You can feed the hungry (that's you) and help house the homeless at the same time. The 85-kr daily special gets you a hot plate, salad, and coffee, or choose the 85-kr salad bar—both

Swedish Cuisine

Most people don't travel to Sweden for the [...] call it Wonder Bready. Though potatoes ar[...] are a focus of the country's cuisine, its vari[...] fish dishes can be surprisingly satisfying. If you don't think you'll like Swedish or Scandinavian food, be sure to splurge at a good-quality place before you pass final judgment.

Every region of Sweden serves different specialties, but you'll always find *svenska köttbullar* on the menu (Swedish meatballs made from beef and pork in a creamy sauce). This Swedish favorite is topped with lingonberry jam, which is served with many meat dishes across Scandinavia. Potatoes, seemingly the only vegetable known to Sweden, make for hearty *kroppkakor* dumplings filled with onions and minced meat. The northern variation, *pitepalt*, is filled with pork. Southern Sweden takes credit for *pytt i panna*, a medley of leftover meat and diced potatoes that's fried and served with an egg yolk on top. And it seems that virtually every meal you'll eat here includes a side of boiled, small new potatoes.

Though your meals will never be short on starch, be sure to try Sweden's most popular baked good, *kanelbulle*, for a not-so-light snack during the day. This pastry resembles a cinnamon roll, but it's made with cardamom and topped with pearl sugar. Enjoy one during *fika*, the daily Swedish coffee break so institutionalized that many locals use the term as a verb (see page 473).

Like those of its Nordic neighbors, Sweden's extensive coastline produces some of the best seafood in the world. A light, tasty appetizer is *gravad lax*, a dill-cured salmon on brown bread or crackers. You'll also likely encounter *Toast Skagen*. This appetizer-spread is made from shrimp, dill, mayonnaise, and Dijon mustard, and eaten on buttered toast.

For a main course, the most popular seafood dish is crayfish. Though only eaten by the aristocracy in the 16th century, these shellfish have since become a nationwide delicacy; they're cooked in brine with dill and eaten cold as a finger food. Traditional crayfish parties take place outdoors on summer evenings, particularly in August. Friends and family gather around to indulge in this specialty with rye bread and a strong cheese. The Swedes also love Baltic herring; try *stekt strömming*, a specialty of the east coast, which is herring fried with butter and parsley. As usual, it's served with potatoes and lingonberry jam. Adventurous diners can have their herring pickled or fermented—or order more unusual dishes like reindeer.

As for beer, the Swedes classify theirs by alcohol content. The higher the number, the higher the alcohol content—and the higher the price. *Klass 1* is light beer—very low-alcohol. *Klass 2* is stronger, but still mild. And *Klass 3* has the most body, the most alcohol, and the highest price.

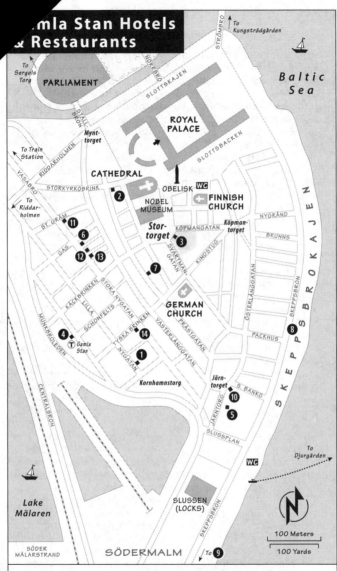

amla Stan Hotels & Restaurants

1. Rica Hotel Gamla Stan
2. Lady Hamilton Hotel
3. Grillska Huset Cafeteria
4. Vapiano Pasta Pizza Bar
5. O'Leary's Sports Bar
6. Hermitage Restaurant
7. Kryp In Restaurant
8. Pontus by the Sea
9. To Mosebacke Beer Garden; Patricia Restaurant & Party Boat
10. Co-op Nära Supermarket
11. Stampen Jazz & R-n-B Pub
12. Wirströms Pub
13. O'Connells Irish Pub
14. The Liffey Irish Pub

available Mon-Fri 11:00-14:00 (café serves sandwiches and salads daily 10:00-18:00, Stortorget 3, tel. 08/787-8605). They also have a fine little bakery.

Vapiano Pasta Pizza Bar, a mod, high-energy Italian place, issues you an electronic card as you enter. Circulate, ordering up whatever you like as they swipe your card. It's fun to oversee the construction of your 100-kr pasta, pizza, or salad. Portions are huge and easily splittable. As you leave, your card indicates the bill. Season things by picking a leaf of basil or rosemary from the potted plant on your table. Because tables are often shared, this a great place for solo travelers. They have Pilsner Urquell on tap but watch out—my glass of Chianti cost more than my pizza (daily 11:00-24:00, Fri-Sat until 1:00 in the morning, right next to entrance to Gamla Stan T-bana station, Munkbrogatan 8, tel. 08/222-940). They also have locations on Östermalm (facing Humlegården park at Sturegatan 12) and Norrmalm (between the train station and Kungsholmen at Kungsbron 15)—for these locations, see the map on page 463.

O'Leary's Sports Bar is a sudsy place that transports you to Ireland. While sloppy, it's good for basic pub grub and beer. And if a game is on, this is the place to be—their motto is, "Better than live" (120-kr meals, Järntorgsgatan 3, tel. 08/239-923).

Hermitage Restaurant serves tasty vegetarian food in a warm communal dining setting. Their daily special (100-kr lunch, 110-kr dinner after 15:00) buys a hot plate, salad, bread, and coffee (Mon-Fri 11:00-20:00, Sat-Sun 12:00-20:00, Stora Nygatan 11, tel. 08/411-9500).

Kryp In, a small, cozy restaurant (the name means "hide away") tucked into a peaceful lane, has a stylish hardwood and candlelit interior, great sidewalk seating, and an open kitchen letting you in on Vladimir's artistry. If you dine well in Stockholm once (or twice), I'd do it here. It's gourmet without pretense. They serve delicious, modern Swedish cuisine with a 445-kr three-course dinner. From June to August, they have weekend lunch specials starting at 120 kr. Reserve ahead for dinner (200-250-kr plates, Mon-Fri 17:00-23:00, Sat 12:30-23:00, open Sun in summer only 12:30-22:00, a block off Stortorget at Prästgatan 17, tel. 08/208-841).

Harborview Dining in Gamla Stan and Östermalm

Pontus by the Sea is a classy restaurant with a long, covered, and heated veranda offering grand harbor views. Pontus is well-respected for its modern mix of French and Swedish cuisine. Half the place is a sofas-on-the-harbor cocktail lounge. Though the restaurant is pricey, their bar menu offers some deals. Call to reserve a harborside table (daily 12:00-24:00, off-season closed Sun, Tullhus 2, tel. 08/202-095).

Djurgårdsbrons Sjöcafe, beautifully situated and greedily soaking up the afternoon sun, fills a woody terrace stretching along the harbor just over the Djurgårdsbron bridge. In summer, this is a fine place for a meal or just a drink before or after your Skansen or *Vasa* visit. They have cheap lunch plates (90 kr, Mon-Fri 11:00-13:00 only); at other times, you'll pay 130-180 kr per plate (order at the bar, daily 11:00-22:00, closed off-season, behind the bike-rental hut, tel. 08/661-4488). For the location, see the map on page 450.

Dinner Cruises: The Palace Park Dinner Cruise sails nightly from Stadshusbron, offering a three-course dinner during a scenic cruise that includes a walking tour of the gardens at Drottningholm Palace (565 kr, drinks extra, three-hour cruise, departs daily in summer 17:30-22:00, tel. 08/1200-4000, www.stromma.se).

In Kungsholmen: Lakefront Behind City Hall

On a balmy summer's eve, **Mälarpaviljongen** is a dreamy spot with hundreds of locals enjoying the perfect lakefront scene, as trendy glasses of rosé shine like convivial lanterns. From City Hall, walk 15 minutes along Lake Mälaren (a treat in itself) and you'll find a hundred casual outdoor tables on a floating restaurant and among the trees on shore. Line up at the cafeteria to order a drink, snack, or complete meal. If it's cool, they have heaters and blankets. The walk along the lake back into town caps the experience beautifully (56-kr beer, 125-kr cocktails, 100-kr lunch plates, 150-200-kr evening plates, open in good weather April-Sept daily 11:00-late, easy lakeside walk or T-bana to Freedomsplace plus a 5-minute walk to Nörr Mälarstrand 63, no reservations, tel. 08/650-8701).

In Södermalm

Just south of Gamla Stan, the Södermalm district is the gritty, funky, proud-to-be-working-class part of town. It's the downscale antidote to the upscale, ritzy areas where most tourists spend their time (Norrmalm, Östermalm, Djurgården, and Gamla Stan). And it's recently in vogue, thanks to the Stieg Larsson's Millennium trilogy of novels, in which Lisbeth Salander and her cohorts represent the "real," hardscrabble Stockholm (all the villains come from the posh north side). While the often-repeated comparison to "Stockholm's Brooklyn" is a stretch (this relatively sterile area lacks the loosey-goosey hipster charm of many such neighborhoods in the US and other parts of Europe), it does have a nice variety of restaurants where locals outnumber tourists. Combine dinner here

Fika: Sweden's Coffee Break

Swedes drink more coffee per capita than just about any other country in the world. The Swedish coffee break—or *fika*—is a ritual. *Fika* is to Sweden what teatime is to Britain. The typical *fika* is a morning or afternoon break in the workday, but can happen any time, any day. It's the perfect opportunity (and excuse) for tourists to take a break as well.

Fika-fare is coffee with a snack—something sweet or savory. Your best bet is a *kanelbulle*, a Swedish cinnamon  bun, although some prefer *pariserbulle*, a bun filled with vanilla cream. These can be found nearly everywhere coffee is sold, including just about any café or *konditori* (bakery) in Stockholm. A coffee and a cinnamon bun in a café will cost you about 40 kr. (Most cafés will give you a coffee refill for free.) But at Pressbyrån, the Swedish convenience stores found all over town, you can satisfy your *fika*-fix for 25 kr by getting a coffee and bun to go. Grab a park bench or waterside perch, relax, and enjoy.

with a stroll through a side of Stockholm many visitors miss. The best areas are along Götgatan (described next) and the zone south of Folkungagatan street—nicknamed "SoFo."

Götgatan: This main drag, leading from Slussen (where Södermalm meets Gamla Stan) steeply up into the heart of Södermalm, is the neighborhood's liveliest artery. Here, mixed between the boutiques, you'll find cafés tempting you to join the Swedish coffee break called *fika*, plus plenty of other eateries. Even if you don't dine in Södermalm, it's worth a stroll here just for the window-shopping fun. At the top you'll pop out into the big square called Medborgarplasten, filled with outdoor restaurant and café tables and fronted by a big food hall. (There's also a T-bana stop here for an easy return home after dinner.) The recommended Kvarnen beer hall (see next) is just around the corner to the left. The big white sphere on the horizon is the Ericsson Globe, a hockey arena.

Classic Swedish Beer Halls: Two different but equally traditional Södermalm beer halls serve well-executed, hearty Swedish grub in big, high-ceilinged, orange-tiled spaces with rustic wooden tables. While both could use a bit more personality, the food is good and the ambience is lively. **Kvarnen** ("The Mill") is a reliable choice that recently enjoyed its 15 minutes of fame as a setting for the Millennium novels (90-120-kr starters, 125-165-kr main dishes, Mon-Fri 11:00-24:00, Sat 12:00-24:00, Sun 12:00-23:00, 87-kr lunch special available Mon-Fri 11:00-14:00, Tjärhovsgatan 4, tel. 08/643-0380). **Pelikan** is an old-school beer hall in a trendy neighborhood a bit deeper into Södermalm (90-125-kr starters, 190-260-kr main dishes, Mon-Thu 16:00-23:00, Fri-Sun 13:00-23:00, Blekingegatan 40, tel. 08/5560-9092).

Nytorget Urban Deli is the epitome of Södermalm's trendy-hipster vibe. It's half fancy artisanal delicatessen—with all manner of ingredients—and half eatery, with indoor and outdoor tables filled with Stockholm yuppies eating well (90-170-kr light meals, 190-225-kr bigger meals, Sun-Tue 8:00-23:00, Wed-Thu 8:00-24:00, Fri-Sat 8:00-1:00 in the morning, Nytorget 4, tel. 08/5990-9180).

Beer Garden: **Mosebacke** is a gravelly beer garden with a grand harbor view, perched high above town just past Slussen in Södermalm. Open only on warm summer evenings and priding itself on its beer rather than its cheap grub, it's a good place to mix with a relaxed young crowd (a block inland from the top of the Katarina viewing platform, occasional live music, Mosebacke Torg 3, tel. 08/556-09890).

Krogen Soldaten Švejk, named for a Czech folk hero, is a lively beer hall with woody ambience, a small pub up front, and a cozy dining room in back. They have several Czech beers on tap and serve heavy, reasonably priced Eastern European food (120-140-kr main dishes, daily 17:00-24:00, Fri-Sat from 16:00, Östgötagatan 35, tel. 08/641-3366).

Patricia **Restaurant and Party Boat** is a fun, raucous place to enjoy a basic Swedish meal surrounded by good-time Swedes. The menu on this old steamer is a fun-loving surf-and-turf mix, with 250-kr plates and a 139-kr lobster feed on Wednesday nights. The boat has one deck packed with dinner tables, a bar on the top deck, and two dance zones below: one that's a *schlager* pop bar and dance floor, and the other that's a late-night disco. The boat really rocks with live music on weekends (music from 20:00, cover charge after 22:00). Consider having dinner here beforehand to get in free (Wed-Thu from 17:00, Fri-Sun from 18:00 until late, gay night on Sun, closed Mon-Tue, 200 yards past Djurgården boat dock, near Slussen at Stadsgårdskajen 152, tel. 08/743-0570, www.patricia.st).

On Norrmalm

Royal *Smörgåsbord* at the Grand Hotel

To stuff yourself with all the traditional Swedish specialties (a dozen kinds of herring, salmon, reindeer, meatballs, lingonberries, and shrimp, followed by a fine table of cheeses and desserts) with a super harbor view, consider splurging at the Grand Hotel's dressy **Grand Veranda Restaurant.** While very touristy and a bit tired, this is the finest *smörgåsbord* in town. The Grand Hotel, where royal guests and Nobel Prize winners stay, faces the harbor across from the palace. Pick up their English flier for a good explanation of the proper way to enjoy this grand buffet (and read about *smörgåsbords* on page 30). Reservations are necessary (425 kr, tap water is free, other drinks extra, nightly 18:00-22:00, Sat-Sun also 13:00-16:00, May-Sept also Mon-Fri 12:00-15:00, no shorts, Södra Blasieholmshamnen 8, tel. 08/679-3586).

At the Royal Opera House

The Operakällaren, one of Stockholm's most exclusive restaurants, runs a little "hip pocket" restaurant called **Backfickan** on the side, specializing in traditional Swedish quality cooking at reasonable prices. It's ideal for someone eating out alone, or for anyone wanting an early dinner (they serve daily specials from 12:00 all the way up to 20:00). Sit inside—at tiny private side tables or at the big counter with the locals—or, in good weather, grab a table on the sidewalk. Choose from two different daily specials (about 150-200 kr), or pay 200-250 kr for main dishes from their regular menu (Mon-Sat 12:00-22:00, closed Sun, on the inland side of Royal Opera House, tel. 08/676-5809).

At or near Hötorget

Hötorget ("Hay Market"), a vibrant outdoor produce market just two blocks from Sergels Torg, is a fun place to picnic-shop. The outdoor market closes at 18:00, and many merchants put their unsold produce on the push list (earlier closing and more desperate merchants on Sat).

Hötorgshallen, next to Hötorget (in the basement under the modern cinema complex), is a colorful indoor food market with an old-fashioned bustle, plenty of exotic and ethnic edibles, and—in the tradition of food markets all over Europe—some great little eateries. The best is **Kajsas Fisk Restaurang,** hiding behind the fish stalls. They serve delicious fish soup to little Olivers who can hardly believe they're getting...more. For 85 kr, you get a big bowl of hearty soup, a simple salad, bread and crackers, butter, and water—plus one soup refill (100-kr daily fish specials, Mon-Fri 11:00-18:00, Sat 11:00-16:00, closed Sun, Hötorgshallen 3, tel. 08/207-262).

Kungshallen, an 800-seat indoor food court across the street from Hötorget, has 14 eateries—mostly chain restaurants and fast-food counters, including Chinese, sushi, pizza, Greek, and Mexican (Mon-Fri 9:00-23:00, Sat-Sun 12:00-23:00).

Drottninghof is a busy place with tables perfectly positioned

STOCKHOLM

for people-watching on the busy pedestrian boulevard (good-value 159-kr dinner specials, hearty 150-250-kr plates, Mon-Thu 11:00-24:00, Fri-Sat 11:00-1:00 in the morning, Sun 12:00-23:00, Drottninggatan 67, tel. 08/227-522).

Near Sergels Torg

The many modern shopping malls and department stores around Sergels Torg all have appealing, if pricey, eateries catering to the needs of hungry local shoppers. **Åhléns** department store has a Hemköp supermarket in the basement (Mon-Fri 8:00-21:00, Sat-Sun 10:00-21:00) and two restaurants upstairs with 80-110-kr daily lunch specials (Mon-Fri 11:00-19:30, Sat 11:00-18:30, Sun 11:00-17:30).

In Östermalm

Saluhall, on Östermalmstorg square (near recommended Hotel Wellington), is a great old-time indoor market with top-quality artisanal producers and a variety of sit-down and take-out eateries. While it's nowhere near "cheap," it's one of the most pleasant market halls I've seen, oozing with upscale yet traditional Swedish class (Mon-Thu 9:30-18:00, Fri until 17:30, Sat until 16:00, closed Sun).

Örtagården, upstairs from the Saluhall, is primarily a vegetarian restaurant and serves a 99-kr buffet weekdays until 17:00 and a larger 129-kr buffet evenings and weekends (Mon-Fri 10:30-22:00, Sat-Sun 11:00-21:00, entrance on side of market building at Nybrogatan 31, tel. 08/662-1728).

Riche, a Parisian-style brasserie just a few steps off Nybroplan at Östermalm's waterfront, serves up pricey but elegantly executed Swedish and international dishes. The seating is tight—either in the winter garden, the bright dining room, or the white-tile-and-wine-glass-chandeliered bar—and it's a high-energy environment (125-225-kr starters, 200-300-kr main dishes, Mon-Fri 7:30-24:00, Sat-Sun 12:00-24:00, Birger Jarlsgatan 4, tel. 08/5450-3560).

Stockholm Connections

By Bus

Unless you have a railpass, long-distance buses are cheaper than trains, such as from Stockholm to Oslo or Kalmar. Buses usually take longer, but have more predictable pricing, shorter ticket lines, and student discounts. Swebus is the largest operator (tel.

0771-21-8218, www.swebus.se); Säfflebussen also has lots of routes, including to Oslo (www.safflebussen.se). It's worth knowing about discount offers: Buy tickets at least 24 hours ahead for Swebus discounts; Säfflebussen cuts ticket prices on low-demand days and times.

From Stockholm by Bus to: Copenhagen (2/day, 9 hours), **Oslo** (3/day, 8 hours), **Kalmar** (4/day, fewer on weekends, 6 hours).

By Train

The easiest and cheapest way to book train tickets is online at www.sj.se. Simply select your journey and pay for it with a credit

card. When you arrive at the train station, print out your tickets at a self-service ticket kiosk (bring your purchase confirmation code). You can also buy tickets at a ticket window in a train station, but this comes with long lines and a 5 percent surcharge. For timetables and prices, check online, call 0771/757-575, or use one of the self-service ticket kiosks.

As with airline tickets and hotel rooms, Swedish train ticket prices vary with demand. For intercity and regional trains, ask for the *"Just nu"* ("Just now") fare, which can earn you up to a 60 percent discount if you book far enough in advance.

For railpass holders, seat reservations are required on express (X2000) and overnight trains, and they're recommended on some other trains (to Oslo, for example). Second-class seat reservations to Copenhagen cost 65 kr (150 kr in first class). If you have a railpass, make your seat reservation at a ticket window in a train station or by phone (not online or at self-service ticket kiosks).

From Stockholm by Train to: Uppsala (1-3/hour, 40 minutes), **Växjö** (every 2 hours, 3.5 hours, change in Alvesta, reservations required), **Kalmar** (12/day, 4.5-5 hours, transfer in Alvesta, reservations required), **Copenhagen** (almost hourly, 5-6 hours on high-speed train, some with a transfer at Lund or Hässleholm, reservations required; overnight train requires a change in Malmö or Lund; all trains stop at Copenhagen airport before terminating at the central train station), **Oslo** (2/day direct Intercity trains, 6 hours; 2/day with change in Kristinehamn, 6 hours; plus a direct 9-hour night train in summer only).

By Overnight Boat

Ferry boat companies run shuttle buses from the train station to coincide with each departure; check for details when you buy your ticket. When comparing prices between boats and planes, remember that the boat fare includes a night's lodging.

From Stockholm to: Helsinki and **Tallinn** (daily/nightly boats, 16 hours, see Helsinki and Tallinn chapters), **Turku** (daily/nightly boats, 11 hours). St. Peter Line connects Stockholm to **St. Petersburg,** but the trip takes two nights—you'll sail the first night to Tallinn, then a second night to St. Petersburg; returning, you'll sail the first night to Helsinki, and the second night to Stockholm (www.stpeterline.com). Note: To visit Russia, American and Canadian citizens need a visa (arranged weeks in advance); for details on the visa requirement and the company, see page 595 in the Helsinki chapter.

By Cruise Ship

For many more details on the following ports, and other cruise destinations, pick up my *Rick Steves' Northern European Cruise Ports* guidebook.

Cruise Ports

Stockholm has two cruise ports: the more central **Stadsgården** port, used mainly by ships that are just passing through, is in Södermalm (just south of Stockholm's Old Town/Gamla Stan); the **Frihamnen** port, used primarily by ships that are beginning or ending a cruise, is three miles northeast of the city center.

Shuttle Bus to Downtown: Most cruise lines offer a shuttle bus that drops you in downtown Stockholm, along the harborfront road next to the Opera House, facing the Old Town/Gamla Stan—an easy walk or public bus/tram ride to various points of interest. While the shuttle bus can be pricey (varies by cruise line, but likely $15/€12 round-trip), it's very convenient and not a bad value in this expensive city, where a single one-way ticket on public transit costs over $5. If you'd rather do it on your own, I've outlined the options below.

Port Details: TI kiosks (with bus tickets, city guides, and maps) open at both ports when ships arrive.

Stadsgården is a long embankment, with cruises arriving at two different areas that flank the busy Viking Line Terminal (used by boats to Helsinki). The nearest transportation hub (with bus and T-bana stops) is Slussen, which sits beneath the bridge connecting the Old Town/Gamla Stan and the Södermalm neighborhood.

Closer to the city, **berth 160** hunkers next to an old red-brick terminal building; from here, it's an easy 10-minute walk to Slussen, and five minutes farther to Gamla Stan.

Farther out (past the Viking Line Terminal), **berths 165/167** are still a walkable distance to town; figure about 25 minutes to Slussen, then five more minutes to Gamla Stan (follow the blue line painted on the pavement to the port gate, then walk with the water on your right, passing the Viking Line Terminal and berth 160 en route). A faster option is the handy **hop-on, hop-off harbor boat tour,** which departs right next to the cruise dock (follow the red line painted on the pavement) and connects several worthwhile downtown areas for a reasonable all-day price of 100 kr (€10 for cruise ship passengers who pay in euros; for more details, see page 429). A **taxi** stand is next to the TI kiosk just outside the port gate (figure 115 kr to the Old Town, 150 kr to City Hall, or 190 kr to the Vasa Museum). Near the taxi stand is the departure point for **hop-on, hop-off tour buses** (pricier than the boat; for details see page 428). You can also take a **public bus,** but the bus stop sits inconveniently on a busy road above the port: Passing the Viking Line Terminal and heading up the ramp to the main road, make a sharp left turn and head up the busy street with the port area on your left, until you reach the Londonviadukten bus stop (from here, any bus starting with #4—such as #401—takes you to Slussen; bus #53 goes to Slussen, Gamla Stan, and the train station; and bus #71 hits Slussen, Gamla Stan, and the Opera House).

Frihamnen is a sprawling, drab industrial port zone used by **cruise liners** as well as overnight boats to Helsinki, Tallinn, St. Petersburg, and other Baltic cities. Fortunately, most of the cruises are concentrated in one part of the port, typically using one of three berths: **Berth 638,** the main dock, has the only dedicated terminal building (with a TI desk and gift shops, but no ATM or Internet access). **Berth 650** is at the next pier over. And **berth 634** shares the same pier as berth 638, but is closer to the mainland. From all three berths, the best strategy is to walk down the pier to reach the main harborfront road (follow the blue line painted on the pavement; figure a 10-minute walk from berth 638, and a 5-minute walk from either of the other two). Along this road you'll find a TI kiosk (red building with white trim); a public bus stop (the best way into town—see next); and hop-on, hop-off bus tours (pricey but convenient, for details see page 428). If you need cash, you'll find an **ATM** upstairs in the Frihamnsterminalen (the terminal building for Tallink Silja and St. Peter Line boats, at the base of the pier for berths 638 and 634).

From **Frihamnen,** the public bus is your most affordable way into the center. From the bus stop along the main road, **bus #76** zips you to several major sights in town, including Djurgårdsbron (at the bridge a short walk from the Vasa Museum and other Djurgården sights), Nybroplan, Kungsträdgården (near the Opera House), Slottsbacken (by the palace in Gamla Stan), Räntmästartrappan (at the southern end of Gamla Stan), and Slussen (4-7/hour Mon-Fri, 2-3/hour Sat, none Sun). On Saturday, you may be better off taking **bus #1,** which cuts across the top of

Östermalm and Norrmalm to the train station (every 5-8 minutes daily). You can't buy bus tickets on board, so be sure to get them before you reach the stop—buy one at either TI (inside the terminal or at the booth near the bus stop), or use the automated machine at the bus stop (accepts credit cards). You can also take a **taxi** (figure about 150 kr to the Vasa Museum/Djurgården, or 235 kr to the Old Town or City Hall).

If your cruise **begins in Stockholm,** you'll probably depart from Frihamnen (but confirm with your cruise line). Figure about 200-250 kr for a **taxi** from downtown. It's much cheaper to take the bus: You can take **bus #1** from the train station (handy if you're riding the train in **from the airport**—see page 422), or **bus #76** from various points downtown (including some close to my recommended hotels—see the list earlier) to the end of the line, Frihamnen. Stepping off the bus, continue straight along the street to the first intersection, and carefully look at the signs directing you to different areas. If you're leaving from berth 650, you'll turn right here; for berth 634 or 638, turn left, then bear right up the pier at Frihamnsterminalen.

By Plane

For information on arriving at Stockholm's airports, see "Arrival in Stockholm," earlier in this chapter.

To Helsinki and Tallinn: Many low-fare airlines are offering flights across the Baltic. For flights from Stockholm to Helsinki, check www.blue1.com; to Tallinn, also visit www.norwegian.com and www.estonian-air.com.

Route Tips for Drivers

Stockholm to Oslo: It's an eight-hour drive from Stockholm to Oslo. **Årjäng,** just before the Norwegian border, is a good place for a rest stop. At the border, change money at the little TI kiosk (on right side). Pick up the Oslo map and *What's On in Oslo,* and consider buying your Oslo Card here.

Near Stockholm: Uppsala

Uppsala is a compact city with a cathedral and university that win Sweden's "oldest/largest/tallest" awards. If you're not traveling anywhere else in Sweden other than Stockholm, Uppsala makes a pleasant day trip. But if you're short on time, Uppsala is not worth sacrificing time in Stockholm or a boat trip through the archipelago. If you visit, allow the better part of a day, including the trip out and back. During summer vacations, this university town is very quiet.

Getting There: Take the train from Stockholm's central station (1-3/hour, 40 minutes, 80 kr, buy tickets at ticket windows). Since the Uppsala station has lockers and is in the same direction from Stockholm as the airport, you could combine a quick visit here with an early arrival or late departure.

STOCKHOLM

Orientation to Uppsala

Tourist Information

The helpful TI, overlooking the canal through the heart of town, has free maps and the informative *What's On Uppsala* magazine (Mon-Fri 10:00-18:00, Sat 10:00-15:00, Sun July-Aug only 11:00-15:00, Fyristorg 8, tel. 018/727-4800, www.uppsala.to).

Arrival in Uppsala

From the train station (lockers-20-30 kr), walk straight out the front door, cross the busy street, and walk two blocks. Turn right along the newly pedestrianized shopping street called Kungsängsgatan. Walk three more blocks (passing the Åhléns department store, with its handy Hemköp grocery downstairs) and you'll run into the town's main square, Stora Torget. From here, you can turn left and cross the canal. The TI is just to the right after the canal, and you can see the cathedral spires (which also mark the university zone) just behind it.

Sights in Uppsala

▲▲Uppsala Cathedral (Domkyrkan)

One of Scandinavia's largest, most historic cathedrals feels as vital as it does impressive. The building was completed in 1453;

the spires and interior decorations are from the late 19th century. The cathedral—with a fine Gothic interior, the relics of St. Erik, and the tomb of King Gustav Vasa—is well worth a visit.

Cost and Hours: Free, open daily 8:00-18:00, tel. 018/187-177, www.uppsaladomkyrka.se.

Tours: Ask inside about **guided tours** in English (mid-June-mid-Aug Mon-Sat at 11:00 and 14:00, Sun at 16:00; off-season call to arrange). Or, just inside the nave, look for the self-service kiosk and buy the handy 10-kr **leaflet** outlining an excellent self-guided tour.

Visiting the Cathedral: Near the entrance is the tomb and memorial to scientist Carolus Linnaeus, who created the formal system for naming different species of plants and animals. Farther into the church you'll find the gorgeously carved, gold-slathered Baroque pulpit, and the transept where today's services take place.

Look high above in the choir area (beyond the transept) to enjoy fine murals that gleam, thanks to a major restoration of the church in the 1970s.

At the far end of the church, don't disturb the woman peering toward the grave in the apse. This eerily lifelike statue from 2005, called *Mary (The Return)*, captures Jesus' mother later in life, wearing a scarf and timeless garb. The chapel she's looking at once housed a shrine to her, but for more than 300 years after the Reformation, images of Mary were downplayed in

this church. In keeping with the Protestant spirit here, this new version of Mary is shown not as an exalted queen, but as an everywoman, saddened by the loss of her child and seeking solace—or answers—in the church.

Follow Mary's gaze into the chapel housing the **tomb of King Gustav Vasa** and his family. Notice that in the sculpture, Gustav is shown flanked by not one, but two wives—his first wife died after suffering a fall; his second wife bore him 10 children. The chapel is ringed with murals of his illustrious life.

Back at the entrance to the church, by the gift shop, you can pay to enter the **treasury** collection. Here you'll find medieval textiles (tapestries and vestments), swords and crowns found in Gustav's grave, and the Nobel Peace Prize won by Nathan Söderblom, an early-20th-century archbishop here (30 kr, Mon-Sat 10:00-17:00, Sun 12:30-17:00). In this same narthex area, notice the debit-card machine soliciting donations: The church doing its same old work in a new way.

University Attractions and Nearby Sights

Scandinavia's first university was founded here in 1477. Two famous grads are Carolus Linnaeus (father of modern taxonomy) and astronomer Anders Celsius (who developed the temperature scale that bears his name). The following two university buildings are interesting and open to non-students.

▲▲**Gustavianum**—Directly across from the cathedral is the university's oldest surviving building, with a bulbous dome that

doubles as a sundial (notice the
gold numbers). Today it houses
a well-presented museum that
features an anatomical theater, a
cabinet filled with miniature curiosities, and Celsius' thermometer.
The collection is unaccountably
engaging for the glimpse it gives
into the mind-set of 17th-century
Europe.

Cost and Hours: 50 kr, June-Aug Tue-Sun 10:00-16:00,
Sept-May Tue-Sun 11:00-16:00, closed Mon year-round, tours
in English Sat-Sun at 13:00, Akademigatan 3, tel. 018/471-7571,
www.gustavianum.uu.se.

Visiting the Gustavianum: Find the elevator (hiding near
the gift shop/ticket desk) and ride it up to the fourth floor, then see
the exhibits as you walk back down. Up top is a collection of artifacts discovered at Valsgärde, a prehistoric site near Uppsala used
for burials for more than 700 years. Archaeologists have uncovered
15 boat graves here (dating from A.D. 600-1050—roughly one per
generation), providing more insight on the Viking Age.

Next you'll find the museum's highlight, the anatomical theater (accessible from the fourth and third floors). Its only show was
human dissection. In the mid-1600s, as the enlightened ideas of
the Renaissance swept far into the north of Europe, scholars began
to consider dissection of the human body the ultimate scientific
education. Corpses of hanged criminals were carefully sliced and
diced here, under a dome in an almost temple-like atmosphere,
demonstrating the lofty heights to which science had risen in
society. Imagine 200 students (and others who'd paid admission) standing tall all around and leaning in to peer intently at the
teacher's scalpel.

Another floor down (on the second floor) is an exhibit on
the history of the university, which is far more interesting than it
sounds. The Physics Chamber features a collection of instruments
from the 18th and 19th centuries that were used by university
teachers. But the most fascinating item is in the room across the
hall: the Augsburg Art Cabinet, a dizzying array of nearly a thousand miniscule works of art and other tidbits held in an ornately
decorated oak cabinet. Built in the 1620s for a bigwig who wanted
to impress his friends, the cabinet's contents are shown in display
cases all around. Find the interactive video screen, where you can
control a virtual tour of the collection. Beyond the cabinet and to
the right is a thermometer once belonging to Celsius.

Rounding out the collection (on the first floor) is the university's collection from the Mediterranean: ancient Greek and Roman

artifacts and Egyptian sarcophagi.

▲**University Library (Universitetsbiblioteket)**—Uppsala University's library, housed in a 19th-century building called the Carolina Rediviva, is just up the hill from the cathedral and Gustavianum. Off the entry hall (to the right) is a small exhibit of treasured old books. Well-displayed and well-described in English, the carefully selected collection is surprisingly captivating. The centerpiece of the exhibit, in its own room, is the sixth-century Silver Bible. Sweden's single most precious book is so named for its silver-ink writing (on purple-colored parchment) in the extinct Gothic language. You'll also see the Carta Marina, the first more-or-less accurate map of Scandinavia, created in 1539. Compare this 16th-century understanding of the region with your own travels.

Cost and Hours: 20 kr, free Oct-May; open Mon-Fri 9:00-20:00, Sat 10:00-17:00, closed Sun, tel. 018/471-3918, www.ub .uu.se.

More Sights near the University—The **Uppland Museum** (Upplandsmuseet), a regional history museum with prehistoric bits and folk-art scraps, is on the river by the waterfall, near the TI (free, Tue-Sun 12:00-17:00, closed Mon, tel. 018/169-100, www.upplandsmuseet.se). Uphill from the university library are the **botanical gardens** and a museum named after Linnaeus, and the 16th-century **Uppsala Castle,** which houses an art museum and runs slice-of-castle-life tours (required 80-kr tour, offered in English only a few weeks each summer Tue-Sun at 13:00 and 15:00, tel. 018/727-2485).

▲Gamla Uppsala

This site on the outskirts of town, which gives historians goose bumps even on a sunny day, includes nine large royal burial

mounds circled by a walking path with English descriptions. Fifteen hundred years ago, when the Baltic Sea was higher and it was easy to sail all the way to Uppsala, the pagan Swedish kings had their capital here. You can simply wander the grounds, or learn more by visiting the attractive Gamla Uppsala Museum, which gives a good overview of early Swedish history and displays items found in the mounds.

Cost and Hours: Grounds—free; museum—60 kr; May-Aug daily 10:00-16:00; Sept-Nov and Jan-April Mon, Wed, and Sat-Sun 12:00-15:00, closed Tue and Fri; closed Dec; includes guided tours in English available May-Aug daily at 15:30, tel. 018/239-300, www.raa.se/gamlauppsala.

Nearby: The venerable **Gamla Uppsala church** dates from the 12th century (free, daily April-Aug 9:00-18:00, Sept-March 9:00-16:00).

Eating at Gamla Uppsala: Gamla Uppsala is great for picnics, or you can recharge at the half-timbered **Odinsborg café,** which serves sandwiches, mead, and buffets—including *smörgåsbord* in summer (café daily 10:00-18:00, restaurant daily 12:00-18:00—reservations required, tel. 018/323-525).

Getting There: From downtown Uppsala, go to the bus stop at Vaksalagatan 7-13 (a block and a half from Stora Torget, the main square) and take bus #2, marked *Gamla Uppsala,* to the last stop (30 kr, buy ticket at nearby Pressbyrån kiosk, 2-4/hour, 15-minute trip). Allow two or three hours for your visit, including the time it takes to bus there and back.

Eating in Uppsala

Eateries abound along the river and in the business district. **Domtrappkällaren,** tucked behind the cathedral, serves up traditional Swedish meals in its characteristic interior or outside at streetside tables (110-kr lunches served Mon-Fri 11:00-14:30, then pricier dinners—100-210-kr starters, 185-325-kr main dishes; open Mon-Fri 11:00-23:00, Sat 17:00-23:00, closed Sun, St. Eriks Gränd, go through the little tunnel behind the cathedral and look left, tel. 018/130-955).

For picnic fixings, stop by **Hemköp,** a grocery located on the ground floor of Åhléns department store (Mon-Fri 7:00-22:00, Sat-Sun 9:00-22:00, on Stora Torget). Enjoy the picnic at one of Uppsala's parks, or join the locals down on the boardwalk along the river, below St. Olof's bridge.

STOCKHOLM'S ARCHIPELAGO

Vaxholm • Grinda • Svartsö • Sandhamm

Some of Europe's most scenic islands stretch 80 miles out into the Baltic Sea from Stockholm. If you're cruising to (or from) Finland, you'll get a good look at this island beauty. If you have more time and want to immerse yourself in all that simple Swedish nature, consider spending a day or two island-hopping.

The Swedish word for "island" is simply *ö*, but the local name for this area is *Skärgården*—literally "garden of skerries," unforested rocks sticking up from the sea. That stone is granite, carved out and deposited by glaciers. The archipelago closer to Stockholm is rockier, with bigger islands and more trees. Farther out (such as at Sandhamn), the glaciers lingered longer, slowly grinding the granite into sand and creating smaller islands.

Locals claim there are more than 30,000 of these islands, and as land here is rising slowly, more pop out every year. Some 150 are inhabited year-round, and about 100 have ferry service. There's an unwritten law of public access in the archipelago. Technically you're allowed to pitch your tent anywhere for up to two nights, provided the owner of the property can't see you from his or her house. It's polite to ask first and essential to act responsibly.

With thousands of islands to choose from, every Swede seems to have a favorite. This chapter covers four very different island destinations that offer an overview of the archipelago. Vaxholm, the gateway to the archipelago, comes with an imposing fortress, a charming fishermen's harbor, and the easiest connections to Stockholm. Rustic Grinda feels like—and used to be—a Swedish summer camp. Sparsely populated Svartsö is another fine back-to-nature experience. And swanky Sandhamn thrills the sailboat set, with a lively yacht harbor, a scenic setting at the far edge of the

archipelago, and (true to its name)
sandy beaches.

The flat-out best way to experience the magic of the archipelago is simply stretching out
comfortably on the rooftop deck
of your ferry. The journey truly is
the destination. Enjoy the charm
of lovingly painted cottages as you
glide by, delicate pairs of lounge

chairs positioned to catch just the right view and sun, the steady
rhythm of the ferries lacing this world together, and people savoring quality time with each other and nature.

Planning Your Time

On a Tour: For the best quick look, consider one of the many
half- or full-day package boat trips from downtown Stockholm
to the archipelago. **Strömma Kanalbolaget** runs several options,
including the three-hour Archipelago Tour (2-4/day, 230 kr), or
the all-day Thousand Island Cruise (departs daily in summer at
9:30, 1,210 kr includes lunch and dinner). Or, to be efficient, combine a three-hour island joyride with a meal—choose between a
lunch, brunch, or dinner cruise (tel. 08/1200-4000, www.stromma
kanalbolaget.com).

On Your Own: For more flexibility, freedom, and a better
dose of the local vacation scene, do it on your own. Any one of the
islands in this chapter is easily doable as a single-day side-trip from
Stockholm. And, because all boats to and from Stockholm pass
through Vaxholm, it's easy to tack on that town to any other one.

For a very busy all-day itinerary that takes in the two most
enjoyable island destinations (Grinda and Sandhamn), consider
this plan: 8:00—Set sail from Stockholm; 9:30—Arrive in Grinda
for a quick walk around the island; 10:50—Catch the boat to
Sandhamn; 11:45—Arrive in Sandhamn, have lunch, and enjoy
the town; 17:00—Catch boat to Stockholm (maybe have dinner on board); 19:05—Arrive back in Stockholm. Depending
on your interests, you could craft a more in-depth route: For
example, for a back-to-nature experience, try Stockholm-
Grinda-Svartsö-Stockholm. For an urban mix of towns, consider
Stockholm-Vaxholm-Sandhamn-Stockholm.

Overnighting on an island really lets you get away from it all
and enjoy the island ambience. I've listed a few island accommodations, but note that mid-range options are few; most tend to be
either pricey and top-end or very rustic (rented cottages with minimal plumbing). Decide up front whether you want to splurge or
rough it.

Stockholm's Archipelago

Don't struggle too hard with the "which island?" decision. The main thing is to get well beyond Vaxholm, where the scenery gets more striking. I'd sail an hour or two past Vaxholm, have a short stop on an island, then stop in Vaxholm on the way home. Again, the real joy is the view from your ferry.

Getting Around the Archipelago

A few archipelago destinations (including Vaxholm) are accessible overland, thanks to modern bridges. For other islands, you'll

take a boat. Two major companies run public ferries from downtown Stockholm to the archipelago: the bigger Waxholmsbolaget and the smaller Cinderella Båtarna.

Tickets: Regular tickets are sold on board. Simply walk on, and at your convenience, stop by the desk to buy your ticket before you disembark (or wait for them to come around and sell you one). Waxholmsbolaget offers a deal that's worthwhile if you're traveling with a small group or doing a lot of island-hopping. You can save 25 percent by buying a 1,000-kr ticket credit for 750 kr (sold only on land; use the splittable credit to buy tickets on the boat). If you're staying in the archipelago for a few days and want to island-hop, consider the Boat Hiking Card. This five-day all-inclusive pass is good on either boat line (420 kr, plus a 40-kr refundable deposit). Buy the card at the Waxholmsbolaget office or at the Strandvägen information office listed below.

Schedules: Check both companies' schedules when planning your itinerary; you might have to mix and match to make your itinerary work. A single, confusing schedule booklet mixes times for both lines. Ferry schedules are complex even to locals, especially outside of peak season.

It's essential to carefully review and confirm your plans, ideally at the information desk in the glassy house on the Strandvägen embankment (see map on page 426). Attendants will help you sort through your options and plan your archipelago visit (May-Sept Mon-Fri 9:00-17:30, Sat-Sun 10:00-16:00; off-season Mon-Fri 10:00-16:00, closed Sat-Sun; Strandvägen Kajplats 18—that's boat landing #18, www.visitskargarden.se).

Note that the departures mentioned below are for summer (mid-June-mid-Aug); the number of boats declines off-season.

Waxholmsbolaget: Their ships depart across from Stockholm's Grand Hotel, at the stop called Stromkäjen (tel. 08/679-5830, www.waxholmsbolaget.se). Waxholmsbolaget boats run from Stockholm to: **Vaxholm** (at least hourly, 75 minutes, 75 kr), **Grinda** (nearly hourly, 2 hours, 90 kr), **Svartsö** (3/day, 2.5 hours, 110 kr), and **Sandhamn** (1/day, Sat-Sun only, 3.5 hours, 130 kr). These destinations are all listed in Waxholmsbolaget's challenging-to-decipher schedule for the Middle Archipelago (Mellersta Skärgården). The same company has routes and schedules for the North and South Archipelago as well.

Cinderella Båtarna: This company focuses its coverage on the most popular destinations. Their ships—generally faster, more comfortable, and a little pricier than their rivals'—leave from near Stockholm's Nybroplan, along Strandvägen (tel. 08/1200-4000, www.cinderellabatarna.com). Cinderella boats sail frequently (4/day Mon-Thu, 5/day Fri-Sun) from Stockholm to **Vaxholm** (50 minutes, 105 kr) and **Grinda** (1.25 hours, 130 kr). After Grinda, the line splits, going either to **Sandhamn** (from Stockholm: 1/day Mon-Thu, 2/day Fri-Sun, 2.75 hours, 155 kr), or Finnhamn, with a stop en route at **Svartsö** (from Stockholm: 2/day, 1.5 hours, 150 kr). These fares are for peak season (mid-June-mid-Aug); Cinderella's fares are slightly cheaper off-season.

On Board: When you board, tell the conductor which island you're going to. Boats don't land at all of the smaller islands unless passengers have requested a stop. Hang on to your ticket, as you'll have to show it to disembark. Some boats have luggage-storage areas (ask when you board).

You can usually access the outdoor deck; if you can't get to the front deck (where the boats load and unload), head to the back. Or nab a window seat inside. For the best seat, with less sun and nicer views, I'd go POSH: Port Out, Starboard Home (on the left side leaving Stockholm, on the right side coming back). As you sail, a monitor on board shows the position of your boat as it motors

ARCHIPELAGO

through the islands.

Food: You can usually buy food on board, ranging from simple fare at snack bars (60-kr sandwiches and basic 85-100-kr meals) to elegant sea-view dinners at fancy restaurants (100-kr starters, 200-kr main dishes). If your boat has a top-deck restaurant and you want to combine your cruise with dinner, make a reservation as soon as you board. Once you have a table, it's yours for the whole trip, so you can simply claim your seat and enjoy the ride, circling back later to eat. You can also try calling ahead to reserve a table for a specific cruise (for Waxholmsbolaget, call 08/243-090; for Cinderella, call 08/1200-4000).

Helpful Hints

Opening Times: All the opening hours I list in this chapter are reliable only for peak season (mid-June–mid-Aug). The rest of the year, hours are flexible and completely weather-dependent; more services tend to be open on weekends than weekdays. Outside the short summer season, many places close down entirely.

Money: Bring cash. The only ATMs are in Vaxholm; farther out, you'll wish you'd stocked up on cash in Stockholm. Fortunately, most vendors do accept credit cards.

Signal for Stop: At the boat landings or jetties on small islands, you'll notice a small signal tower (called a semaphore) that's used to let a passing boat know you want to be picked up. Pull the cord to spin the white disc and make it visible to the ship. Be sure to put it back before boarding the boat. At night, you signal with light—locals just use their mobile phones.

Weather: The weather on the islands is often better than in Stockholm. For island forecasts, check Götland's (the big island far to the south) instead of Stockholm's.

Local Drink: A popular drink here is *punsch*, a sweet fruit liqueur. Stately old buildings sometimes have *punsch-verandas*, little glassed-in upstairs porches where people traditionally would imbibe and chat.

Vaxholm

The self-proclaimed "gateway to the archipelago," Vaxholm (VAX-holm) is more developed and less charming than the other islands.

Connected by bridge to Stockholm, it's practically a suburb, and not the place to commune with Swedish nature. But it also has an illustrious history as the anchor of Stockholm's naval defense network, and it couldn't be easier to reach (constant buses and boats from Stockholm). While Vaxholm isn't the rustic archipelago you might be looking for, you're almost certain to pass through here at some point on your trip. If you have some extra time, hop off the boat for a visit.

Getting There: Boats constantly shuttle between Stockholm's waterfront and Vaxholm (1-2/hour, 1.25 hours, 75-100 kr depending on boat company). **Bus** #670 runs regularly from the Tekniska Högskolan T-bana stop in northern Stockholm to the center of Vaxholm (3/hour Mon-Fri, 2/hour Sat-Sun, 45-minute trip, 72 kr one-way—three zones). Unless you're on a tight budget, I'd take the boat for the scenery.

Orientation to Vaxholm

Vaxholm, with about 11,000 people, is on the island of Vaxön, connected to the mainland (and Stockholm) by a series of bridges. Everything of interest is within a five-minute walk of the boat dock.

Arrival in Vaxholm

Ferries stop at Vaxholm's south harbor (Söderhamnen). The **bus** from Stockholm begins and ends at the bus stop called Söderhamnsplan, a few steps from the boats. To get your bearings, follow my self-guided walk. There are luggage lockers in the Waxholmsbolaget building on the waterfront. The handy electronic departure board (*Nasta Avgang* means "next departure") near the ticket office shows when boats are leaving. For more help, confirm your plans with the person at the ticket office.

Tourist Information

Vaxholm's good TI is well-stocked with brochures about Vaxholm itself, Stockholm, and the archipelago, and can help you with boat schedules (June-Aug Mon-Fri 10:00-18:00, Sat-Sun 10:00-16:00; May and Sept Mon-Fri 11:00-16:00, Sat-Sun 11:00-15:00; Oct-April Mon-Fri 10:00-15:00, Sat-Sun 10:00-14:00; in the Town Hall building on Rådhustorget, tel. 08/5413-1480, www.roslagen .se). They also have pay Internet access.

Self-Guided Walk

Welcome to Vaxholm

This 30-minute, two-part loop will take you to the most charac-teristic corners of Vaxholm. Begin at the boat dock—you can even start reading as you approach.

Waterfront: Dominating Vaxholm's waterfront is the big Art Nouveau Waxholms Hotell, dating from the early 20th century.

Across the strait to the right is Vaxholm's stout fortress, a reminder of this town's strategic importance over the centuries.

With your back to the water, turn left and walk with the big hotel on your right-hand side. Notice the Waxholmsbolaget office building. Inside you can buy tickets, confirm boat schedules, or stow your bag in a locker. After the hamburger-and-hot-dog stand, you'll reach a round-about. Just to your left is the stop for bus #670, connecting Vax-holm to Stockholm. Beyond that, a wooden walkway follows the seafront to the town's private boat harbor (Västerhamnen, or "west harbor"), where you can count sailboats and rent a bike.

But for now, continue straight up Vaxholm's appealing, shop-lined main street, Hamngatan. After one long block (notice the handy Coop/Konsum grocery store across the street), turn right up Rådhusgatan (following signs to *Rådhustorget*) to reach the town's main square. The TI is inside the big, yellow Town Hall building on your left. Continue kitty-corner across the square (toward the granite slope) and head downhill on a street leading to the...

Fishermen's Quarter: This Norrhamnen ("north harbor") is ringed by former fisher-men's homes. Walk out to the dock and survey the charming wooden cottages. In the mid-19th century, Stockholmers considered Vaxholm's herring, called *strömming*, top-quality. Caught fresh here, the

herring could be rowed into the city in just eight hours and eaten immediately, while herring caught farther out on the archipelago, which had to be preserved in salt, lost its flavor.

As you look out to sea, you'll see a pale green building protruding on the left. This is the charming Hembygdsgården homestead museum, with a pleasant indoor-outdoor café. It's worth heading to this little point (even if the museum is closed, as it often is): As you face the water, go left about one block, then turn right down the gravel lane called Trädgårdsgatan (also marked for *Hembygdsgården*). At this corner, look for the *Strömmingslådan* ("herring shop") sign for the chance to buy what herring connoisseurs consider top-notch fish (summer only, Tue-Fri 10:00-16:00, Sat 10:00-14:00, closed Sun-Mon).

Continuing down Trädgårdsgatan lane, you'll run right into the **Hembygdsgården homestead.** The big house features an endearing museum showing the simple, traditional fisherman's lifestyle (free but donation requested, June-Aug Fri-Sun 12:00-16:00, plus Mon in July, otherwise closed). Next door is a fine café serving sweets and light meals with idyllic outdoor seating (both in front of and behind the museum—look around for your favorite perch, taking the wind direction into consideration). This is the best spot in town for coffee or lunch (see listing under "Sleeping and Eating in Vaxholm," later). From here, look across the inlet at the tiny beach (where we're heading next).

Backtrack to the fishermen's harbor, then continue straight uphill on Fiskaregatan road, and take the first left up the tiny gravel lane marked Vallgatan. This part of the walk takes you back in time, as you wander among old-fashioned wooden homes. At the end of the lane, head left; then, when you reach the water, go right along a path leading to a thriving little **sandy beach.** In good weather, this offers a fun chance to commune with Swedes at play. (In bad weather, it's hard to imagine anyone swimming or sunning here.)

When you're done relaxing, take the wooden stairs up to the top of the rock and **Battery Park** (Batteripark)—where giant artillery helped Vaxholm flex its defensive muscles in the late 19th century. As you crest the rock and enjoy the sea views, notice (on your right) the surviving semicircular tracks from those old artillery guns. With a range of 10 kilometers, the recoil from these powerful cannons could shatter glass in nearby houses. Before testing them, they'd play a bugle call to warn locals to stow away their valuables. More artifacts of these defenses are dug into the rock.

To head back to civilization, turn right before the embedded bunker (crossing more gun tracks and passing more fortifications on your left). As you leave the militarized zone, take a left at the fork, and the road will take you down to the embankment—just around the corner from where the boat docks, and our starting point. From along this stretch of embankment, you can catch a boat across the water to Vaxholm Fortress.

Sights in Vaxholm

Vaxholm Fortress and Museum (Vaxholms Kastell/ Vaxholms Fästnings Museum)—Vaxholm's only real attraction is the fortification just across the strait. While the town feels sleepy today, for centuries it was a crucial link in Sweden's nau-

tical defense because it presided over the most convenient passage between Stockholm and the outer archipelago (and, beyond that, the Baltic Sea, Finland, and Russia). The name "Vaxholm" means "Island of the Signal Fire," emphasizing the burg's strategic importance. In 1548, King Gustav

Vasa decided to pin his chances on this location, ordering the construction of a fortress here and literally filling in other waterways, effectively making this the only way into or out of Stockholm... which it remained for 450 years. A village sprang up across the waterway to supply the fortress, and Vaxholm was born. The town's defenses successfully held off at least two major invasions (Christian IV of Denmark in 1612, and Peter the Great of Russia in 1719). Vaxholm's might gave Sweden's kings the peace of mind they needed to expand their capital to outlying islands—which means that the pint-size powerhouse of Vaxholm is largely to thank for Stockholm's island-hopping cityscape.

Cost and Hours: 60 kr, July-Aug daily 11:00-17:00, June daily 12:00-16:00, first and second Sat-Sun in Sept 11:00-17:00, closed off-season, tel. 08/5417-1890, www.vaxholmsfastning.se.

Getting There: A ferry shuttles visitors back and forth from Vaxholm (50 kr round-trip, every 15 minutes when museum is open, catch the boat just around the corner and toward the fortress from where the big ferries put in). Once on the island, hike into the castle's inner courtyard and look to the left to find the museum entrance.

Visiting the Fortress: The current, "new" fortress dates from the mid-19th century, when an older castle was torn down and replaced with this imposing granite behemoth. During the 30

Sleep Code

(7 kr = about $1, country code: 46, area code: 08)
S = Single, **D** = Double/Twin, **T** = Triple, **Q** = Quad, **b** = bathroom, **s** = shower. Unless otherwise noted, all of my listings accept credit cards and include big breakfast buffets. Everyone speaks English.

To help you sort easily through these listings, I've divided the accommodations into three categories, based on the price for a standard double room with bath during high season:

$$$ Higher Priced—Most rooms 1,500 kr or more.
$$ Moderately Priced—Most rooms between 1,000-1,500 kr.
$ Lower Priced—Most rooms 1,000 kr or less.

Prices can change without notice; verify the hotel's current rates online or by email.

years it took to complete the fortress, the tools of warfare changed. Both defensively and offensively, the new fortress was obsolete before it was even completed. The thick walls were no match for the invention of shells (rather than cannonballs), and the high hatches used for attacking tall sailing vessels were useless against new, low-lying, Monitor-style attack boats.

Today, the fortress welcomes guests to wander its tough little island and visit its museum. Presented chronologically on two floors (starting upstairs), the modern exhibit traces the military history of this fortress and of Sweden generally. It uses lots of models and mannequins, along with actual weaponry and artifacts, to tell the story right up to the 21st century. There's no English posted, but you can pick up the good English translations as you enter. It's as interesting as a museum about Swedish military history can be.

Sleeping and Eating in Vaxholm

Since Vaxholm is so close to Stockholm, there's little reason to sleep here. But in a pinch, Waxholms is the only hotel in town.

$$$ Waxholms Hotell's stately Art Nouveau facade dominates the town's waterfront. Inside are 42 pleasant rooms with classy old-fashioned furnishings (peak-season Sb-1,400 kr, Db-1,750 kr; weekends/July Sb-1,150 kr, Db-1,495 kr; free Wi-Fi, loud music some nights in summer—ask what's on and request a quiet room if necessary, Hamngatan 2, tel. 08/5413-0150, fax 08/5413-1376, www.waxholmshotell.se, info@waxholmshotell .se). The hotel has a grill restaurant outside in summer and a fancy dining room inside.

Hembygdsgården ("Homestead Garden") **Café** is Vaxholm's most tempting eatery, serving "summer lunches" (salads and sandwiches) and homemade sweets, with delightful outdoor seating around the Homestead Museum in Vaxholm's characteristic fishermen's quarter. Anette's lingonberry muffins are a treat (40-75-kr light meals, daily mid-June-Aug 11:00-18:00, May-mid-June 11:00-16:00, closed Sept-April, tel. 08/5413-1980).

Grinda

The rustic, traffic-free isle of Grinda—half retreat, half resort—combines back-to-nature archipelago remoteness with easy proximity to Stockholm. The island is a tasteful gaggle of hotel buildings idyllically situated amid Swedish nature—walking paths, beaches, trees, and slabs of glacier-carved granite sloping into the sea. Since Grinda is a nature preserve (owned by the Stockholm Archipelago Foundation, or Skärgårdsstiftelsen), only a few families actually live here. There's no real town. But in the summer, Grinda becomes a magnet for day-tripping urbanites, which can make it quite crowded. Adding to its appeal is the

nostalgia it holds for many Stockholmers, who fondly recall when this was a summer camp island. In a way, with red-and-white cottages bunny-hopping up its gentle hills and a stately old inn anchoring its center, it retains that vibe today.

Orientation to Grinda

Grinda is small and easy to manage. It's a little wider than a mile in each direction; you can walk from end to end in a half-hour. Its main settlement—the historic **Wärdshus building** (a busy hub of tourist activities), hotel, and related amenities—sits next to its harbor, where private yachts and sailboats put in. Public ferries use one of two docks, at opposite ends of the island: Most use Södra Grinda to the south (nearest the hostel and cottages), while a few use Norra Grinda to the north (closer to the campground). From either of these, it's about a 10- to 15-minute walk to the action. Everything on the island is owned and operated by the same company; fortunately, it does a tasteful job of managing the place to keep the island's relaxing personality intact.

Major points of interest are well-signposted in Swedish: *Södra Bryggan* (south dock), *Norra Bryggan* (north dock), *Värdshus* (hotel at the heart of the island), *Gästhamn* (guest harbor); *Affär* (general store); *stuga/stugby* (cottage/s); *Grindastigen* (nature trail); and *Tältplats* (campground).

Tourist Information

The red cottage marked *Expedition* greets arriving visitors just up the hill from the Södra Grinda ferry dock. The staff answers questions, and the cottage serves as a small shop, a place to rent kayaks or saunas, and a reception desk for the island's cottages and hostel (mid-June–mid-Aug daily 9:00-18:00; shoulder season Mon-Fri 10:00-16:00, Sat 10:00-18:00, Sun 10:00-14:00; general info tel. 08/5424-9491, www.skargardsstiftelsen.se).

Sights in Grinda

Grinda is made to order for strolling through the woods, taking a dip, picnicking, and communing with Swedish nature. Watch the boats bob in the harbor and work on your Baltic tan. You can simply stick to the gravel trails connecting the island's buildings, or for more nature, take the Grindastigen trail, which loops to the far end of the island and back in less than an hour (signposted from near the Wärdshus).

You can also rent a kayak or rent the private little sauna hut bobbing in the harbor. There's no bike rental here—and the island is a bit too small to keep a serious biker busy—but you could bring one on the boat from Stockholm.

As you stroll, you might spot a few haggard-looking tents through the trees. The right to pitch a tent here was established by the Swedish government during World War II, to give the downtrodden a cheap place to sleep. Those permissions are still valid, inherited, bought, and sold, which means that Grinda has a thriving community of tent-dwelling locals who camp out here all summer long (April-Oct). While some may be the descendants of those original hobos, these days they choose this lifestyle and live as strange little barnacles attached to Grinda. Once each summer they have a progressive tent-crawl bender before heading to the Wärdshus to blow a week's food budget on a fancy meal.

The island just across from the Södra Grinda dock (to the right) is Viggsö, where the members of ABBA have summer cottages and wrote many of their biggest hits.

Sleeping in Grinda

(7 kr = about $1, country code: 46, area code 08)
You have various options, in increasing order of rustic charm: hotel, hostel, and cottages. You can reserve any of these through the Wärdshus. This hub of operations has a restaurant, bar, free Wi-Fi, and conference facilities (tel. 08/5424-9491, www.grinda .se, info@grinda.se).

Grinda is busiest in the summer, when tourists fill its hotel; in spring and fall, it mostly hosts conferences. If sleeping at the hostel or cottages, arrange arrival details (you'll probably pick up your keys at the *Expedition* shed near the dock). The hostel and cottages charge extra for bed linens. If you have a tent, you can pitch it on the island for 80 kr.

$$$ Grinda Hotel rents 30 rooms (each named for a local bird or fish) in four buildings just above the Wärdshus. These are modern, comfortable, and made for relaxing, intentionally lacking distractions such as TVs or phones (Sb-1,600 kr, Db-2,000 kr, larger suite-2,600 kr, 120 kr less/person if you skip breakfast, extra bed-400 kr, if dining at the restaurant the "Wärdshus package" will save you a few kronor).

$ The 27 **cottages**—most near the Södra Grinda ferry dock—are rentable, offering a rustic retreat (kitchenettes but no running water, shared bathroom facilities outside). From mid-June to mid-August, these come with a one-week minimum and cost more (2-bed cottage-3,000 kr/week, 4-bed cottage-3,500 kr/week, 6-bed cottage-4,000 kr; at other times rentable by the night: 2-bed-1,000 kr, 4-bed-1,100 kr, 6-bed-1,300 kr).

$ Grinda Hostel (Vand-rarheim) is the place to sleep if you wish you'd gone to Swedish summer camp as a kid. The 44 bunks are in simple two- and four-bed cottages, surrounding a pair of fire pits (300 kr/bed regardless of room size, great shared kitchen/dining hall). A small  pebbly beach and a basic sauna are nearby.

ARCHIPELAGO

Eating in Grinda

All your options (aside from bringing your own picnic from Stockholm) are run by the hotel. Fortunately, there are choices for each price range.

Grinda Wärdshus, the inn at the center of the complex, has a good restaurant that combines rural island charm with fine food. You can choose between traditional Swedish meals and contemporary international dishes. Servings are small but thoughtfully designed to be delicious. Eat in the woody dining room or on the terrace out front (1,420 kr/person covers dinner and room, 90-180-kr starters, 180-300-kr main dishes; late June-Aug daily 12:00-24:00; off-season Fri 17:00-23:00, Sat 12:00-23:00, Sun 12:00-18:00, closed Mon-Thu; also closed Fri Dec-early March).

Grindas Framficka ("Grinda's Front Pocket") is a pleasant bistro that serves up basic but tasty food (such as fishburgers and grilled shrimp) right along the guest harbor. Order at the counter, then choose a table to wait for your food (140-170-kr dishes, early June-mid-Aug daily 11:00-22:00, otherwise sporadically open in good weather—especially weekends).

The **general store and café** (Lanthandel) just below the Wärdshus is the place to rustle up some picnic fixings. You'll also find coffee to go, ice cream, 40-kr "one-time grills" for a disposable barbecue, and kayak rentals (early June-mid-Aug daily 8:00-18:00; shoulder season Sat 10:00-18:00, Sun 10:00-16:00, open sporadically Mon-Fri).

Svartsö

The remote and lesser-known isle of Svartsö (svert-show, literally "Black Island"), a short hop beyond Grinda, is the "Back Door" option of the bunch. Unlike Grinda, Svartsö is home to a real community; islanders have their own  school and library. But with only 80 year-round residents, the old generation had to specialize. Each person learned a skill to fill a niche in the community—one guy was a carpenter, the next was a plumber, the next was an electrician, and so on. While the island is less trampled than the others in this chapter (just one B&B and a great restaurant), it is reasonably well-served by ferries. Svartsö feels remote and potentially even boring for those who aren't wowed by simply strolling through meadows. But it's ideal for those who want to slow down and immerse themselves in nature.

Orientation to Svartsö

The island, about five miles long and a half-mile wide, has three docks. The main one, at the southwestern tip, is called Alsvik (with the general store and restaurant). Halfway up is Skälvik (near the B&B), and at the northeastern end is Söderboudd. Most boats stop at Alsvik, but if you want to go to a different dock, you can request a stop (ask the conductor on board, or use the semaphore signal at the dock).

At the **Alsvik dock,** the great little general store, called Svartsö Lanthandel, sells anything you could need and also acts as the town TI, post office, and liquor store (mid-June-mid-Aug Mon-Fri 9:00-19:30, Sat-Sun 10:00-18:00; mid-May-mid-June Mon-Thu 9:00-17:30, Fri 9:00-19:30, Sat-Sun 10:00-14:00; shorter off-season, tel. 08/5424-7325, run by friendly Matte Hedelin). You can rent bikes here; call ahead to reserve in busy times. The little café on the dock sells drinks and light food, and rents cottages (shared showers and toilets, tel. 08/5424-7110).

The island has a few paved lanes and almost no traffic. Residents own three-wheeled utility motorbikes for hauling things to and from the ferry landing. The interior consists of little more than trees. With an hour or so, you can bike across the island and back, enjoying the mellow landscape and chatting with the friendly big-city people who've found their perfect escape.

Svartsö hosts the school for this part of the archipelago. Because Swedish law guarantees the right to education, even kids living on remote islands are transported to class. A school boat trundles from island to island each morning to collect kids headed for the school on Svartsö. If the weather is bad, a hovercraft retrieves them. If it's really bad, and all of the snow days have been used up, a helicopter takes the kids to school.

Eating in Svartsö

If you leave the Alsvik dock to the right and walk five minutes up the hill, you'll find the excellent **Svartsö Krog** restaurant. Opened by a pair of can-do foodies who also run a top-end butcher shop at a Stockholm market hall, this place has a deep respect for the sanctity of meat. Specializing in well-constructed, ingredient-driven dishes, the restaurant brings Stockholm culinary sophistication to a castaway island. Choose one of the three eating zones (each with the same menu): outside, the upscale dining room, or in the original pub interior (an Old West-feeling tavern that the new owner has kept as-is to respect the old-timers). The menu is pricey but good (130-160-kr starters, 200-300-kr main dishes). Their specialty is "golden entrecôte," grilled steak that's been aged for eight weeks (figure a hefty 580 kr but potentially worth it for meat-lovers; June-Aug daily 11:00-1:00 in the morning; May and Sept Thu 16:00-1:00, Fri 15:00-1:00, Sat 12:00-1:00, Sun 12:00-18:00, closed Mon-Wed; closed Oct-April; tel. 08/5424-7255).

Sandhamn

Out on the distant fringe of the archipelago—the last stop before Finland—sits the proud village of Sandhamn (on the island of Sandön). Literally "Sand Harbor," this is where the glacier got hung up and kept on churning away, grinding stone into sand. The town has a long history as an important and posh place. In 1897, the Royal Swedish Sailing Society built its clubhouse here, putting Sandhamn on the map as the yachting center of the Baltic—Sweden's answer to Nantucket. It remains an extremely popular stop for boaters—from wealthy yachties to sailboat racers—as well as visitors simply seeking a break from the big city.

You'll find two halves to Sandhamn: In the shadow of that still-standing iconic yacht clubhouse is a ritzy resort/party zone throbbing with big-money nautical types. But just a few steps away, around the harbor, is an idyllic time-warp Old Town of colorfully painted shiplap cottages tucked between tranquil pine groves. While most tourists come here for the resort, the quieter part of Sandhamn holds the real appeal.

Orientation to Sandhamn

The island of Sandön feels stranded on the edge of the archipelago, rather than immersed in it. On its sheltered side is the town of Sandhamn. Though it's far from Stockholm, Sandhamn is very popular. During the peak of summer (mid-June through late August), it's extremely crowded. Expect to stand in line, and call ahead for restaurant reservations. But even during these times, the Old Town is relatively peaceful and pleasant to explore. If the weather's decent, shoulder season is delightful (though it can be busy on weekends).

Sandhamn's hopes of opening a TI may come to fruition in time for your visit, but don't count on it. (For some information, see www .destinationsandhamn.se.) There's also no ATM in Sandhamn, so bring cash (or use your credit card).

Self-Guided Tour

Welcome to Sandhamn

To get your bearings from the ferry dock, take the following tour. Begin by facing out to sea.

As you look out to the little point across from the dock, notice the big yellow building. In the 18th century, this was built as the **pilot house.** Because the archipelago is so treacherous to navi-

gate—with its tens of thousands of islands and skerries, not to mention untold numbers of hidden underwater rocks—locals don't trust outsiders to bring their boats here. So passing ships unfamiliar with these waters were required to pick up a local captain (or "pilot") to take them safely all the way to Stockholm. The tradition continues today. The orange boats marked *pilot,* moored below the house, ferry loaner captains to oncoming ships. And, since this is the point of entry into Sweden, foreign ships can also be processed by customs here.

The little red shed just in front of the pilot house is home to a humble **town museum** that's open sporadically in the summer, featuring exhibits on Sandhamn's history and some seafaring tales. Just below that, notice the waterfront red barn with the *T* sign. The owner of this boat-repair shop erected this marker for Stockholm's T-bana just for fun.

Just above the barn, look for the yellow building with the blue letters spelling **Sandhamns Värdshus.** This traditional inn, built in the late 17th century, housed sailors while they waited here to set out to sea. During that time, Stockholm had few exports, so ships that brought and unloaded cargo there came to Sandhamn to load up their holds with its abundant sand as ballast. Today the inn still serves good food (see "Eating in Sandhamn," later).

Stretching to the left of the inn are the quaint storefronts of most of Sandhamn's **eateries** (those that aren't affiliated with the big hotel)—bakery, deli, and grocery store, all of them humble but just right for a simple bite or picnic shopping. Local merchants enjoy a pleasantly symbiotic relationship. Rather than try to compete with each other, they attempt to complement what the next shop sells—each one finding just the right niche. (For details, see "Eating in Sandhamn," later.)

The area stretching beyond these storefronts is Sandhamn's **Old Town**—a maze of wooden cottages that's an absolute delight to explore (and easily the best activity in town). Only 50 of Sandhamn's homes (of around 450) are occupied by year-rounders. The rest are summer cottages of wealthy Stockholmers, or bunk-houses for seasonal workers in the tourist industry. Most locals live at the farthest-flung (and therefore least desirable) locations. Imagine the impact of 100,000 annual visitors on this little town.

Where the jetty meets the island, notice (on the right) the old-fashioned telephone box with the fancy *Rikstelefon* logo. It contains the island's lone working pay phone. Just to the right of the phone box, you can see the back of the town's bulletin board, where locals post their classified ads. To the left at the base of the dock is Sandhamns Kiosk, a newsstand selling local and international publications (as well as candy and ice cream). A bit farther to the left, the giant red building with

the turret on top is the **yacht clubhouse** that put Sandhamn on the map, and still entertains the upper crust today with a hotel, several restaurants, spa, mini-golf course, outdoor pool, and more (see page 502). You'll see its proud SSS-plus-crown logo (standing for Svenska Segelsällskapet—Swedish Sailing Society) all over town. In the 1970s, the building was owned by a notorious mobster who made meth in the basement, then smuggled it out beneath the dock to sailboats moored in the harbor.

Spinning a bit farther to the left, back to where you started,

survey the island across the strait (Lökholmen). Just above the trees, notice the copper dome of an observatory that was built by this island's eccentric German oil-magnate owner in the early 20th century. He also built a small castle (not quite visible from here) for his kids to play in.

For a narrated stroll to another fine viewpoint, walk into town and turn left along the water. After about 50 yards, a sign on the right points up a narrow lane to *Post*. This unassuming gravel path is actually one of Sandhamn's most important streets, with the post office, police department (which handles only paperwork—real crimes are deferred to the Stockholm PD), and doctor (who visits town every second Wednesday). While Sandhamn feels remote, it's served—like other archipelago communities—by a crack emergency-response network that can dispatch a medical boat, or in extreme cases, a helicopter. With top-notch hospitals in Stockholm just a 10-minute chopper ride away, locals figure that if you have an emergency here, you might just make it to the doctor faster than if you're trying to make it through congested city streets in an ambulance. At the end of this lane, notice the giant hill of the town's namesake sand.

Continuing along the main tree-lined harborfront strip, you can't miss the signs directing yachters to the *toalett* (toilet) and *sopor* (garbage dump). Then you'll pass the Sandhamns Guiderna office, a **travel agency** where you can rent bikes, kayaks, and fishing gear. (If they've managed to open a TI in time for your visit, this is where you'll find it; travel agency tel. 08/640-8040.) Just after that is the barn for the volunteer fire department (Brandstation). With all the wooden buildings in town, fire is a concern—one reason why Sandhamn restricts camping (and campfires).

Go beneath the skyway connecting the big red hotel to its modern annex. Then veer uphill (right) at the *Badstranden Trouville* sign, looking down at the mini-golf course. After you crest the top of the hill, on the left is a big,

flat expanse of rock nicknamed Dansberget ("Dancing Rock") because it once hosted community dances with a live orchestra. Walk out to enjoy fine **views** of the Baltic Sea—from here, boaters can set sail for Finland, Estonia, and St. Petersburg, Russia. Looking out to the horizon, notice the three lighthouse towers poking up from the sea, used to guide ships to this gateway to the archipelago. The finish line for big boat races stretches across this gap (from the little house on the point to your left). In summer, this already busy town gets even more jammed with visitors, thanks to the frequent sailing races that end here. The biggest annual competition is the Götlandrunt, a round-trip from here to the island of Götland. In 2009, Sandhamn was proud to be one of just 10 checkpoints on the Volvo Ocean Race, a nine-month race around the world that called mostly at bigger cities (such as Boston, Singapore, and Rio).

Our walk is finished. You can head back into town. Or, to hit the beach, continue another 15 minutes to Trouville beach (explained below).

Sights in Sandhamn

Beaches (Stränder)—True to its name, Sandön ("Sandy Island") has some of the archipelago's rare sandy beaches. The closest, and local favorite, is the no-name beach tucked in a cove just behind the Old Town (walk through the community from the main boat dock, then follow the cove around to the little sandy stretch).

The most popular—which can be quite crowded in summer—is Trouville beach, at the opposite end of the island from Sandhamn (about a 20-minute walk). To find it, walk behind the big red hotel and take the right, uphill fork (marked with the low-profile *Badstranden Trouville* sign) to the "Dancing Rock," then proceed along the road. Take a left at the fork by the tennis courts, then walk about 10 minutes through a mysterious-feeling forest until you reach a little settlement of red cottages. Take a right at the fork (look up for the *Till Stranden* sign), and then, soon after, follow the middle fork (along the plank walks) right to the beach zone: Two swathes of sand marked off by rocks, stretching toward Finland.

Sleeping in Sandhamn

(7 kr = about $1, country code: 46, area code 08)
Sandhamn has a pair of very expensive top-end hotels, a basic but comfortable B&B, and little else. If you're sleeping on Sandhamn, the B&B is the best choice.

$$$ Sands Hotell is a stylish splurge sitting proudly at the top of town. While oriented mostly to conferences and private parties, its 19 luxurious rooms also welcome commoners in the summer (Sb-2,100 kr, Db-2,500 kr, free Wi-Fi, elevator, spa in basement, tel. 08/5715-3020, www.sandshotell.se, info@sands hotell.se).

$$$ Sandhamns Seglarhotellet rents 79 nautical-themed rooms in a modern annex behind the old yacht club build-ing (where you'll find the reception). The rooms are fine, but the prices are sky-high (Db-2,390 kr, 200 kr more for balcony, extra bed-400 kr, small apartment-2,590 kr, large apartment-2,890 kr, suite-4,090 kr, free Wi-Fi, loud music from disco inside the club-house—light sleepers should ask for a quieter back room, great gym and pool area in basement, tel. 08/5745-0400, www.sand hamn.com, reception@sandhamn.com).

$ Sandhamns Värdshus B&B rents five rustic but tasteful, classically Swedish rooms in an old mission house buried deep in the colorful Old Town. To melt into Sandhamn and get away from the yachties, sleep here (S-795 kr, D-1,290 kr, mostly twins, all rooms share WC and shower, tiny cottage with its own bathroom for same price, includes breakfast, reception is at the restaurant—see below, tel. 08/5715-3051, www.sandhamns-vardshus.se, info @sandhamns-vardshus.se). The rooms are above a reception hall that is rented out for events, but after 22:00, quiet time kicks in.

Eating in Sandhamn

In the Old Town

Sandhamn's most appealing eateries are along the Old Town side of the harbor.

Sandhamns Värdshus, right on the water, is the town's best eatery. They serve traditional Swedish food in three separate din-ing zones (which mostly share the same menu, but each also has its own specials): out on an inviting deck overlooking the water; upstairs in a salty dining room with views; or downstairs in a simple pub (100-150-kr starters, 100-250-kr main dishes, pub serves cheap lunch deal for 69-89 kr; Easter-Oct daily 11:00-22:30, Nov-Easter Mon-Sat closed 14:00-17:00 & after 21:00, Sun 11:00-18:00; reser-vations possible only in restaurant—otherwise first-come first-served, tel. 08/5715-3051).

To grab a bite or assemble a picnic, browse through these smaller eateries (listed in the order you'll reach them from the boat dock): **Westerbergs Livsmedel** grocery store has basic supplies (Mon-Fri 10:00-13:00 & 16:00-18:00, Sat 10:00-15:00, Sun 10:00-13:00). **Dykarbaren Café** serves meals with indoor and outdoor seating (110-175-kr lunches, 240-300-kr dinners, summer daily 11:00-24:00; May-mid-June and mid-Aug-Sept Wed-Sat 11:00-15:00 & 18:00-24:00, Sun 11:00-15:00, closed Mon-Tue and off-season; tel. 08/5715-3554). **Sandhamns Deli** is a bright, innovative shop where you can buy 45-kr sandwiches and salads, a wide array of meats for grilling, cheeses, cold cuts, drinks, fresh produce, and other high-quality picnic fixings (daily in summer 10:00-19:00, later in good weather, mobile 0709-650-300). Just around the corner (uphill from the harbor and behind the Värdsgasthus) is **Sandhamns Bageriet,** a popular bakery/café serving coffee, sweet rolls, and 50-kr sandwiches (daily in summer 8:00-17:00, "self-service café" opens at 7:00).

Among the Yachties

Sandhamns Seglarhotellet has several eateries, open to guests and non-guests. Out on the dock is the Café Seglar'n, an American-style grill with a take-out window and outdoor tables (40-80-kr dishes, 150-kr combo meals, open in summer in good weather only). Upstairs in the building's main ballroom is an eatery serving good but pricey Swedish and international food. There are two parts—the cheaper, mellow bistro (100-150-kr starters, 200-250-kr main dishes, traditional daily lunch special for 150 kr), and the fancier restaurant (150-200-kr starters, 185-300-kr main dishes). Both parts enjoy fine sea views, and they meet at the bar/dance hall zone in the middle (with loud disco music until 2:00 in the morning nearly nightly in summer). Down on the ground floor is a pub/nightclub (tel. 08/5745-0421).

SOUTHEAST SWEDEN

Växjö • Glass Country • Kalmar • Öland

Ranking Sweden's sights, Stockholm is tops, but the southeastern province of Småland is the top runner-up. More Americans came from this densely forested area than any other part of Scandinavia, and the House of Emigrants in Växjö tells the story well.

Between Växjö and Kalmar is Glass Country, a 70-mile stretch of forest sparkling with glassworks that welcome guests to tour and shop. Historic Kalmar has a rare Old World ambience and the most magnificent medieval castle in Scandinavia. From Kalmar, you can cross one of Europe's longest bridges to hike through the Stonehenge-like mysteries of the strange island of Öland.

Planning Your Time

By train, on a three-week Scandinavian trip, I'd skip this area in favor of the direct, high-speed train from Copenhagen to Stockholm, or the night train from Malmö (just over the Øresund Bridge from Copenhagen) to Stockholm. Side-trips from Stockholm to Helsinki and Tallinn merit more time than this part of Sweden.

But if you have at least three weeks in Scandinavia and a car, the sights described in this section are an interesting way to spend a couple of days. While I'm not so hot on the Swedish countryside (OK, blame my Norwegian heritage), you can't see only Stockholm and say you've seen Sweden. Växjö and Kalmar give you the best possible dose of small-town Sweden. (I find Lund and Malmö, both popular side-trips from Copenhagen, relatively dull. And I'm not old or sedate enough to find a sleepy boat trip along the much-loved Göta Canal appealing.)

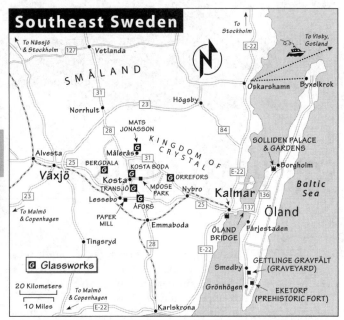

By Car: Drivers can spend three days getting from Copenhagen to Stockholm this way:

Day 1: Leave Copenhagen after breakfast, drive over the bridge to Sweden and on to Växjö, tour Växjö's House of Emigrants, drive into Glass Country, tour Kosta Boda and Transjö glassworks, and arrive in Kalmar in time for dinner.

Day 2: Spend the day in Kalmar touring the castle and Kalmar County Museum, and browsing its people-friendly streets. If you're restless, cross the bridge for a joyride on the island of Öland.

Day 3: 8:00—Begin five-hour drive north along the coast to Stockholm; 10:30—Break in Västervik; 12:00—Stop in Söderköping for picnic lunch and a walk along the Göta Canal; 13:30—Continue drive north; 16:00—Arrive in Stockholm.

Shorten your stops on Day 3 and you'll arrive in Stockholm in time to make the overnight boat to Tallinn or Helsinki. This is an especially good plan on Sunday through Wednesday in the off-season, when boat fares are cheaper. You can see Stockholm on the way back.

By Public Transit: Växjö and Kalmar are easy to visit by train. I'd skip Glass Country and Öland, but if you wouldn't, take the bus (from Växjö to Kosta Boda glassworks, and from Kalmar to Öland).

Växjö

A pleasant, sleepy town of almost 80,000, Växjö (locals say VEK-hwuh; Stockholmers pronounce it VEK-shuh) is in the center of Småland. An important trading town for centuries, its name loosely means "where the road meets the lake." Today an enjoyable three-mile path encircles that lake, and a farmers market enlivens the otherwise too-big and too-quiet main square on Wednesday and Saturday mornings.

While there isn't much heavy-duty sightseeing in Växjö, it does have a trio of visit-worthy attractions (all within a 10-minute walk of the train station): The excellent House of Emigrants, chronicling the plight of Swedes who fled to North America; the Smålands Museum, offering a convenient look at the region's famous glass without a trip to Glass Country; and the cathedral, decorated with fine modern glass sculptures.

In 1996, Växjö set itself a goal to become a fossil-fuel-free city by the year 2050. Now a single biomass power plant provides nearly all the community's heat and hot water, half of its energy comes from renewable sources, and carbon dioxide emissions are down by 34 percent. Växjö earned the title "Greenest City in Europe" when it received the EU's first award for sustainable development in 2007.

Orientation to Växjö

Växjö's town center is compact and pedestrian-friendly; the train station, main square, and two important museums are all within two blocks of each other. Blocks here are short; everything I mention is within about a 15-minute walk of everything else.

Arrival in Växjö

Växjö's modern woody train station has snack stands and lockers (40-50 kr). Pick up a city map at the train station information desk. The station faces the heart of town; walk a few steps straight ahead, and you'll be in the pedestrian shopping zone. Everything in town is in front of you except the two main museums, which are behind the station; to reach these, cross the tracks using the pedestrian overpass.

Tourist Information

The **TI** is inside the municipal building facing the main town square, about a 10-minute walk from the train station. With your back to the station, go straight down the pedestrian walkway two blocks and turn right on Linnégatan (June-Aug Mon-Fri 9:30-18:00, Sat 10:00-14:00, Sun in July only 10:00-14:00—otherwise closed Sun; Sept-May Mon-Fri 9:30-16:30, closed Sat-Sun; free Internet access, room-booking service, Kronobergsgatan 7, tel. 0470/733-280, www.turism.vaxjo.se).

Internet Access: Everlast Internet café, two blocks in front of the train station, has more computers than the TI (30 kr/hour; Mon-Fri 12:00-18:00, Sat 12:00-17:00, closed Sun; Sandgärdsgatan 12, next to recommended Ali Baba restaurant).

Sights in Växjö

Växjö's attractions cluster around the north end of its delightful lake and the surrounding park. You'll find the museums on the hill just behind the train station.

▲**Smålands Museum/Swedish Glass Museum (Sveriges Glasmuseum)**—This instructive museum celebrates the region of Småland and its glassmaking tradition. On the ground floor, the "Six Centuries of Swedish Glass" exhibit traces the history of the substance that still powers the local economy. Upstairs you'll find more on glass, along with displays on the region's prehistory, and a look at Kronoberg County (which includes Växjö) in the 19th century. Temporary exhibits round out your visit. The collection is well-described in English, so this is a handy place to learn a bit about glass if you're not headed deeper into Glass Country. Who knew that the person who designed the original Coca-Cola bottle was a Swede?

Cost and Hours: 50-kr combo-ticket includes House of Emigrants; June-Aug Mon-Fri 10:00-17:00, Sat-Sun 11:00-17:00; Sept-May Tue-Fri 10:00-17:00, Sat-Sun 11:00-17:00, closed Mon; café with 85-100-kr light meals, Södra Järnvägsgatan 2, tel. 0470/704-200, www.smalandsmuseum.se.

▲▲**House of Emigrants (Utvandrarnas Hus)**—If you have Swedish roots, this tidy museum is really exciting. Even if you don't, it's an interesting stop for anyone with immigrant ancestors. While modest, the well-presented, inspiring "Dream of America" exhibit offers powerful insight into the experience of more than one million Swedes who sought refuge in North America in the late 19th and early 20th centuries.

Cost and Hours: 50-kr combo-ticket includes Swedish Glass Museum; June-Aug daily 10:00-17:00; Sept-May Tue-Fri 10:00-17:00, Sat-Sun 10:00-16:00, closed Mon; just down the hill behind

the glass museum, Vilhelm Mobergs Gata 4, tel. 0470/20120, www
.utvandrarnashus.se.

Background: As economic woes wracked Sweden from the
1850s to the 1920s (even a potato famine hit at one point), the
country was caught up in an "American Fever." Nearly 1.3 million
mostly poor Swedes endured long voyages and culture shock to
find prosperity and freedom in the American promised land. In
that period, one in six Swedes went to live in the US. So many left
the country that Swedish authorities were forced to rethink their
social policies and to institute reforms.

Visiting the Museum: In the "Dream of America" exhibit,
well-worded displays—all translated into English—explain various aspects of the immigrant experience.

A display about Ellis Island vividly recounts how 3.8 million new arrivals from around the world entered the US through
Manhattan's Castle Garden processing center between 1886 and
1890. Firsthand accounts recall the entry procedure, including
medical evaluations and an uncomfortable eye exam. (While the
US's immigration policies are more stringent today, even in those
days about 2 percent of would-be Americans were rejected.) The
display's name, "Isle of Hopes, Isle of Tears," evokes the bittersweet experience of leaving a comfortable (if troubled) old home
for an unfamiliar new one.

The model of a poor, potato-famine-stricken village demonstrates why so many Swedes were forced to emigrate. The Swedes
formed enclaves across North America: on farms and prairies,
from New York to Texas, from Maine to Seattle—and, of course,
in Chicago's "Swede Town" (the world's second-biggest Swedish
town in the world in 1900) and in Minnesota's Twin Cities. The
life-size *Snusgatan* re-creates the main street in a Swedish neighborhood—called "Snoose Boulevard," for Swedish snuff. Other
displays trace immigrant lifestyles, religion, treatment in the press,
women's experiences, and the Swedish cultural societies that preserved the traditions of the Old World in the New. Rounding out
the exhibit, homage is paid to prominent Swedish-Americans,
including Charles Lindbergh and the second man on the moon,
Buzz Aldrin.

Don't miss the display about the *Titanic*, which takes pains to
point out that—after Americans—Swedes were the second-largest
group to perish on that ill-fated vessel. On view are a few items
that went to the bottom of the Atlantic with one of those Swedes.

The Moberg Room celebrates local writer Vilhelm Moberg
(1898-1973), who put the Swedish immigrant experience on the
map with his four-novel series *The Emigrants*. (These books—
and two Max von Sydow/Liv Ullmann films based on them,
The Emigrants and *The New Land*—are essential pre-trip reading

and viewing for Swedish-Americans.) Here you'll see a replica of Moberg's "writer's hut," his actual desk, and some original manuscripts.

Powerful as the museum is, it's become even more poignant in recent years, as Sweden—which not long ago scattered its people far and wide—has become known for taking in other countries' emigrants.

Växjö Town Park (Växjö Stadspark)—Directly downhill from the House of Emigrants, you'll reach the big lake called Växjösjön. This is a fine place to relax with a picnic or go for a stroll. The pleasant three-mile path around the lake takes you from manicured flower gardens through forested areas. The top part of the lake borders the delightful Linnéparken next to the cathedral (both described next). The TI has a good *Växjö Town Park* brochure in English that explains your options.

A 10-minute walk around the top of the lake from the House of Emigrants is the town's modern **swimming hall** (*Simhall*, 75-kr base price includes sauna; extra fee if you want to tan, use the exercise room, or rent a towel or locker; 230-kr family ticket, call for open-swim hours, tel. 0470/41204, www.medley.se/vaxjosimhall).

Cathedral (Domkyrka)—Växjö's striking orange church, with its distinctive double-needle steeple, features fine sacred art—in glass, of course. Its austere, bright-white interior is enlivened by gorgeous, colorful, and highly symbolic glass sculptures.

Cost and Hours: Free entry, daily 9:00-18:00.

Visiting the Cathedral: Pick up the thoughtfully written (if evangelical) 15-kr brochure, which offers a detailed self-guided tour. At the back-right corner of the church, find the *Spring of Life* baptistery, which

resembles a spring bubbling up from underground. Near the back-left corner, the *Tree of Life and Knowledge* is a fantastically detailed candelabra shaped like a tree. On one side, find Adam, Eve, and the snake; on the other, Jesus and Mary with arms outstretched. Notice the thematically parallel design—the snake opposite the dove (representing the Holy Spirit); the snake's tempting apple opposite the bunch of grapes (symbolizing the wine of the Eucharist). At the front of the church, the main altar stands before a glass-decorated triptych showing the subtle interplay between light and dark. Explore the other pieces of glass art around the church, and take in its trio of pipe organs. Before you leave, take a look at the ATM-like machine in the lobby that accepts donations from your debit or credit card—the Lord moves in mysterious ways.

Linnéparken—This peaceful park beside the cathedral is dedicated to the great Swedish botanist Carl von Linné (a.k.a. Carolus Linnaeus). It has an arboretum, lots of well-categorized perennials, a cactus garden, and a children's playground.

Sleeping in Växjö

As elsewhere in Scandinavia, hotels charge less on Friday and Saturday nights and from late June through early August.

$$$ Elite Stadshotell is a big, modern, business-class hotel with all the comforts in its 163 rooms. It's in a royal setting on the town's main square (very flexible prices; in peak season usually Sb-1,000 kr, Db-1,400 kr; summer/weekends Sb-550 kr, Db-900 kr; 200 kr more for plush and newly renovated "deluxe" rooms, free Wi-Fi, park on square out front—pay by day but free at night, about a block from the train station's main entrance at Kungsgatan 6, tel. 0470/13400, fax 0470/44837, www.elite.se, info.vaxjo @elite.se).

$$ Hotell Värend is friendly, comfortable, and inexpensive. It has 24 worn but workable rooms at the edge of a residential neighborhood six blocks from the front of the train station along Kungsgatan (Sb-550-700 kr, Db-650-850 kr, Tb-795-1,000 kr, non-smoking, elevator, free Wi-Fi, free parking, a block beyond

---

Sleep Code

(7 kr = about $1, country code: 46, area code: 0470)
S = Single, **D** = Double/Twin, **T** = Triple, **Q** = Quad, **b** = bathroom, **s** = shower. All of these hotels accept credit cards and include breakfast.

To help you sort easily through these listings, I've divided the accommodations into three categories, based on the price for a standard double room with bath during high season:

  $$$ Higher Priced—Most rooms 1,200 kr or more.
   $$ Moderately Priced—Most rooms between 700-1,200 kr.
    $ Lower Priced—Most rooms 700 kr or less.

Prices can change without notice; verify the hotel's current rates online or by email.

N. Esplanaden at Kungsgatan 27, tel. 0470/776-700, mobile 076-769-0700, fax 0470/36261, www.hotellvarend.se, info@hotellvarend.se). If driving, follow *Centrum* signs into town from the freeway. At the Royal Corner Hotel, turn left; 200 yards later, at the first light, turn right onto N. Esplanaden, then left onto Kungsgatan.

$$ Hotel Esplanad, nearby on a busy street, is a bit more modest, with 25 less-expensive rooms, some with private baths on the hall (S-450-650 kr, Sb-550-850 kr, D-700-850 kr, Db-800-1,050 kr, free parking, N. Esplanaden #21A, tel. 0470/22580, fax 0470/26226, www.hotellesplanad.com, info@hotellesplanad.com, Anna). From the train station, walk five blocks up Klostergatan and turn left on N. Esplanaden.

$ *Hostel:* Växjö's fine **Evedal Hostel** is near a lake three miles out of town (200 kr/bed in 2- to 4-bed rooms, D-600 kr, 50 kr cheaper for members, breakfast-60 kr, sheets-75 kr, office open daily 8:00-10:00 & 17:00-19:00, tel. 0470/63070, www.vaxjo vandrarhem.nu, vaxjo.vandrarhem@telia.com). From Växjö's train station, catch bus #7 (June-Aug hourly Mon-Fri, less Sat-Sun and off-season, 15 minutes). A taxi costs 200 kr: Tell them you're going to the hostel for a 10 percent discount (tel. 0470/16000).

Eating in Växjö

After-hours Växjö is not very exciting. Consider livening things up by dining out.

PM is a trendy eatery where a younger crowd stands in line to see and be seen. They have good international cuisine with Swedish flair, a mod black-and-white interior, and nice outdoor tables on the pedestrian mall (110-kr lunch special, 150-190-kr starters, 160-270-kr main dishes, 375-kr three-course dinners, Mon-Sat 11:30-23:00, often later Fri-Sat, closed Sun, Storgatan 24 at corner of Västergatan, tel. 0470/700-444).

Lagerlunden, the elegant, glassed-in restaurant at the recommended Elite Stadshotell, has dinner specials for 150-250 kr (Tue-Sat 18:00-24:00, closed Sun-Mon, Kungsgatan 6, tel. 0470/13400).

Ethnic Options: If you're looking to save money, or if it's a Sunday—when other restaurants are closed—visit one of downtown Växjö's dozen or so Asian restaurants and kebab-and-pizza shops. Of these, **Ali Baba's** is a cut above, with a glitzy, Lebanese-casino vibe and a fun stalactite ceiling (60-100-kr meals, Mon-Thu 10:00-22:00, Fri-Sat 12:00-late, Sun 12:30-22:00, Sandgärdsgatan 10, tel. 0470/27900). **La Gondola,** serving Swedish, Chinese, Thai, and Greek food, is simple and engagingly multinational, and offers seating indoors and out (80-90-kr lunch buffet, 40-65-kr starters, 105-160-kr main dishes, Mon 12:00-15:00, Tue-Wed 11:00-21:00, Thu 11:00-15:00 & 19:00-20:00, Fri-Sun 12:00-

22:00, Storgatan 33, tel. 0470/27632).

Groceries: Visit the **ICA supermarket** at the corner of Sand-gärdsgatan and Klostergatan, one block from the front of the train station (Mon-Sat 8:00-20:00, Sun 11:00-20:00). **Coop/Konsum** is farther away, but bigger and open later (daily 7:00-23:00, about a 7-minute walk left of the train station at Oxtorget 8—look for large parking lot).

Växjö Connections

From Växjö by Bus to Kosta (2-3/day, 1 hour, bus #218 from train station). Växjö does not have good long-distance bus connections.

By Train to: Copenhagen (8/day, 2.5-3 hours), **Stockholm** (every 2 hours, 3.5 hours, change in Alvesta, reservations required), **Kalmar** (12/day, 60-70 minutes). See the Stockholm chapter (page 419) for information on taking trains in Sweden.

Glass Country

Filling the remote-feeling woods between Växjö and Kalmar with busy glassmaking workshops, Sweden's famous Glasriket ("Kingdom of Crystal") is worth ▲▲ for drivers. It's touristy, yes—but it also wins over skeptics. There's something to please everybody here: Shoppers thrill at the chance to pick up deeply discounted factory seconds, art-lovers enjoy seeing all of the creative uses for glass, and engineers are fascinated by the skilled glassblowers who persuade glowing globs of molten glass to become fine pieces of tableware or art.

Visiting a glassworks *(glasbruk)* has three parts: the shop; an exhibition of attractive pieces by local artists; and the hot shop, or *hytta,* where glassblowers are hard at work. At most glassworks, it's possible to walk through the hot shop—close enough to feel the heat from the globs of glass as they're being worked (come before the 15:00 quitting time). The shops and exhibitions are usually free, but sometimes charge a token admission fee. To visit the hot shop, most places technically charge admission—but since there's nobody posted at the hot-shop door at smaller glassworks, in practice you can usually just stroll through for free. Taking a guided tour of at least one hot shop—which costs extra—is a must to really understand the whole process. (For starters, read the "Glassmaking in Sweden" sidebar.)

The glassworks I describe in this chapter are a representative mix of the 15 or so that you can visit in Glass Country, ranging from big corporate factories to charming artistic workshops. On

Glassmaking in Sweden

In the mid-16th century, King Gustav Vasa decided he wanted more fine glass to decorate his palace, so he invited German glassmakers to train his subjects, and the trend took off. It's no surprise that glassmaking caught on here in Sweden. While the very rocky soil makes farming difficult, the resources needed for glass are abundant: vast forests to fire the ovens, and lakes with an endless supply of sand. By the difficult 19th century—when a sixth of Sweden's population emigrated to North America—the iron mills had closed, leaving behind unemployed workers who were highly skilled at working with materials at high temperatures. Glassmaking was their salvation, and by the early 1900s, this region had more than 100 glassworks.

While glassmaking was important throughout Sweden, it was in the area between Växjö and Kalmar (engulfed in a dense forest) that it took hold the strongest, and lasted the longest. When other materials became cheaper than glass (for example, paper cartons instead of glass bottles), the glassmaking industry was hit hard, and it dried up in other parts of Sweden. But here in Glass Country, workers refocused their efforts: They still make some everyday items, but their emphasis is on high-quality art pieces that command top kronor. An Ikea wine glass made in China costs 10 kr, while a handmade Swedish one might cost 150 kr—but consumers interested in quality are willing to pay that premium.

The glassmaking process is fascinating—and hasn't changed much over the centuries. The glass begins as little white pellets that are about 70 percent sand (most of the sand for the clearest-color glass is imported from Belgium). Soda and potash are added to lower the melting point, and limestone and zinc are added to minimize boiling (and the resulting bubbles). The final qualities of the glass are determined by other additives— glassmakers use a different mix for a thin champagne flute than for a thick platter.

You'll see two different types of glass being created: everyday tableware and art pieces. The mass-produced tableware— such as wine glasses—is created by small teams of glassblowers who use an assembly-line system, supervised by a "master," who monitors quality control. Art-glass pieces, however, are never the same. The region has a passel of big-name designers, each with their own aesthetic and all considered local celebrities. Most glass artists conceptualize the design, but leave the actual grunt work to their assistants—you might see the artist hovering off to the side, directing the glassblowers.

As you watch these masters at work, keep in mind they're working with a molten medium that can melt skin. First, a worker places the glass-blowing rod into the furnace (notice the foot pedals used to open and close the doors) and grabs a blob of molten glass. Glassblowers have to move quickly—before the glass hardens too much—but carefully, to avoid shattering the medium or burning their colleagues. After rolling the glass out on a heat-resistant graphite table to give it the desired shape, they blow into the end of the rod to open a space inside. If creating a mass-produced item, they generally stick it into a mold to ensure the correct dimensions. Other appendages are added; for example, if it's a wineglass with a stem and foot, separate pieces of glass are stretched out to the appropriate shape and stuck on the bottom.

For this entire process, the glass is at about 2,100 degrees Fahrenheit. If it gets too hot, glassblowers cool it down with water or air; if the glass needs to be reheated, they use a blow-torch or poke it momentarily back into the furnace. All glass begins clear. To make colored glass, they either add powdered dye during production, or paint the finished piece and then refire it. Finally, the area where the glass was attached to the rod is cut with an industrial diamond, broken off, and ground and polished smooth. When the piece is finished, it's set in a special oven to cool gradually—over a few hours for smaller pieces, or a day or more for large items.

The workday ends around 15:00, when the raw materials for the next day's glass are dumped into giant, custom-made clay pots and placed in the ovens. Overnight, these will gradually melt down to the molten medium the glassblowers will need by tomorrow morning at 7:00.

The last stop is quality control. Only the best pieces are deemed "first quality" *(1:A Sortering)*—you'll pay a premium for these flawless items. Some items, deemed "second quality" *(2:A Sortering)*, have minor imperfections that bring the price down substantially. When shopping, pay close attention to these labels; if you don't need your glass perfect, you can save by looking for second quality. Quite a few items are simply too imperfect—these are dumped into a bin and disposed of. Sorry, budget travelers—these "factory thirds" are trashed, not sold.

SOUTHEAST SWEDEN

the corporate side, the Kosta company dominates; its flagship Kosta Boda complex is the biggest and most accessible of all the glassworks (though its smaller subsidiaries, Åfors and Orrefors, are also tourable). But round out your look at the region with at least one smaller, independent producer as well (Transjö Glashytta is the most appealing, but I've also described Bergdala and Mats Jonasson Målerås). And, for a change of pace, you can learn about traditional papermaking (at the Lessebo mill) and the local moose population. For more tips on which glassworks to visit—and which to skip—see "Planning Your Time," below.

Information: The *Glasriket/Kingdom of Crystal* magazine (available at any TI) and the region's official website (www .glasriket.se) describe the many glassworks that welcome the public. The 95-kr **Glasriket Pass** includes free entry to exhibitions and hot shops, and discounts on tours, shopping, and *hyttsill* dinners (explained on page 525). The pass, sold at glassworks and local TIs, is worthwhile only if you're visiting several hot shops and doing some serious shopping (10 percent discount at certain shops, often with a 500-kr minimum purchase). Note that in Swedish, *glas* is glass, while *glass* is ice cream.

Planning Your Time

Though you can take a bus from Växjö to Kosta, the glassworks aren't worth the time and trouble unless you have a car. Train travelers should instead take a careful look at the glass exhibit in Växjö's Smålands Museum, and then go straight to Kalmar.

With a car, the drive from Växjö to Kalmar is a 70-mile joy—light traffic with endless forest-and-lake scenery punctuated by numerous glassworks. The driving time between Växjö and Kosta is 45 minutes; it's another 45 minutes between Kosta and Kalmar.

Looking at a map, you'll notice the glassworks are scattered around the center of the region. While it would take the better part of a day to loop around and visit them all, distances are relatively short and roads are good. Still, it's smart to be selective. On a tight schedule, I'd visit Kosta and Transjö, possibly Bergdala or Åfors, and maybe the Lessebo paper mill, skipping the rest.

If you're visiting Glass Country en route from Växjö to Kalmar, consider this driving plan: Head southeast from Växjö on highway 25, following signs for *Kalmar*. If you want to visit Bergdala, turn off after Hovmantorp; to skip it, head straight to Lessebo (and its paper mill). In Lessebo, turn north for Kosta and tour the big Kosta Boda glassworks there. Then, if you'd like to visit the Moose Park, detour slightly east (it's just on the outskirts of Kosta, toward Orrefors). From here you can also detour much farther to the Mats Jonasson glassworks, to the northeast in Målerås. Otherwise, from Kosta, head south on highway 28, watching for signs to *Transjö* for the best of the smaller, artsy glassworks. The same road 28 takes you to Eriksmåla, where the Åfors workshop is also worth a visit if you're not glassed out. In Eriksmåla you can pick up highway 25 and make a beeline east to Kalmar.

Sights in Glass Country

These attractions are tied together by the driving tour described above. Don't forget the two non-glass sights (the historic paper mill and Moose Park), described after the glassworks.

Glassworks (Glasbruks)

These are listed in the order you'll reach them, from Växjö to Kalmar. Many glassworks charge admission to watch the hot shop at work, but most aren't set up to actually collect this fee at the door—so curious tourists can simply poke around and might not even have to pay (the entrance fee is waived if you have the 95-kr Glasriket Pass). Also note that many workshops take a lunch break sometime between 10:00 and 11:00, and stop working entirely after about 15:00 or 15:30.

▲**Bergdala Studioglas**—The small, independent Bergdala glassworks, in a village of the same name, has an enjoyably artsy hot shop. Its well-stocked shop is full of its trademark blue-rimmed tableware, and the engaging gallery upstairs shows off a different sampling of local artists every year.

Cost and Hours: Hot shop—20 kr, mid-June-Aug Mon-Fri 7:00-15:30, closed Sat-Sun; gallery—free, mid-June-Aug Mon-Fri 10:00-17:00, Sat 10:00-16:00, Sun 12:00-16:00; shorter hours off-season, tel. 0478/31650, www.studioglas.se.

▲▲**Kosta (a.k.a. Kosta Boda)**—About an hour east of Växjö, the village of Kosta boasts the oldest of the *glasbruks,* dating back to 1742. Today, the sprawling Kosta com-plex—the only real jolt of civilization in this otherwise remote-feeling landscape—includes a modern outlet mall, a factory store (labeled *Kosta Boda*), a fancy new art hotel...and, of course, the glassworks.

The highlight here is unquestionably watching the **glassworks** in action. Argu-ably the best hot-shop tour in the region, this allows you to look over the shoulders of glassblowers crafting both mass-produced, crank-'em-out tableware and high art fit to be shown off in a museum. You can visit the glassworks and its gallery on your own.

But if you know you're coming, call or email ahead to arrange a 45-minute English tour—usually guided by Kristina, whose enthusiasm makes the place meaningful. In the surprisingly modest **exhibition gallery,** each piece is identified with a photo and brief bio (in English) of its designer, which personalizes the art (often offered for sale). You'll also see historical pieces.

Cost and Hours: 30 kr, 20-kr extra for tour; usually open Mon-Fri 10:00-18:00, Sat-Sun 11:00-17:00, last tour departs one hour earlier (hours vary; call or email ahead). The glassworks is much quieter—and less interesting—after about 15:30. From early July to early Aug, when the glassblowers are on vacation, there's less glassblowing and more tourists—and the complex is open daily 11:00-17:00. To reserve a tour call 0478/34529 or email info @kostaboda.se (www.kostaboda.se).

Shopping: In the Kosta Boda **factory outlet shop,** crystal "seconds" (with tiny bubbles or sets that don't quite match) and discontinued models are sold at good prices. This is duty-free shopping, and they'll happily mail your purchases home. Don't confuse this with the big outlet mall across the street (daily 10:00-18:00, until 19:00 mid-June-Aug).

Sleeping and Eating: I ate well at the **cafeteria** inside the outlet mall, which features 85-kr lunch specials. Nearby is the pricey **$$$ Kosta Boda Art Hotel,** designed to impress. Everything's decorated to the hilt with (of course) artistic glass, created in the hot shop across the street. With Växjö and Kalmar so close, there's little reason to sleep here (rooms start at Db-2,500 kr, tel. 0478/34830, www.kostabodaarthotel.se). But if you have a few extra minutes, poke around this surreal, over-the-top, world-of-glass complex, which includes a "glass bar," a mind-bending indoor swimming pool, and a restaurant where, on most evenings, you can watch an actual glassblower at work while you dine (250-kr main dishes in fine-dining section, less in bistro).

▲▲Transjö Hytta—Set up in an old converted farm 10 minutes south of Kosta, this tiny glassworks does expensive but unique fine-art pieces. From the main shop, a canal-like pond (with glass art pieces suspended overhead) leads back to the hopping hot shop. Transjö—started by a pair of highly regarded glass designers—uses up-and-coming artists as apprentices; they imbue it with a youthful vigor. You can feel the art oozing out of the ovens. The tiny glassworks is funkier and less predictable than the big boys; it's most worthwhile if you catch the artists in action.

The gift shop out front sells one-of-a-kind (expensive) art pieces and limited-run production items made on-site (the *elevarbete*/apprentice works are cheaper). Unfortunately the hot shop is often closed (they don't do much glassblowing in warmer weather), but if you follow the canal back to the workshop, you might find the glassblowers in action. If the shop is closed, the glassblowers will often take a break and open it for you.

Cost and Hours: Free, shop usually open early June-mid-Sept daily 9:00-17:00, hot shop hours unpredictable, smart to call or email ahead—tel. 0478/50700, www.transjohytta.com, info@transjohytta.com. To find it, look for *Transjö* signs just south of Kosta.

▲**Åfors**—The Åfors (OH-foss) glassworks is near Eriksmåla, a

charming village south of Kosta and Transjö. While it's part of the Kosta corporate scene, Åfors focuses on individual art pieces rather than mass-produced tableware. This makes it refreshingly intimate, with a looser and more artistic vibe than its assembly-line cousins. You can visit the hot shop as well as a shop/gallery.

Cost and Hours: Hot shop—30 kr, Mon-Fri 10:00-15:30, closed Sat-Sun; shop/gallery—free, Mon-Fri 10:00-18:00, Sat 10:00-16:00, Sun 12:00-16:00; tel. 0481/34274, www.kostaboda.se.

Mats Jonasson Målerås—In the town of Målerås northeast of

Kosta, Mats Jonasson's glassworks specializes in engraving, mixed metal-and-glass sculptures, and necklaces. While it started small, the facility has grown quite big, giving the glassworks a less personal atmosphere. The "design arena" shows off works by other local glass artists.

Cost and Hours: Free; watch glassmaking Mon-Fri 9:00-15:00, also weekends in July-Aug; shop/gallery open June-Aug Mon-Fri 9:00-18:00, Sat 10:00-17:00, Sun 11:00-17:00, shorter hours off-season; tel. 0481/31401, www.matsjonasson.com.

Orrefors—Once a glassworks with its own proud history, Orrefors (OH-reh-fohs) is now part of the Kosta empire and plays second fiddle to the flagship brand. While Kosta does more handmade pieces, Orrefors focuses on machine-made mass production. Orrefors feels drearily industrial and sadly neglected, but might be worth visiting if you know your glass and have a special affinity for their works.

The dazzling **museum** displays its historic art pieces chronologically (from early-20th-century pieces with Art Nouveau flair through works from the 1940s) and includes a "crystal bar." In the **hot shop,** visitors observe the work from platforms. If you're inspired, try one of the glassblowing lessons offered in July and August (245 kr). English tours are available in summer (but the Kosta tour is better). Like Kosta, Orrefors' **shop** sells nearly perfect crystal seconds at deep discounts.

Cost and Hours: Hot shop—30 kr, 20-kr extra for tour (arrange in advance, tel. 0478/34529), Mon-Fri 9:00-15:30, closed Sat-Sun, longer hours in summer; museum—same hours as hot shop; gift shop—Mon-Fri 10:00-18:00, Sat 10:00-17:00, Sun 12:00-17:00; tel. 0481/34189, www.orrefors.com.

Non-Glass Attractions

▲**Lessebo Hand Paper Mill (Handpappersbruket)**—The town of Lessebo has a 300-year-old paper mill (tucked next to a giant modern one) that's kept working for visitors to enjoy. If you've never seen handmade paper produced, this mill is worth a visit. Cotton linters (fibers) are soaked, packed into a frame, pressed, dried, glazed, and hand-torn into the perfect size and shape. This paper is coveted for special purposes: top-of-the-line stationery (for wedding invitations), impossible-to-forge embossed document paper (for certificates or important examinations), and long-lasting archival use (the cotton fibers ensure the paper will stay pristine for decades).

You can pick up the English brochure and visit on your own, but to see papermaking in action, join a 40-minute English tour with one of the craftsmen who still run the place. Watercolor paper and stationery are available for purchase.

Cost and Hours: 20 kr, late June-late Aug Mon-Fri 9:15-17:00, closed Sat-Sun, off-season closes at 16:00 and for lunch 12:00-13:00; 35-kr extra for tour, departures at 9:30, 10:30, 13:00, and 14:15 (no tours off-season); look for black-and-white *Handpappersbruk* sign just after the Kosta turnoff, Storgatan 79, tel. 0478/47691, www.vida.se/handpappersbruket-1.aspx.

Grönåsen's Moose Park (Älgpark)—This offbeat attraction, just outside Kosta, demonstrates the love-hate relationship Swedes feel toward their moose population. (The Swedish word *älg* can be translated both as "moose" and "elk," but these are the same Bullwinkle-type moose you'll find in the northern latitudes of North America.) A third of a million of these giant, majestic beasts live in Sweden. They're popular with hunters but unpopular with drivers, because collisions on backcountry roads have caused fatalities. At this attraction, you'll walk through the moose-happy gift shop before taking a mile-long stroll around the perimeter of a pen holding live moose. Periodic museum exhibits—life-size dioramas with stuffed moose (including one plastered to the hood of a car)—round out the attraction. You can even buy moose sausage. Sure it's a hokey roadside stop, and will hardly be a hit with animal-rights activists, but for many the park is an enjoyable place to learn about Swedish moose.

SOUTHEAST SWEDEN

Cost and Hours: 50 kr, Easter-mid-Nov daily 10:00-18:00, closed off-season, just outside Kosta on the road to Orrefors, tel. 0478/50770, www.moosepark.net.

Eating in Glass Country

You'll find plenty of simple eateries designed for day-trippers. For example, the cafeteria in the outlet mall at the big Kosta complex is the perfect place for fast and cheap, Ikea-style Swedish grub.

If you'd like to linger over a more serious dinner, consider joining one of the special *hyttsill* **dinners** at various glass workshops. Traditionally, a hot shop's fires made it a popular place to convene after hours on frigid winter nights. People would huddle around the ovens and be entertained by wandering minstrel-type entertainers called *luffar*. The food was nothing special (*hyttsill* literally means "hot shop herring," usually served with crispy pork, potatoes, and other stick-to-your-ribs fare), but it was a nice opportunity for a convivial rural community to get together. Today modern glassworks carry on the tradition, inviting tourists on several nights through the summer. They usually have live music and glassblowers working while you dine (figure around 395 kr per person; see complete schedule and reserve at www.glasriket.se).

Kalmar

Kalmar feels like it used to be of strategic importance. In its heyday—back when the Sweden/Denmark border was just a few miles to the south—they called Kalmar Castle the "Key to Sweden." But today Denmark is distant, and Kalmar is a bustling small city of 62,000 (with 9,000 students in its university and maritime academy). Kalmar's salty old center, classic castle, and busy waterfront give it a wistful sailor's charm.

History students may remember Kalmar as the place where the treaty establishing the 1397 Kalmar Union was signed. This "three crowns" treaty united Norway, Sweden, and Denmark against their common enemy: German Hanseatic traders. It created a huge kingdom, dominated by Denmark, that lasted a bit more than a hundred years. But when the Swede Gustav Vasa came to power in 1523, Kalmar was rescued from the Danes, the union was dissolved...and even the European Union hasn't been able to reunify the Scandinavian Peninsula since.

Kalmar town was originally next to the castle but was entirely rebuilt on the nearby island of Kvarnholmen after a huge fire in 1647. There it was encircled by giant 17th-century earthworks and bastions, parts of which still survive.

The town center of Kvarnholmen, the charming Old Town, the castle, and nearby vacation island of Öland are all enjoyable to explore, making Kalmar Sweden's most appealing stop after Stockholm.

Orientation to Kalmar

For a relatively small city, Kalmar has a complicated layout; its many small islands are connected to the mainland—and to each other—by bridges. Kalmar is easily walkable and fun by bike.

The mostly pedestrianized core of town is on the island of Kvarnholmen, walled and with a grid street plan. The Old Town district is between Kvarnholmen and Kalmar Castle, which is on a little island of its own (a 10-minute walk from Kvarnholmen). The train station, TI, and ugly industrial "new harbor" are on a manmade extension just south of Kvarnholmen.

Additional islands make up Kalmar (including charming Ängö and mod Varvsholmen), but most visitors stick to Kvarnholmen, the Old Town, and the castle. If your time is limited, the castle should be your top priority.

Tourist Information

Look for the TI in the big, modern building next to the marina.
The staff hands out helpful brochures and maps of town, including
the *Wander Round Kalmar* self-guided tour booklet (summer usually Mon-Fri 9:00-19:00 or 21:00, Sat-Sun 10:00-16:00 or 17:00;
shorter hours off-season and generally closed Sat-Sun Sept-May;
Ölandskajen 9, tel. 0480/417-700, www.kalmar.com).

The TI has Internet access (60 kr/hour) and can book you a
local hotel room (no booking charge) or a room in a private home
(50-kr fee). Ask about biking tips (you can rent a bike at some
hotels, or at the Baltic shop across the street from the TI). Kalmar,
with its cheery lanes, surrounding parks, and brisk harborfront,
makes for happy biking.

The TI shares a building with the Kalmar Maritime Academy,
which is part of the university. It's built to look like a ship, and the
bridge simulator above is used to train future sailors.

Arrival in Kalmar

Arriving at the combined train and bus station couldn't be easier
(train ticket office open Mon-Fri 6:40-18:00, Sat 8:40-15:00, Sun
10:30-17:00; lockers available). As you walk out the front door,
the town center (Kvarnholmen) is dead ahead. The TI is to your
right (exit station to the right, turn right around the bottom of the
tracks, cross the street to the harbor, and walk to its end). Kalmar
Castle and the Old Town are behind you (follow the tracks to your
left until the first crosswalk, then follow the big tree-lined boulevard to the castle).

Sights in Kalmar

▲▲Kalmar Castle (Kalmar Slott)

This moated castle is one of Europe's great medieval experiences. The imposing exterior, anchored by stout watchtowers and

cuddled by a lush park, houses
a fine Renaissance palace interior. Built in the 12th century,
the castle was enlarged and further fortified by the great King
Gustav Vasa (r. 1523-1560) and
lived in by two of his sons, Erik
XIV and Johan III. In the 1570s,
Johan III redecorated the castle in
the trendy Renaissance style, giving it its present shape. Kalmar
Castle remained a royal hub until 1658, when the Swedish frontier
shifted south and the castle lost its strategic importance. Kalmar

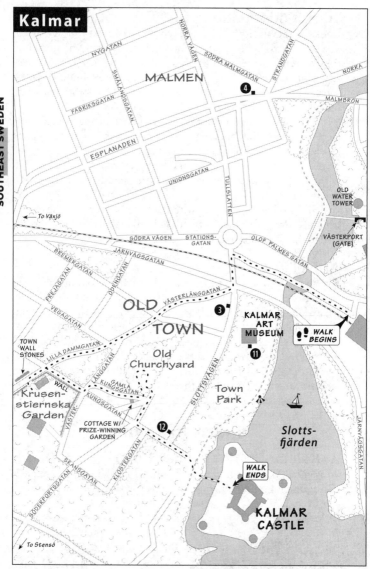

Kalmar

SOUTHEAST SWEDEN

MALMEN

4

OLD
WATER
TOWER

VÄSTERPORT
(GATE)

← To Växjö

3

KALMAR
ART
MUSEUM

WALK
BEGINS

TOWN
WALL
STONES

OLD
TOWN

Old
Churchyard

11

Town
Park

Krusen-
stiernska
Garden

COTTAGE W/
PRIZE-WINNING
GARDEN

12

Slotts-
fjärden

WALK
ENDS

↙ To Stensö

KALMAR
CASTLE

Castle was neglected, then used as a prison, distillery, and granary. Finally, in the mid-19th century, a newfound respect for history led to the castle's renovation.

Cost and Hours: 100 kr (tickets sold in gift shop inside, or sometimes outside the gate in summer); late June-Aug daily 10:00-18:00, May and Sept daily 10:00-16:00, Oct-April generally Sat-Sun only 10:00-16:00; tel. 0480/451-490, www.kalmarslott.se.

SOUTHEAST SWEDEN

1 Calmar Stadshotell
2 Frimurare Hotellet
3 Slottshotellet
4 Hotell Hilda
5 To Hotell Svanen
6 Källaren Kronan Restaurant
7 Calmar Hamnkrog Restaurant
8 Kullzénska Café
9 Pizzeria Italia
10 Co-op/Konsum Grocery
11 Byttan Restaurant
12 Söderportcafé

Getting There: To reach the castle from the center of town, consider taking a short detour to the Old Town and ending your stroll at the castle (route described under "In the Old Town, near the Castle," later).

Tours: Catch the one-hour English tour to hear about the goofy medieval antics of Sweden's kings (included in admission price, offered daily late June-mid-Aug usually at 11:30, 13:30, and

14:30, reconfirm times by phone or on website). A new elevator has made this tour more accessible. You can buy a too-thorough, 45-kr English guidebook, or for the highlights, follow my self-guided tour.

○ Self-Guided Tour: Approaching the castle, you'll cross a wooden drawbridge. Peering into the grassy, filled-in moat, look for sunbathers, who enjoy soaking up rays while the ramparts protect them from cool winds. To play "king of the castle," you can scramble along these outer ramparts (included in castle ticket, or open and free when castle interior is closed).

In the central **courtyard** is the canopied Dolphin Well, a particularly fine work of Renaissance craftsmanship. If you haven't bought your ticket yet, buy one in the gift shop on the left. Then follow the well-marked, one-way tour route.

Near the gift shop, the models and drawings in the **Governor's Quarters** illustrate the evolution of the castle over time. Notice the bulky medieval shape of the towers, before they were capped by fancy Renaissance cupolas; and the Old Town that once huddled in the not-protective-enough shadow of the castle. In the adjoining **Prisoners' Tower,** you can peer down into the dungeon pit. The room was later converted into a kitchen (notice the big fireplace), and the pit became a handy place to dump kitchen waste.

Go through the labyrinth of rooms to the right. Historians are renovating what used to be empty rooms to show daily life at the castle. You may see a reconstruction of the castle kitchen, a room being "painted" by medieval workers in anticipation of a royal visit, and more. Check out the touch-screen terminals with information about the castle and Kalmar.

Then head back to the entrance at the gift shop and look for a red banner marked "Codex." This is the beginning of a stunning exhibit about the **Women's Prison,** a grim 19th-century chapter of the castle's history. Modern black-and-white photographs interpret the prison experience of women incarcerated during the Middle Ages and Renaissance. Images of women in stocks or of an accused "witch" undergoing trial by water will stay in your mind long after the royal rooms fade away.

Then climb the **Queen's Staircase,** up steps made of Catholic gravestones. While this might have simply been an economical way to recycle building materials, some speculate that it was a symbolic move in support of King Gustav Vasa's Reformation, after the king broke with the pope in a Henry VIII-style power struggle.

At the top of the stairs, go through the wooden door into the **Queen's Suite.** The ornate Danish bed (captured from the Danes after a battle) is the only surviving original piece of furniture in the castle. The faces decorating the bed have had their noses chopped off, as superstitious castle-dwellers believed that potentially troublesome spirits settled in the noses. This bed could easily be disassembled ("like an Ikea bed," as my guide put it) and moved from place to place—handy for medieval kings and queens, who were forever traveling throughout their realm. Smaller servants' quarters adjoin this room.

Proceed into the **Checkered Hall.** You'll see reconstructions of a king's coronation robe and a queen's royal dress. Examine the incredibly detailed inlaid wall panels, which make use of 17 different types of wood—each a slightly different hue. The room has an unmistakably Renaissance aesthetic, which strives to achieve symmetry and perspective. Door handles were left off so as not to break up the harmony. (When the queen wanted to go into the next room, she'd clap her hands to alert servants to open the doors for her.)

Speaking of which, continue into the **dining room** (a.k.a. Gray Hall, for the frescoes of Samson and Delilah high on the wall). The table is set for an Easter feast (based on a detailed account by a German visitor to one particular Easter meal held here). For this holiday feast, the whole family was in town—including Gustav Vasa's two sons, Erik XIV and Johan III. The giant birds are for decoration, not for eating. Notice all the fish on the table. Since Erik's wife Katarzyna Jagiellonka was a Polish Catholic (their marriage united Sweden, Poland, and Lithuania into a grand empire), she was abstaining from meat during this holy time. Forks (which resembled the devil's pitchfork) were not used—just spoons, knives, and hands. At the adjacent table, peruse the dessert selection, with marzipan and expensive herbs and spices.

The door in the far corner with the sun above it leads to the **King's Chamber.** Notice the elaborate lock on the door, installed by King Erik XIV because of constant squabbles about succession. The hunting scenes inside have been restored a bit too colorfully, but the picture of Hercules over the window is original—likely painted by Erik himself. Examine more of those elaborate inlaid panels. Peek into the little room (to the left of the fireplace, with a fine castle illustration embedded in its hidden door) to see the king's toilet. Also in here was a secret escape hatch the king could use in case of trouble. Perhaps King Erik XIV was right to be so paranoid; he eventually died under mysterious circumstances, perhaps poisoned by his brother Johan III, who succeeded him as king.

Backtrack through the dining room and continue into the **Golden Hall,** with its gorgeously carved (and painstakingly restored) gilded ceiling. The entire ceiling is suspended from the true ceiling by chains. If you visually trace the ceiling, the room seems crooked—but it's actually an optical illusion to disguise the fact that it's not perfectly square. Find the portraits of the (dysfunctional) royal family whose tales enliven this place: Gustav Vasa, one of his wives, sons Erik XIV and Johan III, and Johan's son Sigismund.

Peek into **Agda's Chamber,** the bedroom of Erik's consort. The replica furniture re-creates how it looked when the king's kept woman lived here. Later, the same room was used for a different type of captivity: as a prison cell for female inmates.

Go to the top of the King's Staircase (also made of gravestones like the Queen's Staircase, and topped by a pair of lions). The big door leads to the grand **Green Hall,** once used for banquets and now for concerts.

At the end of this hall, the **chapel** is one of Sweden's most popular wedding venues (up to four ceremonies each Saturday). As reflected by the language of the posted Bible quotations, the sexes sat separately: men, on the warmer right side, were more literate and could read Latin; women, on the cooler left side, read Swedish. The fancy pews at the front were reserved for the king and queen.

At the far end, near the altar, a door leads to a stairwell with a model ship, donated by a thankful sailor who survived a storm. In the next room is Anita, the stuffed body of the last horse who served with the Swedish military (until 1937); beyond that you might find some temporary exhibits.

The rest of the castle complex includes the vast **Burned Hall,** which—true to its name—feels stripped-down and is not as richly decorated. In summer you may find a temporary art exhibit here: The curators usually choose a modern theme to give visitors a refreshing break from the Renaissance.

The Old Town, near the Castle

The tidy, quiet residential zone between the castle and the town center is actually more rewarding to explore than downtown Kalmar. For centuries, this *was* the town center of Kalmar. But it burned down in 1647, and sat deserted for a century. Now it's a toy village of colorfully painted wooden homes, tidy yards, and perfect picket fences. Locals still call it the Old Town (Gamla Stan), even though almost everything here is newer than the buildings on Kvarnholmen, now the heart of town.

Consider a slight detour strolling through this neighborhood on your way from the town center to the castle. I've connected the sights in this area with some self-guided commentary.

From the train station at the edge of Kvarnholmen, walk along the tracks (toward Växjö) until your first opportunity to cross over. Across the tracks is Slottsvägen, a pleasant, tree-shaded boulevard that leads to the castle. (If you want to visit the castle first, head up this drag to do it now.) At the start of this boulevard, take the angled, cobbled street on the right (Västerlånggatan). The grand mansion you'll walk behind once belonged to the prestigious Jeansson family, who donated the parkland near the castle to the town (now the Slottshotellet, recommended under "Sleeping in Kalmar"). Enjoy the time-passed cottages as you peek over fences into private gardens. At the intersection, continue straight with the cobbles, then follow the path through the middle of the big park. As you cross the road on the other side of the park, you'll pass two lines of stones, a small surviving remnant of Kalmar's town wall on the right.

• *Straight ahead and on the left is the entrance to the...*

▲**Krusenstiernska Gården**—This relaxed, kid-friendly garden, with its breezy café selling traditional homemade cakes, is a treat. Poke inside to discover a manicured world of charming plantings clustered around a well.

Cost and Hours: Free; June-Aug Mon-Fri 11:00-18:00, Sat-Sun 12:00-17:00 except closed Sat in July; Sept Mon-Fri 11:00-16:00, closed Sat-Sun; May Mon-Fri 11:00-17:00, Sat-Sun 12:00-17:00; closed Oct-April; Stora Dammgatan 11, tel. 0480/411-552.

Visiting the Garden: On most weekday afternoons, you can take a guided tour of the early-19th-century upper-middle-class **home** located in the garden. It's lovingly cluttered with old family photos, toys, and Gustavian-style furniture. A helpful English leaflet gives a room-by-room inventory (tour-25 kr; June-Aug Tue-Fri at 13:00, 14:00, and 15:00; no tours Sat-Mon).

On summer evenings, this garden is a venue for a Swedish comedy duo, Allan Svensson and Suzanne Reuter—stars of one of Sweden's most popular sitcoms of all time, the 1990s hit *Svensson, Svensson*. (Think of it as the Swedish *Honeymooners*.) Their sold-out shows here in July and early August flood the town with Swedish comedy fans, bringing new life to this otherwise sedate quarter of town.

• *Leaving the garden, follow the red fence to the right, along the top of the park. At the end of the fence (and park), jog left and squeeze between the yellow and red houses, heading up Gamla Kungsgatan. Immerse yourself in this Swedish village world. At the fork, the yellow cottage on the right, surrounded by an almost huggable flower garden, often wins nationwide garden contests. About 20 yards farther down on the left, you'll reach the...*

Old Churchyard (Gamla Kyrkogården)—Dating from the 13th century, this field scattered with headstones is virtually all that remains of the original Old Town. Look for the monument topped by a statue of a man carrying a boy (St. Christopher, patron of traders and seafarers). Circling this slab, you'll see the floor plan of the original cathedral, an image looking down the cathedral's nave, and a rendering of the town before it was destroyed. The cathedral tower—which had partially survived the 1647 fire—was torn down in 1678 by the Swedes themselves, who wanted to ensure that their enemies (the Danes) couldn't use the tower to launch an attack on the castle.

About 50 yards farther into the yard, the stone slab on the pedestal (marked *Kalmarunionen 600 ar*) commemorates the 600th anniversary of the 1397 Kalmar Union, which united the Nordic states. On June 14, 1997, the contemporary leaders of those same nations—Sweden, Norway, Denmark, Finland, and Iceland—came here to honor that union. You can see their signatures etched in the stone.

• *Exit the churchyard the way you came in, and turn right on the paved street (along the big building). Take the first left (down Kungsgatan) and you'll wind up back on the main boulevard. The castle entrance is just across the boulevard, and on your left is the appealing, recommended Söderportcafé.*

But first, stretching to the left of the castle (across the boulevard) is Kalmar's best public space...

Town Park (Stadsparken)—This entertaining English-style garden is Kalmar's playground. While thoughtfully planned, it's also rugged, with surprises around each corner. Locals brag that their region is a "banana belt" that enjoys a milder climate than most of Sweden; some of the plants here grow nowhere else in the country. This diversity of foliage, and the many sculptures and monuments, make the park a delight to explore.

• *The big, black, mysterious-looking box in the middle of the park is the...*

Kalmar Art Museum (Kalmar Konstmuseum)—Completed in 2008, this bold museum build-ing caused quite a stir in Kalmar, both for its expense and for the way it faces down the fanciful medieval/Renaissance castle with a jolt of staid modernity. Its interior, with clean concrete spaces, is ideal for showing off constantly changing exhibits of modern and contemporary art. Some rooms provide fine views back on the castle. If the exhibits advertised appeal to you—or if you're an art-lover intrigued by the space—it's worth a visit.

Cost and Hours: 50 kr, Tue-Sun 12:00-17:00, Wed until 19:00, closed Mon, Stadsparken, tel. 0480/426-282, www.kalmar konstmuseum.se.

Eating: Attached to the museum—and complementing its style, though it was built some 70 years earlier—is the recommended **Byttan restaurant.** This is a good spot for a meal or a drink, with cozy indoor—or castle-view outdoor—seating.

• *Our walk is finished. The castle is easy to visit from here. If you have time for a long walk (or a bike or car ride), consider exploring the coastline beyond (southwest of) Kalmar Castle, lined with more parks and inviting beaches. About a mile after the castle is the charming little seafront community of **Stensö**, with its own pocket-size harbor, charming fishing cottages, and (another half-mile farther) a lightly forested island with a popular campground (open April-Oct, www.stensocamping.se).*

Kvarnholmen, Kalmar's Town Center

Today, downtown Kalmar is on the island of Kvarnholmen. Get your bearings with the following walk, and then—if you're interested—dig into its museums.

Kvarnholmen Self-Guided Walk—Most action centers on the lively, restaurant-and-café-lined square called **Larmtorget,**

a few steps uphill from the train station. This is the most inviting square in town for outdoor dining—scout your options for dinner later tonight. The fountain depicts David standing triumphantly over the slain Goliath—a thinly veiled allusion to King Gustav Vasa, who defeated the Danes (the fountain's reliefs depict his arrival in Kalmar in 1520). The area just to the north, up Larmgatan, is a charming old quarter (with a restored old water tower and the historic Västerport gate) that's worth exploring.

But for now, we'll stroll straight through town on the main pedestrian shopping street, **Storgatan.** Because Kvarnholmen is a planned Renaissance town (built after the devastating 1647 fire consumed the Old Town), it's laid out on a regular grid plan. This uniformity makes it a bit less appealing than it could be, and a 1960s push to "modernize" the town stripped away whatever Old World character the place once enjoyed. Still, the lack of traffic on most of its central streets makes Kvarnholmen a delightful place to stroll. And some buildings still have stories to tell.

The first major cross-street, Kaggensgatan, leads (to the right) down to the town harbor; a block to the left, on the right-hand side (at #26), is the landmark Kullzénska Café, whose owners refused to let it be torn down to make way for "progress" (it remains a good place for a drink or light meal in a genteel setting—see "Eating in Kalmar," later).

Back on Storgatan, on the right just before the big square (after #20), look for the building marked *1667,* with the cannon-balls decorating the doorway. This was the home of a war profi-teer—a lucrative business in this military-minded town.

Storgatan leads to the main square, **Stortorget.** Built in the 17th century in a grand style befitting a European power, the square tries a little too hard to show off—today it feels too big and too quiet (locals prefer hanging out on the cozier Larmtorget). The numbered spaces in the cobbles show where market stalls were located (though there's no regular market schedule today).

The **cathedral** *(domkyrkan)* dominating the square is the big-gest and (some say) finest Baroque church in Sweden. Its interior, which contains a gigantic 17th-century pulpit and bells from the earlier town cathedral, has been elegantly restored to its original glory. Its architect was inspired by the great Renaissance churches of Rome, and it shows. The interior is all very high church (for such a Lutheran country), with a mag-nificent Baroque altar, carved  tombstones used for flooring, and homogeneous white walls (free, Mon-Fri 8:00-15:30 except Wed until 18:30, Sat-Sun 9:00-16:00, tel. 0480/12300, www.kalmardomkyrka.se).

Facing the cathedral is the decorated facade of the **Town Hall** *(rådhuset).* The biggest windows are on the second (middle) floor, where the courts are located. During the spring (generally May and June), you can duck around the left side of the Town Hall and poke into its courtyard to see the blooming "handkerchief tree" *(Davidia involucrata),* whose flowers have hanky-sized petals.

• *From here, you have two options:*

Beaches and Parks (East): Continue straight through Stor-torget, and proceed three more blocks on Storgatan. The area beyond Östra Vallgatan (the old eastern wall of the city) has a pleasant park and small swimming beach. This area is called Kattrumpan (literally, "cat's rear end") because of the widely held and disturbing notion that Kvarnholmen looks like a cat's skin splayed out. To the left, on a little pier in the water, look for the last remaining *klapphus*—laundry building—in Kalmar. In the mid-1800s, four of these small, wooden structures stood at the seaside. Today the *klapphus* is still occasionally used for washing rugs and carpets; take a peek inside and see if anyone is at work. Across the water is the island neighborhood of Varvsholmen, which once housed an eyesore shipyard but has been converted into a futuristic residential development. Just for fun, imagine if they did this with the grim industrial zone in your hometown. To the left of Varvsholmen is the sleepy residential island neighborhood of Ängö, traditionally home to sailors and fishermen, now one of Kalmar's most desirable areas.

• *Or, also from Stortorget, you can head for the...*

Ramparts and Harbor (South): Turn right on Sjögatan (at the start of Stortorget) and head down to the little square called Lilla Torget, with some fine old wooden homes. Just beyond, the surviving ramparts (free to walk on top of) mark the old harbor line. It's strange to think that these sturdy ramparts became largely irrelevant so soon after they were built, when the Swedish-Danish border shifted dramatically to the south. As you pass through the walls, a modern shopping mall called Baronen is ahead and to the right; beyond it, around the little guest harbor, is the maritime academy building that also houses the TI. To the left are some charming old merchant houses and the stand-alone old Customs House (Tullhuset); beyond those, the waterfront is dominated by giant red-brick buildings—steam mills once used to grind flour and strip rice. Today this complex houses a concert hall and the Kalmar County Museum, worth visiting and described next.

▲▲**Kalmar County (Läns) Museum**—Dedicated to telling the story of Kalmar County, this museum is worth a visit mostly for its excellent exhibit on the royal ship *Kronan*, a shipwrecked 17th-century warship that still sits on the bottom of the Baltic just off the island of Öland. Soggy bits and rusted pieces, well-described in English, give visitors a here's-the-buried-treasure thrill. It's a much more intimate look at life at sea than Stockholm's grander Vasa Museum—though, crucially, this exhibit lacks the boat's actual hull.

Cost and Hours: 80 kr, less off-season; Mon-Fri 10:00-16:00, Wed until 20:00; Sat-Sun 11:00-16:00; Skeppsbrogatan 51, tel. 0480/451-300, www.kalmarlansmuseum.se.

◔ **Self-Guided Tour:** As you enter the building, notice that from the museum's door, you can see the distant half of the long bridge leading to the island of Öland.

Beyond the entry, the first floor has temporary exhibits and shows off the cannons recovered from the *Kronan* wreckage. In those days, cannons were so valuable they were prized the way a Rolls Royce would be today, so each one has its own story (described in English). In the years following the ship's sinking,

SOUTHEAST SWEDEN

these cannons were the only artifacts considered worth recovering.

The stairs and elevator in the center of the building let you zip right to your choice of exhibits. Floor 2 has temporary exhibits, which can be worth a stop if you have extra time.

From the first floor, I'd head to Floor 3, which displays salvage from the *Kronan*. Twice the size of Stockholm's famous *Vasa*, this warship was a floating palace and the most heavily armed vessel in the world. But it exploded and sank about three miles beyond the island of Öland in 1676. The giant illustration at the elevator shows the dramatic event: The *Kronan*'s admiral misjudged conditions and harnessed too much wind, causing the vessel to tip and its gun ports to fill with water. As the ship began to list into the water, a fallen lantern ignited explosives in the hold, and...BLAM! The ship was a goner, and its Danish and Dutch foes—who hadn't fired a shot—watched it sink into the deep. Of the 850 people on board, only about 40 were rescued. The wreck's whereabouts were forgotten until 1980, when it was rediscovered by the same oceanographer who found the *Vasa*.

Head into the exhibit, where you'll view a model of the shipwreck site (press the button for a 7-minute English explanation). You'll see a cross-section of the mighty vessel; a recovered carving of the potbellied Swedish king (one of many such carvings that decorated the ship); a street scene from Kalmar in that era, also illustrated by a good map and model; and an excellent 12-minute film about the ship (push the button for English).

The replica of the middle gun deck leads to the exhibit's most interesting section, which explains everyday life on board. The 850 sailors who manned the ship (about the population of a mid-sized town of that age) represented all walks of life, "all in the same boat." Engaging illustrations, eyewitness accounts, and actual salvage items bring the story to life. You'll see guns, musical instruments, a medicine chest, dishes, and clothing—items that emphasize the nautical lifestyles of the simple, common people who worked and perished on the ship. A treasure chest contains coins from all around the known world at the time, each one carefully identified.

The final exhibit reminds us that the *Kronan* still sits on the sea floor, awaiting funding to be raised to the surface. You'll see the diving bell that was used for very early dives to the site. Today a dedicated crew of scientists and enthusiasts—including, at times, Sweden's King Carl XVI Gustav—continue to dive to recover bits and pieces.

For extra credit, head up to Floor 4 for its exhibit on **Jenny Nyström,** an early-1900s Kalmar artist who gained fame for her cute Christmas illustrations featuring elves and pixies. You'll see some of her children's books and textbooks, as well as some less commercial, more artistic portraits (with a touch of Art Nouveau flair). Ponder Nyström's status as a proto-feminist icon: She was one of the first female artists to support her family by selling her paintings. Nearby are other exhibits and a tiny café serving light lunches.

Maritime History Museum (Sjöfartsmuseum)—This humble, dusty little exhibit sits a long block beyond and behind the Kalmar County Museum. It's a jumble of photos of vessels, model boats, charts, and other seafaring bric-a-brac that traces the nautical story of Kalmar up to modern times. The collection is displayed in three rooms of a former apartment, shuffled between beautiful porcelain stoves left behind by a previous owner. While it's well-explained by an English booklet, the exhibit is really interesting only if you sail.

Cost and Hours: 40 kr, mid-June-mid-Sept daily 11:00-16:00, off-season open only Sun 12:00-16:00, Södra Långgatan 81, tel. 0480/15875.

Sleeping in Kalmar

(7 kr = about $1, country code: 46, area code: 0480)
The TI can nearly always find you a room in a private home (500 kr per double, 50-kr fee per booking, no breakfast). They can also get you special last-minute discounts on fancy hotels.

In the Town Center (Kvarnholmen)

$$$ Calmar Stadshotell is a 126-room business hotel filling a historic shell right on Kalmar's too-big main square, Stortorget. The standard rooms can be rather faded, but the hotel is busy renovating floor-by-floor. Be sure to ask for a redone room when you book (standard Sb-925-1,280 kr, standard Db-1,085-1,495 kr, deluxe "superior" rooms 200-kr extra, all rooms cheaper on winter weekends; elevator, free Wi-Fi in some rooms—request when you reserve, Stortorget 14, tel. 0480/496-900, fax 0480/496-910, www.profilhotels.se, calmarstadshotell@profilhotels.se).

$$ Frimurare Hotellet fills a grand old building overlooking inviting Larmtorget square, just steps from the train station. Warmly run by Jesper, the place has soul and a disarmingly friendly staff. Rich public areas, broad hardwood halls, chandeliers, and pilasters give it a 19th-century elegance. Guests can help themselves to coffee, tea, fruit, and cookies in the lounge anytime. The 35 rooms have been thoughtfully renovated and provide modern comfort amid period decor. Because it's squeezed between a café-packed square and a park that's popular for concerts, it can come with some noise (Sb-850 kr, Db-1,040 kr, Tb-1,240, these special rates promised when you book direct with this book, elevator, pay Wi-Fi, free sauna, bike rental-50 kr/day, 50 yards in front of train station, Larmtorget 2, tel. 0480/15230, fax 0480/85887, www .frimurarehotellet.com, info@frimurarehotellet.se).

Outside the Town Center

$$$ Slottshotellet ("Castle Hotel") is an enticing splurge in the atmospheric Old Town. It's the nicely upgraded but still homey former mansion of a local big shot. The 44 rooms—some in the mansion, others sprinkled throughout nearby buildings—sit across a leafy boulevard from Kalmar's Town Park, just up the street from the castle (standard Sb-1,195-1,395 kr, standard Db-1,395-1,595 kr, bigger "superior" Db-1,595-1,795 kr, free Wi-Fi, Slottsvägen 7, tel. 0480/88260, www.slottshotellet.se, info@slottshotellet.se).

$$ Hotell Hilda has eight good rooms in an updated old house, located in a modern residential zone just over the canal from the town center (Sb-795 kr, Db-1,095 kr, elevator, free Wi-Fi in breakfast room, free parking, Esplanaden 33, tel. 0480/54700, www.hotellhilda.se, info@hotellhilda.se). The ground-floor Kallskänken café, which doubles as the reception, serves good salads and sandwiches (50-kr sandwiches, 75-kr salads, Mon-Fri 7:00-18:00, Sat 8:00-14:00, Sun 10:00-11:00; if checking in outside of these times, call ahead for the door code).

$$ Hotell Svanen, a 15-minute walk or short bus ride from the center in the Ängö neighborhood, is a new breed of budget hotel with a mix of nicer hotel rooms with private bath, cheaper rooms with shared bath, and hostel beds (no more than six beds per room). All guests have access to laundry and kitchen facilities, a TV room, Internet terminal (60 kr/hour), and a sauna. While it's a bit institutional, you can't argue with the value (hotel: S-595 kr, Sb-695-815 kr, D-830 kr, Db-930-990 kr, price depends on size, includes sheets and breakfast; hostel: dormitory bed-195 kr, D-490 kr, Db-590 kr, T-720 kr, Q-960 kr, sheets-55 kr, no member discount, breakfast-75 kr; reception open daily 7:30-21:00, elevator, Rappegatan 1, tel. 0480/25560, fax 0480/88293, www .hotellsvanen.se, info@hotellsvanen.se). You'll see a blue-and-white hotel sign and a hostel symbol at the edge of town on Ängöleden street, a mile from the train station. Catch bus #402 at the station to Ängöleden (2-3/hour, 5 minutes), or take a taxi for about 70 kr. They rent canoes for exploring the small bays around Kalmar (120 kr/half-day, 200 kr/day).

Eating in Kalmar

Kalmar has a surprising number of good dining options for a small city. For lunch, look for the *dagens rätt* (daily special) for 80-100 kr, which gets you a main dish, salad, bread, and usually coffee or a soft drink. Many restaurants in Kalmar offer fixed-price meals at dinner.

In the Town Center (Kvarnholmen)

All of these are in the downtown pedestrian zone.

Källaren Kronan, open only for dinner (except on Sat), is an elegant candlelit cellar restaurant with tables under stone arches. They serve old-time Swedish dishes as well as modern cuisine (85-125-kr starters, 200-300-kr main dishes, 229-kr two-course meals, 279-kr three-course meals, Tue-Fri 18:00-23:00, Sat 12:00-23:00, Sun 17:00-22:00, closed Mon, look for stairwell just inside southern town wall at Ölandsgatan 7, tel. 0480/411-400).

Calmar Hamnkrog is *the* place for a dressy harborview meal among the Swedish sailing set. Its mod white interior creates a cool elegance; call ahead to reserve window seating (145-185-kr starters, 200-300-kr main dishes, Mon-Fri 11:30-14:00 & 18:00-22:00, Sat 17:00-22:00, closed Sun; in peak season open longer hours and on Sun 11:30-16:00; just beyond the Baronen mall at Skeppsbrogatan 30, tel. 0480/411-020).

Kullzénska Café is a cozy, antique-filled eatery in a historic building. Locals adore its cakes and sandwiches (Mon-Fri 10:00-18:30, Sat 10:00-16:00, Sun 12:00-16:30, Kaggensgatan 26 at the corner of Norra Långgatan, go up the stairs, tel. 0480/28882).

Pizzeria Italia, right on the main Storgatan shopping street, is a handy place to get a break from Swedish food. While they serve up yummy pizzas (60-80 kr, or 160-200 kr for family-size), the best deal might be their all-you-can-eat buffet pizza lunch (90 kr on Mon-Fri 11:00-15:30; 110 kr on Sat-Sun 12:00-16:00, includes drinks). Sit inside or out front (open Mon-Fri 11:00-22:00, Sat 12:00-22:00, Sun 12:00-18:00, Storgatan 10, tel. 0480/87087).

Supermarket: In the pedestrian district, you'll find the **Co-op/ Konsum** in the Kvasten mall, at the corner of Kaggensgatan and Storgatan (daily 7:00-22:00, if mall is closed, you can enter supermarket around the corner on Norra Långgatan).

Near the Castle

The castle lawn cries out for a picnic (buy one in the town center before your visit). Or you can grab a bite in the café inside the castle itself. Otherwise, consider one of these options.

Byttan sits in a landmark 1930s functionalist building adjoining the art museum in the leafy Town Park, offering fine dining (or just a coffee break) with views of the castle. Choose between trendy indoor and castle-view outdoor tables. In summer only, their best deal is the all-you-can-eat buffet, offered at lunch (100 kr, available Mon-Fri 11:30-14:30) and at dinner, called the "grill buffet" (250 kr, from 18:00). You can order off the menu anytime (in summer Mon-Fri 11:00-22:00, Sat 12:00-22:00, Sun 12:00-17:00, closed off-season; you'll pass it as you walk to the castle, tel. 0480/16360).

Söderportcafé, just across the street from the castle drawbridge, is handy for a quick, light lunch or afternoon snack. They're well-regarded locally for their live music in the evenings (140-200-kr meals, 200-kr early-evening dinner buffet in summer, Mon-Fri 9:00-23:00, Sat 13:00-23:00, Sun 13:00-22:00, closed Sun off-season, Slottsvägen 1, tel. 0480/12501).

Kalmar Connections

From Kalmar by Train to: Växjö (12/day, 60-70 minutes), **Copenhagen** and its airport (12/day, 3.5-4 hours, transfer in Alvesta), **Stockholm** (12/day, 4.5-5 hours, transfer in Alvesta, reservations required).

By Bus to Stockholm: The bus to Stockholm is much cheaper but slower than the train (4/day, fewer on weekends, 6 hours).

Route Tips for Drivers

Kalmar to Copenhagen: See "Route Tips for Drivers" at the end of the Near Copenhagen chapter.

Kalmar to Stockholm (230 miles, 6 hours): Leaving Kalmar, follow *E-22 Lindsdal* and *Nörrköping* signs. Sweden did a cheap widening job, paving the shoulders of the old two-lane road to get 3.8 lanes. Fortunately, traffic is polite and sparse. There's little to see, so stock the pantry, set the compass on north, and home in on Stockholm. Make two pleasant stops along the way: Västervik and the Göta Canal.

Västervik is 90 miles north of Kalmar, with an 18th-century core of wooden houses (3 miles off the highway, *Centrum* signs lead you to the harbor). Park on the waterfront near the great little smoked-fish market (Mon-Sat).

Sweden's famous **Göta Canal** consists of 190 miles of canals cutting the country in half, with 58 locks *(slussen)* working up to a summit of 300 feet. It was built 150 years ago, with more than seven million 12-hour man-days (60,000 men working about 22 years) at a low ebb in the country's self-esteem—to show her industrial might. Today it's a lazy three- or four-day tour, which shows Sweden's zest for good living.

Take just a peek at the Göta Canal over lunch, in the medieval town of **Söderköping:** Stay on E-22 past where you'd think you'd exit for the town center, then turn right at the *Kanalbåtarna/Slussen*. Look for the *Kanal P* signs leading to a handy canalside parking lot. From there, walk along the canal into the action. The TI on Söderköping's Rådhustorget (a square about a block off the canal) has good town and Stockholm maps, a walking brochure, and canal information (www.ostergotland.info). On the canal is the Kanalbutiquen, a yachters' laundry, shower, shop, and WC, with idyllic picnic grounds just above the lock. From the lock, stairs lead up to the Utsiktsplats pavilion (commanding view).

From Söderköping, E-22 takes you to Nörrköping. Follow *E-4* signs through Nörrköping, past a handy rest stop, and into Stockholm. The *Centrum* is clearly marked. (Viking's ferry terminal for Helsinki is in Södermalm; the Tallink Silja terminal is northeast of town at Värtahamnen harbor—see ferry terminal info in beginning of Helsinki chapter, page 555.)

The Island of Öland

The island of Öland—90 miles long and only 8 miles wide—is a pleasant resort known for its windmills, wildflowers, old limestone buildings, happy birdwatchers, prehistoric sights, roadside produce stands on the honor system, and Swede-filled beaches. This castaway island, with only about 25,000 permanent residents, attracts some 2.5 million visitors annually. It's a top summer vacation destination for Swedes—even the king and queen have their summer home here—due to its climate and tony, Martha's Vineyard vibe. Because of its relatively low rents, better weather, and easy bridge access to the mainland, Öland is also a popular bedroom community for Kalmar. If you've got a car, good weather, and some time to kill—and if the place isn't choked with summer crowds—Öland is a fine destination for a quick joyride. (For a basic map of Öland, see page 510.)

Dubbed the "Island of Sun and Wind," Öland enjoys an even warmer climate than already-mild Kalmar and a steady sea breeze. And, because its top layer of soil was scraped off by receding glaciers, it has a completely different landscape than the pines-and-lakes feel of mainland Sweden. The island's chalky limestone, rich soil, and lush vegetation make it feel almost more Mediterranean than Baltic. Öland is one of Sweden's premier agricultural zones. Some call it "Sweden's Provence." While that's a stretch, skeptical visitors are pleasantly surprised by its colorful wildflowers (in spring) and by the bright sunshine, which works like a magnet both on holidaymakers and on artists.

Centuries ago, the entire island was the king's private hunting ground. Because local famers were not allowed to fell trees, they made their simple houses from limestone. The island's 34 limestone churches, which were also used for defense, have few windows. Stone walls demarcate property and were used to contain grazing livestock.

When built in 1972, the **Öland Bridge** from Kalmar to the island was Europe's longest (free, 3.7 miles). The channel between Kalmar and Öland is filled with underwater rocks, making passage here extremely treacherous—but ideal for the Vikings' flat-bottomed boats. (In fact, "Kalmar" comes from the phrase "stones in water.") The little town of Färjestaden, near the island end of the bridge, was once the "ferry town" where everyone came and went; today it sits sad and neglected.

Getting There: Public transportation is tricky but workable; the island is most worthwhile if you have a car and at least three extra hours to explore. **Drivers** simply head north from Kalmar a few minutes on highway 137 to the Öland Bridge. Once across, highway 136 is the island's main north-south artery. **Buses** regularly connect Kalmar with the town of Borgholm (54 kr, nearly hourly in summer, off-season every 2 hours, 50-60 minutes) and, with less frequency, to other Öland destinations (check www.klt .se). **Bikers** who are in shape might enjoy biking to and around Öland, but note that you're not allowed to ride your bike on the bridge; instead, take the shuttle bus that carries bikers across (20 kr, April-June and Sept, runs early morning and late afternoon only, catch it at the start of the bridge, look for line #408 "Cykelbuss," www.klt.se). It's possible to rent bikes on Öland, including in Borgholm (though hours and quantities are limited—try to call and pre-arrange, see the next page).

Sights on Öland

Visitors can (and do) spend days exploring this giant island's pleasures. But on a quick visit of a few hours, you'll want to narrow your focus. Your basic choices are center/north Öland (more developed and resorty, with royal sights, and easier to reach on a quick visit) or south Öland (more rugged and remote-feeling, with prehistoric sites, and demanding more time). I've outlined a few basic ideas for each area below, but these are just the beginning—there's much more to discover on Öland.

Central/North Öland

On a quick spin to the island, I'd stick with the strip of Öland just north of the bridge. As you drive north along highway 136, keep an eye out for some of Öland's characteristic, old-fashioned windmills. Occasional stone churches dot the landscape (including the one in Räpplinge—just off the main road—where the royals worship when in town).

The island's main town is **Borgholm** (BOY-holm), about a 30-minute drive north of the bridge. Borgholm itself isn't much to see, unless you enjoy watching Swedes at play. It's got a smattering of turn-of-the-century wooden villas, erected here after the royal palace was built nearby (described below). Notice that many of these have a humble shack in the garden: Locals would move into these cottages so they could rent the main villa to vacationing Stockholmers in the summer and make a killing. The traffic-free main drag, Storgatan, is lined with tacky tourist shops and ice-cream parlors (Ölandsglass, at #10, is tops). At the handy **TI**, right on the town's main street, you can get maps and advice for your visit (generally Mon-Fri 9:00-17:00, in summer until 18:00 and also 10:00-16:00 on Sat and sometimes Sun, Storgatan 1, tel. 0485/89000, www.olandsturist.se). To rent a bike, get tips from the TI or try Hallbergs Hojar (mobile 070-514-1937).

A pair of interesting sights sits on the hill just above Borgholm (to reach them, you can either drive or hike—get details at TI). **Borgholm Castle** (Borgholms Slott), which looks like Kalmar Castle with its top blown off, broods on the bluff above town, as if to remind visitors of the island's onetime strategic function. Its hard-fought history has left it as the empty shell you see today—impressive, but not worth the 70-kr entry fee (www.borgholms slott.se).

From near the castle, you can hike down to a more recent and appealing royal sight, the current royal summer residence, **Solliden Palace** (Sollidens Slott). It was built in 1906 in an Italian villa style,

after the tastes of the Austrian-import queen, who hated Sweden. The palace interior is off-limits, but its sprawling, gorgeously landscaped garden is open to us commoners. Divided into Italian (geometrical and regimented), English (rough), and Dutch (flowers) sections, the Solliden garden complex is well worth a wander (75 kr, mid-May-mid-Sept daily 11:00-18:00, last entry at 17:00, closed in winter, on-site café open the same hours, tel. 0485/15356, www.sollidensslott.se).

The Swedish royalty is smart about not testing the patience of their subjects. The palace and garden complex is financially self-sufficient. And locals brag that when the royals come down from Stockholm, they fly commercial. If the first two rows are open when you board your Stockholm-Kalmar flight, you know they'll soon be filled by a royal backside.

South Öland

A 60-mile loop south of the bridge will give you a good dose of the island's more remote, windy rural charm. Head south on highway

136 to experience the savannah-like limestone plain, old grave-yards, and mysterious prehistoric monuments.

Gettlinge Gravfält (off the road about 10 miles up from the south tip, just south of Smedby) is a wonderfully situated, boat-shaped, Iron Age graveyard littered with monoliths and overseen by a couple of creaky old windmills. It offers a commanding view of the windy and mostly treeless island.

Farther south is the **Eketorp Prehistoric Fort** (Eketorps Borg), a reconstructed fifth-century stone fort that, as Iron Age forts go, is fairly interesting. Several evocative huts and build-ings are designed in what someone imagined was the style back then, and the huge rock fort is surrounded by runty Linderöd pigs, a native breed that was common in Sweden 1,500 years ago. A sign reads: "For your convenience and pleasure, don't leave your children alone with the animals" (75 kr, May-Aug daily 11:00-17:00, July-mid-Aug until 18:00, free English tours daily July-mid-Aug—call for times, tel. 0485/662-000, www.eketorp.se). It's near the southern tip of the island, on the eastern side: When you approach Grönhögen on the main road from the north, look for signs on the left.

FINLAND

FINLAND
Suomi

From medieval times to 1809, Finland was part of Sweden. City fires have left little standing from this period, but Finland still has a sizeable Swedish-speaking minority, bilingual street signs, and close cultural ties to Sweden.

In 1809, Sweden lost Finland to Russia. Under the next century of relatively benign Russian rule, Finland began to industrialize, and Helsinki grew into a fine and elegant city. Still, at the beginning of the 1900s, the rest of Finland was mostly dirt-poor and agricultural, and its people were eagerly emigrating to northern Minnesota. (Read Toivo Pekkanen's *My Childhood* to learn about the life of a Finnish peasant in the early 1900s.)

In 1917, Finland and the Baltic states won their independence from Russia, fought brief but vicious civil wars, and then enjoyed two decades of prosperity...until the secret Nazi-Soviet pact of August 1939 assigned them to the Soviet sphere of influence. When Russia invaded, only Finland resisted successfully, its white-camouflaged ski troops winning the Winter War against the Soviet Union in 1939-1940 and holding off the Russians in the Continuation War from 1941 to 1944.

After World War II, Finland was made to suffer for having allied itself for a time with Germany and for having fought against one of the Allied Powers. The Finns were forced to cede Karelia (eastern Finland) and part of Lapland to the USSR, to accept a Soviet naval base on Finnish territory, and to pay huge reparations to the Soviet government. Still, Finland's bold, trendsetting modern design and archi-

tecture blossomed, and it built up successful timber, paper, and electronics industries. All through the Cold War, Finland teetered between the West and the Soviet Union, trying to be part of Western Europe's strong economy while treading lightly and mak-

ing nice with her giant neighbor to the east. The collapse of the Soviet Union has done to Finland what a good long sauna might do to you.

When Moscow's menace vanished, so did about 20 percent of Finland's trade. After a few years of adjustment, Finland bounced back quickly, joining the European Union and adopting the euro currency. Many Finns used to move to Sweden (where they are the biggest immigrant group), looking for better jobs in Stockholm. Some still nurse an inferiority complex, thinking of themselves as poor cousins to the Swedes. But now Finland is the most technologically advanced country in Europe. Home to the giant mobile-phone company Nokia, Finland has more mobile-phone numbers than fixed ones, and ranks fourth among European nations (15th globally) in the number of Internet users per capita.

We think of Finland as Scandinavian, but it's better to call it "Nordic." Technically, the Scandinavian countries are Denmark, Sweden, and Norway—all constitutional monarchies with closely related languages. Add Iceland, Finland, and maybe Estonia— former Danish or Swedish colonies that speak separate languages—and you have the "Nordic countries." Iceland, Finland, and Estonia are also republics, not monarchies. In 1906, Finnish women were the first in Europe to vote. The country's president from 2000 to 2012 was a woman, and today, 40 percent of the Finnish parliament is female.

Finland is known as a nation of few words; Finns value silence, yet are easily approachable. Tourists are not considered a

Finland Almanac

Official Name: Republic of Finland.

Population: Finland is home to 5.2 million people (40 per square mile). The majority are Finnish in descent (93.4 percent). Other ethnicities include Swedish (5.5 percent), Russian, Estonian, Roma, and Sami (less than 1 percent each). The official languages are Finnish, spoken by 91 percent, and Swedish, spoken by 5.5 percent. Small minorities speak Sami and Russian. Finland is 83 percent Lutheran, 1 percent Orthodox, 1 percent other Christian, and 15 percent unaffiliated.

Latitude and Longitude: 64°N and 26°E, similar latitude to Nome, Alaska.

Area: 130,500 square miles (nearly twice the size of Washington state).

Geography: Finland is bordered by Russia to the east, Sweden and Norway to the north, the Baltic Sea to the west, and Estonia (across the Gulf of Finland) to the south. Much of Finland is flat and covered with forests, with the Lapland region extending north of the Arctic Circle. Finland is home to thousands of lakes and encompasses nearly as many islands: It has 187,800 lakes and 179,500 islands (the last time I counted).

Biggest City: Helsinki is the capital of Finland and has a population of 602,000; 1.1 million people—about one in four Finns—live in the Helsinki urban area.

Economy: Finland's Gross Domestic Product is $198 billion and its per-capita GDP is $36,700. Manufacturing, timber, engineering, electronics, and telecommunications are its chief industries, with mobile phones among its top exports.

Currency: €1 (euro) = about $1.30.

Government: Finland has both a president, responsible for foreign policy, and a prime minister, who—along with the 200-member Parliament (Eduskunta)—is responsible for domestic legislation. President Sauli Ninisto began his six-year term in March of 2012. Jyrki Katainen was elected as prime minister in April of 2011.

Flag: The Finnish flag is white with a blue Scandinavian cross. The blue represents the lakes of Finland and the white its winter snow.

The Average Finn: He or she is 43 years old, has 1.73 children, will live to be 79, and is tech savvy; the United Nations' Technology Achievement Index ranks Finland first in the world (the US ranks second).

headache to the locals the way they might be in places like Paris and Munich.

Finnish is a difficult-to-learn Uralic language whose only relatives in Europe are Estonian (closely) and Hungarian (distantly). Finland is officially bilingual, and about 1 in 20 residents speaks Swedish as a first language. You'll notice that Helsinki is called *Helsingfors* in Swedish. Helsinki's street signs list places in both Finnish and Swedish. Nearly every educated young person speaks effortless English—the language barrier is just a road turtle. But to get you started, I've included a selection of Finnish survival

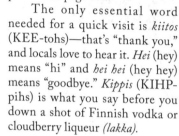

phrases on page 692.

The only essential word needed for a quick visit is *kiitos* (KEE-tohs)—that's "thank you," and locals love to hear it. *Hei* (hey) means "hi" and *hei hei* (hey hey) means "goodbye." *Kippis* (KIHP-pihs) is what you say before you down a shot of Finnish vodka or cloudberry liqueur *(lakka)*.

HELSINKI

The next best thing to being in Helsinki is getting there. Europe's most enjoyable cruise, from Stockholm to Helsinki, starts with dramatic archipelago scenery, a setting sun, and a royal *smörgåsbord* dinner. Dance until you drop and sauna until you drip. Budget travel rarely feels this hedonistic. Sixteen hours after you depart, it's "Hello Helsinki."

The Cruise from Stockholm to Helsinki

Two fine and fiercely competitive lines, Viking Line and Tallink Silja, connect the capitals of Sweden and Finland. Each line offers

state-of-the-art ships with luxurious *smörgåsbord* meals, reasonable cabins, plenty of entertainment (discos, saunas, gambling), and enough duty-free shopping to sink a ship. Of the two, Viking Line has the reputation as the party boat. Tallink Silja is considered more elegant. But both lines—used mostly by locals for a quick getaway and duty-free booze run—have their share of noisy, sometimes-irritating passengers.

The Pepsi and Coke of the Scandinavian cruise industry vie to outdo each other with bigger and fancier boats. The ships are huge—at around 50,000 tons, 200 yards long, and with 2,700 beds, they're the largest (and cheapest) luxury hotels in Scandinavia. Many other shipping lines buy their boats used from Viking Line and Tallink Silja.

Which line is best? You could count showers and compare *smörgåsbords*, but both lines go overboard to win the loyalty of

Sailing the Baltic Sea

100 Kilometers
100 Miles

Gulf of Bothnia

Jyväskylä
Savonlinna

Tampere

FINLAND

RUS.

Lahti

To North Sweden & Trondheim, Norway

Åland Islands

Naantali
Turku

To St. Petersburg

Porvoo

Helsinki

Gulf of Finland

SWEDEN

Mariehamn

Uppsala

Lake Mälaren

Tallinn

To St. Pete.

To Oslo

Archipelago

Stockholm

Hiiumaa

ESTONIA

R U S S I A

Nynäshamn

Göta Canal

Norrköping

Baltic Sea

Saaremaa

Pärnu

Tartu

Söderköping

Gotland

To Kalmar & Copenhagen

Visby

.... Tallink Silja & Viking ships between Stockholm & Helsinki
----- Other ships

LATVIA

Riga

HELSINKI

the nine million duty free-crazy Swedes and Finns who make the

trip each year. Viking Line has an older, less luxurious fleet, but caters better to low-budget travelers, selling cheap "economy" cabins (shower down the hall) and allowing summertime passengers the option of paying for deck passage only and sleeping for free on chairs, sofas, and under the stars or stairs.

Cruise Schedules

Both Viking Line and Tallink Silja sail nightly from Stockholm and Helsinki year-round. In both directions, the boats leave at about 17:00 and arrive the next morning around 10:00. Both companies also sail daily between Stockholm and Turku, Finland. For exact schedules, see www.vikingline.fi and www.tallinksilja.com.

Scenery: During the first few hours out of Stockholm, your ship passes through the *Skärgården* (archipelago). The third hour features the most exotic island scenery—tiny islets with cute red huts and happy people. I'd have dinner at the first sitting (shortly after departure) and be on deck for sunset. But if you don't like cold temperatures, book the second sitting because the deck gets chilly later in the cruise.

Time Change: Finland is one hour ahead of Sweden. Sailing from Stockholm to Helsinki, operate on Swedish time until you're ready to go to bed, then reset your watch. Morning schedules are Finnish time, and vice versa when you return. The cruise-schedule flier in English makes this clear—pick it up as you board.

Cost

Fares vary by season, by day of the week, and by cabin class. Mid-June to mid-August is most crowded and expensive (with prices the same regardless of day). Off-season, Friday is always the most expensive night to travel, while Sunday through Wednesday nights are the cheapest.

In summer, a one-way ticket per person for the cheapest bed that has a private bath (in a below-sea-level, under-car-deck "C" quad) costs about €50-70. Couples will pay a total of about €150-200 for the cheapest double room (with bath) that's above the car deck.

Round-trip cruise fares (across and back on **successive nights,** leaving you access to your bedroom throughout the day) generally cost much less than two one-way trips. (In peak season, the cheapest double cabin round-trip is about €250-300.) The drawback is that this itinerary leaves you with only a few hours on land. But you can get the round-trip fare on **non-successive nights** if you book a hotel through the cruise line for every intervening night. If it fits your schedule, this is a good deal.

The fares are cheap because many locals sail to shop and drink tax-free. It's a huge operation—the boats are filled with about 45 percent Finns, 45 percent Swedes, and 10 percent cruisers from other countries. The average passenger spends as much on booze and tax-free items as on the boat fare. The boats make a midnight stop in the Åland Islands—a self-governing, Swedish-speaking province of Finland that's exempt from the European Union's value-added tax (VAT)—to maintain their tax-free status.

Discounts: Travelers with railpasses that include Sweden or Finland get discounts on both lines. Tallink Silja's discount is 20 percent in high season and 40 percent in low season (available on one-way tickets only, not valid for the more expensive cabins). Viking Line's 50 percent discount applies only to the transport portion of the fare (not the cabin cost), so it averages out to about a 30 percent discount on the cheap economy beds and less on nicer cabins (discounts for early booking, seniors, and families—look for family-cabin rates). Check the cruise lines' websites for specifics.

Age Restrictions: The boat lines do not permit travel on some Stockholm-Finland routes by those aged 18-20 who are not accompanied by a parent or guardian. This applies especially to round-trip cruises on successive nights. One-way tickets are usually exempt from these rules. Websites have more information, but it's really best to contact Viking Line or Tallink Silja by phone or email to clarify your individual situation.

Reservations

For summer or weekend sailings, reserve well in advance. You'll get a reservation number and can then just pick up your boarding card at the port. Try to book online with a credit card. Websites are well-organized and both companies offer online discounts not available elsewhere (www.vikingline.fi, www.tallinksilja.com). Tallink Silja charges a €5 fee if you reserve on the phone or at their offices; Viking Line charges €5 for in-person bookings, but lets you book for free by phone.

If you want to reserve by phone or just have a question, call the companies directly. The Swedish reservations numbers are tel. 08/452-4000 for Viking Line, and tel. 08/222-140 for Tallink Silja. In Finland, both lines have toll numbers that cost extra to call: tel. 0600-41577 for Viking, and tel. 0600-15700 for Tallink Silja. Drop the first zero if calling from North America. Both companies have sales agents in the US: For Viking Line, call 800-843-0602 (www.bortonoverseas.com); for Tallink Silja, call 800-533-3755 ext. 1 (www.tallinksilja.us). But it's easy to deal directly with the Scandinavian offices, which are efficient and English-speaking.

Any travel agent in Scandinavia can also sell you a ticket (with a small booking fee).

Terminals

Locations: In **Stockholm,** Viking Line has its own terminal (squeezed between cruise ships) along the Stadsgården embankment on Södermalm (facing the Old Town/Gamla Stan). To get there, it's easiest to ride Viking Line's shuttle bus from Stockholm's bus station right to the terminal (40 kr, departs according to boat schedule). You can also ride public bus #53 (from the train station or Gamla Stan) or #71 (from the Opera House or Gamla Stan) to the Londonviadukten stop, then hike five minutes down to the terminal. A taxi from the train station will cost you around 150 kr.

Tallink Silja's boats leave from the Frihamnen port, about three miles northeast of the city center. At Frihamnen, Tallink Silja boats use the terminal called Värtahamnen (at the northern end of the sprawling industrial port). To reach the terminal, it's simplest to catch the Tallink Silja shuttle bus from Stockholm's bus station (50 kr, departs according to boat schedule). By public transportation, you can either ride the T-bana to the Gärdet station, then walk about 10 minutes; or you can take public bus #76 all the way from downtown (Mon-Sat only, direction Ropsten, get off at Färjeterminalen stop). Figure about 230-250 kr for a taxi from Gamla Stan, the train station, or other downtown areas.

For Stockholm public transport information, see www.sl.se.

In **Helsinki,** both lines are perfectly central, on opposite sides of the main harbor, a 10-minute walk from the center. See the map on page 560.

Terminal Buildings: These are well-organized, with cafés, lockers, tourist information desks, lounges, and phones. Remember, 2,000-plus passengers come and go with each boat. Boats open 1.5 hours before departure, and you must be checked in 20 minutes before departure.

Parking: Both lines offer safe and handy parking in Stockholm. Ask for details when you reserve your ticket.

Onboard Services

Meals: While ships have cheap, fast cafeterias as well as classy, romantic restaurants, they are famous for their *smörgåsbord* dinners. If you want the *smörgåsbord* experience, board the ship hungry. Dinner is self-serve in two sittings, one at about 17:30, the other around 20:00. You'll save 10 percent if you pay for both the dinner buffet (€36-39) and breakfast buffet (€10) when you buy your ticket. If you board without a reservation, go to the restaurant and make one. Make sure to reserve your table, not just your meal; window seats are highly sought after. The key to eating a *smörgåsbord* is to take small portions and pace yourself. (For more tips, see page 30.) The price includes free beer, wine, soft drinks, and coffee. Of course, you can also bring a picnic and eat it on deck, or eat a standard restaurant meal.

Sauna: Each ship has a sauna (which costs about €8 extra) and other spa facilities. Tallink Silja also offers massage for an extra fee. Reserve sauna time or massage appointments immediately upon boarding.

Banking: Ships take euros and Swedish kronor, and just about every vendor or shop also accepts credit cards. Each boat has a handy exchange desk on board with acceptable rates. None of the boats has an ATM, but all terminals have ATMs and exchange windows.

Tourist Info on Board: Boats generally offer racks of *Stockholm* or *Helsinki This Week* magazines. Grab a copy for some practical bedtime reading.

Options

Tallinn: You can visit Tallinn as a day trip from Helsinki, or Helsinki as a day trip from Tallinn, or you can make a triangle trip on Tallink Silja: Stockholm-Helsinki-Tallinn-Stockholm, or vice versa (this has to be booked as three one-ways). See the Tallinn chapter for details on the Helsinki-Tallinn and Stockholm-Tallinn crossings.

Turku: Both Viking Line and Tallink Silja also sail from Stockholm to Turku in Finland, a shorter crossing (11 hours, departing daily at about 7:00-9:00 and 19:30-21:00). Turku is two hours from Helsinki by bus or train. The boats are usually smaller, with less cruise-ship excitement. The cheaper fare saves you enough to pay for the train trip from Turku to Helsinki.

Helsinki

Helsinki is the only European capital with no medieval past. Although it was founded in the 16th century by the Swedes in hopes of countering Tallinn as a strategic Baltic port, it never amounted to more than a village until the 18th century. Then, in 1746, Sweden built a huge fortress on an island outside its harbor, and the village boomed as it supplied the fortress. After taking over Finland in 1809, the Russians decided to move Finland's capital and university closer to St. Petersburg—from Turku to Helsinki. They hired a young German architect, Carl Ludvig Engel, to design new public buildings for Helsinki and told him to use St. Petersburg as a model. This is why the oldest parts of Helsinki (around Market Square and Senate Square) feel so Russian—stone buildings in yellow and blue pastels with white trim and columns. Hollywood used Helsinki for the films *Gorky Park* and *Dr. Zhivago,* because filming in Russia was not possible during the Cold War.

Though the city was part of the Russian Empire in the 19th century, most of its residents still spoke Swedish, which was the language of business and culture. In the mid-1800s, Finland began to industrialize. The Swedish upper class in Helsinki expanded the city, bringing in the railroad and surrounding the old Russian-inspired core with neighborhoods of four- and five-story apartment buildings, including some Art Nouveau masterpieces. Meanwhile, Finns moved from the countryside to Helsinki to take jobs as industrial laborers. The Finnish language slowly acquired equal status with Swedish, and eventually Finnish speakers became the majority in Helsinki (though Swedish remains a co-official language).

Since downtown Helsinki didn't exist until the 1800s, it was more conscientiously designed and laid out than other European capitals. With its many architectural overleafs and fine Neoclassical and Art Nouveau buildings, Helsinki often turns guests into students of urban design and planning. Good neighborhoods for architecture buffs to explore are Katajanokka, Kruununhaka, and Eira. If you're intrigued by what you see, look for the English-language guide to Helsinki architecture (by Arvi Ilonen) in bookstores.

All of this makes Helsinki sound like a very dry place. It's not. Despite its sometimes severe cityscape and chilly northern latitude, the city bursts with vibrant street life and a joyful creative spirit. In 2012, Helsinki celebrated its stint as a "World Design Capital," seizing the opportunity to spiff up the city with exciting new projects—including the new Helsinki Music Center concert hall, an extensive underground bike tunnel that cuts efficiently beneath congested downtown streets, and an all-around rededication to its already impressive design. While parts of the city may seem dark and drab, splashes of creativity and color hide around every corner—but you'll only discover them if you take the time to look.

Planning Your Time

On a three-week trip through Scandinavia, Helsinki is worth at least the time between two successive nights on the cruise ship—about seven hours. To do the city justice, two days is ideal. (Wear layers; Helsinki can be windy and cold.)

For a quick one-day visit, start with the 1.75-hour orientation bus tour that meets the boat at the dock. Then take my self-guided walking tour through the compact city center from the harbor—enjoying Helsinki's ruddy harborfront market and getting goose bumps in the churches—ending at the underground Temppeliaukio Church. In the afternoon, dive into Finnish culture in the open-air folk museum or take a walk in Kaivopuisto Park. Enjoy a cup of coffee at the recommended Café Kappeli before sailing away.

Orientation to Helsinki

Like most big European cities, Helsinki (pop. 602,000) has a compact core. The city's natural gateway is its main harbor, where ships from Stockholm and Tallinn dock. At the top of the harbor is Market Square (Kauppatori), an outdoor food and souvenir bazaar. Nearby are two towering, can't-miss-them landmarks: the white Lutheran Cathedral and the red-brick Orthodox Cathedral.

Helsinki's grand pedestrian boulevard, the Esplanade, begins right at Market Square, heads up past the TI, and ends after a few blocks in the central shopping district. The broad, traffic-filled Mannerheimintie, a bustling avenue that veers north through town past the train and bus stations, begins at the far end of the Esplanade. For a do-it-yourself orientation to town along this route, follow my "Welcome to Helsinki" self-guided walk on page 566. The "Tram #2/#3 Tour" (see page 571) also provides a good drive-by introduction to the main sights.

Tourist Information

The friendly, energetic **main TI,** just off the harbor, offers great service, and its brochure racks are fun to graze through. It's located a half-block inland from Market Square, on the right just past the fountain, at the corner of the Esplanade and Unioninkatu (May-Sept Mon-Fri 9:00-20:00, Sat-Sun 9:00-18:00, Oct-April closes two hours earlier, free Internet access, tel. 09/3101-3301, www .visithelsinki.fi). Pick up a city map, a public-transit map, and the free *Helsinki This Week* magazine (lists sights, hours, concerts, and events). Also consider these free brochures: the scenic #2/#3 tram route/map, *Helsinki on Foot* (which maps out five well-described walking tours), and *Finnish Design*. If interested, ask about concerts; popular venues are Kallio Church and the Lutheran Cathedral (free organ recitals Sun at 20:00 in summer).

The tiny **train station TI,** which consists of a one-person desk inside the Helsinki Expert office, provides many of the same services and publications.

Helsinki Expert: This private service sells the Helsinki Card (described next), ferry tickets, and sightseeing tours, and also makes hotel bookings. They have one branch in the train station hall, another occupying the front desks in the main TI on Market Square, and a small sightseeing kiosk out on the Esplanade (summer only, not all services). They charge an €8 fee for ferry bookings and for walk-in hotel reservations, though the hotel fee is waived if you email or phone for reservations (main TI branch: June-Aug Mon-Fri 9:00-18:30, Sat-Sun 9:00-17:00; Sept-May Mon-Fri 9:00-16:30, Sat 10:00-16:00, closed Sun; train station branch has similar hours, tel. 09/2288-1500, www.helsinkiexpert.com).

Helsinki Card: If you're planning to visit a lot of museums in Helsinki, this card can be a good deal (€36/24 hours, €46/48 hours, €56/72 hours, €3 less if bought online and picked up on arrival at the downtown TI's Helsinki Expert desk; includes free entry to over 50 museums, fortresses, and other major sights; free use of buses, trams, and the ferry to Suomenlinna; free city bus tour; and a 72-page booklet; sold at all Helsinki Expert locations, most hotels, and both Viking Line and Tallink Silja ferry terminals, www.helsinkicard.com).

For a cheaper alternative, you could buy a public-transit day ticket (see "Getting Around Helsinki," later), take my self-guided tours (the "Welcome to Helsinki" walk and "Tram #2/#3

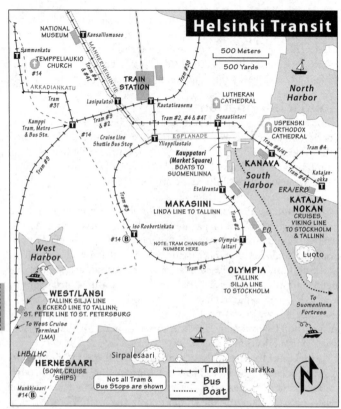

Tour"), visit the free churches (Temppeliaukio Church, Lutheran Cathedral, and Uspenski Orthodox Cathedral), and stop by the free Helsinki City Museum.

Arrival in Helsinki

By Boat: Helsinki's main South Harbor (Eteläsatama) has four terminals *(terminaali)*; for locations, see the map above and the color map in the front of this book. The Olympia and Makasiini terminals are on the south side (to the left as you face inland) of the main harbor. The Katajanokan terminal is on the north side (right) of the main harbor. Most Viking Line boats use the Katajanokan terminal; most Tallink Silja boats use the Olympia terminal. The Makasiini terminal is mostly for fast boats to Tallinn. Trams stop near all the main-harbor terminals (tram #4T near Katajanokan, tram #2 near Olympia).

The Länsi terminal, in Helsinki's West Harbor (Länsistama), is for large car ferries to/from Tallinn and St. Peter Line boats to St. Petersburg. You can get to downtown Helsinki on tram #9 (leaves from right outside the door, zips you to the train station downtown) or by taxi (about €15).

By Cruise Ship: Cruises arrive at any of four different terminals in Helsinki; for all the details, see the end of this chapter.

By Train and Bus: The train station, an architectural landmark, is near the top of the Esplanade, a 15-minute walk from

Market Square. Local buses leave from both sides of the building, trams stop out front, and the Metro runs underneath. The long-distance bus station is two blocks (or one tram stop) away, on the other side of Mannerheimintie; the ticket office and machines are on the ground floor, with bus platforms below.

By Plane: Helsinki Airport is about 10 miles north of the city (airport code: HEL, www.helsinki-vantaa.fi). To get between the airport and downtown Helsinki, take the Finnair bus (€6.20, leaves for airport from platform 30 at Elielinaukio on west side of train station, 3/hour, 35-minute trip, www.finnair.com; stops at some downtown hotels on request) or public bus #615 (€4.50, pay driver, not covered by transit tickets or Helsinki Card, leaves for airport from platform 3 at Rautatientori on east side of train station, 3-6/hour, 45-minute trip, also stops at Hakaniemi). Or take the Yellow Line door-to-door shared van service (€29 for 1-2 people, €45 for 3-4 people, €60 for 5-7 people, tel. 010-00700 or toll tel. 0600-555-555, www.yellowline.fi). An ordinary taxi from the airport runs about €35-40.

Helpful Hints

Bilingual Confusion: Because Finland is officially bilingual, you'll often see both Finnish and Swedish spellings for everything from street names to tram stops and map labels. This can be confusing, especially since the two names often look completely different. For example, the South Harbor—where many overnight boats arrive—is called Eteläsatama in Finnish and Södra Hamnen in Swedish; the train station is Rautatieasema in Finnish, Järnvägsstationen in Swedish.

Time: Finland and Estonia are one hour ahead of Sweden and the rest of Scandinavia.

Money: Finland's currency is the euro. ATM machines are labeled *Otto*.

Telephones: Finland's phone system generally uses area codes, but has some national numbers (starting with 010 or 020) that must be dialed in full when you're calling from anywhere in the country.

Internet Access: The **City Hall,** facing Market Square and the harbor, has six free, fast terminals and speedy Wi-Fi in its inviting lobby (get code from desk, Mon-Fri 9:00-19:00, Sat-Sun 10:00-16:00). At the **train station,** go down the escalators from the main hall and you'll see a bank of red terminals on your right (€2/hour).

Pharmacy: The central **Apteekki Palvelee** faces the TI and City Hall just off Market Square (Mon-Fri 8:00-19:00, Sat 9:00-17:00, Sun 11:00-16:00, Eteläesplanadi 2). A **24-hour pharmacy**—*apteekki*—is located at Mannerheimintie 96 (at Kansaneläkelaitos stop for tram #2, #4/4T, or #10, tel. 020-320-200).

Laundry: PesuNet, primarily a dry-cleaning shop, welcomes travelers to use its half-dozen self-service machines. It's within a few blocks of recommended hotels, and the Iso Roobertinkatu stop for tram #3 is around the corner (€9.30/load, not coin-op—pay staff who will help, Mon-Thu 8:00-20:00, Fri 8:00-18:00, Sat 10:00-15:00, closed Sun, Punavuorenkatu 3, tel. 09/622-1146).

Bike Rental: Try **Greenbike** (one-speed bike-€20/4 hours, €30/24 hours; three-speed bike-€5 more; May-mid-Sept daily 10:00-18:00, until 20:00 in Aug, usually no rentals off-season; Narinkka 3 in front of Kamppi shopping center; mobile 050-404-0400, www.greenbike.fi).

Best View: The **Torni Tower's Ateljee Bar** offers a free panorama view. Ride the elevator from the lobby of the venerable Torni Hotel (built in 1931) to the 12th floor, where you can browse around the perch or sit down for a drink (Sun-Thu 14:00-24:00, Fri-Sat 12:00-24:00, Yrjönkatu 26, tel. 020-123-4604).

Meet the Finns: With **Cozy Finland's** "Meet the Finns" program, you can match your hobbies with a local—and suddenly, you're searching out classic comics at the flea market with a new Finnish friend. Their most popular service involves arranging dinner at a local host's home (around €55); contact Cozy Finland for exact prices (www.cosyfinland.com).

What's With the Slot Machines? Finns just have a love affair with lotteries and petty gambling. You'll see coin-operated games of chance everywhere, including restaurants, supermarkets, and the train station.

Updates to This Book: For news about changes to this book's coverage since it was published, see www.ricksteves.com/update.

Getting Around Helsinki

In compact Helsinki, you won't need to use public transportation as much as in Stockholm.

HELSINKI

By Bus and Tram: With the public-transit route map (available at the TI, also viewable on the Helsinki Region Transport website—www.hsl.fi) and a little

mental elbow grease, the buses and trams are easy, giving you Helsinki by the tail. The single Metro line is also part of the system, but is not useful unless you're traveling to my recommended sauna.

Single tickets are good for an hour of travel (€2.70 from driver, €2.20 at automated ticket machines at a few larger bus and tram stops). A day ticket (€7/24 hours of unlimited travel) pays for itself if you take four or more rides; longer versions are also available (€3.50 per extra 24 hours, 7-day maximum). Day tickets can be bought at the ubiquitous yellow-and-blue R-Kiosks (convenience stores), as well as at TIs, the train station, Metro stations, automated ticket machines at a handful of stops, and on some ferries, but not from drivers. The Helsinki Card also covers public transportation. All of these tickets and cards are only valid within the city of Helsinki, not the suburbs; for example, you pay extra for the public bus to the airport.

Tours in Helsinki

For a fun, cheap tour, take public tram #2/#3—it makes the rounds of most of the town's major sights in an hour. Use my self-guided "Tram #2/#3 Tour" (described later and rated ▲▲) to follow along with what you see, and also pick up the helpful tram #2/#3 explanatory brochure—free at TIs and often on board.

▲▲▲**Orientation Bus Tours**—These 1.75-hour bus tours, run by Helsinki Expert, give an ideal city overview with a look at all of the important buildings, from the recently remodeled Olympic Stadium to Embassy Row. You stay on the bus the entire time, except for a short stop or two (e.g., for 10 minutes at the Sibelius Monument, and when possible, Temppeliaukio Church). You'll learn strange facts, such as how Finns took down the highest steeple in town during World War II so that the Soviet bombers flying in from Estonia couldn't see their target. Tours cost €28, but are free with the Helsinki Card, and are €3 cheaper if you book on the Helsinki Expert website (www.helsinkiexpert.com). Tours get booked up, so it's wise to reserve in advance online (or call 09/2288-1600, email sightseeing@helsinkiexpert.fi, or ask your hotelier to help).

Bus Tours Departing from Boat Dock: Conveniently, tours

depart from the Viking Line and Tallink Silja boat docks at 10:30, soon after the boats arrive from Stockholm. Tours end back at the dock they started from, though you can get off downtown near the end of the tour.

Viking Line tours run daily year-round, with a live guide (who speaks English and Swedish) from June through late August, and an audioguide narration off-season. Tallink Silja has a live guide for a bigger chunk of the year—from mid-April through September—but offers no tours off-season. If you haven't reserved your tour online, buy your ticket (and Helsinki Card, if you wish) on board the ship.

If you want to take the bus tour and end up downtown for an overnight stay, stow your bag on the bus, and get off in the city center before the end of the tour (cost-effectively using the tour for transportation as well as for information).

Bus Tour Departing from the Center: The same 1.75-hour bus tour, with an audioguide, leaves later in the day from the corner of Fabianinkatu and the Esplanade (mid-June–mid-Aug daily at 11:00, 12:00, 13:30, and 15:00; fewer tours off-season, but 11:00 departure runs year-round).

Hop-On, Hop-Off Bus Tours—If you'd enjoy the tour described above, but want the chance to hop on and off at will, consider **Open Top Tours** (owned by Strömma/Helsinki Sightseeing). Their two one-hour, complementary routes—yellow around the southern part of town and to the Hernesaari cruise terminal, and green to points north including the Sibelius Monument and Olympic Stadium—depart every 30-45 minutes (€25 for either route or €30 for both, €35 combo-ticket also includes harbor cruise—see next, all tickets good for 24 hours, May-Sept daily 10:00-16:00, tel. 020-741-8210, www.stromma.fi). A different company, **Sightseeing City Tour,** offers a similar combination of routes for similar prices, but has fewer departures (www.citytour.fi).

Harbor Tours—Three boat companies compete for your attention along Market Square, offering snoozy cruises around the harbor and its islands roughly hourly from 10:00 to 18:00 in summer (typically 1.5 hours for €17-20; www.royalline.net, www.ihalines.fi, www.stromma.fi). The narration is slow-moving—often recorded and in as many as four languages. I'd call it an expensive nap. Taking the ferry out to Suomenlinna and back gets you onto the water for much less money (€5 round-trip, covered by day ticket or Helsinki Card).

Pub Tram—In summer, this antique red tram makes a 50-minute circle through the city while its passengers get looped on the beer for sale on board (€8 to ride, €5.50 beer, mid-May-Aug Tue-Sat 14:00-20:00, no trams Sun-Mon, leaves at the top of each hour

Helsinki at a Glance

▲▲▲**Temppeliaukio Church** Awe-inspiring, copper-topped 1969 "Church in the Rock." **Hours:** June-Sept Mon-Sat 10:00-17:45, Sun 11:45-17:45; closes one hour earlier off-season. See page 577.

▲▲**Uspenski Orthodox Cathedral** Orthodoxy's most prodigious display outside of Eastern Europe. **Hours:** Mon-Fri 9:30-16:00, Sat 9:30-14:00, Sun 12:00-15:00. See page 575.

▲▲**Lutheran Cathedral** Green-domed, 19th-century Neoclassical masterpiece. **Hours:** June-Aug Mon-Sat 9:00-24:00, Sun 12:00-24:00; Sept-May Mon-Sat 9:00-18:00, Sun 12:00-18:00. See page 575.

▲▲**National Museum of Finland** The scoop on Finland, featuring folk costumes, an armory, czars, and thrones; the prehistory exhibit is best. **Hours:** Tue-Sun 11:00-18:00, closed Mon. See page 579.

▲▲**Seurasaari Open-Air Folk Museum** Island museum with 100 historic buildings from Finland's farthest corners. **Hours:** June-Aug daily 11:00-17:00; late May and early Sept Mon-Fri 9:00-15:00, Sat-Sun 11:00-17:00, buildings closed mid-Sept-mid-May. See page 581.

▲▲**Suomenlinna Fortress** Helsinki's harbor island, sprinkled with picnic spots, museums, and military history. **Hours:** Daily May-Sept 10:00-18:00, Oct-April 10:30-16:30. See page 581.

▲**Senate Square** Consummate Neoclassical square, with Lutheran Cathedral. **Hours:** Always open. See page 576.

▲ **Helsinki City Museum** Tells the city's history well and in English. **Hours:** Mon-Fri 9:00-17:00, Thu until 19:00, Sat-Sun 11:00-17:00. See page 577.

▲**Ateneum, The National Gallery of Finland** Largest collection of art in Finland, including local favorites plus works by Cézanne, Chagall, Gauguin, and Van Gogh. **Hours:** Tue and Fri 10:00-18:00, Wed-Thu 10:00-20:00, Sat-Sun 11:00-17:00, closed Mon. See page 579.

▲**Sibelius Monument** Stainless-steel sculptural tribute to Finland's greatest composer. **Hours:** Always open. See page 579.

from in front of the Fennia building, Mikonkatu 17, across from train-station tower, www.koff.net).

Architectural Walk—Archtour's two-hour guided walk shows you a few of Helsinki's late-19th-century architectural highlights, including the university's library and the stock exchange building (€20, mid-June-Aug Mon-Fri at 14:00, no tours on weekends, leaves from middle of Senate Square, tel. 09/477-7300, www.arch tours.com).

Local Guides—**Helsinki Expert** can arrange a private guide (book at least three days in advance, €220/3 hours, tel. 09/2288-1222). **Christina Snellman** is a good, licensed guide (mobile 050-527-4741, chrisder@pp.inet.fi).

Self-Guided Walk

▲▲Welcome to Helsinki

This walk offers a convenient spine for your Helsinki sightseeing. Several points of interest on this walk are described in more detail later, under "Sights in Helsinki."

❶ **Market Square:** Start at the obelisk in the center of the harborfront market. This is the Czarina's Stone, with its double-headed eagle of imperial Russia. It was the first public monument in Helsinki, designed by Carl Ludvig Engel and erected in 1835 to celebrate the visit by Czar Nicholas I and Czarina Alexandra. Step over the chain and climb to the top step for a clockwise spin-tour:

The big, red Viking ship and white Tallink Silja ship are each floating hotels for those making the 40-hour Stockholm-Helsinki round-trip. The brown-and-tan brick building is the old market hall. A number of harbor cruise boats vie for your business. The trees mark the beginning of Helsinki's grand promenade, the Esplanade (where we're heading). Hiding in the leaves is the venerable iron-and-glass Café Kappeli. The yellow building across from the trees is the TI. From there, a string of Neoclassical buildings face the harbor. The blue-and-white City Hall building was designed by Engel in 1833 as the town's first hotel, built to house the czar and czarina. Now it houses a public Internet point, free WCs, and free exhibits on Helsinki history (often photography). The Lutheran Cathedral is hidden from view behind this building. Next is the Swedish Embassy (flying the blue-and-yellow Swedish flag and designed to look like Stockholm's Royal Palace). Then comes the Supreme Court and, in the far corner, Finland's Presidential Palace. Standing proud, and reminding Helsinki of the Russian behemoth to its east, is the Uspenski Orthodox Cathedral.

Explore the colorful outdoor market—part souvenirs and crafts, part fruit and veggies, part fish and snacks (Mon-Fri roughly

6:30-17:00, Sat 6:30-16:00, only tourist stalls on Sun 10:00-16:00). Then, with your back to the water, walk left to the fountain, *Havis Amanda,* designed by Ville Vallgren and unveiled here in 1908. The fountain has become the symbol of Helsinki, the city known as
the "Daughter of the Baltic"—graduating students decorate her with a school cap. The voluptuous figure, modeled after the artist's Parisian mistress, was a bit too racy for the conservative town, and Vallgren had trouble getting paid. But as artists often do, Vallgren had the last laugh: For more than a hundred years now, the city budget office (next to the Sasso restaurant across the street) has seen only her backside.

A one-block detour up Unioninkatu (noteworthy shops listed in "Shopping in Helsinki," later) takes you to the Neoclassical Senate Square and Lutheran Cathedral.

To continue with this walk, backtrack to the TI. In the park across the street is the delightful...

❷ Café Kappeli: If you've got some time, dip into this old-fashioned, gazebo-like oasis of coffee, pastry, and relaxation (get what you like at the bar inside and sit anywhere). In the 19th century, this was a popular hangout for local intellectuals and artists. Today the café offers romantic tourists waiting for their ship a great €3-cup-of-coffee memory. The bandstand in front hosts nearly daily music and dance performances in summer.

❸ The Esplanade: Behind Café Kappeli stretches the Esplanade, Helsinki's top shopping boulevard, sandwiching a park in the middle (another Engel design from the 1830s). The grandiose street names Esplanadi and Bulevardi, while fitting today, must have been bombastic and almost comical in rustic little 1830s Helsinki. To help you imagine this elegant promenade in the 19th century, informative signs (in English) explain Esplanade Park's background and its many statues.

The north side (with the TI) is interesting for window-shopping, people-watching, and sun-worshipping. You'll pass several stores specializing in Finnish design. At #35, Gamla Passage leads to a courtyard hopping with bars and live music at night. Farther up on the right, at #39, is the huge Academic Bookstore (Akateeminen Kirjakauppa), designed by Alvar Aalto, with an extensive map and travel section, periodicals, English books, and Café Aalto (bookstore and café open Mon-Fri 9:00-21:00, Sat 9:00-18:00, also usually open Sun 12:00-18:00).

HELSINKI

HELSINKI

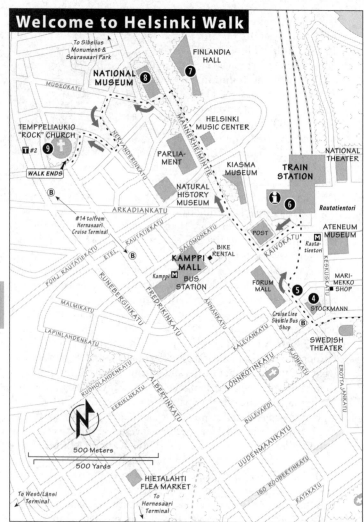

Welcome to Helsinki Walk

❹ Stockmann Department Store: Finally, you'll come to the prestigious Stockmann department store—Finland's answer to Harrods or Macy's. Stockmann is the biggest, best, and oldest department store in town, with a great gourmet supermarket in the basement (see listing in "Shopping in Helsinki"). Just beyond is Helsinki's main intersection, where Esplanade and Mannerheimintie meet. (Mannerheimintie is named for Carl Gustaf Mannerheim, the Finnish war hero who frustrated the Soviets in World War II.)

❺ The *Three Blacksmiths* Statue: Turn right on Manner-

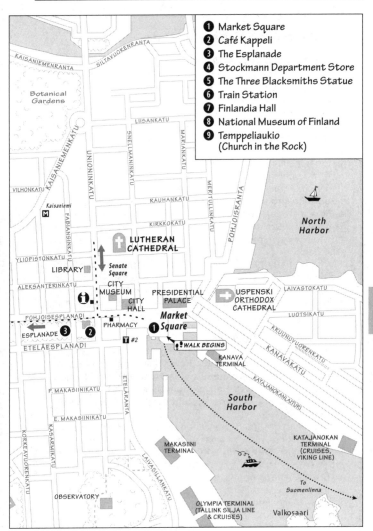

Legend:
1. Market Square
2. Café Kappeli
3. The Esplanade
4. Stockmann Department Store
5. The Three Blacksmiths Statue
6. Train Station
7. Finlandia Hall
8. National Museum of Finland
9. Temppeliaukio (Church in the Rock)

heimintie and at the far side of Stockmann, you'll see the famous *Three Blacksmiths* (from 1932). While there's no universally accepted meaning, most say it celebrates human labor and cooperation and shows the solid character of the Finnish people. Note the rare, surviving bullet damage from World War II on the

Two Men Who Remade Helsinki

Eliel Saarinen (1873-1950)

At the turn of the 20th century, architect Eliel Saarinen burst on the scene by pioneering the Finnish National Romantic style. Inspired by peasant and medieval architectural traditions, his work was fundamental in creating a distinct—and modern—Finnish identity. The château-esque National Museum of Finland, designed by Saarinen and his two partners after winning a 1902 architectural competition, was his first major success (see page 579).

Two years later, Saarinen won the contract to construct the Helsinki train station (completed in 1919). Its design marks a transition into the Art Nouveau style of the early 1900s. The landmark station—characterized by massive male sculptures flanking its entrance, ornate glass and metalwork, and a soaring clock tower—presently welcomes over 300,000 travelers each day.

In the early 1920s, Saarinen and his family emigrated to the US where his son, Eero, would become the architect of such iconic projects as the Gateway Arch in St. Louis and the main terminal at Dulles International Airport near Washington, DC.

Alvar Aalto (1898-1976)

Alvar Aalto was a celebrated Finnish architect and designer working in the Modernist tradition; his buildings used abstract forms and innovative materials without sacrificing functionality. Finlandia Hall in Helsinki, undoubtedly Aalto's most famous structure, employs geometric shapes and sweeping lines to create a striking concert hall, seating up to 1,700 guests. Aalto designed an inclined roof to try to maximize the hall's acoustics, with marginal success.

A Finnish Frank Lloyd Wright, Aalto concerned himself with nearly every aspect of design, from furniture to light fixtures. Perhaps most notable of these creations was his sinuous Savoy Vase, a masterpiece of simplicity and sophistication that is emblematic of the Aalto style. His designs became so popular that in 1935 he and his wife opened Artek, a company that manufactures and sells his furniture, lamps, and textiles to this day (see page 584).

base. The most serious Russian shelling came in February of 1944. Overall, Helsinki emerged from the war with little damage.

Stockmann's entrance on Aleksanterinkatu, facing the *Three Blacksmiths*, is one of the city's most popular meeting points. Everyone in Finland knows exactly what it means when you say: "Let's meet under the Stockmann's clock." Tram #2 also makes a stop right at the clock (see "Tram #2/#3 Tour," page 571). Across the street from the clock, the Old Student Hall is decorated with mythic Finnish heroes.

❻ **Train Station:** Just past the *Three Blacksmiths,* look for a passageway to your right through a shopping arcade. Walking through it, you'll emerge in front of the harsh (but serene) architecture of the train station (by Eliel Saarinen; see sidebar). The four people on the facade symbolize peasant farmers with lamps coming into the Finnish capital. Duck into the main hall and the Eliel Restaurant inside to catch the building's ambience.

Continuing past the post office and the equestrian statue of Mannerheim, return to Mannerheimintie, which passes the Kiasma Museum, Parliament, and Helsinki Music Center on the way to the large, white ❼ **Finlandia Hall,** another Aalto masterpiece. Across the street is the excellent little ❽ **National Museum of Finland** (looks like a château with a steeple), and a few blocks behind that is the sit-down-and-wipe-a-tear beautiful "Church in the Rock," ❾ **Temppeliaukio.** Sit. Enjoy the music. It's a wonderful place to end this walk.

If you want to continue on to the Sibelius Monument, located in a lovely park setting, take bus #24 (direction: Seurasaari) from nearby Arkadiankatu street. The same ticket is good for your return trip (within one hour), or ride it to the end of the line for the bridge to Seurasaari Island and Finland's open-air folk museum. From there, bus #24 returns to the top of the Esplanade.

Self-Guided Tram Tour

▲▲Tram #2/#3 Tour

Of Helsinki's many tram routes, #2/#3 seems made-to-order for a tourist's joyride. In fact, the TI hands out a free little map with the described route, making this tour easier to follow. (Helsinki revised the numbering of some tram routes in summer 2013; old tram line #3T is now #2, and #3B is #3. Signs should be changed over by the time of your visit.)

If you buy a single ticket, just stay on the tram for the entire circuit (€2.70 from driver, €2.20 from ticket machines at a few major stops, good for one hour). Using a day ticket (see "Getting Around Helsinki," earlier) or a Helsinki Card allows you to hop off to tour a sight, then catch a later tram (runs every 10 minutes).

You can't get lost because the route makes a figure-eight, and an hour after you start, you end up back at the beginning. The only confusing thing is that the tram has different names during different parts of the figure-eight; the top-left and bottom-right lobes are #2, the other lobes are #3, and the letter on the tram's sign changes at the north and south ends of the route.

A few departures circle only the top or bottom loop, so

HELSINKI

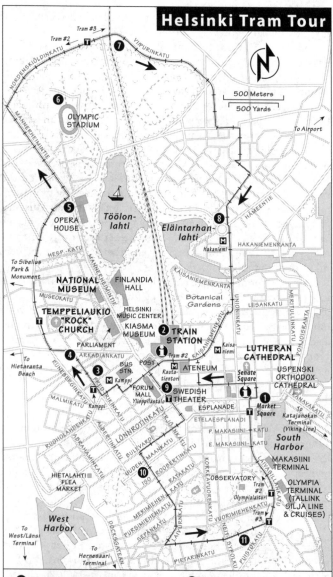

Helsinki Tram Tour

Tram #3
Tram #2

VIIPURINKATU

To Airport

500 Meters
500 Yards

NORDENSKIÖLDINKATU

6 OLYMPIC STADIUM

5 OPERA HOUSE

Töölön-lahti

MANNERHEIMINTIE

HÄMEENTIE

8 Eläintarhan-lahti

Hakaniemi

HAKANIEMENRANTA

HESP.-KATU

To Sibelius Park & Monument

MUSEOKATU

NATIONAL MUSEUM

FINLANDIA HALL

KAISANIEMENRANTA

Botanical Gardens

UNIONINKATU

LIISANKATU

MERITULLINKATU

SILTAVUORENRANTA

TEMPPELIAUKIO "ROCK" CHURCH

HELSINKI MUSIC CENTER

KIASMA MUSEUM

2 TRAIN STATION

Kaisa-niemi

LUTHERAN CATHEDRAL

PARLIAMENT

To Hietaranta Beach

4 ARKADIANKATU

RUNEBERGINKATU

FREDRIKINKATU

BUS STN.

POST

Kamppi

3

9

1

ATENEUM

Rauta-tientori

Senate Square

USPENSKI ORTHODOX CATHEDRAL

MALMINKATU

Kamppi

FORUM MALL
Ylioppilastalo

SWEDISH THEATER

ESPLANADE

1 Market Square

PANAVAKATU

To Katajanokan Terminal

South Harbor

To Tallink (Viking Line)

MEKELININKATU

ALBERTINKATU

LÖNNROTINKATU

BULEVARDI

UUDEN-MAANKATU

FREDRIKINKATU

ROOBERTINKATU

KORKEAVUORENKATU

ETELAESPLANADI

P. MAKASIINI-KATU

E. MAKASIINI-KATU

MAKASIINI TERMINAL

HIETALAHTI FLEA MARKET

10
190

RATAKATU

OBSERVATORY

Tram #2

Olympialaituri

OLYMPIA TERMINAL (TALLINK SILJA LINE & CRUISES)

RUOHOLAHDENK.

ABRAHAMINKATU

West Harbor

DOCKGATEAN

MEKIMIEHEN KATU

PURSIMIEHENKATU

SEPÄNKATU

LAIVURINKATU

VUORIMIEHENKATU

Tram #3

11

LAIVASILLANKATU

TUTIJOKATU

To West/Länsi Terminal

To Hernesaari Terminal

PIETARINKATU

NEITSYTPOLKU

1 Market Square/Senate Square/Shopping Street

2 Finnish National Theater/Train Station

3 Shopping & Entertainment District

4 School of Economics & Trendy Apartments

5 Finnish National Opera House

6 Sports Complex

7 Classic Amusement Park (Linnanmäki)

8 Working-Class District

9 The Three Blacksmiths Statue

10 Funky & Artsy Shops

11 Embassy Row

confirm with the driver before boarding that your tram will make the entire figure-eight.

❶ **Market Square:** While you can hop on anywhere, it's most convenient to start—and end—at Market Square by the TI. Stand at the tram stop that is between the fountain and the market, and wait for one of the frequent #2 trams. Since the tracks split here briefly, it's hard to get on in the wrong direction; still, confirm that the destination listed on the front of the tram is *Eläintarha*, not *Kaivopuisto*. From Market Square, you'll first pass **Senate Square** (with the gleaming white Lutheran Cathedral, a statue of Alexander II—Finland's favorite czar, and many of the oldest buildings in town) and then head up Aleksanterinkatu street. It's Helsinki's Fifth Avenue-type main shopping drag (tram stop: Aleksanterinkatu).

❷ **Finnish National Theater/Train Station:** After the Mikonkatu stop, you'll pass a big square. Fronting it is Finland's granite National Theater, in Art Nouveau style. The statue in the square honors Aleksis Kivi, the father of Finnish literature, who in 1870 wrote *The Seven Brothers*, the first great novel in Finnish. The mid-19th century was a period of national awakening. By elevating the language to high culture, Kivi helped inspire his countrymen to stand strong and proud during a period of attempted "Russification." On the left is the **Ateneum,** Finland's national art gallery. From there (on the right), you'll pass the striking train station—with its iconic countrymen stoically holding their lamps—designed by the great Finnish architect, Eliel Saarinen.

❸ **Shopping and Entertainment District:** Crossing the busy Mannerheimintie boulevard, you'll pass the Kamppi mall (tram and Metro stop: Kamppi, with bus station in basement). The adjacent Tennis Palace is a cultural zone with galleries and movie theaters.

❹ **School of Economics and Trendy Apartments:** After passing the yellow brick buildings of the School of Economics (on your left, note facade—Kauppakorkeakoulut stop), you'll enter a neighborhood with lots of desirable 1920s-era apartments. Young couples start out here, move to the suburbs when they have their kids, and return as empty-nesters. The Temppeliaukio Church (a.k.a. "Church in the Rock"), while out of sight, is just a block uphill from the next stop (Sammonkatu).

❺ **Finnish National Opera House:** Built in 1993, the National Opera House is the white, sterile, shower-tile building on the right (tram stop: Ooppera). The next stop (Töölön halli) is a short walk from the Sibelius Monument and its pretty park (detour along a street called Sibeliuksenkatu).

❻ **Sports Complex:** A statue honors long-distance runner Paavo Nurmi (early 20th-century Finn who won a slew of Olympic gold medals, on left). The white building with the skinny tower (in

HELSINKI

the distance on the right) marks the Olympic Stadium, used for the summer games in 1952. After the Aurorankatu stop, you'll see skateboarders enjoying a park of their own (on the right). At the next stop, Eläintarha, the tram may pause as it changes to become #3 (stay seated).

❼ **Classic Amusement Park: Linnanmäki,** Helsinki's low-end, Tivoli-like amusement park is by far the most-visited sight in town (on the right, free admission to park but rides cost €4-6, open daily until late, tram stop: Alppila, www.linnanmaki.fi). Roller-coaster nuts enjoy its classics from the 1950s.

❽ **Working-Class District:** Next you'll enter an old working-class neighborhood. Its soccer fields (on your left) are frozen into ice rinks for hockey in the winter. You'll pass the striking granite **Kallio Church** (Art Nouveau, on your right) and **Hakaniemi** square, with a big indoor/outdoor market (on your left). Crossing a saltwater inlet, you'll pass Helsinki's **Botanical Gardens** (on the right), and then head back toward the town center. As you return to the train station with its buff lamp-holders, you've completed the larger, top loop of the figure-eight.

❾ **The *Three Blacksmiths* Statue:** After turning left on big, busy Mannerheimintie, you'll pass the most famous statue in town, the *Three Blacksmiths* (on your left), which honors hard work and cooperation. Towering above the smiths is the Stockmann department store. Then (at the Ylioppilastalo stop), the round, white Swedish Theater marks the top of the town's graceful park—the Esplanade—which leads back down to the harbor (where you began this tour). From here, you'll loop through a colorful and artsy district.

❿ **Funky and Artsy Shops:** The cemetery of the church (which dates from 1827) on the right was cleaned out to make a park. It's called the "Plague Park," recalling a circa-1700 plague that killed more than half the population. Coming up, funky small boutiques, cafés, and fun shops line the streets (stops: Fredrikinkatu, Iso Roobertinkatu, and Viiskulma). After the Art Deco brick church (on your right), the tram makes a hard left (at the Eiran Sairaala stop, for a hospital) and enters a district with Art Nouveau buildings. Look down streets on the right for facades and decorative turrets leading to the Baltic Sea.

⓫ **Embassy Row and Back to Market Square:** After the Neitsytpolku stop, spy the Russian Embassy (on left), still sporting its hammer and sickle; it was built to look like London's Buckingham Palace. Across the street is the Roman Catholic church, and beyond that (on the right), a street marked "no entry" leads to an embattled US Embassy. Returning to the harbor, you'll likely see the huge Tallink Silja ship that leaves at 17:00 each evening for Stockholm. Its terminal (the appropriately named Olympiaterminaali) was built for the 1952 Olympics, which inundated Helsinki with visitors. Across the harbor stands the Uspenski Orthodox Cathedral. Then, after passing the cute brick market hall (with several great little eateries), you'll arrive back at Market Square, where you started.

Sights in Helsinki

Near the South Harbor

▲▲**Uspenski Orthodox Cathedral**—This house of worship was built in 1868 for the Russian military back when Finland

belonged to Russia. *Uspenski* is Russian for the Assumption of Mary. It hovers above Market Square and faces the Lutheran Cathedral as Russian culture faces Europe.

Cost and Hours: Free; Mon-Fri 9:30-16:00, Sat 9:30-14:00, Sun 12:00-15:00, Kanavakatu 1.

Visiting the Cathedral: The uppermost "onion dome" represents the "sacred heart of Jesus," while the smaller ones represent the hearts of the 12 apostles. The cathedral's interior is a potentially emotional icon experience. Its rich images are a stark contrast to the sober Lutheran Cathedral. While commonly called the "Russian church," the cathedral is actually Finnish Orthodox, answering to the patriarch in Constantinople (Istanbul). Much of eastern Finland (parts of the Karelia region) is Finnish Orthodox.

The cathedral's Orthodox Mass is beautiful, with a standing congregation, candles, incense, icons in action, priests behind the iconostasis (screen), and timeless music (human voices only—no instruments). In the front left corner, find the icon featuring the Madonna and child, surrounded by rings and jewelry (under glass), given in thanks for prayers answered. Across from the icon is a white marble table with candle holes and a dish of wheat seeds, representing recent deaths. Wheat seeds symbolize that death is not the end, but just a change.

Though the cathedral is worthwhile, the one in Tallinn is even nicer, so skip this one if you're visiting both cities and short on time.

▲▲**Lutheran Cathedral**—With its prominent green dome, gleaming white facade, and the 12 apostles overlooking the city and harbor, this church is Carl Ludvig Engel's masterpiece.

Cost and Hours: Free; June-Aug Mon-Sat 9:00-24:00, Sun 12:00-24:00; Sept-May Mon-Sat 9:00-18:00, Sun 12:00-18:00;

HELSINKI

sometimes closes for events; on Senate Square, www.helsingin seurakunnat.fi. In summer, free organ concerts are held on Sundays at 20:00.

Visiting the Cathedral: Finished in 1852, the interior is pure architectural truth. Open a pew gate and sit, surrounded by

the saints of Protestantism, to savor Neoclassical nirvana. Physically, this church is perfectly Protestant—austere and unadorned—with the emphasis on preaching (prominent pulpit) and music (huge organ). Statuary is limited to the local Reformation big shots: Martin Luther, Philipp Melanchthon (Luther's Reformation sidekick), and the leading Finnish reformer, Mikael Agricola. A follower of Luther at Wittenberg, Agricola brought the Reformation to Finland. He also translated the Bible into Finnish and is considered the father of the modern Finnish language. Agricola's Bible is to Finland what the Luther Bible is to Germany and the King James Bible is to the English-speaking world.

▲**Senate Square**—Once a town square with a church and City Hall, this square's original buildings were burned in 1808. Later, after Finland became a grand duchy of the Russian Empire, the czar sent in architect Carl Ludvig Engel (a German who had lived and worked in St. Petersburg) to give the place some Neo-class. The result: the finest Neoclassical square in Europe.

Survey Senate Square from the top of the Lutheran Cathedral steps. The Senate building (now the prime minister's office) is on your left. The small, blue, stone building with the slanted mansard roof in the far-left corner, from 1757, is one of just two pre-Russian-conquest buildings remaining in Helsinki. On the right, the line of once-grand Russian administration buildings now house the **university** (36,000 students, 60 percent female). Symbolically (and physically), the university and government buildings are connected via the cathedral, and both use it as a starting point for grand ceremonies.

The **statue** in the center of the square honors Russian Czar Alexander II. While he wasn't popular in Russia (he was assassinated), he was well-liked by the Finns. That's because he gave Finland more autonomy in 1863 and never pushed the "Russification" of Finland. The statue shows him holding the Finnish constitution, which he supported. It defined internal independence and affirmed autonomy.

The huge staircase leading up to the cathedral is a popular meeting (and tanning) spot in Helsinki. This is where students from the nearby university gather...and romances are born. Café Engel (opposite the cathedral at Aleksanterinkatu 26) is a fine place for a light lunch or cake and coffee. The café's winter lighting seems especially designed to boost the spirits of glum, daylight-deprived Northerners.

National Library—This fine, purpose-built Neoclassical building is open to the public and worth a look (on Senate Square, immediately to the left as you face the cathedral). In czarist times, the National Library received a copy of every book printed in the Russian Empire. With all the chaos Russia suffered throughout the 20th century, a good percentage of its Slavic texts were destroyed. But Helsinki, which enjoyed relative stability, claims to have the finest collection of Slavic books in the world.

Cost and Hours: Free, July-Aug Mon-Thu 9:00-18:00, Fri 9:00-16:00, closed Sat-Sun; Sept-June Mon-Thu 9:00-20:00, Fri-Sat 9:00-16:00, closed Sun; www.nationallibrary.fi.

▲**Helsinki City Museum**—This interesting museum, a half-block south of Senate Square, gives an excellent, accessible overview of the city's history in English. Unfortunately, it may close or relocate in the future—inquire locally.

Cost and Hours: Free, Mon-Fri 9:00-17:00, Thu until 19:00, Sat-Sun 11:00-17:00, Sofiankatu 4, www.helsinkicitymuseum.fi.

Elsewhere in Central Helsinki

▲▲▲**Temppeliaukio Church**—A more modern example of great church architecture (from 1969), this "Church in the Rock" was blasted out of solid granite. It was designed by architect broth-

ers, Timo and Tuomo Suomalainen, and built within a year's time. Barren of decor except for a couple of simple crosses, the church is capped with a copper-and-skylight dome; it's normally filled with live or recorded music and awestruck visitors. Grab a pew. Gawk upward at a 13-mile-long coil of copper ribbon. Look at the bull's-eye and ponder God. Forget your camera. Just sit in the middle, ignore the crowds, and be thankful for peace...under your feet is an air-raid shelter that can accommodate 6,000 people.

Cost and Hours: Free, June-Sept Mon-Sat 10:00-17:45, Sun 11:45-17:45, closes one hour earlier off-season and for special events and concerts, Lutherinkatu 3, tel. 09/2340-6320, www.helsingin seurakunnat.fi.

Getting There: The church is at the top of a hill in a residential neighborhood, about a 15-minute walk north of the bus station

Sauna

Finland's vaporized fountain of youth is the sauna—Scandinavia's answer to support hose and facelifts. A traditional sauna is a wood-paneled room with wooden benches and a wood-fired stove topped with rocks. The stove is heated blistering hot. Undress entirely before going in. Lay your towel on the bench, and sit or lie on it (for hygienic reasons). Ladle water from the bucket onto the rocks to make steam. Choose a higher bench for hotter temperatures.

The famous birch branches are always available for slapping. Finns claim this enhances circulation and say the chlorophyll released with the slapping opens your sinuses while emitting a refreshing birch aroma. (Follow the lead of the locals around you—tourists merrily flagellating themselves can be really annoying.) Let yourself work up a sweat, then, just before bursting, go outside to the shower for a Niagara of liquid ice. Suddenly your shower stall becomes a Cape Canaveral launch pad, as your body scatters to every corner of the universe. A moment later you're back together and can re-enter the steam room and repeat as necessary. Only rarely will you feel so good. The Finnish Sauna Society's informative website details the history of saunas and sweat baths (www.sauna.fi).

Your hostel, hotel, or the ship you came to Finland on may have a sauna. Ask them when they heat it, and whether it's semi-public (separate men's and women's hours, pay per person) or for private use (book and pay for a 45- to 60-minute time slot, and save money by bringing a group of friends, either mixed or same-sex). Public saunas are a dying breed these days, because most Finns have private saunas in their homes or cabins. But some public saunas survive in rougher, poorer neighborhoods.

For a good, traditional wood-heated sauna with a coarse and local crowd, try the **Kotiharjun Sauna.** There are no tourists and no English signs, but the guy at the desk speaks English and can help: Pay €12 plus €3 for a towel (cash only), find a locker, strip (keep the key on your wrist), and head for the steam. Cooling off is nothing fancy, just a bank of cold showers. A woman in a fish-cleaner's apron will give you a wonderful scrub with Brillo pad-like mitts (€9, only on Tue and Fri-Sat 16:00-19:00). Regulars relax with beers on the sidewalk just outside (open Tue-Sat 14:00-21:30, closed Sun-Mon, last entry 2 hours before closing; men—ground floor, women—upstairs; 200 yards from Sörnäinen Metro stop, Harjutorinkatu 1, tel. 09/753-1535, www.kotiharjunsauna.fi).

or a 10-minute walk behind the National Museum (or take tram #2 to Sammonkatu stop).

▲▲National Museum of Finland (Kansallismuseo)—This pleasant, easy-to-handle collection (covering Finland's story from A to Z, with good English descriptions) is in a grand building designed by three of this country's greatest architects—including Eliel Saarinen—in the early 1900s. The Neoclassical furniture, folk costumes, armory, and portraits of Russia's last czars around an impressive throne are interesting, but the highlight is Finland's largest permanent archaeological collection, covering the prehistory of the country. The fine, new 20th-century exhibit bookends your visit by bringing the story up to the present day. The interactive top-floor workshop is worth a look for its creative teaching.

Cost and Hours: €8, free on Fri 16:00-18:00; open Tue-Sun 11:00-18:00, closed Mon; Mannerheimintie 34, tel. 09/4050-9544 or mobile 040-128-6469, www.nba.fi. The museum café, with a tranquil outdoor courtyard, has light meals and Finnish treats such as lingonberry juice and reindeer quiche (open until 17:00). It's just a five-minute walk from Temppeliaukio Church.

Visiting the Museum: Following the clear English-language descriptions, visit each of the museum's four parts, in chronological order. First, straight ahead from the ticket desk is the **Prehistory of Finland,** where you'll learn how Stone, Bronze, and Iron Age tribes of Finland lived. Back out in the main entrance hall, proceed into **The Realm** (to the left from the ticket desk), which continues upstairs and sends you directly into **A Land and Its People.** Finally, head back down to the ground floor for Finland in **The 20th Century,** starting with the birth of modern Finland in 1917 and its 1918 civil war. Touchscreen tables help tell the story of the fledgling nation, as do plenty of well-presented artifacts (including clothing, household items, vehicles, a typical 1970s living room, and a traditional outhouse). A 15-minute film presents archive newsreel footage from throughout the 20th century.

▲Ateneum, The National Gallery of Finland—This museum showcases Finnish artists on the top floor (mid-18th to 20th century), hosts exhibits, and has a fine international collection including works by Cézanne, Chagall, Gauguin, and Van Gogh.

Cost and Hours: €12, Tue and Fri 10:00-18:00, Wed-Thu 10:00-20:00, Sat-Sun 11:00-17:00, closed Mon, near train station at Kaivokatu 2, tel. 09/173-361, www.ateneum.fi.

▲Sibelius Monument—Six hundred stainless-steel pipes called "Love of Music"—built on solid rock, as is so much of Finland—shimmer in a park to honor Finland's greatest composer, Jean Sibelius. It's a forest of pipe-organ pipes in a forest of trees. The artist, Eila Hiltunen, was forced to add a bust of the composer's face to silence critics of her otherwise abstract work. City

HELSINKI

orientation bus tours stop here for 10 minutes—long enough. Bus #24 stops here (30 minutes until the next bus, or catch a quick glimpse on the left from the bus) on its way to the Seurasaari Open-Air Folk Museum. The #2 tram, which runs more frequently, stops a few blocks away.

Finlandia Hall (Finlandia-Talo)—Alvar Aalto's most famous building in his native Finland means little to the non-architect without a tour. To see the building from its best angle, view it

from the seaside parking lot, not the street—where nearly everyone who looks at the building thinks, "So what?"

Cost and Hours: €11, tours in summer held often at 14:00, call ahead or visit website to check times; hall information shop open Mon-Fri 7:30-17:00, closed Sat-Sun; Mannerheimintie 13e, tel. 09/40241, www.finlandiatalo.fi.

Kiasma Museum—Finland's museum of contemporary art, designed by American architect Steven Holl, hosts temporary exhibitions and doesn't have a permanent collection. Ask at the TI or check online to find out what's showing.

Cost and Hours: €10, Tue 10:00-17:00, Wed-Thu 10:00-20:30, Fri 10:00-22:00, Sat-Sun 10:00-17:00, closed Mon, Mannerheiminaukio 2, near train station, tel. 09/1733-6501, www.kiasma.fi.

Natural History Museum—Recently renovated and run by the University of Helsinki, this museum has about eight million animal specimens, the largest collection of its kind in Finland. Displays range from spiders to dinosaurs, all with English descriptions.

Cost and Hours: €6, free on Thu 16:00-18:00; open Tue-Fri 9:00-16:00 except Thu until 18:00, Sat-Sun 10:00-16:00, closed Mon, Pohjoinen Rautatiekatu 13, www.luomus.fi.

Outer Helsinki

A weeklong car trip up through the Finnish lakes and forests to Mikkeli and Savonlinna would be relaxing, but you can actually enjoy Finland's green-trees-and-blue-water scenery without leaving Helsinki. Here are three great ways to get out and go for a walk on a sunny summer day. If you have time, do at least one of them during your stay.

▲▲Seurasaari Open-Air Folk Museum

Inspired by Stockholm's Skansen, also on a lovely island on the edge of town, this is a collection of 100 historic buildings from

every corner of Finland. It's wonderfully furnished and gives rushed visitors an opportunity to sample the far reaches of Finland without leaving the capital city. If you're not taking a tour, get the €1.20 map or the helpful €6 guidebook. You're welcome to bring a picnic, or you can have a light lunch (snacks and cakes) in the Antti farmstead at the center of the park. Off-season, when the buildings are closed, the place is empty and not worth the trouble.

Cost and Hours: Free park entry, €8 to enter buildings; June-Aug daily 11:00-17:00; late May and early Sept Mon-Fri 9:00-15:00, Sat-Sun 11:00-17:00; closed mid-Sept-mid-May; tel. 09/4050-9660, www.seurasaari.fi.

Tours: English tours are free with €8 entry ticket, offered mid-June-mid-Aug generally at 15:00, and take one hour (confirm times on their website).

Getting There: To reach the museum, ride bus #24 (from the top of the Esplanade, 2/hour) to the end (note departure times for your return) and walk across the quaint footbridge.

▲▲Suomenlinna Fortress

The island guarding Helsinki's harbor served as a strategic fortress for three countries: Finland, Sweden, and Russia. It's now a popular park with several museums and a visitors center located about five minutes from the boat dock. The free Suomenlinna guidebook (stocked at the Helsinki TI, ferry terminal, and the visitors center) covers the island thoroughly.

Cost and Hours: Visitors center-free, Suomenlinna Museum-€6.50, both open daily May-Sept 10:00-18:00, Oct-April 10:30-16:30, tel. 09/684-1850, www.suomenlinna.fi. The island has several skippable smaller museums, including a toy museum and several military museums (€3-4 each, open summer only).

Suomenlinna Timeline

1748—Construction began.

1788—The fort was used as a base for a Swedish war against Russia.

1808—It was surrendered by Sweden to Russia.

1809—Finland became part of the Russian Empire and the fort was used as a Russian garrison for 108 years.

1855—French and British navies bombarded the fort during the Crimean War, inflicting heavy damage.

1917—Finland declared independence.

1918—The fort was annexed by Finland and renamed Suomenlinna.

1939—The fort served as a base for the Finnish navy.

1973—The Finnish garrison moved out, the fort's administration was transferred to the Ministry of Education, and the fort was opened to the public.

Tours: The museum's film on the island's history runs twice hourly (last showing 30 minutes before closing; pick up English translation of exhibits by entrance). The English-language island tour, which runs daily in summer (otherwise only on weekends), departs from the visitors center (€8, free with Helsinki Card, June-Aug daily at 11:00 and 14:00, Sept-May Sat-Sun only at 13:30).

Getting There: Catch a ferry to Suomenlinna from Market Square. Walk past the high-priced excursion boats to the public HKL ferry (€5 round-trip, covered by day ticket and Helsinki Card, 15-minute trip, May-Aug 2-3/hour—generally at :00, :20, and :40 past the hour, but pick up schedule to confirm; Sept-April every 40-60 minutes). If you'll be taking at least two tram rides within 24 hours of visiting Suomenlinna, it pays to get a day ticket instead of a round-trip ticket. A private ferry, JT Line, also runs to Suomenlinna from Market Square in summer (at least hourly, €6.50 round-trip, tel. 09/534-806, www.jt-line.fi).

Background: The fortress was built by the Swedes with French financial support in the mid-1700s to counter Russia's rise to power. (Peter the Great had built his new capital, St. Petersburg, on the Baltic and was eyeing the West.) Named Sveaborg ("Fortress of Sweden"), the fortress was Sweden's military pride and joy. With five miles of walls and hundreds of cannons, it was the second strongest fort of its kind in Europe after Gibraltar. Helsinki, a small community of 1,500 people before 1750, soon became a boomtown supporting this grand "Gibraltar of the North."

The fort, built by more than 10,000 workers, was a huge investment and stimulated lots of innovation. In the 1760s, it had the world's biggest and most modern dry dock. It served as a key naval base during a brief Russo-Swedish war in 1788-1790. But in 1808, the Russians took the "invincible" fort without a fight—by siege—as a huge and cheap military gift.

Visiting Suomenlinna: Today, Suomenlinna has 1,000 permanent residents, is home to Finland's Naval Academy, and is most appreciated by locals for its fine scenic strolls. The island is large—actually, it's four islands connected by bridges—and you and your imagination get free run of the fortifications and dungeon-like chambers. When it's time to eat, you'll find a half-dozen cafés and plenty of picnic opportunities.

Across from the ferry landing are the Jetty Barracks, housing a convenient WC, free modern art exhibit, and the pricey Panimo Brewery restaurant. From here, start your stroll of the island. The garrison church, which was Orthodox until its 20th-century conversion to Lutheranism, doubled as a lighthouse. A five-minute walk from the ferry brings you to the visitors center, which houses the worthwhile Suomenlinna Museum, where the island's complete history is presented in a fascinating 25-minute "multi-vision" show.

From the visitors center, climb uphill to the right into Piper Park, past its elegant 19th-century café, up and over the ramparts to a surreal swimming area. See the King's Gate on the far side of the island before heading back to the ferry.

Peninsula Promenade

For a breezy, salty seaside walk, consider this promenade around the Kaivopuisto Park peninsula. Allow 1.5 hours at a leisurely pace. From Market Square, wander past the old brick market hall and Tallink Silja terminal (with its huge ship likely at the dock) and follow the shoreline pedestrian path. The first island you come to, Valkosaari, hosts the local yacht club—NJK—the oldest in Scandinavia, with a classy restaurant (daily 17:00-24:00). The next island, Luoto, is home to the posh Palace Kämp by the Sea restaurant (with shuttle boat service). During a typical winter, the bay freezes (18 inches of ice is strong enough to allow cars to drive to the islands—in the past there was even a public bus route that extended to an island during the winter). The fortress island of Suomenlinna is in the distance. The hill you're circling (on the right) is home to several embassies; ahead, Ursula Café, with its fine harbor views, is good for a coffee break.

Around the corner, the next island, Uunisaari, belonged to the military until the 1980s. Its unique plant life (much studied by local students) is believed to have hitched a ride all the way to

Finland from Siberia on the boots of Russian soldiers. The odd-looking pier nearby is a station for washing rugs (those are not picnic tables). Saltwater brightens the rag rugs traditionally made by local grandmas. While American men put on aprons and do the barbeque, Finnish men wash the carpets. After the scrub, the rugs are sent through big mechanical wringers and hung on nearby racks to dry in the wind. The posted map shows 11 such stations scattered around Helsinki. Buy an ice cream at the nearby stand and watch the action (best in the morning).

In the distance looms Helsinki's big new West Harbor port, hosting 300 cruise ships a year. From here you can follow Neitsytpolku street back to the town center, keeping an eye out for fun Art Nouveau buildings.

Near Helsinki

Porvoo, the second-oldest town in Finland, has wooden architecture that dates from the Swedish colonial period. This coastal town can be reached from Helsinki by bus (one hour) or by excursion boat from Market Square.

Turku, the historic capital of Finland, is a two-hour bus or train ride from Helsinki. Overall, Turku is a pale shadow of Helsinki, and there is little reason to make a special trip. It does have a handicraft museum in a cluster of wooden houses (the only part of town to survive a devastating fire in the early 1800s), an old castle, a fine Gothic cathedral (this was the first part of Finland to be Christianized, in the 12th century), and a market square. Viking and Tallink Silja boats sail from Turku to Stockholm every morning and evening, passing through the especially scenic Turku archipelago.

Naantali, a cute, commercial, well-preserved medieval town with a quaint harbor, is an easy 20-minute bus ride from Turku.

Shopping in Helsinki

The Esplanade: The Esplanade is capped by the enormous, eight-floor **Stockmann** department store, arguably Scandinavia's most impressive (Mon-Fri 9:00-21:00, Sat 9:00-18:00, open most Sundays 12:00-18:00, great basement supermarket, Aleksanterinkatu 52B, www.stockmann.fi).

The rest of the Esplanade is lined with smaller stores ideal for window-shopping. Keep an eye out for sleek Scan-design gifts. Consider the purses, scarves, clothes, and fabrics from **Marimekko,** the well-known Finnish fashion company famous for striped designs (at #33, plus a new larger branch nearby at the corner of Aleksanterinkatu and Keskuskatu; www.marimekko.com).

The **Artek** store (#18), founded by designers Alvar and Elissa Aalto, showcases expensive, high-end housewares in the modern, practical style that Ikea commercialized successfully for the mass market (www.artek.fi). **Aarikka** (#25) and **Iittala** (#27) also have Finnish housewares and ceramics. Bookworms enjoy the impressive **Academic Bookstore** just before Stockmann (#39, same hours as Stockmann).

Fans of Tove Jansson's Moomin children's stories will enjoy the **Moomin Shop,** on the second floor of the Forum shopping mall at Mannerheimintie 20, across from Stockmann (Mon-Fri 9:00-21:00, Sat 9:00-18:00, Sun 12:00-18:00, www.moomin.fi).

Bus Station: For less glamorous shopping needs, the **Kamppi** mall above and around the bus station is good.

Market Square: This harbor-front square is packed not only with fishmongers and producers, but also with stands selling Finnish souvenirs and more refined crafts (roughly Mon-Fri 6:30-17:00, Sat 6:30-16:00, only tourist stalls open on Sun 10:00-16:00). Sniff the stacks of trivets, made from cross-sections of juniper twigs—an ideal, fragrant, easy-to-pack gift for the folks back home (they smell even nicer when you set something hot on them).

Flea Market: If you brake for garage sales, Finland's biggest flea market, the outdoor **Hietalahti Market,** is worth the 15-minute walk from the harbor or a short ride on tram #6 from Mannerheimintie to the Hietalahdentori stop (June-Aug Mon-Fri 9:00-19:00, Sat 8:00-16:00, Sun 10:00-16:00; less action, shorter hours, and closed Sun off-season). The stalls in the adjacent red-brick indoor market specialize in antiques (Mon-Fri 10:00-17:00, Sat 10:00-15:00, closed Sun).

Unioninkatu: This short street (connecting the harbor with the Lutheran Cathedral) has a few fun shops. **Kalevala Jewelry,** at #25, sells quality made-in-Finland jewelry. Some pieces look modern, while others are inspired by old Scandinavian, Finnish, and Sami themes (VAT refunds available, Mon-Fri 10:00-18:00, Sat 10:00-16:00, closed Sun, tel. 020-761-1380, www.kalevalakoru.com).

Fishermen head next door to #23, where the **Schröder** sporting goods store shows off its famous selection of popular Finnish-made Rapala fishing lures—ideal for the fisherfolk on your gift list.

Sleeping in Helsinki

You have three basic money-saving options: modest but comfortable smaller hotels; discounted big-hotel rooms in summer and on weekends; and unusually comfortable hostels and student dorms that rent plenty of twin-bedded rooms. Also remember that some of the cheapest beds in Helsinki are on the cruise ships to Stockholm.

At most Helsinki hotels, rates vary by the day of the week—with deep discounts on Friday and Saturday nights, and higher rates the rest of the week. From late June to early August, rooms are discounted every day of the week. A few hotels extend the weekend discount to Sunday nights as well. When two prices are listed, the first is for weeknights, the second for weekends and summer.

Of course, hotels play a complicated game of price discrimination with computer programs that tell them exactly how much to charge for a room based on demand, so prices can range above and below what I list. Check the hotel website for exact rates, and shop around to see if someone is offering an especially good deal.

Helsinki Expert's hotel-booking service, with branches at the TI and the train station, can reserve a hotel room for you (€8 booking fee for walk-ins, no fee for requests by phone or email, www.helsinkiexpert.com, also see page 559).

Central Hotels

$$ Hotel Anna is comfortable and feels like home. Its 64 rooms are efficiently run as a fundraiser for the Finnish Free Church. For more air in the rooms, ask at the desk for a key to open the larger windows (Sb-€110/€80, Db-€145/€115, extra bed-€15, reserve by email and mention this book for these prices, often €15-25 per room cheaper in winter or when slow, worth checking website for deals, free Wi-Fi and Internet access, non-smoking, 4 blocks south of the top of the Esplanade—take tram #2/#3 to Iso Roobertinkatu, Annankatu 1, tel. 09/616-621, fax 09/602-664, www.hotelanna.fi, info@hotelanna.fi).

$$ Hotel Arthur, a five-minute walk from the train station on a quiet street, is run by the YMCA, with 182 forgettable, industrial-strength rooms (S-€65/€55, Sb-€110/€80, small twin Db-€130/€100, nicer Db-€150/€120, extra bed-€20, weekend rates also valid Sun night, free Wi-Fi, sauna-€6/hour, non-smoking, by Kaisaniemi tram stop at Vuorikatu 19, tel. 09/173-441, fax 09/626-880, www.hotelarthur.fi, reception@hotelarthur.fi).

$$ Hotelli Finn is inexpensive, newly renovated, and wonderfully central. It's stowed quietly on the sixth floor of an office building near the top of the Esplanade. It's also consciously short

> ## Sleep Code
>
> **(€1 = about $1.30, country code: 358)**
> **S** = Single, **D** = Double/Twin, **T** = Triple, **Q** = Quad, **b** = bathroom,
> **s** = shower. Unless otherwise noted, credit cards are accepted,
> English is spoken, and breakfast is included.
>
> To help you sort easily through these listings, I've divided
> the accommodations into three categories, based on the full
> (non-weekend) price for a standard double room with bath
> during high season:
>
> **$$$ Higher Priced**—Most rooms €150 or more.
> **$$ Moderately Priced**—Most rooms between €80-150.
> **$ Lower Priced**—Most rooms €80 or less.
>
> Prices can change without notice; verify the hotel's
> current rates online or by email.

on amenities: no shower curtains in the tiny bathrooms, no desks or chairs in the rooms, no breakfast (though a nearby bakery offers a €7 buffet spread), no real lobby or common space. The price and location are right, though, and it's a good value for a quick stay when other places aren't discounting (Sb-€69, Db-€79-99, third or fourth person-about €15, best to reserve on website, free Wi-Fi, Kalevankatu 3B, tel. 09/684-4360, fax 09/6844-3610, www.hotelli finn.fi, info@hotellifinn.fi).

$ Omena Hotelli ("Apple Hotel"), with three equally handy 100-room locations in downtown Helsinki, is the newest concept in budget slumbermills. Omena's hotels are entirely automated: You book on the Web, they bill you, and you receive a room access code. The rooms, while spartan, are perfectly good, with flat-screen TVs, refrigerators, microwaves, and modern bathrooms. Because the price is for the room, and each room comes with a double bed and two petite hide-away beds, this can be a fine value for families. But keep in mind that you can't check in until 16:00 (Qb-€45-85, breakfast at nearby cafés runs €6-8, free Wi-Fi, Lönnrotinkatu 13, Eerikinkatu 24, or Yrjönkatu 30, toll booking tel. 0600-18018—only answered Mon-Fri 9:00-16:00, www.omena.com). Check their website for deals and details.

Expensive Hotels with Great Weekend Deals

On Friday and Saturday nights and from late June to early August, Helsinki's more expensive hotels usually have great room deals. Checking the websites of the following places can save you a bundle. Prices sometimes get even better if you agree to a nonrefundable reservation.

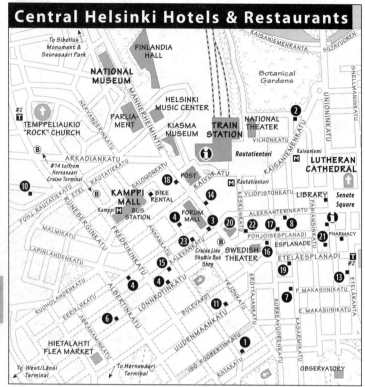

Central Helsinki Hotels & Restaurants

$$$ **Scandic Grand Marina,** a huge 462-room, impersonal four-star hotel filling a big, brick warehouse building near the Viking cruise ship terminal, discounts its doubles from about €190 down to €105 (free Wi-Fi, Katajanokanlaituri 7, tel. 09/16661, www.scandichotels.com/grandmarina, grandmarina@scandic hotels.com).

$$$ **GLO Hotel Art** has 170 modern rooms behind a striking Art Nouveau facade that makes it feel like a stony medieval château has landed in the middle of Helsinki (Db-€154-300, drops to €104-151 in summer and on weekends, air-con, free Wi-Fi, Lönnrotinkatu 29, tel. 010-344-4100, fax 010-344-4101, www.glo hotels.fi, art@glohotels.fi).

$$$ **Hotel Rivoli Jardin** is a cozy 55-room place tucked away right off the Esplanade. Warm and personal, it has an inviting lounge and modern, comfortable rooms (Db-about €190, discounted to around €110 in summer and weekends, extra bed-€20, air-con, pay Wi-Fi, Kasarmikatu 40, tel. 09/681-500, fax 09/656-988, www.rivoli.fi, rivoli.jardin@rivoli.fi).

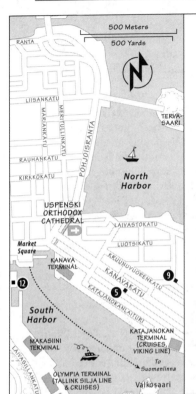

500 Meters
500 Yards

RANTA

LIISANKATU

MARIANKATU
MERTULLINKATU

POHJOISRANTA

TERVA-
SAARI

RAUHANKATU

KIRKKOKATU

USPENSKI
ORTHODOX
CATHEDRAL

North
Harbor

LAIVASTOKATU

Market
Square

LUOTSIKATU

KANAVA
TERMINAL

KRUUNUVUORENKATU

KANAVAKATU

KATAJANOKANLAITURI

South
Harbor

MAKASIINI
TERMINAL

LAIVASILANKATU

KATAJANOKAN
TERMINAL
(CRUISES
VIKING LINE)

To
Suomenlinna

OLYMPIA TERMINAL
(TALLINK SILJA LINE
& CRUISES)

Valkosaari

1. Hotel Anna
2. Hotel Arthur
3. Hotelli Finn
4. Omena Hotelli (3)
5. Scandic Grand Marina Hotel
6. GLO Hotel Art
7. Hotel Rivoli Jardin
8. GLO Hotel Kluuvi
9. Hotel Katajanokka & Eurohostel
10. Academica Summer Hostel
11. Erottajanpuisto Hostel
12. Market Hall Eateries
13. Sundmans Krog Bistro
14. Zetor Restaurant
15. Lappi Restaurant
16. Teatterin Grilli
17. Strindberg Restaurant
18. Lasipalatsi Café
19. Savoy Restaurant
20. Stockmann Dep't Store
21. Café Kappeli
22. Café Aalto (in Academic Bookstore)
23. Ateljee Bar (in Torni Tower)

HELSINKI

$$$ GLO Hotel Kluuvi, which has 144 rooms and a well-designed spa-type quality, gives you an appreciation for how an extremely wealthy society manages to survive a long, dark winter. It's perfectly located just north of the Esplanade (Db-€180-200, but often discounted to €150 or so, air-con, free Wi-Fi, Kluuvikatu 4, tel. 010-3444-400, www.glohotels.fi).

$$$ Hotel Katajanokka is a former red-brick prison built in 1888. Its last prisoner checked out in 2002, and it was converted in 2007 into a four-star, business-class hotel. Its 106 rooms are very quiet—the walls are so thick that the hotel provides free Internet cables rather than Wi-Fi. While the windows no longer have bars (thanks to the local fire code) and walls have been removed so that two or three cells make a room, you can still imagine the guards strolling up and down the corridors (Db-€200, around €140 in summer and on weekends, Sb-€30 less, air-con, bike rental-€10/day, by Vyökatu stop of tram #4 near the Viking cruise ship terminal, Merikasarminkatu 1A, tel. 09/686-450, fax 09/670-290, www.bwkatajanokka.fi, sales@bwkatajanokka.fi).

Hostels

Helsinki's hostels are unusually comfortable. While they offer €3 discounts for those with hostel cards, all ages are welcome with or without a hostel membership. Eurohostel and Academica are more like budget hotels than hostels.

$ Eurohostel, a modern hostel with 255 beds, is 400 yards from the Viking ferry terminal and a 10-minute walk from Market Square. The more expensive rooms have been renovated and come with TVs. It's packed with facilities, including a laundry room, a members' kitchen with unique refrigerated safety-deposit boxes for your caviar and beer, a restaurant, and plenty of good budget-travel information. While generally fully booked in advance, they release no-show beds at 18:00 (S-€45-50, D-€54-61, T-€72-92, family room with up to 4 kids under age 15-€65-73, shared twins or triples-€27-31 per person, includes sheets; breakfast-€8, free morning sauna, evening sauna-€7.50, private lockable closets, pay Wi-Fi, laundry-€3/load, Vyökatu stop for tram #4 is around the corner, Linnankatu 9, tel. 09/622-0470, fax 09/6220-4747, www .eurohostel.fi, eurohostel@eurohostel.fi).

$ Academica Summer Hostel is a university dorm that's professionally run as a hostel from June through August. Finnish university students have it good—the 200 rooms are hotel-quality with private baths and kitchenettes, though all doubles have twin beds. Guests can have a morning sauna and use the swimming pool for free (Sb-€55, Db-€67, Tb-€90, extra bed-€23, bed in shared 2-3-person room-€27, prices include sheets, breakfast-€6.50, safe deposit box, free Wi-Fi and Internet access by reception, laundry-€5/load; tram #2 to the Kauppakorkeakoulut stop, then walk 5 minutes to Hietaniemenkatu 14, tel. 09/1311-4334, fax 09/441-201, www.hostelacademica.fi, hostel.academica@hyy.fi).

$ Erottajanpuisto is a smaller, friendly, centrally located hostel, on the third floor of a 19th-century apartment building. This is a better place to stay than Eurohostel if you're looking to meet fellow travelers in the common room and don't mind lugging your bags up the stairs (15 rooms with 2-8 beds, dorm bed-€27, S-€54-57, D-€68-72, T-€90-96, includes sheets, breakfast-€7, lockers-€2, free Wi-Fi and Internet access, kitchen, no elevator, Uudenmaankatu 9, tel. 09/642-169, fax 09/680-2757, www.erotta janpuisto.com, info@erottajanpuisto.com).

Eating in Helsinki

Helsinki's many restaurants are smoke-free and a good value for lunch on weekdays. Finnish companies get a tax break if they distribute lunch coupons (worth €9) to their employees. It's no surprise that most downtown Helsinki restaurants offer weekday lunch specials that cost exactly the value of the coupon. These low prices evaporate in the evenings and all day Saturday and Sunday, when picnics and Middle Eastern kebab restaurants are the only budget options. Dinner reservations are smart at nicer restaurants.

Fun Harborfront Eateries

Stalls on Market Square: Helsinki's delightful and vibrant square is magnetic any time of day...but especially at lunchtime. This really is the most memorable, casual, quick-and-cheap lunch place in town. A half-dozen orange tents (erected to shield diners from bird bombs) serve fun food on paper plates until 18:00. It's not unusual for the Finnish president to stop by here with visiting dignitaries. There's a crêpe place, and at the far end—my favorites—several salmon grills (€8-9 for a good meal). The only real harborside dining in this part of town is picnicking. While these places provide picnic tables, you can also have your food foil-wrapped to go and grab benches right on the water down near Uspenski Orthodox Cathedral.

Market Hall: Just beyond the harborside market is a cute, red-brick, indoor market hall (Mon-Fri 8:00-18:00, Sat 8:00-16:00, closed Sun). Today, along with produce stalls, it's a hit for its fun, inexpensive eateries. The tiny, four-table **Soppakeittiö** ("Soup Kitchen") serves big bowls of filling, tasty seafood soup for €8.50, including bread and water (Mon-Fri 11:00-16:00, Sat 11:00-15:00—except closed Sat in summer, closed Sun year-round). A sushi place is across the lane. In the middle of the hall, the only slightly larger **Snellman** café is popular for its €3.50 meat pies *(lihapirakka)* and €2.70 pastries called "apple pigs" *(munkkipossu)*.

Sundmans Krog Bistro is sedate and Old World but not folkloric, filling an old merchant's mansion facing the harbor. As it's the less fussy and more affordable (yet still super-romantic) little sister of an adjacent, posh, Michelin-rated restaurant, quality is assured. A rare and memorable extra is their Baltic fish buffet—featuring salmon, Baltic sprat, and herring with potatoes and all the toppings—€14 as a starter, €19 as a main course. The €18 lunch special (Mon-Fri 11:00-15:00) includes the buffet plus the main dish of the week—often more fish (€21-25 main courses, €42-49 three-course dinners, Mon-Fri 11:00-22:00, Sat 12:00-22:00, Sun 13:00-22:00, Eteläranta 16, tel. 09/6128-5450).

Finnish-Themed Dining: Tractors and Lapp Cuisine

Zetor, the self-proclaimed *traktor* restaurant, mercilessly lampoons Finnish rural culture and cuisine (while celebrating it deep down). Sit next to a cow-crossing sign at a tractor-turned-into-a-table, in a "Finnish Western" atmosphere reminiscent of director

Aki Kaurismäki's movies. For lunch or dinner, main courses run €14-20 and include reindeer, vendace (small freshwater fish), and less exotic fare. This place, while touristy and tacky, can be fun. It gets loud after 20:00 when the dance floor gets going (daily 12:00-24:00, 200 yards north of Stockmann department store, across street from McDonald's at Mannerheimintie 3-5, tel. 010-766-4450).

Lappi Restaurant is a fine place for Lapp cuisine, with an entertaining menu (they smoke their own fish) and creative decor that has you thinking you've traveled north and lashed your reindeer to the hitchin' post. The friendly staff serves tasty Sami dishes in a snug and very woody atmosphere. Dinner reservations are strongly recommended (€23-39 main courses, Mon-Fri 12:00-24:00, Sat 13:00-24:00, closed Sun, off Bulevardi at Annankatu 22, tel. 09/645-550).

Venerable Esplanade Cafés

Highly competitive restaurants line the sunny north side of the Esplanade—offering enticing and creative lunch salads and light meals in their cafés (with fine sidewalk seating), plush sofas for cocktails in their bars, and fancy restaurant dining upstairs.

Teatterin Grilli, next to the landmark Swedish Theater, has fine, park-side seating indoors and out. Order a salad from the café counter (€9 with bread, choose two meats or extras to add to crispy base, Caesar salad option). The long cocktail bar is popular with office workers yet comfortable for baby-boomer tourists; there's also a dressy restaurant (café counter open Mon-Sat 11:00-20:00, June-mid-Aug Sun 11:00-20:00, closed Sun off-season, at the top of the Esplanade, Pohjoisesplanadi 2, tel. 09/6128-5000).

Strindberg is also popular (at the corner of the Esplanade and Mikonkatu). Downstairs is an elegant café with outdoor and indoor tables great for people-watching (€8-9 sandwiches and salads). The upstairs cocktail lounge—with big sofas and bookshelves giving it a den-like coziness—attracts the after-work office crowd. Also upstairs, the inviting restaurant has huge main dishes for €18-26, with fish, meat, pasta, and vegetarian options; reserve in advance to try to get a window seat overlooking the Esplanade (restaurant open Mon 11:00-23:00, Tue-Sat 11:00-24:00, closed Sun; café open Mon 9:00-23:00, Tue-Sat 9:00-24:00, Sun 10:00-22:00, Pohjoisesplanadi 33, tel. 09/681-2030).

Functional Eating

Lasipalatsi, the renovated, rejuvenated 1930s Glass Palace, is on Mannerheimintie between the train and bus stations. The café (with a youthful terrace on the square out back) offers a self-service lunch buffet for €12 on weekdays and a €15 brunch on weekends; there are always €5 sandwiches and €4 cakes (lunch/brunch served 11:00-15:00, café open Mon-Fri 7:30-22:00, Sat 9:00-23:00, Sun 11:00-22:00, more expensive restaurant upstairs—closed Sun, across from post office at Mannerheimintie 22-24, tel. 09/612-6700).

Dressy Splurge Dinners

Savoy Restaurant, where locals go for a special occasion, is expensive, formal, and drenched in Alvar Aalto design. Everything—from the chairs and lampshades to the doors—is 1937 original. The food is Continental with a Finnish touch. While the glassed-in terrace offers a great eighth-floor, rooftop view, the interior is where you'll experience a classic Finnish atmosphere (€39-44 main courses, €80 three-course meal, €110-120 four- to five-course meal, Mon-Fri 11:30-14:30 & 18:00-23:00, Sat 18:00-23:00, closed Sun, Eteläesplanadi 14, tel. 09/6128-5300).

Picnics

In supermarkets, buy the semi-flat bread (available dark or light) that Finns love—every slice is a heel. Finnish liquid yogurt is also a treat (sold in liter cartons). Karelian pasties, filled with rice or mashed potatoes, make a good snack. A beautiful, upscale supermarket is in the basement of the **Stockmann** department store—follow the *Delikatessen* signs downstairs (Mon-Fri 9:00-21:00, Sat 9:00-18:00, open most Sun 12:00-18:00, Aleksanterinkatu 52B). Two blocks north, a more workaday, inexpensive supermarket is **S Market,** under the Sokos department store next to the train station (Mon-Sat 7:00-22:00, Sun 10:00-22:00).

Helsinki Connections

By Bus or Train

From Helsinki, it's easy to get to **Turku** (hourly, 2 hours by either bus or train) or **St. Petersburg, Russia** (see options later). For train info, visit www.vr.fi. For bus info in English, consult www.matkahuolto.fi.

By Overnight Boat

Tallink Silja and Viking Line ships sail nightly from Helsinki to **Stockholm** (see beginning of this chapter for details) and **Tallinn** (ferries and—in summer only—fast boats travel the 50 miles many times a day; see the Tallinn chapter for details). See "Arrival in Helsinki" for terminal locations.

By Cruise Ship

For more details on the following ports, and other cruise destinations, pick up my *Rick Steves' Northern European Cruise Ports* guidebook.

Cruise Ports

Cruises arrive in Helsinki at various ports circling two large harbors—West Harbor (Länsistama) and South Harbor (Eteläsatama). Each individual cruise berth is designated by a three-letter code (noted later, along with each terminal's name in both Finnish and Swedish). For a map, see www.portofhelsinki.fi.

Getting Downtown: In addition to the public transit and/or walking options outlined later, many cruise lines offer a **shuttle bus** into downtown (likely €8 one-way, €12 round-trip; especially worth considering if you arrive at the farther-flung West Harbor). This bus usually drops you off across the street from Stockmann department store (near the corner of Mannerheimintie and Lönnrotinkatu). To reach the top of the Esplanade, cross the busy Mannerheimintie boulevard and proceed down the street between the huge, red-brick Stockmann and the white, round Swedish Theater (Svenska Teatern). Another option is to take a **hop-on, hop-off bus tour;** these meet arriving ships at Hernesaari terminal, and are easy to find around the South Harbor (for details, see "Tours in Helsinki," earlier).

West Harbor (Länsistama/Västra Hamnen)

This ugly industrial port is about a mile and a half west of downtown. From either of the two cruise ports here, it's about a €15-20 taxi ride into town.

Hernesaari Terminal (Ärtholmen in Swedish): The primary cruise port for Helsinki sits on the eastern side of West Harbor. It has two berths (Quay B, code: LHB; and Quay C, code: LHC) and a handy TI kiosk where you can pick up free maps and brochures, buy a day ticket for public transit, or use the free Wi-Fi. It's a five-minute walk to the stop for **bus #14,** which takes you downtown: Head through the parking lot, turn left at the street, take the next right, and look for the bus stop (3-6/hour). From here, ride bus #14 to Kamppi (a 10-minute walk from the train station area and the Esplanade) or continue to Kauppakorkeakoulut (near Temppeliaukio, the Church in the Rock—get off the bus, walk straight ahead one block, then turn right up Luthernikatu to find the church). In summer, there's also a **ferry** that goes from Hernesaari to Market Square (€7 one-way, €10 all day, only 3/day starting at 9:30, late June-early Aug daily, early-late June and early-late Aug Sat-Sun only, 30 minutes, mobile 040-736-2329, www.seahelsinki.fi).

West Terminal (Länsiterminaali/Västra Terminalen):
From the cruise berth at Melkki Quay (code: LMA), you'll walk
10 minutes through dull shipyards (follow the green line on the
pavement) to the Länsiterminaali building, with ATMs and other
services. From right in front of this terminal, tram #9 zips into
town (6/hour, handiest downtown stop is Rautatieasema, at the
train station).

South Harbor (Eteläsatama/Södra Hamnen)

This centrally located harbor, which fans out from Market Square,
is an easy walk from downtown (taxis are unnecessary here, but
if you take one, figure €10-15 to most points in the city center).
Ringing this harbor are several terminals for both cruises and
overnight boats; two are most commonly used by cruise ships.

Katajanokan Terminal (Skatudden in Swedish): The harbor's northern embankment has two cruise berths (codes: ERA
and ERB). A third berth (code: EKL), used more by overnight
boats than cruise ships, is closer to town. The Viking Line terminal in this area has ATMs, other services, and—across the street—
the stop for **tram #4T**, which zips you right into town (stops at
City Hall, Senate Square, Lasipalatsi near the train station, and
National Museum). Or you can simply **walk** 15 minutes to Market
Square (stroll between brick warehouses, with the harbor on your
left, toward the white-and-green dome).

Olympia Terminal: Smaller cruise ships use this terminal
(code: EO), along the southern embankment. Inside the terminal
are ATMs and other services; out front is a stop for **tram #2,** which
takes you to Senate Square, then the train station (Rautatieasema
stop), then the Sammonkatu stop near Temppeliaukio (the Church
in the Rock). It's also easy to **walk** into town from here—figure
about 15 minutes (head around the harbor, with the water on your
right, to the white-and-green dome).

The South Harbor berths that are closest to downtown
(**Kanava terminal** and **Makasiini terminal**) are used mostly by
overnight boats, though occasionally overflow cruise ships may
end up there. Either one is an easy five-minute walk to Market
Square.

Connecting Helsinki and St. Petersburg

Many visitors use Helsinki as a launch pad for a visit to St.
Petersburg, Russia—just 240 miles east. For more details on
St. Petersburg, consider my *Rick Steves' Snapshot St. Petersburg,
Helsinki & Tallinn.*

Visa Requirements: American and Canadian travelers to
Russia need a visa, which must be arranged weeks in advance.
You'll need to secure an official "invitation" in St. Petersburg and

HELSINKI

mail your passport to the Russian consulate (for details, US citizens should see www.russianembassy.org; Canadians can consult www.rusembassy.ca). Given the logistical headaches, it's smart to enlist an agency to help obtain an invitation and process your paperwork (I've had a good experience with www.passportvisas express.com). It's not cheap: Plan on $180 for the visa, around a $55 fee for the processing agency, plus around $55 to securely mail your passport to the embassy and back.

Visa Exceptions: If you arrive in St. Petersburg **on a cruise,** the visa requirement is waived provided you contract with a local tour operator (or join one of your cruise line's excursions) for a guided visit around the city—you'll have no free time. But there is an exception that gives you time on your own: If you go to St. Petersburg on a St. Peter Line ship (see below), then pay for a "shuttle service" from the dock into the city (typically €25 round-trip), you can technically stay up to 72 hours before returning with a St. Peter Line shuttle and boat. Although this is not a guided visit, it's treated as the "cruise exception" explained above—at least, it is as of this writing (in late 2012). **Important:** As this loophole may well be closed in the future—and all aspects of the Russian visa situation (especially how far ahead you'll need to apply) change frequently—carefully confirm these details before planning your trip.

By Land: You have two options. The **bus** is slower and cheaper (3/day—departing at 9:00, 12:00, and 23:00; 8-9 hours, €40, less for students, www.matkahuolto.fi); the Allegro **train,** operated by Finnish Railways, is much faster (4/day, 3.5 hours, €76-97 depending on demand, no student discount, www.vr.fi, book ahead by email at international.tickets@vr.fi). There's also a daily overnight train to **Moscow.**

By Sea: Many Baltic Sea **cruises** include a stop in St. Petersburg. But if you're on your own, a relatively new service called **St. Peter Line** can take you there from Helsinki. Their *Princess Maria* sails every other day (3-4/week), departing from Helsinki's West Harbor (from the West/**Länsi terminal**) at 19:00; 14.5 hours later, it reaches St. Petersburg (where it turns around and, at 19:00, heads back to Helsinki). In high season (July-late Aug), the cheapest bunk in a shared four-bed cabin costs €27 one-way; a round-trip "cruise" starts at €150. St. Peter Line's ship *Anastasia* connects St. Petersburg to Tallinn about once weekly, then continues on to Stockholm. For details, see www.stpeterline .com; Helsinki Expert also has information.

ESTONIA

ESTONIA

Eesti

 Estonians are related to the Finns and have a similar history—first Swedish domination, then Russian (1710-1918), and finally independence after World War I. In 1940, Estonians were at least as affluent and as advanced as the Finns, but they could not preserve their independence from Soviet expansion during World War II. As a result, Estonia sank into a 50-year communist twilight from which it is still emerging. In 2004, Estonia took a significant step forward when it joined the European Union. Estonia switched its currency from the krooni to the euro in January of 2011.

Estonia will always face both West, across the Baltic; and East, into the Russian hinterlands. After the Cold War, the pendulum has swung further West. EU membership seemed like a natural step to many Estonians; they already thought of themselves as part of the Nordic world. Language, history, religion, and twice-hourly ferry departures connect Finns and Estonians. Only 50 miles separate Helsinki and Tallinn, and Stockholm is just an overnight boat ride away. Finns visit Tallinn to eat, drink, and shop more cheaply than at home. While some Estonians resent how Tallinn becomes a Finnish nightclub on summer weekends, most people on both sides are happy to have friendly new neighbors.

One problematic legacy of the Soviet experience is Estonia's huge Russian population. Most Estonian Russians' parents and grandparents were brought to Estonia in the 1950s and 1960s to work in now-defunct factories in Tallinn and the northeastern cities. Twenty-five percent of Estonia's population is now ethnically Russian. Making Russians feel at home in Estonia while building a distinctly Estonian culture and identity is one of independent Estonia's biggest challenges. In 2007, Tallinn made international headlines when it controversially relocated a giant "Liberation Monument" depicting a WWII-era Russian soldier (as well as actual remains of Soviet soldiers) from the city center to a cemetery on the outskirts of town. This sparked protests in both Tallinn and Moscow. In retaliation, Estonia suffered a flurry of cyber attacks

Estonia Almanac

Official Name: Eesti Vabariik—the Republic of Estonia—or simply Estonia.

Population: Estonia is home to 1.3 million people (77 per square mile). Nearly three in four are of Estonian heritage, and about one-quarter are of Russian descent, with smaller minorities of Ukrainians, Belarusians, and Finns. About 70 percent speak the official language—Estonian—and nearly 30 percent speak Russian. The majority of Estonians are unaffiliated with any religion. About 14 percent are Lutheran and 13 percent are Orthodox.

Latitude and Longitude: 59°N and 26°E, similar latitude to Juneau, Alaska.

Area: 17,500 square miles, about the size of New Hampshire and Vermont combined.

Geography: Between Latvia and Russia, Estonia borders the Baltic Sea and Gulf of Finland. It includes more than 1,500 islands and islets, and has the highest number of meteorite craters per land area in the world.

Biggest City: The capital of Estonia, Tallinn, has 400,000 people (500,000 in the metropolitan area).

Economy: Estonia's transition to a free-market system included joining the World Trade Organization and the European Union. Once a Baltic tiger, its economy was hard-hit by the recent economic downturn. But Estonia is making a comeback: It now has the highest GDP growth rate in Europe and boasts a per-capita GDP of $20,600—the highest of the Baltic states. Its three major trading partners are Finland, Sweden, and Germany; its strengths are electronics and telecommunications (the country is so wired that its nickname is E-stonia).

Currency: €1 (euro) = about $1.30.

Government: Estonia is a parliamentary democracy, with a president elected by parliament (Toomas Hendrik Ilves, since October of 2006) and a prime minister (Andrus Ansip, since April of 2005). The 101-member parliament (Riigikogu) is elected by popular vote every four years.

Flag: The pre-1940 Estonian flag was restored in 1990. It has three equal horizontal bands with blue at the top, black in the middle, and white on the bottom. The blue represents Estonia's lakes and sea, and the loyalty and devotion of the country to its people. The black symbolizes the homeland's rich soil and the hardships the people have suffered. The white represents hope and happiness.

The Average Estonian: He or she is 40 years old, has 1.4 children, and will live to be 72. About 58 percent of the population are women (they live longer), and when she sings the national anthem, she uses the same melody as Finland.

in which many of its governmental, political, and business websites were crippled. Many of the attacks originated within Russia, leading some to allege that the Kremlin was waging "cyber war." Since then, Estonia has taken an international leadership role in Internet security.

But despite a sometimes fitful adjustment to its post-Soviet reality, Estonia is a welcoming place. Younger Estonians speak English—it's the first choice these days at school. Estonian is similar to Finnish and equally difficult. Only a million people speak Estonian worldwide. Two useful phrases to know are *"Tänan"* (TAH-nahn; "Thank you") and *"Terviseks!"* (TEHR-vee-sehks; "Cheers!"). If you'd like to learn a few more phrases, see the Estonian survival phrases on page 693. The farther you go beyond the touristy zones, the

more you see that Russian is still Estonia's second language. If you know some Russian, use it. It's the mother tongue of more than 40 percent of Tallinners (many of whom have no intention of learning Estonian).

TALLINN

Tallinn is a rising star in the tourism world, thanks to its strategic location (an easy boat ride from Stockholm, Helsinki, and St. Petersburg); its perfectly preserved, atmospheric Old Town, bursting with quaint sightseeing options; and its remarkable economic boom since throwing off Soviet shackles just over two decades ago. Easily the most accessible part of the former USSR, Estonia was only the third post-communist country to adopt the euro (in 2011) and has weathered recent Europe-wide economic crises like a champ. While the city still struggles to more effectively incorporate its large Russian minority, Tallinn feels ages away from its Soviet past—having eagerly reclaimed its unique Nordic identity. Estonian pride is in the air...and it's catching.

If you're pondering a cultural detour on your Nordic vacation, Tallinn is a logical choice—Estonia is quite different from the Scandinavian countries, and Tallinn is easily reached on a night cruise from Stockholm, a fast boat ride from Helsinki, or a quick flight from any Scandinavian capital. Tallinn has great restaurants, affordable shopping (rare in this expensive corner of Europe), and atmosphere in spades. While it can be seen on a quick side-trip from Helsinki, Tallinn is mobbed with day-trippers (mostly cruise passengers) and rewards those who spend the night. While its Old Town is (understandably) a magnet for visitors, there's also a lot to see outside its ancient walls. Give yourself a few extra days for a stopover in Tallinn, or do both Tallinn and Helsinki as a triangular side-trip from Stockholm.

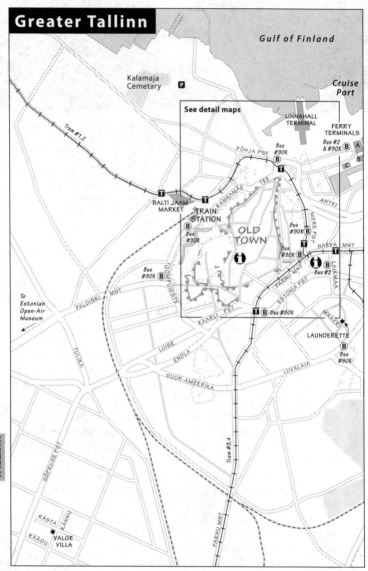

Getting to Tallinn

You have two basic options (both described in detail next): A slow overnight boat ride from Stockholm, or a fast daytime boat from Helsinki.

Sailing from Stockholm to Tallinn

Tallink Silja's ships leave Stockholm at 17:45 every evening and

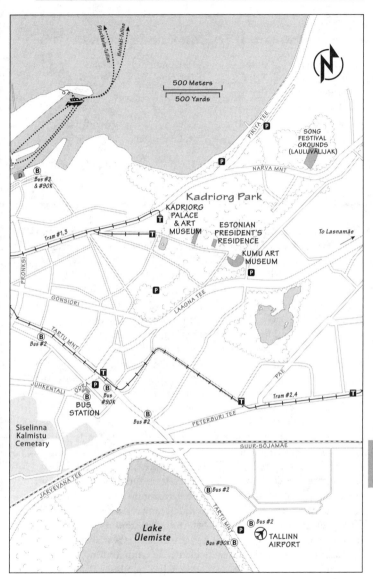

arrive in Tallinn at 10:00 the next morning. Return trips leave Tallinn at 18:00 and arrive in Stockholm at 10:00. All times are local (Tallinn is an hour ahead of Stockholm).

Fares vary by the day and season—higher on Friday and Saturday nights and from July 1 to August 15, and lower on Sunday through Thursday nights the rest of the year. A one-way berth in a four-person, sex-segregated cabin with a private bath costs

Helsinki/Tallinn Connections

Company	Ship Type	Helsinki Terminal	Helsinki Phone #
Tallink Silja	Ferries	Länsi	0600-15700
Linda Line	Catamarans	Makasiini	0600-668-9700
Eckerö Line	Ferries	Länsi	09/228-8544
Viking Line	Ferries	Katajanokan	09/12351

Note: Finland's country code is 358 (drop initial zero of area code when calling Finland internationally).

€52 (weekends and summer) or €39 (weeknights). Couples can travel in a private cabin for €200 (weekends and summer) or €150 (weeknights).

An onboard breakfast is €10, and the *smörgåsbord* dinner is €30. Reserve your meal (and even, if possible, a window table) when you buy your ticket. The boats have exchange offices with acceptable rates for your leftover euros or Swedish kronor.

Online bookings are encouraged, and the sophisticated website lets you reserve extras such as hotels and excursions. The website is also the place to check for bargains. Booking by phone or in person at downtown offices costs €5 extra. If you just have questions, the reservations lines will answer them for free (Swedish tel. 08/222-140, Estonian tel. 640-9808, www.tallinksilja.com).

In Stockholm, Tallink Silja ships leave from the Värtahamnen harbor. To get there from downtown Stockholm, take the Tallink Silja shuttle bus from the train station (50 kr, departs according to boat schedule), or take the T-bana (subway, 36 kr) to the Gärdet station, then walk 10 minutes to the harbor. On Mondays through Saturdays, public bus #76 (direction: Ropsten) takes you directly to the terminal (leaves from several downtown locations, including Kungsträdgården; get off at Färjeterminalen stop). For Stockholm public transit information, see page 425 and www.sl.se/english. In Tallinn, Tallink Silja ships dock at D-Terminal (see "Arrival in Tallinn," later).

Age Restrictions: Travelers ages 18-20 are not permitted on the Stockholm-Tallinn route unless accompanied by a parent or guardian. Exceptions may be possible with a permission form or documented reason. Before making plans, contact Tallink Silja by phone or email to clarify your individual situation.

Speeding Between Helsinki and Tallinn

Four different companies—shown in the table above—offer ferry

TALLINN

Company	Tallinn Terminal	Tallinn Phone #	Website
Tallink Silja	D	640-9808	www.tallinksilja.com
Linda Line	Linnahall	699-9333	www.lindaline.ee
Eckerö Line	A	664-6000	www.eckeroline.fi
Viking Line	A	666-3966	www.vikingline.fi

Note: Estonia's country code is 372 (dial number in full when calling Estonia internationally).

trips between Helsinki and Tallinn. Fares run €20-55 one-way (evening departures from Helsinki and morning departures from Tallinn tend to be cheaper; student and senior discounts available). Their websites have all the latest information and prices. If you travel round-trip on the same day, your ticket will cost barely more than a one-way fare, but you'll have just a few hours on shore. Prices differ only slightly from company to company— base your choice on the most convenient departure times and ferry terminal locations. Make sure you know which terminal your boat leaves from and how to get to it (for descriptions of Helsinki's terminals, see page 555; for Tallinn's, see "Arrival in Tallinn," later).

Unless you're bringing a car, the Linda and Viking lines are usually the most convenient, as their docks in Helsinki and Tallinn are easy to reach by foot or public transport. **Linda Line** uses 400-passenger, Australian-made catamarans that zip across the Gulf of Finland in just 1.5 hours (6-7/day March-Oct, 3-5/day Nov-Feb). Boats leave from the Makasiini terminal in Helsinki's South Harbor (Eteläsatama), just five minutes' walk from Market Square, and arrive in Tallinn at the Linnahall terminal. Catamarans lack the spacious party atmosphere of larger boats, and are slightly more expensive (but they're the only ones that offer discounts on non-same-day round-trips). Cancellations, which can occur in stormy conditions, rarely happen in summer; still, if you have a plane to catch, play it safe and take a regular ferry. **Viking Line** leaves from the other side of Helsinki's South Harbor (Katajanokan terminal), and arrives at Tallinn's A-Terminal. Viking offers a more traditional experience on a big ferry with restaurants and shops (2/day, 2.5-hour crossing, generally a few euros less than Linda Line).

Tallink Silja and **Eckerö Line** leave from the relatively inconvenient Länsi terminal at Helsinki's West Harbor (Länsistama), which you can reach on tram #9 (catch it at Kamppi mall in downtown Helsinki; the terminal is the end of the line). At the other end of the journey, Tallink Silja uses Tallinn's D-Terminal—the farthest from the Old Town, making it a bit less convenient but still walkable. On the other hand, Tallink Silja's ferries are frequent and fast (6-7/day, 2-hour crossing). Eckerö Line has just one slow, inexpensive sailing per day (3.5-hour crossing).

Slower boats—all except Linda Line—have *smörgåsbord* buffets (€10 for breakfast, €26 for dinner). The slower the boat, the more likely it is to be filled with "four-legged Finns" crazy about cheap booze, slot machines, and karaoke.

Advance reservations aren't essential, but usually save a little money, ensure your choice of departure, and provide peace of mind. The boat lines encourage online booking with small discounts and, increasingly, have only toll phone numbers—something to keep in mind if you need to talk to a real person. You can also buy tickets at the port or at travel agencies. The helpful **Helsinki Expert** desk in the Helsinki TI sells tickets (€8 fee per booking) and posts a sheet clearly explaining departures and costs. The TI in Tallinn posts a list but does not sell tickets, though you'll find travel agencies in the Old Town that do (see "Helpful Hints," later).

Tallinn

Among Nordic medieval cities, there's none nearly as well-preserved as Tallinn. Its mostly intact city wall includes 26 watchtowers, each topped by a pointy red roof. Baroque and choral music ring out from its old Lutheran churches. I'd guess that Tallinn (with 400,000 people) has more restaurants, cafés, and surprises per capita and square inch than any city in this book—and the fun is comparatively cheap.

Though it's connected by an easy boat trip to Helsinki and Stockholm, Tallinn feels a world removed from those cities. Yes, Tallinn's Nordic Lutheran culture and language connect it with Scandinavia, but two centuries of tsarist Russian rule and 45 years as part of the Soviet Union have blended in a distinctly Russian flavor.

As a member of the Hanseatic League, the city was a medieval stronghold of the Baltic trading world. (For more on the Hanseatic League, see the sidebar on page 372.) In the 19th and early 20th centuries, Tallinn industrialized and expanded beyond its walls. Architects encircled the Old Town, putting up broad streets of public buildings, low Scandinavian-style apartment buildings, and single-family wooden houses. After 1945, Soviet planners ringed the city with stands of now-crumbling concrete high-rises where many of Tallinn's Russian immigrants settled. Like Prague and Kraków, Tallinn has westernized at an astounding rate since the fall of the Soviet Union in 1991. Yet the Old World ambience within its walled town center has been beautifully preserved.

Tallinn is still busy cleaning up the mess left by the communist experiment. New shops, restaurants, and hotels are bursting out of old buildings. The city

changes so fast, even locals can't keep up. The Old Town is getting a lot of tourist traffic now, so smart shopping is wise. You'll eat better for half the price by seeking out places that cater to locals.

Tallinn's Old Town is a fascinating package of pleasing towers, ramparts, facades, *striptiis* bars, churches, shops, and people-watching. It's a rewarding detour for those who want to spice their Scandinavian travels with a Baltic twist.

Planning Your Time

On a three-week tour of Scandinavia, Tallinn is certainly worth a day. Get oriented with either the official walking tour or my self-guided walk. Check concert schedules if you'll be around for the evening.

Day-Trippers: Whether arriving from Helsinki or Stockholm, hit the ground running by following my self-guided walk right from the ferry terminal. Enjoy a nice restaurant in the Old Town for lunch. Then spend the afternoon shopping and browsing (or out at the Estonian Open-Air Museum if you enjoy folk history, or at the Kumu Art Museum if you like art).

Note that Tallinn can be inundated with cruise passengers and other day-trippers; if the Old Town is simply too jammed, consider getting out of town (Kadriorg Park is pleasant) and coming back when it's less crowded.

Remember to bring a jacket—Tallinn can be chilly even on sunny summer days. And, given that locals call their cobbled streets "a free foot massage," sturdy shoes are smart, too.

Orientation to Tallinn

Tallinn's walled Old Town is an easy 15-minute walk from the ferry and cruise terminals, where most visitors land (see "Arrival in Tallinn," later). The Old Town is divided into two parts (historically, two separate towns): the upper town (Toompea), and the

lower town, with Town Hall Square. A remarkably intact medieval wall surrounds the two towns, which are themselves separated
by another wall.

Town Hall Square (Raekoja Plats) marks the heart of the
medieval lower town. The main TI is nearby, as are many sights
and eateries. Pickpockets have become a problem in the more
touristy parts of the Old Town, so keep valuables carefully stowed.
The area around the Viru Keskus mall and Hotel Viru, just east
of the Old Town, is useful for everyday shopping (bookstores and
supermarkets), practical services (laundry and Internet café), and
public transport.

Tourist Information

The hardworking, English-speaking **TI** has maps, concert listings, and free brochures. It also sells *Tallinn in Your Pocket* and
the Tallinn Card, both described later (May-Aug Mon-Fri 9:00-
19:00—until 20:00 mid-June-Aug, Sat-Sun 9:00-17:00—until
18:00 mid-June-Aug; Sept-April Mon-Fri 9:00-18:00, Sat-Sun
9:00-15:00; a block off Town Hall Square at Kullassepa 4, tel. 645-
7777, www.tourism.tallinn.ee, turismiinfo@tallinnlv.ee).

Travellers' Tent isn't an official information center, but a creative service offered by young people for young visitors. Working
from a tent in the park immediately
in front of the TI, the friendly staff
is a great source for backpacker info,
youthful tours, bike rental, and cheap
accommodations (daily June-Aug
10:00-18:00, mobile 5837-4800).
Their free map is packed with fun
tips to enjoy Tallinn down, dirty, and
on the cheap. While their map and
information services are free, they

appreciate donations. Consider their inexpensive and spirited tours
(see "Tours in Tallinn," later).

Tallinn in Your Pocket is the best city guidebook on Tallinn
(may be free at your hotel, otherwise €2.20 all over town, on ships,
at airport newsstands, and at the TIs). It's worth buying for its
complete restaurant, hotel, and sight listings that go far beyond
what's in this book (for pre-trip planning, use the online edition at
www.inyourpocket.com).

Tallinn Card: This card—sold at the TIs, airport, train station, travel agencies, ferry ports, and big hotels—gives you free
use of public transport and entry to more than 40 museums and
major sights (€12/6 hours, €24/24 hours, €32/48 hours, €40/72
hours, comes with good info booklet, www.tallinncard.ee). From
the 24-hour level up, it includes one tour of your choice, plus a 50

percent discount on any others—by bus, by bike, or on foot (see "Tours in Tallinn," later, for specifics). If you're planning to take one of these tours (otherwise €13-20) and to visit several sights (otherwise €3-6), this card will likely save you money. Add up the cost of your intended sightseeing to confirm. But don't buy the card primarily for its public transport benefits, as transit passes are much cheaper.

Arrival in Tallinn

For advice on taking taxis, and more details on the public transportation options mentioned below, see "Getting Around Tallinn," later.

By Boat or Cruise Ship: Tallinn has four terminals lettered A through D, a fifth one called Linnahall (used only by the fast Linda Line boat), and a dedicated cruise terminal. A-Terminal, B-Terminal, and C-Terminal are clustered together; the cruise terminal is just to the north; D-Terminal is a 10-minute walk to the east (and the farthest from Old Town); the Linnahall terminal is a 10-minute walk to the west (just over the large stairway). Each terminal offers baggage storage. Be sure to confirm which terminal your return boat will use. The main cruise pier can accommodate two large ships; when more are in town, they may use one of the other terminals.

If you have no luggage, you can **walk** 15 minutes to reach the center of town—just follow signs to the city center and set your sights on the tallest spire in the distance (or follow my self-guided walk, later). If you have bags, it's best to grab a **taxi**—otherwise your rolling suitcase will take a pounding on the Old Town's cobbled streets and gutter-ridden sidewalks. While the legitimate taxi fare to anywhere in or near the Old Town should be less than €5, unscrupulous cabbies may try to charge double or triple.

To get into town by bus, you have several options: Public **bus #2** goes from A-Terminal and D-Terminal directly to the "A. Laikmaa" stop—behind Hotel Viru and the Viru Keskus mall, just south of the Old Town—then continues to the airport (2/hour, buy transit pass or €1 ticket from kiosks in terminals). The privately run bus **#90K** also carries travelers between A-Terminal, D-Terminal, and downtown, but costs a bit more and takes a different route: It loops around the northern end of the Old Town, stopping at the train station, then curls to the south (stopping at major hotels en route) before heading to the bus station and airport (€2, 3/hour, get off at the Viru stop, www.hansabuss.ee). From the Linnahall terminal, Linda Line provides a **shuttle bus** (€2) to major downtown points for its passengers. Cruise lines sometimes also offer a shuttle bus into town (to the Russian Cultural Center, near Hotel Viru), but—since it's so easy to just stroll from the port into town—this isn't worth paying for.

By Plane: The convenient Tallinn airport (Tallinna Lennu-jaam), just three miles southeast of downtown, has a small info desk (airport code: TLL, www.tallinn-airport.ee, tel. 605-8888). A **taxi** to the Old Town should cost €8-10. Public **bus #2** runs every 20-30 minutes from the lower entrance (floor 0) into town; the seventh stop, "A. Laikmaa," is behind the Viru Keskus mall, a short walk from the Old Town (departs from curb in front of airport arrivals area, buy transit pass or €1 ticket from kiosk in terminal). Alternatively, the privately run **bus #90K** does a loop from the airport, with stops near the Old Town, the port's D- and A-terminals, and the train station.

By Train and Bus: While Tallinn has a sleepy and cute little train station (called Balti Jaam), few tourists will need to use it. The station, a five-minute walk across a busy road from the Old Town, is adjacent to the big, cheap Hotel Shnelli and the colorful Balti Jaam Market. Tallinn's long-distance bus station *(autobussi-jaam)* is midway between downtown and the airport, and served by bus #2 and trams #2 and #4, as well as by bus #90K.

Helpful Hints

Money: Estonia uses the euro. You'll find ATMs (sometimes marked *Otto*) at locations around Tallinn.

Telephones: In case of a medical emergency, dial 112. For police, dial 110. Most Estonian phone numbers are seven to eight digits with no area codes. Tallinn numbers begin with 6, and mobile phones (more expensive to call) begin with 5. (From outside Estonia, you'll first dial the country code: 372; for more on dialing, see page 657.)

Internet Access: Metro 24 is on the lower level of the Viru Keskus mall, where city buses depart (across from platform 6; €2.60/hour, Mon-Fri 7:00-23:00, Sat-Sun 10:00-23:00, tel. 610-1519). The **main TI** has one terminal where you can briefly check your email for free. There are open Wi-Fi networks literally all over town; look for the orange-and-black "wifi.ee" logo in shop windows. Every hotel I list offers free Wi-Fi, and some have a computer for guests to use.

Laundry: Pesumaja Sol is just walkable from the Old Town, beyond the Viru Keskus mall and Kaubamaja department store (or take tram #2 or #4 to the Paberi stop, a few blocks away—see map on page 602). Choose between self-serve (€5/load, ask staff to interpret Estonian-only instructions) or full-service (€9.50/load, Mon-Fri 7:00-20:00, Sat 8:00-16:00, closed Sun, Maakri 23, tel. 677-1551).

Travel Agency: Estravel, at the corner of Suur-Karja and Müürivähe, is as good as any. It's handy and sells boat tickets

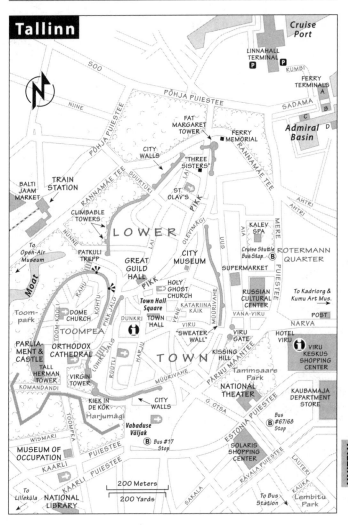

for no extra fee (Mon-Fri 9:00-18:00, closed Sat-Sun, Suur-Karja 15, tel. 626-6233).

Bike Rental: Head for **City Bike,** at the north end of the Old Town near the ferry terminals (one-speeds-€7.50/6 hours, €10/24 hours; better bikes-€10/6 hours, €13/24 hours; includes helmet and reflective vest; daily May-Sept 9:00-19:00, Oct-April 9:00-17:00, Uus 33, mobile 511-1819, www.citybike.ee). They also do bike tours (see "Tours in Tallinn," later).

Parking: The Port of Tallinn has a cheap lot by D-Terminal (€5/day, www.portoftallinn.com). Old Town parking is very expensive.

Getting Around Tallinn

By Public Transportation: The Old Town and surrounding areas can be explored on foot, but use public transit to reach outlying sights (such as Kadriorg Park, Kumu Art Museum, or Estonian Open-Air Museum). Tallinn has buses, trams, and trolleys (buses connected to overhead wires)—avoid mistakes by noting that they reuse the same numbers (bus #2, tram #2, and trolley #2 are totally different lines). Maps and schedules are posted at stops, or visit http://soiduplaan.tallinn.ee (for an overview of transit stops useful to visitors, see the "Greater Tallinn" map on page 602).

Stop by any yellow-and-blue R Kiosk convenience store (found all over town) to buy a ticket, then stamp it in the machine on board. Single tickets cost €1; a pack of 10 is €8. A 24-hour pass (valid from the moment it's stamped) is handy and costs €4. The 72-hour (€6) and 120-hour (€7) passes are even better deals. Drivers grudgingly sell single tickets on board for €1.60, but not passes.

Bus #2 (Moigu-Reisisadam) is helpful on arrival and departure, running every 20-30 minutes between the ferry port's A-Terminal and the airport. En route it stops at D-Terminal; at "A. Laikmaa," next to the Viru Keskus mall (a short walk south of the Old Town); and at the long-distance bus station.

Bus #90K is also convenient, connecting many of the same stops—and additional ones—in a different order (airport, southern end of Old Town, D-Terminal, A-Terminal, train station, northern and western ends of Old Town, then back to the airport); however, since it's privately run, it is not covered by regular bus tickets or passes (€2, 3/hour, www.hansabuss.ee).

By Taxi: Taxis in Tallinn are handy, but it's easy to get ripped off. The safest way to catch a cab is to order one by phone (or ask a trusted local to call for you)—this is what Estonians usually do. Tulika is the largest company, with predictable, fair prices (€3.10 drop charge plus €0.65/kilometer, €0.77/kilometer from 23:00-6:00, tel. 612-0001 or 1200, check latest prices at www.tulika.ee). Cabbies are required to use the meter and to give you a meter-printed receipt. If you don't get a receipt, it's safe to assume you're being ripped off and legally don't need to pay. Longer rides around the city (e.g., from the airport to the Old Town) should run around €8-10.

If you must catch a taxi off the street, go to a busy taxi stand where lots of cabs are lined up. It's also OK to use the stands at the airport and ferry terminals. Before doing *anything* else, take a close look at the yellow price list on the rear passenger-side door; the base fare should be around €3.10 and the per-kilometer charge under €1. If it's not, keep looking. Glance inside—a photo ID license should be attached to the middle of the dashboard. Don't negotiate or ask for a price estimate; let the driver use the meter. Rates must be posted by law, but are not capped or regulated, so the most common scam—unfortunately widespread, and legal—is to list an inflated price on the yellow price sticker (as much as €3/kilometer), and simply wait for a tourist to hop in without noticing. Singleton cabs lurking in tourist areas are usually fishing for suckers, as are cabbies who flag you down ("Taxi?")—give them a miss. It's fun to play spot-the-scam as you walk around town.

Tours in Tallinn

Bus and Walking Tour—This thoroughly enjoyable, narrated 2.5-hour tour of Tallinn comes in two parts: first by bus for an overview of sights outside the Old Town such as the Song Festival Grounds and Kadriorg Park, then on foot to sights within the Old Town (€20, pay driver; covered by 24-hour or longer Tallinn Card—not the 6-hour version; in English and Finnish; daily morning and early afternoon departures from A-Terminal, D-Terminal, and major hotels in city center, later afternoon trip added in summer, tel. 610-8634—to see the schedule, go to www.tourism.tallinn.ee and type "official sightseeing tour"—without quotes—in search box).

Local Guides—**Mati Rumessen** is a top-notch guide, especially for car tours inside or outside town (€32/hour for driving or walking tours, mobile 509-4661, www.tourservice.ee, mati700@hot.ee). Other fine guides are **Antonio Villacis** (mobile 5662-9306, antonio.villacis@gmail.com) and **Miina Puusepp** (€20/hour, mobile 551-7028, miinap@hot.ee).

Tallinn Traveller Tours—These student-run tours show you the real city without the political and corporate correctness of official tourist agencies. All tours start from the Travellers' Tent, across from the main TI; reserve by dropping by the tent, by calling (mobile 5837-4800), or online (www.traveller.ee). Their **City Introductory Walking Tour** is free, but tips are encouraged (around €5/person if you enjoy yourself, daily at 12:00, 2 hours, English only, runs year-round; off-season, this tour meets at the corner just outside the TI). The **Tallinn Ghost and Legends Tour** promises a spooky evening of ghost stories (€13, Tue, Thu, and Sat at 21:00). On the **Funky Bike Tour,** you'll pedal through industrial zones and offbeat residential districts, learn about the divide between Estonian and Russian speakers, and visit an old prison (€13, June-Aug daily at 12:00, 3.5 hours). The **Beautiful Bike Tour** takes you to the Song Festival Grounds, Kadriorg, and more (€13, June-Aug daily at 16:00, 3.5 hours). They also offer a minibus excursion to the **Western Coast** and the Soviet military town of Paldiski (€39, daily at 10:00, 7 hours), and one to **Lahemaa**

Tallinn at a Glance

▲▲▲**Tallinn's Old Town** Well-preserved medieval center with cobblestoned lanes, gabled houses, historic churches, and turreted city walls. **Hours:** Always open. See page 615.

▲▲**Kumu Art Museum** The best of contemporary Estonian art displayed in a strikingly modern building. **Hours:** May-Sept Tue-Sun 11:00-18:00, closed Mon; Oct-April Wed-Sun 11:00-18:00, closed Mon-Tue; open Wed until 20:00 year-round. See page 627.

▲**Museum of Occupation** Estonia's tumultuous, sometimes secret history under Soviet and Nazi occupiers from 1940 to 1991. **Hours:** June-Aug Tue-Sun 10:00-18:00, Sept-May Tue-Sun 11:00-18:00, closed Mon year-round. See page 625.

▲**Kadriorg Park** Vast, strollable oasis with the palace gardens, Kumu Art Museum, and a palace built by Tsar Peter the Great. **Hours:** Park always open. See page 626

▲**Song Festival Grounds** National monument and open-air theater where Estonians sang for freedom. **Hours:** Open long hours. See page 630.

▲**Estonian Open-Air Museum** Authentic farm and village buildings preserved in a forested parkland. **Hours:** Late April-Sept—park open daily 10:00-20:00, buildings open until 18:00; Oct-late April—park open daily 10:00-17:00 but buildings closed. See page 631.

Town Hall and Tower Gothic building with history museum and climbable tower on the Old Town's main square. **Hours:** Museum—July-Aug Mon-Sat 10:00-16:00, closed Sun and rest of year; tower—May-mid-Sept daily 11:00-18:00, closed rest of year. See page 625.

National Park east of town (€49, daily at 10:00, 9 hours). Both excursions go year-round but require at least two people to run. You can also book any one of these tours for your own small group for the same per-person price (4-person minimum).

Hop-on, Hop-off Bus Tours—Tallinn City Tours offers three different one-hour bus tours—you can take all three (on the same day) for one price. Aside from a stop near Toompea Castle, the routes are entirely outside the Old Town, and the frequency is low (just 5/day May-Sept, 2/day Oct-April, so you need to coordinate your sightseeing to the infrequent departures). But if you want to rest your feet and listen to a fairly good recorded commentary, the tours do get you to outlying sights such as Kadriorg and the towering Russalka Monument. You can catch the bus at the port terminals and near the Viru Turg clothing market (€16, free with Tallinn Card valid for 24 hours or more, 5 daily departures May-Sept plus some summer evening trips, 2 daily departures Oct-April, tel. 627-9080, www.citytour.ee). **CitySightseeing Tallinn** also runs three similar routes, with a similarly sparse frequency (€16, or €13 for just one "basic" line, www.citysightseeing.ee).

City Bike Tours—City Bike offers a two-hour, nine-mile **Welcome to Tallinn** bike tour that takes you outside the city walls to Tallinn's more distant sights: Kadriorg, Song Festival Grounds, the beach at Pirita, and more (€16, free with Tallinn Card valid 24 hours or more; includes helmet and reflective vest, daily at 11:00 year-round, weather permitting, departs from their office at Uus 33 in the Old Town). They also run a **Soviet Bike Tour** with an emphasis on Tallinn's USSR connection, stopping at Kadriorg Park, the Song Festival Grounds, the Lasnamäe suburb, and the Maarjamäe WWII Memorial (€13, free or discounted with Tallinn Card, daily May-Sept at 16:00, same departure point). They also do €49 day trips (car and bike) to **Lahemaa National Park** (see page 631) and will arrange multiday, self-guided bike tours around Estonia (mobile 511-1819, www.citybike.ee).

Toomas the Tourist Train—This red choo-choo train, mostly for kids and their parents, leaves (when full) from the top of Town Hall Square (€5, June-Aug daily 12:00-17:00, May and Sept Sat-Sun only, doesn't run Oct-April, look for *Rong Toomas* sign).

Self-Guided Walk

▲▲▲Welcome to Tallinn

This walk explores the "two towns" of Tallinn. The city once consisted of two feuding medieval towns separated by a wall. The upper town—on the hill, called Toompea—was the seat of government ruling Estonia. The lower town was an autonomous Hanseatic trading center filled with German, Danish, and Swedish merchants who hired Estonians to do their menial labor. Many of the Old Town's buildings are truly old, dating from the boom times of the 15th and 16th centuries. Decrepit before the 1991 fall of the Soviet Union, the Old Town has been slowly revitalized, though there's still plenty of work to be done.

Two steep, narrow streets—the "Long Leg" and the "Short Leg"—connect Toompea and the lower town. This walk winds through both towns, going up the short leg and down the long leg. The walk starts near the ferry terminals. If you're coming from elsewhere in Tallinn, take tram #1 or #2 to the Linnahall stop, or

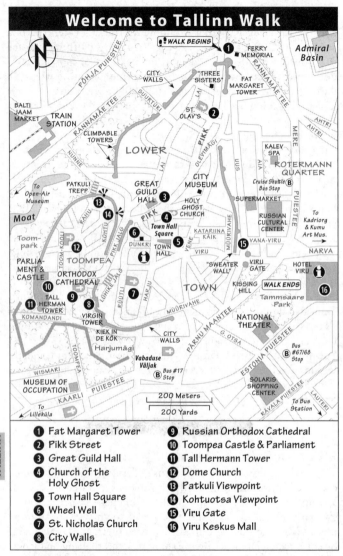

Welcome to Tallinn Walk

- ① Fat Margaret Tower
- ② Pikk Street
- ③ Great Guild Hall
- ④ Church of the Holy Ghost
- ⑤ Town Hall Square
- ⑥ Wheel Well
- ⑦ St. Nicholas Church
- ⑧ City Walls
- ⑨ Russian Orthodox Cathedral
- ⑩ Toompea Castle & Parliament
- ⑪ Tall Hermann Tower
- ⑫ Dome Church
- ⑬ Patkuli Viewpoint
- ⑭ Kohtuotsa Viewpoint
- ⑮ Viru Gate
- ⑯ Viru Keskus Mall

TALLINN

just walk out to the Fat Margaret Tower from anywhere in the Old Town.

① To Fat Margaret Tower and Start of Walk: From the ferry terminals, hike toward the tall tapering spire, go through a small park, and enter the Old Town through the archway by the squat Fat Margaret Tower (Paks Margareeta). Just outside the tower on a bluff overlooking the harbor is a broken black arch, a memorial to 852 people who perished in September of 1994 when the

Estonia passenger-and-car ferry sank in stormy conditions during its Tallinn-Stockholm run. The ship's bow visor came off, and water flooded into the car deck, throwing the boat off-balance. Only 137 people survived. The crew's maneuvering of the ship after it began taking on water is thought to have caused its fatal list and capsizing.

Fat Margaret Tower (so-called for its thick walls) guarded the entry gate of the town in medieval times (the sea once came much closer to this point than it does today). The relief above the gate dates from the 16th century, during Hanseatic times, when Sweden took Estonia from Germany. The Estonian Maritime Museum in the tower is paltry (€4, Wed-Sun 10:00-18:00, closed Mon-Tue, tel. 641-1408).

Just inside the gate, you'll feel the economic power of those early German trading days. The buildings nicknamed "Three Sisters" (on the right), now a hotel, are textbook examples of a merchant home/warehouse/office from the 15th-century Hanseatic Golden Age. The charmingly carved door near the corner evokes the wealth of Tallinn's merchant class.

• *Head up Pikk (which means "long") street.*

TALLINN

❷ **Pikk Street:** The medieval merchants' main drag, leading from the harbor up into town, is lined with interesting buildings—many were warehouses complete with cranes on the gables. After a block, you'll pass St. Olav's Church (Oleviste Kirik, a Baptist church today), notable for what was once the tallest spire in the land. Its plain whitewashed interior is skippable, though climbing 234 stairs up the tower rewards you with a great view (church-free entry, daily 10:00-18:00, July-Aug until 20:00; tower-€2, open April-Oct only; www.oleviste.ee).

While tourists see only a peaceful scene today, locals strolling this street are reminded of dark times under Moscow's rule. The KGB used the tower at St. Olav's Church to block Finnish TV signals. The once-handsome building nearby at Pikk 59 (the second house after the church, on the right) was, before 1991, the sinister local headquarters of the KGB. "Creative interrogation methods" were used here. Locals well knew that the road of suffering started here, as Tallinn's troublemakers were sent to Siberian gulags. The ministry building was called the "tallest" building in town (because "when you're in the basement, you can already see Siberia"). Notice the bricked-up windows at foot level and the plaque (in Estonian only).

A few short blocks farther up Pikk (after the small park), the fine house of the **Brotherhood of the Black Heads** (on the left, at #26, with the extremely ornate doorway) dates from 1440. For 500 years, until Hitler invited Estonian Germans back to their historical fatherland in the 1930s, this was a German merchants' club.

Until the 19th century, many Estonians lived as serfs on the rural estates of the German nobles who dominated the economy. In Tallinn, the German big shots were part of the Great Guild, while the German little shots had to make do with the Brotherhood of the Black Heads. This guild or business fraternity was limited to single German men. In Hanseatic towns, when a fire or battle had to be fought, single men were deployed first, because they had no family. Because single men were considered unattached to the community, they had no opportunity for power in the Hanseatic social structure. When a Black Head member married a local woman, he automatically gained a vested interest in the town's economy and well-being. He could then join the more prestigious Great Guild, and with that status, a promising economic and political future often opened up.

Today the hall is a concert venue. Its namesake "black head" is that of St. Maurice, an early Christian soldier-martyr, beheaded in the third century A.D. for his refusal to honor the Roman gods. Reliefs decorating the building recall Tallinn's Hanseatic glory days.

Architecture fans enjoy several fanciful facades along here (including the boldly Art Nouveau #18 and the colorful, eclectic building across the street). Just ahead, pause at the big yellow building on the right.

❸ **Great Guild Hall (Suurgildi Hoone):** With its wide (and therefore highly taxed) front, the Great Guild Hall (#17) was the epitome of wealth. The interior is less grand and houses a museum

(Eesti Ajaloomuuseum) covering the basics of Estonian history as well as the Guild Hall's past. (But I'd spend time in the nearby Tallinn City Museum instead—closed Tue; see page 625.) The Guild Hall does have a fun "time capsule" in the cellar where you can insert your face into videos illustrating episodes in local history (€5, May-Aug daily 10:00-18:00, Sept-April closed Wed, tel. 641-1630, www.ajaloomuuseum.ee).

Across the street, at #16 (look for *Kalev* awnings), the famous and recommended Maiasmokk ("Sweet Tooth") coffee shop, in business since 1864, remains a fine spot for a cheap coffee-and-pastry break.

❹ **Church of the Holy Ghost (Pühavaimu Kirik):** Sporting an outdoor clock from 1633, this pretty medieval church is worth a visit. (The plaque on the wall just behind the ticket desk is in Estonian and Russian, but not English; this dates from before 1991, when things were designed for "inner tourism"—within the USSR). The church retains its 14th-century design. Flying from the back pillar, the old flag of Tallinn—the same as today's red and white Danish flag—recalls 13th-century Danish rule. (The name "Tallinn" means "Danish Town.") The Danes sold Tallinn to the German Teutonic Knights, who lost it to the Swedes, who lost it to the Russians. The windows are mostly from the 1990s (€1, Mon-Sat 9:00-17:00, closed Sun to non-worshippers, Pühavaimu 2, tel. 646-4430, www.eelk.ee). The church hosts English-language Lutheran services Sundays at 15:00.

• *Leading alongside the church, tiny Saiakang lane (meaning "White Bread"—bread, cakes, and pies have been sold here since medieval times) takes you to...*

❺ **Town Hall Square (Raekoja Plats):** A marketplace through the centuries, with a cancan of fine old buildings, this is

the focal point of the Old Town. The square was the center of the autonomous lower town, a merchant city of Hanseatic traders. Once, it held criminals chained to pillories for public humiliation and knights showing off in chivalrous tournaments; today it's full of Scandinavians savoring cheap beer, children singing on the bandstand, and cruise-ship groups following the numbered paddles carried high by their well-scrubbed local guides.

The 15th-century Town Hall (Raekoda) dominates the square; it's now a museum, and climbing its tower earns you a commanding view (see photo on top of next page; for details see page 625). On the opposite side of the square, across from #12 in

TALLINN

the corner, the pharmacy (Raeapteek) dates from 1422 and claims—as do many—to be Europe's oldest. With decor that goes back to medieval times, the still-functioning pharmacy welcomes visitors with painted ceiling beams, English descriptions, and long-expired aspirin (Tue-Sat 10:00-18:00, closed Sun-Mon). Town Hall Square is ringed by inviting but touristy eateries, a few of which are still affordable, such as Troika and the Kehrwieder cafés. The TI is a block away (behind Town Hall).

• *Facing the Town Hall, head right up Dunkri street one block to the...*

❻ **Wheel Well:** The well is named for the "high-tech" wheel, a marvel that made fetching water easier.

• *Turn left on Rataskaevu street (which soon becomes Rüütli) and walk two blocks to...*

❼ **St. Nicholas (Niguliste) Church:** This 13th-century Gothic church-turned-art-museum served the German merchants

and knights who lived in this neighborhood 500 years ago. On March 9, 1944, while Tallinn was in German hands, Soviet forces bombed the city, and the church and surrounding area—once a charming district, dense with medieval buildings—were burned out; only the church was rebuilt (€3.50, Wed-Sun 10:00-17:00, closed Mon-Tue; organ concerts Sat and Sun at 16:00 are included in admission).

• *At the corner opposite the church, climb uphill along the steep, cobbled, Lühike Jalg ("Short Leg Lane"), home to a few quality craft shops. Pass through the giant stone tower, noticing the original oak door—one of two gates through the wall separating the two cities. This passage is still the ritual meeting point of the mayor and prime minister whenever there is an important agreement between town and country.*

Climb up through the gate and pop out on the street above. Turn left up the street, then hook left for a good view of the fortifications around the city.

❽ **City Walls:** The imposing city wall once had 46 towers—the stout, round tower is nicknamed "Kiek in de Kök." (While fun to say, it means "Peek in the Kitchen" in Low German.) It was situated so that "peek" is exactly what guards could do. It's now

TALLINN

a small museum with cannons and other relics from the 16th-century Livonian wars.

Above you is the so-called "Danish King's Garden." Tallinn is famous among Danes as the birthplace of their flag. According to legend, the Danes were losing a battle here. Suddenly, a white cross fell from heaven and landed in a pool of blood. The Danes were inspired and went on to win. To this day, their flag is a white cross on a red background.

• *You're standing at the back of Tallinn's onion-domed Russian cathedral. Circle around to the far side (facing the pink palace) to enjoy a great view of the church, and to find the entrance.*

❾ Russian Orthodox Cathedral: The Alexander Nevsky Cathedral was built here in 1900 smack in Tallinn's political

power center and over the supposed grave of a legendary Estonian hero, Kalevipoeg; a statue of Martin Luther was also taken down to make room. While it's a beautiful building, its placement was a crass attempt to flex Russian cultural muscle during a period of Estonian (and German) national revival, and there were plans (later shelved) to remove

it in the 1920s after Estonia became independent. The church has been exquisitely renovated inside and out. Step inside for a sample of Russian Orthodoxy. It's OK to visit discreetly during services (daily at 10:00 and 18:00), when you'll hear priests singing the liturgy in a side chapel. More than 40 percent of Tallinn's population is ethnic Russian (church free and open daily 8:00-19:00, icon art in gift shop).

• *Across the street is the...*

❿ Toompea Castle (Toompea Loss): The pink palace is an 18th-century Russian addition onto the medieval Toompea Castle. Today, it's the Estonian Parliament (Riigigoku) building, flying the Estonian flag—the flag of both the first (1918-1940) and second (1991-present) Estonian republics. Notice the Estonian seal: three lions for three great battles in Estonian history, and oak leaves for strength and stubbornness. Ancient pagan Estonians, who believed spirits lived in oak trees, would walk through forests of oak to toughen up. (To this day, Estonian cemeteries are in forests. Keeping some of their pagan sensibilities, they believe the spirits of the departed live on in the trees.)

• *Facing the palace, go left through the gate into the park to see the...*

⓫ Tall Hermann Tower (Pikk Hermann): This tallest tower of the castle wall is a powerful symbol here. For 50 years, while Estonian flags were hidden in cellars, the Soviet flag flew from Tall Hermann. As the USSR was unraveling, Estonians proudly and defiantly replaced the red Soviet flag here with their own black, white, and blue flag.

• *Backtrack and go uphill, passing the Russian church on your right. Climb Toom-Kooli street to the...*

⓬ Dome Church (Toomkirik): Estonia is ostensibly Lutheran, but few Tallinners go to church. A recent Gallup Poll showed Estonia to be the least religious country in the European Union—only 14 percent of respondents identified religion as an important part of their daily lives. Most churches double as concert venues or museums, but this one is still used for worship. Officially St. Mary's Church but popularly called the Dome Church, it's a perfect example of simple Northern European Gothic, built in the 13th century during Danish rule, then rebuilt after a 1684 fire. Once the church of Tallinn's wealthy German-speaking aristocracy, it's littered with more than a hundred coats of arms, carved by local masters as memorials to the deceased and inscribed with German tributes. The earliest dates from the 1600s, the latest from around 1900. For €5, you can climb 140 steps up the tower to enjoy the view (church entry free, daily 9:00-18:00, www .eelk.ee/tallinna.toom).

• *Leaving the church, turn left and hook around the back of the building. You'll pass the slanted tree and the big, green, former noblemen's clubhouse on your right (vacated when Germans left Estonia in the 1930s), then go down cobbled Rahukohtu lane. Government offices and embassies have moved into the buildings and spruced up the neighborhood. But as you pass under the yellow Patkuli Vaateplats arch, notice a surviving ramshackle bit of the 1980s. Just a few years ago, the entire city looked like this.*

Belly up to the grand...

⓭ Patkuli Viewpoint: Survey the scene. On the far left, the Neoclassical facade of the executive branch of Estonia's govern-

ment enjoys the view. Below you, a bit of the old moat remains. The *Group* sign marks Tallinn's tiny train station, and the clutter of stalls behind that is the rustic market. Out on the water, ferries shuttle to and from Helsinki (just 50 miles away). Beyond the lower town's medieval wall and towers stands the green spire of St. Olav's Church, once 98 feet taller and, locals claim, the world's tallest tower in 1492. Far in the distance is the 985-foot-tall TV tower (much appreciated by Estonians for heroically keeping the people's airwaves open during the harrowing days when they won independence from the USSR). During Soviet domination, though, Finnish TV was even more important, as it gave Estonians their only look at Western lifestyles. Imagine: In the 1980s, many locals had never seen a banana or pineapple—except on TV. People still talk of the day that Finland broadcast the soft-porn movie *Emmanuelle*. A historic migration of Estonians purportedly flocked from the countryside to Tallinn to get within rabbit-ear's distance of Helsinki and see all that flesh on-screen. The TV tower was recently refurbished and opened to visitors.

• *Go back through the arch, turn immediately left down the narrow lane, turn right (onto Toom-Rüütli), take the first left, and pass through the trees to...*

⓮ Kohtuotsa Viewpoint: On the far left is St. Olav's Church, then the busy cruise port and the skinny white spire of the Church

of the Holy Ghost. The narrow gray spire farther to the right is the 16th-century Town Hall tower. On the far right is the tower of St. Nicholas Church. Below you, visually trace Pikk street, Tallinn's historic main drag, which winds through the Old Town, leading from

Toompea down the hill (from right to left), through the gate tower, past the Church of the Holy Ghost, behind St. Olav's, and out to the harbor. Less picturesque is the clutter of Soviet-era apartment blocks on the distant horizon. The nearest skyscraper (white) is Hotel Viru, in Soviet times the biggest hotel in the Baltics, and infamous as a clunky, dingy slumbermill. Locals joke that

Hotel Viru was built from a new Soviet wonder material called "micro-concrete" (60 percent concrete, 40 percent microphones). Underneath the hotel is the modern Viru Keskus, a huge shopping mall and local transit center, where this walk will end. To the left of Hotel Viru, between it and the ferry terminals, is the Rotermann

Quarter, where old industrial buildings are being revamped into a new commercial zone.

• *From the viewpoint, descend to the lower town. Go out and left down Kohtu, past the Finnish Embassy (on your left). Back at the Dome Church, the slanted tree points the way, left down Piiskopi ("Bishop's Street"). At the onion domes, turn left again and follow the old wall down Pikk Jalg ("Long Leg Lane") into the lower town. Go under the tower, then straight on Pikk street,* and after two doors turn right on Voorimehe, which leads into Town Hall Square.

⓯ **Through Viru Gate:** Cross through the square (left of the Town Hall's tower) and go downhill (passing the kitschy medieval Olde Hansa Restaurant, with its bonneted waitresses and merry men). Continue straight down Viru street toward Hotel Viru, the blocky white skyscraper in the distance. Viru street is old Tallinn's busiest and kitschiest shopping street. Just past the strange and modern wood/glass/stone mall, Müürivahe street leads left along the old wall, called the "Sweater Wall." This is a colorful and tempting gauntlet of women selling knitwear (anything with images and bright colors is likely machine-made). Beyond the sweaters, Katariina Käik, a lane with glassblowing shops, leads left. Back on Viru street, pass the golden arches and walk through the medieval arches—Viru Gate—that mark the end of old Tallinn. Outside the gates, opposite Viru 23, above the flower stalls, is a small park on a piece of old bastion known as the Kissing Hill (come up here after dark and you'll find out why).

• *Use the crosswalk to your right to reach the...*

⓰ **Viru Keskus Mall:** Here, behind Hotel Viru, at the end of this walk, you'll find the real world: branch TI, Internet café, basement supermarket, ticket service, bookstore, and many bus and tram stops. If you still have energy, you can cross the busy street by the complex and explore the nearby Rotermann Quarter (see page 626).

Sights in Tallinn

In or near the Old Town

Central Tallinn has dozens of small museums, most suitable only for specialized tastes (complete listings in *Tallinn in Your Pocket*). The following sights are the ones I'd visit first.

Town Hall (Raekoda) and Tower—This museum, facing Town Hall Square, has exhibits on the town's administration and history, along with an interesting bit on the story of limestone. The tower, the place to see all of Tallinn, rewards those who climb its 155 steps with a wonderful city view.

Cost and Hours: Museum—€4, entrance through cellar, July-Aug Mon-Sat 10:00-16:00, closed Sun and Sept-June; tower—€3, May-mid-Sept daily 11:00-18:00, closed rest of year; tel. 645-7900, www.tallinn.ee/raekoda.

Tallinn City Museum (Tallinna Linnamuuseum)—This humble museum features Tallinn history from 1200 to the 1950s. Well described in English, it offers some intimate looks at local lifestyles and a few exhibits on the communist days.

Cost and Hours: €3.20, March-Oct Wed-Mon 10:30-18:00, Nov-Feb Wed-Mon 10:00-17:30, closed Tue year-round, last entry 30 minutes before closing, Vene 17, at corner of Pühavaimu, tel. 615-5183, www.linnamuuseum.ee.

▲Museum of Occupation (Okupatsioonide Muuseum)—It's said that Estonia didn't formally lose its independence from 1940 to 1991, but was just "occupied"—first by the Soviets, then by the Nazis, and then again by the USSR. Built with funding from a wealthy Estonian-American, this compact museum tells the history of Estonia during those years.

Cost and Hours: €4, skip the amateurish €3 audioguide, June-Aug Tue-Sun 10:00-18:00, Sept-May Tue-Sun 11:00-18:00, closed Mon year-round, Toompea 8, at corner of Kaarli Puiestee, tel. 668-0250, www.okupatsioon.ee.

Visiting the Museum: It's organized around seven TV monitors screening documentary films in English and Estonian, each focusing on a different time period. Among the artifacts displayed are suitcases, a reminder of people who fled the country. Exhibits and videos tell how the Soviets kept the Estonians in line. Surveillance was a part of daily life, as Estonians were tough to bring into the Soviet fold. Prison doors evoke the countless lives lost to detention and deportation. In the basement by the WCs is a collection of Soviet-era statues of communist leaders—once they lorded over the people, now they're in the cellar guarding the toilets. The ticket desk sells a well-chosen range of English-language books on the occupation years.

Rotermann Quarter—Sprawling between Hotel Viru and the port, this 19th-century industrial zone is being redeveloped
into shopping, office, and living
space. To see the first completed
section, start at Hotel Viru, cross
busy Narva Maantee and walk
down Roseni street. At #7 you'll
find the hard-to-resist Kalev
chocolate shop, selling Estonia's
best-known sweets (Mon-Sat
10:00-20:00, Sun 11:00-18:00).

Kadriorg Park and the Kumu Museum

▲**Kadriorg Park**—This expansive seaside park, home to a summer
royal residence and the Kumu Art Museum, is just a five-minute

tram ride or a 25-minute
walk from Hotel Viru. After
Russia took over Tallinn
in 1710, Peter the Great
built the cute, pint-sized
Kadriorg Palace for Tsarina
Catherine (the palace's
name means "Catherine's
Valley"). Stately, peaceful,
and crisscrossed by leafy
paths, the park has a rose garden, duck-filled pond, playground
and benches, and old tsarist guardhouses harkening back to the
days of Russian rule. It's a delightful place for a stroll or a picnic.
If it's rainy, duck into one of the cafés in the park's art museums
(described below).

Getting There: Reach the park on tram #1 or #3 (direction:
Kadriorg; catch at any tram stop around the Old Town). Get off
at the Kadriorg stop (the end of the line, where trams turn and
head back into town), and walk 200 yards straight ahead and up
Weizenbergi, the park's main avenue. Peter's summer palace is on
the left; behind it, visit the formal garden (free). At the end of the
avenue is the Kumu Art Museum, the park's most important sight.
A taxi from Hotel Viru to this area should cost €5 or less.

Visiting Kadriorg Park: The palace's manicured **gardens**
(free to enter) are a pure delight; on weekends, you'll likely see
a steady parade of brides and grooms here, posing for wedding
pictures. The summer palace itself is home to the **Kadriorg Art
Museum** (Kadrioru Kunstimuuseum), with very modest Russian
and Western European galleries (€4.50; May-Sept Tue-Sun
10:00-17:00, Wed until 20:00; Oct-April Wed-Sun 10:00-17:00,

closed Tue; closed Mon year-round; tel. 606-6400, www.kadrioru muuseum.ee/en).

The fenced-off yard directly behind the garden is where you'll spot the local "White House" (although it's pink)—home of **Estonia's president**. Walk around to the far side to find its main entrance, with the seal of Estonia above the door, flagpoles flying both the Estonian and the EU flags, and stone-faced guards.

A five-minute walk beyond the presidential palace takes you to the Kumu Art Museum, described next. For a longer walk from here, the rugged park rolls down toward the sea.

▲▲**Kumu Art Museum (Kumu Kunstimuuseum)**—This main branch of the Art Museum of Estonia brings the nation's

best art together in a striking modern building designed by an international (well, at least Finnish) architect, Pekka Vapaa-vuori. The entire collection is accessible, well-presented, and engaging, with a particularly thought-provoking section on art from the Soviet period. The museum is well worth the trip for art lovers, or for anyone intrigued by the unique spirit of this tiny nation—particularly when combined with a stroll through the nearby palace gardens (described earlier) on a sunny day.

Cost and Hours: €5.50, or €4.20 for just the permanent collection, audioguide-€3.20; May-Sept Tue-Sun 11:00-18:00, closed Mon; Oct-April Wed-Sun 11:00-18:00, closed Mon-Tue; Wed until 20:00 year-round; trendy café, tel. 602-6000, www.kumu.ee.

Getting There: To reach the museum, follow the instructions for Kadriorg Park, above; Kumu is at the far end of the park. To get from the Old Town to Kumu directly without walking through the park, take bus #67 or #68 (each runs every 10-15 minutes, #68 does not run on Sun); both leave from Teatri Väljak, on the far side of the pastel yellow theater, across from the Solaris shopping mall. Get off at the Kumu stop, then walk up the stairs and across the bridge.

➋ **Self-Guided Tour:** Just off the ticket lobby, the **great hall** has temporary exhibits; however, the permanent collection on the third and fourth floors is Kumu's main draw. While you can rent an audioguide, I found the free laminated sheets in most rooms enough to enjoy the collection. The maze-like layout on each floor presents the art chronologically.

The **third floor**, which focuses on classics of Estonian art, starts with 18th-century portraits of local aristocrats, moves through 19th-century Romanticism (including some nice views of

Tallinn and idealized images of Estonian peasant women in folk costumes), winds through several rooms of local Expressionists and other Modernist painters, and ends with art produced during World War II. One very high-ceilinged room has a wall lined with dozens of expressive busts by sculptor Villu Jaanisoo.

The **fourth-floor exhibit,** called "Difficult Choices," is an interesting survey of Estonian art from the end of World War II until "re-independence" in 1991. Some of the works are mainstream, while others are by dissident artists.

Estonian art parted ways with Western Europe with the Soviet takeover in 1945. The Soviets insisted that artworks actively promote the communist struggle, and to that end, Estonian artists were forced to adopt the Stalinist formula, making paintings that were done in the traditional national style but that were socialist in content—in the style now called **Socialist Realism.**

Socialist Realism had its roots in the early 20th-century Realist movement, whose artists wanted to depict the actual conditions of life rather than just glamour and wealth—in America, think of John Steinbeck's novels or Walker Evans' photographs of the rural poor. In the Soviet Union, this artistic curiosity about the working class was perverted into an ideology: Art was supposed to glorify labor and the state's role in distributing its fruits. In a system where there was ultimately little incentive to work hard, art was seen as a tool to motivate the masses, and to support the Communist Party's hold on power.

In the collection's first room, called "A Tale of Happiness," you'll see syrupy images of what Soviet leadership imagined to be the ideal of communist Estonia. In *Agitator Amongst the Voters* (1952), a stern portrait of Stalin in the hazy background keeps an eye on a young hotshot articulating some questionable ideas; his listeners' reactions range from shudders of horror to smirks of superiority. *The Young Aviators* (1951) shows an eager youngster wearing a bright-red neckerchief (indicating his membership in the Pioneers, the propaganda-laden communist version of Scouts) telling his enraptured schoolmates stories about a model airplane.

The next room shows canvases of miners, protesters, speechifiers, metalworkers, and more all doing their utmost for the communist society. You'll also see paintings of industrial achievements (like bridges), party meetings, and, of course, the great leader Stalin himself. Because mining was big in Estonia, miners were portrayed as local heroes, marching like soldiers to their glorious labor. Women were depicted toiling side by side with men, as equal partners. (Though they're not always on display here, posters were a natural fit, with slogans exhorting laborers to work hard on behalf of the regime.)

While supposedly a reflection of "real" life, Socialist Realism

Estonia's Singing Revolution

When you are a humble nation of just a million people lodged between Russia and Germany (and tyrants such as Stalin and Hitler), simply surviving is a challenge. Estonia was free from 1920 to 1939. Then they had a 50-year Nazi/Soviet nightmare. Estonians say, "We were so few in numbers that we had to emphasize that we exist. We had no weapons. Being together and singing together was our power." Singing has long been a national form of expression in this country; the first Estonian Song Festival occurred in 1869, and has been held every five years since then.

Estonian culture was under siege during the Soviet era. Moscow wouldn't allow locals to wave their flag or sing patriotic songs. Russians and Ukrainians were moved in, and Estonians were shipped out in an attempt to dilute the country's identity. But as cracks began to appear in the USSR, the Estonians mobilized—by singing.

In 1988, 300,000 Estonians—imagine...a third of the population—gathered at the Song Festival Grounds outside Tallinn to sing patriotic songs. On August 23, 1989—the 50th anniversary of a notorious pact between Hitler and Stalin—the people of Latvia, Lithuania, and Estonia held hands to make "the Baltic Chain," a human chain that stretched 360 miles from Tallinn to Vilnius in Lithuania. Some feared a Tiananmen Square-type bloodbath, but Estonians kept singing.

In February of 1990, the first free parliamentary elections took place in all three Baltic states, and pro-independence candidates won majorities. In 1991, hard-line communists staged a coup against Soviet leader Mikhail Gorbachev, and Estonians feared a violent crackdown. The makeshift Estonian Parliament declared independence. Then, the coup in Moscow failed. Suddenly, the USSR was gone, and Estonia was free.

Watch the documentary film *The Singing Revolution* before your visit (www.singingrevolution.com) to tune into this stirring bit of modern history and to draw inspiration from Estonia's valiant struggle for freedom.

TALLINN

art was formulaic and showed little creative spirit. Though some Estonian artists flirted with social commentary and the avant-garde, a few ended up in Siberia as a result.

Later, in the Brezhnev years, Estonian artists managed to slip Surrealist, Pop, and Photorealist themes into their work (for example, Rein Tammik's large painting *1945-1975*). Estonia was the only part of the USSR that recognized Pop Art. As the Soviets would eventually learn, change was unstoppable.

The rest of the museum is devoted to temporary exhibits, with contemporary art always on the **fifth floor** (where there's a nice view back to the Old Town from the far gallery). It's also worth admiring the mostly successful architecture—the building is partly dug into the limestone hill, and the facade is limestone, too.

Outer Tallinn

▲Song Festival Grounds (Lauluväljak)—At this open-air theater, built in 1959 and resembling an oversized Hollywood Bowl, the Estonian nation gath-  ers to sing. Every five years, these grounds host a huge national song festival with 25,000 singers and 100,000 spectators. While it hosts big pop-music acts, too, it's a national monument for the compelling role it played in Estonia's fight for independence.

Since 1988, when locals sang patriotic songs here in defiance of Soviet rule, these grounds have taken on a symbolic importance to the nation. Locals vividly recall putting on folk costumes knitted by their grandmothers (some of whom later died in Siberia) and coming here with masses of Estonians to sing. Overlooking the grounds from the cheap seats is a statue of Gustav Ernesaks, who directed the Estonian National Male Choir for 50 years through the darkest times of Soviet rule. He was a power in the drive for independence, and lived to see it happen.

Cost and Hours: Free, open long hours, bus #1A, #5, #8, #34A, or #38 to Lauluväljak stop.

Lasnamäe Neighborhood—In its attempt to bring Estonia into the Soviet fold, Moscow moved tens of thousands of Russian  workers into Tallinn, using the promise of new apartments as an incentive. Today, two generations later, Tallinn has a huge Russian minority (about 40 percent of the city's population) and three huge, charmless suburbs of ugly, Soviet-built apartments: Mustamäe, Õismäe, and Lasnamäe. Today, about one of every two Tallinners lives in one of these Brezhnev-era suburbs of massive, cookie-cutter apartment blocks (many now privatized). Seventy percent of the residents who live in Lasnamäe are Russian-speaking. Some parts are poor, rough, and edgy (not comfortable after dark), with blue lights in the public toilets so that junkies can't see their veins. Other sections are nicer, and by day, you can visit here without fear.

Forging Russians and Estonians into a single society, with the Estonian language dominant, was an optimistic goal in the early

1990s. Ethnic Russians grumbled, but knew they probably had a brighter economic future in Estonia than in Russia. Now, with a new generation of children learning both languages in school and everyone enjoying reasonable prosperity, peaceful ethnic coexistence (like between Swedes and Finns in Helsinki) seems achievable.

For a quick look at Lasnamäe, hop bus #67 or #68 (each runs every 10-15 minutes); both leave from Teatri Väljak, on the far side of the pastel yellow theater from the Old Town, across from the Solaris shopping mall. You'll see carefully dressed young women, track-suited men, grass that needs mowing, cracked paving stones, grandmothers pushing strollers, and lots of new, boxy shops. Ride to the last stop (about 25 minutes), then return to town.

▲Estonian Open-Air Museum (Vabaõhumuuseum)— Influenced by their ties with Nordic countries, Estonians are

enthusiastic advocates of open-air museums. For this one, they salvaged farm buildings, windmills, and an old church from rural areas and transported them to a park-like setting just outside town (4 miles west of the Old Town). The goal: to both save and share their heritage. Attendants are posted in many houses, but to really visualize life in the old houses, rent the audioguide (€7/3 hours). The park's Kolu Tavern serves traditional dishes. You can rent a bike (€3/hour) for a breezy roll to quiet, faraway spaces in the park.

Cost and Hours: Late April-Sept: €6, park open daily 10:00-20:00, historic buildings until 18:00; Oct-late April: €3, park open daily 10:00-17:00 but historic buildings closed. Tel. 654-9100, www.evm.ee.

Getting There: Take bus #21 from the train station to Rocca al Mare stop—because buses back to Tallinn run infrequently, check the departure schedule as soon as you arrive, or ask staff how to find the Zoo stop, with more frequent service, a 15-minute walk away.

Lahemaa National Park (Lahemaa Rahvuspark)—This vast, flat, forested coastal preserve on the Gulf of Finland is only a one-hour drive east of Tallinn. While it is a popular tour destination and the nature is pristine, the park's charms are modest. I had a great guide, and it was a fascinating day out. But with an average guide, it could be a snore. Highlights include the thick forest (including cemeteries, because Estonians bury their dead in the woods), bog walks, rich berry and mushroom picking, rebuilt manor homes, and peaceful fishing villages surrounded by the evocative ruins of Soviet occupation. City Bikes and Tallinn Traveller Tours organize day trips out (€49/person; see "Tours in Tallinn," page 613). For hiking and cycling trail descriptions, check online (www.keskkonnaamet.ee/lahe-eng) or stop at the park's visitor center when you arrive (mid-April-mid-Oct daily 9:00-18:00, later hours in summer; mid-Oct-mid-April Mon-Fri 9:00-17:00; tel. 329-5555).

Shopping in Tallinn

With so many cruise-ship tourists inundating Tallinn, the Old Town is full of trinkets, but it is possible to find good-quality stuff. Wooden goods, like butter knives and juniper-wood trivets, are a good value. Marvel at the variety on sale in Tallinn's liquor stores, popular with visiting Scandinavians. Tucked into the Old Town are many craft and artisan shops where prices are lower than in Nordic countries.

The **"Sweater Wall"** is a fun place to browse sweaters and woolens, though few are hand-knitted by grandmothers these days. Find the stalls under the wall on Müürivahe street (daily 10:00-17:00, near the corner of Viru street, described on page 624). From there, explore **Katariina Käik,** a small alley between Müürivahe and Vene streets, which has several handicraft stores and workshops selling pieces that make nice souvenirs.

The cheery **Navitrolla Gallerii** is filled with work by the well-known Estonian artist who goes just by the name Navitrolla. His whimsical, animal-themed prints are vaguely reminiscent of *Where the Wild Things Are* (Mon-Fri 10:00-18:00, Sat 10:00-17:00, Sun 10:00-16:00, Sulevimägi 1, near Tallinn Backpackers, tel. 631-3716, www.navitrolla.ee).

The **Rahva Raamat** bookstore in the Viru Keskus mall (floors 3-4) has plenty of English books mixed throughout its shelves (daily 9:00-21:00).

Balti Jaam Market, Tallinn's bustling traditional market, is behind the train station and has little of touristic interest besides wonderful photo ops. That's why I like it. It's a great time-warp scene, fragrant with dill, berries, onions, and mush-rooms. You'll hear lots of Russian. The indoor sections sell meat, clothing, and gadgets (look for the Jaama Turg gate beyond track 9, Mon-Fri 8:00-18:00, Sat-Sun 8:00-17:00, better early).

For something tamer, the **Viru Turg outdoor market,** a block outside the Old Town's Viru Gate, has a lively, tourist-oriented collection of stalls selling mostly clothing and textiles (daily May-Sept 9:00-17:00, Oct-April 10:00-16:00, north of Viru street at Mere Puiestee 1).

Entertainment in Tallinn

Music: Tallinn has a dense schedule of classical music perfor-mances, especially during the annual Old Town Days, generally at the beginning of June (www.vanalinnapaevad.ee). Choral sing-ing became a symbol of the struggle for Estonian independence after the first Estonian Song Festival in 1869 (still held every five years—next one in 2014).

Even outside of festival times, you'll find many performances in Tallinn's churches and concert halls, advertised on posters around town or at the TI, and in the free *Tallinn This Week* bro-chure (www.ttw.ee). Tickets are usually available at the door or through the Piletilevi booth in the Viru Keskus mall (daily 9:00-21:00, www.piletilevi.ee). Watch for performances by Hortus Musicus, one of Estonia's finest classical ensembles, or concerts featuring the work of Arvo Pärt, Veljo Tormis, or Erkki-Sven Tüür, who are among Estonia's best modern choral composers and arrangers. Estonian groups have put out a lot of good CDs; you'll find a good music shop on the top floor (A5) of the Kaubamaja department store (daily 9:00-21:00, behind Viru Keskus mall).

Swimming: The indoor water park and 50-meter pool at the **Kalev Spa** is lots of fun. It's at the edge of the Old Town; many Finns come here on fitness travel packages (€10.50/2.5 hours, €8.50/1.5 hours, €6.50/1.5 hours weekdays after 15:00; Mon-Fri 6:45-21:30, Sat-Sun 8:00-21:30; Aia 18, tel. 649-3370, www .kalevspa.ee).

Sleeping in Tallinn

Tallinn has a good selection of hotel choices. There are some bar-gains in the Old Town, but even more if you're willing to stay a short walk or bus ride away.

More than in most cities, it's important to start your search on hotel websites. Room prices vary with current demand. Many hotels, especially the bigger ones, list their best price on the web-site and offer walk-in individuals only the inflated rack rates—the

---

Sleep Code

(€1 = about $1.30, country code: 372)

S = Single, **D** = Double/Twin, **T** = Triple, **Q** = Quad, **b** = bathroom, **s** = shower. Credit cards are accepted and breakfast is included unless otherwise noted.

To help you sort easily through these listings, I've divided the accommodations into three categories, based on the full price for a standard double room with bath during high season:

$$$ Higher Priced—Most rooms €90 or more.
$$ Moderately Priced—Most rooms between €60-€90.
$ Lower Priced—Most rooms €60 or less.

Prices can change without notice; verify the hotel's current rates online or by email.

---

bulk of their business comes from agencies anyway.

Summer is high season (Tallinn has more tourists than business travelers), and prices almost always drop from October to April, except around Christmas and New Year's. I've listed high-season, summer prices here. When I give a range, expect the higher rate during busy times (typically Friday and Saturday nights) and the lower price on slow days.

Use a taxi to get to your hotel when you arrive, and then figure out public transportation later.

In and Around the Old Town

$$$ Baltic Hotel Imperial is a fine four-star hotel set in a lovely park-like spot under the Old Town wall. Its 32 rooms are modern and small, while the public spaces have a spacious, professional ambience. Though it feels like a chain (and is), when it's discounted, it's the best Old Town, top-end value I've found (Sb-€89-119, Db-€99-129, website shows best rates, elevator, air-con, free Wi-Fi, sauna-€19/hour, kids' playroom, Nunne 14, tel. 627-4800, fax 627-4801, www.imperial.ee, imperial@baltichotelgroup.com).

$$$ My City Hotel fills a handsome 1950s building on the south edge of the Old Town with 68 rooms and spacious common areas. Along with the Sõprus cinema across the street, it's in Stalinist Classical style—Soviet stars and sheaves of wheat still adorn the facade (Sb-€79-120, Db-€80-144, extra bed-€25, children 12 and under free in parents' room, non-smoking, elevator, air-con, free Internet access and Wi-Fi, sauna-€20-30/hour, Vana-Posti 11/13, tel. 622-0900, fax 622-0901, www.mycityhotel.ee, booking@mycityhotel.ee).

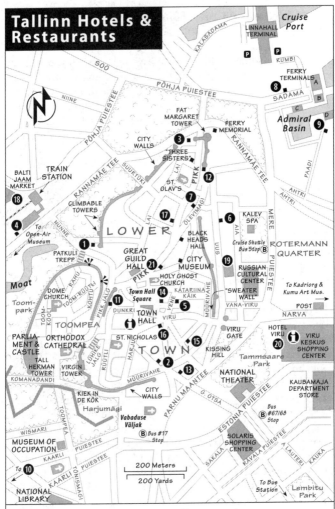

Tallinn Hotels & Restaurants

① Baltic Hotel Imperial
② My City Hotel
③ Meriton Old Town Hotel
④ Hotel Shnelli
⑤ Villa Hortensia & Pierre Chocolaterie
⑥ Old House Guesthouse/Hostel
⑦ Tallinn Backpackers Hostel
⑧ Tallink Express Hotel
⑨ City Hotel Portus
⑩ To Valge Villa
⑪ Vanaema Juures, Restaurant Aed & Von Krahli Baar

⑫ Leib Restaurant
⑬ Mekk Restaurant
⑭ Troika Restaurant
⑮ Must Lammas Restaurant & Eat Dumpling Café
⑯ Olde Hansa Restaurant & Peppersack Restaurant
⑰ Hell Hunt Pub
⑱ Balti Jaama Kohvik
⑲ Rimi Supermarket
⑳ Viru Keskus Supermarket
㉑ Kolmjag "Everything" Grocery & Maiasmokk Café

$$ Meriton Old Town Hotel sits grandly (for a hotel in its category) at the tip of the Old Town, not far from the ferry terminals. Its 41 small rooms are mostly doubles with twin beds and showers, and some could be noisy if you sleep with the window open. But the price is right and the location convenient. Don't let them move you to the nearby, similarly named, more expensive Meriton Old Town Garden Hotel (Db-€70-90, non-smoking, elevator, free Internet access and Wi-Fi, Lai 49, tel. 614-1300, fax 614-1311, www.meritonhotels.com, reservations@meriton hotels.com).

$$ Hotel Shnelli, a big, high-rise "efficiency hotel" adjacent to the sleepy little train station (a 5-minute walk from the Old Town in a neighborhood that feels a bit seedy at night), rents 124 Ikea-mod rooms. It fronts a noisy street, so request a quiet room in the back—these overlook the tracks, but no trains run at night (Db-€60-65, sometimes €10-20 more on weekends, connecting family rooms, elevator, pay Internet access, free Wi-Fi, Toompuiestee 37, tel. 631-0100, fax 631-0107, www.gohotels.ee, reservations@gohotels.ee).

Budget Beds in the Old Town

$$ Villa Hortensia rents six simple, creaky-floored rooms with kitchenettes above a sophisticated little café in a courtyard close to Town Hall Square. The three twin-bed rooms and one single-bed room are furnished sparsely (no TV), with beds in a sleeping loft. The "deluxe" room comes with a double bed and a small balcony. The apartment is on two floors, with a double bed upstairs and a foldout sofa bed in the living room. Named after the home of a group of down-and-outs in a famous Estonian novel, the hotel is creatively run by jewelry designer Jaan Pärn. It's a decent, inexpensive choice if you don't mind the ramshackle feeling and the fact that the rooms aren't serviced every day. Jaan's jewelry shop, across the courtyard, serves as the reception (Sb-€40, Db-€55, deluxe Db-€80, apartment Db-€105 or Tb-€130, no breakfast, no elevator, free Internet access and Wi-Fi, 50 yards from the corner of Vene and Viru streets at Vene 6, look for *Master's Courtyard* and *Chocolaterie* signs, mobile 504-6113, www.hoov.ee, jaan.parn @mail.ee).

$ Old House Guesthouse and Hostel is small and snug, split between two buildings halfway between Town Hall Square and the ferry terminals. There's street noise in many rooms, so bring earplugs (bed in 6-person dorm-€15, S-€30, D-€44, Quint-€75, see their website for deals, includes sheets and towel, breakfast-€4, no lockout, shared shower and WC, kitchen facilities, free Wi-Fi, free parking—reserve ahead, Uus 26, tel. 641-1464, fax 641-1604, www.oldhouse.ee, info@oldhouse.ee).

$ **Tallinn Backpackers,** a block from the Old House Guesthouse, is a leave-your-shoes-at-the-door place renting 30 beds in four rooms to backpackers. Smoothly run and fun for the right crowd, it has a friendly party vibe (dorm bed–€17, less off-season, kitchen, lockers, free Internet access and Wi-Fi, laundry–€3.50/load, Olevimägi 11, tel. 644-0298, www.tallinn backpackers.com, tallinnbackpackers@gmail.com).

Near the Ferry Terminals

If you're cruising in, these two places right next to the ferry terminals are almost too convenient. They are inexpensive, but without character.

$$ **Tallink Express Hotel** is a few steps from the A, B, and C ferry terminals, close to Linnahall terminal, and a short walk from the Old Town. It's a modern, cheery Motel 6-type place with excellent prices and 163 comfortable cookie-cutter rooms. The rooms can be stuffy in hot weather, as windows don't open very far and there's no air-conditioning. Walk-in rates are much higher than the website prices I give here (Sb/Db–about €89, about €63 in winter, can run higher on busy weekends, extra bed–€25, children under 17 sleep free on sofa beds in family rooms, request a non-smoking floor, elevator, free Internet access and Wi-Fi, free parking, Sadama 9, tel. 630-0808, fax 630-0861, www.hotels.tallink .com, hotelbooking@tallink.ee).

$$ **City Hotel Portus,** with 107 rooms, is in an utterly charmless location right across from D-Terminal. Its motto is "young at heart," and the theme is rock and roll, with Muzak and posters throughout. While it's perfectly comfortable, the only good reason to stay here is if you're traveling via D-Terminal, especially at odd hours (Sb–about €62-84, Db–about €65-95, reserve on website for best deals, free Wi-Fi, Uus-Sadama 23, tel. 680-6600, fax 680-6601, www.tallinncityhotelportus.com, portus@tallinn hotels.ee).

In Lilleküla, Outside the Center

Lilleküla is a quiet, green, and peaceful residential area of single-family houses, small Soviet-era apartment blocks, and barking dogs. For a clearer understanding of Estonian life, stay here. You'll save money without sacrificing comfort. The downside: It's a 15-minute, €1 bus ride into the center.

$ **Valge Villa** ("White Villa"), a homey guesthouse set in a great garden run by Anne and Andres Vahtra and their family, does everything right. It's worth the commute for its competitive prices and 10 spacious, wood-paneled, well-furnished rooms. They like you to book and pay a 10 percent advance deposit on their website (Sb-€35, Db-€45, small suite-€56, larger suite-€63, suite-apartments-€80, extra bed-€16, kids under 12 stay free in same room, every fifth night free, free Internet access and Wi-Fi, free parking, bikes-€14/day, sauna-€19, laundry-€8/load; take bus #17 to Räägu stop, or trolley bus #2, #3, or #4 to Tedre stop; Kännu 26/2, between Rästa and Räägu streets—see map on page 602, tel. 654-2302, www.white-villa.com). I'd take a taxi here to check in (about €9 from the ferry port), and figure out the public-transit options later.

Eating in Tallinn

The Old Town's thriving restaurant culture serves not just tourists but also locals, who like to meet downtown after work. In the obvious, high-traffic locations, such as Town Hall Square

and Viru street, prices have risen to Western European levels, and average main dishes can cost €15-20. Instead, roam at least a block or two off the main drags, where you can find great food at what seems like fire-sale prices. Some restaurants have good-value lunch specials on weekdays (look for the words *päeva praad*). Tipping is not required, but if you like the service, round your bill up by 5-10 percent when paying. Reserving ahead for dinner is a smart idea.

A few years ago it was hard to find authentic local cuisine, but now Estonian food is trendy—a hearty Northern mixture of meat, potatoes, root vegetables, mushrooms, dill, garlic, bread, and soup. Pea soup is a local specialty. You usually get a few slices of bread as a free, automatic side dish (as in the rest of the ex-USSR). A typical pub snack is Estonian garlic bread *(küüslauguleivad)*—deep-fried strips of dark rye bread smothered in garlic and served with a dipping sauce. Estonia's Saku beer is good, cheap, and on tap at most eateries. Try the nutty, full-bodied Tume variety.

Dining in the Old Town
Estonian Restaurants
Vanaema Juures ("Grandma's Place"), an eight-table cellar restaurant, serves homey, traditional Estonian meals, such as pork roast with sauerkraut and horseradish. This is a fine bet for local cuisine,

and dinner reservations are strongly advised. No tacky medieval stuff here—just good food at fair prices in a pleasant ambience, where you expect your waitress to show up with her hair in a bun and wearing granny glasses (€8-17 main dishes, Mon-Sat 12:00-22:00, Sun 12:00-18:00, Rataskaevu 10/12, tel. 626-9080, Ava mothers you).

Restorant Aed is an elegant, almost gourmet, health-food eatery calling itself "the embassy of pure food." While not vegetarian, it is passionate about serving modern, organic Estonian cuisine in a woody, romantic setting (€7-14 main dishes, Mon-Sat 12:00-22:00, Sun 12:00-18:00, Rataskaevu 8, tel. 626-9088).

At **Leib**, at the seaside end of the Old Town, you enter up steps into a fun garden under the medieval walls, and can sit indoors or out. As at other reasonably-priced places, a great three-course meal costs no more than €20: Try pea soup (€4.50), followed by free-range chicken (€10) and a €4 dessert (daily 12:00-23:00, Uus 31, tel. 611-9026).

Mekk is a small, fresh, more upscale place whose name stands for "modern Estonian cuisine." They offer two great deals: artful weekday lunch specials for just €5, and a €30 four-course set-price menu for serious eaters. Young, elegant locals take their lunch breaks here (€16-25 main dishes, Mon-Sat 12:00-23:00, closed Sun, Suur-Karja 17/19, tel. 680-6688).

Russian and Caucasian Food

As about a third of the local population is enthusiastically Russian, there are plenty of places serving Russian cuisine (see also under "Budget Eateries," next page).

Troika is my choice for Russian food. Right on Town Hall Square, with a folkloric-costumed waitstaff, they serve €6-9 *bliny* (pancakes) and *pelmeni* (dumplings), and €12-20 main dishes. Sit out on the square (reserve for dinner), down in the trippy, trendy cellar, or in the more casual tavern (ground level out back, prices 15 percent lower). A balalaika player usually strums and strolls after 19:00 (daily 12:00-23:00, Raekoja Plats 15, tel. 627-6245).

Must Lammas is straightforward and elegant, focusing on just plain tasty Caucasian food from Georgia, Armenia, and Azerbaijan (€9 lunch specials, €10-18 main dishes, Mon-Sat 12:00-23:00, Sun 12:00-18:00, Sauna 2, tel. 644-2031).

Medieval Cuisine

Two well-run restaurants just below Town Hall Square specialize in re-creating medieval food (from the days before the arrival of the potato and tomato from the New World). They are each grotesquely touristy, complete with gift shops where you can buy your souvenir goblet. Both have street seating, but you'll get all the tourists and none of the atmosphere.

Olde Hansa, filling three creaky old floors and outdoor tables with tourists, candle wax, and scurrying medieval waitresses, can be quite expensive (€13-35 main dishes, daily 10:00-24:00, musicians circulate nightly after 18:00, a belch below Town Hall Square at Vana Turg 1, reserve in advance, tel. 627-9020). **Peppersack,** across the street, tries to compete (Vana Turg 6, tel. 646-6800).

Pubs in the Old Town

Young Estonians eat well and affordably at pubs. In some pubs, you go to the bar to look at the menu, order, and pay. Then find a table, and they'll bring your food out when it's ready.

Hell Hunt Pub ("The Gentle Wolf") was the first Western-style pub to open after 1991, and it's still going strong, attracting a mixed expat and local crowd with its tasty food. Consider making a meal from the great pub snacks (€2.50-€4.50) plus a salad (€5-6). Choose a table in its convivial interior or in the rustic courtyard across the street (€4.50 soups, €6-10 main dishes, daily 12:00-1:00 in the morning, Pikk 39, tel. 681-8333).

Von Krahli Baar serves cheap, substantial Estonian grub—such as potato pancakes *(torud)* stuffed with mushrooms or shrimp (€5)—in a big, dark space that doubles as a center for Estonia's alternative theater scene; there's also seating in the tiny court-yard where you enter. It started as the bar of the theater upstairs, then expanded to become a restaurant, so it has a young, avant-garde vibe. You'll feel like you're eating backstage with the stage-hands (€4-7 main dishes, Mon-Sat 12:00-22:00, Sun 12:00-18:00, Rataskaevu 10/12, a block uphill from Town Hall Square, near Wheel Well, tel. 626-9090).

Budget Eateries

Eat, a laid-back, cellar-level student hangout with a big foosball table and a book exchange, serves the best-value lunch in town. Its menu is very simple: three varieties of *pelmeenid* (dumplings), plus sauces, beet salad, and pickles. You dish up what you like and pay by weight (€2-3/big bowl). Ask for an education in the various dumplings and sauces and then go for the complete experience. Enjoy with abandon—you can't spend much money here, and you'll feel good stoking their business (Mon-Sat 11:00-21:00, closed Sun, Sauna 2, tel. 644-0029).

Balti Jaama Kohvik, at the end of the train station near the Balti Jaam Market, is an unimpressive-looking 24-hour diner with no real sign (look for a red awning and *Kohvik avatud 24 tundi*—"café open 24 hours"—on the door). The bustling stainless-steel kitchen cranks out traditional Russian/Estonian dishes—the cheapest hot food in town. While you won't see or hear a word of English here, the glass case displays the various offerings and prices (€3 meals, €1.60 soups, dirt-cheap-yet-wonderful savory pancakes, and tasty *beljaš*—a kind of pierogi). Unfortunately, the area feels dangerous after dark.

Supermarkets: For picnic supplies, try the **Rimi** supermarket just outside the Old Town at Aia 7, near the Viru Gate (daily 8:00-22:00). A larger, more upscale supermarket in the basement of the **Viru Keskus** mall (directly behind Hotel Viru) has convenient, inexpensive take-away meals (daily 9:00-22:00). The handy little **Kolmjag "Everything"** grocery is a block off Town Hall Square (daily 24 hours, Pikk 11, tel. 631-1511).

Breakfast and Pastries

The **Maiasmokk** ("Sweet Tooth") café and pastry shop, founded in 1864, is the grande dame of Tallinn cafés—ideal for dessert or breakfast. Even through the Soviet days, this was *the* place for a good pastry or a glass of herby Tallinn schnapps ("Vana Tallinn"). Point to what you want from the selection of classic local pastries at the counter, and sit down for breakfast (€3 omelets) or coffee on the other side of the shop. Everything's reasonable (Mon-Fri 8:00-22:00, Sat 9:00-22:00, Sun 9:00-21:00, Pikk 16, across from church with old clock, tel. 646-4079). They also have a marzipan shop (separate entrance).

Pierre Chocolaterie at Vene 6 has scrumptious fresh pralines, sandwiches, and coffee in a courtyard filled with craft shops (daily 8:30-late, tel. 641-8061).

Tallinn Connections

TALLINN

The bus is usually the best way to travel by land from Tallinn. The largest operator, with the most departures, is Lux Express (tel. 680-0909, www.luxexpress.ee); there's also Ecolines (tel. 614-3600 or mobile 5637-7997, www.ecolines.net) and the spiffy Hansabuss (with onboard Wi-Fi, tel. 627-9080, www.hansabuss.ee). The bus station *(autobussijaam)* is at Lastekodu 46, a short taxi ride from the Old Town, or a few stops on trams #2 or #4 to the Autobussijaam stop (direction: Ülemiste). Not much English is spoken at the station; reserving online is recommended.

From Tallinn to: Rīga (12 buses/day, 4.5 hours, no train option), **Vilnius** (2 buses/day at 10:00 and 22:30, 10 hours), **St. Petersburg** (11 buses/day, 6.5-8 hours; also possible by overnight cruise—about 1/week, 14.5 hours, www.stpeterline.com; for details, see page 595), **Moscow** (take the overnight train—daily at 17:20, 16-hour trip, www.gorail.ee—or fly). Americans and Canadians must obtain a visa to travel to Russia and need to plan long in advance (for more information on visa requirements, see page 595 in the Helsinki chapter; www.russianembassy.org or www.rusembassy.ca).

For the latest bus and train schedules, see the helpful binders at the TI or consult *Tallinn in Your Pocket*.

SCANDINAVIAN HISTORY

On your trip, you'll see reminders everywhere of Scandinavia's long history. Eerie graves, carved rune stones, and horned helmets bring to mind *Lord of the Rings*-style warriors of old who worshipped Thor and Odin. You'll see the ships and weapons of their descendants—the Vikings—who terrorized Europe with their fierce, pagan culture. Evocative wooden-stave churches show how Christianity slowly seeped into the region.

You'll visit the harbors of these seafaring peoples and tour the stark castles of nobles who fought for control of Baltic trade. As modern nations emerged, absolute monarchs built luxurious palaces intended to rival Versailles. Today's streets and main squares are studded with statues and monuments honoring great kings and their battles, great patriots who lobbied for national independence, and great writers and musicians who enriched Scandinavian culture. Scandinavian museums are filled with paintings that capture the beauty of the landscape and celebrate its people. You'll hear bittersweet stories of the millions of 19th-century Scandinavians who left their homes for better lives in America. You'll learn about those who suffered under WWII Nazi occupation, and the heroes who organized resistance and sheltered Jewish people. And you'll experience the richness of Scandinavia today—its wealth, its liberal policies, and its global outlook.

Want to hear more of the Scandinavian story? Read on.

Prehistory and Hunters with Spears (c. 8000 B.C.-A.D. 1)

Scandinavia became habitable when the glaciers receded at the end of the last ice age. Stone Age hunters moved north, chasing valuable deer, elk, and fish. Among these were the forebears of the Sami—or Laplanders—of northern Scandinavia, some of whom continue to herd reindeer and live a nomadic lifestyle today. For more on the Sami, visit Oslo's National Historical Museum (page 254) or Norwegian Folk Museum (page 261), or Stockholm's Nordic Museum (page 454). The early Scandinavians began farming (c. 4000 B.C.) and eventually developed tools and weapons made of bronze (c. 1800 B.C.). We know these people mainly by their graves—either burial mounds (as on the island of Öland, Sweden, page 543) or the heavy stone tombs called dolmens (as on Denmark's isle of Ærø, page 159).

Iron-Age Warriors with Horned Helmets (A.D. 1-800)

Isolated from the Continent and unconquered by the Romans, Scandinavia kept close to its prehistoric past. The 2,000-year-old Grauballe Man—whose corpse was preserved in a peat bog (and is now displayed at the Moesgård Museum just outside Aarhus, page 202)—was a contemporary of Julius Caesar. But in his world, people spoke not Latin but a Germanic language, wore animal-horned helmets, and used ceremonial curvy-shaped *lur* horns. They forged iron implements decorated with the gods of their pagan religion (such as the Gundestrup Cauldron displayed in Copenhagen's National Museum, page 86). They commemorated heroic deeds with large stones carved with the angular alphabet known as runes (see the rune stones at Copenhagen's National Museum, page 86, and at Jelling, Denmark, page 211). One of their most sacred sites is at Gamla Uppsala near Stockholm (page 485), where mighty chieftains were buried along with their worldly possessions—weapons, jewels, dogs, horses, and even slaves. This distinct, pre-Christian Scandinavian culture thrived in the first centuries A.D. and continued even as the rest of Europe fell under the sway of Rome's Latin culture and, later, Christianity.

Though isolated, the Scandinavians made fleeting contact with Roman Europe, trading furs and amber (a petrified tree sap, used in jewelry) for crucial tool-making metals from the Continent. Eventually, the Scandinavians learned to extract their own bronze and iron. With better tools, they became productive farmers and shipbuilders. The population boomed due to a warmer climate and better nutrition. The Scandinavians were soon eyeing Europe and the North Atlantic as a source for new resources and for potential expansion of their clans.

Vikings with Ships (800-1000)

Scandinavia's entrance onto the European stage was swift, dramatic, and unforgettable. On January 8, 793, a fleet of Scandinavian pirates came ashore on the northeast coast of England and sacked the Lindisfarne monastery, slaughtering monks, burning buildings, and plundering sacred objects. Word spread like wildfire of brutal pirates who seemed to come from nowhere, looted and pillaged with extreme prejudice, then moved on. Their victims called them *Normanni, Dani, Rus,* or worse, but the name they gave themselves came from the inlets and bays *(vik)* where they lived: the Vikings.

For the next 200 years, hardy Viking sailors plundered and explored the coasts of northern Europe. Vikings from Norway primarily went west to the British Isles and settled Iceland, Greenland, and beyond; Swedes ventured east to the Baltic states, navigated the Russian rivers, and reached Constantinople; and Danes headed south (to England, France, Spain, and Italy).

The Vikings attacked in fleets of sleek, narrow, open-topped ships a hundred feet long, called *drakkars.* (See them for yourself at the Viking Ship Museums in Oslo, page 262, or Roskilde, page 141.) Rigged with square sails and powered by dozens of men at the oars, they could attack at 15 miles an hour and land right on the beach, where they would pour out, brandishing their weapons.

Each Viking was decked out with a coat of mail, a small shield, and a helmet (though not one with horns, which by Viking times were merely ceremonial). Each warrior specialized in a particular kind of warfare: sword, spear, battle-axe, or bow-and-arrow. At the battle's crucial moment, the Vikings might send in their secret weapon—the so-called *berserkers.* These warriors attacked with a seemingly superhuman (and possibly drug-induced) frenzy, scaring the leotards off their enemies and giving us our English word "berserk."

Despite their reputation as ruthless pirates, most Vikings were settlers who established towns, married the locals, farmed the land, hunted in the forests, and traded with their neighbors. They spread Scandinavian culture and rune stones far and wide. In Northern France, the region of "Normandy" was settled by the "North-men." Eric the Red, a Norwegian Viking, was an early settler in Iceland, and his son Leif Eriksson sailed as far as the coast of North America around A.D. 1000.

To the dismay of Roman Catholic bishops, while the rest of Europe became Christian, the Vikings held onto their pagan gods, many of whom were, like themselves, warriors: Odin, the king of the gods (who gave us our word for Wednesday), and Thor with his hammer, the god of war (and of Thursday). Believing in an afterlife, the Vikings buried their dead ceremonially along with their possessions. Some were interred beneath large mounds of dirt (such as the Gamla Uppsala burial mounds described on page 485). Others were laid to rest in ships that were buried underground, or in graves marked with stones placed upright in the shape of a full-size ship.

Typical Castle Architecture

Castles were fortified residences for medieval nobles. Castles come in all shapes and sizes, but knowing a few general terms will help you understand them.

Barbican: A fortified gatehouse, sometimes a stand-alone building located outside the main walls.

Crenellation: A gap-toothed pattern of stones atop the parapet.

Drawbridge: A bridge that could be raised or lowered, using counterweights or a chain and winch.

Great Hall: The largest room in the castle—serving as throne room, conference center, and dining hall.

Hoardings (or Gallery or Brattice): Wooden huts built onto the upper parts of the stone walls. They served as watch towers, living quarters, and fighting platforms.

The Keep (or Donjon): A high, strong stone tower in the center of the castle complex that was the lord's home and refuge of last resort.

Loopholes: Narrow slits in the walls (also called embrasures, arrow slits, or arrow loops) through which soldiers could shoot arrows at the enemy.

Machicolation: A stone ledge jutting out from the wall, fitted with holes in the bottom. If the enemy was scaling the walls, soldiers could drop rocks or boiling oil down through the holes and onto the enemy below.

Moat: A ditch encircling the wall, often filled with water.

Parapet: Outer railing of the wall walk.

Portcullis: A heavy iron grille that could be lowered across the entrance.

By the year 1000, Scandinavian society was gradually changing—unifying, Christianizing, and assimilating into European culture. Scattered Nordic peoples coalesced into kingdoms, united under the banner of Christianity. In Norway, there was King (later "Saint") Olav II (c. 1020). Among the Svea people (Sweden), King Olof Skotkonung (c. 968-1020) unified and Christianized the land. The Danes were united by King Harald Bluetooth (c. 980), who commemorated Denmark's Christian conversion on a now-famous rune stone (located in Jelling, page 211)—although in reality, Bluetooth's "conversion" was a ploy to keep the German-Catholic bishops and missionaries at bay. Under Harald's grandson, King Canute, Denmark ruled a large empire that included parts of southern England (c. 1020). One of Canute's battles there inspired the nursery song "London Bridge Is Falling Down."

By 1100, the last pagans were gathering at Gamla Uppsala to put on their ceremonial horned helmets, worship the sun, bury fallen heroes, and retell the sagas of their ancestors. Viking culture blended into the European mainstream, but we still see traces of it

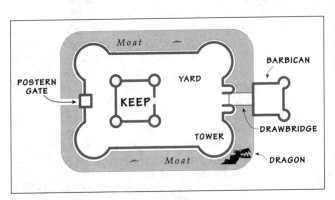

Postern Gate: A small, unfortified side or rear entrance used during peacetime. In wartime, it became a "sally-port" used to launch surprise attacks, or as an escape route.

Towers: Tall structures serving as lookouts, chapels, living quarters, or the dungeon. Towers could be square or round, with either crenellated tops or conical roofs.

Turret: A small lookout tower projecting up from the top of the wall.

Wall Walk (or Allure): A pathway atop the wall where guards could patrol and where soldiers stood to fire at the enemy.

The Yard (or Bailey or Ward): An open courtyard inside the castle walls.

today—in rune stones and burial sites; in surviving tools, weapons, and jewelry; and in the dragon-prowed designs found on Christian stave churches and even on contemporary Scandinavian coins.

Medieval Christians, Bickering Nobles, and German Businessmen (1000–1400)

In the Middle Ages, three separate (if loosely united) kingdoms emerged: Denmark, Sweden, and Norway. They were Christian and feudal, with land worked by peasants who owed allegiance to a petty noble sworn to the king. Towns sprang up, including what would become the main cities: Oslo (1048), Copenhagen (1165), and Stockholm (1255). Rulers began flying flags featuring a cross, which eventually became the main motif in each country's national flag.

Christianity dominated. Some of the region's oldest churches (especially in Norway) are wooden stave, made with vertical planks and ornamented with dragons and other semi-pagan figures to ward off evil and ease the transition to Christianity (see page 221).

Devout Christians laid the cornerstones for huge cathedrals, such as the skyscraping Uppsala Cathedral in 1287, Aarhus Cathedral in 1201, and Stockholm Cathedral in 1306.

Finland entered the Scandinavian sphere when zealous Swedes launched a series of crusades to forcibly convert their pagan neighbors to the east, farm their lands, and fish in their lakes. They conquered and assimilated the region (c. 1200), making it a part of their own country for the next 600 years. Even today, Swedish is spoken on Finland's southern coast. Danish and German "warrior monks" fought a similar crusade against the loosely organized Estonian people, divvying up that region between themselves.

The many castles that dot Scandinavia attest to the civil warfare between nobles. A strong central government headed by a dominant king was still centuries away.

Sea trade between the Scandinavian neighbors boomed. The lucrative trade was controlled by enterprising German businessmen who organized Scandinavia's ports into a free-trade zone known as the Hanseatic League (c. 1200-1400). Under German direction, Scandinavia became a powerful player in overseas commerce with the Continent. Cities such as Bergen, Norway, reaped big rewards under the Hanse (see Håkon's Hall on page 374). German settlers emigrated to Scandinavia, influencing the culture and language. By 1370, these German businessmen were so rich that they wielded more actual power than any Scandinavian king. It took a queen to break them.

Dominant Danes: Wars and Reformation (1400-1600)

When Margrethe I of Denmark married the Norwegian king in 1363, Norway came under Danish control (where it would remain for the next 450 years). Denmark emerged as the region's main power. In 1397, Margrethe took on the Hanseatic League by uniting Norway, Denmark, and Sweden against the league with the Treaty of Kalmar. The German monopoly was broken, and Scandinavia gained control of its own wealth. But after Margrethe, the union faltered. For a century, Swedish nobles chafed and occasionally rebelled against Danish domination.

In 1520, Denmark invaded Sweden and—in the notorious Stockholm Bloodbath—massacred 80 rebellious Swedish nobles in the city's main square, Stortorget (see page 432). Gustav Vasa rallied the enraged Swedes and drove out Denmark's King Christian (known as Christian II in Denmark and as Christian the Tyrant in Sweden). Vasa was crowned king of Sweden on June 6, 1523 (now Sweden's flag day). He centralized the Swedish government and Protestantized the country, seizing church property to form a strong nation-state. In many ways, this was the birth of modern

Sweden (and the origin of the name for Wasa flatbread).

By the 1500s, all of Scandinavia had converted to Lutheran-style Protestantism. They'd been primed by the influence of German Hanseatic traders and preachers. And their kings jumped at the chance to confiscate former church property and authority.

For the next century, Denmark and Sweden—the region's two powerhouses—battled for control of the Baltic's lucrative trade routes, particularly for the Øresund, the crucial strait between Denmark and Sweden that connects the Baltic with the North Sea (and is now spanned by a modern bridge—see sidebar on page 155). It was during this period that much of Estonia fell under control of the Swedish empire.

Swedish Superiority: Absolute Monarchs (1600-1800)

By 1600, Denmark-Norway was still the region's superpower, but Sweden-Finland-Estonia was rising fast. Denmark's one-eyed, high-living King Christian IV was spending centuries' worth of acquired wealth building lavish castles—including Rosenborg and Frederiksborg—and putting a Renaissance face on Copenhagen and Oslo (see page 97 and the sidebar on page 52). Meanwhile, his wars with Sweden and others were slowly sapping the country, emptying its coffers, and undermining Danish superiority. Christian IV even sold the Orkney and Shetland Islands to England to raise funds.

Sweden emerged under the inspired military leadership of King Gustavus Adolphus (1594-1632). The "Lion of the North" roared southward, conquering large chunks of Russia, Poland, Germany, and Denmark during the Thirty Years' War. The vast *Vasa* ship in Stockholm, which the king commissioned in 1628, trumpeted the optimism of the era—but sank ignominiously on its maiden voyage in the middle of Stockholm harbor (see page 452).

Sweden's supreme moment came under Gustavus' great-grandson, Charles X Gustav (1622-1660). In 1657, Charles invaded Denmark through the back door—from the south. The winter was extremely cold, and the seas froze between several of Denmark's islands. In one of the most daring maneuvers in military history, Charles X Gustav led his armies across the ice between the islands—from Funen to Langeland to Lolland to Zealand—then sped toward Copenhagen. The astonished Danes surrendered, signing the humiliating Treaty of Roskilde (1658). The treaty gave Sweden a third of Danish territory, plus shared control of the Øresund Strait. Denmark would never again dominate, while Sweden became a major European power, with an imposing fleet and a Baltic empire that included Finland, Estonia, Latvia, and parts of Poland, Russia, and Germany.

In the 1660s, the kings of Denmark-Norway and Sweden-Finland-Estonia—following the trend set by Louis XIV in France—declared themselves to be absolute, divinely ordained monarchs. For the next 50 years, these kings scuffled with each other (and neighboring countries) for superiority in the Baltic. By 1720, the wars had drained both countries, at the very time that France and England were on the rise. Sweden ceded Estonia to the Russians, and Scandinavia sank back into relative obscurity.

For the rest of the 1700s, Denmark-Norway and Sweden-Finland mostly avoided war while trying to modernize and expand their economies. But the French Revolution (1789) and the Europe-wide wars that followed stirred up this relative peace, awakening a desire for democracy, ethnic recognition, and national independence.

Patriots, Artists, Industrialists, and Emigrants (1800s)

As Europe's monarchs ganged up on Revolutionary France under Napoleon, Scandinavia was forced to take sides. Through a series of complicated alliances, Denmark ended up backing the loser (France), while Sweden backed the winners (Britain and others). At war's end, Denmark was forced to cede Norway to Sweden in the 1814 Treaty of Kiel. Meanwhile, Sweden had just lost Finland to Russia in 1809. Thus began the nation-building process that, a century later, would result in the five independent nations we have today.

The wars also gave Sweden a new king—a French soldier who spoke not a word of Swedish, was not Scandinavian, and had not a drop of noble blood. But Jean-Baptiste Bernadotte, a career military man in Napoleon's army, was loved by Sweden's childless king, admired by Sweden's soldiers for his fighting prowess, and popular with the people for treating Swedish prisoners well during the wars. The bizarre choice of a French commoner was a surprise, but everyone said *oui-oui*, and Jean-Baptiste was crowned Sweden's King Karl Johan XIV (and Karl Johan III in Norway). During his reign (1818-1844), Bernadotte brought peace, prosperity, and fresh DNA, founding the royal dynasty that would produce the current monarchs of Sweden—and, by intermarriage, of Norway and Denmark.

The French Revolution (and Napoleon) spread the idea throughout Europe that people should embrace their ethnic roots and demand self-rule. Norwegians—having been ruled for centuries by Danes, and now Swedes—met at Eidsvoll Manor (outside Oslo—see page 272), drafted a constitution with a parliament, elected a king, and demanded independence. Though the country was still too weak to make this a political reality, the date of May

17, 1814, has become the country's Fourth of July, celebrated today with plenty of flag-waving and folk costumes by Norwegians both in and out of Norway.

Culturally (if not politically), nationalism flourished, producing artists like J. C. Dahl, who captured the beauty of the Norwegian countryside and the simple dignity of its people. (You can see his works at Oslo's National Gallery, page 247.) Playwright Henrik Ibsen realistically portrayed the complexities of a changing Norwegian society. And composer Edvard Grieg used music to convey the majesty of the landscape near his home in Bergen (Troldhaugen, page 380).

In Denmark, nationalism inspired the German-speaking majority in the provinces of Schleswig and Holstein to call for autonomy (1848-1851). The region was finally taken by force from Denmark by Prussia (1864) and incorporated into the new state of Germany. The resulting nationwide sense of humiliation and self-critique actually spurred a cultural golden age. Philosopher Søren Kierkegaard captured the angst of an age when traditional certainties were crumbling. Storyteller Hans Christian Andersen (*The Ugly Duckling, The Emperor's New Clothes, The Little Mermaid,* and others) gained a Europe-wide reputation. And sculptor Bertel Thorvaldsen, who studied and worked in Rome, decorated Copenhagen with his realistic, Neoclassical statues (at Copenhagen's Cathedral of Our Lady, page 73; and the Thorvaldsen's Museum, page 91).

Throughout the 1800s, Scandinavia was modernizing. The Industrial Revolution brought trains, factories, and larger cities. While some got rich, millions of poor farmers were forced to emigrate from Sweden, Norway, and Finland to America between 1850 and 1920, due to the changing economy, overpopulation, and famine. (The House of Emigrants museum in Växjö, Sweden, tells their story—see page 512.) As in other European countries, Scandinavia saw the steady advance of democracy, parliaments, labor unions, and constitutional monarchies. The 20th century would quicken that pace.

Independence and World Wars (1900-1945)

In 1905—after five and a half centuries of Danish and Swedish rule—Norway finally was granted independence when it voted overwhelmingly to break from Sweden. National pride ran high, as Oslo's own Roald Amundsen became the first person to reach the South Pole (in 1911—for more, see the Fram Museum on page 263). In 1919, Finland and Estonia—after centuries of Swedish and Russian rule—won their independence while Russia was distracted by the Bolshevik Revolution.

The Scandinavian nations remained neutral through World

War I. But when Hitler's Nazi Germany began its European conquest in World War II, it was impossible for Scandinavians—try as they might—to remain uninvolved. While officially neutral, Sweden allowed Nazi troops "on leave" to march through. (Sweden's neutrality later provided a safe haven for Danish Jews and a refuge for the Danish and Norwegian resistance movements.)

Germany invaded Denmark and Norway on April 9, 1940, with Operation Weserübung. Scattered fighting at the Danish border was quickly put down, and Denmark capitulated and officially cooperated with the Nazis until 1943, when the Germans took over the government. Danish resistance groups harried the Nazis and provided intelligence to the Allies (see the Museum of Danish Resistance, page 95). In 1943, a German diplomat informed Copenhagen's rabbi that the Jews were about to be deported. Danish citizens quickly hid and eventually evacuated all but 500 of Denmark's Jews to neutral Sweden.

Norway's army held out a few weeks longer, allowing time for King Håkon VII to flee and organize a vital resistance movement (memorialized at Oslo's Norwegian Resistance Museum, page 246). Norway spent the war chafing under a Nazi puppet government headed by Vidkun Quisling, whose surname has become synonymous with "traitor."

Denmark, Sweden, and Norway came out of the war without the horrendous damage and loss of life suffered elsewhere in Europe—in part, probably, because Hitler wanted to turn the Scandinavian countries into model states. After all, these were the people Germany was trying to emulate: tall, blonde, blue-eyed symbols of the Aryan race.

Finland and Estonia's fate were more complicated. During the war, the Finns valiantly battled Russian invaders, at one point allying with Hitler against the Russians. By war's end, Finland had fought both the Soviets and the Nazis. Estonia, meanwhile, was occupied first by the Soviets and later by the Nazis.

As postwar Europe was divvied up between the communist East and the democratic West, Estonia wound up in the Soviet sphere of influence. Finland avoided this fate through a compromise policy called "Finlandization." The Finns paid lip service to Soviet authority, censored their own media, acted as a buffer against military invasion from the West, rejected rebuilding money from the US (the Marshall Plan), and avoided treaties with the West. In return, Finland remained a self-ruling capitalist democracy and a firm part of the Nordic world. They imported raw materials from the Soviets, then shipped them back as manufactured products, in a mutually beneficial trade agreement.

Meanwhile, Norway and Denmark stood with the West, joining NATO and participating in the Marshall Plan. Sweden

Little Maria...or Metallica?

Scandinavia is viewed as one of the most liberal corners of Europe, so Americans are often surprised to learn there are government restrictions on what parents can name their children. Historically, parents in Denmark, Norway, Sweden, and Finland were required to choose their child's name from a published list of acceptable monikers. Any variations had to be approved by a government board. One intent of the rules was to prevent commoners from using royal names and to ban names considered ridiculous, inappropriate, potentially harmful to the child, or just not Scandinavian enough. A Norwegian mom even spent two days in jail in the '90s for naming her son Gesher (it means "bridge" in Hebrew). But following a recent series of court rulings, Scandinavian countries are relaxing parts of their naming laws. Denmark has allowed some Legolas's and Gandolfs, and in Sweden there's a little girl named Metallica and a little boy named Q.

Estonia took a different approach: In the 1930s it encouraged its citizens to change their Swedish-sounding names to the Estonian equivalent.

took a more neutral approach, and Sweden's Dag Hammarskjöld served as the UN's Secretary General from 1953 to 1961. Estonia was submerged into the Soviet Union as one of the 15 "republics" of the USSR, only regaining its independence with the breakup of the Soviet Union in 1991.

The Social Welfare State (1946-Present)

In the decades since World War II, the Scandinavian countries have made themselves quite wealthy following a mixed capitalist-socialist model. In the late 1960s, Norway discovered oil in the North Sea, instantly transforming itself into a rich nation. Citizens across Scandinavia have come to take for granted cradle-to-grave security—health care, education, unemployment benefits, welfare, and so on—all financed with high taxes. In social policies, Scandinavia has often led the way in liberal attitudes toward sexuality, drug use, and gay rights. For more on current-day Scandinavia, see page 38.

Immigration in the late 20th century brought many citizens from non-European nations. While adding diversity, it also threatened the homogenous fabric of a society whose roots have traditionally been white, Christian, European, democratic, and blonde. Far-right parties gained support with anti-immigration platforms, but reaction to the July 2011 massacre in Norway (see page 270) seems to have weakened those movements, at least in the short term.

Today, Finland, Sweden, Denmark, and Estonia are all members of the European Union. Norway has stayed outside (a decision still hotly debated by Norwegians, though an association agreement gives the country most of the benefits of membership). While Finland and Estonia have embraced the euro, Norway, Sweden, and Denmark have preserved their own currencies (though Denmark's is pegged to the euro).

As the Scandinavian people forge into the 21st century, they are adamant about preserving their culture, traditions, and high standard of living while competing in a global economy.

APPENDIX

Contents

Tourist Information

The Scandinavian Tourist Board's office in **the US** is a wealth of information on Norway, Denmark, Sweden, Finland, and Iceland. Before your trip, get the free general information packet and request any specifics you want (such as regional and city maps and festival schedules). Call 212/885-9700 or visit www.goscandinavia .com (info@goscandinavia.com). Estonia doesn't have a tourist office in the US, but you can check their website (www.visitestonia .com, tourism@eas.ee).

In Scandinavia, your best first stop in every town is generally the tourist information office (abbreviated **TI** in this book). Throughout Scandinavia, you'll find TIs are usually well-organized and always have an English-speaking staff. Most TIs are run by the government, which means their information isn't colored by a drive for profit. (The big exception is the commercially operated Copenhagen TI, which dubs itself "Wonderful Copenhagen.")

TIs are good places to get a city map and advice on public transit (including bus and train schedules), walking tours, special events, and nightlife. Many TIs have information on the entire country or at least the region, so try to pick up maps for destinations you'll be visiting later in your trip. If you're arriving in town after the TI closes, call ahead or pick up a map in a neighboring town.

Most big cities publish a *This Week in...* or *What's On...* guide (to Oslo, Bergen, Stockholm, Helsinki, and Tallinn, but not Copenhagen). These are free, found all over town, and packed with all the details about each city (24-hour pharmacy, embassies, tram/bus fares, restaurants, sights with hours/admissions/phone numbers), plus a useful calendar of events and a map of the town center.

While TIs are eager to book you a room, they're a good deal only if you're in search of summer and weekend deals on business hotels. A TI can help you find small pensions and private homes, but you'll save yourself and your host money by going direct with the listings in this book.

Communicating

Hurdling the Language Barrier

In Scandinavia, English is all you need. These days every well-educated Scandinavian seems to speak English. Still, knowing the key words in the language of the country you are visiting is good style and helpful.

Each country has its own language. Danish, Norwegian, and Swedish are so closely related that locals can laugh at each other's TV comedies. The languages are similar to English but with a few extra letters (Æ, Ø, Ö, Å, Ä). These letters barely affect pronunciation, but do affect alphabetizing. If you can't find, say, Årjäng in a map index, look after Z. Finnish and Estonian are vastly different from the other Scandinavian languages and English; in fact, Finnish has more in common with Hungarian than with Swedish (see page 551).

Here are a few words you'll see and hear a lot (these are all Norwegian; the Danish and Swedish versions differ slightly): *takk* (thanks), *gammel* (old), *lille* (small), *stor* (big), *slot* (palace), *fart* (trip), *centrum* (center), *gate* (street), *øl* (beer), *forbudt* (not allowed), and *udsalg*, *salg*, or *rea* (sale). For more, see the survival phrases later in the appendix. Give it your best shot. The locals will appreciate your efforts.

Telephones

Smart travelers use the telephone to reserve or reconfirm rooms, get tourist information, reserve restaurants, confirm tour times, or phone home. Generally the easiest, cheapest way to call home is to use an international phone card purchased in Scandinavia. This section covers dialing instructions, phone cards, and types of phones (for more in-depth information, see www.ricksteves.com /phoning).

How to Dial

Calling from the US to Scandinavia, or vice versa, is simple—once you break the code. The European calling chart in this chapter will walk you through it.

Dialing Domestically in Scandinavia

The following instructions apply to dialing from a landline (such as a pay phone or your hotel-room phone) or from a Scandinavian mobile phone.

Denmark, Estonia, and **Norway** use a direct-dial system (no area codes). To call anywhere within one of these countries, just dial the number. For example, the number of one of my recommended Copenhagen hotels is 33 13 19 13. To call the hotel from anywhere in Denmark (including Copenhagen), simply dial 33 13 19 13.

Sweden and **Finland,** on the other hand, use area codes. To make domestic calls anywhere within these countries, punch in just the phone number if you're dialing locally, and add the area code if calling long distance. For example, Stockholm's area code is 08, and the number of one of my recommended Stockholm hotels is 723-7250. To call the hotel within Stockholm, just dial 723-7250. To call it from Kalmar (in southeast Sweden), dial 08/723-7250. Be aware, however, that if you're calling a mobile or toll-free number, you'll need to dial the whole number, regardless of where you are calling from.

Don't be surprised that Scandinavian phone numbers may vary in length; for instance, a hotel can have a six-digit phone number and an eight-digit fax number.

If you're making calls within Scandinavia using your **US mobile phone,** you may need to dial as if it's a domestic call, or you may need to dial as if you're calling from the US (see "Dialing Internationally," next). Try it one way, and if it doesn't work, try it the other way.

Dialing Internationally to or from Scandinavia

If you want to make an international call, follow these steps:

• Dial the international access code (011 if you're calling from the US or Canada, 00 if you're calling from Europe—except in

European Calling Chart

Just smile and dial, using this key:
AC = Area Code, LN = Local Number.

European Country	Calling long distance within ...	Calling from the US or Canada to ...	Calling from a European country to ...
Austria	AC + LN	011 + 43 + AC (without the initial zero) + LN	00 + 43 + AC (without the initial zero) + LN
Belgium	LN	011 + 32 + LN (without initial zero)	00 + 32 + LN (without initial zero)
Bosnia-Herzegovina	AC + LN	011 + 387 + AC (without initial zero) + LN	00 + 387 + AC (without initial zero) + LN
Britain	AC + LN	011 + 44 + AC (without initial zero) + LN	00 + 44 + AC (without initial zero) + LN
Croatia	AC + LN	011 + 385 + AC (without initial zero) + LN	00 + 385 + AC (without initial zero) + LN
Czech Republic	LN	011 + 420 + LN	00 + 420 + LN
Denmark	LN	011 + 45 + LN	00 + 45 + LN
Estonia	LN	011 + 372 + LN	00 + 372 + LN
Finland	AC + LN	011 + 358 + AC (without initial zero) + LN	999 (or other 900 number) + 358 + AC (without initial zero) + LN
France	LN	011 + 33 + LN (without initial zero)	00 + 33 + LN (without initial zero)
Germany	AC + LN	011 + 49 + AC (without initial zero) + LN	00 + 49 + AC (without initial zero) + LN
Gibraltar	LN	011 + 350 + LN	00 + 350 + LN
Greece	LN	011 + 30 + LN	00 + 30 + LN
Hungary	06 + AC + LN	011 + 36 + AC + LN	00 + 36 + AC + LN
Ireland	AC + LN	011 + 353 + AC (without initial zero) + LN	00 + 353 + AC (without initial zero) + LN

European Country	Calling long distance within ...	Calling from the US or Canada to ...	Calling from a European country to ...
Italy	LN	011 + 39 + LN	00 + 39 + LN
Montenegro	AC + LN	011 + 382 + AC (without initial zero) + LN	00 + 382 + AC (without initial zero) + LN
Morocco	LN	011 + 212 + LN (without initial zero)	00 + 212 + LN (without initial zero)
Netherlands	AC + LN	011 + 31 + AC (without initial zero) + LN	00 + 31 + AC (without initial zero) + LN
Norway	LN	011 + 47 + LN	00 + 47 + LN
Poland	LN	011 + 48 + LN	00 + 48 + LN
Portugal	LN	011 + 351 + LN	00 + 351 + LN
Slovakia	AC + LN	011 + 421 + AC (without initial zero) + LN	00 + 421 + AC (without initial zero) + LN
Slovenia	AC + LN	011 + 386 + AC (without initial zero) + LN	00 + 386 + AC (without initial zero) + LN
Spain	LN	011 + 34 + LN	00 + 34 + LN
Sweden	AC + LN	011 + 46 + AC (without initial zero) + LN	00 + 46 + AC (without initial zero) + LN
Switzerland	LN	011 + 41 + LN (without initial zero)	00 + 41 + LN (without initial zero)
Turkey	AC (if there's no initial zero, add one) + LN	011 + 90 + AC (without initial zero) + LN	00 + 90 + AC (without initial zero) + LN

- The instructions above apply whether you're calling a land line or mobile phone.

- The international access code (the first numbers you dial when making an international call) is 011 if you're calling from the US or Canada. It's 00 if you're calling from virtually anywhere in Europe (except Finland, where it's 999 or another 900 number, depending on the phone service you're using).

- To call the US or Canada from Europe, dial 00, then 1 (the country code for the US and Canada), then the area code and number. In short, 00 + 1 + AC + LN = Hi, Mom!

Finland, which uses 999 or another 900 number depending on the phone service you're using). If you're dialing from a mobile phone, you can replace the international access code with +, which works regardless of where you're calling from. (On many mobile phones, you can insert a + by pressing and holding the 0 key.)

• Dial the country code of the country you're calling.

• Dial the area code (if applicable) and the local number, keeping in mind that calling many countries requires dropping the initial zero of the area code or local number. (For specifics per country, see the European calling chart in this chapter.)

Calling from the US to direct-dial countries (Denmark, Estonia, and Norway): To call the Copenhagen hotel from the US, dial 011 (US access code), 45 (Denmark's country code), then 33 13 19 13 (the hotel's local number).

Calling from the US to area-code countries (Sweden and Finland): To call the Stockholm hotel from the US, dial 011, 46 (Sweden's country code), 8 (Stockholm's area code minus the initial zero), then 723-7250 (local number).

Calling from any European country to the US: To call my office in Edmonds, Washington, from anywhere in Europe, I dial 00 (Europe's access code), 1 (US country code), 425 (Edmonds' area code), and 771-8303. Remember that Finland has different international access codes.

Mobile Phones

Traveling with a mobile phone is handy and practical. Whether you're using a smartphone or a conventional cell phone, the basics for how to make calls and send texts are the same. For specifics on using your smartphone to get online, see the sidebar.

Roaming with Your Mobile Phone: Your US mobile phone works in Europe if it's GSM-enabled, tri-band or quad-band, and on a calling plan that includes international calls. Phones from AT&T and T-Mobile, which use the same GSM technology that Europe does, are more likely to work overseas than Verizon or Sprint phones (if you're not sure, ask your service provider). Most US providers will charge you $1.29-1.99 per minute to make or receive calls while roaming internationally, and 20-50 cents to send or receive text messages. If you sign up for an international calling plan with your provider, you'll save a few dimes per minute. Though pricey, roaming on your own phone is easy and can be a cost-effective way to keep in touch—especially on a short trip or if you won't be making many calls.

Buying and Using SIM Cards in Europe: You'll pay much cheaper rates if you put a European SIM card in your mobile phone; to do this, your phone must be electronically "unlocked" (ask your provider about this, buy an unlocked phone before you leave, or get one in Europe—see "Other Mobile-Phone Options," next). Then, in Europe, you can buy a fingernail-size **SIM card,** which gives you a European phone number. SIM cards are sold at mobile-phone stores and some newsstand kiosks for $5–10, and often include at least that much prepaid domestic calling time (making the card itself almost free). When you buy a SIM card, you may need to show ID, such as your passport. I've had good luck with the following SIM cards: Lebara in Denmark, Telenor in Norway, and Comviq in Sweden.

Insert the SIM card in your phone (usually in a slot behind the battery or on the side) and it'll work like a European mobile phone. Before purchasing a SIM card, always ask about fees for domestic and international calls, roaming charges, and how to check your credit balance and buy more time. When you're in the SIM card's home country, domestic calls average 10-20 cents per minute, and incoming calls are free. Rates are higher if you're roaming in another country, and you may pay more to call a toll number than you would dialing from a fixed line.

Other Mobile-Phone Options: Many travelers like to carry two phones: both their own US mobile phone (allowing them to stay reachable on their own phone number) and a second, unlocked European phone (which lets them do all their local calling at far cheaper rates). You could either bring two phones from home, or get one in Europe. If you have an old mobile phone sitting around, ask your provider for the "unlock code" so it can be used with European SIM cards. Or buy a cheap, basic phone before you go (search your favorite online shopping site for "unlocked quad-band GSM phone").

In Europe, basic phones are sold at mobile phone stores, at hole-in-the-wall vendors at many airports and train stations, and at phone desks within larger department stores. Phones that are "locked" to work with a single provider start around $40; "unlocked" phones (which work with any SIM card) start around $60. Regardless of how you get your phone, remember that you'll need a SIM card to make it work.

Car-rental companies and mobile-phone companies offer the option to rent a mobile phone with a European number. While this seems convenient, hidden fees (such as high per-minute charges or expensive shipping costs) can really add up—which usually makes it a bad value. One exception is Verizon's Global Travel Program, available only to Verizon customers.

Calling over the Internet
Some things that seem too good to be true...actually are true. If you're traveling with a laptop, tablet, or smartphone, you can make free calls over the Internet to another wireless device, anywhere in

Smartphones and Data Roaming

I take my smartphone to Europe, using it to make phone calls (sparingly) and send texts, but also to check email, listen to audio tours, and browse the Internet. If you're clever, you can do all this without incurring huge data-roaming fees. Here's how.

Many smartphones, such as the iPhone, Android, and BlackBerry, work in Europe (though some older Verizon iPhones don't). For voice calls and text messaging, smartphones work like any mobile phone (as described under "Roaming with Your Mobile Phone," earlier)—unless you're connected to free Wi-Fi, in which case you can use Skype, Google Talk, or FaceTime to call for free (or at least very cheaply; see "Calling over the Internet," previous page).

The (potentially) *really* expensive aspect of using smartphones in Europe is not voice calls or text messages, but sky-high rates for using data: checking email, browsing the Internet, streaming videos, using certain apps, and so on. If you don't proactively adjust your settings, these charges can mount up even if you're not actually using your phone—because the phone is constantly "roaming" to update your email and such. (One tip is to switch your email settings from "push" to "fetch," so you can choose when to download your emails rather than having them automatically "pushed" over the Internet to your device.)

The best solution: Disable data roaming entirely, and use your device to access the Internet only when you find free Wi-Fi (at your hotel, for example). Then you can surf the net to your heart's content, or make free (or extremely cheap) phone calls via Skype. You can manually turn off data roaming on your phone's menu (check under the "Network" settings). For added security, you can call and ask your service provider to temporarily suspend your data account entirely for the length of your trip.

Some travelers enjoy the flexibility of getting online even when they're not on free Wi-Fi. But be careful. If you simply switch on data roaming, you'll pay exorbitant rates of about $20 per megabyte (figure around 40 cents per email downloaded, or about $3 to view a typical web page)—much more expensive than it is back home. If you know you'll be doing some data roaming, it's far more affordable to sign up for a limited international data-roaming plan through your carrier (but be very clear on your megabyte limit to avoid inflated overage charges). In general, ask your provider in advance how to avoid unwittingly roaming your way to a huge bill.

the world, for free. (Or you can pay a few cents to call from your computer to a telephone.) The major providers are Skype, Google Talk, and (on Apple devices) FaceTime. You can get online at a Wi-Fi hotspot and use these apps to make calls without ringing up expensive roaming charges (though call quality can be spotty on slow connections). You can make Internet calls even if you're traveling without your own mobile device: Many European Internet cafés have Skype, as well as microphones and webcams, on their terminals—just log on and chat away.

Landline Telephones

As in the US, these days most Europeans make the majority of their calls on mobile phones. But you'll still encounter landlines in hotel rooms and at pay phones.

Hotel-Room Phones: Calling from your hotel room can be great for local calls and for international calls if you have an international phone card (described later). Otherwise, hotel-room phones can be an almost criminal rip-off for long-distance or international calls. Many hotels charge a fee for local and sometimes even "toll-free" numbers—always ask for the rates before you dial. Incoming calls are free, making this a cheap way for friends and family to stay in touch (provided they have a long-distance plan with good international rates—and a list of your hotels' phone numbers).

Public Pay Phones: There are no pay phones in Estonia, and they're becoming hard to find in Scandinavian countries as well. You're likely to see them only in railway stations, airports, and medical facilities. To make calls from public pay phones, you'll need a prepaid phone card, described next.

Types of Telephone Cards

There are two types of phone cards: insertable (for pay phones) and international (cheap for overseas calls and usable from any type of phone). A phone card works only in the country where you bought it, so if you have a live card at the end of your trip, give it to another traveler to use—most cards expire three to six months after the first use.

Insertable Phone Cards: This type of card can only be used at public pay phones. It's handy and affordable for local and domestic calls, but more expensive for international calls. Insertable phone cards are sold at post offices, newsstands, and tobacco shops. To use the card, physically insert it into a slot in the pay phone. These cards only work in the country where you buy them (so your Swedish phone card is worthless in Denmark), and aren't available in Estonia (which has no public pay phones).

APPENDIX

International Phone Cards: With these cards, phone calls from Scandinavia to the US can cost less than a nickel a minute. The cards can also be used to make local calls, and they work from any type of phone, including your hotel-room phone or a mobile phone with a European SIM card. To use the card, dial a toll-free access number, then enter your scratch-to-reveal PIN code.

The cards are sold at some post offices, newsstands, mini-marts, and shops serving immigrants. Ask the clerk which of the various brands has the best rates for calls to the US. Buy a lower denomination in case the card is a dud. Some shops also sell card-less codes, printed right on the receipt. Since you don't need the actual card or receipt to use a card account, you can write down the access number and code and share it with friends.

Most merchants promise that the cards work throughout Scandinavia (cards are generally printed with local access numbers for each country), but often they don't work in neighboring countries, leaving you stuck with extra minutes that you can't use. (It can be difficult to find international phone cards in Finland and they aren't available in Estonia.)

When using an international calling card, the area code must be dialed even if you're calling across the street. Usually the prompts are in fairly concise English, but if you hear a Scandinavian language, or worse, an interminable English sales pitch, experiment: Dial your code, followed by the pound sign (#), then the number, then pound again, and so on, until it works. Sometimes the star (*) key is used instead of the pound sign.

US Calling Cards: These cards, such as the ones offered by AT&T, Verizon, and Sprint, are a rotten value, and are being phased out. Try any of the options outlined earlier.

Useful Phone Numbers
Emergencies
In all the countries in this book, dial 112 for medical or other emergencies. For police, dial 112 everywhere except Estonia (dial 110).

US Embassies
Embassies are located in all the capital cities.

In Denmark: Dag Hammarskjölds Allé 24, Copenhagen, passport services by appointment, info tel. 33 41 71 00 (Mon-Fri 14:00-16:00), emergency tel. 33 41 74 00, http://denmark.usembassy.gov

In Estonia: Kentmanni 20, Tallinn, passport services Mon-Fri 9:00-12:00 & 14:00-17:00, tel. 668-8128, emergency tel. 509-2129, http://estonia.usembassy.gov

In Finland: Itäinen Puistotie 14B, Helsinki, passport services by appointment, info tel. 40/140-5957 (Mon-Thu 14:00-16:00), emergency tel. 09/616-250, http://finland.usembassy.gov

In Norway: Henrik Ibsens Gate 48, Oslo, passport services by appointment, info tel. 21 30 85 58 (Mon-Fri 15:00-16:30), emergency tel. 21 30 85 40, http://norway.usembassy.gov

In Sweden: Dag Hammarskjölds Väg 31, Stockholm, passport services by appointment, info tel. 08/783-4375 (Mon-Tue and Thu 13:00-14:00), emergency tel. 08/783-5300, http://stockholm.us embassy.gov

Canadian Embassies

In Denmark: Kristen Bernikowsgade 1, Copenhagen, passport services Mon-Fri 8:30-12:00 & 13:00-16:30, tel. 33 48 32 00, www.canada.dk

In Estonia: Toomkooli 13, Tallinn, passport services Mon-Fri 8:30-17:00, tel. 627-3311, www.canada.ee

In Finland: Pohjoisesplanadi 25B, Helsinki, passport services Mon-Fri by appointment only, tel. 09/228-530, www.canada.fi

In Norway: Wergelandsveien 7, Oslo, passport services Mon-Fri 8:30-12:30, tel. 22 99 53 00, www.canada.no

In Sweden: Klarabergsgatan 23, Stockholm, passport services Mon-Fri 9:00-12:00, tel. 08/453-3000, www.canadaemb.se

Travel Advisories

US Department of State: tel. 202/647-5225, www.travel.state.gov

Canadian Department of Foreign Affairs: Canadian tel. 800-267-6788, www.dfait-maeci.gc.ca

US Centers for Disease Control and Prevention: tel. 800-CDC-INFO (800-232-4636), www.cdc.gov/travel

Internet Access

It's useful to get online periodically as you travel—to confirm trip plans, check train or bus schedules, get weather forecasts, catch up

on email, blog or post photos from your trip, or call folks back home (explained earlier, under "Calling over the Internet").

Your Mobile Device: The majority of accommodations in Scandinavia offer Wi-Fi, as do many cafés, making it easy to get online with your laptop, tablet, or smartphone. Access is often free, but sometimes there's a fee.

Some hotel rooms and Internet cafés have high-speed Internet jacks that you can plug into with an Ethernet cable. A cellular modem—which lets your device access the Internet over a mobile network—provides more extensive coverage, but is much more expensive than Wi-Fi.

Public Internet Terminals: Many accommodations offer a computer in the lobby with Internet access for guests. If you ask politely, smaller places may let you sit at their desk for a few minutes just to check your email. If your hotelier doesn't have access, ask to be directed to the nearest place to get online.

Security: Whether you're accessing the Internet with your own device or at a public terminal, using a shared network or computer comes with the potential for increased security risks. Be careful about storing personal information online, such as passport and credit-card numbers. If you're not convinced a connection is secure, avoid accessing any sites that could be vulnerable to fraud (e.g., online banking).

Mail

You can mail one package per day to yourself worth up to $200 duty-free from Europe to the US (mark it "personal purchases"). If you're sending a gift to someone, mark it "unsolicited gift." For details, visit www.cbp.gov and search for "Know Before You Go."

The postal service works fine throughout Scandinavia, but for quick transatlantic delivery (in either direction), consider services such as DHL (www.dhl.com). You can get stamps at the neighborhood post office, newsstands within fancy hotels, and some mini-marts and card shops.

Transportation

Getting to Scandinavia

Copenhagen is usually the most direct and least expensive Scandinavian capital to fly into from the US (Icelandair serves Copenhagen as well as Stockholm, Oslo, and Helsinki). Copenhagen is also Europe's gateway to Scandinavia from points south. There are often cheaper flights from the US into Frankfurt and Amsterdam than into Copenhagen, but it's a long, rather dull, one-day drive (with a 45-minute, $90-per-car ferry crossing at Puttgarden, Germany—www.scandlines.dk). By train, Copenhagen is an easy overnight ride from Amsterdam, Cologne, or Frankfurt. The base ticket price ($200 or more) is covered if you have a Global Pass or a railpass covering the particular countries. Another option is flying into London and then hopping to Copenhagen on a low-cost, no-frills airline, such as easyJet or Ryanair.

By Car or Public Transportation?

Cars are best for three or more traveling together (especially families with small kids), those packing heavy, and those scouring the

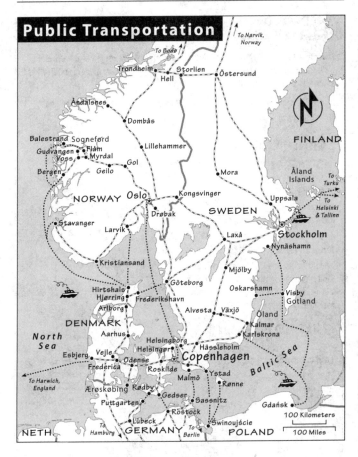

countryside. Trains, buses, and boats are best for solo travelers, blitz tourists, and city-to-city travelers; those with an ambitious, multi-country itinerary; and those who don't want to drive in Europe. While a car gives you more freedom—enabling you to search for hotels more easily and carrying your bags for you—trains, buses, and boats zip you effortlessly and scenically from city to city, usually dropping you in or near the center, often near a TI. Cars are an expensive headache in places like Copenhagen and Stockholm.

Public Transportation

Trains

With a few exceptions, trains cover my recommended Scandinavian destinations wonderfully.

Schedules and Tickets: Pick up train schedules from stations as you go. While most information is given both in the

Railpasses

Prices listed are for 2012 and are subject to change. For the latest prices, details, and train schedules (and easy online ordering), see my comprehensive *Guide to Eurail Passes* at www.ricksteves.com/rail.

Note that youth prices apply to those under age 26. Some two-country combinations are also available.

SCANDINAVIA PASS

	Individual 2nd Cl.	Saver 2nd Cl.	Youth 2nd Cl.
4 days in 2 months	$335	$285	$252
5 days in 2 months	370	316	279
6 days in 2 months	422	359	317
8 days in 2 months	467	398	351
10 days in 2 months	518	441	390

Covers Denmark, Norway, Sweden, and Finland. Saver price per person for two or more traveling together. Kids 4–11 half adult or saver price. Kids under 4 free.

FINLAND PASS

	1st Cl.	2nd Cl.
3 days in 1 month	$259	$175
5 days in 1 month	344	232
10 days in 1 month	467	314

Children 6-16 half price, under 6 free.

DENMARK PASS

	Adult 1st Cl.	Adult 2nd Cl.	Youth 2nd Cl.
3 days in 1 month	$205	$134	$102
7 days in 1 month	298	195	147

Kids 4-11 half adult or saver price. Kids under 4 free.

Map key:

Approximate point-to-point one-way standard-class fares in US dollars. First class costs 50 percent more. Add up fares for your itinerary to see whether a railpass will save you money.

NORWAY PASS

	Individual 2nd Cl.	Saver 2nd Cl.	Youth 2nd Cl.
3 days in 1 month	$258	$220	$194
4 days in 1 month	279	238	210
5 days in 1 month	309	263	232
6 days in 1 month	351	299	264
8 days in 1 month	391	333	394

Saver price per person for two or more traveling together. Kids 4–11 half adult or saver price. Kids under 4 free.

SWEDEN PASS

	Individual 1st Cl.	Saver 1st Cl.	Individual 2nd Cl.	Saver 2nd Cl.	Youth 2nd Cl.
3 days in 1 month	$335	$286	$259	$221	$195
4 days in 1 month	360	306	278	237	210
5 days in 1 month	400	341	309	263	233
6 days in 1 month	453	385	350	298	263
8 days in 1 month	505	430	390	332	294

Saver price per person for two or more traveling together. Kids 4–11 half adult or saver price. Kids under 4 free.

SELECTPASS

This pass covers travel in three adjacent countries. Please visit **www.ricksteves.com/rail** for four- and five-country options.

	Individual 1st Class	Saver 1st Class	Youth 2nd Class
5 days in 2 months	$372	$317	$243
6 days in 2 months	410	349	268
8 days in 2 months	484	413	316
10 days in 2 months	561	478	366

"Saver" prices are per person for two or more people traveling together. Kids 4–11 pay half of adult individual or Saver fare; under 4 free.

country's language and in English, it's good to know the word for "delayed"—*forsinket* in Danish and Norwegian, and *försenad* in Swedish.

To study ahead on the Web, check www.bahn.com (Germany's excellent Europe-wide timetable). Local train companies also have their own sites with fare and timetable information, and even online booking in English; see www.dsb.dk or www.rejseplanen.dk (Denmark), www.nsb.no (Norway), www.sj.se (Sweden), www.vr.fi (Finland), and www.gorail.ee (Estonia).

Railpasses: One of the great Nordic bargains, the Eurail Scandinavia pass is your best railpass deal for a trip limited to Scandinavia. Although Eurail Scandinavia passes are available only for second-class seats, Scandinavian second class is plenty comfortable. Some trains, including those that cover part of the popular Norway in a Nutshell route (see page 290), do not offer first class. For options and prices, see the railpass chart in this chapter and www.ricksteves.com/rail.

If your trip extends south of Scandinavia, consider the flexible Select Pass, which allows you to choose three, four, or five adjoining countries connected by land or ferry (for instance, Germany-Sweden-Finland). A more expensive Global Pass is a good value only for those spending more time throughout Europe. A three-week first-class Global Pass costs about $950 (if you travel with a companion, you'll save about 15 percent apiece with a Global saverpass).

Railpasses give you discounts on some boat tickets (such as Stockholm to Helsinki) and cover almost all trains in the region (though you'll need 50-kr reservations for long rides and express trains, plus a 180-kr supplement for Norway's Myrdal-Flåm ride—part of the Norway in a Nutshell route). If you'll be taking a popular train on a busy day and want to be assured of having a seat, a reservation can be a good investment even if it's not required.

Buses

Don't overlook long-distance buses, which are usually slower but have considerably cheaper and more predictable fares than trains. (In Denmark, however, the train system is excellent and nearly always the better option.) On certain routes, such as between Stockholm and Oslo, the bus is cheaper and only slightly slower than the train. Scandinavia's big bus carriers are Norway's Nor-Way Bussekspress (www.nor-way.no), Denmark's public buses (www.rejseplanen.dk), Sweden's Swebus (www.swebusexpress.se), and Finland's Matkahuolto (www.matkahuolto.fi). Estonia has several carriers, of which Lux Express is the largest (www.lux express.ee).

Boats

Boats are romantic, scenic, and sometimes the most efficient—or only—way to link destinations in coastal Scandinavia. But boats can often be more expensive than other options, although some routes may be covered or discounted if you have a railpass. Note that short-distance ferries may take only cash, not credit cards.

Advance reservations are recommended for overnight boats, especially in summer or on weekends. The main links are Oslo to Copenhagen (www.dfdsseaways.com), Stockholm to Helsinki (www.vikingline.fi and www.tallinksilja.com), and Stockholm to Tallinn (www.tallinksilja.com).

Several companies speed between Helsinki and Tallinn in 2-3 hours (see page 604). Other worthwhile routes connect Norway and Denmark (Kristiansand and Hirtshals several times daily, Stavanger and Hirtshals by overnight boat; see page 410, www .fjordline.com and www.colorline.com). Ferries are essential for hopping between the mainland and Scandinavia's many islands, such as Ærø in central Denmark (drivers should reserve in advance for weekends and summer, www.aeroe-ferry.dk), or Stockholm's archipelago. Boats are both a necessary and spectacular way to travel through Norway's fjords or along its coast (www.fjordtours

.no, www.fjord1.no, and www.tide.no). Bergen, in Norway, is a departure point for boats to the Arctic (www.hurtigruten.com).

Renting a Car

If you're renting a car in Scandinavia, bring your driver's license. It's recommended, but not required, that you also have an International Driving Permit (sold at your local AAA office for $15 plus the cost of two passport-type photos, see www.aaa.com); however, I've frequently rented cars in Scandinavia and traveled problem-free with just my US license.

The minimum age to rent a car varies by country and rental company (you must be 21 in Denmark and Estonia, and 19 in Sweden, Norway, and Finland). Drivers under the age of 25 may incur a young-driver surcharge, and some rental companies do not rent to anyone 75 and over. If you're considered too young or old, look into leasing (explained later), which has less-stringent age restrictions.

Research car rentals before you go. It's cheapest to arrange most car rentals from the US. Call several companies, and look online to compare rates, or arrange a rental through your home-town travel agent.

Most of the major US rental agencies (including National, Avis, Budget, Hertz, and Thrifty) have offices throughout Europe. Also consider the two major Europe-based agencies, Europcar and Sixt. It can be cheaper to use a consolidator, such as Auto Europe (www.autoeurope.com) or Europe by Car (www.ebctravel.com), which compares rates at several companies to get you the best deal. However, my readers have reported problems with consolidators, ranging from misinformation to unexpected fees; because you're going through a middleman, it can be more challenging to resolve disputes that arise with the rental agency.

Regardless of the car-rental company you choose, always read the contract carefully. The fine print can conceal a host of common add-on charges—such as one-way drop-off fees, airport surcharges, or mandatory insurance policies—that aren't included in the "total price," but can be tacked on when you pick up your car. You may need to query rental agents pointedly to find out your actual cost.

For the best deal, rent by the week with unlimited mileage. To save money on fuel, ask for a diesel car. I normally rent the smallest, least-expensive model with a stick shift (cheaper than an automatic). An automatic transmission adds about 50 percent to the car-rental cost over a manual transmission. Almost all rentals are manual by default, so if you need an automatic, you must request one in advance; beware that these cars are usually larger models (not as maneuverable on narrow, winding roads).

For a three-week rental, allow about $900 per person (based on 2 people sharing the car) for a small economy car with unlimited mileage, including tolls, fuel, and insurance. For trips of this length, look into leasing; you'll save money on insurance and taxes.

Be warned that international trips—say, picking up in Copenhagen and dropping off in Oslo—can be expensive (it depends partly on distance). As a rule, always tell your car-rental company up front exactly which countries you'll be entering. Some companies levy extra insurance fees for trips taken in certain countries with certain types of cars (such as BMWs, Mercedes, and convertibles). Double-check with your rental agent that you have all the documentation you need before you drive off.

You can sometimes get a GPS unit with your rental car or leased vehicle for an additional fee (around $15/day; be sure it's set to English and has all the maps you need before you drive off). Or, if you have a portable GPS device at home, consider taking it with you to Europe (buy and upload European maps before your trip). GPS apps are also available for smartphones, but downloading maps on one of these apps in Europe could lead to an exorbitant data-roaming bill (for more details, see the sidebar on page 662).

Big companies have offices in most cities; ask whether they can pick you up at your hotel. Small local rental companies can be cheaper but aren't as flexible.

Compare pickup costs (downtown can be less expensive than the airport) and explore drop-off options. When selecting a location, don't trust the agency's description of "downtown" or "city center." In some cases, a "downtown" branch can be on the outskirts of the city—a long, costly taxi ride from the center. Before choosing, plug the addresses into a mapping website. You may find that the "train station" location is handier. Returning a car at a big-city train station or downtown agency can be tricky; get precise details on the car drop-off location and hours, and allow ample time to find it. Note that rental offices usually close from midday Saturday until Monday morning.

When you pick up the rental car, check it thoroughly and make sure any damage is noted on your rental agreement. Find out how your car's lights, turn signals, wipers, and fuel cap function, and know what kind of fuel the car takes. When you return the car, make sure the agent verifies its condition with you.

In some cases, I prefer to connect long distances by train or bus, then rent cars for a day or two where they're most useful (I've noted these places throughout this book).

Car Insurance Options

When you rent a car, you are liable for a very high deductible, sometimes equal to the entire value of the car. Limit your financial

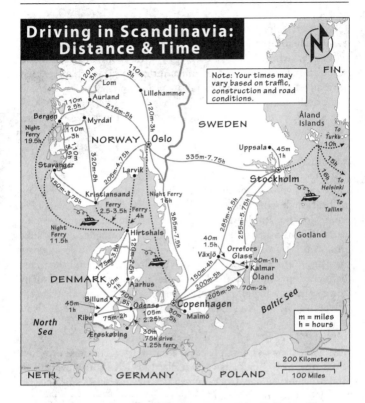

Driving in Scandinavia: Distance & Time

Note: Your times may vary based on traffic, construction and road conditions.

m = miles
h = hours

200 Kilometers
100 Miles

risk by choosing one of these three options: Buy Collision Damage Waiver (CDW) coverage from the car-rental company, get coverage through your credit card (free, if your card automatically includes zero-deductible coverage), or buy coverage through Travel Guard.

CDW includes a very high deductible (typically $1,000-1,500). Though each rental company has its own variation, basic CDW costs $15-35 a day (figure roughly 30 percent extra) and reduces your liability, but does not eliminate it. When you pick up the car, you'll be offered the chance to "buy down" the basic deductible to zero (for an additional $10-30/day; this is sometimes called "super CDW").

If you opt for **credit-card coverage,** there's a catch. You'll technically have to decline all coverage offered by the car-rental company, which means they can place a hold on your card (which can be up to the full value of the car). In case of damage, it can be time-consuming to resolve the charges with your credit-card company. Before you decide on this option, quiz your credit-card company about how it works.

Finally, you can buy collision insurance from Travel Guard

($9/day plus a one-time $3 service fee covers you up to $35,000, $250 deductible, tel. 800-826-4919, www.travelguard.com). It's valid everywhere in Europe except the Republic of Ireland, and some Italian car-rental companies refuse to honor it. Note that various states differ on which products and policies are available to their residents.

For more fine print about car-rental insurance, see www.rick steves.com/cdw.

Leasing

For trips of three weeks or more, consider leasing (which automatically includes zero-deductible collision and theft insurance). By technically buying and then selling back the car, you save lots of money on tax and insurance. Leasing provides you a brand-new car with unlimited mileage and a 24-hour emergency assistance program. You can lease for as little as 21 days to as long as six months. Car leases must be arranged from the US, and cars must be picked up and dropped off outside Scandinavia. One of many companies offering affordable lease packages is Europe by Car (US tel. 800-223-1516, www.ebctravel.com).

Driving

Except for the dangers posed by scenic distractions and moose crossings, Scandinavia is a great place to drive. But never drink and drive—even one drink can get a driver into serious trouble.

Road Rules: Seat belts are mandatory, and young children need a child-safety seat in Norway, Finland, and Estonia—age 4 and under; Denmark—age 6; Sweden—age 7). Be aware of typical European road rules; for example, many countries require headlights to be turned on at all times, and it's generally illegal to drive while using your mobile phone without a hands-free headset. In Europe, you're not allowed to turn right on a red light, unless there is a sign or signal specifically authorizing it. Ask your car-rental company about these rules, or check the US State Department

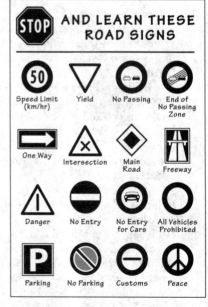

STOP **AND LEARN THESE ROAD SIGNS**

Speed Limit (km/hr) · Yield · No Passing · End of No Passing Zone

One Way · Intersection · Main Road · Freeway

Danger · No Entry · No Entry for Cars · All Vehicles Prohibited

Parking · No Parking · Customs · Peace

website (www.travel.state.gov, click on "International Travel," then specify your country of choice and click "Traffic Safety and Road Conditions").

Fuel: Gas is expensive—often more than $8 per gallon. US credit and debit cards likely won't work at pay-at-the-pump stations, but are generally accepted (with a PIN code) at staffed stations. Carry cash just in case. Diesel rental cars are common; make sure you know what type of fuel your car takes before you fill up.

On the Road: Roads are good (though nerve-rackingly skinny in western Norway). Bikes tend to whiz by close and quiet in cities, so be on guard. In the countryside, traffic is generally sparse, and drivers are civil. Signs and road maps are excellent. Local road etiquette is similar to that in the US. There are plenty of good facilities, gas stations, and scenic rest stops. Snow is a serious problem off-season in the mountains.

Tolls: You'll encounter one-way tolls of €20-45 on major bridges including the Øresund Bridge between Sweden and Denmark, the Svinesund Bridge between Sweden and Norway, and the Storebælt Bridge between the Danish islands of Zealand and Funen. Cities such as Oslo, Bergen, and Stockholm charge tolls for entering the city center.

To minimize tolls in Norway, register as a visitor at www.autopass.no. By prepaying a lump sum with your credit card and specifying when you'll be on the road, you won't need to buy a sticker or pay manually at toll plazas; you can even register up to 14 days after you've driven through your first toll point. Any remaining balance will be credited back to your card three months later.

Parking: Parking on the street is a headache only in major cities, where expensive garages are safe and plentiful. Denmark uses a parking windshield-clock disk (free at TIs, post offices, and newsstands; set it when you arrive and be back before your posted time limit is up). Even in the Nordic countries, thieves break into cars. Park carefully, use the trunk, and show no valuables.

Signage: As you navigate, you'll find town signs followed by the letters *N, S, Ø* (*Ö* in Sweden), *V,* or *C.* These stand for north *(nord),* south *(sud),* east *(øst),* west *(vest),* and center *(centrum),* respectively; understanding them will save you lots of wrong turns. Due to recent changes, some maps have the wrong road numbers. It's safest to navigate by town names.

Cheap Flights

This book covers far-flung destinations separated by vast stretches of mountains and water. While boats and trains are more romantic, cheap flights can provide an affordable and efficient way to connect the dots on a Scandinavian itinerary.

The best comparison search engine for both international and intra-European flights is www.kayak.com. For inexpensive flights within Europe, try www.skyscanner.com or www.hipmunk.com. If you're not sure who flies to your destination, check its airport's website for a list of carriers.

SAS, the region's dominant airline, operates a low-cost Finnish subsidiary called Blue1 (hubs in Helsinki and Stockholm, www.blue1.com) and is affiliated with Oslo-based Widerøe Air (www.wideroe.no). Other options are Norwegian Airlines (hubs in Oslo and Bergen, www.norwegian.no); the Denmark-based Cimber Sterling (specializes in connecting Scandinavian capitals such as Oslo and Copenhagen with sunny destinations in southern Europe, www.cimber.com); and Tallinn-based Estonian Air (www.estonian-air.com). Well-known cheapo airlines easyJet (www.easyjet.com) and Ryanair (www.ryanair.com) fly into Scandinavia.

Be aware of the potential drawbacks of flying on the cheap: nonrefundable and nonchangeable tickets, minimal or nonexistent customer service, treks to airports far outside town, and stingy baggage allowances with steep overage fees. If you're traveling with lots of luggage, a cheap flight can quickly become a bad deal. To avoid unpleasant surprises, read the small print before you book.

Resources

Resources from Rick Steves

Rick Steves' Scandinavia is one of many books in my series on European travel, which includes country guidebooks, city guidebooks (Rome, Florence, Paris, London, etc.), Snapshot guides (excerpted chapters from my country guides), Pocket Guides (full-color little books on big cities), and my budget-travel skills handbook, *Rick Steves' Europe Through the Back Door*. Most of my titles are available as ebooks. My phrase books—for German, French, Italian, Spanish, and Portuguese—are practical and budget-oriented. My other books include *Northern European Cruise Ports* and *Mediterranean Cruise Ports* (how to make the most of your time in port), *Europe 101* (a crash course on art and history), and *Travel as a Political Act* (a travelogue sprinkled with advice for bringing home a global perspective). A more complete list of my titles appears near the end of this book.

Video: My public television series, *Rick Steves' Europe*, covers European destinations in 100 shows, with nine episodes on

Begin Your Trip at www.ricksteves.com

At our travel website, you'll discover a wealth of free information on European destinations, including fresh monthly news and helpful tips from thousands of fellow travelers. You'll find my latest guidebook updates (www.ricksteves.com/update), a monthly travel e-newsletter (easy and free to sign up), my personal travel blog, and my free Rick Steves Audio Europe smartphone app (if you don't have a smartphone, you can access the same content via podcasts). You can even follow me on Facebook and Twitter.

Our **online Travel Store** offers travel bags and accessories that I've designed specifically to help you travel smarter and lighter. These include my popular carry-on bags (roll-aboard and backpack versions), money belts, totes, toiletries kits, adapters, other accessories, and a wide selection of guidebooks, planning maps, and DVDs.

Choosing the right **railpass** for your trip—amidst hundreds of options—can drive you nutty. We'll help you choose the best pass for your needs and ship it to you for free.

Want to travel with greater efficiency and less stress? We organize **tours** with more than three dozen itineraries and more than 500 departures reaching the best destinations in this book...and beyond. We offer a 14-day Best of Scandinavia tour featuring the big-city highlights of Stockholm, Copenhagen, and Oslo as well as quieter Nordic nooks such as the Danish island of Ærøskobing and a scenic cruise through the fjords; and a nine-day tour of Tallinn, Helsinki, and St. Petersburg. You'll enjoy great guides, a fun bunch of travel partners (with small groups of generally around 24-28), and plenty of room to spread out in a big, comfy bus. You'll find European adventures to fit every vacation length. For all the details, and to get our Tour Catalog and a free *Rick Steves Tour Experience* DVD (filmed on location during an actual tour), visit www.ricksteves.com or call us at 425/608-4217.

Scandinavia. To watch episodes online, visit www.hulu.com; for scripts and local airtimes, see www.ricksteves.com/tv.

Audio: My weekly public radio show, *Travel with Rick Steves,* features interviews with travel experts from around the world. All of this free audio content is available at Rick Steves Audio Europe, an extensive online library organized by destination. Choose whatever interests you, and download it via the free Rick Steves Audio Europe smartphone app, www.ricksteves.com/audioeurope, iTunes, or Google Play.

Maps

The black-and-white maps in this book are concise and simple, designed to help you locate recommended places and get to local TIs, where you can pick up more in-depth maps of cities and regions (usually free). Better maps are sold at newsstands and bookstores. Before you buy a map, look at it to be sure it has the level of detail you want.

Train travelers can use a simple rail map (such as the one that comes with your train pass). But drivers shouldn't skimp on maps—get one good overall road map for Scandinavia (either the Michelin *Scandinavia* or the Kummerly & Frey *Southern Scandinavia* 1:1,000,000 edition). The Collins Road Atlas is also good. The only detailed map worth considering is the *Southern Norway-North* (*Sør Norge-nord,* 1:325,000) by Cappelens Kart (about €30 in Scandinavian bookstores).

Other Guidebooks

If you're like most travelers, this book is all you need. But if you're heading beyond my recommended destinations, $40 for extra maps and books is money well spent.

The following books are worthwhile, though most are not updated annually; check the publication date before you buy. Lonely Planet's *Scandinavian Europe* is thorough, well-researched, and packed with good maps and hotel recommendations for low- to moderate-budget travelers. The similar *Rough Guide to Scandinavia* is hip and insightful, written by British researchers. Culture Shock's guides to Norway, Denmark, and Sweden help travelers to better understand local customs and etiquette. Older travelers enjoy guides from Frommer's, even though, like the Fodor's guide, they ignore alternatives that enable travelers to save money by dirtying their fingers in the local culture.

The popular, skinny green Michelin Guides are excellent, especially if you're driving. Michelin Guides are known for their city and sightseeing maps, dry but concise and helpful information on all major sights, and good cultural and historical background. English editions are sold in Europe at gas stations and tourist shops.

The Eyewitness series—which covers Denmark, Norway, and Sweden—is popular for great, easy-to-grasp graphics and photos, 3-D cutaways of buildings, aerial-view maps of historic neighborhoods, and cultural background. But written content in Eyewitness is relatively skimpy, and the books weigh a ton. I simply borrow them for a minute from other travelers at certain sights to make sure that I'm aware of that place's highlights.

Those staying longer in Stockholm, Oslo, Bergen, or Helsinki might consider the Insight guides to those cities. The British entertainment publication *Time Out* sells well-researched guides with up-to-date coverage on Copenhagen and Stockholm, including the latest on hotels, restaurants, and nightlife (www.timeout .com).

For Estonia, consider the *Bradt Guide to Estonia* (published by Globe Pequot Press).

Recommended Books and Movies

To learn about Scandinavia past and present, check out a few of these books and films.

Nonfiction

For a solid grasp of Scandinavia's past, try *A History of Scandinavia: Norway, Sweden, Denmark, Finland, and Iceland* (Derry) or *Scandinavia Since 1500* (Nordstrom). The history of the Swedish people from feudalism to democracy is recorded in *Sweden: The Nation's History* (Scott). *The Vikings* (Else Roesdhal) offers a Scandinavian perspective on this complex Nordic society.

For insight into Hans Christian Andersen, try his autobiography, *The Fairy Tale of My Life*, and Jens Andersen's biography *Hans Christian Andersen: A New Life. Scandinavian Folk and Fairy Tales* (Boos) is a good compilation. In *My Childhood*, Roivo Pekkanen perceptively recalls his family's working-class life in early-20th-century Finland. Peter Tveskov combines historical fact with childhood memories of Denmark under German occupation during World War II in *Conquered, Not Defeated*. Norwegian biologist Thor Heyerdahl records his historic 1947 journey from Peru to Polynesia on a balsa-wood raft in *Kon-Tiki*.

Fiction

Read a collection of Hans Christian Andersen's classic fairy tales: *The Little Mermaid, The Little Match Girl, The Princess and the Pea, The Steadfast Tin Soldier*, and many more. Also beloved by children of all ages are the *Pippi Longstocking* books by Sweden's Astrid Lindgren.

Swede Selma Lagerlöf was the first woman to win the Nobel Prize for Literature (in 1909) for her fantastical children's novel, *The Wonderful Adventures of Nils*. Nobel Prize winners by Norwegians include Knut Hamsun's influential *Growth of the Soil* (w. 1920) and Sigrid Undset's epic *Kristin Lavransdatter* (w. 1928).

Music and Silence by Rose Tremain captures 17th-century Denmark through the eyes of a lute-player at court. *The Emigrants* is the first of Vilhelm Moberg's four-volume epic about Swedish immigrants settling the American frontier. The multigenerational saga *Hanna's Daughters* by Marianne Fredriksson traces a Swedish family from the 1870s through World War II. Norwegian playwright Henrik Ibsen's controversial plays explore the role of women in the 19th century (try *A Doll's House* or *Hedda Gabler*). A 19th-century Frenchwoman takes refuge in Denmark in *Babette's Feast* by Karen Blixen.

Stieg Larsson's Millennium trilogy (*The Girl with the Dragon Tattoo*, *The Girl Who Played with Fire*, and *The Girl Who Kicked the Hornet's Nest*)—with its themes of violence against women and government corruption—put Swedish crime fiction on the map. His bestselling novels have been translated into some 30 languages. Other thrillers include *Smilla's Sense of Snow* by Dane Peter Høeg, and *Faceless Killers*, the first of several Kurt Wallender mysteries by Swede Henning Mankell. *Sophie's World* by Norwegian Jostein Gaarder is a metaphysical mystery wrapped in the history of philosophy.

Films

Watch any of Oscar-winning Swedish director Ingmar Bergman's films, especially *The Seventh Seal* (1957, a knight questions the meaning of life), *Smiles of a Summer Night* (1955, turn-of-the-century frolic), and *Fanny & Alexander* (1983, children overcome father's death).

Song of Norway (1970) is a musical based on the life of Norwegian composer Edvard Grieg. Bergman alums Max von Sydow and Liv Ullmann star in *The Emigrants* and *The New Land* (1971, 1972) based on the Moberg novels. The bittersweet *My Life as a Dog* (1985) shows Sweden in the 1950s, while the "original foodie movie," *Babette's Feast* (1988), is set in rural 19th-century Denmark (and based on the book by Karen Blixen cited above). *Pelle the Conqueror* (1988) examines Swedish immigration to Denmark in the 19th century, and *Kristin Lavransdatter* (1995) is a much-condensed version of the epic novel. The midnight sun plays a role in the Norwegian thriller *Insomnia* (1997, later adapted by American filmmakers). A young Finnish boy is evacuated to

Sweden during World War II in *Mother of Mine* (2005).

Julia Ormond plays the title role in the dramatic film adaptation of *Smilla's Sense of Snow* (1997). For lighter fare, try comedies such as *Italian for Beginners* (2000, Danish thirtysomethings learn Italian), *Together* (2000, life in a 1970s Stockholm commune), *Elling* (2001, oddballs make it on their own), and *Dalecarlians* (2005, big-city sister returns to rural hometown). The quirky *Cool & Crazy* (2001) is an uplifting documentary about a Norwegian men's choir, while *As It Is in Heaven* (2004) recounts a Swedish conductor's search for happiness. *The Singing Revolution* (2006) is an enjoyable documentary about Estonia's musical fight for freedom (www.singingrevolution.com).

Norway's resistance against the Nazi occupation is dramatized in *Max Manus* (2008), which traces the exploits of the Norwegian war hero and his comrades in Oslo during World War II. Trolls wreak havoc in modern-day Norway in *Trollhunter* (2010), a fun fantasy-thriller that explains the real purpose of those power lines in the Norwegian mountains.

Legendary Norwegian explorer Thor Heyerdahl epically crossed the Pacific on a balsa-wood raft in 1947 (he wanted to prove the possibility of South American settlement of Polynesia). Norwegian filmmakers have catalogued his exploits in two films called *Kon-Tiki:* an Academy-Award-winning documentary (1950) and a blockbuster historical drama (2012).

Let the Right One In (*Låt den Rätte Komma in,* 2008), a Swedish vampire flick, is becoming a cult classic—especially for anyone who's dealt with a bully. The Swedish film versions of Stieg Larsson's Millennium novels (with Noomi Rapace as Lisbeth) are as compelling as the novels. Hollywood released its version of Larsson's *The Girl with the Dragon Tattoo* in 2011, starring Daniel Craig and Rooney Mara.

Holidays and Festivals

This list includes selected festivals in major cities, plus national holidays observed throughout Scandinavia. Many sights and banks close down on national holidays—keep this in mind when planning your itinerary. Before planning a trip around a festival, verify its dates at the festival's website or TI sites (www.goscandinavia.com; for Estonia, check www.visitestonia.com).

Jan 1	New Year's Day, all countries
Feb	Winter Jazz Festival (www.jazz.dk), Copenhagen, Denmark
Feb 24	National Day, Estonia
Good Friday	March 29 in 2013, April 18 in 2014
Easter	March 31 in 2013, April 20 in 2014
April 30	Walpurgis Night (bonfires, choirs), Sweden and Finland
May 1	May Day (parades, some closures), Scandinavia
Common Prayer Day	April 26 in 2013, May 16 in 2014, Denmark (businesses closed)
Ascension Day	May 9 in 2013, May 29 in 2014
May 15	St. Hallvard's Day, Oslo, Norway
Mid-May	Stavanger International Jazz Festival ("MaiJazz"; www.maijazz.no), Stavanger, Norway
Mid-May	Folk Festival (www.odensefolkfestival .dk), Odense, Denmark
May 17	Constitution Day (parades, closures), Norway
Whitsunday and Whitmonday	May 19-20 in 2013, June 8-9 in 2014
Late May	Dragon Boat Festival (Chinese boat races), Bergen, Norway, and Stockholm, Sweden
Late May-Early June	Bergen International Festival (concerts, ballet, opera, theater; www.fib.no), Bergen, Norway
June 5	Constitution Day (businesses closed), Denmark
June 6	National Day (parades), Sweden
Early June	Archipelago Boat Day (steamboat parade, (www.skargardstrafikanten.se), Stockholm, Sweden
Early June	Old Town Days (music), Tallinn, Estonia
Early June	Taste of Stockholm (outdoor food vendors; www.smakapastockholm.se), Stockholm, Sweden
Mid-June	Norwegian Wood Rock Music Festival (www.norwegianwood.no), Oslo, Norway
Mid-June	Bergenfest (rock, pop, hip hop, and folk music; www.bergenfest.no), Bergen, Norway

Mid-June	Medieval Festival ("Middelalderfestival," www.oslomiddelalderfestival.org), Oslo, Norway
Mid-June–Mid-Aug	Fløyen Concert Festival (classical music), Bergen, Norway
Late June	Midsummer Solstice Eve (celebrations, bonfires), Scandinavia
Late June–Aug	Grieg in Bergen Festival (summer-long concert series; www.grieginbergen.com), Bergen, Norway
July 4	Fourth of July festivities, Stockholm, Sweden
Early July	Copenhagen Jazz Festival (www.jazz.dk), Copenhagen, Denmark
Early July	Roskilde Festival (music and culture, www.roskilde-festival.dk), Roskilde, Denmark
Early July–Late Aug	Savonlinna Opera Festival (www.operafestival.fi), Savonlinna, Finland
Mid-Late July	International Jazz Festival (www.jazzfest.dk), Aarhus, Denmark
Late July	Food Festival ("Gladmat," www.gladmat.no), Stavanger, Norway
Late July–Mid-Aug	Hans Christian Andersen Festival (www.hcandersenfestspil.dk), Odense, Denmark
Early Aug	International Chamber Music Festival (www.icmf.no), Stavanger, Norway
Mid-Aug	Chamber Music Festival (www.oslokammermusikkfestival.no), Oslo, Norway
Mid-Aug	Jazz Festival (www.oslojazz.no), Oslo, Norway
Mid-Late Aug	Helsinki Festival (music, dance, film, theater; www.helsinkifestival.fi), Helsinki, Finland
Late Aug–Sept	Aarhus Festival (music, dance, theater; www.aarhusfestuge.dk), Aarhus, Denmark
Mid-Sept	Ultima Contemporary Music Festival (www.ultima.no), Oslo, Norway
Mid-Oct	DølaJazz Festival (www.dolajazz.no), Lillehammer, Norway
Mid-Nov–Dec 23	Christmas Fair (Tivoli Garden), Copenhagen, Denmark

APPENDIX

Dec 6	Independence Day (candlelit windows), Finland
Dec 10	Nobel Peace Prize Award Ceremony, Oslo, Norway
Dec 13	St. Lucia Day (festival of lights), Sweden
Dec 25	Christmas, Scandinavia
Dec 26	Boxing Day, Scandinavia

Conversions and Climate

Numbers and Stumblers

- Europeans write a few of their numbers differently than we do. 1 = 1, 4 = 4, 7 = 7.
- In Europe, dates appear as day/month/year, so Christmas is 25/12/2014.
- Commas are decimal points and decimals commas. A dollar and a half is 1,50, one thousand is 1.000, and there are 5.280 feet in a mile.
- When counting with fingers, start with your thumb. If you hold up your first finger to request one item, you'll probably get two.
- What Americans call the second floor of a building is the first floor in Europe.
- Scandinavians number their weeks. Instead of saying, "Spring break is the third week in March," they'd say, "Spring break is week 12."
- On escalators and moving sidewalks, Europeans keep the left "lane" open for passing. Keep to the right.

Metric Conversions

A kilogram is 2.2 pounds, and 1 liter is about a quart, or almost four to a gallon. A kilometer is six-tenths of a mile. I figure kilometers to miles by cutting them in half and adding back 10 percent of the original (120 km: 60 + 12 = 72 miles, 300 km: 150 + 30 = 180 miles).

1 foot = 0.3 meter	1 square yard = 0.8 square meter
1 yard = 0.9 meter	1 square mile = 2.6 square kilometers
1 mile = 1.6 kilometers	1 ounce = 28 grams
1 centimeter = 0.4 inch	1 quart = 0.95 liter
1 meter = 39.4 inches	1 kilogram = 2.2 pounds
1 kilometer = 0.62 mile	32°F = 0°C

Clothing Sizes

When shopping for clothing, use these US-to-European comparisons as general guidelines (but note that no conversion is perfect).

- Women's dresses and blouses: Add 30
  (US size 10 = European size 40)
- Men's suits and jackets: Add 10
  (US size 40 regular = European size 50)
- Men's shirts: Multiply by 2 and add about 8
  (US size 15 collar = European size 38)
- Women's shoes: Add about 30
  (US size 8 = European size 38-39)
- Men's shoes: Add 32-34
  (US size 9 = European size 41; US size 11 = European size 45)

Climate

First line, average daily high; second line, average daily low; third line, average days without rain. For more detailed weather statistics for destinations in this book (as well as the rest of the world), check www.worldclimate.com.

	J	F	M	A	M	J	J	A	S	O	N	D
DENMARK • Copenhagen												
	37°	37°	42°	51°	60°	66°	70°	69°	64°	55°	46°	41°
	29°	28°	31°	37°	45°	51°	56°	56°	51°	44°	38°	33°
	14	15	19	18	20	18	17	16	14	14	11	12
ESTONIA • Tallinn												
	25°	25°	32°	45°	57°	66°	68°	66°	59°	50°	37°	30°
	14°	12°	19°	32°	41°	50°	54°	52°	48°	39°	30°	19°
	12	12	18	19	19	20	18	16	14	14	12	12
FINLAND • Helsinki												
	26°	25°	32°	44°	56°	66°	71°	68°	59°	47°	37°	31°
	17°	15°	20°	30°	40°	49°	55°	53°	46°	37°	30°	23°
	11	10	17	17	19	17	17	16	16	13	11	11
NORWAY • Oslo												
	28°	30°	39°	50°	61°	68°	72°	70°	60°	48°	38°	32°
	19°	19°	25°	34°	43°	50°	55°	53°	46°	38°	31°	25°
	16	16	22	19	21	17	16	17	16	17	14	14
SWEDEN • Stockholm												
	30°	30°	37°	47°	58°	67°	71°	68°	60°	49°	40°	35°
	26°	25°	29°	37°	45°	53°	57°	56°	50°	43°	37°	32°
	15	14	21	19	20	17	18	17	16	16	14	14

APPENDIX

Temperature Conversion:
Fahrenheit and Celsius

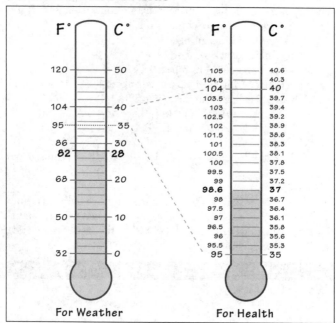

Scandinavia takes its temperature using the Celsius scale, while we opt for Fahrenheit. For a rough conversion from Celsius to Fahrenheit, double the number and add 30. For weather, remember that 28°C is 82°F—perfect. For health, 37°C is just right.

Packing Checklist

Whether you're traveling for five days or five weeks, here's what you'll need to bring. Pack light to enjoy the sweet freedom of true mobility. Happy travels!

- ❏ 5 shirts: long- and short-sleeve
- ❏ 1 sweater or lightweight fleece
- ❏ 2 pairs of pants
- ❏ 1 pair of shorts
- ❏ 5 pairs of underwear and socks
- ❏ 1 pair of shoes
- ❏ 1 rainproof jacket with hood
- ❏ Tie or scarf
- ❏ Sleepwear
- ❏ Swimsuit
- ❏ Money belt
- ❏ Money—your mix of:
  - ❏ Debit card
  - ❏ Credit card(s)
  - ❏ Hard cash ($20 bills)
- ❏ Documents plus photocopies:
  - ❏ Passport
  - ❏ Printout of airline eticket
  - ❏ Driver's license
  - ❏ Student ID, hostel card, etc.
  - ❏ Railpass/train reservations/ car-rental voucher
  - ❏ Insurance details
- ❏ Guidebooks and maps
- ❏ Address list for postcards
- ❏ Notepad and pen
- ❏ Journal
- ❏ Daypack
- ❏ Electronics—your choice of:
  - ❏ Camera (and related gear)
  - ❏ Mobile phone
- ❏ Portable media player (iPod or other)
- ❏ Laptop/netbook/tablet
- ❏ Ebook reader
- ❏ Headphones or earbuds
- ❏ Chargers for each of the above
- ❏ Plug adapter(s)
- ❏ Alarm clock
- ❏ Earplugs
- ❏ Toiletries kit
  - ❏ Toiletries
  - ❏ Medicines and vitamins
  - ❏ First-aid kit
  - ❏ Glasses/contacts/ sunglasses (with prescriptions)
- ❏ Sealable plastic baggies
- ❏ Laundry soap
- ❏ Clothesline
- ❏ Small towel/washcloth
- ❏ Sewing kit

If you plan to carry on your luggage, note that all liquids must be in 3.4-ounce or smaller containers and fit within a single quart-size sealable baggie. For details, see www.tsa.gov.

Hotel Reservation

To: _____   _____
              hotel   *email or fax*

From: _____   _____
                name   *email or fax*

Today's date: _____ / _____ / _____
                        day   *month*   *year*

Dear Hotel _____ ,
Please make this reservation for me:

Name: _____

Total # of people: _____   # of rooms: _____   # of nights: _____

Arriving: _____ / _____ / _____   My time of arrival (24-hr clock): _____
                day *month* *year*   (I will telephone if I will be late)

Departing: _____ / _____ / _____
                 day *month* *year*

Room(s): Single___   Double ___   Twin ___   Triple ___   Quad___

With: Toilet ____   Shower ____   Bath ____   Sink only ___

Special needs: View___   Quiet___   Cheapest ___   Ground Floor___

Please email or fax confirmation of my reservation, along with the type of
room reserved and the price. Please also inform me of your cancellation
policy. After I hear from you, I will quickly send my credit-card information
as a deposit to hold the room. Thank you.

_____
Name

_____
Address

_____
City   *State*   *Zip Code*   *Country*

Before hoteliers can make your reservation, they want to know the information listed above. You can use this form as the basis for your email, or you can photocopy this page, fill in the information, and send it as a fax (also available online at www.ricksteves.com/reservation).

Danish Survival Phrases

The Danes tend to say words quickly and clipped. In fact, many short vowels end in a "glottal stop"—a very brief vocal break immediately following the vowel. While I haven't tried to indicate these in the phonetics, you can listen for them in Denmark...and (try to) imitate. Three unique Danish vowels are æ (sounds like the *e* in "egg"), ø (sounds like the German *ö*—purse your lips and say "oh"), and å (sounds like the *o* in "bowl"). The letter *r* is not rolled—it's pronounced farther back in the throat, almost like a *w*. A *d* at the end of a word sounds almost like our *th*; for example, *mad* (food) sounds like "math." In the phonetics, Ī / ī sounds like the long *i* sound in "light."

Hello. (*formal*)	Goddag.	goh-DAY
Hi. / Bye. (*informal*)	Hej. / Hej-hej.	hī / hī-hī
Do you speak English?	Taler du engelsk?	TAY-lehr doo ENG-elsk
Yes. / No.	Ja. / Nej.	yeah / nī
Please. (May I?)*	Kan jeg?	kan yī
Please. (Can you?)*	Kan du?	kan doo
Please. (Would you?)*	Vil du?	veel doo
Thank you (very much).	(Tusind) tak.	(TOO-sin) tack
You're welcome.	Selv tak.	sehl tack
Can I help (you)?	Kan jeg hjælpe (dig)?	kan yī YEHL-peh (dī)
Excuse me. (to pass)	Undskyld mig.	OON-skewl mī
Excuse me. (Can you help me?)	Kan du hjælpe mig?	kan doo YEHL-peh mī
(Very) good.	(Meget) godt.	(MĪ-ehl) goht
Goodbye.	Farvel.	fah-VEHL
one / two	en / to	een / toh
three / four	tre / fire	tray / feer
five / six	fem / seks	fehm / sehks
seven / eight	syv / otte	syew / OH-deh
nine / ten	ni / ti	nee / tee
hundred	hundrede	HOON-reh
thousand	tusind	TOO-sin
How much?	Hvor meget?	vor MĪ-ehl
local currency: (Danish) crown	(Danske) kroner	(DAHN-skeh) KROH-nah
Where is...?	Hvor er..?	vor ehr
..the toilet	..toilettet	toh-ee-LEH-teht
men	herrer	HEHR-ah
women	damer	DAY-mah
water / coffee	vand / kaffe	vehn / KAH-feh
beer / wine	øl / vin	uhl / veen
Cheers!	Skål!	skohl
Can I have the bill?	Kan jeg få regningen?	kan yī foh RĪ-ning-ehn

*Because Danish has no single word for "please," they approximate that sentiment by asking "May I?", "Can you?", or "Would you?", depending on the context.

Norwegian Survival Phrases

Norwegian can be pronounced quite differently from region to region. These phrases and phonetics match the mainstream Oslo dialect, but you'll notice variations. Vowels can be tricky: *å* sounds like "oh," *æ* sounds like a bright "ah" (as in "apple"), and *u* sounds like the German *ü* (purse your lips and say u). Certain vowels at the ends of words (such as *d* and *t*) are sometimes barely pronounced (or not at all). In some dialects, the letters *sk* are pronounced "sh." In the phonetics, Ī / ī sounds like the long i in "light."

Hello. (formal)	**God dag.**	goo dahg
Hi. / Bye. (informal)	**Hei. / Ha det.**	hī / hah deh
Do you speak English?	**Snakker du engelsk?**	SNAHK-kehr dew ENG-ehlsk
Yes. / No.	**Ja. / Nei.**	yah / nī
Please.	**Vær så snill.**	vayr soh sneel
Thank you (very much).	**(Tusen) takk.**	(TEW-sehn) tahk
You're welcome.	**Vær så god.**	vayr soh goo
Can I help you?	**Kan jeg hjelpe deg?**	kahn yī YEHL-peh dī
Excuse me.	**Unnskyld.**	EWN-shuld
(Very) good.	**(Veldig) fint.**	(VEHL-dee) feent
Goodbye.	**Farvel.**	fahr-VEHL
one / two	**en / to**	ayn / toh
three / four	**tre / fire**	treh / FEE-reh
five / six	**fem / seks**	fehm / sehks
seven / eight	**syv / åtte**	seev / OH-teh
nine / ten	**ni / ti**	nee / tee
hundred	**hundre**	HEWN-dreh
thousand	**tusen**	TEW-sehn
How much?	**Hvor mye?**	voor MEE-yeh
local currency: (Norwegian) crown	**(Norske) kroner**	(NORSH-keh) KROH-nehr
Where is...?	**Hvor er...?**	voor ehr
..the toilet	**...toalettet**	toh-ah-LEH-teh
men	**menn** Or: **herrer**	mehn / HEHR-rehr
women	**damer**	DAH-mehr
water / coffee	**vann / kaffe**	vahn / KAH-feh
beer / wine	**øl / vin**	uhl / veen
Cheers!	**Skål!**	skohl
The bill, please.	**Regningen, takk.**	RĪ-ning-ehn tahk

Swedish Survival Phrases

Swedish pronunciation (especially the vowel sounds) can be tricky for Americans to say, and there's quite a bit of variation across the country; listen closely to locals and imitate, or ask for help. The most difficult Swedish sound is *sj*, which sounds roughly like a guttural "*h*w" (made in your throat); however, like many sounds, this is pronounced differently in various regions—for example, Stockholmers might say it more like "shw."

Hello. (formal)	**Goddag!**	goh-DAH
Hi. / Bye. (informal)	**Hej. / Hej då.**	hey / hey doh
Do you speak English?	**Talar du engelska?**	TAH-lahr doo ENG-ehl-skah
Yes. / No.	**Ja. / Nej.**	yaw / nay
Please.	**Snälla. / Tack.***	SNEHL-lah / tack
Thank you (very much).	**Tack (så mycket).**	tack (soh MEE-keh)
You're welcome.	**Ingen orsak.**	EENG-ehn OOR-sahk
Can I help you?	**Kan jag hjälpa dig?**	kahn yaw JEHL-pah day
Excuse me.	**Ursäkta.**	OOR-sehk-tah
(Very) good.	**(Mycket) bra.**	(MEE-keh) brah
Goodbye. (formal)	**Adjö.**	ah-YEW
one / two	**en / två**	ehn / tvoh
three / four	**tre / fyra**	treh / FEE-rah
five / six	**fem / sex**	fehm / sehks
seven / eight	**sju / åtta**	*h*woo / OH-tah
nine / ten	**nio / tio**	NEE-oh / TEE-oh
hundred	**hundra**	HOON-drah
thousand	**tusen**	TEW-sehn
How much?	**Hur mycket?**	hewr MEE-keh
local currency: (Swedish) kronor	**(Svenske) kronor**	(svehn-SKEH) KROH-nor
Where is...?	**Var finns...?**	vahr feens
..the toilet	**...toaletten**	toh-ah-LEH-tehn
men	**man**	mahn
women	**kvinna**	KVEE-nah
water / coffee	**vatten / kaffe**	VAH-tehn / KAH-feh
beer / wine	**öl / vin**	url / veen
Cheers!	**Skål!**	skohl
The bill, please.	**Kan jag få notan, tack.**	kahn yaw foh NOH-tahn tack

*Swedish has various ways to say "please," depending on the context. The simplest is *snälla*, but Swedes sometimes use the word *tack* (thank you) in the way we use "please."

Finnish Survival Phrases

In Finnish, the emphasis always goes on the first syllable. Double vowels (e.g., *ää* or *ii*) sound similar to single vowels, but are held a bit longer. The letter *y* sounds like the German *ü* (purse your lips and say "oo"). In the phonetics, Ī / ī sounds like the long i in "light."

Good morning. *(formal)*	**Hyvää huomenta.**	HEW-vaah HWOH-mehn-tah
Good day. *(formal)*	**Hyvää päivää.**	HEW-vaah PĪ-vaah
Good evening. *(formal)*	**Hyvää iltaa.**	HEW-vaah EEL-taah
Hi. / Bye. *(informal)*	**Hei. / Hei, hei.**	hey / hey hey
Do you speak English?	**Puhutko englantia?**	POO-hoot-koh EN-glahn-tee-yah
Yes. / No.	**Kyllä. / Ei.**	KEWL-lah / ay
Please.	**Ole hyvä.**	OH-leh HEW-vah
Thank you (very much).	**Kiitos (paljon).**	KEE-tohs (PAHL-yohn)
You're welcome.	**Kiitos.** *Or:* **Ei kestä.**	KEE-tohs / ay KEHS-tah
Can I help you?	**Voinko auttaa?**	VOIN-koh OWT-taah
Excuse me.	**Anteeksi.**	AHN-teek-see
(Very) good.	**(Oikein) hyvä.**	(OY-kayn) HEW-vah
Goodbye.	**Näkemiin.**	NAH-keh-meen
one / two	**yksi / kaksi**	EWK-see / KAHK-see
three / four	**kolme / neljä**	KOHL-meh / NEHL-yah
five / six	**viisi / kuusi**	VEE-see / KOO-see
seven / eight	**seitsemän / kahdeksan**	SAYT-seh-mahn / KAH-dehk-sahn
nine / ten	**yhdeksän / kymmenen**	EW-dehk-sahn / KEWM-meh-nehn
hundred	**sata**	SAH-tah
thousand	**tuhat**	TOO-haht
How much?	**Paljonko?**	PAHL-yohn-koh
local currency: euro	**euro**	AY-oo-roh
Where is...?	**Missä on...?**	MEE-sah ohn
..the toilet	**..WC**	VAY-say
men	**miehet**	MEE-ay-heht
women	**naiset**	NĪ-seht
water / coffee	**vesi / kahvi**	VEH-see / KAHKH-vee
beer / wine	**olut / viini**	OH-luht / VEE-nee
Cheers!	**Kippis!**	KIHP-pihs
The bill, please.	**Saisinko laskun, kiitos.**	SĪ-seen-koh LAHS-kuhn KEE-tohs

Estonian Survival Phrases

Estonian has a few unusual vowel sounds. The letter *ä* is pronounced "ah" as in "hat," but *a* without the umlaut sounds more like "aw" as in "hot." To make the sound *ö*, say "oh" and purse your lips; the letter *õ* is similar, but with the lips less pursed. Listen to locals and imitate. In the phonetics, Ī / ī sounds like the long *i* in "light."

Hello. (formal)	**Tervist.**	TEHR-veest
Hi. / Bye. (informal)	**Tere. / Nägemist.**	TEH-reh / NAH-geh-meest
Do you speak English?	**Kas te räägite inglise keelt?**	kahs teh RAAH-gee-the EEN-glee-seh kehlt
Yes. / No.	**Jah. / Ei.**	yah / ay
Please. / You're welcome.	**Palun.**	PAH-luhn
Thank you (very much).	**Tänan (väga).**	TAH-nahn (VAH-gaw)
Can I help you?	**Saan ma teid aidata?**	saahn mah tayd Ī-dah-tah
Excuse me.	**Vabandust.**	VAW-bahn-doost
(Very) good.	**(Väga) hea.**	(VAH-gaw) HEY-ah
Goodbye.	**Hüvasti.**	HEW-vaw-stee
one / two	**üks / kaks**	ewks / kawks
three / four	**kolm / neli**	kohlm / NAY-lee
five / six	**viis / kuus**	vees / koos
seven / eight	**seitse / kaheksa**	SAYT-seh / KAW-hehk-sah
nine / ten	**üheksa / kümme**	EW-hehk-sah / KEW-meh
hundred	**sada**	SAW-daw
thousand	**tuhat**	TOO-hawt
How much?	**Kui palju?**	quee PAWL-yoo
local currency: (Estonian) crown	**(Eesti) krooni**	(EH-stee) KROO-nee
Where is...?	**Kus asub...?**	koos ah-SOOB
..the toilet	**...tualett**	TOO-ah-leht
men	**mees**	mehs
women	**naine**	NĪ-neh
water / coffee	**vesi / kohvi**	VAY-see / KOHKH-vee
beer / wine	**õlu / vein**	OH-loo / vayn
Cheers!	**Terviseks!**	TEHR-vee-sehks
The bill, please.	**Arve, palun.**	AHR-veh PAH-luhn

INDEX

INDEX

INDEX

MAP INDEX

Audio Europe

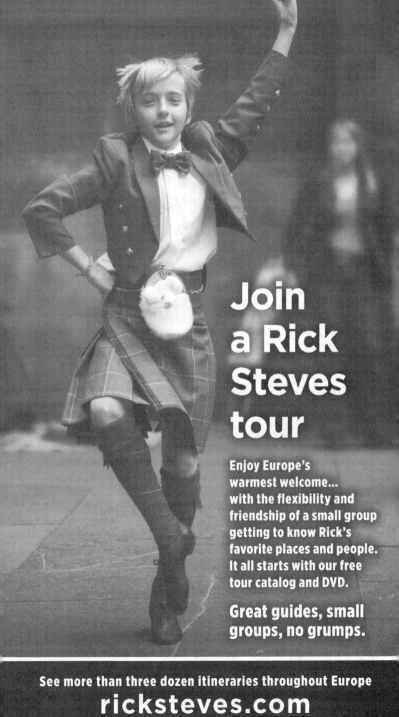

Join a Rick Steves tour

Enjoy Europe's warmest welcome... with the flexibility and friendship of a small group getting to know Rick's favorite places and people. It all starts with our free tour catalog and DVD.

Great guides, small groups, no grumps.

Free information and great gear to

▶ Plan Your Trip

Browse thousands of articles and a wealth of money-saving tips for planning your dream trip. You'll find up-to-date information on Europe's best destinations, packing smart, getting around, finding rooms, staying healthy, avoiding scams and more.

▶ Eurail Passes

Find out, step-by-step, if a railpass makes sense for your trip—and how to avoid buying more than you need. Get free shipping on online orders

▶ Graffiti Wall & Travelers Helpline

Learn, ask, share—our online community of savvy travelers is a great resource for first-time travelers to Europe, as well as seasoned pros.

Rick Steves' Europe Through the Back Door, Inc.

Rick Steves

www.ricksteves.com

NOW AVAILABLE:
eBOOKS, DVD & BLU-RAY

TRAVEL CULTURE

Europe 101
European Christmas
Postcards from Europe
Travel as a Political Act

eBOOKS

*Nearly all Rick Steves guides
are available as eBooks. Check
with your favorite bookseller.*

RICK STEVES' EUROPE DVDs

10 New Shows 2011–2012
Austria & the Alps
Eastern Europe
England & Wales
European Christmas
European Travel Skills & Specials
France
Germany, BeNeLux & More
Greece & Turkey
Iran
Ireland & Scotland
Italy's Cities
Italy's Countryside
Scandinavia
Spain
Travel Extras

BLU-RAY

Celtic Charms
Eastern Europe Favorites
European Christmas
Italy Through the Back Door
Mediterranean Mosaic
Surprising Cities of Europe

PHRASE BOOKS & DICTIONARIES

French
French, Italian & German
German
Italian
Portuguese
Spanish

JOURNALS

Rick Steves' Pocket Travel Journal
Rick Steves' Travel Journal

PLANNING MAPS

Britain, Ireland & London
Europe
France & Paris
Germany, Austria & Switzerland
Ireland
Italy
Spain & Portugal

Credits

Researchers
To help update this book, Rick relied on...

Tom Griffin

Tom edits and researches guidebooks for Rick Steves. As a young lad, he acquired an affinity for all things Scandinavian, thanks to Ingmar Bergman movies, Nordic skiing, and Danish pastries. For this book, he researched Norway and Sweden. He lives in Seattle with his wife, Julie.

Cameron Hewitt

Cameron writes and edits guidebooks for Rick Steves, specializing in Eastern Europe. For this book, he spent a week in Denmark, cycling on the isle of Ærø, nibbling candy floss at Tivoli, and storming Frederiksborg Castle. When he's not traveling, Cameron lives in Seattle with his wife, Shawna.

Ian Watson
Ian has worked with Rick's guidebooks since 1993, after starting out with Let's Go and Frommer's guides. He studied Scandinavian linguistics in college and has traveled widely throughout the region. Originally from upstate New York, Ian now lives with his family in Reykjavík, Iceland.

Contributor
Gene Openshaw

Gene is the co-author of 10 Rick Steves books. For this book, he wrote material on Europe's art, history, and contemporary culture. When not traveling, Gene enjoys composing music, recovering from his 1973 trip to Europe with Rick, and living everyday life with his daughter.

Acknowledgments
Thanks to Thor, Hanne, Geir, Hege, and Kari-Anne, our Norwegian family. Special thanks to Jane Klausen for her expertise in all things Danish. Thanks to these translators for their help with the survival phrases: Marita Bergman, Unni-Marie Kvikne, Mati Rummessen, and Christina Snellman. And in loving memory of Berit Kristiansen, whose house was my house for 20 years of Norwegian travel.

Chapter Images

The following list identifies the chapter-opening images and credits their photographers.

Location	Photographer
Front color matter: Copenhagen-Nyhavn	Rick Steves
Introduction: Archipelago	Cameron Hewitt
Scandinavia: Viking Ships	David C. Hoerlein
Denmark: Copenhagen's Højbro Plads	Rick Steves
Copenhagen: Nyhavn	Cameron Hewitt
Near Copenhagen: Frederiksborg Castle	David C. Hoerlein
Central Denmark: Ærøskøbing	Rick Steves
Jutland: Den Gamle By	Rick Steves
Norway: Sognefjord	Rick Steves
Oslo: Vigeland Sculpture Garden	Rick Steves
Norway in a Nutshell: Aurlandsfjord	Cameron Hewitt
More on the Sognefjord: Balestrand	Cameron Hewitt
Gudbrandsdal Valley and Jotunheimen Mountains: Maihaugen Open-Air Folk Museum	Rick Steves
Bergen: Bryggen	Cameron Hewitt
South Norway: South Norway Port Town	Rick Steves
Sweden: Archipelago	Rick Steves
Stockholm: Drottningholm Palace	Rick Steves
Archipelago: Vaxholm	Cameron Hewitt
Southeast Sweden: Kalmar Castle	Rick Steves
Finland: Helsinki's Lutheran Cathedral	Cameron Hewitt
Helsinki: Helsinki Harbor	Cameron Hewitt
Estonia: Tallinn	Cameron Hewitt
Tallinn: Old Town Square	Cameron Hewitt

Avalon Travel
a member of the Perseus Books Group
1700 Fourth Street
Berkeley, CA 94710

Printed in Canada by Friesens. Updated for second printing April 2013.

ISBN 978-1-61238-192-3
ISSN 1084-7206

For the latest on Rick's lectures, guidebooks, tours, public radio show, and public television series, contact Europe Through the Back Door, Box 2009, Edmonds, WA 98020, 425/771-8303, fax 425/771-0833, www.ricksteves.com, rick@ricksteves.com.

Europe Through the Back Door

Managing Editor: Risa Laib
Editors: Jennifer Madison Davis, Glenn Eriksen, Tom Griffin, Cameron Hewitt, Suzanne Kotz, Cathy Lu, John Pierce, Carrie Shepherd, Gretchen Strauch
Editorial Interns: Valerie Gilmore, Rebekka Shattuck, Amanda Zurita
Researchers: Tom Griffin, Cameron Hewitt, Ian Watson
Graphic Content Director: Laura VanDeventer
Maps & Graphics: David C. Hoerlein, Twozdai Hulse, Lauren Mills

Avalon Travel

Senior Editor & Series Manager: Madhu Prasher
Editor: Jamie Andrade
Assistant Editor: Nikki Ioakimedes
Copy Editor: Patrick Collins
Proofreader: Kelly Lydick
Indexer: Stephen Callahan
Production & Typesetting: McGuire Barber Design
Cover Design: Kimberly Glyder Design
Maps & Graphics: Kat Bennett, Mike Morgenfeld, Brice Ticen

Cover Photo: Sognefjord © Rick Steves
Front Matter Color Photos: p. i, Copenhagen, Denmark © Rick Steves; p. ii (left) © Sonja Groset; (right) © Rick Steves; p. iii © Rick Steves; p. xi-xii © Dominic Bonucelli and © Pat O'Connor
Additional Photography: Dominic Bonuccelli, Tom Griffin, Sonja Groset, Cameron Hewitt, David C. Hoerlein, Lauren Mills, Rick Steves, Renee Van Drent, Ian Watson, Chris Werner

ABOUT THE AUTHOR

RICK STEVES

Since 1973, Rick Steves has spent 100 days every year exploring Europe. Along with writing and researching a bestselling series of guidebooks, Rick produces a public television series *(Rick Steves' Europe)*, a public radio show *(Travel with Rick Steves)*, and an app and podcast *(Rick Steves Audio Europe)*; writes a nationally syndicated newspaper column; organizes guided tours that take over 10,000 travelers to Europe annually; and offers an information-packed website (www.ricksteves.com). With the help of his hardworking staff of 80 at Europe Through the Back Door—in Edmonds, Washington, just north of Seattle—Rick's mission is to make European travel fun, affordable, and culturally enlightening for Americans.

Connect with Rick:

facebook.com/RickSteves   twitter: @RickSteves